Total 1-2-3

Release 2.2

PETER G. RANDALL
AND
STEVEN J. BENNETT

Brady
New York

Brady

Simon & Schuster, Inc.
15 Columbus Circle
New York, NY 10023

Distributed by Prentice Hall Trade

Manufactured in the United States of America

1 2 3 4 5 6 7 8 9 10

Library of Congress Cataloging-in-Publication Data
Randall, Peter G., 1951–
Total 1-2-3, release 2.2/Peter G. Randall and Steven J. Bennett.
p. cm.
ISBN 0-13-926130-3:$24.95
1. Lotus 1-2-3 (Computer program) 2. Business—Data processing.
3. Electronic spreadsheets. 4. IBM Personal computers.
I. Bennett, Steven J., 1951– . II. Title
HF5548.4.L67R358 1989
650'.028'55369—dc20 89-22269
CIP

ACKNOWLEDGEMENTS

First and foremost, we want to thank our editor, Susan Hunt for guiding us through another project. Her insights once again helped us see things in a new light

We are also grateful to the Brady support staff for their clerical assistance, and to Geraldine Ivins and Mia McCroskey who helped make sure that the book was produced on time. We are also deeply indebted to Michael Mellin, Vice President, Simon & Schuster Technical Reference, for his support during the project.

In addition, we'd like to express our gratitude to the people at Lotus Development Corp. who helped during the Release 2.2 beta phase, in particular Susan Earabino, Alexandra Trevelyan, and Lisa Kosciak. Without their help, this project would have been much more difficult.

Finally, we thank to the people at PageWorks—Donna Merrell-Chernin, Lee Busch, and Ron Creamer—for working long and hard hours to produce this book in a timely fashion.

PRODUCTION NOTE

This book was produced at PageWorks, Inc, in Cambridge Massachusetts. It was formatted on a network of Macintosh computers with Quark Xpress, and output on a Varityper 4300p.

LIMITS OF LIABILITY AND DISCLAIMER OF WARRANTY

TRADEMARK ACKNOWLEDGEMENTS

Contents

Introduction

A PROGRAM FOR ALL MACHINES

In early 1989, Lotus Development Corporation stunned the computing world when it announced its plans to introduce Release 2.2, which was designed for IBM PC's, XT's, and compatibles. The immediate response was: "Is Release 2.2 a minor enhancement of earlier versions?" "Is it just for users who don't have the horsepower needed to run Release 3?"

The answer is an emphatic "No" to both questions. Release 2.2 represents far more than a simple upgrade to earlier versions. It's packed with powerful new features and capabilities that will excite even the most demanding user. Release 2.2 holds its own for most spreadsheet applications, and even outshines Release 3 in terms of its printing capabilities. In fact, even those who own high-power 286- or 386-based computers, Release 2.2 may well be the program of choice.

If you've never used a spreadsheet program, Release 2.2 is an ideal way to get started. You can easily use it to translate your manual systems into electronic worksheets that can be used for automating just about any task that involves numerical computations. As your computing skills grow, Release 2.2 will supply you with plenty of power to handle your most complex worksheet needs.

If you're an experienced 1-2-3 user, you'll find yourself right at home with Release 2.2. The program reads and writes .WK1 files so you can use your existing worksheets and graphs without any modifications—compatibility guaranteed. You'll also find Release 2.2's new features and enhancements welcome additions to earlier releases. In a sense, the program represents everything that Lotus has learned from its users about the shortcomings of its earlier product. With Release 2.2 you'll be able to build more complex models and generate better looking reports and graphs than you could in the past.

Here's a capsule summary of the new features of Release 2.2.

WHAT'S NEW AND IMPROVED IN RELEASE 2.2

The first thing you'll notice when you start Release 2.2 is that it's fast; very fast compared to its predecessors. If you used to take a stretch break while your old version of 1-2-3 loaded, you better find some other way to limber up; depending on your hardware, the program now loads in the blink of an eye. You'll also find that recalculation times are significantly faster, thanks to the use of the optimal recalculation technique (also known as "minimal recalc") that enables Release 2.2 to perform calculations only on those cells in which data has changed since the last recalculation took place.

Presentation Quality Reports Release 2.2 contains an add-in printing program called Allways, which Lotus calls a spreadsheet publisher. Allways provides a what-you-see-is-what-you-get environment and allows you to quickly and easily print a worksheet with a variety of fonts, lines, and shading. It also enables you to print a worksheet and a graph on the same page.

Undo Even the most experienced user occasionally regrets issuing a command that destroys or does extensive damage to a worksheet. With the UNDO key (ALT-F4), help is but a keystroke away. If you have enough memory in your computer, you can restore your worksheet to the state it was in prior to making your last keyboard entry (unless you've used one of the file commands).

File Linking Release 2.2 allows you make references in your worksheet to cells in other worksheets on disk. These "links" to source cells in other worksheets are updated each time you load your worksheet or use the /File Admin Link-Refresh command.

New Macro Features Users of 1-2-3's macro command language will appreciate the new macro Learn feature, which captures and records your keystrokes in a worksheet range. You can play back the recorded keystrokes or modify them for inclusion in other macros. Other enhancements in this area include new macro commands, an expanded macro-naming facility, and the ability to keep macro libraries in memory.

Easier Graphing Alas, PrintGraph is *still* a separate program that must be run outside of 1-2-3. (Although you can print graphs without leaving 1-2-3 by using Allways.) Despite this minor inconvenience, Release 2.2 still offers superior graphing capabilities by allowing one step-selection of graph data ranges, one-step selection of data labels, and one-step selection of graph legends.

Automatic Execution of Add-Ins If you use third party add-ins, such as @base, Look & Link, or other programs that extend 1-2-3 functionality and capabilities, you no longer have to use the add-in manager to modify your 123.set file. Release 2.2 lets you control up to eight add-ins right from 1-2-3's main menu.

Other modifications include the display of "settings sheets," which show you the various options you have selected for data sorts and queries and other commands. 1-2-3 also offers several new global default settings, the ability to create backup files, and the ability to use the program in a network environment.

A BOOK FOR ALL USERS

Total 1-2-3/Release 2.2 is designed to serve the novice and the experienced 1-2-3 user. We suggest the following reading paths.

New User

Begin with Chapter 1, which covers installation, then skip to Chapters 3 through 11. These chapters cover the basics of 1-2-3 in detail and assume no knowledge of earlier versions. When you have the basic principles under your belt, read through Chapter 12, which provides hands-on instruction for building a 1-2-3 worksheet based on a tested model. You'll learn how to use the various commands and functions to develop a basic worksheet model. You'll also learn how to carry out "what-if" analyses and to print out your worksheets as high quality reports and graphs.

At this point, you can stop reading and begin using Release 2.2 for your own purposes. Later, when you are completely familiar with the program and wish to develop more sophisticated worksheets, you can return to the discussion of macros in Chapter 13.

The Reference section of the book is meant to serve as your "1-2-3 Bible." It provides detailed information about every 1-2-3 command. Even when you graduate to the level of worksheet expert, you'll probably find yourself turning back to the reference section for reminders and tips.

Experienced 1-2-3 Users

Even if you know your way around 1-2-3, please begin with Chapter 1, which covers installation; it will save you time and aggravation. Next, move to Chapter 2, which describes the new features of Release 2.2.

We recommend that you read or skim through Chapters 11, which discusses Allways, and Chapter 12, which is devoted to creating a 1-2-3 cash flow model, and explores the use of the various 1-2-3 commands and functions.

Make sure that you read the discussion about macros and the new macro commands in Chapter 13. Turn to the Reference section for detailed information about all the commands and @ functions used in Release 2.2. Each command is explained in depth and many are illustrated with examples of proper usage.

LEARN BY DOING

Regardless of what reading path you choose, you will benefit the most from *Total 1-2-3/Release 2.2* by experimenting as you read along. Take some time to try the various approaches to worksheet building, formatting, and usage described in the various sections. Stop and enter your own data if you are following the tutorial, or develop your own model if you are inventing your own reading path through the book.

Whatever method you choose, we believe that *Total 1-2-3/Release 2.2* will help you master the principles of worksheet computing quickly and easily. One final bit of advice before you launch into the exciting world of possibilities opened up by Release 2.2: Don't try to learn everything at once. No one becomes a 1-2-3 expert overnight—there are simply too many commands, rules, and principles to take in during one sitting. Focus on specific areas and work at them until you feel confident, then move on. The best approach to tackling Release 2.2 (or any complex program) is to learn what you need to know to accomplish the tasks at hand. As your needs change, you can build upon a solid foundation of knowledge, adding more complex and "exotic" techniques for manipulating data.

No matter how you learn Release 2.2, be aware that the program is extremely addictive. Once you dig into its wealth of features, you'll only want to find new ways of unleashing its awesome power.

Peter G. Randall
Philadelphia, PA

Steven J. Bennett
Cambridge, MA

1 Installation

This chapter explains how to install Release 2.2 on your system. The process involves four steps with a floppy drive system, and five with a hard disk system. The steps are:

1. Checking to make sure you have the required hardware and software;
2. Initializing your disks;
3. Backing up your disks;
4. Copying the files to your hard disk, if you have one;
5. Running the Install program.

It is important to understand that running 1-2-3's Install program is the last step in the installation process. The Install program does not "install" 1-2-3 in the conventional sense; that is, it does not transfer files from your floppy disks to your hard disk. Rather, it tailors 1-2-3 to your hardware; in the Install program you are asked to select the appropriate "driver" files for your monitor and printer. These driver files contain information that tells 1-2-3 how to display graphics on your screen, and what control codes to send to your printer so that reports are properly printed. All driver information for 1-2-3 is stored in files called "driver sets," or .SET files.

Before you run the Install program, you must go through several other procedures. If you are an experienced 1-2-3 user, you need to be concerned primarily with step 2, initializing your copy of 1-2-3. This is new to Release 2.2 (and 3.0). If you simply copy the program without first initializing your System Disk, 1-2-3 will not run at all. Therefore, be sure to follow the initialization instructions before going any further.

The Advanced Options section of this chapter explains how to use the Advanced Installation options to modify existing driver sets (you can change your equipment specifications as many times as you like), and how to add equipment drivers to 1-2-3 that are not currently supplied with the program.

STEP 1: PRE-INSTALLATION CHECKLIST

Before you attempt to install Release 2.2, make sure that your system meets the following hardware and software requirements.

Required Hardware

- Any IBM, Compaq, AT&T, or 1-2-3 certified compatible. If you're not sure whether your computer is 1-2-3 certified, contact your dealer or Lotus Development Corporation.
- A monochrome or color monitor (you must have a monitor with graphics capabilities if you want to display graphs).
- Two floppy drives, or a hard disk and at least one floppy drive. In order to use Allways, the "spreadsheet publisher" add-in included with the program, you must have a hard disk.

Optional Hardware

A printer. You can use 1-2-3 with or without a printer, although its value will be severely compromised if you have no access to a printer.

Memory Requirements

To use 1-2-3 without Allways, you must have at least 320K of main memory. Release 2.2 will support up to 4 megabytes of expanded memory. To use Allways, you will need at least 512K of main memory RAM.

Other

Release 2.2. runs on any version of DOS above 2.0. Release 2.2. does *not* run under OS/2; Release 3 is currently the only version of 1-2-3 designed to run under OS/2. You can, however, run Release 2.2 within OS/2's DOS window.

STEP 2: INITIALIZATION

You're probably aware that Lotus Development Corporation has done away with copy protection, so you might be tempted to immediately copy your program disks onto your hard disk and prepare for the installation. Don't. 1-2-3 won't run if the system disk has not been initialized. Initialization permanently encodes your name and company name onto the disk, so that they appear on the title screen every time the program is loaded.

To initialize your copy of 1-2-3, insert the System Disk into your A drive. (Users with a high-density A drive may wish to use a low-density drive; otherwise, once you complete the initialization process you might not be able to read the System disk in a 360K drive again.) Type:

```
init
```

and press ENTER. Now type in your name, and 1-2-3 will display a screen prompting you to confirm your name. Press Y to confirm that your name is correct, or N to re-enter your name. The initialization program will then display a similar screen that prompts you to enter your company name. As you did with your personal name, confirm your entry by entering Y, or edit it after selecting N. Once you press Y, the program will display your name and company name, and ask you to confirm again whether they are correct.

If both are correct, press ENTER. If not, press and hold the CTRL key, and then press the Break key. This will interrupt the initialization program. You can then start over by typing `init` again and repeating the procedure.

If you do press ENTER to confirm your choices, 1-2-3 will encode your entries onto the System Disk, the initialization will be complete, and the DOS prompt will be redisplayed.

Once you complete the process you won't have to do it again. In fact, you *can't* once your name is on the disk; it's there to stay, so make sure the information is correct.

STEP 3: BACKUP YOUR ORIGINAL DISKETTES

Before you go any further, make a copy of the diskettes supplied with your 1-2-3 package. This is important if your original diskettes get damaged, and you need to reinstall 1-2-3 at a later date. If you have a dual floppy system, use the DOS DISKCOPY command; type:

```
DISKCOPY A: B:
```

If you only have one floppy drive, type:

```
DISKCOPY A: A:
```

Either way, your computer will instruct you when and in which drive to insert the source diskette (i.e., the original supplied by Lotus Development Corporation), and the target diskette (i.e., the blank disk on which the files will be copied).

NOTE If you back up your original system disk before you initialize it, the copy will not do you any good. You can't initialize a copied system disk; and without an initialized System Disk, 1-2-3 won't run.

STEP 4: COPYING THE FILES TO YOUR HARD DISK

If you have a two-drive system, skip this section and move on to step 5. If you have a hard disk, you will need to copy your original program diskettes to your hard disk. First, though, you should create a directory for your 1-2-3 program files and a second dirctory for your 1-2-3 data files (i.e., the files that you create when you use the program and save a worksheet). It is best to avoid mixing the program files and data files on your hard disk in one directory (i.e., location); large numbers of files quickly become confusing and difficult to manage. You may create directories or locations with the DOS md (make directory) command.

For the sake of simplicity, create a program directory for 1-2-3 and call it "123". At the C:\ prompt (in the root directory), type:

```
md 123
```

Now create a data directory called "123data" by typing:

```
md 123data
```

You're now all set to copy your program files to your 1-2-3 directory. Before doing so, move to the 1-2-3 program directory location with the DOS cd (change directory) command. Type:

```
cd \123
```

Now that you are in your 123 program directories, you are ready to copy the program files from your floppies to your hard drive. Place the system diskette in your A drive and use the DOS Copy command. Type:

```
copy a:*.*
```

and press ENTER to have all the files in drive A copied one-by-one to the 123 directory (your current directory) on your hard disk. Do this for every program diskette, except those marked "Allways." The Allways installation procedure is described separately below.

Installing Allways

There's no need to copy every one of the Allways program files to your hard disk; many are device-specific and you'll waste a lot of space storing files that your system doesn't need. Instead, place the Allways Setup disk into your A drive. Make the A drive your current drive and at the A> prompt type:

```
awsetup
```

Select First Time Installation from the menu and follow the on-screen setup instructions regarding your equipment. Allways will copy only those files that you need to run the program.

The next and final step in the 1-2-3 installation process actually involves running the 1-2-3 Install program. You can actually use 1-2-3 without having run the Install program—as long as you do not need to display any graphs or print any data.

STEP 5: RUNNING THE INSTALL PROGRAM

The Install program supplied with Release 2.2 creates a driver set that contains information about your monitor and printer; the driver set is saved in a file called 123.SET. Creating a driver set involves three separate steps: selecting a monitor, selecting a text and graphics printer, and naming the driver set. As explained below, you can also create and name additional driver sets to run alternative monitor and printer configurations.

Starting Install from the DOS Prompt

Floppy Drive Users

Insert the disk labeled INSTALL into your A drive. Make the A drive your current drive. At the A> prompt type:

```
install
```

During the install, 1-2-3 will ask you to insert various disks into your drive, so that it can read certain files. Follow the prompts, and place the correct disk in the drive as you are instructed. Eventually, the Install program title screen will be displayed. Press ENTER to continue. Refer to the install menu system below for explanations of the various steps used to select monitors and printers.

Hard Disk Users

Assuming that you have copied all the files from your original floppies to your hard disk, make the directory containing your 1-2-3 files the current directory (e.g., type cd \123). Then, at the DOS prompt, type:

```
install
```

The Install program will then load. Press ENTER, and a series of menus will be displayed, as described below.

Starting Install from 1-2-3's Access System

An alternative way of running the Install program is to use the Lotus Access System. This program offers a menu with options to start 1-2-3, run the Install program, print 1-2-3 graphs, or use the translate utility (which converts 1-2-3 data into formats usable by other programs or vice versa). Floppy users can start the Access System by placing the System Disk in drive A and typing:

```
lotus
```

Hard disk users should change to the 1-2-3 program directory and type `lotus` at the DOS prompt. Either way, 1-2-3 will display the Access System menu. Select the Install option and the Install program will begin.

What's the difference in starting the Install program from the DOS prompt or through the Access System? None, except that when you finish using Install from the Access System, you can start 1-2-3 without having to return to the DOS prompt. The minor disadvantage is that the Access System takes a few extra moments to load. It's a matter of personal preference.

The Install Main Menu

The Main Menu of Install contains four options, listed at the left of the opening screen (see Figure 1.1). Use the Up and Down cursor keys to move the highlight bar up and down the menu choices. At any point during the installation, you can return to the Install Main Menu by pressing the F9 key. You can also review the choices you've already made by pressing the F10 key. Finally, you can always backtrack to a previous menu by pressing the ESC key. (All keystroke options are listed at the bottom of the screen.)

When the Main Menu is first displayed, the option First-Time Installation will be highlighted. If this is your first time running the Install program, press ENTER to begin the installation. (If you need to change various equipment options that you specified previously, choose Change Selected Equipment. If you wish to add new driver sets (or use drivers other than those supplied in the 1-2-3 menu selections), or if you wish to modify any driver sets on disk, select Advanced Options. (See discussion below).

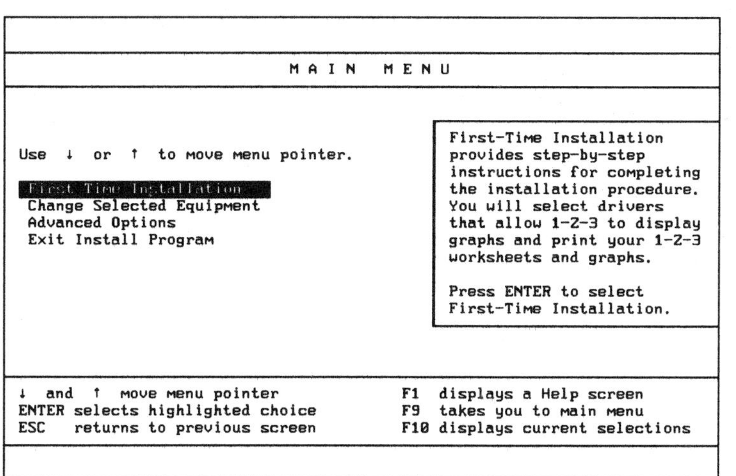

```
MAIN MENU

Use ↓ or ↑ to move menu pointer.

 First-Time Installation
 Change Selected Equipment
 Advanced Options
 Exit Install Program

First-Time Installation
provides step-by-step
instructions for completing
the installation procedure.
You will select drivers
that allow 1-2-3 to display
graphs and print your 1-2-3
worksheets and graphs.

Press ENTER to select
First-Time Installation.

↓ and ↑ move menu pointer          F1  displays a Help screen
ENTER selects highlighted choice   F9  takes you to main menu
ESC   returns to previous screen   F10 displays current selections
```

Figure 1.1. Main Menu of Install Program.

Selecting a Monitor

After you select First Time Installation, 1-2-3 displays an opening instruction screen. Read it, press ENTER, and you will be asked whether your computer can display graphs.

If you have a monochrome monitor, select No, and you will proceed immediately to the text printer selection menu. If you select Yes, 1-2-3 will ask you how many monitors you have, one or two.

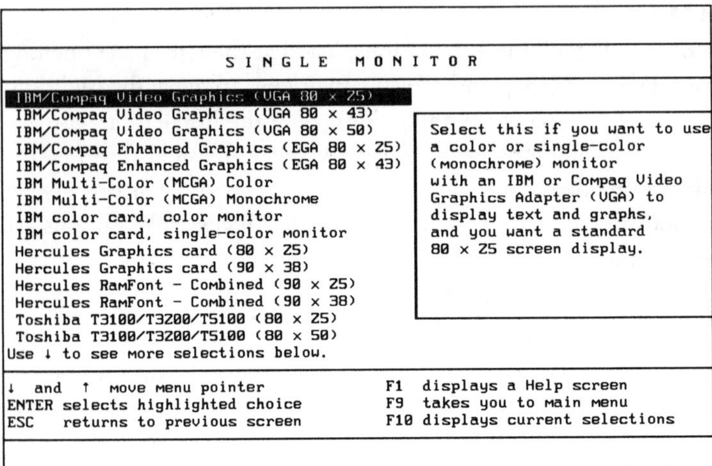

Figure 1.2a Single Monitor Selection Menu.

One Monitor Select One Monitor regardless of whether you have one or two monitors. (The option should have been probably labeled First Monitor). 1-2-3 will display a list of monitors and/or graphics card devices. (The list is two screens long; see Figure 1.2a.) Highlight your monitor type and press ENTER. (You can scroll through the list with the Down cursor or the PgDn key.) If you have two monitors, select the monitor type that you wish to use for text display as your First Monitor.

The dimensions specified after the monitor types refer to the number of columns and rows that can be displayed on your screen. For example, the "IBM/Compaq Video Graphics (VGA 80 x 50)" selection will display 80 columns and 50 rows of data. The normal number of rows for a standard monitor is 24 lines, so 50 lines will cram about twice as many rows on your screen. The trade-off, though is that the characters are half as large, and may be hard to read. Experiment to determine which selection works best for you.

Two Monitors After you have selected one monitor for text display, you may wish to designate a second monitor (if you have one) for displaying graphs. For example, suppose you have a monochrome monitor that you wish to use for text display, and that you also selected the "Hercules Graphics card (90 x 38)" option (from the One Monitor menu) to display the maximum amount of characters on your monochrome screen. If you also have an IBM color card and a color monitor connected to your computer, it would be preferable to display your graphs as you create them—in color, standard size—on that second monitor. To do so, select the Two Monitors option (it would have been better labeled Second

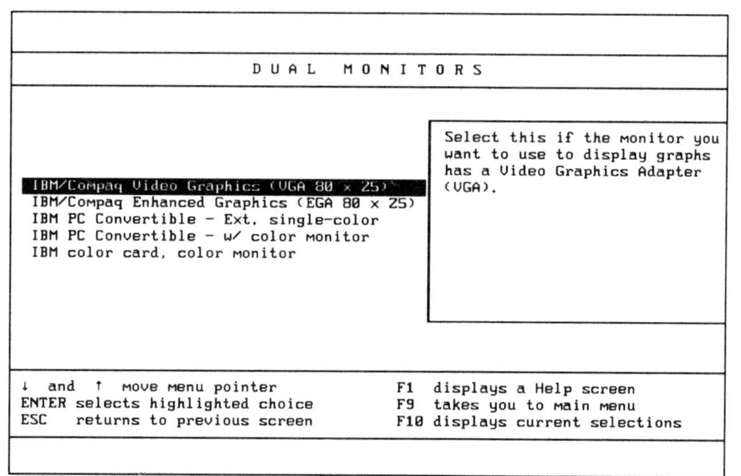

Figure 1.2b. Second Monitor Selection Menu.

Monitor), highlight the "IBM color card, color monitor" option and press ENTER. (See Figure 1.2b.)

You will notice that the selection list for two monitors shown in Figure 1.2b is rather short. Lotus has determined that for graphics display on a second monitor, these drivers are compatible with the first monitor options shown in Figure 1.2a. You can, in fact, designate other monitors for graphics display with the Advanced Options selection on the Main Menu (see below). If you choose an incompatible mix of first and second monitors, though, your screen might blank out when you attempt to run 1-2-3.

Selecting a Text Printer(s)

After you select your monitor options, 1-2-3 asks whether you have a text printer. (If you select No, 1-2-3 will go on to ask whether you want to print graphs.) If you choose Yes, you will be given a list of printer brand names (two screens long) to select from (see Figure 1.3a).

Highlight your brand of printer and press ENTER. 1-2-3 will display a list of specific models. For example, if you selected HP (for Hewlett-Packard), 1-2-3 would display the model choices shown in Figure 1.3b. (Use the "2686 LaserJet Series" for all HP LaserJet printers.)

Once you select a text printer, 1-2-3 will ask if you have another one. Selecting Yes repeats the process to specify a second text printer. If you select No, you will be asked to specify a graphics printer.

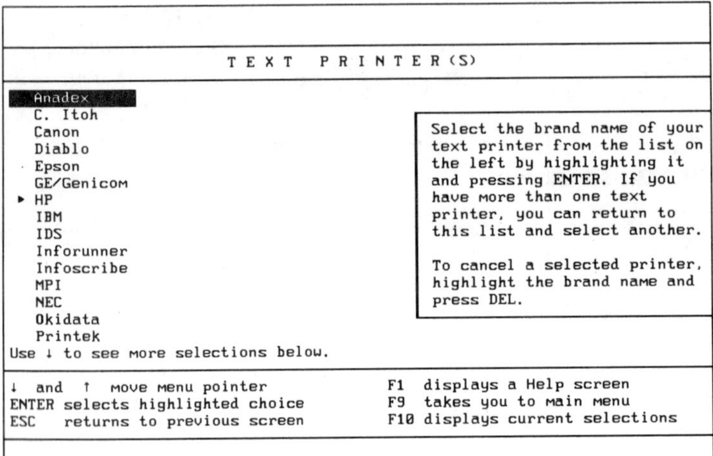

Figure 1.3a. Text printer selection by manufacturer.

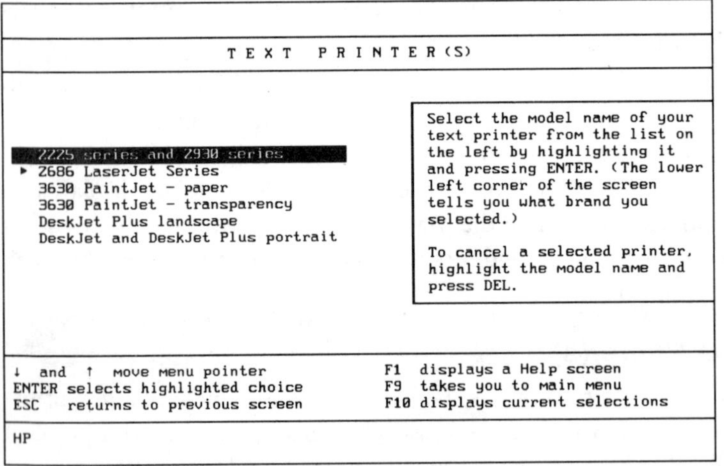

Figure 1.3b. Printer Model Selection Screen.

Selecting a Graphics Printer

Once you finish selecting the text printer(s), 1-2-3 will ask if you want to print graphs and if you have a graphics printer. Choose Yes to include a graphics printer in your driver set. 1-2-3 will display a list of manufacturers to select from, followed by a list of specific models. This process is identical to that used for selecting a text printer. (If you are using an HP laser printer, you must distinguish between the original LaserJet, and the LaserJet+/LaserJet Series II models. The original LaserJet does not have enough memory to print full page graphics at the highest possible resolution.) When you're done choosing a graphics printer, 1-2-3 will ask if you want to select another one. Either repeat the process for a second graphics printer, or select No to complete the next phase of the installation routine.

Naming Your Driver Set

After you have completed the selection of a second graphics printer (or after you select No at any point during the graphics printer selection process), 1-2-3 will ask whether you want to name your driver set (see Figure 1.4a).

If you select No, 1-2-3 automatically assigns the name 123.SET to the file containing your equipment specifications. In fact, in order to start 1-2-3 at all, Lotus must be able to find a driver file named 123.SET. You can, however, change the file name (not the extension—it must be .SET) by selecting Yes. If you do so, 1-2-3 will display the screen shown in Figure 1.4b.

At the bottom of the screen, you will see the default name, "123." You can modify or overwrite the name and substitute one of your own if you choose.

Why would you want to change the name of the driver set? If you're performing a first-time installation, you probably won't. Later, however, you might want to use other special equipment. Perhaps you want a dot-matrix printer for draft, and a laser printer for final output. Occasionally, however, you want to use an ink jet printer for graphs. You could create an additional driver set using the ink jet printer, and call it "inkjet." Substitute inkjet for the default name 123, and

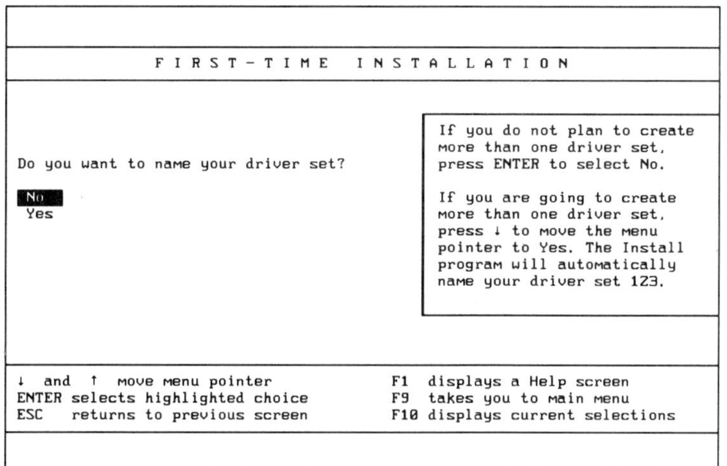

Figure 1.4a.
Driver Naming Option.

```
                    S A V I N G   C H A N G E S

Give your driver set a name of no more than eight characters.  Do not type
an extension: the Install program adds the extension .SET automatically.
You can specify a path if you want to save your driver set in a different
directory.  The name of the driver set itself should not contain:

                  [ ] ; , . / ? * : " + = - < > \ |

If you want to use the name displayed in the highlight, just press ENTER.
To use another name, type the name you want.  The name in the highlight will
disappear as soon as you start typing.  If you use a name other than 123,
you will have to type that name whenever you start 1-2-3.

Press ENTER or type a new name for your driver set

123

─────────────────────── Press ENTER to continue ───────────────────────
```

Figure 1.4b
Driver Naming Screen.

1-2-3 will automatically add the .SET extension, the driver file will be named INKJET.SET.

Then, whenever you wish to run 1-2-3 with the inkjet driver set, you would start 1-2-3 by typing `123 inkjet` at the command line, rather than simply `123`.

As another example, perhaps you normally wish to display text in VGA 80 x 25 mode. For certain budget worksheets, however, you want to display more rows. You could create a second driver set called "50lines," which includes the VGA 80 x 50 driver. You would start 1-2-3 from the command line by typing: `123 50lines`.

Completing the Installation Process

After you have specified a filename for the driver set, Lotus will save your equipment selections on disk. By following the prompts you will arrive at the exit screen. Select Yes to return to the DOS prompt (or to the Access System). Selecting No will bring you back to the Main Menu of the Install program.

To confirm that you have indeed selected the correct equipment options, you may review your choices before you exit by pressing the F10 key. 1-2-3 will display as shown in Figure 1.5.

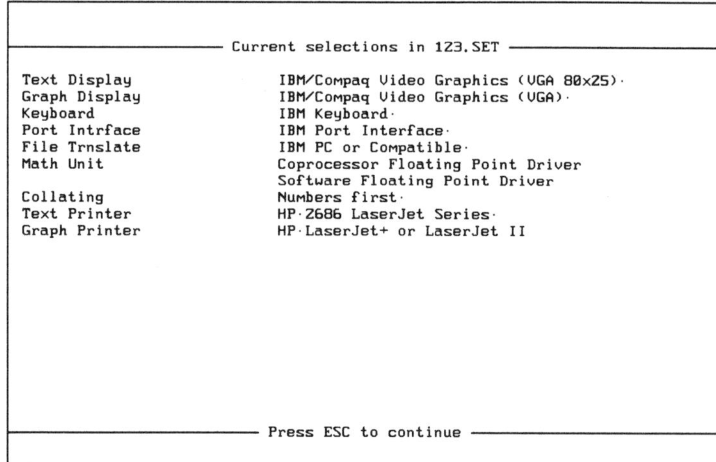

Figure 1.5.
Current options, displayed by pressing the F10 key.

CHANGING YOUR DRIVER SET/ADDING A DRIVER SET

If you acquire a new piece of equipment, you'll probably want to modify your current driver set (123.SET) or create a new one. To do so, run the Install program and choose the option, "Change Selected Equipment" from the Main Menu. Repeat the procedures described above to account for your new monitor and/or printer. You can either overwrite your existing driver set by retaining the name 123.SET, or, if you want to create an additional driver set, enter another name. If you do create an additional driver set, you can access it by referencing the driver set name when you start 1-2-3 (by typing 123 inkjet at the DOS prompt, see above).

ADVANCED OPTIONS

Use the "Advanced Options" selection on the Main Menu of Install if you need to modify driver sets other than the current set; if you wish to make changes to certain drivers that you cannot make through the Install menus themselves; or, if you have new equipment with its own driver files (.DRV) and you wish to add these new drivers to the 1-2-3 driver library. Advanced Options offers five choices (see Figure 1.6a).

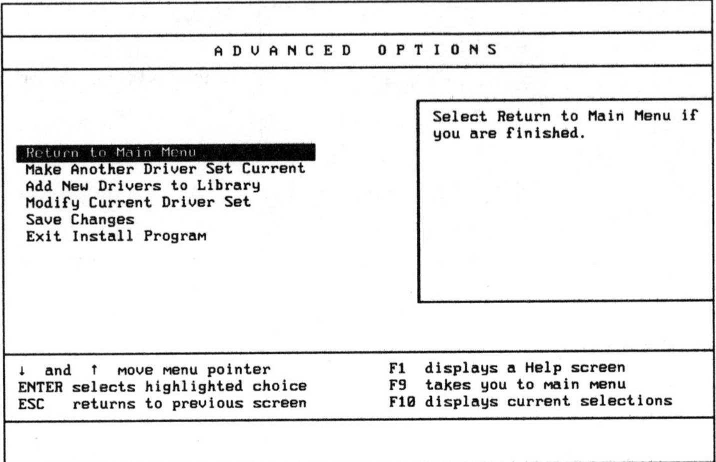

Figure 1.6a. Advanced Options Menu.

```
To change a driver, highlight the driver type and press ENTER.  Only drivers
that you can change appear.  If you don't know how to combine Text and
Graph Display drivers, use the Change Selected Equipment, main menu option.

Return to menu             Leave driver list
Text Display               IBM/Compaq Video Graphics (VGA 80x25)·
Graph Display              IBM/Compaq Video Graphics (VGA)·
Port Intrface              IBM Port Interface·
Math Unit                  Coprocessor Floating Point Driver
                           Software Floating Point Driver
Collating                  Numbers first·
Text Printer               HP·2686 LaserJet Series·
Graph Printer              HP·LaserJet+ or LaserJet II
```

Figure 1.6b. Current driver set selections.

Modifying Driver Sets

The "Modify Current Driver Set" option lets you specify text and graphics driver combinations that are not available through the Install Main Menu. (The drivers that you select, however, must be compatible; 1-2-3 warns that not all text and graphics display drivers will work together.)

In order to modify an alternative driver set on disk, you must first make that set current. Select "Make Another Driver Set Current," and 1-2-3 will prompt you for the name of the driver you wish to modify. Do not type in the .SET extension. Now, select the "Modify Current Driver Set" option. 1-2-3 will display the settings (now current) of the driver you requested.

Highlight the option that you wish to modify (e.g., Text Display or Graph Display, etc.) and press ENTER. 1-2-3 will then display a list of alternative selections. Highlight your choice and press ENTER. Make other changes to the Current Options display as necessary. When you are done changing equipment specifications, press ESC, and then choose "Save Changes." 1-2-3 will prompt you to name the new driver set. Press ENTER to accept the current name, and thus update the driver set. You can also create another driver set by typing in a different name and pressing ENTER. Either way, 1-2-3 will save the changes.

Adding New Drivers to Library

1-2-3 has special provisions for adding new drivers to 1-2-3's "driver library" (named SINGLE.LBR). The library contains driver files for the most commonly used equipment. Some equipment, such as high-resolution monitors and "brand X" printers, for example, may have their own special 1-2-3 drivers. A valid 1-2-3 driver must have the extension .DRV. To add the new driver to your library, first copy the new driver into your Install program directory. Then, to incorporate your new driver into Install's selection lists, choose "Add New Drivers to Library." 1-2-3 will copy the new driver to the appropriate directory or disk. You will then be able to select the driver through the normal installation routine and use your special equipment with 1-2-3.

This completes the discussion of 1-2-3's installation options. At this point you are ready to begin using the program. You can continue with the next chapter, which summarizes the new features in Release 2.2 or skip to Chapter 3 for an introduction to spreadsheets.

The New Features in Release 2.2

If you're an experienced 1-2-3 user, read this chapter to learn about the new features and enhancements contained in Release 2.2. The way the new Release 2.2 features operate is not always obvious. Thus, to avoid potential problems, and to get the most out of the enhancements and improvements in Release 2.2, we strongly suggest that you experiment with each of the features described in this chapter before you apply them to your existing worksheets.

GLOBAL DEFAULTS

Release 2.2 offers several new options for global default settings; while individually they may seem like small enhancements, together they give you a significantly greater ability to customize your 1-2-3 environment. As with previous 1-2-3 releases, you can make changes to your global settings effective permanently or for the current session only. To use your setting changes temporarily, select Quit from the /Worksheet Global Default menu after you make your selection. This avoids saving the changes to the .CFG file on disk. To change your global defaults permanently, select Update from the /Worksheet Global Default menu; the new settings will be saved in your configuration file. The new Global Default settings include:

Display labels in cells that evaluate to zero. You can now display a label of your choosing in cells with zero values rather than simply suppressing the display of zeros. You could, for example, display the words "none," "not applicable," "N/A," or "Nil" instead of zero. This feature can be very useful in applications where zeros are annoying or meaningless. To designate what text you want displayed, select /Worksheet Global Zero Label; type in a maximum of 240 characters. If you don't specify an alignment prefix, 1-2-3 will right justify the text within the cell.

Control the autoexec macro. You now have a choice of whether or not 1-2-3 will automatically run an autoexecuting macro (named \0) when you retrieve a file. As shipped, the program will run the autoexecute macro. If you don't want to run the autoexecute macro, select /Worksheet Global Default Autoexec No. This is useful when you're trying to fix a bug in an autoexec macro that is preventing your worksheet from loading. If you turn off the autoexec option, you can load the worksheet and edit the macro. It is also useful if you wish to load a file simply for quick reference or to update its linked-cell references.

Silence your computer. If you don't like having 1-2-3 beep at you each time an error occurs, select /Worksheet Global Default Other Beep No.

Select automatic add-in control. 1-2-3 has built an add-in manager into the program. No longer do you have to use a separate add-in manager for each add-in. You can instruct 1-2-3 to automatically attach up to eight add-in programs with the /Worksheet Global Default Other Add-In Set command. When you choose the Set option, 1-2-3 displays a menu that prompts you to assign a number to the add-in program. This is used to specify the order for loading the add-ins. Once you've indicated a number, 1-2-3 will display a list of all add-ins (*.ADN files) that you have installed on disk. Select the desired add-in, press ENTER; then, if you wish, you can specify an ALT-key combination to invoke the program. You may also elect to auto-invoke one of your add-ins. (See the Reference Section under /Add-In for more information.)

Change the display of negative numbers. Release 2.2 allows you to display negative numbers in two ways: enclosed in parentheses or preceded by a minus sign (no parentheses). Select /Worksheet Global Default Other International Negative and you will be given the options Parentheses or Sign. Note that your choice only affects numbers in ranges that have been formatted with the currency or comma (,) options.

Display the worksheet file name. You can now have 1-2-3 display the current worksheet filename in the lower-left corner of the screen instead of the time and

Place
First Class
Postage
Here
Post Office
Will Not
Deliver
Without Postage

Brady Books
One Gulf+Western Plaza
New York, NY 10023

date indicator. Select /Worksheet Global Default Other Clock Filename to specify a filename indicator. (The date and time will still appear in files that are as yet unnamed.) You can revert to the time/date display by selecting the Clock option; on the same menu you can also clear the indicator altogether with the None option .

Enable or disable Undo. The new Undo feature defaults to enabled. You can conserve memory by using /Worksheet Global Default Other Undo Disable. (See below for an in-depth discussion of the Undo feature.)

WORKSHEET FEATURES

In addition to the new global default options, Release 2.2 provides a number of new worksheet features and functions; perhaps the most significant addition is the Undo feature.

Undo

The new Undo feature allows you to "undo" your last command and restore your worksheet to its prior state. For example, if you erase a particular range by mistake or, even a whole worksheet, you can recover your work with the UNDO key (ALT-F4).

The same holds for formatting commands. Suppose you had painstakingly formatted a large range with a variety of percentage and currency formats, and later you accidentally reset the range to General. Pressing UNDO immediately afterward would restore your original format selections.

You can even salvage mistakes made with the /Copy and /Move commands, where you may have overwritten the contents and formatting of the target cell or range. You might copy the value 10 formatted for percentage, one decimal place from cell A21 to cell B24; cell B24 contained the number 456, formatted as currency, no decimal places. If you press the UNDO (ALT-F4) key, the original value in the target cell, 456, is redisplayed in cell B24, along with its original formatting—currency, no decimal places.

Had you used the /Move command in the above example, the formatting of the source cell (A21) would have been changed to General, and B24 would have adopted the formatting of A21 (percentage, one decimal place). Pressing UNDO (before keying in anything else) will restore the original values of the source and target cells, as well as their formats. This applies to ranges as well as individual cells.

If you want to undo your last Undo command, press ALT-F4 again; provided that you have not entered any data or commands in between, the worksheet will be restored to its state prior to the first Undo command. This feature is extremely useful for comparing two different values or results during "what-if" analysis by showing what if cell A12 had value X, and what if it had value Y. The UNDO key can even be used to undo a /File Retrieve command; thus you can instantly move between one file and another and compare them. Be aware, though, that 1-2-3 only provides one level of backup; once you invoke the main menu to issue another command, you cannot undo *any* previous command (including Undo itself).

When You Can't Use Undo

To better understand how the Undo command operates, and how much you can actually rely on it, you must know how 1-2-3 backs up your worksheet. Each time you enter data into a cell, or you press the slash (/) key to invoke a menu, the TABLE (F8) key, or the CALC (F9) key, 1-2-3 "takes a picture" of your worksheet in memory in a special area called the "Undo buffer" (when Undo is enabled, of course). Once you update the picture, the previous version is gone for good. If you press ESC after pressing the slash key, you cannot go back and restore the worksheet to its state prior to your last command. This is because 1-2-3 will have just made a copy of your worksheet as you pressed the slash (/) key and will have overwritten the previous copy in memory.

Also, once a worksheet is saved to disk, the previous version of that worksheet is overwritten. Undo cannot restore your previous disk version. You must be sure to keep backup copies of important worksheets. In fact, Undo will not "un-write" *any* file that has been written to disk. Therefore, the /File Save and /File Xtract commands, which write current data to disk cannot be undone. Undo also does not work with the new Add-In commands, the System command, or any of the PrintGraph commands.

In addition, you cannot undo actions initiated with the following keys:

BACKSPACE

ENTER

DEL

INS

ESC

CTRL-BREAK

Any function key other than F8 or F9

Any function key combination (e.g., ALT-F2, which invokes the macro STEP mode).

Finally, using Undo with macros has some unforeseen effects, because Undo treats macros as if they were single commands. If you use Undo with a macro that alters your worksheet data or settings, it will restore the worksheet to its condition prior to the execution of the entire macro, not to the state induced by the macro's last command. For example, if you executed a macro that successively copied columns of numbers and pressed Undo when the macro was finished, you would not simply restore the last column to its condition prior to running the macro. Rather, you would restore the data in *all* columns (as well as all worksheet settings).

Enabling/Disabling Undo—Memory Constraints

As shipped, Release 2.2's Undo feature is enabled; it automatically makes a temporary backup copy of your worksheet in memory according to the rules described above, and the UNDO indicator is on (at the bottom of your screen, slightly to the left of the center). The price for this protection can be approximately half of the conventional memory that is available on your system after 1-2-3 is loaded. If you have expanded memory (above 640K), 1-2-3 will attempt to place the entire Undo buffer there. (It will be one-half the size of the total memory available, conventional plus expanded.) If it can't do so, either because you don't enough expanded memory or because you have other programs operating in higher memory, 1-2-3 will place as much of the buffer in expanded memory as it can, and place the rest in conventional memory.

The consequence of giving up half of your memory is that you may not be able to run very large worksheets and Undo at the same time. If you run into this problem, you have two choices. One is to Disable Undo by selecting /Worksheet Global Default Other Undo Disable. You can leave Undo disabled just for the remaining 1-2-3 session by quitting from the /Worksheet Global Default menu, without updating your 123.CFG file. In this case, Undo will be enabled the next time you load 1-2-3. You can also make disable the default setting by selecting Update. When you select Update, Undo will be disabled each time you load 1-2-3 until you again select /Global Default Other Undo Enable. Remember, if you change your Undo global default setting in between commands, the Undo buffer is immediately cleared. Even if you change your mind and re-enable the Undo function, you will not be able to restore the worksheet to its former state.

A second option is to simply keep going until 1-2-3 runs out of space for the Undo buffer, at which point it will abandon the buffer in favor of your worksheet. If you try to use Undo at that point, 1-2-3 will display the prompt:

```
You will not be able to undo this action—do you wish
to proceed? (Y/N)
```

In other words, 1-2-3 will not hamper your efforts to build the largest possible worksheet that your system can handle. But you may lose Undo during the process.

NOTE If 1-2-3 has suspended your current operation to announce that you don't haveve enough memory to use Undo, you can either select N when prompted whether you wish to proceed, or press CTRL-BREAK. You can then decide whether you want to pare down your worksheet or take your chances by going without a backup in memory.

Setting Column Widths

In previous releases of 1-2-3, you had to change column widths one column at a time. With Release 2.2, you can set the column width for a range of columns using the new /Worksheet Column Range command. When you select /Worksheet Column Range you are given two options: Set-Width and Reset-Width. You can set column widths from 1 to 240 characters. The Reset-Width option returns the columns in the specified range to their default setting.

Linking Worksheets

With earlier versions of 1-2-3, you could use data from files on disk in the current worksheet by means of the /File Combine command. As a means of copying ranges from one worksheet into another, /File Combine is sufficient. But for updating active data or "daisy chaining" a series of worksheets together, it is cumbersome and slow. With Release 2.2, you can create a link between your current worksheet and another worksheet on disk. You can reference a *source* cell in the worksheet on disk in a *target* cell in the current worksheet. (To link them the other way around you must go to the cell that you intend to use as your target—i.e, in another worksheet—and reference the cell in your current worksheet as its source.) In the future, whenever the worksheet containing the target cell is retrieved, or whenever the new /File Admin Link-Refresh command is executed, the target cell is updated. You can link only single cells between files. You cannot link a range in one worksheet, for example, to a range in another; you must explicitly reference each individual cell.

To create a link from one cell to another, all you have to do is reference the file containing the source cell in angle brackets <<>>, followed by the address of the source cell. For example, let's say that your current worksheet is called CASHFLOW.WK1, and it uses the totals from another file on disk called REVENUE.WK1. To reference cell A12 from REVENUE.WK1 in cell C12 of CASHFLOW, you would move the cell pointer to C12, then enter the formula: +<<REVENUE>>A12.

If the files are not in the same directory as your target file, you will have to specify its full path name, as in +<<D:\BUDGET\REVENUE>>C12 or +<<B:\EXPENSE>>E2. If you reference a non-existent file, 1-2-3 will display the message "File does not exist" in the lower left-hand corner of the screen, and a flashing error message in the upper right-hand corner. Press ESC to continue, and either enter the correct name or create the missing file.

NOTE You cannot reference more than one file in the same cell. For example, +<<REVENUE>>C12+<<EXPENSE>>C12 is an invalid formula. To obtain the sum of cell C12 from the two files, you would have to reference each of them in separate cells of the current worksheet, and then add the two cells together.

Limitations for Floppy Users

You can reference as many files as you wish in the current worksheet, although the more links you create, the slower the file will load into memory when you next retrieve it. If you are using a floppy system and you reference multiple files, be especially patient since 1-2-3 will have to read each file one by one. Also, with a floppy system you must make sure that all of the source files are on the same floppy; otherwise, when you retrieve the file, 1-2-3 will report an error for any cell referencing the file(s) that cannot be found.

Refreshing Links

One of the beauties of the new linking system is that you can instantly update linked worksheets without having to physically transfer the data to target areas, as was required with earlier releases. The new command, /File Admin Link-Refresh, lets you automatically update all formulas that reference cells in source worksheets on disk. Of course, if you haven't updated your data in the source worksheets, your results may be incorrect; be sure to keep track of what worksheets require updating, so that a series of linked worksheets will produce the correct results.

NOTE Let's say you have three worksheets, and worksheet A depends on worksheet B, and worksheet B depends on worksheet C. If you modify worksheet C and it has a material effect on worksheet B, you must load, recalc, and resave worksheet B before loading worksheet A. Otherwise, the results reported in Worksheet A may be incorrect.

Listing Linked Files

To help you keep track of your source and target worksheets, Release 2.2 provides a new file listing facility. By selecting /File List Linked, the source files associated with the current worksheet will be displayed on your screen, as shown in Figure 2.1.

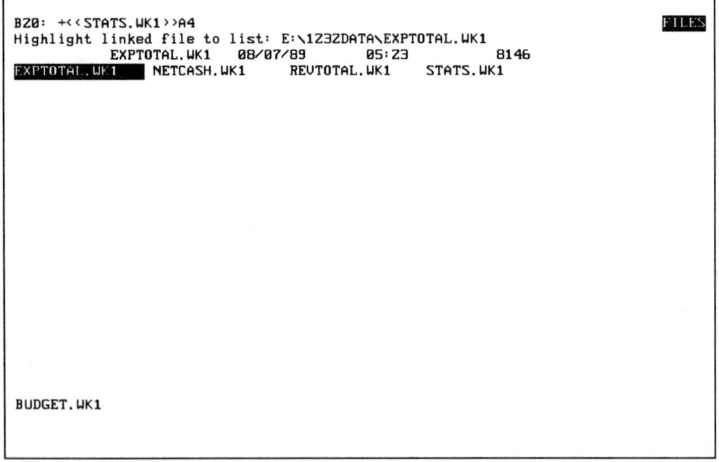

Figure 2.1
Source files.

The display is a bit confusing, because the file information seems redundant—when each linked file is highlighted, it is displayed in three places. The list of linked files actually begins on the fourth line of the screen. When you highlight a file in this area by using the cursor keys, the full drive and path of the file will be displayed on the second line of the screen (and the filename is shown in a different color or intensity, depending on your monitor). The file directory listing is displayed on the third line, including the date and time of creation and its size in bytes. To list another file, highlight it with the cursor.

The order in which linked files are listed will depend on the cell in which the pointer is positioned when the /File Linked List command is issued. The file referenced in the current cell will be the first file listed on the screen. Press ESC to return to the /File menu.

Recalculating Formulas

Release 2.2 uses minimal (also called "optimal") recalculation to streamline the processing of formulas. This means that it recalculates only those cells that have been altered since the last recalculation. Cells that depend on the altered cells are also recalculated. Minimal recalc is activated when /Worksheet Global Recalculation is set for Natural order (rather than Columnwise or Rowwise); none of the other recalculation mode options use the minimal recalc technique.

Be aware that 1-2-3 *always* recalculates cells that contain certain @functions, as well as their dependent cells, even if the recalculation mode is set for Natural. This is because the results generated by these @functions can (and often will) change even though various worksheet values themselves have not been altered. These include @functions that provide cell and range attribute information, or time and date values, or @functions that convert values to strings and vice versa, and @ functions that test for add-in @functions.

@@

@CELL

@CELL POINTER

@DATEVALUE

@ISAFF

@ISAPP

@NOW

@RAND

@STRING

@TIMEVALUE

@VALUE

Add-in @functions

Using Search and Replace

Release 2.2 allows you to search and replace text, much like a word processor. This can be extremely helpful when you need to find a record in a database table, change a commonly used label in a large worksheet, or find a cell linked to a particular worksheet. For example, you could instantly locate a record for the ABC Company by using the Search command, rather than sorting the database or scrolling through it. If ABC Company later changed its name to XYZ Corp, with a few keystrokes you could use the Replace function and change all instances of ABC Company to XYZ Corp. with just a few keystrokes. Here's how the search and replace function works.

1. Select /Range Search and specify the range that you wish to search. (Enter an address or an existing range name for the range.)
2. 1-2-3 will ask you to type in the string you want to search for. Type in the string (1-2-3 will only search for numbers if they are part of string, as in JAN89). Remember, too, that the Search function is *not* case-sensitive.
3. 1-2-3 offers you the choice of searching for the string in Formulas, Labels, or in Both. Use formulas if you are looking for a particular formula or range name or file reference, such as TOTAL in @IF(TOTAL>1,J11,0). If you only want to look for the word in a label, select Labels. Select Both to find all occurences of the string.
4. Next, 1-2-3 will display a menu with two options, Find and Replace. Find moves the cell pointer to the first occurrence of the string; from there you can move to the Next occurrence of the string, or Quit and return to READY mode.

   Replace first asks you to specify a replacement string for the search (or Find) string. Replace then moves the cell pointer to the first occurrence of the search string. You can Replace the current cell with the designated replacement string, replace All occurrences of the string with the replacement string, or Skip the replacement of the current cell and move on to the Next occurence. Quit ends the Search and Replace process.
5. When 1-2-3 reaches the last occurrence of the search string, selecting Next from the menu will display the error message: `String not found.` Press ESC to return to READY mode.

GRAPH COMMANDS

Release 2.2 offers a number of subtle improvements to 1-2-3's graphic output, especially bar graphs. First, on color monitors, 1-2-3 now *outlines* the bars in the bar graph display for clearer viewing. In monochrome displays, adjacent hatch patterns do not run together and are clearly distinguishable; default hatch patterns are automatically accepted on a dark to light scale. Also, grid lines no longer pass through the bars (as though they were superimposed). Finally, now there is air between the graph frame and the first and last bars in a bar chart so they they no longer collide with the graph boundary. On all graphs, long X-axis labels are staggered instead of overlapping, and the Y-axis tic marks are placed within the graph frame (rather than jutting out from it). Long legends wrap onto two lines, for improved appearance.

In addition to the built-in improvements, Release 2.2 makes it easier to create and format graphs through a series of new commands described below.

One-Step Graph Data Range Selection

In earlier versions, each data range (X, A-F) had to be selected individually. Release 2.2's new /Graph Group function allows you to specify all graph data ranges with one command (assuming they are properly set up). You can arrange your data in rows or columns, with the X-axis labels first, followed by the A-F data ranges. All data columns and rows must be contiguous because 1-2-3 interprets any blank column or row as a range with zero values. Once the worksheet is properly set up (see Figure 2.2a), use the following procedure:

1. Choose /Graph Group and specify the entire graph data range that you wish to graph. In the case of our example, it would be B4..G7.
2. Next specify whether the data range is to be read columnwise or rowwise In our example, should 1-2-3 consider the X range to be B4..G7 (columnwise) or B4..G4 (rowwise)? Choose Rowwise since the graph range is intended to be interpreted in rows—the X-axis labels are lined up in row 4 and the corresponding data is located in rows 5 through 7 (see Figure 2.2b).
3. Select View to display the graph on your screen. Figure 2.2b shows the resulting graph.

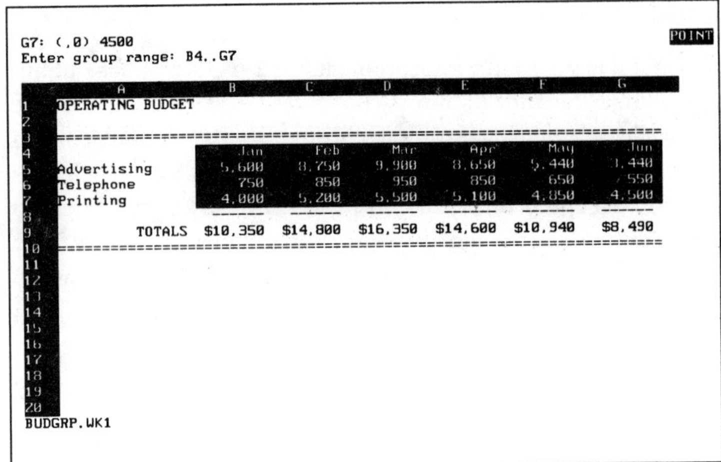

Figure 2.2a
Data ranges organized for group graphing.

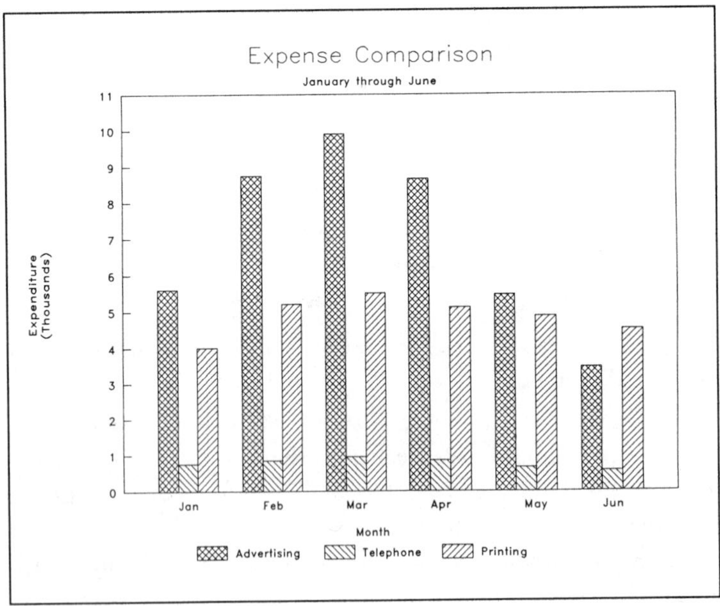

Figure 2.2b
Graph ranges correctly chosen with rowwise option.

One-Step Graph Data Labels

Data labels are most often used to specify the precise numerical values in a graph. (You can also specify text labels if you like.) When actual values, rather than overall trends, are significant, data labels can lead viewers to quickly grasp the meaning of a graph. With Release 2.2, you can select data labels for your A-F data range with one command sequence, rather than specifying each one individually.

1. Select /Graph Options Data-Labels Group.
2. Specify the range that encompasses all of the data labels by name, by address, or by painting it. (In the example above, if we were to graph Expense Totals per month, it would be B9..G9.)
3. Specify whether to interpret the graph data range columnwise or rowwise.
4. Select the position where the labels are to appear: on the data points (Center), to the left of the data points (Left), to the right of the data points (Right), on top of the data points (Above), or underneath the data points (Below). (These positions will vary, depending on your graph type.)

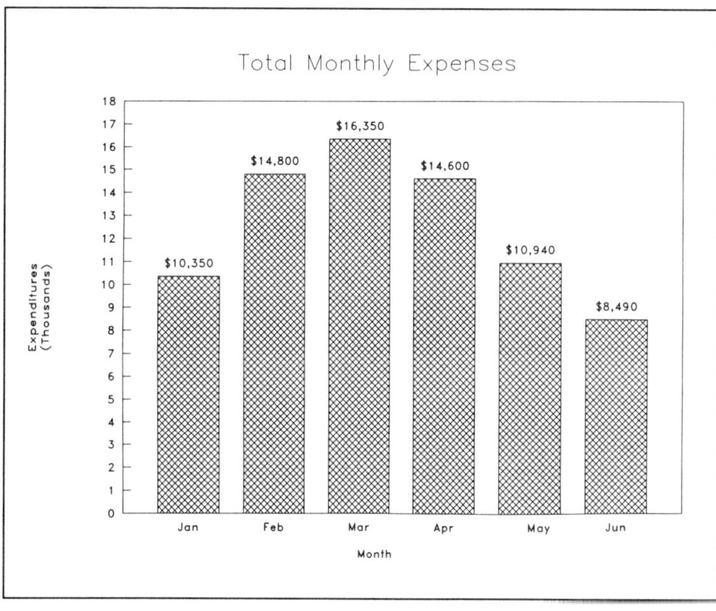

Figure 2.3
Graph using data labels.

One-Step Selection Graph Legends

With Release 2.2, you can specify legends for the entire graph with one command sequence. First, type in the legends you wish to use (in order) in a column or row. Select /Graph Options Legend Range, and specify the range address (or paint it). 1-2-3 will assign the labels to the appropriate data ranges.

New Graph Options for Clearing Settings

Release 2.2 allows you to clear the current graph data ranges without clearing the remaining graph settings with the /Graph Reset Ranges command. Conversely, you can also clear all graph settings without clearing data ranges with the /Graph Reset Options command.

New Graph Name Table

A handy new feature in Release 2.2 is the ability to create a list of named graphs. A graph name table (similar to the range name table) is created with the /Graph Name Table command. 1-2-3 simply prompts you for the range in which to display the table. The table will occupy three columns; it displays the graph name, the graph type, and the first title line of the graph. Be sure that you allow enough space in your worksheet for the table, as it will overwrite existing data. Figure 2.4 shows a sample Graph Name Table.

FILE COMMANDS

Several new additions and capabilities have been added to 1-2-3's repertoire of file commands.

Backup Files

Previously, when you saved a file that already existed on disk (using /File Save), 1-2-3 would ask you if you wanted to replace it. Release 2.2 adds a new option to the /File Save menu: Backup. When you choose Backup, 1-2-3 not only saves the updated version of the worksheet with the .WK1 extension, but it creates a copy of the original file adding a .BAK extension. If, for any reason, you find that you need that .BAK file (i.e., you overwrote the original in error), you can always rename the .BAK file to a .WK1 file.

To list your backup files within 1-2-3, select /File List Other, and then press ESC. Edit the drive and path prompt so it includes the *.BAK file specification, as in `C:\123data\*.BAK` and all .BAK files in the specified directory will be displayed.

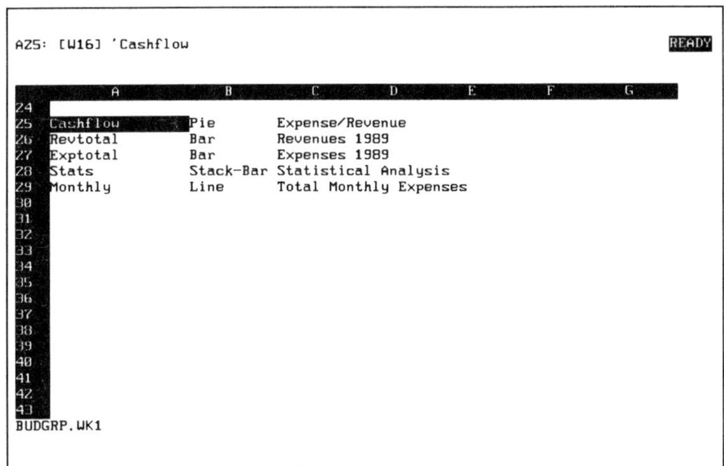

Figure 2.4
Sample graph name table.

File Tables

Release 2.2 allows you to create a comprehensive listing or "table" of all your files in a particular data directory. To create a file table:

1. Select /File Admin Table, and 1-2-3 will prompt you for the directory for which you want a listing. Press Enter to accept the current directory, or edit the current directory name as appropriate.
2. Specify a range in which to put the file table. The table will occupy four columns, so make sure you have enough vertical and horizontal space; the table will overwrite any existing data.
3. Select the type of file you want to list. You can choose from Worksheet (.WKS, .WK1), Print (.PRN and ENC—encoded), Graph (.PIC), Other (any file specification you wish, e.g., *.BAK, *.adn, etc.), and Linked (files that are linked to the current worksheet.)

The resulting table will show the filename and extension, the date and time each file was last modified, and the size in bytes.

Remember, if you don't format the date and time columns, the listings will appear as serial data and time numbers (see Figure 2.5a). Once formatted, the table will appear in the familiar date and time display, as in Figure 2.5b.

Automatic File Retrieve

With Release 2.2, you can automatically retrieve a file when you load the program by specifying the file name at the command line. The file name must be

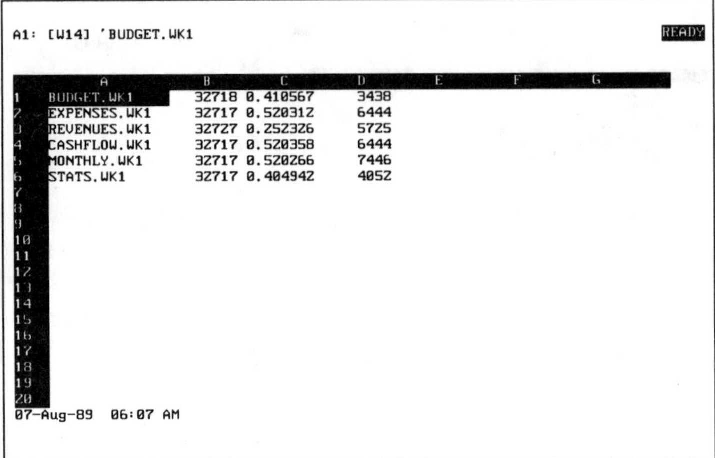

Figure 2.5a
File table listing without date and time formatting.

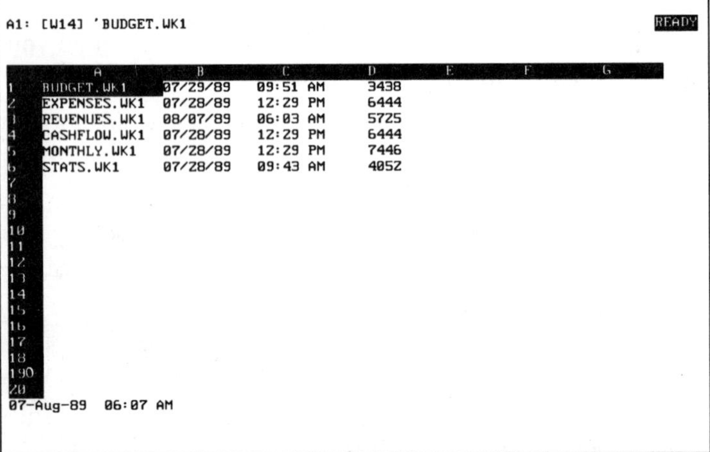

Figure 2.5b
File table listing with date in Format 4 (Long Intn'l) and time in Format 2 (HH:MM AM/PM).

preceded by the -w parameter. Typing `123 -wc:\123data\revenue` at the DOS prompt, for example, instructs 1-2-3 to retrieve the file named revenue in the directory 123data as soon as the main program has loaded. This is convenient when you know exactly which file you will be using. Also, if you are going to be using the same file for a number of sessions, you may wish to write a batch file to retrieve your worksheet automatically.

PRINTING

Allways

One of the most exciting aspects of Release 2.2 is that the spreadsheet publisher, Allways, is now built into the program. Allways allows you to use up to eight different fonts on a page, bold and underline text, add shading, print boxes around cells or ranges of cells, change column widths and row heights, include graphs on your worksheet printouts, and print in color if you have a printer or plotter capable of color output. Figures 2.6a and 2.6b display the dramatic difference between a worksheet printed with Allways and one printed with the standard 1-2-3 printing commands. With Allways, you can create elegant, professional looking documents that clearly convey your message.

NOTE Allways is strictly a program for printed output. If you need to modify your spreadsheet data (e.g., correct the spelling of a label, change a value of a cell, or the format of a cell), you must return to 1-2-3.

To do Allways justice requires a full chapter, but if you'd like to get started immediately, you can use the following crash course to explore Allways' basic features. (This assumes that you have installed and set up Allways for your hardware.) See Chapter 11 for details about the program.

1. Create or retrieve a worksheet.
2. Attach Allways by using the Add-In function from the main menu. Select Attach, highlight Allways, press ENTER, and then assign a function key combination, if you like, say ALT-F8.
3. Now invoke Allways by pressing the assigned key (e.g., ALT-F8). (If you chose No-Key instead of 8, you will need to select /Add-In Invoke, then highlight ALLWAYS.ADN and press ENTER to start the program manually.)
4. Press the slash (/) key to display the Allways main menu. Select items as you would with 1-2-3. Instead of displaying more than one level of submenus in the conventional Lotus-style menu format, Allways uses "pull-down" menus (see Figure 2.7) for certain commands. Use the cursor to highlight the desired options from the pull-down menus.

OPERATING BUDGET						
	Jan	Feb	Mar	Apr	May	Jun
Rent	3,500	3,500	3,500	3,500	3,500	3,500
Payroll	12,932	12,932	12,932	12,932	12,932	12,932
Advertising	5,600	8,750	9,900	8,650	5,440	3,440
Telephone	1,234	850	950	850	650	550
Courier	4,343	650	750	700	690	550
Leases	2,354	765	765	765	765	765
Printing	4,000	5,200	5,500	5,100	4,850	4,500
Office Supplies	250	350	350	350	300	250
TOTALS	$34,213	$32,997	$34,647	$32,847	$29,127	$26,487

Figure 2.6a
A document produced in 1-2-3 without Allways.

OPERATING BUDGET						
	Jan	Feb	Mar	Apr	May	Jun
Rent	3,500	3,500	3,500	3,500	3,500	3,500
Payroll	12,932	12,932	12,932	12,932	12,932	12,932
Advertising	5,600	8,750	9,900	8,650	5,440	3,440
Telephone	1,234	850	950	850	650	550
Courier	4,343	650	750	700	690	550
Leases	2,354	765	765	765	765	765
Printing	4,000	5,200	5,500	5,100	4,850	4,500
Office Supplies	250	350	350	350	300	250
TOTALS	$34,213	$32,997	$34,647	$32,847	$29,127	$26,487

Figure 2.6b
The same document in 2.6a after formatting with Allways.

The Allways main menu options include: Display, which changes the size and appearance of the worksheet on your screen; Format, which allows you to change the font in a cell or range, or to add underlining, shading, lines, or colors; Graph, which allows you add or remove a graph from the worksheet; and Layout, which controls the page size, margins, headers, and footers, and other page-related options.

5. You can apply Allways commands to your worksheet by selecting a command and then specifying a range, or by specifying a range first and then

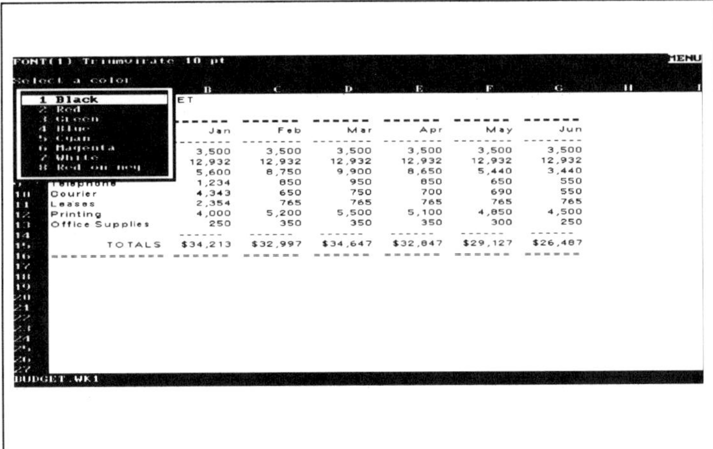

Figure 2.7
Sample "pull-down" menu.

choosing a command. For example, you might select the command Format and then Font. Allways will display a list of available typefaces and point sizes. (You can change the list of available fonts, as explained in Chapter 11). Once you select a typeface, Allways will prompt you for a range. Highlight the range or type in the range name or address, and then press ENTER. All text or numbers in that range will appear on screen in the selected typeface (provided that you have a graphics monitor, otherwise you will not be able to see the font changes and various formatting changes that will appear on your printed report).

Alternately, you might specify a range before you issue a command. Move the cell pointer to the upper left-hand corner of the range, anchor the pointer with a period, and then paint the range with the cursor key. When you have finished highlighting the range do *not* press ENTER; rather, press the slash key to invoke the menu, then select the command you wish to use. The command you choose will apply to the contents of all cells in the specified range.

6. To incorporate a graph, select the /Graph option, then choose Add. Allways will display a list of available graphs. (To print graphs with Allways, graphs must be saved *within* 1-2-3 first with the /Graph Save option. This will create a file on disk with the .PIC extension.) Once you select a graph from the list of .PIC files, Allways will prompt you for the range in which the graph is to appear. When you press ENTER after

identifying the range, Allways will display the specified graph—if you have a graphics monitor. (You can also define the range first, and then choose the Graph command. After you select the graph to be printed, Allways will simply redisplay the specified range.)

NOTE Be sure to define a large enough range to accommodate the graph, and to create a range with the proper proportions; Allways will fit the graph into whatever space is available, so you can potentially create graphs with peculiar proportions.

Whichever method you choose to incorporate a graph, you will find the /Graph option a powerful tool for combining text and graphs or simply printing graphs by themselves. You may even find yourself using PrintGraph less because of the built-in convenience of Allways.

7. To return to 1-2-3, either press ESC, press the ALT-Function Key combination you used to start Allways, or select /Quit from the Allways main menu.

This is but a brief sampling of Allways' capabilities; after your initial experimentation, we strongly recommend that you read Chapter 11 to learn about its full potential.

New 1-2-3 Print Features

Within 1-2-3 itself, you'll find several minor modifications to enhance worksheet printing. You can now incorporate the contents of a cell in headers and footers, for example, with the /Print [Printer File] Options Header or Footer option. Rather than retyping in text from a worksheet cell, type a backslash followed by the cell address, or the range name of that cell.

A new margin setting is also available, called None. By selecting /Print [Printer File] Options Margins None, you automatically set the left, top, and bottom margins to 0, and set the right margin to 240. This is useful when you have to print a worksheet to an ASCII text file because you can reduce the likelihood that lines will wrap.

MACROS

Release 2.2 provides several important new macro features and functions that make it easier than ever to create and use macros. These include a built-in Learn mode (incorporating the spreadsheet add-in, Learn), enhanced macro debugging, named macros, and, most importantly, an add-in Macro Manager that lets you store macros off the worksheet (in hyperspace).

Macro Recorder—Learn Mode

You can have Release 2.2 "watch" over your shoulder as you enter commands and data into the computer, and then store your keystrokes in an area of the worksheet that you designate as the "learn range." Once the macro keystrokes are stored in the learn range, you can name and run the macro any time you wish. To create a macro with the learn feature, use the following procedure:

1. Select /Worksheet Learn Range. Specify a *single* column range long enough to contain each keystroke in the macro (one stroke per cell).
2. Press the LEARN key (ALT-F5) to initiate the learn mode—the LEARN indicator will be displayed on the bottom of the screen.
3. Execute whatever series of keystrokes you wish to incorporate into the macro, then press ALT-F5 again to turn off the learn feature. Your keystrokes will be translated into 1-2-3's special macro language, one command per row in the learn range. (Don't assume, however, that your macros will be foolproof.)
4. Name the macro using the /Range Name Create command. (See below for new naming conventions.) Run it by pressing ALT-F3 and then selecting the assigned macro name; or initiate the macro with the "traditional" ALT + key combination if you assigned it a backslash-letter range name.

New Macro Naming Procedure

Rather than being limited to naming macros with one of the alphabetic characters, as in earlier releases, Release 2.2 allows you to name macros with words of your own choosing. Each macro name can be up to 15 characters in length. To activate a named macro, press the RUN key (ALT-F3). 1-2-3 will display a list of macro names. Highlight the desired name, or type in the name manually. When you press ENTER, the macro will be executed. (You can still run macros with the "traditional" ALT + key combination, provided that you assigned the macro a range name consisting of a backslash (\) followed by a single alphabetic character. (e.g., \a or \m to the macro.)

New Macro Commands

Release 2.2 offers eight new macro commands, four modified versions of existing commands, and three new macro key names. A capsule summary of each is provided below. (See the Macro Command Reference for a complete discussion of the proper use of each macro command.)

New Commands

{BORDERSOFF} Turns off the worksheet borders, (e.g., the column letter and row numbers); this is useful for controlling custom input and help screens. The borders will be suppressed until 1-2-3 encounters a {BORDERSON} command in the macro, or until it reaches the end of the macro.

{BORDERSON} Counters the {BORDERSOFF} command and turns the column letter and row numbers back on.

{BREAK} Brings you to READY mode; it produces the same effect as pressing CTRL-BREAK in the middle of 1-2-3's MENU mode. (Note that this does not discontinue the processing of the macro itself.)

{FRAMEOFF} Identical to {BORDERSOFF}.

{FRAMEON} Redisplays the worksheet frame after it has been turned off with {FRAMEOFF}.

{GRAPHON} Displays the current graph in full screen view during macro execution. {GRAPHON graphname} (e.g., followed by the name of a named graph) causes 1-2-3 to adopt the settings of that named graph, and to display the graph in full view. {GRAPHON graphname, nodisplay} will have 1-2-3 adopt the graph settings of the named graph without displaying it. In all cases when the {GRAPHON} command is used to display a graph, the graph remains on screen until 1-2-3 encounters a {GRAPHOFF} command, or a command that displays a menu or prompt in the control panel, or until the macro ends.

{GRAPHOFF} Switches from the graph display initiated by the {GRAPHON} command to the standard worksheet display.

{SYSTEM} Mimics the effects of the /System command. The argument for {SYSTEM} can be any DOS or batch command. Once the command is finished, control returns to 1-2-3. The system command is useful for allowing the user to format or backup a floppy disk from a 1-2-3 menu. It also adds the capabilities of batch file processing to your macros.

Modified Commands

{INDICATE} No longer limits the mode indicator text to 5 characters, thus allowing you to include custom indicator messages. For example, you could change the WAIT indicator to PROCESSING DATA, PLEASE WAIT. The indicator message can contain up to 240 characters.

{PANELOFF} Now includes a new argument, clear, which clears the control panel and status line before locking the control panel display. The combination of the {BORDERSOFF} command and {PANELOFF clear} allows you to create screens that appear totally independent of the 1-2-3 screen so that the user will not recognize that he or she is within the program.

{WINDOWSOFF} This command freezes the screen during macro execution to reduce the annoying "light show" and speeds up 1-2-3's execution because it doesn't have to regenerate the screen display each step. This command is especially useful, too, because it eliminates the appearance of the new setup sheets for graphs, printing, data queries, etc.

{WINDOWSON} This command returns the display to normal after a {WINDOWSOFF} command has been issued.

New Macro Key Names

{HELP} You can now give users access to Help screens that you have designed for a custom template or macro.

{U}, {D}, {L}, {R} These one-letter cursor movement keys are abbreviations of Up, Down, Left, and Right.

{WINDOW} This key name has the same effect as pressing F6 (Window key). You can use it to switch setting sheet displays on or off.

Macro Library Manager

In addition to Allways, Release 2.2 includes one other add-in program: the Macro Library Manager (also known as Hyperspace). This program (which is approximately 13K) allows you to load and store macros into a reserved portion of memory called a "library"; they are whisked away from the worksheet into conventional RAM. This special library file is given an .MLB extension. You can have up to 16,376 cells per library. The advantage of the library system is that you can use your macros with many different worksheets, rather than having to re-create or copy them every time you build a new worksheet. The library even lets you store data in memory, so that you can retrieve or create another worksheet file, and then transfer the data. Remember to use *range names* only in your libraries and not cell addresses. You can access any macro in Hyperspace with the ALT-F3 key.

To use the library manager:

1. Make sure that the Macro Library Manager is attached as an add-in. (Attach the file MACROMGR.ADN, and assign it a key if you like.)
2. Invoke the macro manager (via the Add-In menu or with your assigned key combination). Your menu options are as follows: Load a macro library into memory (Load); Save a worksheet range into a library (Save); transfer the macros in a macro library into the current worksheet so you can edit them (Edit); delete a macro library from memory (Remove); list the libraries used in the current worksheet (Name-List); or return to READY mode (Quit).

There are several details, rules, and cautions for using the Macro Library Manager to your best advantage; see the Reference Section for more information on the Macro Library Manager.

MISCELLANEOUS

Add-In Commands

As mentioned above, you no longer need to use the various add-in managers that are supplied with third-party 1-2-3 products. When you select /Add-In from the 1-2-3 main menu or press ALT-F10 (assuming no add-ins are assigned to the

F10 key), 1-2-3 will give you the choice of loading an add-in program (Attach); removing an add-in from memory (Detach); starting an add-in (Invoke), and removing all add-ins from memory (Clear). See the Reference Section for a complete discussion of the Add-In function.

Setting Sheets

Release 2.2 brings another valuable addition to 1-2-3 in the form of "setting sheets," that display your values and options selected for global defaults, graphs, data queries, and print jobs (see Figures 2.8a–2.8b). Setting sheets are critical in helping you to keep track of your current values for graph ranges, data queries, print ranges, global defaults, etc.

Setting sheets are automatically displayed when you first select a major command (i.e., /Graph, /Data Sort, /Data Query, etc). To redisplay the Worksheet, press F6. Press F6 again to view the setting sheet again. The setting sheets are automatically updated as you make changes through the menu system.

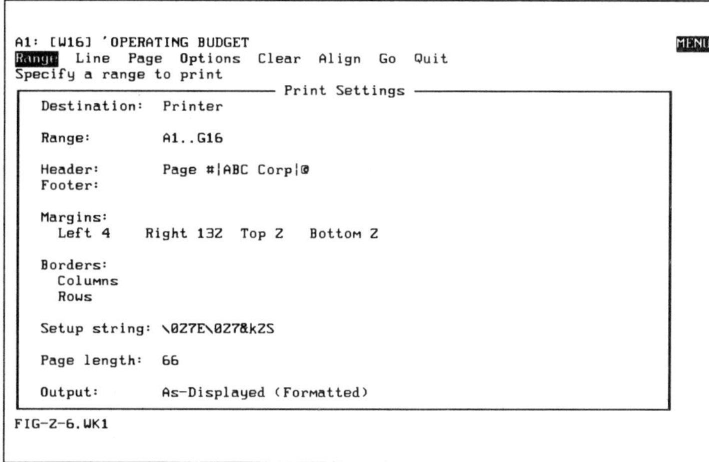

Figure 2.8a

Settings sheet for /Print Command.

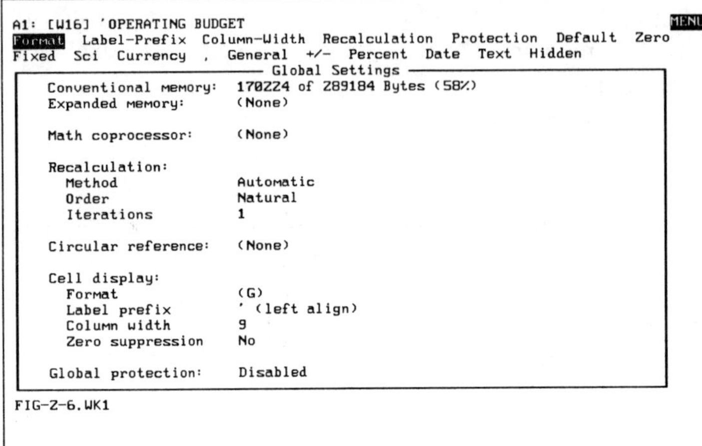

Figure 2.8b
Global Settings Sheet.

File Sharing

Release 2.2 can read files created with 1-2-3 Releases 1A, 2.0, and 2.01, and Release 3.0 (if you have used the translate utility to eliminate commands that Release 2.2 can't recognize.) Release 2.2 files can be read by Release 3.0 without any translation, and by Release 2.0 and 2.01 if the file has been converted with the translation utility.

At this point, you should have a general understanding of Release 2.2's new functions. We suggest that you experiment a bit with each feature, and turn to the Reference section as you need more detail. If you would like to see many of the features used in context, read Chapter 12 on building and using a 1-2-3 model.

Introduction to Spreadsheet Computing

The cornerstone of 1-2-3 is the spreadsheet. All of 1-2-3's many powerful capabilities—including its data management and graphics features—are added to enhance the power and usefulness of the spreadsheet.

CHAPTER OVERVIEW

This chapter describes the basic principles of the 1-2-3 spreadsheet in form and function. It begins with a description of the electronic spreadsheet, and then covers the primary elements of a 1-2-3 spreadsheet. Once the spreadsheet is defined, the chapter explains how to use the cursor and special key combinations to move around the spreadsheet space. The chapter concludes with a discussion of data entry rules and techniques.

If you're completely new to 1-2-3, or you've entered data in 1-2-3 but have never created a spreadsheet from scratch, you should read the chapter from beginning to end. Ideally, you'll turn on your computer, load 1-2-3, and work with the program and the book simultaneously.

ABOUT ELECTRONIC SPREADSHEETS

The traditional spreadsheet tool used by those who need to record numerical data is an accounting pad: a two-dimensional gridsheet that consists of columns running from top to bottom, and rows running horizontally from left to right. The grid is used to present a listing of values, as in a monthly budget, a balance sheet, or a sales report. Each unit in the grid contains a numerical entry, or a text label; each unit can be assigned a column *and* a row reference. The spreadsheet shown in Figure 3.1 should be familiar to just about everyone—it's a checkbook register. As you can see, the register is divided into eight columns. Each column contains a label at the top. Checks and deposits are recorded on individual lines, and the running balance is computed in the last column. The spreadsheet continues as long as you write checks.

RECORD ALL CHARGES OR CREDITS THAT AFFECT YOUR ACCOUNT

NUMBER	DATE	DESCRIPTION OF TRANSACTION	PAYMENT/DEBIT (-)	√ T	FEE (IF ANY) (-)	DEPOSIT/CREDIT (+)	BALANCE
							$ 5023 22
125	8/10	PAGEWORKS	$ 1000 –		$	$	
							4023 22
126	8/12	DONNA CHERNIN	808 21				
							3215 01
127	8/15	LEE F. BUSCH	722 –				
							2493 01
128	8/18	STAR MARKET	52 01				
							2441 00

Figure 3.1

A common spreadsheet; a checkbook register.

Like the accountant's pad, the *electronic spreadsheet* displayed on your computer screen also consists of columns and rows in which you can enter numbers and text by means of your keyboard. In addition to numbers and text, you can type in mathematical formulas that instruct the program to perform various calculations on your numbers, and that will automatically update the spreadsheet each time you add or change any numbers. (We'll discuss formulas in a later section.) In the case of the checkbook register, for example, each time you entered a check amount, the spreadsheet would automatically subtract the amount from the balance. Each time you entered a deposit amount, the spreadsheet would automatically add the amount to your balance.

The ability to include formulas gives the electronic spreadsheet its enormous power. Not only do you eliminate the need to carry out tedious manual calculations, you can also perform instant "what-if" scenarios and analyze your results.

Let's say you have created a monthly budget worksheet that includes anticipated revenues. If you want to find out the impact of decreasing overhead in January by 8 percent, all you have to do is multiply the overhead figure by .08, and the bottom line for each month will be calculated immediately. Imagine how much time it would take to recalculate the monthly profit or loss manually!

From these simple examples, you can see that electronic spreadsheets are valuable time savers. But the real power of spreadsheets extends well beyond basic "time saving"; as you'll discover later in this book, electronic spreadsheets are capable of analyses that are virtually impossible to do by hand. In the next sections we'll explore the basic components of an electronic spreadsheet, and describe how to enter numbers, text, and formulas. Note that from now on we will refer to electronic spreadsheets as "worksheets"; this is the standard terminology used in 1-2-3.

ANATOMY OF A 1-2-3 WORKSHEET

1-2-3's electronic worksheet consists of columns, identified (at the top of the screen) by capital letters, and rows (at the left of the screen), identified by numbers. Since your computer screen is limited in the number of columns and rows it can display at one time, you're limited in how much of the 1-2-3 worksheet you can see in a given instance. In Figure 3.2, for example, you can only see columns A through H, and rows 1 through 20. (In general, the display depends on the size and display capabilities of your monitor.) The worksheet could actually extend on the right from columns J and K, all the way through to column IV, which is the two hundred fifty-sixth column. (The columns after Z are labeled AA, AB, etc. the ones after AZ are called BA, BB, etc. the ones after BZ are called CA, CB, etc. and so forth until IV.) The worksheet could also extend downward to row 8,192. In order to view different parts of a 1-2-3 worksheet on your screen, you must move the worksheet left and right or up and down "behind" your screen display window.

While you could theoretically create a worksheet that consisted of 256 columns by 8,192 rows, in practice a worksheet that size would require an enormous amount of memory, and in all probability considerably more than you have in your computer. It also would be quite unwieldy and disorienting to move around in. Lotus has provided this extended worksheet size capability so that you can develop the largest possible worksheet you need to accomplish your task.

As you examine the top-left corner of a worksheet on your screen, you will notice several distinct areas, as in the screen shown in Figure 3.2.

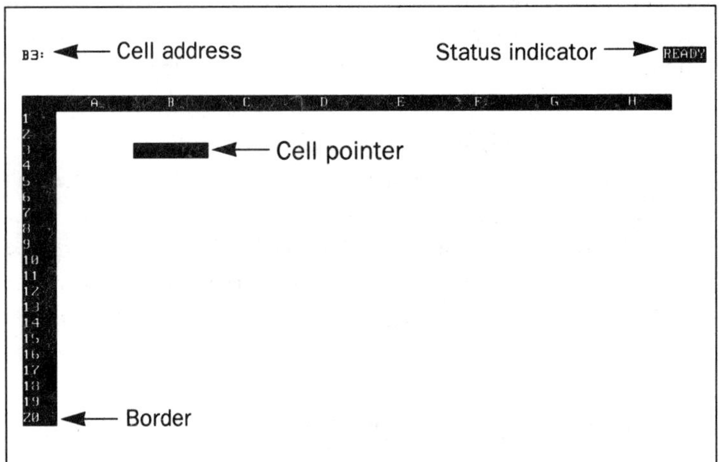

Figure 3.2
A 1-2-3 worksheet, ready for data.

The Worksheet Borders The top and left side of the worksheet are defined by two borders. The alphabetic characters embedded in the top border designate individual columns, starting on the left with column A, and continuing (off the right side of the screen) to column IV. Numbers embedded in the left border indicate rows, starting at the top with row 1, and continuing (off the screen down the page) to row 8,192.

Worksheet Live Area Within the worksheet borders you will find the "live" area, where numbers, labels, and formulas are entered. Each number, label, or formula occupies one spreadsheet unit, referred to as a *cell.* Each cell marks the intersection of a column and row. A cell's *address* (location on the worksheet) consists of the column and row number, so that the address of the cell located at the intersection of column A and row 1 is A1. Similarly, the cell underneath cell A1 is A2, since it sits at the intersection of column A and row 2, and the cell to the immediate right of cell A1 is called B1. By looking at the column and row coordinates, you can immediately pinpoint a cell's location on the worksheet.

One cell in the live area will always be covered with a highlighted bar called the *cell pointer*. The cell pointer indicates the *current cell*, i.e., the cell in which you are currently performing an action such as entering data or formulas, editing data or formulas, and many other things.

The top-left corner of the screen always shows the address of the current highlighted cell, along with all the information about that cell, including its contents. In Figure 3.2, for example, you see the address "B3:". If you type a word or number into that cell and then press ENTER, you will see that cell's contents displayed on the top line, following the address indicator, A1. The address display is very useful when the cell pointer is not immediately adjacent to the right or top border. In fact, when the cell pointer is in the middle of the screen or lower right-hand portion of the screen, it is often quite difficult to determine the cursor's row position.

To change the location of the cell pointer or to move to another cell in the worksheet (and make it your current cell), use the cursor movement keys. (In the following section on worksheet navigation, you will learn a variety of other means for moving the cell pointer.) As you move the pointer, the cell address indicator will change accordingly.

Status Indicator The Status indicator tells you 1-2-3's current operating mode. READY means you can enter data into a cell or call up a menu of command functions. (You do this by pressing the slash / key.) The word in the indicator box will change as your type of action changes. For instance, when you are working in 1-2-3's menus, you are in *menu mode* and the status indicator will display MENU; when you edit the contents of a cell, the indicator will change to EDIT; when you make an error the indicator will flash and change to ERROR; when the program is busy, the flashing indicator WAIT will appear; and so on.

Other Indicators Several other indicators are also used in the worksheet. If you are using the Undo feature, which allows you to restore the worksheet to its condition prior to your previous command, the UNDO indicator will be displayed at the bottom of the screen. If you turn on your Caps Lock key, the CAPS indicator will appear at the bottom right of the screen. Error messages are also displayed on the bottom line of the screen. Other indicators will be explained later in the book.

Clock/File Display You can choose to display the current date and time on the bottom left of the screen, or you can display the name of the worksheet file you are working on (if you have already named and saved the worksheet to disk). You can also select to have neither the date/time or the file name displayed.

Control Panel The three lines above the top border are referred to as the *control panel.* Each line has a specific purpose in the display. We have seen that line one contains the address and contents of the current cell as well as any special cell or column formatting information. The second line displays the characters you are typing in or editing at the time. Note that when you type in numbers the mode indicator changes to VALUE, and when you type in text, the mode indicator changes to LABEL. (We will discuss the rules for value and label entries below.)

Several other types of information appear within the control panel during 1-2-3 command operations. When you call up 1-2-3's main menu by pressing the slash (/) key, for example, the mode indicator changes to MENU and 1-2-3 displays the two-line main menu shown in Figure 3.3.

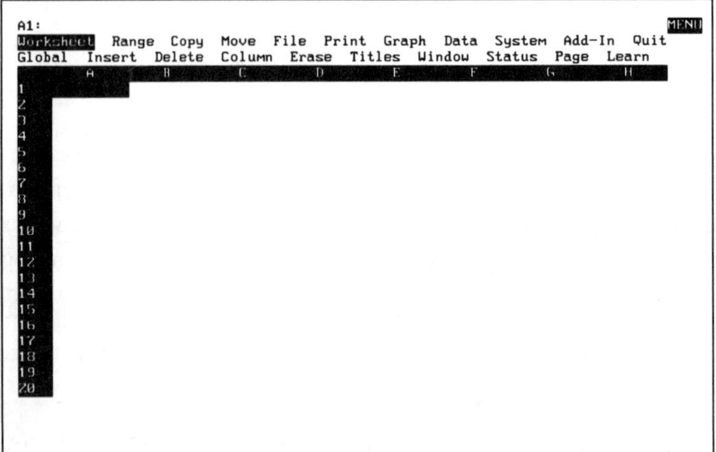

Figure 3.3
1-2-3 Main Menu.

The first line of the menu contains your command options, while the second line briefly defines each choice that you highlight (or identifies the submenu options for that choice.) See Chapter 4 for a full discussion of 1-2-3 menus and refer to the command guide poster at the back of the book to see the many-levelled structure of 1-2-3's menus and submenus.

The control panel is also used when 1-2-3 requests certain information from you, such as the "source" and "target" cells when you copy or move cells from location in the worksheet to another (The Copy and the Move commands are explained in the Reference Section.)

At this point, you are familiar with the key components of the worksheet, and are probably ready to enter data. To get the most out of the remaining material in this section, follow along with 1-2-3 running on your computer, and re-create the various keystrokes and commands as we discuss them.

The first step in creating a worksheet is to move your cell pointer or cursor to the location in which you wish to enter data. The keystrokes for moving the cursor are described in the following section.

NAVIGATING WITHIN A WORKSHEET

As in most every computer program, the basic keys for moving the cell pointer are the up, down, left, and right arrow keys (or the cursor movement keys) on the numeric keypad. As long as you hold down the arrow keys, the cursor will continue to move up, down, left, or right one cell at a time. However, if this were the only way of moving around a large 1-2-3 worksheet it would be pretty inconvenient. Fortunately, 1-2-3 offers a number of short-cut keys and key combinations for cursor movement. The following table describes various ways of moving the cursor to a new location. Note that certain navigation keystrokes require two keys, as in CTRL-Right Cursor. This means press and hold the CTRL key, while simultaneously pressing the Right arrow key. The same holds for any combination involving CTRL and another key.

Table 3.1 Cursor Movement Keys

Cell Pointer Action	Key(s)
Move one cell at a time	Cursor keys
Move one full screen to the left	CTRL - ← or SHIFT - TAB
Move one full screen to the right	CTRL - → or TAB
Move up one full screen	PgUp
Move down one full screen	PgDn
Move down to the last cell in a column that contains data or the final cell in the column.	END - ↓

Table 3.1 (Continued)

Cell Pointer Action	Key(s)
Move up to the last cell in a column that contains data or the final cell in the column.	END - ↑
Move right to the last cell in a row that contains data or the last cell in the row.	END - →
Move left to the last cell in a row that contains data or the last cell in the row.	END - ←
Move to cell A:A1	HOME
Move to the lower-right corner of active area of the worksheet	END - HOME

Experiment with all these cursor movement keys and key combinations until you feel comfortable getting around your worksheet. You may want to take one of the sample files included with the program and try out the various End key combinations—they can be a little confusing. Once you get used to using the End key for cursor movement, you'll find that it is a quick way to move between blocks of data in your worksheet.

The Goto Key

One other shortcut for moving the cell pointer is the special function key, F5, located on the left side or top of your keyboard. When you press the GOTO key, 1-2-3 will prompt you in the second line or a control panel to type in an address to "goto." (The current cell address will appear at the prompt.) Type in the desired address, and 1-2-3 will instantly move the cell pointer to the specified cell. In this way, F5 functions as an "express" means of moving the cell pointer.

Be aware that you don't need to use every available navigational key combination—you can use whatever subset feels most natural to you. Whatever method you choose to move the cell pointer, the next step is to begin entering data. The rules for data entry follow.

ENTERING DATA

All data is typed into 1-2-3 by means of the worksheet cell. 1-2-3 keeps track of all entered data with its column-row cell address system. To type data into a particular cell you must move the cursor to that cell, making it the current cell. Then, if the READY indicator is displayed in the upper right-hand corner of the screen, you are ready to enter data. (If anything other than READY is displayed, press ESC until READY is displayed.)

In READY mode, you can type in all kinds of data into the worksheet. First, though, let's define how 1-2-3 interprets "data." For 1-2-3, "data" consists of labels (i.e., text), values (i.e., numbers), and formulas. As you type in text, the mode indicator changes to LABEL; as you type in numbers or formulas, the mode indicator changes to VALUE. 1-2-3 automatically determines the kind of data you are entering by the first character that you type in.

Whenever you type in any data into a worksheet cell, it does not immediately appear in the current cell as you type. Rather 1-2-3 displays the characters that you are typing in, in the second line of the Control Panel, above the border. For example, if you highlight cell B2, and type in the word "Budget," it will appear as shown in Figure 3.4. Only when you press ENTER or any one of the cursor keys, will it actually be entered (and displayed) in the actual cell.

Each data type has its own entry rules; described below. You will probably get the most out of the following discussion if you duplicate the examples as you read along.

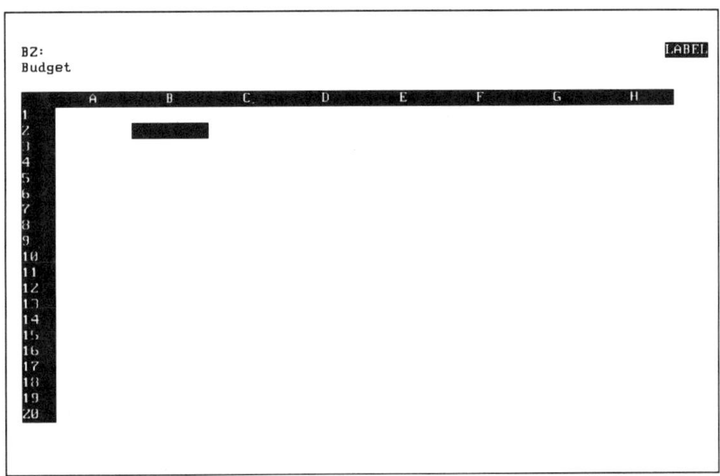

Figure 3.4
Data entry via the control panel.

Labels

A label can consist of text (i.e., Expense Summary), combined text and numbers (i.e., 1989 Budget Summary), and combined text and characters (i.e., J&B Associates). All text must be preceded by a *label prefix* that aligns text within the cell. Three label prefixes are available (see Figure 3.5):

- Single Quote ('), which left-aligns text.
- Carat (^), entered by pressing SHIFT-6, which centers text.
- Double quote ("), which right-aligns text.

Any entry that begins with an alphabetic character is considered a label and is automatically assigned the default label prefix ' (single quote). The numeric characters zero through nine and special formula characters . (period), ((parenthesis), @ (@function), # (pound sign), and $ (dollar sign) are considered *values.* Thus, if you simply enter text without entering any label prefix at all, it will be left-aligned. To center or right-align the text, you must type in the appropriate prefix manually.

Notice that if you type in address labels that begin with a number, such as "238 Main Street," 1-2-3 assumes that you are typing in a value. You must therefore manually insert a label prefix so that 1-2-3 will accept the entry as a label.

Values

If you start your entry with a numeric character, 1-2-3 determines that it is a value and the READY mode indicator will change to VALUE. All numbers entered are right-aligned in the cell, as shown in Figure 3.5. You can change the alignment of a number by using the prefixes as explained above, but if you do so, the number will be converted from a value to a label. That means you will not be able to use it in any mathematical formulas or operations. Let's say that you want to add the contents of cell A1 and cell B1, and display them in cell C1 (see below). If A1 contains the value 1, and B1 contains the value 1, then 2 will be displayed in cell C1. If, however, you preceded the contents of cell B1 with a label prefix, ',", or ^, 1-2-3 would evaluate B1 to be 0 (all labels are considered zeros), and the value of 1 would be reported in cell C1.)

The fact that values can be converted to labels is very important if you wish to combine text and numbers: for typing in addresses, P.O order numbers, identification numbers, etc. If you forget to include a label prefix in front of an entry that begins with a number and contains spaces or alphabetic characters, Lotus will not accept the entry. When you press ENTER to complete the entry, 1-2-3

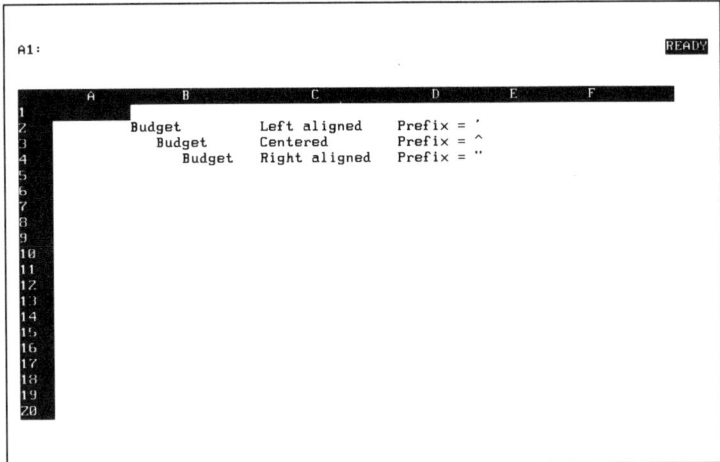

Figure 3.5
Three types of label alignment.

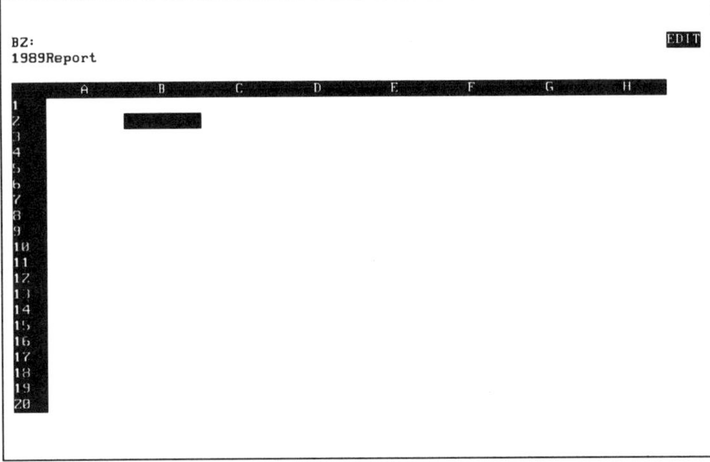

Figure 3.6
1-2-3 switches to EDIT mode when you enter an invalid numeric format.

will switch to EDIT mode, beep, and place the cursor under the first offending character or space in the entry. (See Figure 3.6)

Formulas

The power of 1-2-3 derives from its ability to perform mathematical functions and logical formulas. Like a calculator, you can type in formulas such as 128*1333, press ENTER and 1-2-3 will display the result in the current cell. Besides numbers, certain other initial characters in your entry indicate the presence of a formula, and automatically switch 1-2-3 into VALUE mode. They are:

@ $, #, (, or +. (See Chapter 6 for an in-depth discussion of how and when to use formulas). For example, you might wish to add the numbers in the two cells A1 and B1, and place the sum in cell B2. To do this, you would move to B2 and type in the formula +A1+B1. Notice the plus (+) sign in front of the first cell address. If you had entered A1 without the plus sign, 1-2-3 would have assumed that you were typing in a label and no addition will take place. Alternately, you could have surrounded the formula with parentheses, as in (A1+B1). Since the left parenthesis and the plus sign are considered value characters, 1-2-3 knows you are about to enter a formula.

Figure 3.7 illustrates how simple addition is used in a worksheet. Notice that the cell contents—the formula in cell B2—are displayed in the control panel, while the actual results of the formula are displayed in the cell itself.

1-2-3 also provides a number of special built-in formulas called *@functions,* which begin with the @ character. The formula @SUM(A1..A30), for example, would sum up all the values in cells A1 through A30. When you begin your entry with an @ character, 1-2-3 immediately displays the VALUE indicator, since the data will be considered numerical. The full range and usage of 1-2-3's @functions are explained later, in Chapter 6.

You might want to stop at this point and enter various types of data into a blank worksheet. Try typing text, numbers, and combinations of numbers until you are comfortable with the data entry rules.

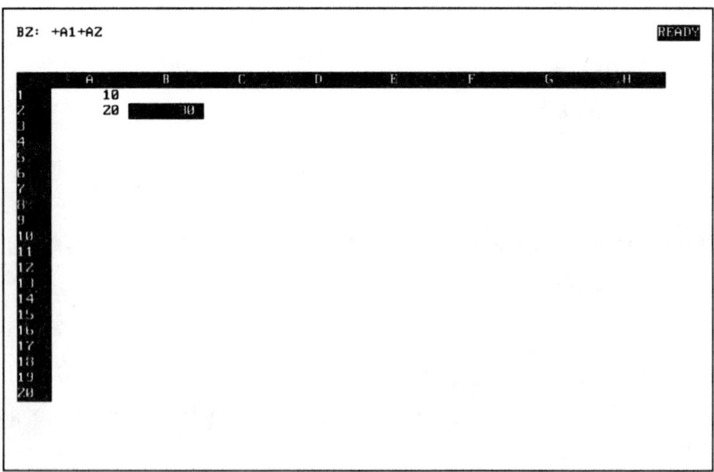

Figure 3.7
The formula is displayed in the control panel, while the resulting value is displayed in the cell.

This chapter describes the basic 1-2-3 rules and procedures for entering data and moving around a worksheet. These are the conventions that underlie every worksheet, whether it contains a few simple formulas or a web of complex, interrelated formulas and functions. If you have the basics under your belt, you're ready to move on to the next chapter, which describes the fundamental tools used to construct 1-2-3 worksheets and to format your data in the worksheet.

1-2-3 Basic Command Tools

INTRODUCTION

In the last chapter, you learned about the basic nature of worksheets, how to enter data into them, and move around them. The next step in developing a worksheet is to learn how to use 1-2-3's built-in commands. The commands are primarily accessed through 1-2-3's extensive menu system, and to a lesser extent through the function keys, located on the left side or the top portion of your keyboard and labeled F1 through F10 or F12. Let's begin by taking a look at how the menu system works, and the major commands you will use to build worksheets. We'll discuss the /Copy, /Move, and some of the /Range commands, which offer you the essentials for arranging your data in the worksheet. Next, we will discuss the /File commands; these are critical for saving your work so you can return to it later. At the end of the chapter, you'll find a description of the special function keys.

USING 1-2-3'S MENUS

You often hear the phrase "Lotus-style" or "1-2-3-style" menus touted as a feature of various software programs. The reason is that 1-2-3's many-tiered menu system is intuitively easy to use. Once you've seen one menu, you can probably

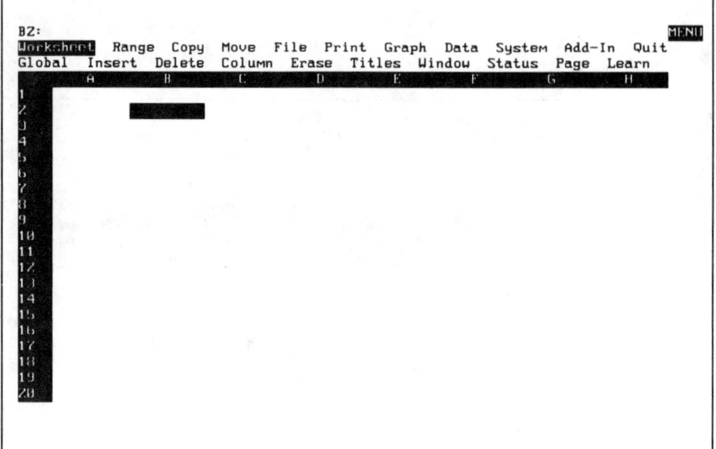

Figure 4.1 Main (Worksheet) menu.

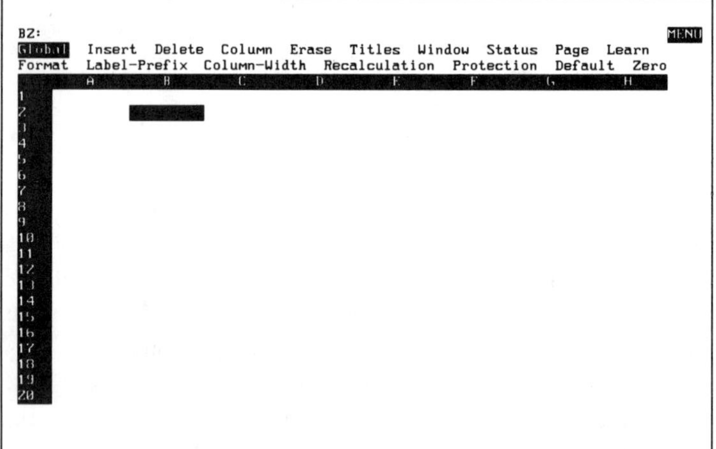

Figure 4.2 Submenu choices for /Worksheet.

find your way throughout the entire menu tree without any difficulty. To bring the Lotus menu system to the screen, press the slash (/) key. The primary menu will be displayed, as shown in Figure 4.1; the status indicator in the control panel will switch to MENU. The first line of the menu contains the available command choices, starting with Worksheet at the left. To select a command, move the cursor highlight to your choice, and press ENTER. Notice as you move the highlight that it cycles around on a continuous loop; if you move it beyond the leftmost choice, Worksheet, it will "wrap around" and highlight the last option on the menu, Quit. Similarly, when Quit is highlighted, pressing the right cursor will return the highlight bar to Worksheet.

The second line of the main menu displays a second level of options, options associated with the currently highlighted main menu command. For example, if you highlight Worksheet and press ENTER, 1-2-3 will display a second level menu (or submenu). The choices that were previously on the second line of the primary menu are now available to choose from. The second line of the Worksheet submenu in Figure 4.2 shows a third level menu associated with the highlighted option, Global. (See Figures 4.1 and 4.2.)

The entire menu system consists of a hierarchy of primary menus and submenus. As you move through the hierarchy, the submenu choices become primary menus and new submenu choices appear. Some of 1-2-3's menus extend five and six levels down from the primary menu. The poster enclosed in this book shows the entire menu tree structure for all 1-2-3 commands. (Be careful how you remove it, so you don't tear the corner. Pull out the poster by grasping it near the glued edge, then gently separating it from the book binding.)

Let's return to the top level, or primary menu again—you can backtrack through the levels of the menu system by pressing ESC. Each time you press ESC, you will move up one level until you reach the top level or "Worksheet" menu. If you press ESC again while at the Worksheet level, you will return to READY mode.

Before moving on, note that some of the menu items on the primary menu do not contain submenu choices, but rather list a brief description of what the items do. These include the commands listed in Table 4.1.

Table 4.1 Worksheet Menu Commands

Command	Description
Copy	"Copy a cell or range of cells."
Move	"Move a cell or range of cells."
System	"Leave 1-2-3 temporarily and use operating system." This "shell" command allows you to return to your DOS prompt and leave your work in 1-2-3 intact. It is invaluable when you need to format a disk, copy a file, or quickly check a series of directories to locate a file. When you are done, type `exit` at the DOS prompt and you will return to 1-2-3 where you left off.

Table 4.1 *continued*

Command	Description
Quit	"End the 1-2-3 session." This option branches into two submenu choices: No and Yes. If you select No, you will return to READY mode; Yes ends your 1-2-3 session and returns you to the DOS prompt.

NOTE Whenever 1-2-3 offers you an option with particularly disastrous consequences (like quitting), it will ask you to confirm your choice in a submenu, defaulting to No. This is to help you avoid making hasty choices that you might later regret.

Alternate Method for Selecting Menu Options

We have described one way of choosing a command from the 1-2-3 menu—highlight it and press ENTER. You can achieve the same result by typing the first letter of the command option—you don't even need to press ENTER. This method is much more efficient when you are dealing with multiple menu levels. For example, to set your right margin for printing, you would normally select /Print Printer Options Margins Right and then type in your margin setting. It is considerably more efficient to type `/ppomr` than it is to slide the cursor from left to right as each menu appears. In fact, for this very reason, Lotus has carefully named the commands on each level of the menu so that they start with unique letters. Therefore, as you learn the commonly used commands, try getting into the habit of selecting menu options by the first letter method—you'll save considerable time during the course of your work with 1-2-3.

At this point, you are ready to invoke any of the commands available through the menu system. First, though, read the next section, which describes one of the main building blocks for using 1-2-3 commands—the range.

RANGES

One of 1-2-3's most important tools for constructing a worksheet is its ability to work with groups of cells as a unit. These cell conglomerates are called *ranges*.

A range is a contiguous, rectangular area within a worksheet, defined by the cell in the upper-left corner of the rectangle and its opposite counterpart—the cell in the lower-right corner of the rectangle. Figure 4.3 shows a range that spans the cells beginning with B4 in the upper-left corner to E11 in the lower-left corner. We've already been dealing with the smallest possible range: a single cell. A range can also span many columns and rows; it can be a single column of any length, a single row of any width, a block of any length or width. The only criterion for a range is that it must consist of a cell or a group of contiguous, adjacent cells.

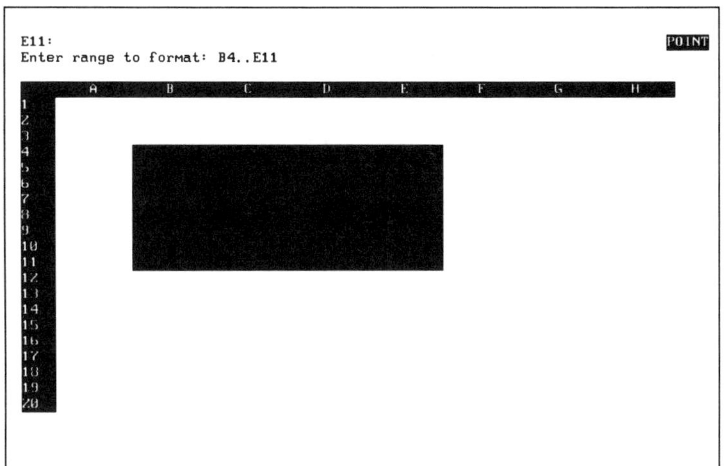

Figure 4.3
Range extending from B4..E11.

Once you have defined a group of cells as a range, you can carry out various actions, calculations, or commands on them en masse. For example, you can select all cells within a range to display numbers in dollar sign format or as percents. You can erase all cells within a range in one fell swoop. Or you can copy or move all cells within a range to another location.

By analogy, most word processors have a block function that allows you to bold, underline, or delete a group of words or sentences with a single command. The range is 1-2-3's equivalent. In addition, ranges have another unique function in 1-2-3; you can use them in formulas. As you'll see in Chapter 6, 1-2-3 provides special built-in functions to perform mass calculations on the contents of ranges. With the @SUM function, for example, you can total all numbers in the range. @AVG will yield the average value of all numbers in a range, and @STD calculates the standard deviation of all numbers in a range.

Any command that operates on a range of cells will prompt you to identify the range you want to work with; you can do this in two ways. Either type in the range address, or the coordinates of the range (that is, the top-left corner cell of the rectangle, followed by a period and then the lower-right corner cell of the rectangle) or "paint" the rectangle with the cursor keys (this is known as using POINT mode).

If you wish to paint the range, the first step is to place your cursor in any cell that will constitute a corner of the range. If the cell pointer is not already located in one of the corner cells in the range, press ESC at the prompt and move it to the desired location. Next, "anchor" the cell in the range corner by entering a period. Then use the cursor keys to highlight all the cells that you wish to include in the range. As you move the cursor from cell to cell, the coordinates will be displayed in the prompt response area at the top of the screen. When the cell pointer is located in the opposite corner cell of the range, press ENTER.

Why paint a range when you can just type in its coordinate address? Because it's generally faster and more accurate. Thinking in two dimensions can be tricky, especially when the range scrolls off the screen. The choice is yours, although Lotus Development Corporation has found that most people prefer painting to entering coordinate addresses.

Not only can you identify a range by its address or by painting it, you can name ranges you frequently use. We can begin to explore some of the ways in which ranges are named and used to build a worksheet by looking at the /Range command menu. To display the commands, select /Range from the Main Menu and a submenu with 11 options will be displayed.

Range Naming Commands

In addition to defining ranges by address or by cursor highlight, 1-2-3 lets you assign names to ranges, so that you can refer to them by name in your formulas or in response to 1-2-3 prompts. In terms of navigation, for example, let's say you have a large worksheet, and one of many cells that you frequently need to adjust or view contains your total revenue figure, cell C92. Rather than constantly having to remember that the total you need is in cell C92, you could assign the range name REVTOTAL to the cell, use the GOTO (F5) key, and type in `REVTOTAL` at the prompt. Substituting a range name for a particular range address applies to various other worksheet building commands, as we'll see below.

You can include range names in your formulas too. Instead of instructing 1-2-3 to find the minimum value in a range using the range address, as in @MIN(B22..G45), you can simply assign the range name TOTAL (if that were

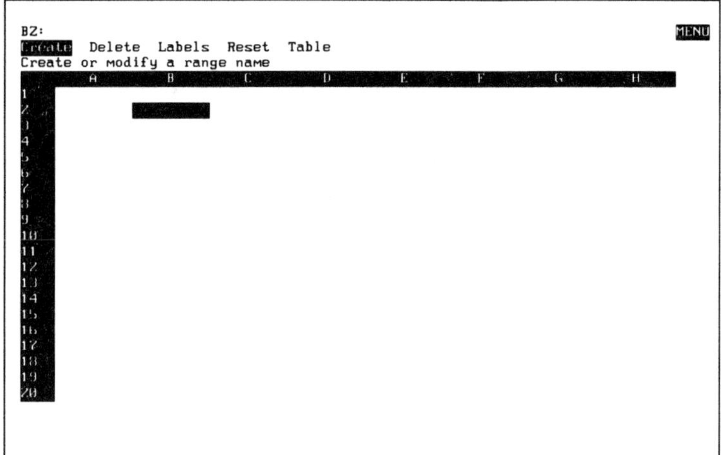

Figure 4.4
Range name menu.

appropriate), and write the formula @MIN(TOTAL). The advantages are twofold. First, it's a lot easier to remember meaningful range names than numerical coordinates. Second, using ranges lessens the chance of error, since you'll be typing in plain English rather than abstract coordinates.

Here's how you go about naming ranges. First, select the /Range Name command. 1-2-3 will then display the submenu shown in Figure 4.4.

Select Create, and 1-2-3 will prompt you to enter the range name. Type in the name, in this case, we'll say REVTOTAL. Next, 1-2-3 will prompt you to enter the range coordinates. You can either paint the range as described above, or type in its coordinates. Remember, a range can be a single cell or any rectangular collection of contiguous cells. When you press ENTER, the name will be assigned to the cell or cells that you specified.

The next time you go to the /Range Name Create menu to name a range, 1-2-3 will display a list of the existing range names. At this time, you can reassign an existing name to a different cell or group of cells if you wish, or you can add a new name to the list by typing it in at the prompt. The /Range Name Delete command does exactly what the command name suggests. When you select the Delete command, 1-2-3 will display a list of the existing range names. Highlight the name you wish to delete and press ENTER. Selecting /Range Name Reset deletes all range names in one keystroke—use it wisely!

A useful command on the /Range Name menu is the Table command, which creates a table in your worksheet, listing all your named ranges. When you select

Table, 1-2-3 prompts you to assign a location in your worksheet for the table. (You need only point to the top-left corner of the area that you want to use.) It is important to designate a clear space, since the table will overwrite any data that might lie in its way. Therefore, before using it, make sure that you have a big enough area for the table display: It occupies two columns and as many rows as you have range names. (If you aren't sure how many rows you'll need, select /Range Name Create and count your ranges.) As you begin to use range names regularly, you'll soon find the Table command is indispensible. It is critical that you document your range names—describing their contents and listing the formulas that reference them—so you or someone else will be able to follow your work afterward. A sample range name table is shown in Figure 4.5.

The /Range Name menu also includes a Label option. This feature lets you take a range of labels and use those labels as range names for their adjacent cells (one cell right, left, up, or down). Thus, you can instantly assign a series of range names to their adjacent cells without having to create each one individually. See the Reference section for more details.

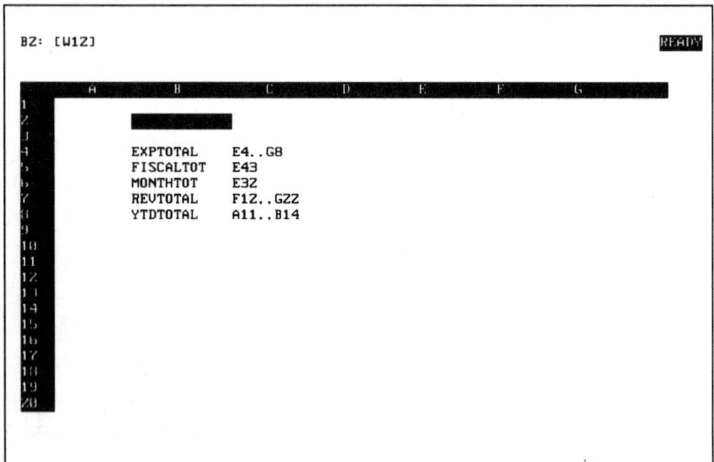

Figure 4.5
Range name table.

Erasing Ranges

One of the first commands that you might use on a range (named or unnamed) is Erase, just as you would delete a block of text in a word processor. The Erase option on the /Range menu is an essential worksheet construction and modification command. In fact, it's the only way to empty the contents of a cell or range. To erase a range, select /Range Erase, and then, at the prompt, identify the range you want to erase: by address, by name, or by painting it. If you just want to erase the current cell, press ENTER.

If you get cold feet about erasing a cell or range, press ESC until you return to a higher-level menu or READY mode. If you are using Undo (see Chapter 5) you can rest a bit easier when you invoke the /Range Erase command.

THE /COPY COMMAND

1-2-3's ability to work with ranges is the key to nearly every 1-2-3 command. One of the most commonly used commands in the program is the /Copy command. /Copy allows you take text or formulas from one section of the worksheet—the *source range*—and duplicate them in another part of the worksheet—the *target range*. Let's say that you have to create a worksheet that reports five months of a department budget. Instead of retyping all the budget categories five times, you could type them in once and then copy them to the next months. This maintains consistency in your data, and saves a great amount of time. To use the /Copy command in such circumstances, you would select /Copy, and see the prompt: `Enter range to copy FROM:`. (The prompt is followed by the current cell address displayed as a range: e.g., A1..A1.) Press ENTER if you simply want to use the current cell as your source range; otherwise, type in the coordinates of the copy source range (use pairs of opposite corners, e.g., A1..C5), or paint the range (move the cursor to one corner of the range, press the period key to anchor the range, then move the cursor to the opposite corner of the range). Of course you can also type in a range name, if you have assigned one.

As soon as you press ENTER, 1-2-3 will show a second prompt: `Enter range to copy TO:` (this, too, is followed by the current cell address). Specify your target cell or range by typing in its coordinates, by painting it, or by entering a range name (if you have assigned one). 1-2-3 will then proceed to duplicate the contents of the source range in the target range. The cursor will then return to the address of the cell from which you initially called up the /Copy command.

Note that if your source range is a single cell, or a single column or row of cells, you can make a series of copies. For example, if you wish to copy a single cell into one or more rows, you would simply specify those rows as your target range, press ENTER, and your single cell will be replicated in each cell of the target range. The same principle holds if you want to copy a row or column into several adjacent rows or columns.

Bear in mind the following characteristics of the /Copy command:

1. The source data will overwrite anything in the target area. If you do not have UNDO enabled (see Chapter 5), make sure that your target range is correctly identified or you may lose hours worth of work. If you want to cancel a /Copy command, you can press ESC at any time during the process until you've pressed ENTER and accepted the target range. At that point, the command will be executed.
2. When you copy data from a source to a target range, 1-2-3 also copies the format of the source area as well, so you may have to make some adjustments to your display. For example, if you copy data to an area of the worksheet in which the columns are narrower than the columns in the source range, you may have to widen the target area columns. Otherwise, numbers and dates may appear as asterisks, and text may overlap into adjacent cells or be truncated by adjacent cells until you do so. We will be discussing formatting and setting column widths later in this chapter.
3. The procedure for copying ranges that contain formulas (e.g., the formula that would sum the contents of cells A1 through A3, @SUM(A1.A3) is similar to the procedure described above. However, 1-2-3 does some very interesting and useful things to the cell addresses in the formula. These are explained in Chapter 6 under Relative and Absolute Cell Addresses.

Repeating Characters

Another special use of the /Copy command is to quickly create separator lines in your worksheet. Separator lines split text and labels apart, making your worksheets more attractive and easier to read. Compare the worksheets in Figures 4.6a and b. The top worksheet contains no separator lines, and the data runs together making it quite difficult to read. The bottom worksheet uses separator lines to highlight labels and separate totals. See Chapter 12 for additional hints for designing more useful and appealing worksheets.

To create a separator line, enter a backslash (\)—this is the repeating character label prefix—in a cell, followed by the character you wish to repeat. A dash produces a good single line, and an equal sign produces a good double line. (You can also use plus signs, asterisks, or periods—it's a matter of personal choice). The character will immediately repeat itself, filling out the entire width of the cell. You can then copy the cell with the repeating character to the entire range of cells that will contain the separator line.

OPERATING BUDGET						
	Jan	Feb	Mar	Apr	May	Jun
Rent	3,500	3,500	3,500	3,500	3,500	3,500
Payroll	12,932	12,932	12,932	12,932	12,932	12,932
Advertising	5,600	8,750	9,900	8,650	5,440	3,440
Telephone	750	850	950	850	650	550
Courier	350	650	750	700	690	550
Leases	765	765	765	765	765	765
Printing	4,000	5,200	5,500	5,100	4,850	4,500
Office Supplies	250	350	350	350	300	250
TOTALS	$28,147	$32,997	$34,647	$32,847	$29,127	$26,487

Figure 4.6a

Note how much harder it is to read the worksheet without separator lines.

OPERATING BUDGET						
	Jan	Feb	Mar	Apr	May	Jun
================	======	======	======	======	======	======
Rent	3,500	3,500	3,500	3,500	3,500	3,500
Payroll	12,932	12,932	12,932	12,932	12,932	12,932
Advertising	5,600	8,750	9,900	8,650	5,440	3,440
Telephone	750	850	950	850	650	550
Courier	350	650	750	700	690	550
Leases	765	765	765	765	765	765
Printing	4,000	5,200	5,500	5,100	4,850	4,500
Office Supplies	250	350	350	350	300	250
	------	------	------	------	------	------
TOTALS	$28,147	$32,997	$34,647	$32,847	$29,127	$26,487
================	======	======	======	======	======	======

Figure 4.6b

This worksheet is easier to interpret and more pleasing to view.

THE /MOVE COMMAND

The /Move command, another frequently used command in 1-2-3, is also extremely useful for arranging data in your worksheet. You'll often find that a worksheet is growing and you need to move a range of text, values, or formulas elsewhere. Equally likely, as you get better at using 1-2-3, you'll have several brainstorms for enhancing or embellishing your worksheets. What started off as a simple invoicing worksheet might turn into a full-blown general ledger system;

what started out as a simple budget worksheet might evolve into a master cash flow planning system. Beware! You too will probably be smitten with the complexity bug. In these instances, you will probably want to rearrange your worksheet many times, rather than erasing and re-entering data when you want it to appear elsewhere on your worksheet. The /Move command will be your salvation.

/Move is identical to /Copy, except that it transfers the data from the source range to the target range; it leaves the source range empty, rather than duplicating it. The /Move command prompts are identical, too, except that the words "copy FROM" and "copy TO" are replaced with "move FROM" and "move TO." Also like /Copy, moving data overwrites anything in the target range, so make sure you really want to do it, especially if you don't have Undo enabled. You can back out by pressing ESC at any point in the process.

When you move data from a source range to a target range, the target range adopts the format of the data you are moving. The source range returns to the /Worksheet Global Format setting. Finally, as with the /Copy command, you may have to stretch or narrow the column widths in the target area to accommodate the text and numbers of the source range.

The /Move command seems straightforward. There are some curious details, however, if you try to move parts of named ranges, or if the data that you move overwrites the top-left or bottom-right corner of a named range. See the Reference section for a complete discussion.

FILE SAVING TOOLS

Once you've created a worksheet, you'll probably want to save it so that you can retrieve it and refer to it at a later date. In fact, you should save your worksheets to disk frequently as you work rather than waiting until you are finished for the day. Remember, until your worksheet has been saved onto your hard or floppy disk, it exists only in the computer's memory and is very vulnerable to hardware and power failures. Also, while Undo might be able to undo your last mistake, it cannot undo a series of mistakes. Nothing is more frustrating than to spend hours creating a worksheet or entering data into a worksheet and then seeing your work evaporate because of a mindless error or a short in the power supply.

1-2-3's /File menu provides essential commands for saving and retrieving files: Save and Retrieve. Any new user will need to use and understand these commands at once. The /File menu also contains a number of other useful, related commands, which are briefly mentioned after the Save and Retrieve commands.

Saving Worksheets

To save a file, select /File Save. 1-2-3 will prompt you for the name of the file. On the third line of the control panel, a list of all existing worksheet—i.e., .WK1—files in the directory are displayed; you can cycle through them with the cursor keys.

If you have created a file from scratch and have never saved it, 1-2-3 displays the current directory name followed by *.WK1 at the prompt. Type in a file name, with a maximum of eight characters. Do not use spaces or punctuation marks. (See your DOS manual for a complete discussion of "legal" file name characters.) Also, you must *not* add an extension (1-2-3 will affix its own .WK1 file extension). Once the file has been saved to disk, 1-2-3 will return to READY mode in the current worksheet.

If you have already saved the file once, 1-2-3 displays the current file name at the prompt. Again, the third line of the control panel lists all existing files in the current directory. If you wish to save the file using the current file name, press ENTER at the prompt. This will update and overwrite the old version of the file. If you wish to save the file under a new name, type in the new name at the prompt. (This will keep the original version of the file intact, and allow you to keep a version of the file under the new name.) You may also highlight and use any file name from the list of existing files. That file will be overwritten by the current worksheet.

As a safety precaution, before 1-2-3 ever overwrites any file on disk, it will display a menu with three choices: Cancel, Replace, and Backup. This is a second-chance confirmation to make sure that you don't overwrite anything inadvertently. The Cancel option returns you to READY mode, Replace takes the contents of the current worksheet in RAM and overwrites the contents of the file on disk with the same name. Backup updates the file on disk and also creates a backup copy of the earlier file, adding a .BAK extension.

If you choose Backup, and discover that you really hadn't wanted to overwrite the original file, you can resort to the backup. To load it, however, you will have to rename it with a new file name and a .WK1 extension, using the DOS rename command, e.g., rename `TOTAL89.BAK TOTAL89.WK1`. (See your DOS manual.) Be aware that Backup will only keep you out of trouble for one file save routine—the next time you select Backup, 1-2-3 will update the old .BAK file with a new .BAK version. 1-2-3 does not maintain a history of several backup versions of your files.

Retrieving Worksheets

To load a worksheet file into memory from your disk, select /File Retrieve. 1-2-3 will then display a list of existing files in the current directory. The files are in alphabetical order and numbers precede alphabetic characters. If you have many files, you may wish to press the F3 NAME key to see them on the full screen. Either highlight the desired file on the list and press ENTER, or type in the name of the file. 1-2-3 will load that worksheet into memory.

Note that when you load a file from disk it "pushes" your current worksheet out of memory; unless you have saved the current worksheet, all your work will be erased. 1-2-3 will do this without any warning. If you wish to keep your current worksheet, save it before using the /File Retrieve command.

At this point, let's digress for a moment and point out that you can specify for 1-2-3 where it should look for your files. If you keep most of your data files in one directory, select /Worksheet Global Default Directory; type in the drive and directory name that the program should look to automatically each time you select one of the /File commands. (Floppy users should enter `B:\` when prompted to enter the default directory.) After you've typed in your choice for the default directory, select Update to update your configuration file, 123.CNF. From that point on, 1-2-3 will always look to your default directory location when you try to save or retrieve a file.

If you retrieve a file from a directory other than the default directory, however, 1-2-3 expects that you will want to save the file in the same directory from which it was retrieved. It will not automatically save that file to the default directory. If you wish to retrieve a file from a subdirectory of the current directory, highlight the appropriate subdirectory and a listing of worksheet files for that directory will appear. Highlight your choice and press ENTER. If you wish to retrieve a file from another directory altogether, press ESC at the file retrieve prompt and type in the file name, including the drive and full directory path.

Other /File Commands

You may wish to save or retrieve your files in other, more specialized ways. For example, you might want to save and retrieve portions of files, or load in a worksheet and add or subtract all of its values from your current worksheet. These options are also available through the /File menu. We list these other /File command options below in brief; for detailed information, see the Reference section.

Combine /File Combine allows you to load a range from another worksheet on disk (or another entire worksheet on disk), into your current worksheet. The current cursor position will serve as the upper left-hand corner of the specified combine range, or file. /File Combine offers three options: Copy, Add, or Subtract. Copy lets you copy the range or file to be combined into your current file (overwriting any data in its way). Add lets you take in the values from the combine range or file and add them to the values in your current worksheet. Subtract lets you take in the values from the combine range or file and subtract them from the values in your current worksheet. (The Add and Subtract options affect only the cells with numbers or blanks.)

Xtract This command allows you to copy a portion of your worksheet to a separate file on disk. You will be able to load the extract as a worksheet file on its own. Xtract gives you the choice of copying your formulas and keeping them intact in the new file, or copying just the formula results (or values) to the new file. When you use this command, 1-2-3 prompts you for a file name for the extract, and then for the extract range. Type in the range address, or name, or paint the range. Note that your current worksheet is unaffected—1-2-3 merely copies the range to its own file.

Import The Import command enables you to retrieve ASCII files created in other programs such as word processors. Be aware that when a file is imported as text, you often have to "noodle" with it to get your data in the right place. When you import an ASCII file, you have the choice of importing it as Text or as Numbers. If you import it as Text, 1-2-3 will import each line in the file as one long label. If you are importing a delimited file from a database, use the Numbers option; that way your data will be separated into appropriate columns and rows.

Erase When you select this command, 1-2-3 gives you the choice of erasing various types of files. They are categorized by extension: Worksheet files (.WK1), print files (.PRN), graph files (.PIC), or "other" files—you can type in your own extension. Select the type of file you wish to erase and 1-2-3 will display all the files of that type. Highlight the desired file, and press ENTER, then enter the confirmation prompt. You can only erase one file at a time. This technique is slow and a bit clumsy; you are better off cleaning house from DOS with the DEL or ERASE command. (To erase the file that is currently loaded, use the /Worksheet Erase command.)

List This command provides a file directory from within 1-2-3. After selecting the file type, the worksheet border clears and the files are listed in five columns. Highlight the file you want to list, and, on the third line of the screen, 1-2-3 will show you the date and time that the file was last saved, and the byte size. Alternatively, you can use the

/System command and view the data directory from DOS.

Directory The ability to temporarily switch data directories is a very useful. If you have many different types of worksheets, think about making separate directories for various worksheet groups. Use the File Directory command to switch from various file groups during your 1-2-3 session.

Admin This command is used with networks, for controlling file access, and for updating formula links between the current worksheet and worksheets on disk.

ERASING WORKSHEETS FROM MEMORY

Sometimes you may wish to erase the current worksheet from memory—because it is incorrect, because you just needed it for a quick calculation, or because it contained confidential data. (/File Delete can only be used to delete files that are already stored on disk.) By selecting /Worksheet Erase and then confirming, Yes, you will "flush" the worksheet from RAM. You will face a blank worksheet with the cursor in cell A1 as though you were starting from scratch.

Remember that when you erase a worksheet in this fashion, you are only erasing it from RAM—any existing copies of the worksheet that have been previously saved to disk will be unaffected.

QUITTING 1-2-3

To end a 1-2-3 session, select /Quit. 1-2-3 will then ask you to confirm your choice with a No or Yes. (The No option appears first so that you don't thoughtlessly press ENTER and quit the program unintentionally.) If you have saved your worksheet, and haven't made any changes since the save, you will be brought back to the DOS prompt (or to the 1-2-3 Access System). If you haven't saved your worksheet after making changes, 1-2-3 will warn you:

```
WORKSHEET CHANGES NOT SAVED! End 1-2-3 anyway?
```

answer Yes or No as appropriate.

SPECIAL FUNCTION KEYS

In addition to the commands that you've just learned, you should familiarize yourself with 1-2-3's function keys, which offer additional built-in functionality. Here's a summary of what each function key does:

F1 **Help** In READY mode, F1 calls up the help index. In MENU mode, it displays help screens relevant to whatever menu option is highlighted. If you press F1 while in the midst of a command, it will display information about that command.

If you enter @ and then press F1, 1-2-3 displays an index of @functions. Highlight the one you're interested in and press ENTER; 1-2-3 will provide explanations of the @function in question.

Enter { and press F1, and 1-2-3 displays an index of macro commands. Highlight a command, press ENTER, and 1-2-3 will display the appropriate help screen. Finally, you can get help with specific macro commands by entering { followed by the macro command, and then pressing F1.

ALT-F1 **Compose** Use this key combination to create foreign characters (such as the Yen sign ¥ or the Pound £ sign) and other special characters that are not available from your keyboard. The keystroke sequence for creating the characters are listed in Appendix C. To create a Yen sign for example, you would press the ALT-F1, combination, then type `y=`. The Yen sign would then appear in the cell. The Pound sign is created by pressing ALT-F1 followed by `l=`.

F2 **Edit** Use F2 to modify a cell without retyping its entire contents, as explained in Chapter 3.

ALT-F2 **Step Mode** Use STEP mode to debug "macros," automated sequences of keystrokes (see Chapter 13). In STEP mode, each automated keystroke is displayed one at a time, so you can see exactly where a problem is occurring. To turn off STEP mode, press ALT-F2 again.

F3 **File name** While in POINT or VALUE mode, this key lists the names of ranges in the worksheet. During File List (see below), it toggles between a full screen listing of the files, or a horizontal list in standard menu format.

ALT-F3 **Macro run** This combination is used to run a macro by name (see Chapter 13).

F4 **Absolute reference** While used in EDIT mode, or as you are typing in cell references. F4 will convert the cell reference at the cursor in a cyclical fashion from relative to absolute to mixed back to relative (see Chapter 6).

ALT-F4 **Undo** One of Release 2.2's most important features is that it lets you restore a worksheet to its state prior to your last com-

	mand (provided that the command didn't involve a file save or deletion). Note: Using the Undo feature requires additional available memory. (See Chapter 5).
F5	**Goto** The F5 key serves as an express ticket to a particular cell or a range. To go to a cell, press F5 followed by the cell address. To go to a range, simply press F5 and type in the name. Alternately, you can also press F5 followed by F3, which will display the named ranges in the worksheet.
ALT-F5	**Learn** This key combination instructs 1-2-3 to "look over your shoulder" and record your series of keystrokes. You can use the recorded keystrokes to create a macro for data entry or command repetitions.
F6	**Window control** The WINDOW key toggles back and forth between windows created with the /Worksheet Window command.
F7	**Data query/find** This repeats the most recent "data query" or "find." In which you isolate or identify selected entries in a database.
F8	**Data table** The F8 key repeats the most recent /Data Table command. /Data Table commands are used to evaluate multiple variables with a single formula.
F9	**Calc** In some cases, as explained in Chapter 3, you will not want 1-2-3 to automatically recalculate formulas whenever new data is entered. When Recalculation is set to manual, you will need to press F9 to recalculate formulas when new data has been entered.
F10	**Graph** This key is used to display the current graph while 1-2-3 is in graph MENU mode or READY mode.

This chapter covered the basic commands you need to know in order to build your worksheets and save your work. Once you gain expertise with these commands, we recommend that you browse through the menu tree and experiment with the commands covered in this chapter, as well as those that were only explained briefly. The Reference section documents every command in the program, so you'll always have a guide, even when you explore the most remote regions of the program.

The next chapter covers worksheet layout and formatting with the /Worksheet and /Range commands, and builds on the concepts covered here.

5 The Worksheet Format and Display

Thus far we have discussed the use of ranges and three of the most essential 1-2-3 commands for manipulating data in ranges: /Range Erase, /Copy, and /Move. It is time now to cover some of the techniques for structuring the worksheet and your working environment; these include setting global defaults, setting column widths, working with split-screen displays, using Undo, etc. From there, we will move on to discuss the options for formatting your numerical data, using the format options that are available under the /Range and the /Worksheet command menus.

The commands for these kind of adjustments are found on the /Worksheet menu. The /Worksheet commands operate on the worksheet as a whole, or on entire columns and rows.

WORKSHEET DEFAULT SETTINGS

One of the key options on the /Worksheet menu, is the Global option. As the name implies, *global* means affecting every cell in the worksheet. When you select the /Worksheet Global menu, a global "settings sheet" is displayed, covering your worksheet data. Settings sheets are displayed with several of 1-2-3's menu options, and show your default settings for the currently selected command; that is, the values and settings 1-2-3 will use by default unless you specifically override them. Settings sheets will appear, for example, when you print, graph, or query data—all of which we will discuss further on. You can press the WINDOW key (F6) to turn any settings sheet on and off.

The default settings that are automatically displayed when you select options on the /Worksheet Global menu are particularly important, because these are settings that apply to the worksheet in general—default settings for cell formatting, cell protection, cell alignment, time and date displays, recalculation methods, and much more. For a complete description of the many /Worksheet Global options and suboptions, refer to the Reference section. At this point, let's go on to explore the key worksheet structuring tools.

/WORKSHEET COLUMN COMMANDS

One of the first things you'll want to do to structure your worksheet is set the widths of your columns. (On your settings sheet for /Worksheet Global, you'll notice that the default setting for the column-width is 9.) The reason is threefold. First, watch what happens when you enter 18 characters of text in a column that is 9 characters wide. If the cell to the right is empty, the full text will be displayed, spanning both columns (see Figure 5.1a). But as soon as you enter data into the adjacent cell (text, values, or formulas), any text that had "spilled over" from the cell on the left will no longer be displayed (Figure 5.1b). The contents of the first cell will appear truncated. Note that the original text has not been deleted; it is simply no longer displayed. If you erase the contents of the cell in the right column (with /Range Erase), 1-2-3 will once again display the original text.

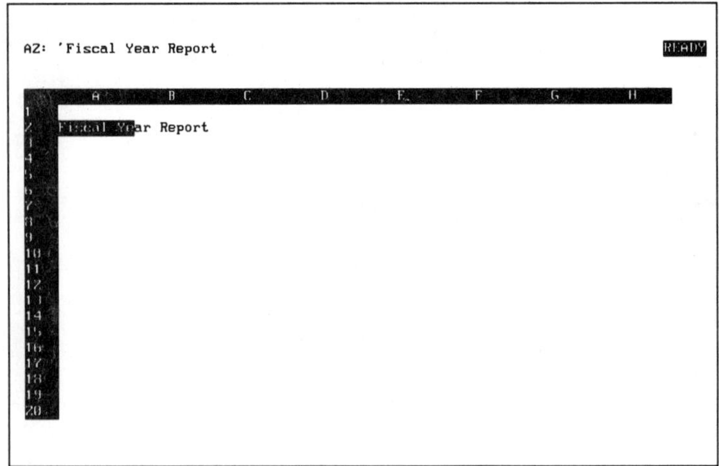

Figure 5.1a

Text that is too long for the current cell will overlap into the adjacent cell, provided that the adjacent cell is empty.

Figure 5.1b
When text is entered into the adjacent cell, the overlapping text from the cell to the left is masked.

If you enter a number with 15 digits into a column that is 9 characters wide, 1-2-3 will display a row of asterisks, rather than truncate it in the display (see Figure 5.2). The same applies to dates; if you select a date format (see below) that requires 12 characters, and the column is only 9 characters wide, 1-2-3 will fill the cell with asterisks.

The second reason for adjusting column widths is to help you print out an entire worksheet on whatever width paper your printer supports. If you have 10

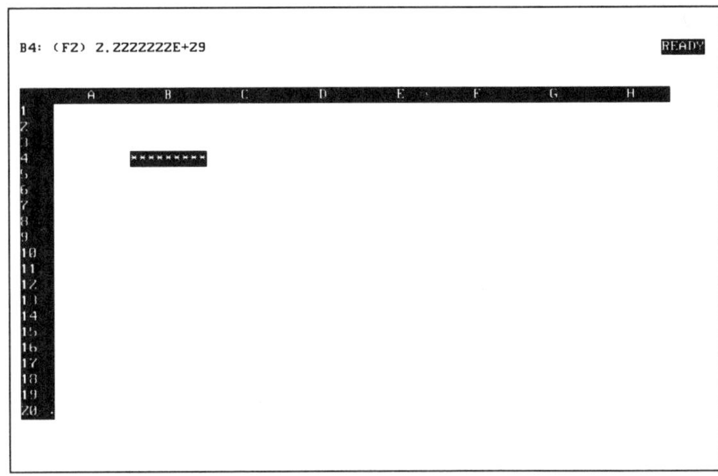

Figure 5.2
If you attempt to enter a number that is too long for the column, 1-2-3 fills the cell with asterisks.

columns of 9 characters each, and you want to print in picas (10 characters per inch) on an 8 1/2 inch wide piece of paper, your worksheet won't fit (10 characters per inch times 8.5 inches = 85 characters). You may, however, be able to adjust the column widths in such a way that the overall width of the worksheet shrinks to 75 characters, allowing a 5 character border on each side.

Also, you may wish to fit an entire worksheet on your screen display, rather than using the cursors to scroll to the right. Sometimes a minor adjustment in column widths will allow you to see the entire worksheet.

Finally, column width adjustment is critical to constructing a visually pleasing worksheet. If several of your wide worksheet columns only have 1 character, but the column width is set for 9 characters, you will create gaps of space that can make the worksheet look unbalanced and even harder to read when it is printed (see Figures 5.3a and 5.3b).

Setting Column Width

You can change the width of a single column or a series of adjacent columns, or all the columns in a worksheet. To change the width of the current column, select the /Worksheet Column Set-Width command. 1-2-3 will prompt you to: `Enter column width (1...240):9`. This means that the current column is now set to 9 characters wide. (All columns are 9 characters wide to begin with.) You can change the column width by typing in an alternative number of characters or by pressing the right or left cursor. Each time you press the right cursor, the column will expand by one character; each time you press the left cursor, the column will contract by one character.

To change the width of a group of adjacent columns move to the left-most or right-most column in the series you wish to adjust, and select the /Worksheet Column Column-Range Set-Width command. 1-2-3 will first ask you to: `Enter range for column width change:` (the prompt will be followed by the address of the current cell). This means to identify for 1-2-3 what group of columns you want to resize. You can use the right or left cursor keys to highlight the appropriate columns and press ENTER.

In addition to painting the column range with the cursor keys, you can simply type in the columns that you wish to change by typing in a set of coordinates, as in E1..J1. (The row number coordinate is irrelevant.) This method has the advantage that you can set the column widths for any series of columns in the worksheet, without having to move the cell pointer.

Invoice Aging Report

Customer	#	Sts	Inv #	Billed	Paid	Age
F. Gerard	12	1	123	03/12/89	03/21/89	9
B. Smith	13	1	124	03/14/89	03/22/89	8
K. Roth	16	0	125	03/14/89		23
F. Locke	22	1	126	03/16/89	03/28/89	12
P. Parnell	33	1	127	03/17/89	03/31/89	14
J. Watts	44	0	128	03/18/89		19
K. Westfall	21	0	129	03/22/89		15
G. Jericho	26	0	130	03/22/89		15

Figure 5.3a

Note the unnecessary gaps in the worksheet.

Invoice Aging Report

Customer	#	Sts	Inv #	Billed	Paid	Age
F. Gerard	12	1	123	03/12/89	03/21/89	9
B. Smith	13	1	124	03/14/89	03/22/89	8
K. Roth	16	0	125	03/14/89		23
F. Locke	22	1	126	03/16/89	03/28/89	12
P. Parnell	33	1	127	03/17/89	03/31/89	14
J. Watts	44	0	128	03/18/89		19
K. Westfall	21	0	129	03/22/89		15
G. Jericho	26	0	130	03/22/89		15

Figure 5.3b

This worksheet is more compact, easier to read, and more attractive.

Either way, once you've specified the group of columns to be formatted, 1-2-3 will ask you for the new column width setting. Type in the desired number and press ENTER.

To change the column width globally (i.e., for the whole worksheet), go to the /Worksheet Global menu and select Column-Width. 1-2-3 will ask you to: `Enter global column width (1..240):9`. When you indicate the desired width (with the cursor keys or by typing in a number all columns in the worksheet will be set to the selected value. Be aware, however, that any individual columns that you have *previously* set with either of the above methods will not be affected by the globally defined column width.

Regardless of how you change various column width settings, once you explicitly set a column width (even if it is set to the same number of characters as the default) the new column width overrides the default and is displayed in in square brackets in the top line of the upper left-hand corner, following the address (see Figure 5.4). The width of column A is indicated by [W11]. If you haven't ever set the width of a particular column, no width setting is displayed; this indicates that it simply follows the default setting.

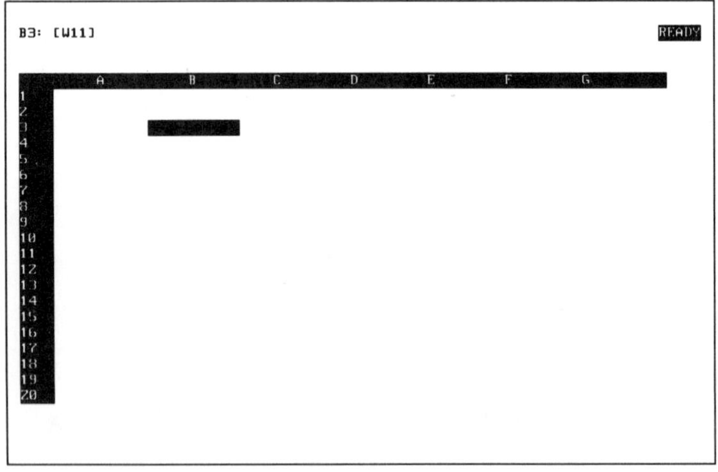

Figure 5.4
Once a column width has been altered, the new width setting appears in the upper left-hand corner of the worksheet.

Finally, you can change the width of a column or group of columns back to the worksheet default (so that no special width-setting is displayed in the control panel). To reset a single column back to the default width, place the cell pointer in the column you wish to change, and then select /Worksheet Column Reset-Width. To reset a group of columns, select /Worksheet Column Column-Range Reset-Width. Specify the range of contiguous columns to reset (use the cursor keys or type in the column coordinates) and press ENTER.

Using Hide and Display

There are a few other commands of interest on the /Worksheet Column menu: Hide and Display. If you wish to suppress the display of a particular column or series of columns in your worksheet, use the Hide command. This command is especially useful when you are printing out your worksheets; you can block the display of various columns that are irrelevant to your printed report. Simply hide the unnecessary portions of the worksheet and then use the /Print command. When you select Hide, 1-2-3 asks you to specify the columns to hide; use the cursor to move to the first column you want hidden, press the period key to anchor the range, move the right or left cursor to highlight the range of columns to hide and press ENTER. You can also simply type in the range of the columns to be hidden (e.g., E1..I1), and press ENTER. Either way, 1-2-3 will remove the columns from view, as shown in Figure 5.5. (Don't worry, your data is still there—you just can't see it). To "unhide" a column (or columns) use the Display command. Specify which columns should be unhidden (or redisplayed) and press ENTER; they will be restored to view.

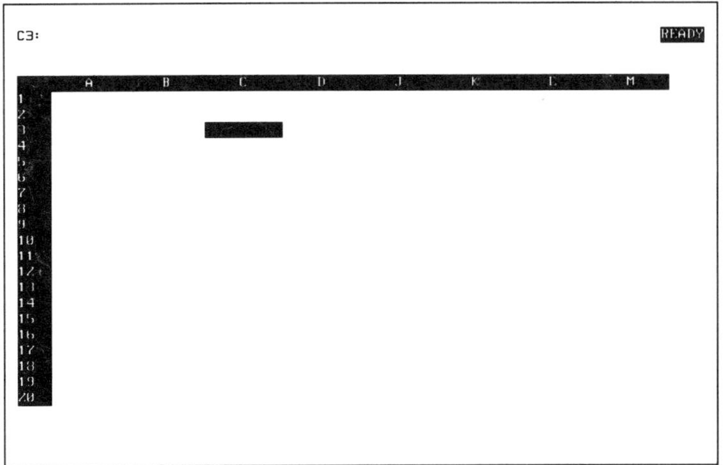

Figure 5.5
Columns E through I are hidden, as you can see from the top border.

INSERTING AND DELETING COLUMNS OR ROWS

Besides affecting your worksheet display by hiding and redisplaying columns, you may wish to actually insert new rows or columns in your worksheet or delete various rows or columns. Adding blank columns or rows can substantially improve a worksheet's appearance, by spacing out crowded data, or highlighting important data. The Column/Row Insert and Delete commands, however, should both be used with extreme caution, especially if Undo is not in effect (see below for a complete discussion of Undo). Insertions may seem harmless, but in fact they can cause unexpected results by confusing formulas that you've entered or macros that you've written, etc.

Deletions, of course, can wipe out whole rows or columns of formulas and data that took hours to think up or enter. (Also, with a deletion you can unwittingly erase a corner of a named range and thus cause 1-2-3 to report an error.) In short, be careful. When in doubt, back out of the command with the ESC key and reconsider your action.

Insertions

To insert one or more columns or rows, select the /Worksheet Insert Column/Row command, 1-2-3 will prompt you for an "insert range." Suppose the pointer was located in column B when you issued the /Worksheet Insert Column command; and you wanted to insert three columns. To do this, press the right cursor two times (there is no need to anchor the range with a period). Columns B, C, and D are highlighted as in Figure 5.6a. When you press ENTER, 1-2-3 will insert three new columns, as shown in Figure 5.6b. What has happened, in fact, is that you've blasted a "hole" in the worksheet, shoving all text and numbers from column B over to the right. Inserted columns appear to the left of the starting column. Thus, the data that was previously located in column B is now located in column E, the data in column C is now located in column F, and so on.

The same principles apply to row insertions. Inserted rows appear above the specified range. Note that when you insert columns or rows, all formulas (relative, mixed, or absolute) are adjusted to reflect the change; and when you insert columns or rows into any named ranges, the ranges expand or shrink accordingly.

Deletions

The /Worksheet Delete Column/Row commands work in just the opposite fashion as the Insert commands—entire columns or rows are stripped from the worksheet and the remaining gap is closed up. When you use either /Worksheet Delete command, 1-2-3 prompts you for the range of columns (or rows) to delete. Type in the coordinates, or paint the range with the cursors. When you press ENTER, the columns or rows will be deleted. Note that you cannot delete parts of worksheet columns or rows from the /Worksheet menu. You can erase (or empty the contents of) portions of the worksheet by using the /Range Erase command.

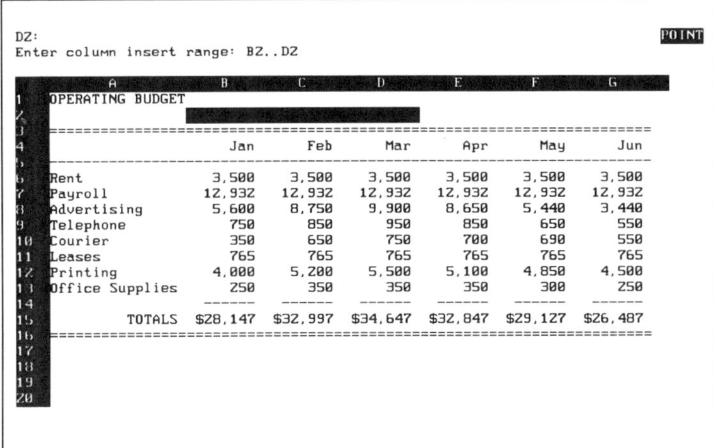

D2: POINT
Enter column insert range: B2..D2

	A	B	C	D	E	F	G
1	OPERATING BUDGET						
2							
3	========	========	========	========	========	========	========
4		Jan	Feb	Mar	Apr	May	Jun
5	--------	--------	--------	--------	--------	--------	--------
6	Rent	3,500	3,500	3,500	3,500	3,500	3,500
7	Payroll	12,932	12,932	12,932	12,932	12,932	12,932
8	Advertising	5,600	8,750	9,900	8,650	5,440	3,440
9	Telephone	750	850	950	850	650	550
10	Courier	350	650	750	700	690	550
11	Leases	765	765	765	765	765	765
12	Printing	4,000	5,200	5,500	5,100	4,850	4,500
13	Office Supplies	250	350	350	350	300	250
14		------	------	------	------	------	------
15	TOTALS	$28,147	$32,997	$34,647	$32,847	$29,127	$26,487
16	========	========	========	========	========	========	========
17							
18							
19							
20							

Figure 5.6a

Column insert range.

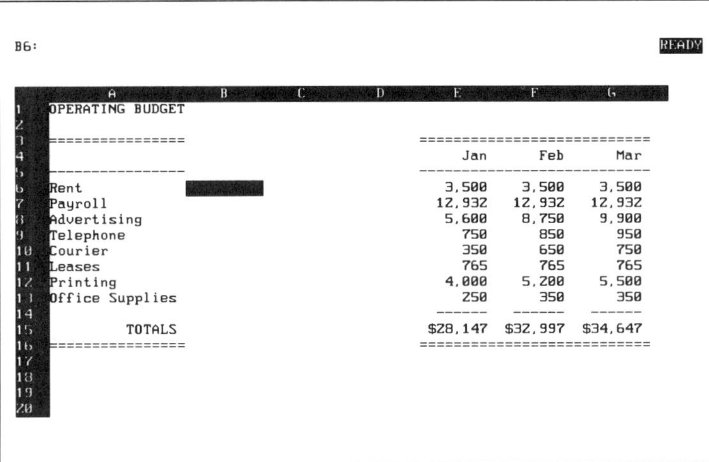

B6: READY

	A	B	C	D	E	F	G
1	OPERATING BUDGET						
2							
3	========				========	========	========
4					Jan	Feb	Mar
5	--------				--------	--------	--------
6	Rent				3,500	3,500	3,500
7	Payroll				12,932	12,932	12,932
8	Advertising				5,600	8,750	9,900
9	Telephone				750	850	950
10	Courier				350	650	750
11	Leases				765	765	765
12	Printing				4,000	5,200	5,500
13	Office Supplies				250	350	350
14					------	------	------
15	TOTALS				$28,147	$32,997	$34,647
16	========				========	========	========
17							
18							
19							
20							

Figure 5.6b

Results of inserting three columns.

WORKSHEET DISPLAY TOOLS

As your worksheets grow larger and more complicated with time, you may be frustrated that you cannot see the entire spreadsheet on screen at once. The /Worksheet command menu offers two different solutions to this problem: locking titles and the split screen.

Titles Lock

As you add columns beyond the right edge of the screen, you might find it difficult to enter new data without seeing your identifying labels to the left in column A.

The same can occur as you add more line items into your worksheet rows; without the column titles in view, you may lose track of which columns are which. The solution to this problem is to lock in place the rows or columns containing labels so that they stay on the screen for reference. Then, even as you move to the right or down, the locked columns or rows will stay in place.

To lock a row in place, position the cursor under the row you want to remain stationary, and select /Worksheet Titles Row. To lock a column in place, move the cursor to the right of the column you want to lock, and select /Worksheet Titles Column. You can lock the row and the column in place by selecting /Worksheet Column Both. If you do so, make sure the cursor is positioned at the top-left corner of the moveable space, so that the desired row and column will be locked in place. To remove the titles lock, select /Worksheet Titles Clear.

Dual Display with Worksheet Windows

Another display tool is the Worksheet Window, which splits the screen horizontally (Figure 5.7a) or vertically (Figure 5.7b) at the position of the cell pointer, giving you a view of two parts of the worksheet.

To move from one window to the other, press the WINDOW (F6) key. As an additional feature, you can control whether the contents of the window are synchronized (/Worksheet Windows Sync—the default), so that moving the cursor up, down, right, or left causes the position of the worksheet in the second window to shift accordingly, or whether the two move independently (/Worksheet Windows Unsync.)

To remove the windowing structure, select /Worksheet Window Clear. For more details about the window feature, see the Reference section.

FORMATTING THE DATA IN YOUR WORKSHEET

There are ten formats to select from when you display (or print) your data, including percentage, currency, date and time formats, etc. These ten formatting options allow considerable flexibility in the presentation of your numerical results. Thus, while you cannot type in numbers with commas (1-2-3 will not accept them) you can adjust your display so that commas separate the thousands places. Whatever the formatting you choose, it affects only the display of your data; the values that 1-2-3 actually stores in each cell and uses in its calculations are based on the exact, full values (no rounding), with up to 15 decimal points in accuracy.

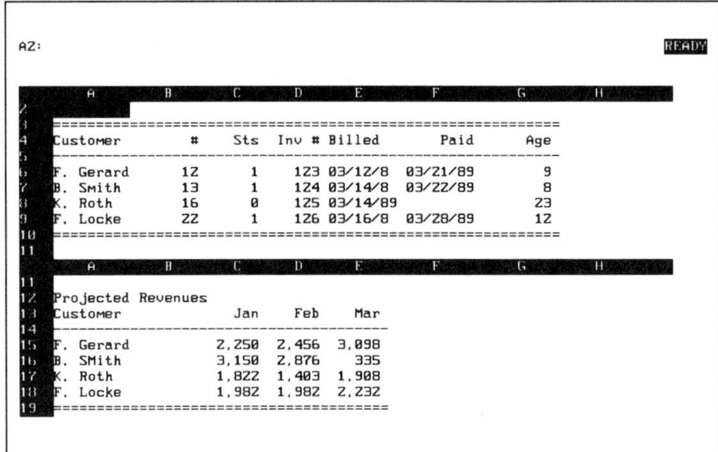

Figure 5.7a
Horizontal window.

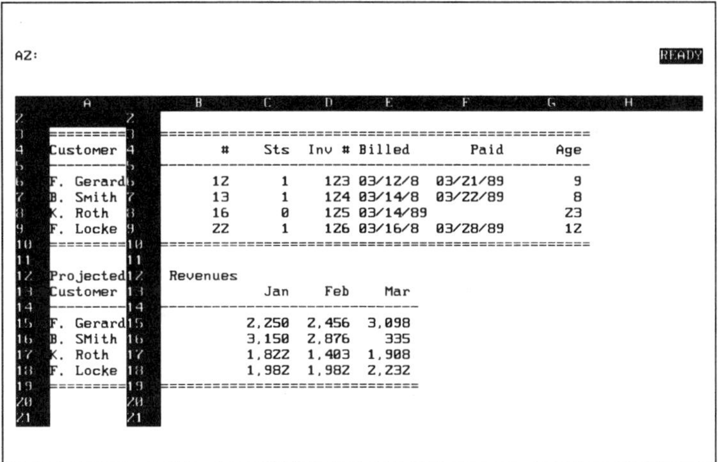

Figure 5.7b
Vertical window.

There are two Main Menu commands from which you make your formatting selections: /Worksheet and /Range. The /Worksheet Global Format commands let you specify a default format for your entire worksheet. Usually the default is General, because most worksheets require a variety of formats. The /Range Format commands on the other hands let you specify formats for various portions of the Worksheet. Any format assignments that are issued through the /Range Format Command take precedence over the worksheet's default format. When you assign a specific format to a cell or range, that format assignment is registered in square brackets in the top line of the control panel.

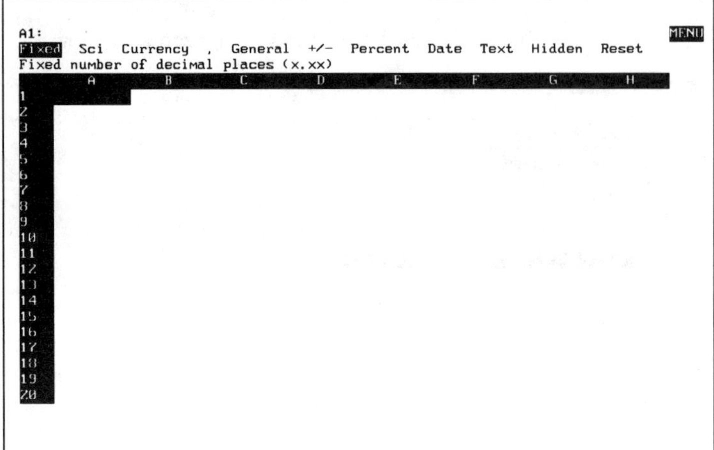

Figure 5.8
/Range Format menu.

The /Range Format Commands

The format options in the /Range Format menu in Figure 5.8 are described below. In many cases, 1-2-3 will ask you to specify the number of decimal places it should include in the display. In all cases, the program will prompt you for the range to format. Either type in the range address or name, or "paint" the range. See the Reference section for an illustration of each format option.

Fixed Displays numbers with no commas, dollar signs, or other symbols. Negative numbers are displayed with a minus sign, unless you select the /Worksheet Global Default Other International Negative Parentheses command, in which case negative numbers appear in parentheses. The fixed format allows you to set the number of decimal places displayed by each number in the range. A leading 0 is placed before decimal numbers (e.g., .45 is displayed as 0.45). If the numbers to the right of the decimal point exceed the number of decimal places specified, 1-2-3 will round the number.) (Note that the default General format, on the other hand, eliminates the display of additional zeros to the right of the decimal point and will truncate any numbers to the right of the decimal that will not fit into the column.) If a cell is formatted as Fixed, with two decimals, the top line of the control panel will display (F2).

Sci Displays numbers in exponential notation. For example, the value 20,000 would be represented as 2.0E+04. In the decimal portion of the number, you can have up to 15 digits. The exponent may range from −99 to 99. If a cell is formatted as Scientific, with 4 decimals, the top line of the control panel will display (S4).

Currency Precedes numbers with a dollar sign, and includes commas separating the thousands places. You can include other currency symbols before or after the number (e.g., 18,000£), but you must specify your alternative currency symbol under /Worksheet Global Default Other International Currency. See the Reference section for details.

, (comma) Adds commas to separate the thousands places. This format is often a good alternative to the Currency format; too many dollar signs on a page can make a worksheet look cluttered. When a cell is formatted as , (comma) with two decimal places, the top line in the control panel will display (,2).

General Displays numbers without commas and without trailing zeros; this is 1-2-3's default format. If the number preceding the decimal point exceeds the column width, 1-2-3 will use scientific notation to display it. If the number of characters following the decimal point exceeds the column width, 1-2-3 will truncate the number rather than rounding it.

+/– Displays the integer value of the cell as a series of plus or minus signs; plus signs designate positive numbers and minus signs designate negative numbers. The number 3 is displayed as +++. The number 2.7 is displayed as +++, The number –1.8 is displayed as –. Values falling between –1 and 1 are represented by a period (.), and values greater than the column width are displayed as asterisks. A cell that is formatted as +/–, displays (+) in the top line of the control panel.

Percent Displays values as percentages with a trailing percent sign (e.g., 10%). Note that when a range is formatted for percent, 1-2-3 will automatically multiply by 100. Therefore to enter 10 percent, enter .1; to enter 100 percent, enter 1. When a cell is formatted for Percent, with two decimal places, the top line of the control panel displays (P2).

Date Converts 1-2-3's serial date numbers to five different date formats: DD-MMM-YY, DD-MMM, MMM-YY, MM/DD/YY, and MM/DD. (The display for the last two options, Long Intn'l and Short Intn'l, can be reordered or adjusted through /Worksheet Global Default Other International Date). The date range is January 1, 1900 (this is 1-2-3's serial date number 1) to December 31, 2099 (1-2-3's serial date number 73050). Date values out of this range are displayed as asterisks.

If you don't know the serial number that corresponds to the date you wish to use (serial numbers are generated during computations), 1-2-3 offers a convenient function that will do it for you. Enter dates in the following manner:

```
@date(YY,MM,DD)
```

The resulting date display will appear in whatever format you have selected for the range. To display the current system date, enter @NOW, and the current date will appear in the format you have chosen. Once in serial date number format, you can add or subtract dates as you would numbers. For example, to generate an invoice aging value, you could use a date billed that was placed in cell C12, formatted for date and subtract it from today's system date with the formula:

```
@NOW-C12.
```

The /Range Format Date command also has an option called Time. 1-2-3 calculates every hour, minute, and second as a fraction of the twenty-four hour clock; 3 AM, for example, is represented as .125. Formatting a cell for Time converts the decimal portion of a value into one of four time formats: HH:MM:SS (AM/PM), 14:00:01 PM; HH:MM (AM/PM), 14:00 PM; HH:MM:SS (24 hour), and HH:MM (24 hour). (The last two display options, Long Intn'l and Short Intn'l, can be adjusted through the /Worksheet Global Default Other International Time command.) As with dates, entering @NOW in a cell formatted for a Time display will show the current system time.

An obvious use of the combined date and time function is to document when reports were printed. If, in the upper corner of your worksheet, you place @NOW in two cells, and format one for date, and one for time, your worksheet will always show the current date and time when you print it out.

Text Displays formulas as they are entered, without evaluating or computing them. The formulas will still be "active," and perform the appropriate calculations, but their results appear elsewhere. This feature is particularly useful when using /Data Table commands (see the /Data Table portion of the Reference Section). When 1-2-3 generates tables of data, several series of input variables are fed to the formula for calculation in sequence, and the results are displayed in an output table range. In such circumstances the formula is displayed as text to clearly identify the operation taking place. Formatting a range of values as text can also be a good way to pick out any cells with formulas in your worksheet. When a cell is formatted as text, the top line of the control panel displays (T).

Hidden Masks the contents of a cell or range from the screen without actually removing the data. The contents of the cell, however, are displayed in the control panel. To blank the cell contents from the control panel as well, you must also protect the cell using /Range Protect, as described below, (and also make sure that protection is activated with /Worksheet Global Protect Enable). This has the additional benefit of preventing anyone from accidentally overwriting the contents of the hidden cell(s) that appear to be empty. See the Reference section for more details. When a cell is formatted as Hidden, the top line of the control panel displays (H).

To unhide a cell or range, use /Range Format Reset. You will then have to reformat the range for the style in which you want to represent numerical values.

Try entering values into several cells and change the format. As you'll see, 1-2-3 will instantly change the display format while leaving the underlying numbers intact. The Reset option on the /Range Format menu returns a range to whatever default settings have been specified with the /Worksheet Global Format command.

Other Formatting Options on the /Range Menu

The /Range menu offers several more speciallized commands that can affect the formatting and layout of your data. We mention them briefly here, but refer you to the Reference section for full details.

The /Range Label command allows you to specify how you want the labels in a range to be aligned: Left, Right, or Center. Note that this command only affects text that is already in the cells of the range. Any new text that you type in will follow the default label prefix, usually left-aligned.

/Range Justify is used to adjust a column of text of variable line lengths to a justified, word-wrapped column. You can specify the width (up to 240 characters) for the justified rendition of your original text. This feature can be particularly useful when you are importing ASCII text files into the spreadsheet.

The /Range Value command is used as a special kind of Copy. It copies one range to another range but instead of copying the formulas and their cell references to the new location, /Range Value copies the current values of the formulas.

/Range Trans is another special kind of copy. You can use transpose to change a row of data into a column of data and vice versa. Note that when you transpose data that contains formulas, they are converted to their current value. Be sure to recalculate your worksheet if recalc is not set to manual before using this command.

Finally, /Range Search will search for, and replace, text within a range just like an ordinary word processor.

PROTECTING THE WORKSHEET

Often several users besides yourself may have to enter data into your worksheet. In these cases, you may want to "protect" your work so that all your efforts will not be obliterated in the hands of an inexperienced user.

Protecting a worksheet involves the Protection option under the /Worksheet Global menu in conjunction with the /Range Prot and /Range Unprot commands. When you first load in a worksheet "global" protection is disabled. This allows you to enter in all your data, edit it, and rearrange it freely. However, once you have set up the worksheet to your satisfaction, you may want to turn /Worksheet Global Protection on to prevent any inadvertent changes to your work. When /Worksheet Global Protection is on, every cell in the worksheet displays a PR in the top line of the control panel unless it is explicity unprotected with the /Range Unprot command.

THE SAFETY NET: UNDO

In several instances we've mentioned the existence of Undo, which gives you a chance to "undo" your last command and restore your worksheet to its prior state. For example, if you erase a particular range (with /Range Erase) by mistake or, even a whole worksheet (with /Worksheet Erase), you can recover your work with the UNDO key (ALT-F4).

Undo applies to formatting commands as well. Suppose you had painstakingly formatted a large range with a variety of percentage and currency formats, and later you reset the range to General accidentally. If you press UNDO immediately afterward, your original format selections would be restored.

You can even salvage mistakes made with the /Copy and /Move commands, where you may have overwritten the contents and formatting of the target cell or range. You might copy the value 10, formatted for percentage, one decimal place, from cell A21 to cell B24; cell B24 contained the number 456, formatted as currency, no decimal places. If you press the UNDO (ALT-F4) key, the original value in the target cell, 456, is redisplayed in cell B24, along with its original formatting—currency, no decimal places.

If you want to undo your last Undo command, press ALT-F4 again; provided that you have not entered any data or commands in between, the worksheet will be restored to its state prior to the first Undo command. This feature is extremely useful for comparing two different values or results during "what-if" analysis by showing what if cell A12 had value X, and what if it had value Y. The UNDO key can even be used to undo a /File Retrieve command; thus you can instantly move between one file and another and compare them. Be aware, though, that 1-2-3 only provides one level of backup; once you enter the Main Menu to issue another command, you cannot undo *any* previous command (including Undo itself).

When You Can't Use Undo

To better understand how the Undo command operates, and how much you can actually rely on it, you must know how 1-2-3 backs up your worksheet. Each time you enter data into a cell, or you press the slash (/) key to invoke a menu, the TABLE (F8) key, or the CALC (F9) key, 1-2-3 "takes a new picture" of your worksheet and records it in memory in a special area called the "undo buffer" (when Undo is enabled, of course). The Undo buffer is then updated again the next time you enter new data or issue a command; the previous version is gone for good. Once you press the slash key to enter the menu system, for example, you cannot go back and restore the worksheet to its state prior to your last command. This is because 1-2-3 will have just made a copy of your worksheet as you pressed the slash(/) key and will have overwritten the previous copy in memory.

Also, once a worksheet is saved to disk the previous version of that worksheet is overwritten. Undo cannot restore previous disk versions of your worksheets. You must be sure to keep backup copies of important worksheets. In fact, Undo will not "un-write" any file that has been written to disk. Therefore, the /File Save and /File Xtract commands that write current data to disk, cannot be undone. Undo also does not work with the new /Add-In commands, the /System command, or any of the PrintGraph commands.

In addition, you cannot undo actions initiated with the following keys:

BACKSPACE

ENTER

DEL

INS

ESC

CTRL-BREAK

Any function key other than F8 or F9

Any function key combination (e.g., ALT-F2, which invokes the macro STEP mode).

Finally, using Undo with macros has some unforeseen effects, because Undo treats macros as if they were single commands. If you use Undo with a macro that alters your worksheet data or settings, it will restore the worksheet to its condition prior to the execution of the entire macro, not to the state induced by the macro's penultimate command. For example, if you executed a macro that successively copied columns of numbers and pressed Undo when the macro was finished, you would not simply restore the last column to its condition prior to running the macro. Rather, you would restore the data in all columns (as well as all worksheet settings).

Enabling/Disabling Undo—Memory Constraints

As shipped, Release 2.2's Undo feature is enabled. It automatically makes a temporary backup copy of your worksheet in memory according to the rules described above and the UNDO indicator is on (at the bottom of your screen, slightly to the left of the center). The price for this protection can be approximately half of the conventional memory that is available on your system after 1-2-3 is loaded. If you have expanded memory (above 640K), 1-2-3 will attempt to place the entire undo buffer there. (It will be one-half the size of the total memory available, conventional plus expanded.) If it can't do so, either because you don't enough expanded memory or because you have other programs operating in higher memory, 1-2-3 will place as much of the buffer in expanded memory as it can, and place the rest in conventional memory.

The consequence of giving up half of your memory is that you may not be able to run very large worksheets and Undo at the same time. If you run into this problem, you have two choices. One is to Disable Undo by selecting /Worksheet Global Default Other Undo Disable. You can leave Undo disabled just for the remaining 1-2-3 session by quitting from the /Worksheet Global Default menu, without updating your 123.CFG file. In this case, Undo will be enabled the next time you load 1-2-3. You can also make disabled the default setting by selecting Update. When you select Update, Undo will be disabled each time you load 1-2-3 until you again select /Global Default Other Undo Enable. Remember, if you change your Undo global default setting in between commands, the Undo buffer is immediately cleared. Even if you change your mind and re-enable the Undo function, you will not be able to restore the worksheet to its former state.

The second option is to simply keep going until 1-2-3 runs out of space for the Undo buffer, at which point it will abandon the buffer in favor of your worksheet. If you try to use Undo at that point, 1-2-3 will display the prompt:

```
You will not be able to undo this action—do you wish to
proceed? (Y/N)
```

In other words, 1-2-3 will not hamper your efforts to build the largest possible worksheet that your system can handle. But you may lose Undo during the process.

NOTE If 1-2-3 has suspended your current operation to announce that you don't have enough memory to use Undo, you can either select N when prompted whether you wish to proceed, or press CTRL-BREAK. You can then decide whether you want to pare down your worksheet or take your chances by going without a backup in memory.

This chapter introduced the commands you need for formatting worksheets and for working the display and structure of your data.

The next chapter covers formulas, and builds on the concepts covered here. You might try setting up a worksheet shell of your own, say a check register or a monthly budget, using the worksheet development and formatting commands discussed above. As you read the following chapter, energize it with the necessary formulas and give it functionality. That procedure—structure→format→formulas—is how the data in all worksheets come to life.

6 Formulas and Functions

OVERVIEW

We mentioned that the real power of 1-2-3 lies in the use of formulas that link cells or groups of cells, formulas that rely on the results in other cells in the current worksheet, and even cells in other worksheets. This chapter describes how to write formulas, and goes on to explain the basic usage of 1-2-3's built-in @functions, many of which are really predefined (often complex) formulas that can offer you tremendous calculation power.

Without formulas, 1-2-3 would be little more than a special word processor/calculator; you would simply lay down your numbers and the appropriate text in various regions of the worksheet. Not only can you calculate formulas with literal numbers (such as 5*(4+3) for example), but 1-2-3 formulas allow you to use cell references and to incorporate them in your mathematical statements. These results can in turn be used for further calculations, and so on, so that an elaborate linking system is created.

USING CELL REFERENCES

Let's first briefly discuss cell referencing in formulas. If you were to use 1-2-3 just as a calculator, you might type in formulas using just numbers, like 7+3, 679*473/45, etc., and 1-2-3 would certainly provide the correct results. But the whole point of 1-2-3's column/row address system is that you can refer to numbers by their location in the worksheet. For example, say that you have specified a unit cost figure—$1.92—in the cell B2 of your worksheet; and suppose that several of your spreadsheet calculations are based on that unit cost. Rather than typing in $1.92 in several places, you can simply refer to the cell B2. (You do this by typing in the cell address preceded by a + sign, e.g., +B2; the plus sign indicates that this is a formula, and not a label.) Not only is a cell reference easier to type in, but it also offers you the opportunity to change the unit cost to different values and see how the calculations throughout your worksheet are affected.

Making Cell References to Other Worksheets

Release 2.2 offers a way to make cell references to another worksheet, thus linking files to the current worksheet. The *source* cell is in the worksheet on disk; the *target* cell is in the current worksheet. Worksheets are linked by cell-to-cell connections that are "live." Whenever a worksheet with links to other files is loaded, 1-2-3 automatically checks all referenced source cells, and updates the target cells with the latest data.

To create a link in your worksheet, all you have to do is reference the file containing the source cell in angle brackets <<>>, followed by that source cell's address. For example, let's say that your current worksheet is called CASHFLOW.WK1, and it uses the totals from another file on disk named REVENUE.WK1. To reference cell A12 from REVENUE in cell C12 of CASHFLOW, you would move the cell pointer to C12, then enter the formula:

```
+<<REVENUE>>A12
```

If the files are not in the same directory as your target file, you will have to specify its full path name, as in:

```
+<<D:\BUDGET\REVENUE>>A12
```

or

```
+<<B:EXPENSE>>E2
```

If you reference a nonexistent file, 1-2-3 will display the message "File does not exist" in the lower left-hand corner of the screen, and a flashing error message in the upper right-hand corner. Press ESC to continue, and either enter the correct name or create the missing file.

You cannot reference more than one file in the same cell. For example,

```
+<<REVENUE>>A12+<<EXPENSE>>A12
```

is an invalid formula. To obtain the sum of cell C12 from the two files, you would have to reference each of them in separate cells of the current worksheet, and then add the two cells together.

You can reference as many files as you wish in the current worksheet, although the more links you create, the more slowly the file will load into memory the next time you retrieve it. If you are using a floppy system and you reference multiple files, be especially patient since 1-2-3 will have to read each file one by one. Also, with a floppy system you must make sure that all of the source files are on the same floppy; otherwise, when you retrieve the file, 1-2-3 will report an error for any cell referencing file(s) that cannot be found.

Refreshing Links to Other Worksheets

One of the beauties of the new linking system is that you can instantly update the linked cells in your worksheet with a special option on the /File menu. When you select /File Admin Link-Refresh, 1-2-3 automatically updates all cells that have references to cells in other worksheets, returning the latest results. Of course, if you haven't updated your data in the source worksheets, your results may still be incorrect, so it is important to keep track of which worksheets need to be updated for a series of linked worksheets to produce correct results.

Listing Linked Files

To help you keep track of your source and target worksheets, Release 2.2 also provides a linked-file listing facility. By selecting /File List Linked, all the source files associated with the current worksheet will be displayed on your screen.

The order in which linked files are listed will depend on the cell in which the pointer is positioned when the /File Linked List command is issued. The file referenced in the current cell will be the first file listed on the screen. Press ESC to return to MENU mode.

MATHEMATICAL FUNCTIONS IN FORMULAS

Having discussed some of the advantages of using cell references in formulas, it is time to review the basic mathematical operations available in 1-2-3. Mathematical functions are carried out using the mathematical operators shown in Table 6.1. The table contains examples using cell references and then range names.

Table 6.1 Mathematical Functions

Operator	Operation	Cell References	Range Names
+	addition	+A11+B11	+REVENUE+EXPENSES
-	subtraction	+C34–D45	+ANNUAL–100
*	multiplication	+F54*J44	+MONTHLY*12
/	division	+Y87/H88	+ANNUAL/MONTHLY
^	exponentiation	+A3^3	+ANNUAL^3

These five operations can be used and combined endlessly to create formulas.

A formula may simply involve just two cells and a single operation—such as +A1+A2—or it may involve many cells, ranges, and mathematical expressions at once. Some complex formulas can be very long and look very difficult.

Even experts must take care in constructing such formulas. Because computations within parenthesis are performed first, and proceed "outward" to the outermost pair, the correct placing of parentheses is key to getting reliable results. In fact, one of the most common errors in entering formulas is the omission of the required punctuation. Let's begin with the rules for writing formulas.

WRITING FORMULAS: GROUND RULES

Regardless of whether you are writing a mathematical formula, or using a built-in @function, you must observe a certain set of ground rules. The following basic rules apply to all formula types:

1. If a formula doesn't begin with a number, 1-2-3 will mistake it for a label, unless you precede it with one of the characters in Table 6.2. This is particularly useful when you must begin your formula with a cell reference (e.g., A1, B2, etc.) or a range name.

Tabel 6.2 Value Prefixes

Value Prefix	Examples
+	+A13+B14
–	–B22/G3
@	@IF(d33>0,A2,H:23)
(	(D12+E34)/2
$	$REVENUE–EXPENSES
#	#NOT#S23=0 (which means, "the contents of cell S23 does not equal zero")

2. A formula can contain up to 240 characters; it must not contain spaces.
3. 1-2-3 has a well-defined order of precedence when it performs calculations. (The following list shows the order, with Exponentiation being the highest level of precedence and the first calculation performed.)

   Exponentiation (^)
   Positive/negative number identification (+, –)
   Multiplication and division (*, /)
   Addition and subtraction (+,–)
   Test for equal to and not equal to (=, <>)
   Test for less-than and greater than (<, >)
   Test for less-than-or-equal-to (<=)
   Test for greater-than-or-equal-to (>=)
   Test for logical-NOT (#NOT#)
   Test for logical-AND and logical-OR (#AND#,#OR#)
   String concatenation (&)

When you want to control or override the absolute sequence of calculation, you must use parentheses to specify your alternative order. For example, 1+2*3 yields 7, because multiplication precedes addition. Likewise, 12–4/2 results in 10 because division precedes subtraction. If you had intended the first formula to yield 9, as in 1+2=3 and then 3*3=9, then you must enclose 1+2 in parentheses, as in (1+2)*3, this tells 1-2-3 to treat 1+2 as a unit and forces the addition to take place before the multiplication. 1-2-3 will always calculate operations that are enclosed in parentheses first. (When there are parentheses within parentheses, 1-2-3 will evaluate the innermost set of nested parentheses first.) The examples in Table 6.3 show how the use of parentheses can affect the outcome of a formula.

Table 6.3 How Parentheses Affect Formulas

Formula	Value
(1–2+3*4/5^6)	–0.999232
((1–2)+3*4/5^6)	–0.999232
(1–(2+3)*4/5^6)	0.99872
(1–2+(3*4)/5^6)	–0.999232
(1–2+3*4/(5^6))	–0.999232

Table 6.3 *continued*

Formula	Value
((1−2+3)*4/5^6)	0.000512
(1−(2+3*4)/5^6)	0.999104
(1−2+(3*4/5)^6)	190.102976
(1−2+3*(4/5^6))	−0.999232
((1−2+3*4)/5^6)	0.000704
(1−2+(3*4/5^6))	−0.999232
(1−2+(3*4/5)^6)	190.102976

At this point, you should be in command of the basic rules necessary for creating your own 1-2-3 formulas. If you've never written formulas before, consider the following two hints:

- Write formulas on paper first. Jot down what the formulas mean and what you intend to do with the results.
- Keep your formulas simple. Using named ranges can be very helpful in this regard, since your formulas will be more meaningful. For example, +REVENUE−EXPENSES is much easier to understand than +B12−F12.

Now that you know the basic rules for writing formulas in 1-2-3, and have a sense of how useful it is to include cell references in your formulas, you can begin to write more sophisticated formulas. There is another aspect to working with formulas that relies on a key feature of 1-2-3's cell address system. In fact, a formula can reference a particular cell by writing its address in one of three ways: as a relative address, as an absolute address, or as a mixed address. This flexibility of the cell reference system is particularly powerful when you start to copy formulas and reuse them in different parts of the worksheet.

RELATIVE/MIXED/ABSOLUTE ADDRESSES

Relative Cell References

By default, when you include cell addresses in your formulas, 1-2-3 treats them as *relative* references. That is, 1-2-3 understands the referenced cells in terms of their locations relative to the cell that contains the formula. For example, if you enter the formula +B5+B6 in cell B7, it actually means "take whatever values are in the first and second cells above the current formula cell, and add them."

When you copy formulas with relative addresses to a new location, the cell references are changed to adapt to the formula's new position. The new cell references maintain the same relative position to the formula cell. For example, if you copy the formula in B7 to C7, you will see that the cells referenced by the formula change to +C5+C6—so that the first and second cells above the new formula cell are added. (See Figure 6.1) If you copy the formula to cell D7, you'll see that the formula changes to +D5+D6, and so on. Relative addressing allows you to copy one formula and "spread" it across a worksheet and have the references change properly in each column or row.

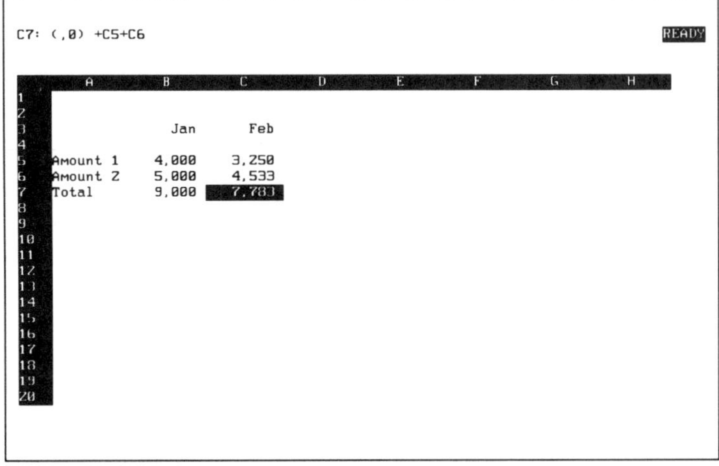

Figure 6.1
Relative address are adjusted with the /Copy command.

Absolute Cell Addresses

As powerful as the relative address function may be, there are times when it is desirable to fix the cell references in your formulas, so that they do *not* adapt to a new position. 1-2-3 lets you include *absolute* or "locked" cell references in your formulas so that the address does not change when the formula is copied.

To continue with the example above, let's say you had to create totals for January through August; and in addition you had to adjust all these monthly totals (labelled "Principal" in this case) to compensate for a certain interest rate factor, a rate that constantly changed from day to day. (See Figure 6.2.) You reserve the cell B1 for holding the interest rate of the day, whatever it is; it is conveniently at the head of the worksheet and immediately tells the viewer what the totals below are based on.

To calculate the interest rate on the principal amount for January, you would

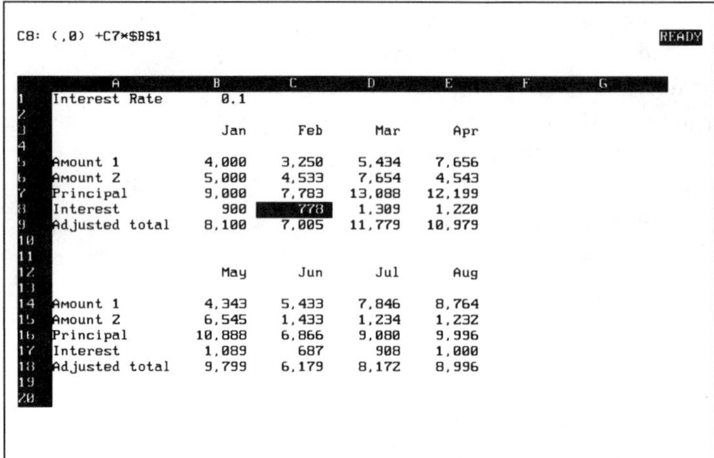
C8: (,0) +C7*$B$1 READY

	A	B	C	D	E	F	G
1	Interest Rate	0.1					
2							
3		Jan	Feb	Mar	Apr		
4							
5	Amount 1	4,000	3,250	5,434	7,656		
6	Amount 2	5,000	4,533	7,654	4,543		
7	Principal	9,000	7,783	13,088	12,199		
8	Interest	900	778	1,309	1,220		
9	Adjusted total	8,100	7,005	11,779	10,979		
10							
11							
12		May	Jun	Jul	Aug		
13							
14	Amount 1	4,343	5,433	7,846	8,764		
15	Amount 2	6,545	1,433	1,234	1,232		
16	Principal	10,888	6,866	9,080	9,996		
17	Interest	1,089	687	908	1,000		
18	Adjusted total	9,799	6,179	8,172	8,996		
19							
20							

Figure 6.2
Using Absolute addresses with the /Copy command.

place the formula +B7*B1 in cell B8. (This allows you to calculate an adjusted total (+B7–B8) in B9.

Then if you copied the formula in B8 to C8 to calculate the interest for February the new formula in C8 would read +C7*C1. That clearly is not what you intended; the cell C1 is empty. The way to avoid this, and keep a fixed reference to the interest rate in B1, is by making the address absolute. To designate a reference as absolute, precede the column letter and row number with a dollar sign character ($). Thus, the formula in B8 should read (B7*$B$1). When you try again to copy this formula to C8 through E8, and then to B17 through E17, you will see that the reference to B1 remains fixed: the formula in C8 is (C7*$B$1), the formula in D8 is (D7*$B$1), the formula in B17 is (B16*$B$1), and so on.

Mixed Addresses

1-2-3 also lets you use *mixed* addresses, where just the column or just the row coordinate in a cell address is fixed and the other dimension is treated as relative. At the head of the worksheet, reserve the cell B1 for the percentage rate again so that the viewer knows what percentage rate you are working with. This time you need to find interest rates for a single row of figures (row 7) as shown in Figure 6.3. You wish to multiply all the numbers in row 7 (B7 through E7) by the percentage figure in B1; you want the adjusted totals placed in row 8. Proceed by entering the formula B7*B1 in cell B8. If you copied the formula as is, into C8, the formula would be changed to C7*C1, to compensate for the new location one column over. This is, of course, not what you want. You need to make the

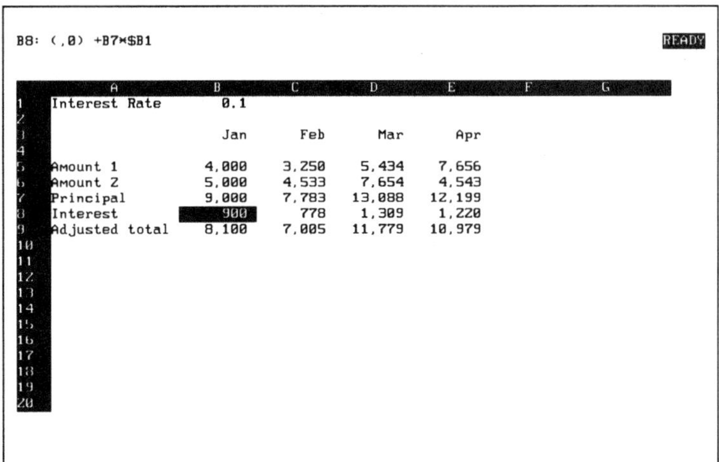

Figure 6.3
Using Mixed References with the /Copy command.

column coordinate "absolute" in the original formula by preceding it with a dollar sign, as in +B7*$B2 and then copy it into C8..E8.

Since you are only copying the formula *across* the worksheet in a single row (row 7), the row number in the formula will not change, and you can leave the formula as a mixed reference. If you were to copy the formula in a single column *down* the worksheet, rather than across the worksheet, you would make the row coordinate absolute, as in +B7*B$1.

In addition to typing out your absolute and mixed references, you can use the F4 special function key, as described in the next section.

Using the F4 Key to Change Cell References

As discussed, you can change the reference in a cell by means of the F4 key as well as by manually entering dollar signs in the appropriate places.

Let's return to the original formula used in the absolute and mixed address sections. Go to cell B8, and press F2 to edit the formula.

```
+B7*B1
```

Press F4, and the address becomes absolute:

```
+B7*$B$1
```

Press F4 again, and the cell address will become mixed, with the column address remaining relative and the row coordinate becoming absolute: (B7*B$1). If you press F4 another time, the address will remain mixed, but now with the column absolute and the row relative: B7*$B1

Finally, pressing F4 again will return the address to relative address (B7*B1). If you had wished to change the relative cell reference, B7, you could simply have moved the cursor to the B, the 7, or immediately to the right of B7 and pressed F4 in the same manner.

This concludes the formula writing discussion. At this point, you should experiment with your own formulas before going onto the next section, which concerns the use of @functions.

@FUNCTIONS—GENERAL USAGE

@Functions are predefined formulas, some of them simple, others complex. @Functions save you the time of typing out otherwise tedious mathematical and statistical formulas and also reduce the possibility of errors. The @functions are usually grouped into seven categories: Mathematical, Date and Time, Financial, Statistical, Logical, String, and Special. We will first run through the rules for using @functions and then review the kinds of tasks you can accomplish with each @function category. The Reference section on @functions (organized alphabetically) covers each function in detail.

Rules for Using @Functions

All @functions begin with the @ sign, followed by the name of the function (in upper- or lowercase) and one or more arguments. The function name describes the action that 1-2-3 is to take while the argument(s) pinpoint the data to be manipulated. For example, "@AVG(A12..F23)" calculates the average of all the numerical entries in the range from A12 through F23. The *function name* is AVG; the function *argument* is (A12..F23).

Arguments can include a simple value, a cell or cells, a range name, a string, or a condition; they must immediately follow the function name (no spaces are allowed in formulas) and they must be placed in parentheses.

Conditional arguments often use the logical operators <,>,=,<>, >=,<=. In addition you can use the Boolean operators NOT, AND, or OR, bracketed by pound signs (#) as in #NOT#. In addition, conditional arguments can consist of numbers, numeric formulas, string formulas, literal strings, or cell references.

String arguments can use a literal string (enclosed in quotes so that 1-2-3 will not try and interpret the string), string formulas, or the range name or cell address of a cell that contains a label or string formula.

Location Arguments for @Functions

To illustrate the use of @functions, we'll look at the simplest @function @SUM. If you understand how the @SUM formula operates, you can apply your knowledge to any of the other @functions that require an address or range name as an argument. Let's say that you want to add all the cells in column C, from C6 to C17, and enter the total in C18. You could do this by enter the following formula in C18:

```
C6+C7+C8+C8+C9+C10+C11+C12+C13+C14+C15+C16+C17
```

A much easier way of proceeding would be to use the @function @SUM, with the argument (C6..C17):

```
@sum(C6..C17)
```

You even could have painted in your range argument by using the following procedure:

1. Move the cell pointer to C18.
2. Type: `@SUM(`
3. Press the up arrow and you'll see the second line of the control panel display: `@SUM(C17.`
4. Anchor the range by pressing the period (.) key. Then press the up arrow key until the painted range includes cell C6.
5. Type the concluding right parenthesis. The cell pointer will return to cell C18. The completed formula @SUM(C17..C6) will appear in the control panel.

NOTE: You do not have to paint a range directly adjacent to the cell in which you are entering the formula. You can move the cell pointer to any cell and press the period (.) key to anchor the range.

If painting in your range seems like a lot of steps, in practice it can be much faster than entering explicit argument locations, especially when the range covers numerous rows and cells. In general, most people prefer painting a range to typing in range coordinates. It is also more accurate, since you give yourself a visual confirmation of the coordinates.

Other @functions require more complicated arguments that include strings, dates, or logical functions, and for those refer to the Reference section. The several categories of @functions have their own special requirements, and we recommend familiarizing yourself with them as specific needs arise. There's no point in learning about every function available in 1-2-3, since you may only use a few of them often and some very rarely, if at all. Start off with @sum, which has almost universal applicability, then expand your repertoire until you are creating ever more sophisticated worksheets to meet your analytical and reporting needs.

Mathematical and Statistical Functions Use these whenever you want to quickly and easily perform a calculation on a column of numbers, a row of numbers, or a named range. For example, you might have a range called CONTRIB, which contains contribution amounts made to your organization. Let's say that CONTRIB spans 500 rows in 40 contiguous columns. Manually calculating the average contribution would take a platoon of bookkeepers armed with calculators. By using the @AVG function with your range name CONTRIB, as in @AVG(CONTRIB), you could instantly calculate the average contribution, and report it in the cell containing the @AVG formula. Other @ functions perform similarly useful mathematical and statistical operations, such as summing a total (@SUM), finding a square root (@SQRT), determining the maximum and minimum value in a range (@MAX and @MIN), and the population standard deviation of the values in a range (@STD).

Date Functions Sometimes you might need to compute a future date, or perform date arithmetic to compute another value. For example, you could determine the date 57 days from today by using the formula @NOW+57, in which @NOW refers to the current system date. Or you could subtract the date of invoice billing from @NOW to generate an invoice aging calculation.

Another useful date function is @DATEVALUE, used to convert dates that have been imported from another programs as labels, into 1-2-3 date values. For example, @DATEVALUE("25-May-89") will generate a serial date number for 25-May-89 that can be displayed in one of the 1-2-3 date formats and then used in subsequent formulas and calculations. Suppose, for instance, that you imported a series of text dates (in 1-2-3 date format) from your database program into column A. You could place the formula @DATEVALUE(A1) in cell B1 to convert the date in cell A1. If you copy the formula down the B column, you can convert all the dates in column A.

Financial Functions 1-2-3 offers a solid selection of financial and accounting calculations for values associated with loans, depreciation, annuities, and cash flows. @PV with the arguments (payment,interest,term), for example, calculates the present value of a future stream of periodic payments discounted at a specified interest rate. For instance, if you won the lottery and were given the option of receiving $400,000 today or $100,000 a year for the next five, which is worth more in today's dollars, assuming an interest rate of 12 percent? @PV (100000, .12,5) tells you to quickly take the cash. The future payments are only worth $360,477.

Other financial functions can be used to determine loan payments, net present value, periodic interest rate, and related values.

Database Functions It is frequently desirable to analyze the numerical components of database records. 1-2-3 offers a number of built-in @D functions specifically designed for database analysis. These allow you to greatly expand upon the usefulness of the basic @functions described above. For example, let's say that you have constructed a 1-2-3 database of donors who have given to the West Side Aquarium, and you want to find out the average contribution by people from New York. You could set up a criteria range establishing the field named State as equal to NY, and then use @DAVG to look at each record in the database where State=NY, and calculate the average contribution of those records. You could vary the criteria, and select other @D functions, such as @DSUM or @DMAX. These formulas are extremely powerful and can be used to quickly to perform sophisticated analyses of 1-2-3 databases.

String Functions Several @functions can be used to manipulate labels or "strings" that you specify within quotation marks. You can add labels together, split them, or extract pieces of them. Suppose you imported a list of names and addresses from another program, and the records contained all capital letters. Nevertheless, you want the names in the worksheet to use proper case (initial capital letters only) instead of uppercase letters. Rather than editing every word in every cell—a time-consuming and tedious task—you could use the @PROPER function, which would instantly convert all words to initial caps only.

For example, if your worksheet contains a list of names in uppercase in column A, beginning with A1, in cell B1 you could enter the formula @PROPER(A1). This will display the contents of cell A1 in proper case form in cell B1. If you then copied the formula down through column B until the last name, all of the uppercase names in column A would be displayed in column B as initial capital letters only. Other string functions allow you to manipulate text in various ways, such as inserting strings into other strings, which would be useful when you want modify a series of part numbers or ID codes, or trimming strings, which is useful for concatenating first and last names in a mailing label and you want to eliminate trailing spaces.

Logical Functions These functions base their results on true or false conditions; 1 if true, 0 if false. If you want to test for a logical condition and then instruct 1-2-3 to follow a certain course of action, for example, you could use the logical function @IF with the arguments (condition,true result,false result). Let's say that you want to compute the aging of your invoices, but only for those that are unpaid. You have established one column, column D, for payment status (1 for paid, 0 for unpaid). Now imagine that your billing date was in column E, the receipt date in Column F, and the Aging was reported in Column G. In Column G you would place the formula:

```
@IF(D1=0,@NOW-E1,F1-E1)
```

and copy it down the column. This instructs 1-2-3: "if the status is 0 (unpaid), then subtract the billing date from today's date. If the status is not 0 (i.e. 1, or paid), then subtract the billing date from the receipt date (i.e., calculate the value of the lapse between the bill date and the receipt date).

In the next chapter, you will learn the basics of the "3" part of 1-2-3: its database capabilities. As you'll quickly see, databases are an extension of the worksheet concepts you've learned so far, and have their own special set of built-in @functions to help you analyze and manipulate data.

Creating and Using a 1-2-3 Database

INTRODUCTION

Databases constitute the "3" in 1-2-3. (The "1" refers to worksheets, and the "2" refers to graphs.) In fact, a 1-2-3 database is simply a special application of the 1-2-3 spreadsheet.

A database is a collection of information arranged in a specific order. An address book, for example, is a database. The complete name and address entry for each individual is called a record, and the specific components of each entry such as "name," "address," "city," etc. are called *fields*.

An address book is usually organized alphabetically. If each name and address entry were placed on a card (as in a Rolodex), you could reorder the cards by state, zip code, profession, or by any other criteria. Of course, it would be a time-consuming task to reshuffle the card file by hand every time you wanted to arrange the names and addresses in a different order. That's one of the advantages of an electronic database—you can quickly resort the record entries any number of ways. With a 1-2-3 database this is easily accomplished by using the built in /Data Sort commands, which allow you to order records according to several different criteria. By switching the Sort criteria, the records will be rearranged in the desired pattern.

Besides sorting and resorting records, 1-2-3's /Data Query commands allow you to find, delete, or extract records from a database. You can search for records that have like attributes (e.g., everyone who lives in Ohio, everyone who has the zip code 02138, everyone who lives in New York and has donated over $1,000, etc.).

Databases, of course, can be used to manage much more than address book information. You could, for example, create a 1-2-3 database of inventory parts, customer invoices, library records, etc. In fact, anything that you would normally keep track of with an index card file can be more efficiently organized with a database.

In this chapter we'll explore the basic features of a 1-2-3 database, and describe the powerful commands and functions that allow you to manipulate and analyze database records. As with other topics in this introductory section of the book, you can find more detailed information in the Reference section.

ANATOMY OF A 1-2-3 DATABASE

As mentioned, a database consists of individual records; each record consists of pieces of information in a specific order that is organized into fields. In a 1-2-3 database, records occupy individual rows. Each column in the row constitutes a field. The titles at the head of each column indicate the name of each field. Figure 7.1 shows a typical 1-2-3 database.

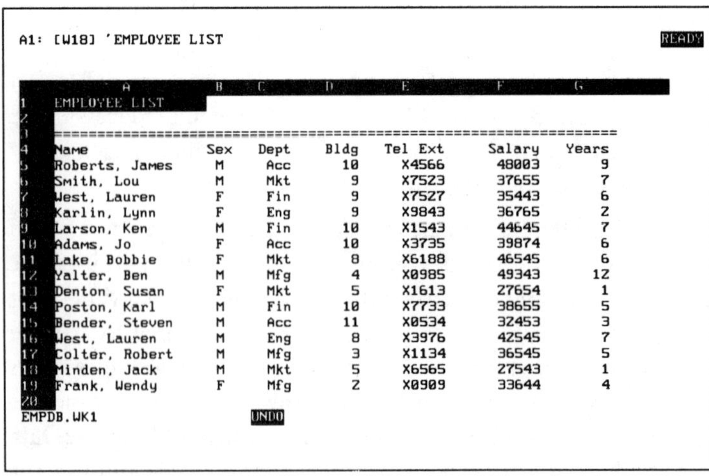
A1: [W18] 'EMPLOYEE LIST READY

EMPLOYEE LIST

Name	Sex	Dept	Bldg	Tel Ext	Salary	Years
Roberts, James	M	Acc	10	X4566	48003	9
Smith, Lou	M	Mkt	9	X7523	37655	7
West, Lauren	F	Fin	9	X7527	35443	6
Karlin, Lynn	F	Eng	9	X9843	36765	2
Larson, Ken	M	Fin	10	X1543	44645	7
Adams, Jo	F	Acc	10	X3735	39874	6
Lake, Bobbie	F	Mkt	8	X6188	46545	6
Yalter, Ben	M	Mfg	4	X0985	49343	12
Denton, Susan	F	Mkt	5	X1613	27654	1
Poston, Karl	M	Fin	10	X7733	38655	5
Bender, Steven	M	Acc	11	X0534	32453	3
West, Lauren	M	Eng	8	X3976	42545	7
Colter, Robert	M	Mfg	3	X1134	36545	5
Minden, Jack	M	Mkt	5	X6565	27543	1
Frank, Wendy	F	Mfg	2	X0909	33644	4

EMPDB.WK1 UNDO

Figure 7.1
1-2-3 employee list database.

The database consists of fifteen records with seven fields including: the employee's name, gender, department, building location, salary, and years with the company. The following sections explain how you can use 1-2-3's various data commands to manipulate and analyze the records of this database. The most elementary /Data command is the Sort command, used to rearrange the records in the database.

SORTING THE DATABASE

1-2-3 provides a very easy-to-use and quick routine for sorting database records according to standards (or criteria) that you specify. When you select /Data Sort, the program will display the submenu shown in Figure 7.2, along with a blank sort settings sheet (assuming you have not already performed a /Data Sort for the current file).

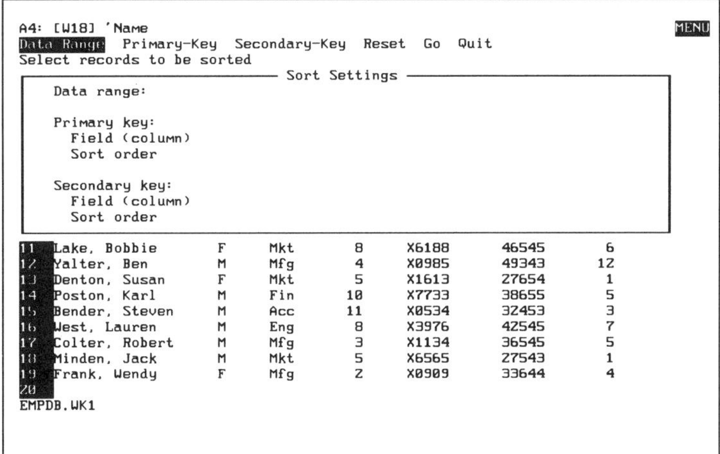

```
A4: [W18] 'Name                                                              MENU
Data-Range  Primary-Key  Secondary-Key  Reset  Go  Quit
Select records to be sorted
 ---------------------------- Sort Settings -----------------------------
   Data range:

   Primary key:
     Field (column)
     Sort order

   Secondary key:
     Field (column)
     Sort order
 ------------------------------------------------------------------------
11 Lake, Bobbie        F      Mkt      8    X6188      46545      6
12 Yalter, Ben         M      Mfg      4    X0985      49343     12
13 Denton, Susan       F      Mkt      5    X1613      27654      1
14 Poston, Karl        M      Fin     10    X7733      38655      5
15 Bender, Steven      M      Acc     11    X0534      32453      3
16 West, Lauren        M      Eng      8    X3976      42545      7
17 Colter, Robert      M      Mfg      3    X1134      36545      5
18 Minden, Jack        M      Mkt      5    X6565      27543      1
19 Frank, Wendy        F      Mfg      2    X0909      33644      4
20
EMPDB.WK1
```

Figure 7.2

/Data Sort menu and setting sheet.

The first step in sorting a database is to specify the *data range*—the range containing the records that you want to rearrange. Move the cell pointer to the upper left-hand corner of the range, select Data-Range, and at the prompt enter a period (.) to anchor the left corner, then paint the range down to the cell in the bottom-right corner, and press ENTER. This will highlight the selected range. (If you have named the range, you can type in the range name.) Make sure that you *don't* include the column headings or any horizontal separator rules in the

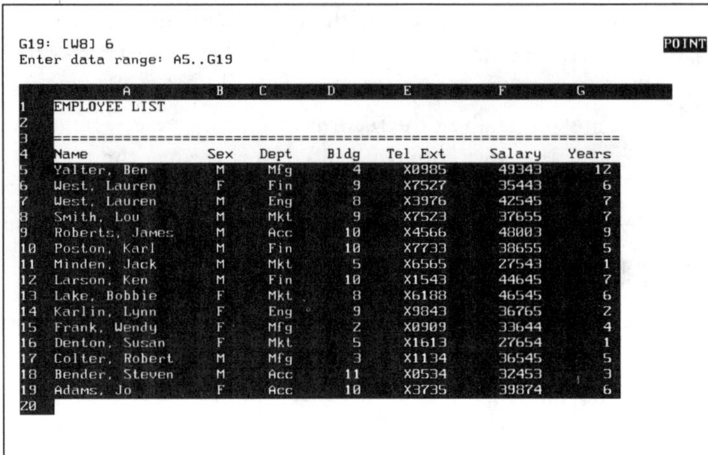

	A	B	C	D	E	F	G
1	EMPLOYEE LIST						
2							
3	==========						
4	Name	Sex	Dept	Bldg	Tel Ext	Salary	Years
5	Yalter, Ben	M	Mfg	4	X0985	49343	12
6	West, Lauren	F	Fin	9	X7527	35443	6
7	West, Lauren	M	Eng	8	X3976	42545	7
8	Smith, Lou	M	Mkt	9	X7523	37655	7
9	Roberts, James	M	Acc	10	X4566	48003	9
10	Poston, Karl	M	Fin	10	X7733	38655	5
11	Minden, Jack	M	Mkt	5	X6565	27543	1
12	Larson, Ken	M	Fin	10	X1543	44645	7
13	Lake, Bobbie	F	Mkt	8	X6188	46545	6
14	Karlin, Lynn	F	Eng	9	X9843	36765	2
15	Frank, Wendy	F	Mfg	2	X0909	33644	4
16	Denton, Susan	F	Mkt	5	X1613	27654	1
17	Colter, Robert	M	Mfg	3	X1134	36545	5
18	Bender, Steven	M	Acc	11	X0534	32453	3
19	Adams, Jo	F	Acc	10	X3735	39874	6
20							

Figure 7.3
Data range for employee database.

data range; otherwise they will get mixed in and sorted with the records. Figure 7.3 shows the data range for the sample employee database.

Next, select the *primary sort key*—the field that will be used as a criteria for organizing the records. If you want to reorder the database according to Name, you would select column A. Either move the cursor to column A, or enter a coordinate that contains column A (it doesn't matter what row you use). Similarly, you could organize the database according to salary by making column F the primary sort key, and so on. Once you've indicated a primary sort key, 1-2-3 will prompt you to enter the sort order for that key. D means descending, i.e. (Z to A, 10 to 1, etc.) and A means ascending (A to Z, 1 to 10, etc.).

Assuming that you want to alphabetize the database, select column A as the primary sort key, then Ascending as your sort order (for A to Z), and then select Go from the /Data Sort menu. The database will be reorganized as shown in Figure 7.4.

You can further refine your sorting method by using a *secondary* sort key, which will serve as a tie breaker for records that have identical data in the primary sort field. In the sample database, two people have the name Lauren West. Let's say that you chose Dept (Column C) as your secondary sort key, and Ascending as the sort order. The two Lauren Wests would appear together, but the one in engineering (Eng) would appear before the one in Finance (Fin), as shown in Figure 7.5. While in this simple example the tie breaker may not seem to add much, in a large database the secondary sort key can make the difference between a highly useful database and a semi-useful listing.

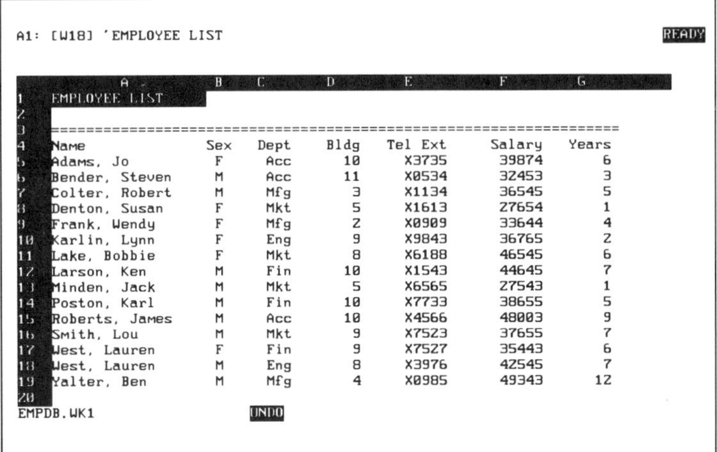

A1: [W18] 'EMPLOYEE LIST READY

	A	B	C	D	E	F	G
1	EMPLOYEE LIST						
2							
3	==========						
4	Name	Sex	Dept	Bldg	Tel Ext	Salary	Years
5	Adams, Jo	F	Acc	10	X3735	39874	6
6	Bender, Steven	M	Acc	11	X0534	32453	3
7	Colter, Robert	M	Mfg	3	X1134	36545	5
8	Denton, Susan	F	Mkt	5	X1613	27654	1
9	Frank, Wendy	F	Mfg	2	X0909	33644	4
10	Karlin, Lynn	F	Eng	9	X9843	36765	2
11	Lake, Bobbie	F	Mkt	8	X6188	46545	6
12	Larson, Ken	M	Fin	10	X1543	44645	7
13	Minden, Jack	M	Mkt	5	X6565	27543	1
14	Poston, Karl	M	Fin	10	X7733	38655	5
15	Roberts, James	M	Acc	10	X4566	48003	9
16	Smith, Lou	M	Mkt	9	X7523	37655	7
17	West, Lauren	F	Fin	9	X7527	35443	6
18	West, Lauren	M	Eng	8	X3976	42545	7
19	Yalter, Ben	M	Mfg	4	X0985	49343	12
20							

EMPDB.WK1 UNDO

Figure 7.4

Database sorted in alphabetical order by name, ascending order.

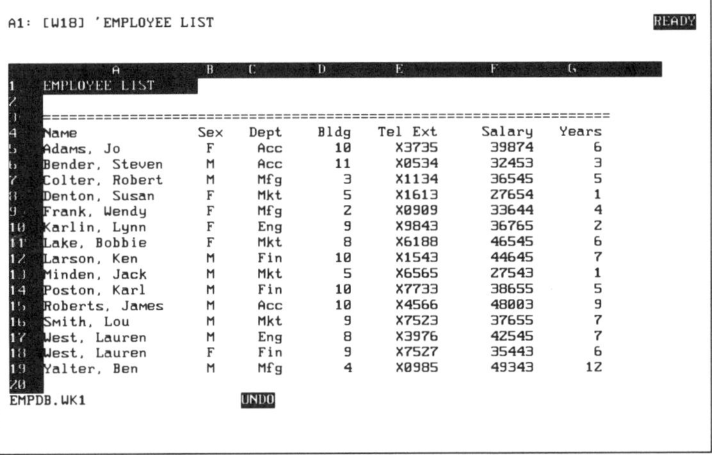

A1: [W18] 'EMPLOYEE LIST READY

	A	B	C	D	E	F	G
1	EMPLOYEE LIST						
2							
3	==========						
4	Name	Sex	Dept	Bldg	Tel Ext	Salary	Years
5	Adams, Jo	F	Acc	10	X3735	39874	6
6	Bender, Steven	M	Acc	11	X0534	32453	3
7	Colter, Robert	M	Mfg	3	X1134	36545	5
8	Denton, Susan	F	Mkt	5	X1613	27654	1
9	Frank, Wendy	F	Mfg	2	X0909	33644	4
10	Karlin, Lynn	F	Eng	9	X9843	36765	2
11	Lake, Bobbie	F	Mkt	8	X6188	46545	6
12	Larson, Ken	M	Fin	10	X1543	44645	7
13	Minden, Jack	M	Mkt	5	X6565	27543	1
14	Poston, Karl	M	Fin	10	X7733	38655	5
15	Roberts, James	M	Acc	10	X4566	48003	9
16	Smith, Lou	M	Mkt	9	X7523	37655	7
17	West, Lauren	M	Eng	8	X3976	42545	7
18	West, Lauren	F	Fin	9	X7527	35443	6
19	Yalter, Ben	M	Mfg	4	X0985	49343	12
20							

EMPDB.WK1 UNDO

Figure 7.5

Database sorted in alphabetical order by name, then by department.

With the two sort keys, you can order your database in many different ways. For example, you could list people by gender and then by department to get a list of all women and men in the company; by department and then by salary to view earning ranges by department (Figure 7.6a); by years at the company and then by salary to see the relationship between tenure and earnings (Figure 7.6b); or by salary and then by sex to demonstrate any relationship between gender and earnings. Other combinations are possible, too; the above sorts merely show how, with two sort keys, you can generate many useful views of a database.

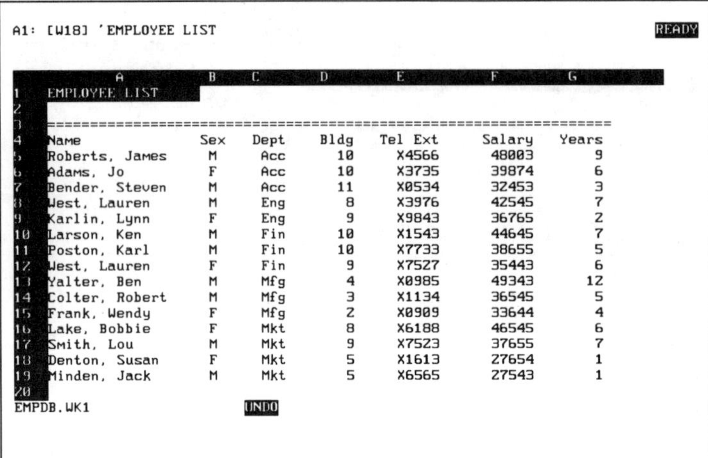

A1: [W18] 'EMPLOYEE LIST READY

	A	B	C	D	E	F	G
1	EMPLOYEE LIST						
2							
3	==========	=====	=====	=====	=======	======	=====
4	Name	Sex	Dept	Bldg	Tel Ext	Salary	Years
5	Roberts, James	M	Acc	10	X4566	48003	9
6	Adams, Jo	F	Acc	10	X3735	39874	6
7	Bender, Steven	M	Acc	11	X0534	32453	3
8	West, Lauren	M	Eng	8	X3976	42545	7
9	Karlin, Lynn	F	Eng	9	X9843	36765	2
10	Larson, Ken	M	Fin	10	X1543	44645	7
11	Poston, Karl	M	Fin	10	X7733	38655	5
12	West, Lauren	F	Fin	9	X7527	35443	6
13	Yalter, Ben	M	Mfg	4	X0985	49343	12
14	Colter, Robert	M	Mfg	3	X1134	36545	5
15	Frank, Wendy	F	Mfg	2	X0909	33644	4
16	Lake, Bobbie	F	Mkt	8	X6188	46545	6
17	Smith, Lou	M	Mkt	9	X7523	37655	7
18	Denton, Susan	F	Mkt	5	X1613	27654	1
19	Minden, Jack	M	Mkt	5	X6565	27543	1
20							

EMPDB.WK1 UNDO

Figure 7.6a
Primary Sort Key: Dept, ascending order; Secondary Sort Key: Salary, descending order.

A1: [W18] 'EMPLOYEE LIST READY

	A	B	C	D	E	F	G
1	EMPLOYEE LIST						
2							
3	==========	=====	=====	=====	=======	======	=====
4	Name	Sex	Dept	Bldg	Tel Ext	Salary	Years
5	Yalter, Ben	M	Mfg	4	X0985	49343	12
6	Roberts, James	M	Acc	10	X4566	48003	9
7	Larson, Ken	M	Fin	10	X1543	44645	7
8	West, Lauren	M	Eng	8	X3976	42545	7
9	Smith, Lou	M	Mkt	9	X7523	37655	7
10	Lake, Bobbie	F	Mkt	8	X6188	46545	6
11	Adams, Jo	F	Acc	10	X3735	39874	6
12	West, Lauren	F	Fin	9	X7527	35443	6
13	Poston, Karl	M	Fin	10	X7733	38655	5
14	Colter, Robert	M	Mfg	3	X1134	36545	5
15	Frank, Wendy	F	Mfg	2	X0909	33644	4
16	Bender, Steven	M	Acc	11	X0534	32453	3
17	Karlin, Lynn	F	Eng	9	X9843	36765	2
18	Denton, Susan	F	Mkt	5	X1613	27654	1
19	Minden, Jack	M	Mkt	5	X6565	27543	1
20							

EMPDB.WK1 UNDO

Figure 7.6b
Primary Sort Key: Years, descending order; Secondary Sort Key: Salary, descending order.

If you forget your sort keys, all you have to do is select the /Data Sort command, and the Sort Settings sheet will display your current choices (see Figure 7.7). The Sort Settings sheet will be updated every time you enter or change the data range or the sort keys. To clear or redisplay the settings sheet from the screen, press the F6 window toggle key. The Sort Settings sheet will reappear each time you select /Data Sort.

Be wary of blanks or blank rows in your data range. Blanks precede alphabetic characters (as do numeric characters). If you sort in ascending order, you

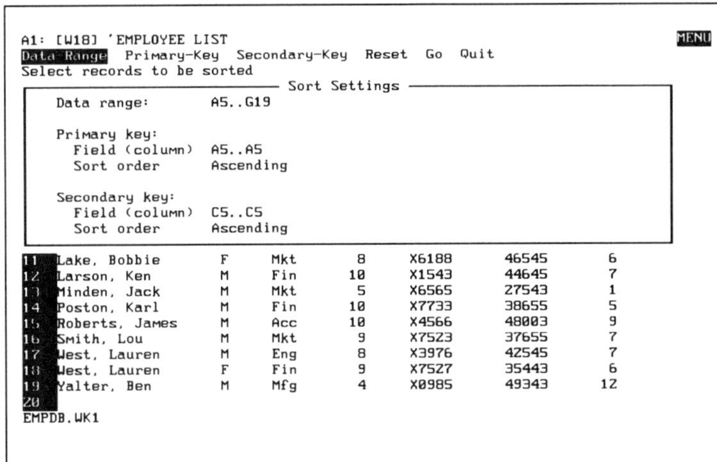

Figure 7.7

Sort Settings sheet.

may have a number of annoying blank rows preceding your data rows or blank fields at the head of a column. Sorting in descending order will place the blanks or blank rows at the bottom of the database.

NOTE You can actually use the Sort command to help close up blanks in a database in which you have been deleting records. By sorting alphabetically, you can isolate all blank rows at the top of the database, and then use the /Worksheet Delete Row command to delete them. If you have formulas or worksheet features that may be disturbed by the row deletion, you can use the Move command to move up all data rows, thereby occupying the blank space.

Resetting a /Data Sort

We have seen that 1-2-3 "remembers" its last data sort. In fact, even when you save the file and quit 1-2-3, your last sort criteria will still be displayed in the Sort Settings sheet when you next retrieve the file. 1-2-3 stores your Sort settings with the file.

To clear out all your Sort settings, select Data Sort Reset. When you do so, all settings will be made blank. To reset just the data range or just a sort key, you are best off simply respecifying that item rather than clearing all your settings with /Data Sort Reset.

Potential Problems

While sorting is simple in principle, in practice it is easy to run into difficulties. In general, it is always a good idea to save a database before sorting it. That way, if you ruin it, you can simply retrieve your presorted version. Another solution (if you don't want to depend on Undo) is to add a field to your database and use the /Data Fill command to fill the column with integers and thus number your records in their current order. You will always be able to retrieve your original order by resorting the database using that column of integers as your primary sort key.

You *must* avoid including headings or any other text that is not in itself a record in the database. Otherwise, the extraneous text will be counted as data rows and you may have some serious surgery to perform on the database—extracting the foreign objects and putting them where they belong.

A second area of caution is sorting a database that contains formulas. In general, formulas that refer to other cells in the same row (or record) should use relative addresses. Formulas that refer to cells outside the data range should use absolute addresses so that values will not be altered in the new sort order.

Finally, be sure to extend your data range far enough to the right to include all data; otherwise 1-2-3 will sort first part of your database and not the second. The result will be a hybrid monstrosity that may be beyond repair. To avoid such problems, always scroll to the right to make sure you haven't forgotten any fields when you define your data range.

This concludes the discussion of the /Data Sort command. In the next section, you will learn how to use other /Data commands that allow you to find and extract records within a database that meet criteria. These commands fall under the umbrella of the /Data Query menu.

/DATA QUERY COMMANDS

1-2-3 provides a number of database querying commands; they let you search for and manipulate database records that match a certain set of criteria. The /Data Query commands include: Find, which allows you to locate (and edit) records that meet your criteria; Extract, which copies matching records to another part of the worksheet; Unique, which is like the Extract command, but which will not duplicate any records in the output range; and Delete, which actually removes records from your database according to your criteria. To use any of the /Data Query commands, you must provide two or three key pieces of information for

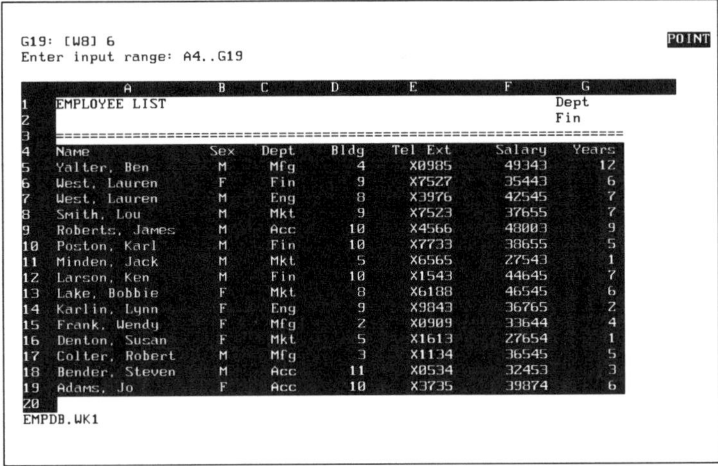

G19: [W8] 6
Enter input range: A4..G19 POINT

	A	B	C	D	E	F	G
1	EMPLOYEE LIST						Dept
2							Fin
3	================						
4	Name	Sex	Dept	Bldg	Tel Ext	Salary	Years
5	Yalter, Ben	M	Mfg	4	X0985	49343	12
6	West, Lauren	F	Fin	9	X7527	35443	6
7	West, Lauren	M	Eng	8	X3976	42545	7
8	Smith, Lou	M	Mkt	9	X7523	37655	7
9	Roberts, James	M	Acc	10	X4566	48003	9
10	Poston, Karl	M	Fin	10	X7733	38655	5
11	Minden, Jack	M	Mkt	5	X6565	27543	1
12	Larson, Ken	M	Fin	10	X1543	44645	7
13	Lake, Bobbie	F	Mkt	8	X6188	46545	6
14	Karlin, Lynn	F	Eng	9	X9843	36765	2
15	Frank, Wendy	F	Mfg	2	X0909	33644	4
16	Denton, Susan	F	Mkt	5	X1613	27654	1
17	Colter, Robert	M	Mfg	3	X1134	36545	5
18	Bender, Steven	M	Acc	11	X0534	32453	3
19	Adams, Jo	F	Acc	10	X3735	39874	6
20							

EMPDB.WK1

Figure 7.8
Input range, employee database.

1-2-3: an input range, a criteria range, and (for the Extract and Unique options) an output range. (See the Query Settings sheet below in Figure 7.9.)

Input Range

Each database query needs an *input range*; the input range simply tells 1-2-3 where it should look for matching records. The input range that you specify will be all or part of your database; it must include the field headings at the top of each column in the database. If you have two-line field headings, only include the bottom row in the input range; if you include both lines, the query command will not operate properly.

To specify an input range, select /Data Query. 1-2-3 will display a blank Query Settings sheet, (assuming this is your first query for the current worksheet). Now select Input, and 1-2-3 will prompt you to enter the range. Type in the address or range name of your database table (or paint the range as in Figure 7.8). When you press ENTER, 1-2-3 will redisplay the Query Settings sheet, this time with the coordinates of the input range you selected (see Figure 7.9).

Criteria Range

Every query must also specify a *criteria range*, which tells 1-2-3 how records should be selected for the query operation. A criteria range consists of two or more rows; the smallest possible criteria range is two vertical cells. The top cell must contain the field heading (from the database) that you would like to use as a basis for your criteria; the cell underneath it should contain the criteria specifica-

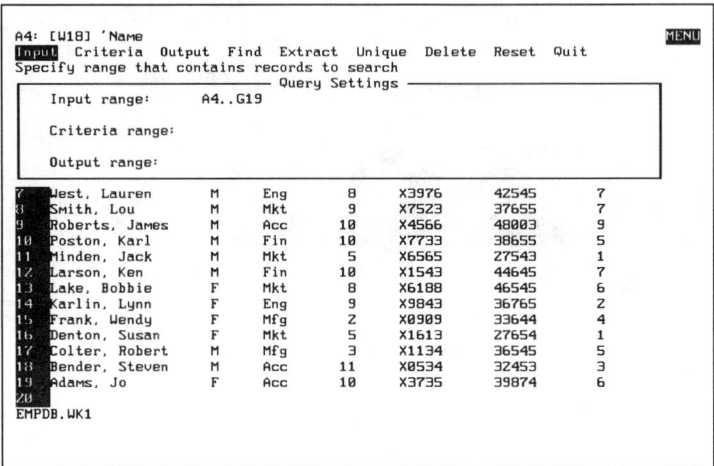

Figure 7.9
/Data Query Settings Sheet with input range address.

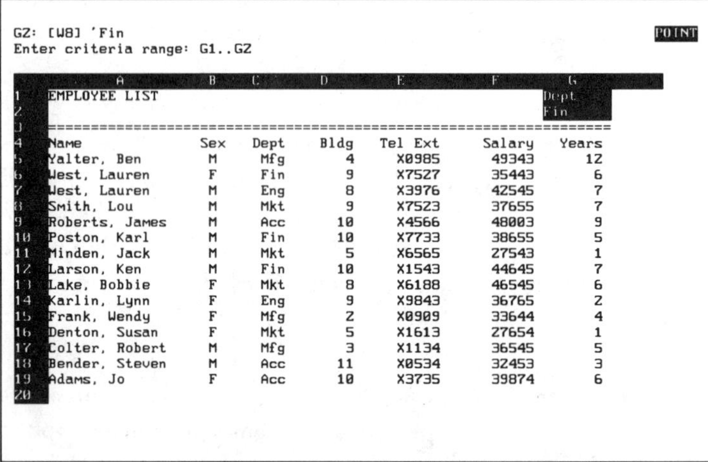

Figure 7.10
Criteria range G1..G2 specifying employees in the Finance department.

tion. You may specify more than one criteria and field heading according to the fields that are relevant to your search. Many find it convenient to copy all the field headings from the database to their criteria range. This prevents spelling errors in the top row of the criteria range and lets you perform several queries in a row by simply exchanging one criteria for another.

In Figure 7.10, a simple criteria range is G1..G2. The top cell contains the field heading "Dept"—spelled exactly as it appears in the database—and the actual criteria is "Fin." This tells 1-2-3 to find any record that has "Fin" in the column with the heading "Dept" and consider it a match. With the /Data Query Find command, 1-2-3 would highlight the first matching record in the database and you would move from matching record to matching record with the up and down arrow keys. With the /Data Query Delete command, all matching records would be deleted from the database.

You might add to the criteria in Figure 7.10 and search for all males in the Finance Department. Simply redefine the criteria range to include cells F1 and F2 along with G1 and G2. In cell F1, type in the field heading Sex; in cell F2, type in the criteria, M. (See Figure 11.a). Note that in this new criteria range F1..G2, the criteria M and Fin appear together in the same row. Any criteria conditions that are specified in the same row are connected by a logical AND. Here, for example, this means that you want to locate all workers who are male and work in the Finance department. There are two: Karl Poston and Ken Larson. But what if you had wanted to find all male workers *or* workers in the Finance department? In 1-2-3, criteria conditions that are specified in separate rows are connected by a logical OR. Thus, if you had added M to the row below—in cell F3 rather than F2 (see Figure 11.b)—and extended your criteria range accordingly (F1..G3), you could carry out a search for all workers who are male *or* workers in the Finance deparment.

To specify a criteria range, select /Data Query Criteria and 1-2-3 will prompt you for the range. You can type in the range address, or coordinates, or a range name, or you can paint the range. Either way, once you press ENTER, 1-2-3 will

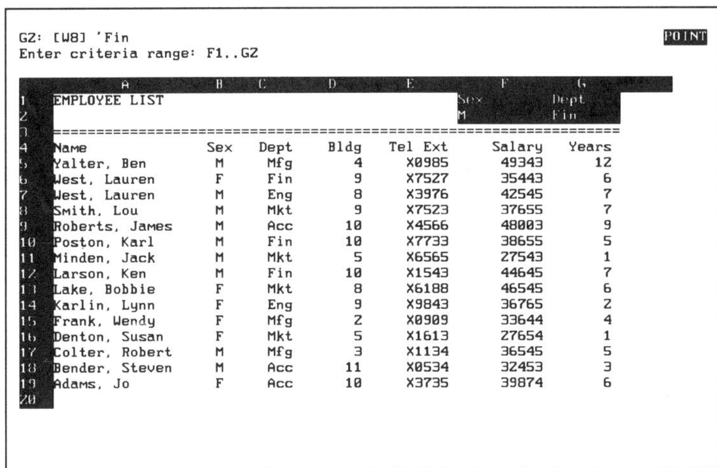

```
G2: [W8] 'Fin                                                   POINT
Enter criteria range: F1..G2

      A                 B       C          D          E        F        G
1   EMPLOYEE LIST                                           Sex      Dept
2                                                           M        Fin
3   ==================================================================
4   Name               Sex    Dept      Bldg    Tel Ext     Salary   Years
5   Yalter, Ben         M      Mfg         4      X0985      49343      12
6   West, Lauren        F      Fin         9      X7527      35443       6
7   West, Lauren        M      Eng         8      X3976      42545       7
8   Smith, Lou          M      Mkt         9      X7523      37655       7
9   Roberts, James      M      Acc        10      X4566      48003       9
10  Poston, Karl        M      Fin        10      X7733      38655       5
11  Minden, Jack        M      Mkt         5      X6565      27543       1
12  Larson, Ken         M      Fin        10      X1543      44645       7
13  Lake, Bobbie        F      Mkt         8      X6188      46545       6
14  Karlin, Lynn        F      Eng         9      X9843      36765       2
15  Frank, Wendy        F      Mfg         2      X0909      33644       4
16  Denton, Susan       F      Mkt         5      X1613      27654       1
17  Colter, Robert      M      Mfg         3      X1134      36545       5
18  Bender, Steven      M      Acc        11      X0534      32453       3
19  Adams, Jo           F      Acc        10      X3735      39874       6
20
```

Figure 7.11a

Criteria range F1..G2 for finding all male employees in the Finance department.

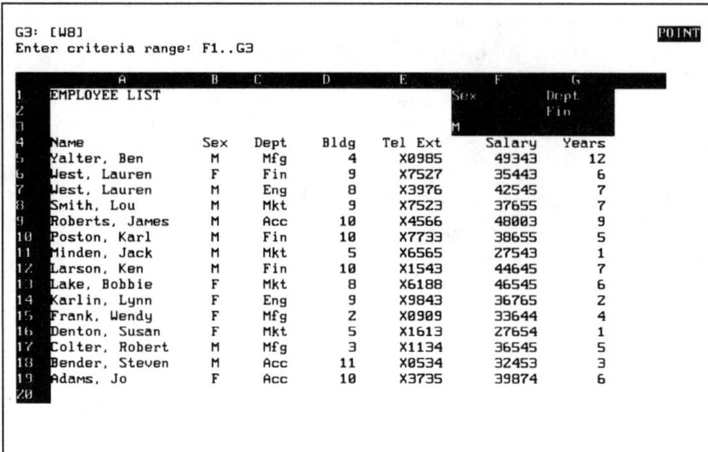

G3: [W8]
Enter criteria range: F1..G3 POINT

	A	B	C	D	E	F	G
1	EMPLOYEE LIST					Sex	Dept
2							Fin
3						M	
4	Name	Sex	Dept	Bldg	Tel Ext	Salary	Years
5	Yalter, Ben	M	Mfg	4	X0985	49343	12
6	West, Lauren	F	Fin	9	X7527	35443	6
7	West, Lauren	M	Eng	8	X3976	42545	7
8	Smith, Lou	M	Mkt	9	X7523	37655	7
9	Roberts, James	M	Acc	10	X4566	48003	9
10	Poston, Karl	M	Fin	10	X7733	38655	5
11	Minden, Jack	M	Mkt	5	X6565	27543	1
12	Larson, Ken	M	Fin	10	X1543	44645	7
13	Lake, Bobbie	F	Mkt	8	X6188	46545	6
14	Karlin, Lynn	F	Eng	9	X9843	36765	2
15	Frank, Wendy	F	Mfg	2	X0989	33644	4
16	Denton, Susan	F	Mkt	5	X1613	27654	1
17	Colter, Robert	M	Mfg	3	X1134	36545	5
18	Bender, Steven	M	Acc	11	X0534	32453	3
19	Adams, Jo	F	Acc	10	X3735	39874	6
20							

Figure 7.11b
Criteria range F1..G3 for finding male employees OR employees in the Finance department.

redisplay the /Data Query menu, and your criteria range address will be shown in the Query Settings sheet. Be sure that you do not include any extra blank lines in your criteria range—1-2-3 will interpret that as no criteria at all, and will therefore match every record in the database.

Using Formulas as Search Criteria

The real advantage in 1-2-3's /Data Query command lies in the ability to include formulas as search criteria. For example, with the employee database, you could instruct 1-2-3 to select records with values above 35,000 in the Salary column (column F). To do so, you would type in the formula anywhere under the field name (or the row of field names) in the criteria range. You write the formula with reference to the column that contains the field of interest (e.g., Salary), and to the first record in the input range (e.g., row 5). The formula in the criteria range for the employee database would be listed as: +F5>35000.

When you type in the formula, it appears in the control panel, although 1-2-3 displays either a 1 or a 0 in the criteria cell itself. 1-2-3 displays 1 if the formula is true for the referenced cell (e.g., F5), and 0 if it is false. In the case of our example, F5 happens to meet the formula criterion of the formula, so a 1 is displayed in cell G2 (see Figure 7.12). This true/false indicator is only for the first record in the database; all other records will be evaluated during the actual /Data Query command according to whether they match the criteria. You can format the cell containing the formula as text with /Range Format so it displays the actual criteria formula instead of 1 or 0.

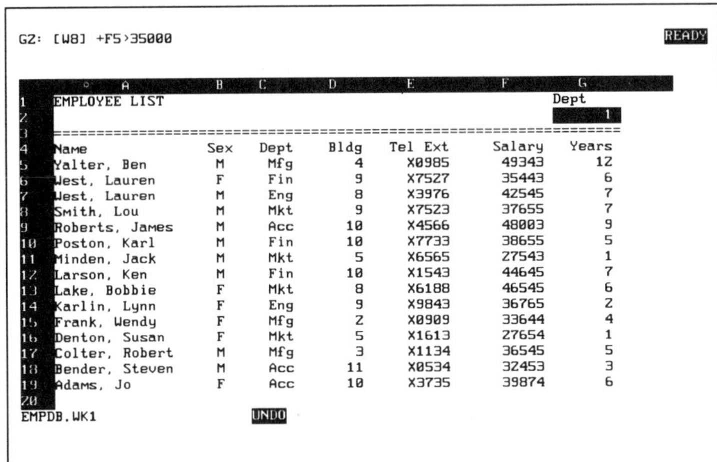

G2: [W8] +F5>35000 READY

	A	B	C	D	E	F	G
1	EMPLOYEE LIST						Dept
2							1
3	========	========	========	========	========	========	========
4	Name	Sex	Dept	Bldg	Tel Ext	Salary	Years
5	Yalter, Ben	M	Mfg	4	X0985	49343	12
6	West, Lauren	F	Fin	9	X7527	35443	6
7	West, Lauren	M	Eng	8	X3976	42545	7
8	Smith, Lou	M	Mkt	9	X7523	37655	7
9	Roberts, James	M	Acc	10	X4566	48003	9
10	Poston, Karl	M	Fin	10	X7733	38655	5
11	Minden, Jack	M	Mkt	5	X6565	27543	1
12	Larson, Ken	M	Fin	10	X1543	44645	7
13	Lake, Bobbie	F	Mkt	8	X6188	46545	6
14	Karlin, Lynn	F	Eng	9	X9843	36765	2
15	Frank, Wendy	F	Mfg	2	X0909	33644	4
16	Denton, Susan	F	Mkt	5	X1613	27654	1
17	Colter, Robert	M	Mfg	3	X1134	36545	5
18	Bender, Steven	M	Acc	11	X0534	32453	3
19	Adams, Jo	F	Acc	10	X3735	39874	6
20							

EMPDB.WK1 UNDO

Figure 7.12
Formula in criteria range.

In addition to using simple comparative operators such as >, >=, etc. in your formulas, you can use the more complex logical operators AND, OR, and NOT with formulas. These must be separated from each formula criteria by a pound sign on either side. For example, if you wanted to select all records for people whose salary is greater than $35,000 and who have been with the company more than 5 years, you could enter this formula in the criteria range:

```
+F5>35000#AND#G5>5
```

1-2-3 will then search for all records in the database that match the criteria. See the Reference section for many more complex examples using formulas in a criteria range.

Output Range

The third component of a data query is the *output range*, which is used for the /Data Query Extract and /Data Query Extract Unique commands. The output range is the area of the worksheet into which any records matching your criteria will be copied during the data extract process. To create an output range, select a *blank* area of the worksheet; when records are copied to the output range, they will overwrite any existing data.

After selecting an area of your worksheet, copy the column headings from your database so that they become the first row of the output range. You do not have to copy every heading from your original database, just those fields that you want displayed in the output range. Nor do you have to maintain the same order of heading as in the original.

Next, select /Data Query Output, and specify the range by address or name, or by painting it. If you specify just the row of field labels, 1-2-3 will copy all matching records that it finds in the rows below. (Be aware that any data below the field headings down to the last row in the worksheet will be erased.) If you specify a two-dimensional range, 1-2-3 will limit its extract to that range; in this case, be sure to make your range large enough to accommodate all the matching records that 1-2-3 will find.

You are now prepared to learn more details of each /Data Query command, using the various ranges described above.

Locating Records with /Data Query Find

The Find command quickly locates all records that meet your criteria, so that you can view them or modify them. For example, let's say that you wanted to find all records in the employee database for people who work in building 10. To do so, you would first select an input range as described above. Then, for your criteria range, you have two choices. Either substitute the formula +D5=10 in cell G2 of the example; or type in "Bldg" as the field name in the top of the criteria range (Cell G1) and type in 10 as your criteria in the bottom cell of the criteria range. 1-2-3 will then locate the records for each worker in building 10.

Here's what actually happens when you issue a /Data Query Find command. 1-2-3 first displays the status indicator FIND and looks for the first record that matches the criteria range. When it finds a match, it highlights the entire record. You can use the left and right arrow keys to edit the contents of the various fields within the record. When you are done viewing or modifying a record, use the down arrow to move to the next matching record, and so on. (The up arrow key will return you to the previous match.) You can switch from FIND mode to READY mode by pressing the ESC key repeatedly to back up from FIND mode, or you can press CTRL-BREAK.

Obviously, in the small employee database that we've been using to illustrate the basic query concepts, the Find command is no faster than visually scanning through the worksheet. But imagine a database with a thousand records and think how much faster it would be to use this technique.

The Extract Command

Now let's say that you don't want to just view selected records in your database, you actually want to copy the records to another area of your worksheet—the output range—so that you could print out the results as a separate report. With our sample employee database, for example, you might create a telephone directory for each building, starting with building 10. To do so, you would first establish your input range, and then specify the criteria formula just used for the Find command above.

Next, you would copy the database field headings to the output range area and define the output range (include the field headings). Finally, you would select /Data Query Extract, and 1-2-3 would copy all records for people in building 10 over to the output area.

Often you won't know exactly how many records will be extracted, and it is difficult to gauge the size of the output range. One solution is just to designate the row containing the field labels as the output range. 1-2-3 will then take up whatever space is required. If you do so, be aware that all rows down to the bottom of the worksheet below the row of labels will be erased—even if 1-2-3 doesn't find any records to extract. This is particularly dangerous if you have not enabled Undo. A second solution is simply to make your best guess as to how large the output range should be. 1-2-3 will not overwrite any data outside the allotted output range.

Once records are extracted to an output range, you can then perform various mathematical or statistical operations on them. Extracted data can serve innumerable purposes. For instance, if you had created an invoice database with an aging column (@now–[Date Billed]), you could select all records that are older than 30 days and extract them to the output range. The extract then becomes a past due report. Similarly, in a fund-raising database, you could extract people who donated more than $50,000 to a cause. The extract list becomes your "heavy hitter" prospect list for the next campaign solicitation.

Data can also be manipulated by eliminating or rearranging the field names in output range. For example, if you were to construct a telephone list based on an extract from the employee database, you would probably want to eliminate the Sex, Salary, and Years fields. No problem—don't include those fields in your output range. The results are shown in Figure 7.13.

NOTE It is generally not a good idea to place your output range under your input database in case your database should expand. Also, if you plan on using only a subgroup of fields in your extract, you should place your output range to the right of your database. If you place it under the database, the column width settings are likely to be inappropriate for the new arrangement of fields; and if you adjust the width for the extracted data, you will alter the widths of your original database as well.

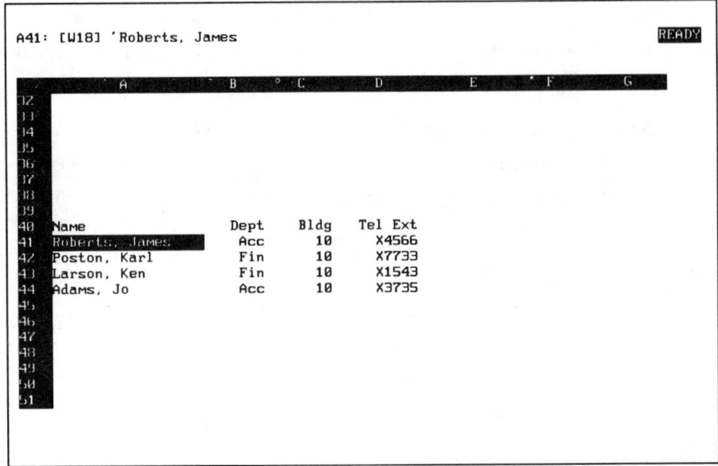

Figure 7.13 Modified Extract of records for Building 10.

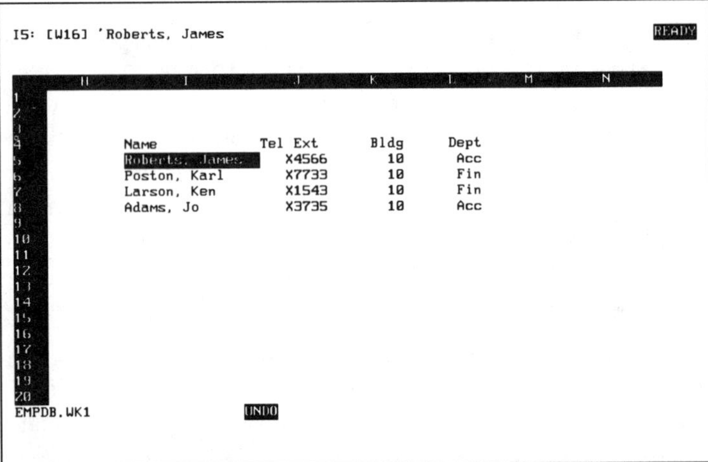

Figure 7.14 Modified field name order for extracted records.

You can also rearrange the order of your field headings in the extract range you need. You might, for instance, wish to create an extract in which the fields of the record appear in the following order: Name, Tel Ext, Bldg, and Dept. The results are shown in Figure 7.14.

Armed with the above information, you can create your own sophisticated extracts to isolate records you would like to group together.

The Unique Command

The /Data Query Unique command is the same as Extract, with one exception: It will not duplicate any records in the extract or output range. This can be valuable, for example, if you wanted to produce a list of all the buildings represented in the employee database. You would define the input range as in the above example; your criteria range would contain a blank criteria cell (simply meaning all records); and your output range would contain the single column labeled "bldg." When you select /Data Query Unique, 1-2-3 will generate a list showing each building represented in the database. Notice that even though the database contains 15 records, only eight building numbers are reported. The Unique command "weeded" out duplicate entries, i.e., entries with the same building number. /Data Query Unique is useful, too, if you have a database with many repeating entries. Say your database logged every donation that had been contributed to your organization for the past three years, and some of your donors had given money two, three, and more times over the years. If you were sponsoring a donor's reception and you wanted to create a mailing list, you could use /Data Query Unique to extract unique donor names and addresses and generate a mailing list without duplicates.

The Delete Command

The last /Data Query command, Delete, is dangerous, especially if you haven't enabled Undo. (Save your file before you delete.) Specify the input and criteria range, and then select Delete. 1-2-3 offers a confirmation prompt to Cancel or Delete the specified records. If you select Cancel, 1-2-3 returns to the Data Query command. If you select Delete, 1-2-3 removes any record that meets the specified criteria. It also closes up all spaces in the database.

USING @FUNCTIONS FOR DATABASE ANALYSIS

Now is a good time to experiment with the Query commands, if you haven't done so already. The next section covers special built-in @functions specifically designed for database analysis.

The @D Functions

In Chapter 5, you saw how 1-2-3's built-in @functions make it easy to perform mathematical operations on ranges of data. 1-2-3 also provides a set of special @functions (they all begin with @D) for use with databases. They are similar to the statistical @functions, but they work a bit differently. For example, while @AVG calculates the average of all values in a range, @DAVG calculates the average of all values in a database for records that match the specified criteria. The following "@D" functions are available:

@DSUM	Totals values for specified records in a database.
@DMIN	Calculates the minimum value for specified records in a database.
@DMAX	Calculates the maximum value for specified records in a database.
@DAVG	Calculates the mean of specified values in a database.
@DSTD	Calculates the standard deviation of specified values in a database.
@DVAR	Calculates the variance of specified values in a database.
@DCOUNT	Calculates the number of entries for specified records in a database.

An @D function contains the following arguments:

```
@Dfunction(input range, offset, criteria range)
```

The input range indicates the database that is to be analyzed. As with the /Data Query commands, the column titles must be included in the input range and, if you have multiple line headings, you only include the bottom row of the heading. For purposes of illustration, we'll use the employee database with the same input range specified in the above examples.

The offset indicates which field (or column) is to be analyzed by the function. An offset of 0 corresponds to the first column in the database. With the employee database, two columns contain values that are worth analyzing: the sixth column, which is represented by an offset of five, and the seventh column, represented by an offset of six.

The criteria range consists of at least two rows: The top row contains one or more field headings, and criteria specifications appear in the rows below. The criteria range is used to specify what records are to be included in the analyisis. The criteria range works exactly as it does for the /Data Query commands.

Putting it All Together

An @D Function can be placed anywhere within the worksheet. In Figure 7.15, the @DAVG formula is located in cell E1, adjacent to the label Average Salary. The formula, with its three arguments, would be written as follows:

```
@DAVG(A4..G19,5,G1..G2)
```

The input range (A4..G19) covers all records in the database, including the column headings. The offset (5) refers to the sixth column of the database, the Salary field. The criteria range is empty, meaning that there are no criteria, or that all records are to be included.

The criteria range could have been modified to include only records above $40,000, by including the formula +F5>40000 in the criteria range.

You could also have modified the criteria range to find the average salary of all employees who have worked for more than four years. Replace the formula +F5>40000 with +G5>4. What about the minimum salary for any employee who has worked for more than four years? We could use the @DMIN function:

```
@DMIN(A4..G19,5,G1..G2)
```

The analysis reveals that the minimum salary for anyone who's worked longer than four years is $35,443.

The @DFunctions are extremely powerful, and they enable you to carry out sophisticated analyses of database records. As simple as the rules may be for using the @DFunctions, three common errors can cause you to stare at the screen wondering what went wrong:

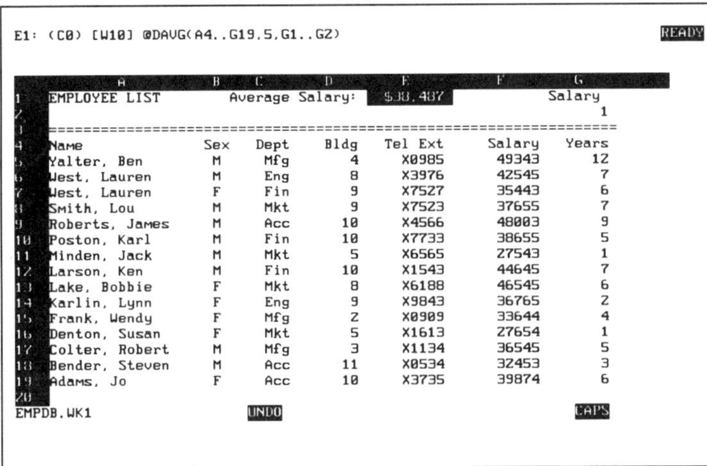

E1: (C0) [W10] @DAVG(A4..G19,5,G1..G2) READY

	A	B	C	D	E	F	G
1	EMPLOYEE LIST		Average Salary:		$38,487		Salary
2							1
3	======						
4	Name	Sex	Dept	Bldg	Tel Ext	Salary	Years
5	Yalter, Ben	M	Mfg	4	X0985	49343	12
6	West, Lauren	M	Eng	8	X3976	42545	7
7	West, Lauren	F	Fin	9	X7527	35443	6
8	Smith, Lou	M	Mkt	9	X7523	37655	7
9	Roberts, James	M	Acc	10	X4566	48003	9
10	Poston, Karl	M	Fin	10	X7733	38655	5
11	Minden, Jack	M	Mkt	5	X6565	27543	1
12	Larson, Ken	M	Fin	10	X1543	44645	7
13	Lake, Bobbie	F	Mkt	8	X6188	46545	6
14	Karlin, Lynn	F	Eng	9	X9843	36765	2
15	Frank, Wendy	F	Mfg	2	X0909	33644	4
16	Denton, Susan	F	Mkt	5	X1613	27654	1
17	Colter, Robert	M	Mfg	3	X1134	36545	5
18	Bender, Steven	M	Acc	11	X0534	32453	3
19	Adams, Jo	F	Acc	10	X3735	39874	6
20							

EMPDB.WK1 UNDO CAPS

Figure 7.15
@DAVG function used to yield average salary.

1. Incorrect offset. It's easy to forget that the column offset number starts with 0, not 1.
2. The input database range cannot contain a separator line between the column headings and the records. A separator line will cause the function to evaluate to 0.
3. Incorrect input range or criteria range addresses. You can minimize errors by assigning range names rather than typing in coordinates. Also, make sure that your ranges include the field label headings at the top of each column. If the database contains two line headings, only the bottom heading can be included in the input range. If both lines are included, the @DFunction will evaluate to 0.

OTHER DATA FUNCTIONS

While Sort and Query are the most commonly used data functions, a number of other useful commands are available in 1-2-3. We will mention them briefly here; refer to the Reference section for details.

Fill Automatically creates a series of values to fill a specific range. With /Data Fill, 1-2-3 prompts you to give a starting value, an incremental step, and a stopping value. The /Data Fill command is especially useful for generating tables of data, with values increasing or decreasing in equal intervals.

Table Used for "what if" analyses. Takes a list of values and substitutes those values one by one into a given formula. This process automatically generates a table of formula results.

Two forms of the /Data Table command are available. /Data Table 1 substitutes values for a single variable in one or more formulas. /Data Table 2 substitutes values for two independent variables in a formula (only one formula permitted).

Distribution Given a range of data, in no particular order, /Data Distribution will calculate a frequency distribution for various value ranges. For example, given data that recorded average temperatures each day of the year, you could determine how many days the temperature fell between 20–30, 30–40, 40–50, etc.

Matrix Used to solve simultaneous equations in inverting and multiplying data matrices. There are two matrix commands: Matrix Invert and Matrix Multiply.

Regression Performs multiple linear regressions. Regressions analysis can also be used to show correlations between a dependent and one or more independent variables.

Parse Used when you import non-delimited ASCII text data from another program. In 1-2-3, the data will show up as a single column of long labels; the data is not automatically split apart into multiple fields. With /Data Parse, the fields can be separated into separate columns.

This completes our tour of the /Data commands. While they may seem intimidating, start off simply and gradually try more complex data queries and analyses—you'll probably find yourself creating many 1-2-3 databases for managing your information.

In the next chapter, you'll learn how to use 1-2-3's printing capabilities to print out your worksheets and databases. Warm up your printer.

Printing a Worksheet or Database

ABOUT THE /PRINT COMMANDS

The /Print menu includes a number of options for printing out your worksheets and databases. (You can also print exceptionally fine looking documents using Allways; this will be discussed in Chapter 11). Whenever you call up the /Print menu, 1-2-3 first asks whether you intend to use your printer, or whether you want to create a print file. Print files can be printed at a later time or imported to another program (such as a word processor). The first section of this chapter deals with printing hard copies of reports; the final section covers the /Print File option.

Our discussion follows the progressive steps required to print a document. The printing procedure starts with the specification of a print range (the portion of the document to be printed), and the selection of various options such as margins, page length, etc. The final step entails issuing an Align and Go command.

Step 1: Defining the Print Range

After you select /Print and then choose your print destination—Printer or File—1-2-3 displays a nearly blank Print Settings sheet (assuming that you have not printed anything yet in the current file). The settings sheet will only contain certain default values for margins, page length, and format, as shown in Figure 8.1. Most of these default values are the ones you specified in the /Worksheet Global Default Printer options menu.

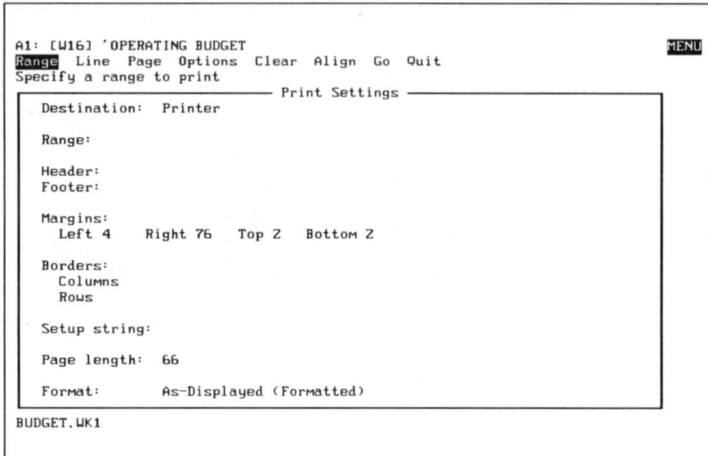

Figure 8.1
Default Printer Settings.

The first blank on the Print Settings sheet is called Range. In order to print all or part of your worksheet, you must tell 1-2-3 what to print; that is, you must define a print range. To do so, select Range from the main /Print menu and type in the range name or address or paint it (see Figure 8.2). Press ENTER, and the Print Settings sheet will be redisplayed, this time with the coordinates of the print range included (see Figure 8.3).

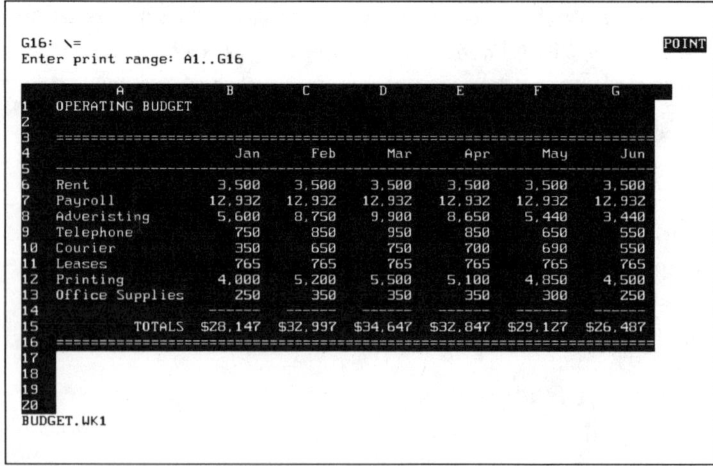

Figure 8.2
Print range defined.

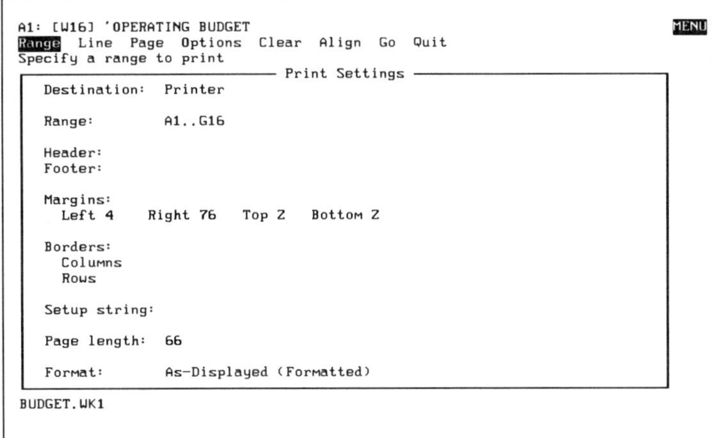

Figure 8.3
Print Settings sheet with range.

At this point, you could print out the worksheet —by selecting Align from the main /Print menu (this sets 1-2-3's internal line count in synch with your printer's top of page), followed by Go, which instructs the printer to begin printing. This can produce a perfectly acceptable printout—a basic report with no page numbers or special headings. However, if the worksheet is too wide or too long for the specified margins, any columns that extend beyond the right side of the page and any rows that extend below the bottom of the page will "spill over" onto a second sheet of paper, generally creating an unusable report (unless you're good with scissors and tape). In most cases, you will want to use one or more of the Print command options to tailor the print specifications to the worksheet at hand.

NOTE If ever there is an opportunity to use range names, it is with the /Print commands. If you have assigned range names to portions of worksheets, it will greatly facilitate your printing sessions. Instead of repainting the range each time you want to print a different portion of a worksheet, you could simply identify the range with common English names such as "budget," "cashflow," or "january."

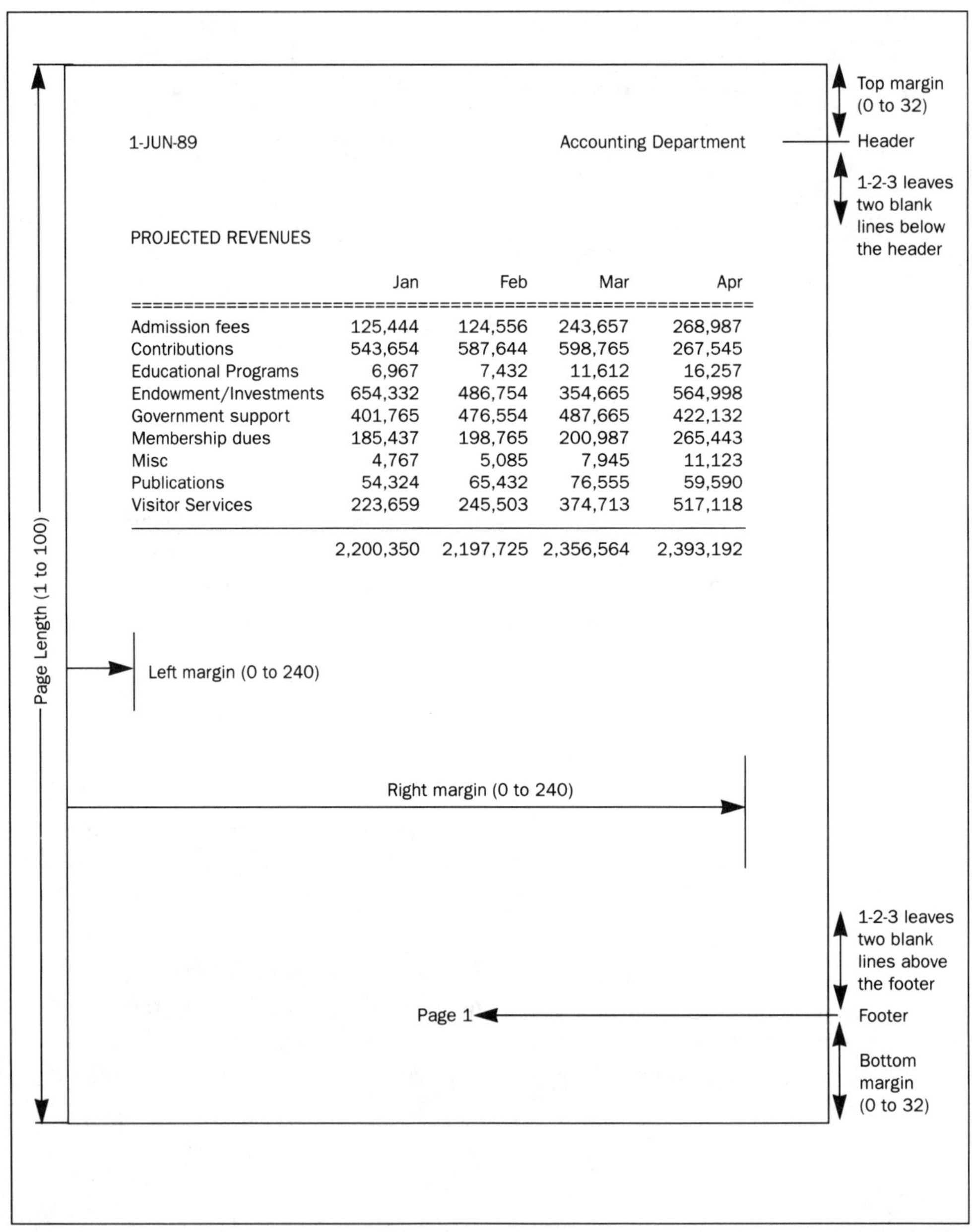

Figure 8.4 Basic page formatting in 1-2-3.

Step 2: Selecting Print Options

The /Print Printer Option command displays a submenu with eight options to set up and customize your report. The sample page in Figure 8.4 should help you visualize how page layout can be controlled using the eight elements of the Options menu. These options include:

Header The header in a print job is the text that appears at the top of each printed page. The header is printed one line below the top margin you have assigned. 1-2-3 skips two lines between the header and the top row of your print range. You can position a header to the left, right, or center of each page using one or two vertical bar (¦) symbols. In effect, the two vertical bars are used to split the heading line into three parts: left¦center¦right. Thus header text that is to be left-aligned, for example, is typed in without any vertical bar indicator. Header text that is to be centered is preceded by one vertical bar; `¦SUMMARY`, for example would center the heading SUMMARY at the top of each page. A heading specification such as ¦¦ `Review` would right-justify the header, Review.

You can include an @ sign in the header to print out today's date in the header; you can also include a # sign to print with automatically incrementing page numbers. For example, the centered header ¦Page #¦ would appear on page one of the report as Page 1, and on page two of the report as Page 2, and so on.

To put it all together, a header specification such as `Page #¦ABC Corp.¦@` would display the page number in the upper left-hand corner of the page, the title ABC Corp. in the top center of the page, and the current date in the upper right-hand corner of the page.

If you want the header to retrieve the contents of a particular cell in the worksheet, type a backslash followed by the address of the relevant cell (e.g. \A25) at the prompt for the header. Or if you want to use the first cell in a named range as a header, type in a backslash followed by the range name as in \ABCTOTAL.

Once you have finished specifying the header information it will appear in the Print Settings sheet.

Footer A footer works exactly like a header, except that the text appears on the bottom of each page, one line above the specified bottom margin. Two blank lines separate the footer from the printed report.

Margins Use Margins when you need to override the /Worksheet Global Default Printer Margin Settings. The left and right margins can be 0 to 240 characters wide. The top and bottom margins can be 0 to 32 lines. If you want to clear all margin settings, select None—this sets Left, Top, and Bottom to 0, and Right to 240. The None option is especially useful when you are printing to ASCII files on disk; the file can be imported by a word processor without having extra line breaks and hard carriage returns.

Borders If your report is more than one page long, you will often want to use the Borders option. Borders allows you to specify a row (or rows) or a column (or columns) in your worksheet to use as a top or left border on a page—a border that is repeated on each page of your print job. (You can use row and column headings as well if you like.) Choose Column, for example, if you are printing out a very wide range; it will create vertical headings on the left side of each page of your report. The repeated label headings on the left will orient the user on the subsequent pages of the printout. Choose Row if you are printing out a very long range; it will create horizontal headings at the top every page of your report.

Setup 1-2-3 allows you to send an initial setup string (or printer command code) to your printer. This lets you take advantage of many of your printer's features—features that you cannot otherwise access with 1-2-3's selection of print options. For example, you can instruct your printer to change fonts, or change to boldface text, or to change the line spacing. Different printers use different setup strings; to find out what setup strings you can use with your printer, see the manual supplied by the printer manufacturer. (A complete list of LaserJet setup strings can be found in Appendix D. For a complete discussion of laser printers and setup strings, see *The LaserJet Handbook* by Bennett and Randall, Brady.)

Use /Print Options Setup to override any setup string that you may have specified with /Worksheet Global Default Printer Setup. When you type in the setup string you need, it must be preceded with a backslash (\), followed by the ASCII value for the first character in the setup string. Because most printer control codes begin with the Escape key, many setup strings will begin with: \027. 027 is the ASCII value for the Escape key. (It is not necessary to use ASCII code values for the alphanumeric characters in the setup string—just type them in as is.)

With the Hewlett-Packard LaserJet Series II, for example, you could type in a setup string that will tell your printer to use the very small built-in line printer typeface by entering the code:

```
\027E\027&k2S
```

To take advantage of the small print you have chosen with this setup string however, you will have to adjust your right margin. Your margin calculation should be based on how many characters of your typeface fit into a linear inch.

Standard or "pica" print is 10 characters per inch (cpi). An 8.5-inch piece of paper will therefore allow you to print 85 characters, with no margins. With margins of, say, 4 on the left and 5 on the right, you have a total of 76 characters, so you'd want to set your right margin for 76. With the condensed LaserJet print, you will get 16.6 characters per inch, which translates into 141 characters per page, with no margins. Subtract 9 for the margins, and you should set your right margin for 132 characters. Do the same kind of calculation with whatever type fonts your printer is capable of producing.

You may also have to adjust the page length for proper page breaks to occur. For most non-laser printers, 66 lines per inch (lpi) is standard. Laser printers, however, should be set to 60 lpi for 10 pitch type; from there, you will have to adjust the page length for smaller fonts according to your printer manual.

If a standard sheet of paper can't accommodate your print range, even when you print in small or condensed fonts, you will either have to use wider paper (with dot-matrix or daisy-wheel printers) or switch to "landscape" (i.e., "width-wise") orientation (with laser printers). The code for printing in landscape mode on a HP LaserJet Series II, with the line printer fonts, is:

```
\027E\027&l1O\027&k2S
```

This printer setup string allows you to set a right margin of 176 characters, and a page length of 45 lines.

You can see that setup strings give you considerable flexibility in controlling your printer. However, it may often be a lot of work to get exactly the results you want. Also, when entering setup strings, be sure you type them in exactly as they are shown in your printer manual. With laser printer setup strings, for example, uppercase and lowercase letters are critical. Also, don't confuse lower case L's and 1's, or upper case O's and zeros.

If you frequently use one typeface, say the LaserJet Line Printer face, you can make it your global default setup string. Select the /Worksheet Global Default Printer Setup command and enter the string. Select Quit and then Update, and 1-2-3 will use Line Printer as the default font. (From now on, each time you call up the /Print main menu, the Print Settings sheet will display the string you entered through the /Global Default Printer command, unless you specifically designate an alternate setup string through the /Print Printer Options menu.)

Pg-Length Page length is determined by lines per inch. If you're using an 11-inch long sheet of paper and printing at 6 lines per inch (this is most common), your page length will be 66 lines; this is the initial 1-2-3 default. 1-2-3 allows you to enter an alternative page length value between 1 and 100. Use the Pg-Length option to override your /Worksheet Global Default Printer Pg-Length setting.

Most laser printers are designed to print at 60 lines per page in the default Courier font, and not 66 lines per page. If you use a laser printer, you should set your global default page length to 60 lines per page. As mentioned above in Setup, check your printer manual for the page length settings that are best for your printer.

Other There are four choices on the Other menu. In effect there are actually two options—and each option can be switched on and off. The first pair of options, As-Displayed or Cell-Formulas, lets you specify what cell contents you want to send to the printer. As-Displayed prints out the text and values—just as you see them on the screen. This is the default setting. Cell-Formulas, on the other hand, prints out the text of any formulas in the print range, rather than just their results. Labels and numbers are printed normally. The Cell-Formulas options lets you create a listing that records the contents of each cell; a printout using the Cell-Formulas option allows others to reconstruct your work. (Appendix B, for example, contains a printout of the model used in Chapter 12; it was printed using the Cell-Formulas option.)

The second pair of options, Formatted and Unformatted, lets you control whether to print the headers, footers and borders, specified in the current print settings. Unformatted is usually used when you print to an ASCII file; in most cases you want to strip off repeating headers, footers, borders, and page breaks. Formatted restores all headers, footers, and borders defaults if the Unformatted command has been previously selected.

The Quit option on the Other menu returns you to the main /Print menu.

As you specify your print options, they are recorded on your Print Settings sheet. When you save your worksheet, the current settings on this sheet will be saved with the file. Figure 8.5 shows a completed settings sheet for a fully configured print job.

Step 3: Align the Printer and Issue a Go Command

With the worksheet range defined and all options selected, you are nearing the final step—issuing the Go print command. Before that, however, you must reset 1-2-3's internal (or logical) page and line count to the top of page one, using the Align command. Select Align before you print, regardless of what kind of printer

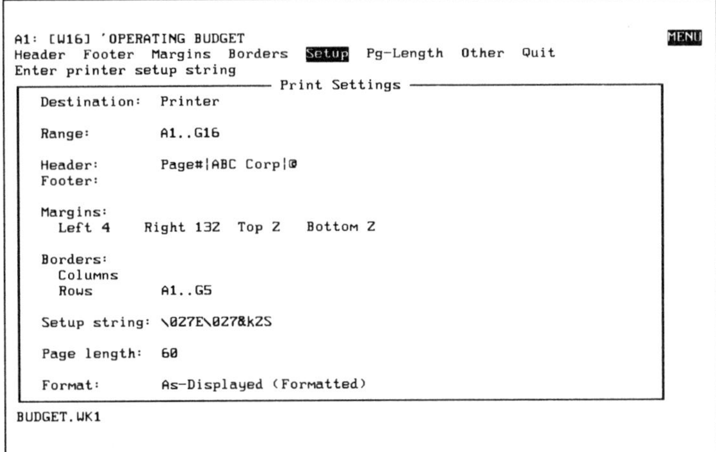

Figure 8.5
Completed Printer Settings Sheet.

you have; this will ensure that all headers, footers, and page breaks are properly positioned when you print.

When you select Align, also be sure that the paper is aligned with the print head and that the printer is at its top of page. If you have a laser printer, check that its buffer is empty (i.e., that the form feed light is off.) If not, take the printer off line and press feed to eject the page and clear the buffer.

After pressing Align, you are ready to instruct the printer to begin the print job. This is done by selecting Go. If the printer is on line, your worksheet will soon appear in hardcopy. If the printer is not on line, or if it runs out of paper in the middle of a print job, 1-2-3 will display a flashing ERROR indicator in the upper right hand corner, and the message "printer error" in the lower left corner. Press ESC or CTRL-BREAK to return to READY mode.

Paper Advance Commands

You may wish to advance the paper by lines or by pages to include extra space between print ranges when you are making a series of print requests. The /Print Printer Line command moves the paper one line each time it is issued. The /Print Printer Page command advances the paper to the top of the next page, as determined by the page length setting. (Laser printer users: Remember to set your default page length to 60 lines per page!) The Page command is particularly useful if you have printed a range that does not reach the end of the page. When you select the Page command, the printer will space down to the bottom of the page, print the appropriate footer, and then eject the page.

In general, it is best to use the Print menu's built-in line feed and page eject commands instead of the buttons or knobs on your printer. This way, 1-2-3 can continue to keep track of the page and line count so that headers, footers, and borders are correctly placed in subsequent print requests.

Be aware that issuing a Page command while 1-2-3 is printing a page does not cause a page break; rather it simply issues a page advance at the end of the current print job. If you issue 10 Page commands while the print job is in progress, 1-2-3 will pump out 10 blank pages after it prints out the specified range.

In order to include a page break command within your worksheet print range, use the /Worksheet Page command. The page break command should appear in the leftmost column of your print range, in a row by itself, wherever you want the page break to occur. When you select /Worksheet Page, 1-2-3 inserts a new row into the worksheet and includes a page break symbol—two colons (|::)—at the current cursor position. (You may also enter the page break symbol manually.) When 1-2-3 encounters the page break symbol in the print range, it begins a new page. 1-2-3 does not print any data that is in a row that begins with a page break symbol.

PRINTER TIPS

Dot-matrix and daisy-wheel printers are line printers, which means that they print each line of data as it is sent from the computer. Laser printers, however, are page printers; they wait until an entire page of data has been transmitted before beginning the printing process. Thus, when you print a small worksheet on a laser printer (or if the last page of your report is a partial page), your data does not fill up the whole page in the buffer; the printer will sit (apparently idle) and wait for more data to be transmitted from the computer before it begins to print that page. With the Hewlett-Packard Laserjet Series printers, the on-line and form feed lights are on in such instances. At this point, you must use 1-2-3's Page command to "push" the partial page through the printing process. Again, be sure that your page length option is set at 60 for the Laserjet (*not* at the default 66). Otherwise, even the Page command will send the printer beyond the top of the next page, and you will have to reset the page length, select Align to put your printer and 1-2-3 in synch, and start the print request over again.

One handy way of avoiding conflicts between 1-2-3's line and page counts and your printer's is to embed a printer control code—an eject command, not just a page break—within your print range. If you are using a Laserjet, the eject command is issued by placing

```
||\012
```

in the left column of the print range, underneath the last row of data. Make sure that you include the row containing the eject command in your print range. This way you can concatenate a whole series of print ranges, one on top of the other, and separate them with embedded eject commands. When you enter the eject command into a cell, 1-2-3 will only display *one* of the vertical bars (see Figure 8.5).

Clearing Print Settings

You will often want to clear out your print specifications when you perform a wide variety of print jobs. A certain portion of a worksheet may require a landscape orientation or a different font; another may require a unique configuration of margins. To wipe the slate clean, select /Print Printer Clear All. A less drastic way of cleaning house is to select Clear Range, Clear Borders, or Clear Format (i.e. set margins, page length, and setup strings back to the default settings).

PRINTING TO A FILE

In some cases, instead of printing out a hard copy of your worksheet, you may want to convert it into a file that you can import into your word processor or desktop publishing program. For this purpose, 1-2-3 can create an ASCII text file out of your worksheet. (All major word processors can read ASCII files.) ASCII files contain no graphs, and no printer control codes or formatting instructions. They can contain any borders, headers, footers, margins, and page breaks that you have specified in your print job, although you may want to dispense with such options. ASCII files can be typed on the screen by using the DOS TYPE command (i.e. `type filename.PRN`). They can also be printed from DOS using the DOS PRINT command (i.e., `print filename.PRN`).

To create an ASCII file, select /Print File, and 1-2-3 will prompt you to type in a filename for the print file. Type in the name, but do not give it an extension; when 1-2-3 creates the ASCII file, it automatically adds a .PRN extension (to indicate print file). If you have already created any .PRN files, they will be displayed in the control panel below the prompt (just as the /File Retrieve command displays existing files). If you want to overwrite an existing .PRN file, highlight it and press ENTER. 1-2-3 will ask if you want to Cancel the command or Replace the file. Respond appropriately.

Next, select the print range, just as though you were going to generate hard copy. If you wish to include headers, footers, borders, or page breaks in the ASCII file, you can use the default setting—Formatted—on the /Print File Options Other menu. If you wish to avoid all page break spaces and repeating headers and footers, select Unformatted from the /Print File Options Other menu. (If you have specified a printer setup string, it will have no effect.)

When you are finished, issue an Align and a Go command. 1-2-3 will create a .PRN file in the current data directory. You can then copy the file to whatever directory contains your word processing or desktop publishing data files.

This concludes our discussion of 1-2-3's built-in printing commands. If you have a laser printer, you may waste a pile of paper before you get your reports looking just right. It's okay to save a tree by recycling your failures through the printer (each piece of paper has two sides). As long as the paper is not excessively curled, it should still feed through the paper path. In Chapter 11, you'll learn how to use the more powerful set of "spreadsheet publishing" tools contained in Allways.

Creating Graphs in 1-2-3

USING GRAPHS TO ENHANCE YOUR WORKSHEETS

The old Chinese proverb, "A picture is worth a thousand words," might be hackneyed, but it is still true. A well conceived graph can instantly convey the significance of a worksheet full of numbers; a single graph may tie together what might otherwise be an indecipherable mass of data.

This chapter describes 1-2-3's most useful graph features in detail, provides guidelines for using the various graph types and options, and walks you through building a graph, step-by-step. You'll get the most out of the information if you build a graph yourself as you read, so you can see the effects of each command and/or option described. For details on each /Graph command and feature in 1-2-3, see the Reference section under /Graph Commands.

CREATING GRAPHS WITH 1-2-3

The essential steps for creating a graph involve selecting a graph type, assigning various values to be graphed (or assigning data ranges), and selecting various presentation or display options. To actually print a graph, you must use the separate PrintGraph program (see discussion in Chapter 10), or Allways (see Chapter 11).

Step 1: Selecting Graph Types

When you select Type from the /Graph menu, 1-2-3 offers five options: Line, Bar, XY, Stack-Bar, and Pie. The key to taking advantage of Release 1-2-3's graphing abilities is to use the right graph for the right occasion. Here are definitions and some suggestions for using each of these graph types.

Line Graph Line graphs are used when you need to demonstrate changes in numeric data over time. As such, they are particularly effective for pinpointing trends and projecting into the future. Line graphs are most telling when you need to graph more than one range of data across a particular time interval and compare the performances of each data range. (1-2-3 allows you to include up to six data ranges in a single line graph.) Line graphs are typically used in business for depicting financial trends, sales trends, income trends, cash flow and other statistics that change over time. Figure 9.1 shows how a line graph was used with a budget worksheet to compare advertising costs between January and June.

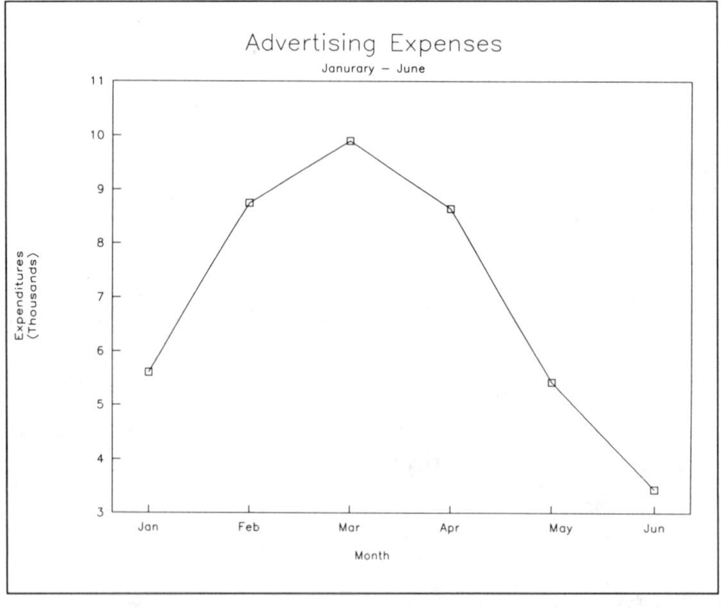

Figure 9.1
Line graph.

Bar Graph Bar Graphs are used to compare two or more entities at a fixed point in time (e.g., a particular month, or year, etc.), or at a series of fixed points in time (first quarter, second quarter, etc.). Bar graphs that use more than one bar to represent more than one data range are sometimes called "clustered" bar graphs. (1-2-3 does not give you the option of clustering bars—it does this for you automatically.) Typical business uses of bar graphs include comparing: sales

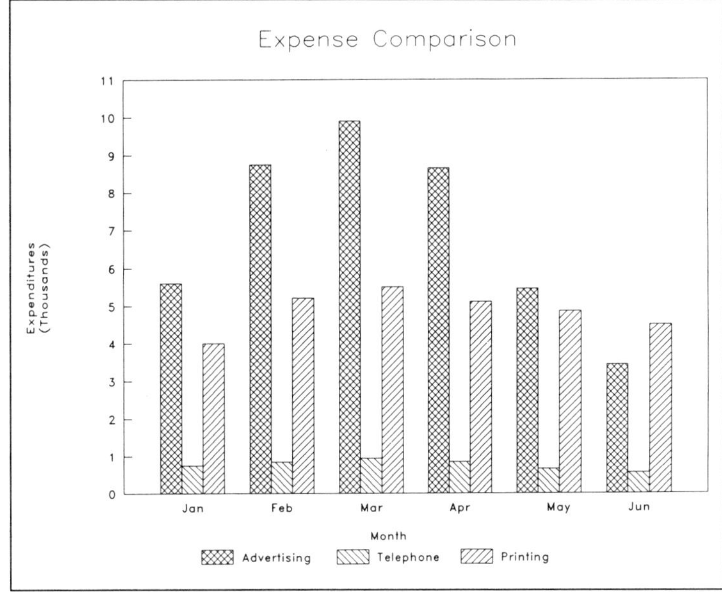

Figure 9.2
Clustered Bar graph.

figures for different product lines or salesperson; sales by month or by year; total inventory by item; total revenue by month, quarter, and year; and customer satisfaction by divisions. Figure 9.2 shows how a bar graph was used to compare advertising, telephone, and printing expenses for each month.

XY Graph The XY graph is similar to a line graph, but uses a numeric scale for the X-axis, rather than a set of fixed labels. That means each point on an XY graph is determined by a pair of X and Y coordinates. The XY graph helps you visualize the relationship between two changing variables (or sets of data values). This is useful when you want to correlate two different types of data, such as customer service ratings and on-time delivery performance, daily customer attendance and daily gross revenues, etc. Figure 9.3 shows net profit versus sales volume plotted as an XY graph.

Stacked Bar Graph Whereas bar graphs are used to compare the values of individual entities, stacked bars compare multiple values "layered" in each bar. This allows you to visualize the relationship of each data value to the total value. At the same time, the stacked bar enables you to compare each data value to the other data values in the graph. For example, a stacked bar graph might consist of the revenue contributions from various departments in a given year. One stacked bar might represent 1986, another 1987, and a third 1988. By comparing the three bars side-by-side, you can get an instant view of the contribution to revenue that

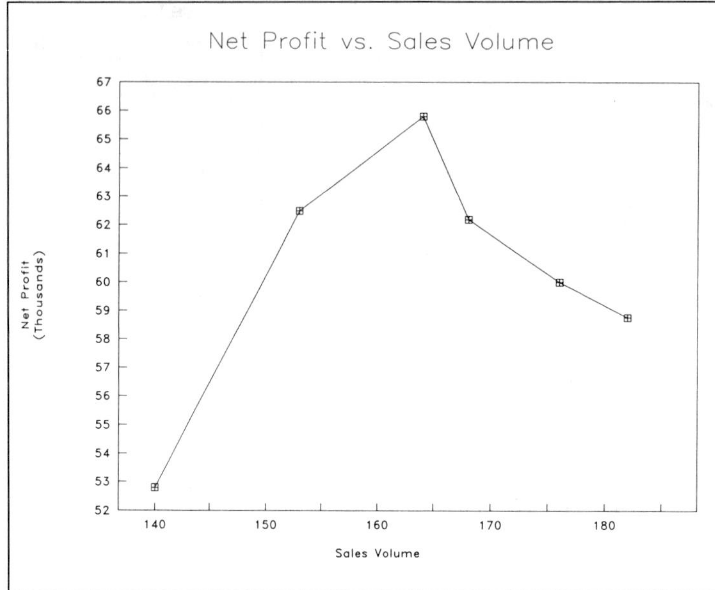

Figure 9.3
XY graph.

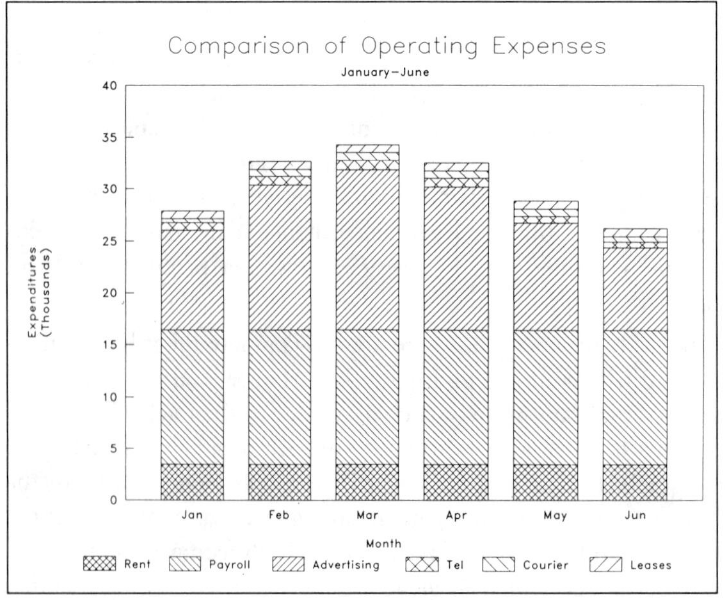

Figure 9.4
Stacked bar graph.

each department has made during the three-year period. You can also see the relative contribution of each department in a given year, and a single department's contribution trend from year to year. Applied to a budget model, the layers in each bar might represent the relative contribution that various line items make to overall monthly expenses. This is shown in Figure 9.4.

Pie Chart The pie chart relates parts to a whole in terms of percentages or absolute values. Each piece of the pie is proportional in size with respect to the total value; a value of 25 percent, for example, would be associated with a piece one-quarter the size of the overall pie. 1-2-3 allows you to enhance a pie chart by *exploding* one or more slices. Exploding means slightly removing the piece from the rest of the diagram so it stands out. Figure 9.5 shows a pie chart for a budget worksheet. Pie charts are typically used when you want to compare a set of component values at a fixed point in time, such as the contribution of various product lines to overall sales revenues or the breakdown of costs for an item or department.

Step 2: Selecting the X-Axis Data Range

Once you've selected a graph type, the next step is to specify the graph data ranges—the values to be graphed. First, select X to specify the X-axis data range. The X-axis data range consists of values or labels in a single row or column. The

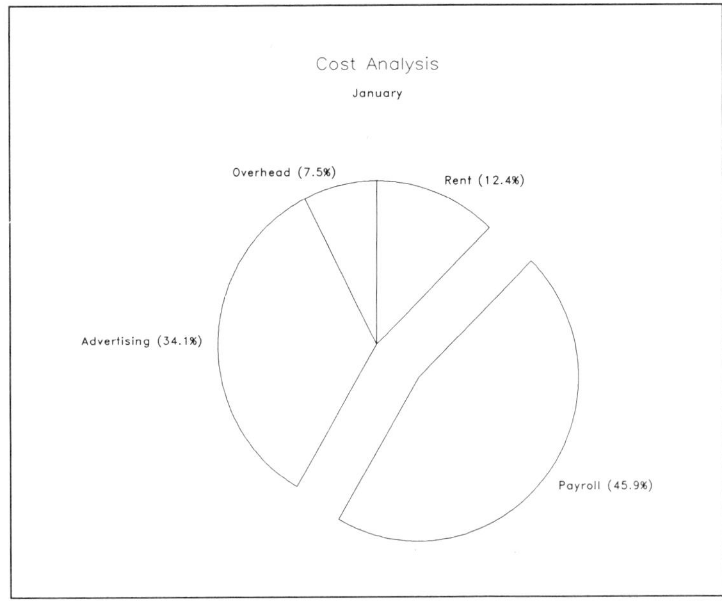

Figure 9.5
Pie chart.

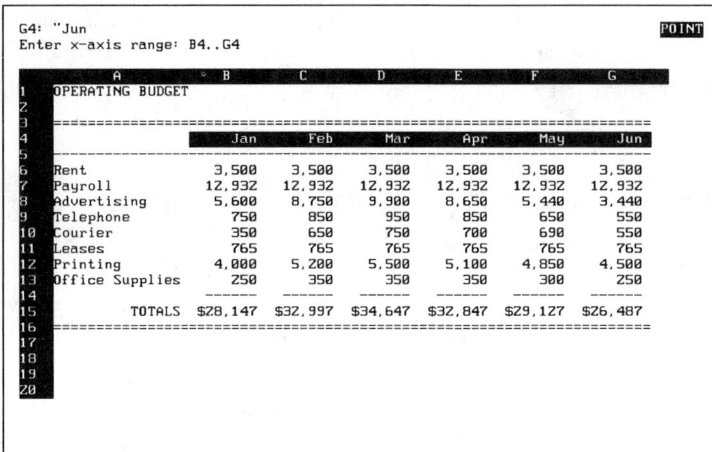

G4: "Jun
Enter x-axis range: B4..G4 POINT

OPERATING BUDGET

	Jan	Feb	Mar	Apr	May	Jun
Rent	3,500	3,500	3,500	3,500	3,500	3,500
Payroll	12,932	12,932	12,932	12,932	12,932	12,932
Advertising	5,600	8,750	9,900	8,650	5,440	3,440
Telephone	750	850	950	850	650	550
Courier	350	650	750	700	690	550
Leases	765	765	765	765	765	765
Printing	4,000	5,200	5,500	5,100	4,850	4,500
Office Supplies	250	350	350	350	300	250
TOTALS	$28,147	$32,997	$34,647	$32,847	$29,127	$26,487

Figure 9.6

X range, budget worksheet.

contents of the X-axis range is used differently for various graph types. For example, the month labels in range B4 through G4 of the budget worksheet would constitute the X-axis range for a line, bar or stacked bar graph. (Refer to the X range specified in Figure 9.6 and then to the corresponding graph in Figure 9.2).

Once you've specified the X data range, the coordinates will appear in your Graph Settings sheet. As you add other features to the graph, they too will appear in the settings sheet, so you can keep tabs on what your graph will look like as you construct it.

The X data range assignment above applies to line, bar, and stacked bar graphs. For pie charts, which obviously have no X-axis, the contents of the cells in the X data range are used as the labels for each pie slice. For XY graphs, the X-axis data range must be numeric, since the X-axis values are used to position the values in the A–F data ranges.

Step 3: Selecting the A–F Data Ranges

After you select an X data range, you are ready to specify the data ranges to be graphed. 1-2-3 allows you to graph a maximum of six sets of data values (A through F). Let's say we want to use a bar graph to compare three line items in each of the six months represented in the budget worksheet: advertising, telephone, and printing. To review the procedures: In Step 1 we select Bar as our graph type, and in Step 2 we select our X range B4 through G4 with monthly labels and then:

1. Select A on the /Graph menu option to define the first data range, advertising.
2. Paint the range of data from B8 to G8, as row 8 contains the advertising expenditures.
3. Repeat the above procedure for the other two data ranges B and C. Use the telephone expenditures in B9 through G9 as the B range, and the printing expenses in B12 through G12 as the C range.
4. Finally, select /Graph View (or F10 in READY mode) to temporarily move the worksheet from view and display the graph. The resulting graph is shown in Figure 9.2.

Alternate to Steps 2 and 3: Group Range Selection

A new feature in Release 2.2 is the /Graph Group option, which allows you to assign all data ranges, including the X-axis data range, in one fell swoop. To do so, all data ranges that you wish to use in the graph must be arranged contiguously; you can organize the data ranges columnwise (side by side) or rowwise (one above the other). The X data range must be the first row or column in the series of ranges, and the subsequent data ranges, A through F, must be adjacent and aligned in that order. Here's how to use the Group command:

1. Select /Graph Group.
2. Paint or specify (by address or name) the entire data range that you want 1-2-3 to automatically assign to separate graph ranges.
3. Select Columnwise or Rowwise. Columnwise, as the name suggests, means that the columns are used to assign graph ranges; rowwise means that rows are used to assign graph ranges.

NOTE If your group data range includes a blank column or a column containing labels, that column will appear as a blank or 0 in your graph. This could throw off your entire graph. For example, if you are creating a clustered bar graph, it will leave a blank between bars. Also, for the Group option the pie chart follows slightly different rules: The values for the pie are assigned to the A range; the pattern specifications (or color and other options) for the pie are assigned to the B range; and the labels for each slice, as we have seen, are assigned to the X range.)

Now let's go back to the bar graph we set up in steps 2 and 3 above. The worksheet has been modified so that the Group command is easily used (see Figure 9.7). The labels in B4 through G4 are used to define the X range, the values in cells B5 through G5 are used for range A, the values in cells B6 through G6 are used for range B, and the values in cells B7 through G7, are used for range C. In this way, all of the data for this graph is located in a single range: B4 through G7 (see Figure 9.7).

By selecting the Group option and then specifying Rowwise, 1-2-3 will automatically take the data in the first row in the range, and assign it to the X-axis range. It will then take the data in the next row, B5 to G5, and assign it to range A, and so on. In this way, you can instantly assign graph data ranges with only a few keystrokes. When you design a worksheet, this quick method is an inducement to make sure that columns and rows are organized in a fashion that allows you to use the /Graph Group command.

Caution: If you select columnwise when you assign graph ranges to a worksheet that contains data in rows, the results will be meaningless. Figure 9.8 shows what would result if you were to select Columnwise for the group range B4 through G7 in Figure 9.7.

Step 4: Adding Options to Improve Appearance and Readability

A number of options are available to make your graphs more informative and attractive. For example, the addition of titles and legends makes it easier for the reader to instantly grasp the message you're trying to convey. This is important,

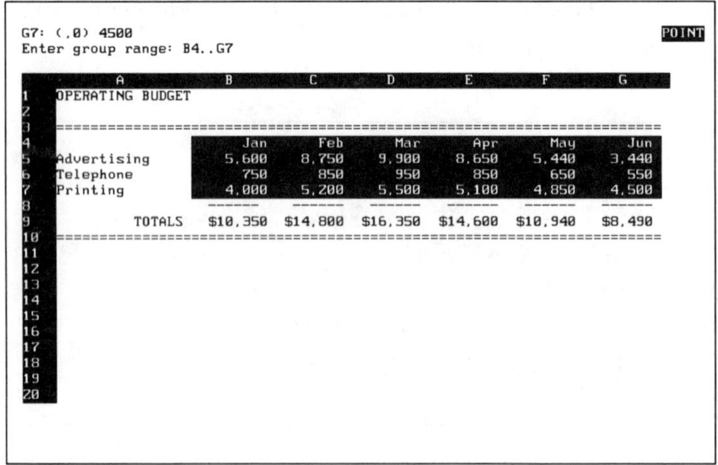

Figure 9.7
Graph range for group assignment.

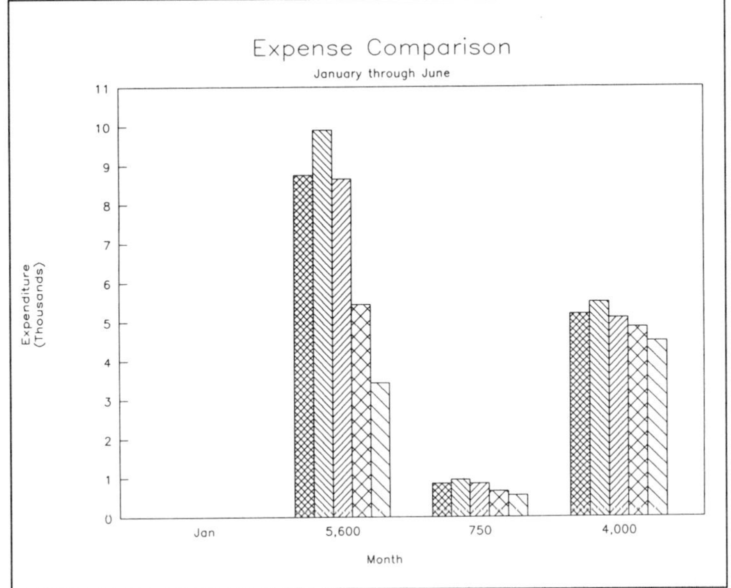

Figure 9.8
Nonsensical graph created by using columns instead of rows with group command.

because the whole point of a graph is to give the viewer an immediate grasp of the significance of the numerical data. The more a viewer has to study the graph, the less effective it will be. If, on the other hand, the meaning of the data is so striking that it "jumps off the page," you've achieved your goal. The following features enable you to fine tune and enhance your 1-2-3 graphs. They are all selected from the /Graph Options menu. Refer to Figure 9.9, which shows a selection of sample elements that can be added to your graphs through the Options menu.

Legend

Explanatory legends can be added below your graph to identify one or more of the graphed data ranges (A through F) according to its pattern or color representation. You can use numbers or labels as legends. Legends enable the viewer to immediately discern what data is being graphed. They can be assigned to the data ranges one by one or all at once, as a range. To designate the first legend for your graph, select one of the data ranges (A–F) from the menu, press ENTER, and type in the text for the legend (e.g., 1989, Advertising, January, etc.). 1-2-3 will create a legend consisting of a sample of the hatching pattern (or color) used for the data range, followed by the legend text that you have just assigned. In Figure 9.2, for example, the legends for Advertising, Telephone, and Printing have been included in the graph.

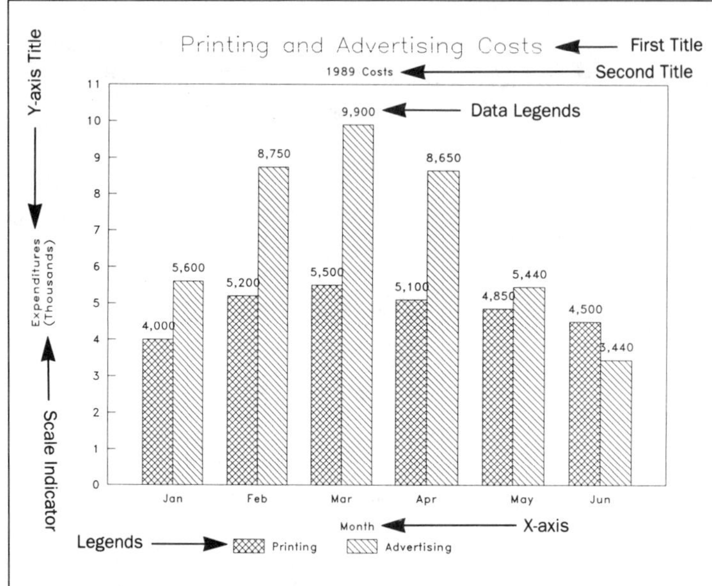

Figure 9.9 Available Graph Options.

If you have a range in your worksheet that contains appropriate text for all the legends in the proper sequence, you can use the special Range option on the Legend menu to assign the legend text to all the data ranges at once. (This is similar to the /Graph Group command.) Select Range, and then specify the range that contains the legend text—by name or address.

For example, using the modified worksheet in Figure 9.7, you could specify the range A5..A7 as the legend range, and 1-2-3 would know that the Advertising legend is to be assigned to the A range (and hence represented by the hatching pattern for the A range), that the Telephone legend is for the B range, and that the Printing legend is for the C range. As you saw in Figure 9.2, the legends contribute to an instant understanding of the data.

Titles

A graph can have up to four titles. At the top of your graph, you can include a first line and a second line heading (First and Second titles) to identify the graph. The First title is printed in a larger type size than any of the other titles. You can also add X-axis and Y-axis titles to the graph to identify what is being measured in each case. All of the graphs we have created thus far have included First and Second titles, as well as X-axis and Y-axis titles, except for the pie chart, which doesn't have X or Y axes. Each graph title consists of one line of text (up to

39 characters long). As you specify the text for your titles, they will appear on the current graph setting sheet. You can use the contents of a particular worksheet cell for any title. At the prompt for the title text, simply enter a backslash (\) followed by the address or range name of the cell that contains the appropriate text.

Scale

On occasion you may need to control the scaling method used for the Y-axis values in your graph. (For XY graphs, you may also need to specify scaling for the X-axis values). In addition, the Scale option allows you to specify the format of the numbers that appear on either axis. A final option on the Scale menu—Skip—lets you define a Skip factor for X-axes that use labels; for example, when you have a large number of X-axis entries you can specify a Skip factor of 2 and include only every other label in the X data range.

When you first select Scale, you are given three options: X-Scale, Y-Scale and Skip (described above). If you choose the X- or Y-scale options, you can set a scaling method for each axis individually. The choices are:

Automatic The automatic scaling method is the default. 1-2-3 automatically establishes a scale that is based on the lowest and highest values in your data range.

Manual If you prefer to set your own upper and lower limits, choose the Manual option. (Any data outside the limits you specify will not be included in the graph.)

Format To set the format for the values that are displayed along the X- or Y-axis in your graph, choose Format. You can select from the full range of 1-2-3 formats: Comma, Percent, Fixed, Scientific, Currency, etc.

Indicator A scale indicator for either axis appears just under the title assigned to that axis. In most of our graphs we have included the scale indicator "(Thousands)". Indicator has three options. Yes maintains the current scale indicator as automatically determined by 1-2-3. The None option hides the scale indicator; and Manual prompts you for your own text.

Data-Labels

You may wish to to label the exact value represented by each data element in the graph. For example, if you have six bars in a graph representing total monthly expenses from January to June, the Data-Labels option would allow you to place the exact figure just over each bar on the graph (see Figure 9.9). This way the graph offers the viewer more than just a visual estimation of the expenses for each month.

When you select Data-Labels, you will have the choice of specifying the labels for each data range (A–F) individually, or selecting the Group option, which allows you to assign your data labels in a single range.

After you select the labels that will be placed on your graph, 1-2-3 will give you five position options: Center, Left, Above, Right, and Below. Choose whichever option best fits your graph. Then use Quit to return to the Options menu.

In general, data labels and grids (see below) don't mix, since they serve similar purposes. Grids guide your eye to a specific Y-axis or X-axis value. Data labels place a precise value on the graph. The mixture of the two renders each visual aid less effective.

Grid

A grid is used to guide the viewer's eye to an accurate reading of the data measurements in a graph. The grid is particularly useful when there are many data elements that need to be aligned with an X-axis or Y-axis value or label. The three grid options can also be used to create aesthetically pleasing graphs. You can place a horizontal or vertical grid in the background of a graph (using the Horizontal or Vertical options). The Both option places a vertical and a horizontal grid on the graph, giving it a "graph paper" appearance (see Figure 9.10). To remove the grid, select Clear.

Format

The Format option applies to line graphs and XY graphs. Format allows you to control how data points are represented in linear graphs, and to determine whether or not the data points should be connected with a line. You can display the data points for each data range with a different symbol; you can connect data points with lines; you can do both of the above, or neither. In addition, you can set the format for all lines in the graph at once (using the Graph option on the Format menu), or you can format one or more lines individually (selecting each data range—A, B, C, D, E or F—and specifying its format).

Data points can be represented by symbols with the Symbol option. 1-2-3 assigns a different symbol to each different range. Data points can also be connected with lines, with the Lines option. The Both option connects data points with lines and assigns symbols (see Figure 9.11), and the Neither option leaves data points as small dots and with no connecting lines or differentiating symbols, producing a "scatter" diagram.

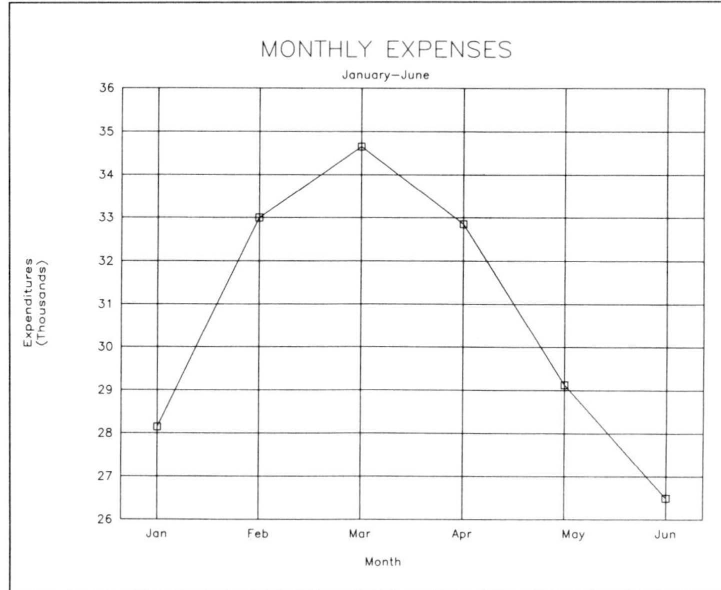

Figure 9.10
Horizontal and vertical grid with line graph.

The last two options on the /Graph Options menu simply allow you to set your display to black and white or color.

Color Displays the graph in color as opposed to the next option, (B&W) Black & White. This is effective only if you have a color display.

B&W Shifts the display to black and white and assigns cross-hatching instead of colors.

Step 5: Naming and Saving Graphs

Once you have gone through the efforts of creating a graph, chances are you want to keep your graph intact—either for printing or for later reference. 1-2-3 allows you to name and save graphs. The distinction is critical and not at all obvious. The Name option is used to *save* your current graph settings and ranges; the Save option is used to *export* the image for use with other programs, such as PrintGraph and Allways. When you name a graph you save the settings for that graph including all options and range specifications; the settings for all named graphs are saved with the current file. This is the only way to save a graph so that you can subsequently recall and modify it. The Save option on the other hand (see below), strange as it may seem, does not save the graph and or any of the data that was gathered to create the graph. Rather, it saves the graph *image* in a file format

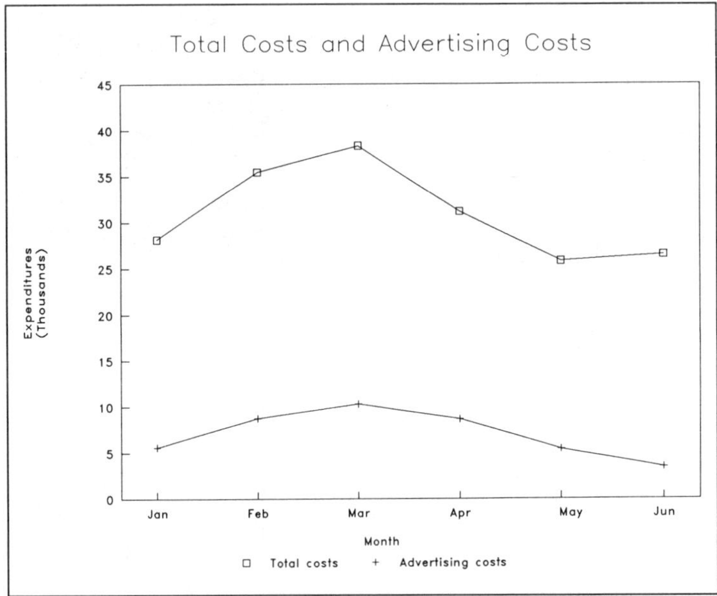

Figure 9.11
Line graph with symbols and lines.

suitable for export only, for use with PrintGraph or programs from other publishers. 1-2-3 cannot even import and read its own exported graph!

Naming Graphs

To name a graph after you've specified its data ranges and applied various options, select /Graph Name. Also select /Graph Name to recall a named graph. /Graph Name enables you to:

Create a graph name When you select the Create option, 1-2-3 displays a list of all currently named graphs. If you want to update (and replace) an existing named graph, highlight the name and press ENTER. If you want to save the current settings under a new name, type in the new name and press ENTER.

Use a named graph The Use option lets you retrieve a named graph that is associated with the worksheet. Select Use and 1-2-3 displays a list of named graphs in the file. Highlight the named graph you wish to recall and press ENTER. The graph will be displayed on your screen as the current graph, and the Graph Settings sheet will now reflect those of the selected graph. The named graph that you retrieved will also overwrite the graph on the screen (or the current graph). So if you have a current graph on the screen and you want to save its range and option settings, name it with /Graph Name Create before calling up another named graph.

Delete a named graph Choose Delete and 1-2-3 will display a list of named graphs in the file. Highlight the name you wish to delete and press ENTER.

Reset all named graphs Select Reset and 1-2-3 will purge all named graphs from the file.

Table The Table option creates a list or a table in your worksheet of all existing graph names associated with the file, and includes the graph type and title for each graph. This is an extremely useful way to keep track of your named graphs, and to document your worksheet for other users. If you have a large worksheet with many named graphs, you should print out the Graph Name Table and keep it nearby for easy reference. Make sure you have a clear area available for the Graph Name Table—the table occupies three columns and as many lines as you have named graphs. The table will overwrite anything in its way.

NOTE You must be sure to save the worksheet file in order to save your named graphs. If you create a complex graph, name it, then erase the worksheet or quit without saving, all your hard work will be lost.

Saving Graphs for Use with PrintGraph and Allways

To save the current graph image so it can be printed with PrintGraph (see next chapter), or Allways (see Chapter 11) use the /Graph Save command. Once a graph is saved, you can use it with PrintGraph, Allways, or any other program that can handle .PIC files.

At this point, you've been exposed to most of the graph options available in 1-2-3. If it seems a bit overwhelming, be assured that you don't have learn or use all of them at once. As with other aspects of the program, start small and build. Add various features as you go along, using those that enhance the graphs value and readability.

After you go hog wild trying out every conceivable graphing feature, back off and ask yourself how you can put your new-found power to the best use. Above all, remember that complex is not always better; sometimes simple images have the biggest impact.

From here we will go on to discuss 1-2-3's utility program—PrintGraph—that lets you print graphs that you have saved using the /Graph Save command.

Using the PrintGraph Program

ABOUT PRINTGRAPH

In the last chapter we discussed procedures for creating and saving graphs. This chapter focuses on the PrintGraph utility program, which enables you to print out the .PIC files you saved in 1-2-3. PrintGraph is not built into 1-2-3, you must quit from 1-2-3 to use it.

It is important to realize that PrintGraph does not enable you to modify graphs; to do so, you must return to 1-2-3, retrieve the worksheet in which the graphs were created, select the /Graph Name Use command, highlight the named graph, and then edit it as necessary. And if your printer is not a graphics printer it won't be able to print graphs, PrintGraph or no PrintGraph. A good clue as to whether your printer will work or not is whether it appears on the list of graphics printers displayed during the install program (see Chapter 1).

STARTING PRINTGRAPH

To start PrintGraph, go to your 1-2-3 program directory with the DOS cd command: `cd\[directory containing 1-2-3 files]`. From there you can load PrintGraph by typing `pgraph` at the prompt. Alternatively, you can start

PrintGraph from the Lotus Access Manager. Go to your 1-2-3 program directory and type `lotus` at the DOS prompt. The Access Manager screen will be displayed, as shown in Figure 10.1. Highlight the PrintGraph option and press ENTER; and PrintGraph will load.

Once the PrintGraph logo has been displayed (it may stay on the screen for a few moments, depending on the speed of your computer), the PrintGraph Main Menu will be displayed (see Figure 10.2). Select options from the menu just as you would in 1-2-3.

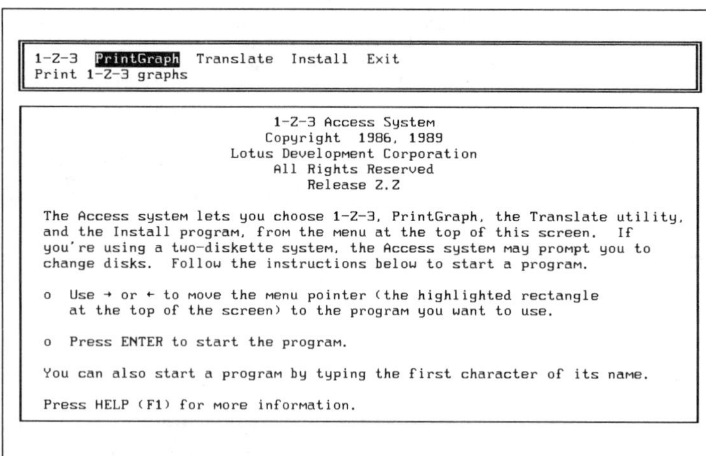

Figure 10.1
Lotus Access Manager.

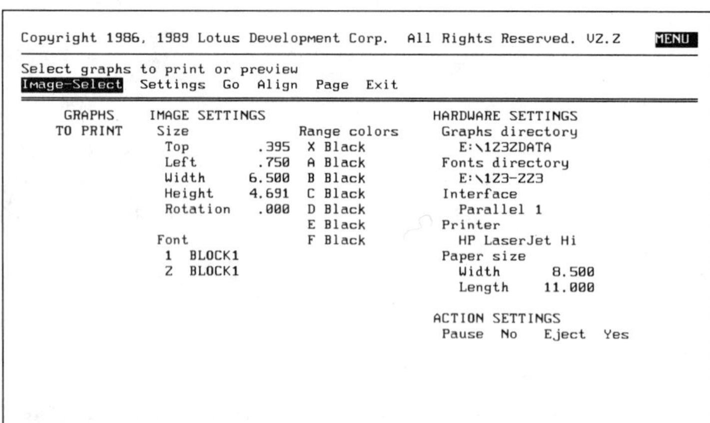

Figure 10.2
PrintGraph Main Menu.

We will proceed by describing the various PrintGraph menu options in the sequence you'll probably use them.

CONFIGURING PRINTGRAPH

PrintGraph offers several important setting options for your hardware, and for your images—including fonts, color, proportions, and rotation. While you might want to modify these settings on occasion, for special graphs or print requests, Lotus assumes that once you decide on certain key settings, you will want to use them most of the time. When you specify appropriate settings for your default Hardware, Action, or Image settings, be sure that you save them in the PrintGraph configuration file. (To do this, use Setting Save option on the main PrintGraph menu.) The settings options include the following:

Hardware

The first thing you'll want to do, if you haven't used PrintGraph before, is to configure the program to your hardware. Select Settings, then Hardware, and the following options will be available to you.

Graphs-Directory You will have to specify the directory in which your graph (or .PIC) files have been saved. Whenever you save a graph, 1-2-3 automatically adds the .PIC extension to the filename and places the .PIC file in the current data directory. If you have multiple data directories in 1-2-3, you will need to specify for PrintGraph which data directory contains the graphs you wish to print.

Fonts Directory When you print out graphs, you use PrintGraph's own font files. Normally, these font files (they have the extension .FNT) are kept in the same directory as your 1-2-3 program files. If, for some reason, you separate your fonts into a different directory, use this option to indicate where the fonts are located.

Printer When you install Lotus, 1-2-3 configures PrintGraph for any graphics printer that you select through the Install program. PrintGraph's Printer option allows you to choose a printer from the list of installed graphics printers (see Figure 10.3). Whenever you install additional graphics printer drivers, the list is updated to reflect the new devices.

For any given print request, you can select only *one* device. To do so, highlight the printer you wish to use and press the space bar. This will place a pound (#) sign before the printer. (Press the space bar again to remove the pound sign

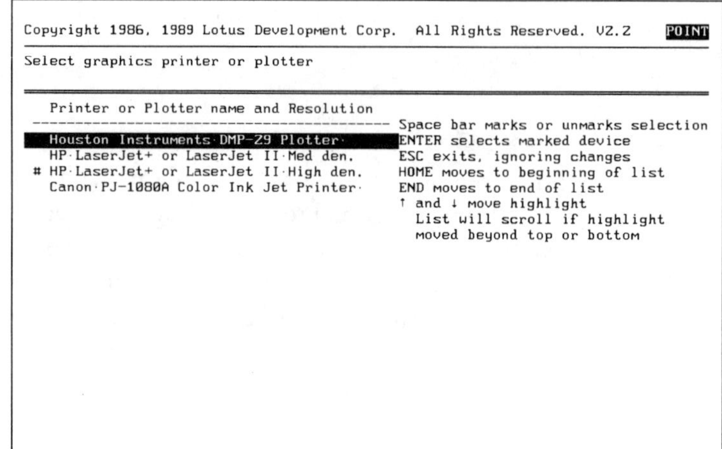

Figure 10.3
PrintGraph shows all graphics printers selected during the Install program.

and unselect the printer.) When you press ENTER, you will be returned to the Main Menu, and the printer you just selected will appear as the default on the settings screen.

Even though you may specify only one printer during the Install program, you may find two options for that printer on the PrintGraph Printer list—one for low density and one for high density. Generally, the low-density option is for faster printouts in draft quality mode. The higher-density option means a higher quality printout but more time. If, for example, you specified a LaserJet+/LaserJet Series II printer during installation, you will find two printer options listed in PrintGraph, shown in Figure 10.3; one for medium density, and one for high density. Medium density produces graphs at 150 dots per inch (dpi), while high density prints at 300 dpi. The difference in resolution is dramatic, as you can see by comparing Figures 10.4a, which shows medium density, and 10.4b, which shows high density. The catch, though, is that to print a full-sized graph at 300 dpi, your laser printer must have sufficient memory. If you cannot print full page graphics at 300 dpi, either reduce the graph size with the Image-Size command (see below), buy some extra memory for your printer, or lower the resolution.

Interface If you have selected multiple printers, you will need to specify the interface whenever you change output devices. For example, say you have a LaserJet Series II printer running from LPT1: (Parallel 1, option 1 on the Interface menu), and you have a plotter connected to the serial port COM2:

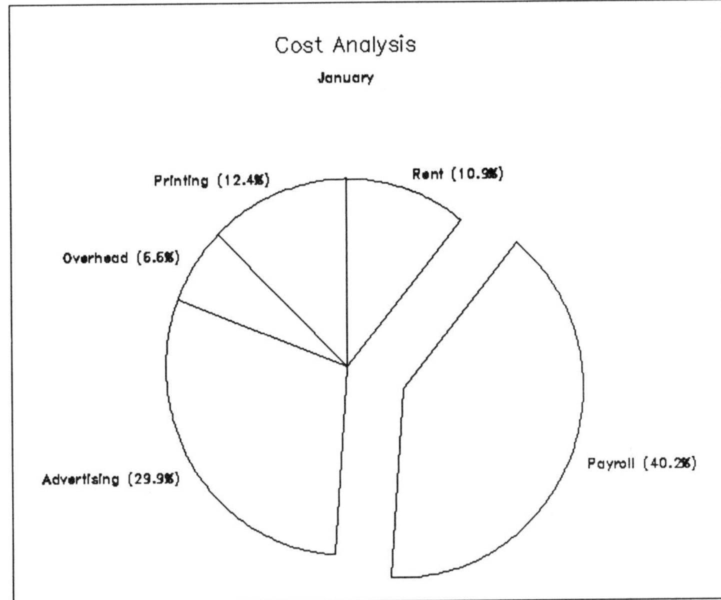

Figure 10.4a

This figure was printed on a LaserJet Series II set for medium resolution (150dpi).

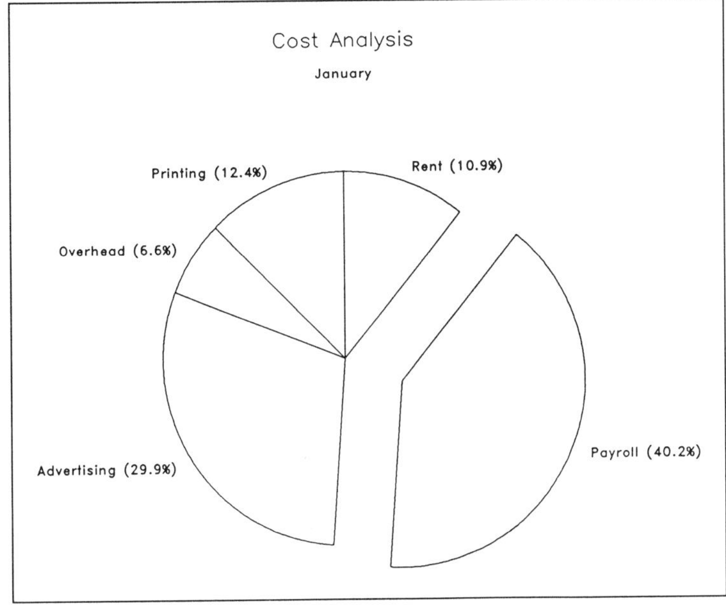

Figure 10.4b

The same graph was printed with the same LaserJet set for high resolution.

(Serial 2, option 4 on the Interface menu). Each time you change printers, you will have to instruct PrintGraph which interface it should use. The Interface menu allows you to choose from two serial and two parallel devices, and also provides options for printers on a network. (See the Reference section for complete details.)

Size-Paper The default paper size is 8.5 by 11 inches. If you are using a different size sheet of paper, this option allows you to specify a new length and width in inches. Note that changing the size of the paper does not in any way affect the size of the graph.

Page Control—the Action Settings Menu

The Action option under the PrintGraph Settings menu allows you to control two options: whether PrintGraph should pause before printing each graph and whether it should print only one graph per page, advancing automatically to the next page when each graph is done. These two options are not mutually exclusive.

Pausing

When you're printing a batch of graphs, you may need to pause in between so you can insert a new piece of paper or adjust your printer. This is typically used with plotters or sheet-fed printers. If you want PrintGraph to pause between graphs, select Yes for the Pause option. During the pause, PrintGraph will beep until you press the space bar to continue printing.

Ejecting Pages

When you select Yes for the Eject option, each graph will be placed on a separate sheet of paper. If you are using continuous feed paper, the paper will advance to the top of the next page after each graph is printed. With sheet-fed printers you will be asked to insert a new piece of paper. If you select No for the Eject option, PrintGraph will attempt to print your graphs out sequentially, one after the other on the same sheet of paper, changing sheets only at page breaks.

Image Settings

PrintGraph offers several important options for tailoring each graph image—including fonts, color, proportions, and rotation. The following Image settings are available.

Size

If you do not specify a setting for the graph size, PrintGraph automatically scales the graph so it occupies a full page width-wise on an 8.5 by 11 inch sheet, i.e., in "portrait" mode. The exact dimensions of the graph are shown underneath the PrintGraph menu in the Image Settings column (refer to Figure 10.2). If you wish, you can select a half page graph size, with the Half command.

You can designate your own length and width measurements with Manual option on the Size menu. Manual also lets you to set the Top and Left margins for the graph (in inches), and to rotate the graph by a specified number of degrees. You would choose 180 degrees, for example, to print the graph in landscape mode, or across the long side of the page. (Note that if parts of your graphs are getting cut off when you use a plotter, you may have to adjust the margins to provide enough area for the plotter to create the image.

Font

1-2-3 allows you to use choose two different fonts per graph. Font 1 is used for the first line title. Font 2 is used for all other text in the graph (i.e., for the second line of the title, the X- and Y-axis titles, as well as the legends and data labels). When you select either 1 or 2 for the first and second font, respectively, PrintGraph will display a list of available fonts (see Figure 10.5). Use the cursor keys to highlight a font from the list and press the space bar to select it. A pound sign (#) will appear beside the specified font. To unselect a font and choose another, press the space bar again. You can only choose one first font and one second font.

PrintGraph can only use its own fonts; your printer's fonts are *not* available. A sample of PrintGraph fonts is shown in Figure 10.6. You may notice that sev-

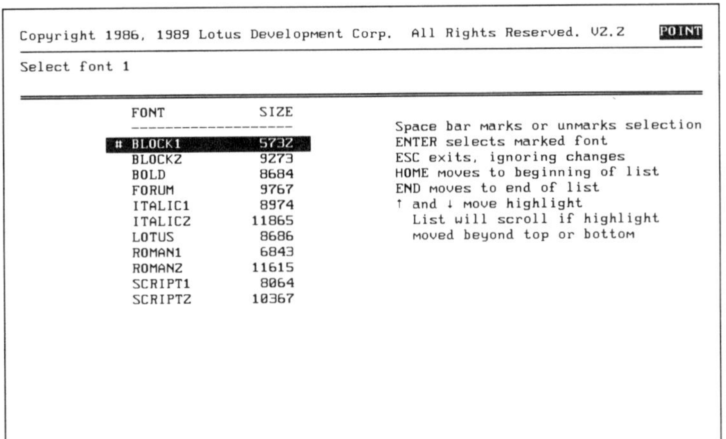

Figure 10.5 Graph font selection list.

eral fonts appear in two versions, (e.g., Roman1 and Roman2); the second version of these fonts is simply a heavier version of the first. Generally, the heavier fonts should be used only with high-resolution printers. The final choice of fonts is up to you, although the simple fonts Block1, Block2, Bold, and Forum are most commonly used for graphs and are by far the clearest. At the other end of the spectrum, Lotus has included some rather gaudy fonts, Script1 and 2; they may be of use for graphs relating to weddings, Barmitzvahs, and funerals.

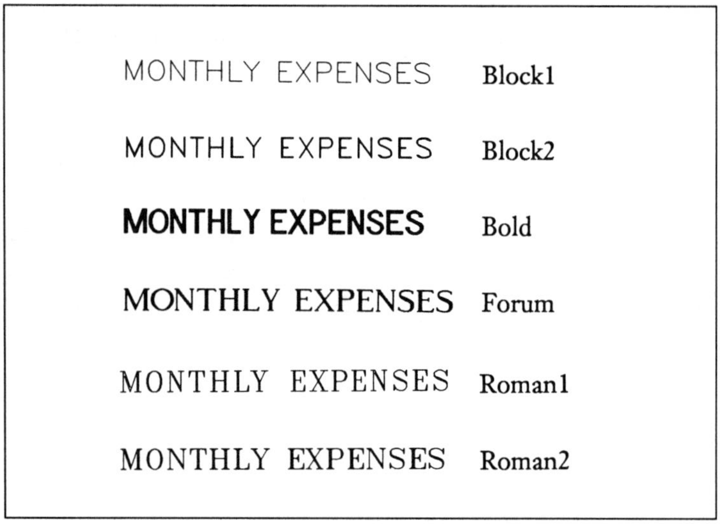

MONTHLY EXPENSES	Block1
MONTHLY EXPENSES	Block2
MONTHLY EXPENSES	Bold
MONTHLY EXPENSES	Forum
MONTHLY EXPENSES	Roman1
MONTHLY EXPENSES	Roman2

Figure 10.6
Sample of PrintGraph fonts.

Range-Colors

If your printer can only print in black, this option will not apply; the choices for each range will only be black. If your printer can produce colors, PrintGraph will display a list of available colors for each range, depending on the printer's characteristics. For example, if you have a basic color printer, such as the Canon PJ-1080 Color Ink Jet printer, your choices for each range will be: black, red, green, yellow, blue, magenta, or cyan.

With a more sophisticated plotter, such as the Houston Instruments DMP-2, you choices for each range will be: black, brown, blue, red, green, violet, orange, lime, yellow, or turquoise.

As you assign colors for ranges X and A through F, they will be reported in the Range Colors column on the PrintGraph Settings sheet (refer to Figure 10.2). Note that there are a few intricacies involved in assigning colors with Pie Charts; see the Reference section for details.

Saving Your PrintGraph Settings

Use the Save command to store your settings for future use. The settings are stored in a PrintGraph configuration file called PGRAPH.CNF. Whenever you load PrintGraph, it will use whatever settings it finds in the configuration file. During a session, you may wish to change some of these configuration settings temporarily—for a particular graph. When you've finished printing that graph and wish to restore the default settings, select Reset.

CHOOSING GRAPHS TO PRINT

To select a graph, choose Image-Select from the Main Menu. PrintGraph will display a list of .PIC files in the current graph directory (Figure 10.7). You can select one or more graphs from the list; highlight each file name you want to print and press the space bar. PrintGraph will place a pound sign (#) in front of each graph you select. (To unselect a graph, highlight its name and press the space bar again—the pound sign will disappear.)

You can preview any graph from the list by highlighting it and pressing the F10 GRAPH key. (This is extremely useful; it ensures that you are selecting the right graph.) Press ESC to return from the graph preview to the graph file list. After you have made all your selections, press ENTER and the Main Menu will be displayed. All of the selected graphs will appear in the left column, "GRAPHS TO PRINT" on the PrintGraph settings screen.

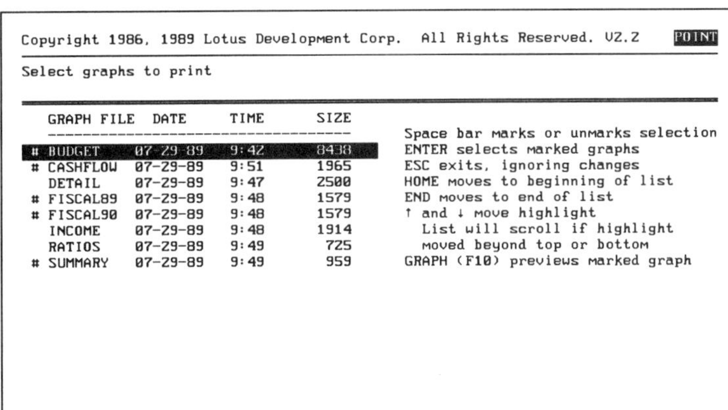

Figure 10.7
Available graph files.

PRINTING A GRAPH

Once you've selected graphs to be printed and have selected the appropriate Hardware, Action, and Image setting, you can begin the printing process. Select Align, to reset the top of the page, followed by Go; Go actually commences the print job. If you selected a group of graphs, and have selected Action Pause No, the entire batch will print consecutively.

If you are using continuous feed paper and are printing a single graph, you can advance the paper to the next page by selecting the Page command (this is an alternative to setting Action to Eject). To interrupt the printing process, press CTRL-BREAK.

EXITING PRINTGRAPH

When you select Exit from the Main Menu, you will return to DOS if you started the program from DOS. If you started PrintGraph from the Access Manager, you will return to the Access Manager screen, from which you can load 1-2-3 or exit to DOS (or install a new graphics printer driver with Install).

While PrintGraph gives you a great deal of control over the graph printing process, you may want to explore an alternative program, Allways, which can be used to print graphs from within 1-2-3. We discuss Allways in detail in the following chapter.

For all the "spreadsheet publishing" features that Allways offers, however, it does not supplant PrintGraph; it is complementary. For batch printing jobs, PrintGraph is still the program of choice.

Advanced Printing: Using Allways

Release 2.2 includes a powerful printing program called Allways, which is designed to run on hard disk systems. If you have a dual drive system, skip to the next chapter, or upgrade to a hard disk system (it's worth it just to be able to use Allways). With Allways, you can create spreadsheet reports that look as good as documents created with a desktop publishing system. In fact, Lotus refers to Allways as a *spreadsheet publisher.* If you have a graphics monitor (monochrome or color), Allways will allow you to see exactly what your printed page will look like, fonts, shading, and all.

INSTALLING ALLWAYS

Allways is a separate add-in program, with its own series of diskettes. You can copy all of the Allways floppy disks to your hard disk, but that would be a tremendous waste of space; the disks contain many printer-specific drivers that you will never use. Therefore, take a few minutes to install Allways by using the following procedure.

First-Time Installation

You must install Allways from a floppy disk. Therefore, place the Allways Setup Disk in your A drive and type:

```
A:
awsetup
```

Allways will display the installation title screen.

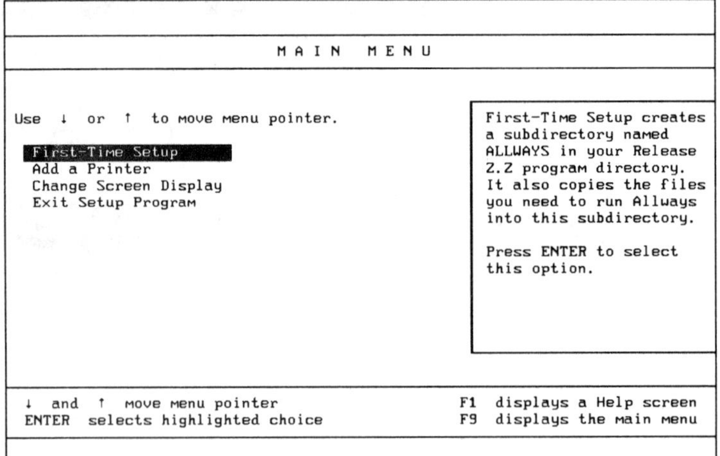

Figure 11.1
Allways Installation Main Menu Screen.

Press ENTER, and you will see the Main Menu shown in Figure 11.1. This is similar to the Main Menu you saw in 1-2-3's Install program. You can return to the Main Menu at any time during the installation, by pressing F9. You can also back up menu by menu with the ESC key until you reach the Main Menu.

Select the First-Time Setup option, and Allways will display a brief instruction screen, telling you what to expect during the installation. To continue press ENTER and you will be asked to type in the name of the drive and directory that contains your 1-2-3 program files. Specify the directory and press ENTER. Allways will proceed to make a subdirectory within your 1-2-3 program directory. The subdirectory, called Allways, will contain your Allways files.

Next, Allways will show the type of monitor display card it has detected with your system. If the display type is correct, select Yes. If not, select No and Allways will present you with a list of screen display cards. Select yours by highlighting it and then press ENTER. If none of the cards in the list match yours, select No Graphics Card.

Once you've selected a display card, Allways will prompt you to specify a printer from a long list of makes and models. Highlight yours, and press ENTER. (If you make a mistake, press DEL.) If your printer is not shown on the list, contact Lotus for information about which printer from the list best matches yours.

Allways will go on to ask if you have another printer. If so, select Yes and repeat the printer selection procedure. If not, select No and Allways will begin to copy the program files (along with the correct monitor and printer driver files) to the Allways subdirectory. You will be instructed to insert various disks, depending on the printer(s) you selected. When all the necessary files have been copied, you are informed that the installation was successful. Press ENTER to return to the Main Menu, then choose Exit to return to DOS.

Changing Equipment

As you acquire new hardware, you may need to update your Allways driver files. Repeat the above procedure to start the setup routine. At the Main Menu shown in Figure 11.1, select Add a Printer to configure Allways for a new printer, or to delete an old one. If you have a new monitor, select Change Screen Display and choose the appropriate card. Again, you can return to the Main Menu at any point by pressing F9, or press ESC to back up to previous menus.

ATTACHING AND INVOKING ALLWAYS

To use Allways (or any other add-in program), you need to understand two issues. First, add-in programs must be *attached* to 1-2-3 before they can function. In other words, you must inform 1-2-3 that the add-in is present and available for use. This is done through the Add-In command located on 1-2-3's main menu.

Second, once an add-in is attached, you must actually *invoke* it (i.e., start it) in order to use it in a 1-2-3 session. This can be done manually by selecting the 1-2-3's /Add-In Invoke command (or by pressing a special key combination that you have assigned to that particular add-in.). You can also invoke an add-in automatically; this entails setting your global defaults to invoke Allways every time 1-2-3 loads, though this is not recommended.

To Attach and Invoke Allways—Instructions

Allways, like any other add-in, must be attached (loaded into memory) before you can invoke it. This can be done automatically each time 1-2-3 is loaded, or manually via the /Add-in Attach command. (If you have a memory constraint you may want to use the manual technique.) The following discussion explains both procedures. Setting the program for automatic attachment will provide the greatest convenience. To set up Allways for auto-attach, use the following procedure:

1. Select /Worksheet Global Default Other Add-in Set. 1-2-3 will then display a Default Settings sheet similar to the one shown in Figure 11.2.
2. You can select up to eight add-ins that 1-2-3 will automatically attach during each session.
3. Select the first available number (which will be 1 if you haven't already selected any add-ins for auto-attach). 1-2-3 will then display a list of available add-ins. Choose Allways.
4. 1-2-3 will display a list of available function keys or "No Key." These keys are numbered 7 through 10 corresponding to the ALT-F7 through ALT-F10 function key combinations used to invoke an add-in program. Note that only those add-in key combinations not already assigned will be displayed.
5. Once you've indicated a key, 1-2-3 will ask if you want to automatically invoke Allways. You are best off selecting No for everyday use; there's no point in starting Allways if you have a blank worksheet. You can't format a worksheet in Allways until it's been created in 1-2-3.

   Whether you select Yes or No for auto-invoke, Allways will load, after which the settings screen will indicate that Allways is the first add-in, along with the designated start key combination. (See Figure 11.3.)
6. Assuming that you selected No for auto invoke, as recommended, you will have to press the ALT-key combination you selected during the default setting process or use the /Add-In Invoke command from the main menu. Either way, Allways will be activated and ready for use. Now you're ready to do some spreadsheet publishing.

NOTE: While you are best off using the assigned function key for everyday use, we suggest using the /Add-In Invoke command for macro use, since you can invoke the program by name, regardless of the assigned function key.

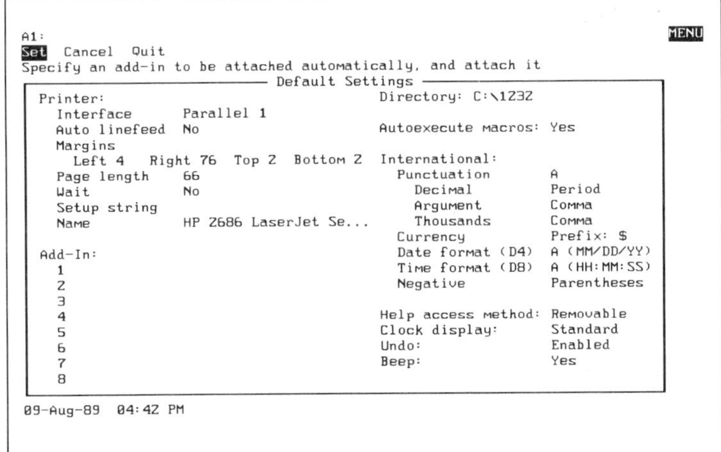

Figure 11.2 Default Settings Sheet.

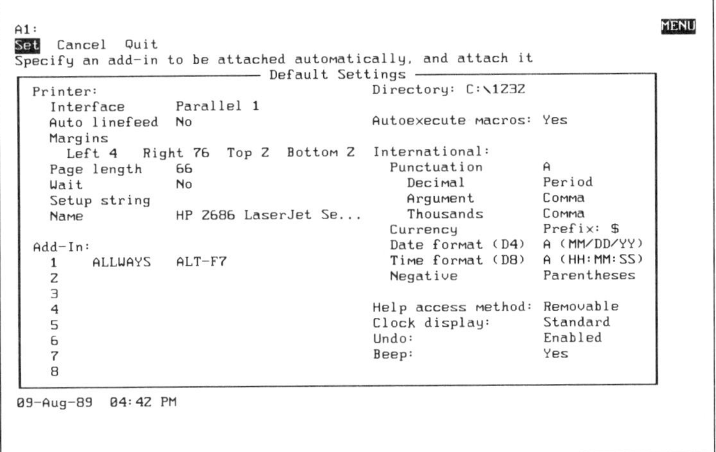

Figure 11.3 Default Settings Sheet with Allways set to be invoked automatically.

GETTING STARTED WITH ALLWAYS

The Screen

However you chose to invoke Allways, the first thing you'll notice is that the screen arrangement is very similar to 1-2-3, although there are several important differences. First, the ALLWAYS indicator is displayed in the upper-right hand corner. The upper-left corner displays the cell address, and above it you'll see the type font selected for the current cell.

If you've selected special formatting options, such as bold, underline, or shading, these will also be indicated after the font. The file name or the date/time will be displayed under the row border.

The Allways Main Menu

Like 1-2-3, you invoke the Allways main menu by pressing the slash key (/). The command options will appear in the control panel, with explanatory text for each option (see Figure 11.4). As with 1-2-3, the indicator in the upper right-hand corner changes to MENU when you press the slash key.

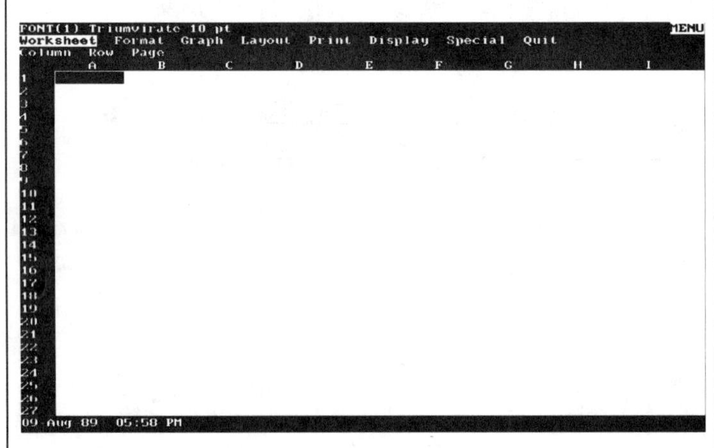

Figure 11.4
Allways Main Menu.

Function Keys

In addition to the menu system, Allways takes advantage of the special function keys. The following keys are used with the program:

F1 Help If Allways is not in MENU mode, when you press F1 the HELP mode title screen will be displayed. Press any cursor key, and the words "Help Index" at the bottom of the screen will be highlighted. Press ENTER, and the index will be displayed. Select a topic by highlighting it and press ENTER.

Each help screen will contain a highlighted phrase. Press any cursor key, and the highlight bar will move to the bottom of the screen where there are additional topics to chose from, including the help index. If the help screen contains more than one key phrase, the additional phrases will be displayed in a different font (depending on your monitor). Each time you press the Down or Right cursor key, the highlight will move down to the next topic. If you press the Left or Up cursor key, the highlight will move backward to the previous topic.

Pressing the Up cursor while the highlight is covering the first topic will move the highlight to the choices along the bottom of the screen. Pressing the Right or Down cursor while the highlight is covering the last topic on the page will also move the highlight to the top row of options.

If Allways is in MENU mode when you press F1, a help screen pertaining to the menu choices will be displayed, rather than the help title screen. Press ESC to return to the Allways screen.

F3 This key will display a list of named ranges when it is pressed after the GOTO (F5) key, or when any Format command is selected, or when Files are selected during the print process.

F4 Each time you press F4, the size of the cells will be reduced, so that more rows and columns appear on the screen.

ALT-F4 or Shift-F4 These combinations enlarge the size of the cells each time the Shift-F4 or ALT-F4 is pressed.

F5 GOTO key F5 works just as it does in 1-2-3.

F6 Display mode Pressing F6 toggles the Allways screen between graphics and text mode.

F10 GRAPH Key This key toggles between graph display mode, in which the actual graph appears, and cross-hatched display, which shows where the graph will appear on the worksheet.

Special Keys

Allways provides a number of special key combinations that enable you to bypass the menu system for formatting cells and ranges. Once you get familiar with the program, you'll find these keys much more efficient than using the menu.

The special keys work in two ways: Either they *toggle* between the format on and the format off options, or they *cycle* through various format options. The ALT-B key combination is a toggle, for example. Pressing ALT-B (i.e., pressing and holding the ALT key and then pressing the B key simultaneously) sets a cell or range to boldface. Pressing ALT-B again returns the cell or range to its non-bold condition. Pressing ALT-S, on the other hand, successively cycles the cell or range through light shading, dark shading, solid fill, and no shading. The full range of key combinations includes:

ALT B	Boldface. (Toggles *on/off.*)
ALT G	Grid Lines. (Toggles *on/off.*)
ALT L	Lines. (Cycles through *outline on:* a rule around a range of cells/*outline on all:* a rule around each cell in a range/*no rules anywhere.*)
ALT S	Shade. (Cycles through *light/dark/solid/no shading.*)
ALT U	Underline. (Cycles through *single/double/no underlining.*)
ALT 1–8	Selects fonts 1 through 8.

This completes our tour of the Allways superstructure. Now let's see how to use the add-in to create professional looking documents.

USING ALLWAYS

At this point you're probably wondering how you compose a worksheet from within Allways. In fact, you don't. To use Allways, you must first create a worksheet within 1-2-3, then switch to Allways to change fonts, add rules, graphs, etc. To edit the worksheet, you must return to 1-2-3 by pressing ESC or /Quit from Allways. This is definitely a nuisance, but is somewhat offset by the fact that Allways stays in synch with 1-2-3; if you move the cell pointer in 1-2-3 to cell B11 and then invoke Allways, the pointer will appear in B11 on the Allways screen. In fact, Allways is really creating a formatted mirror image of the 1-2-3 worksheet with special formatting commands. When you save your 1-2-3 worksheet, Allways automatically creates a file with the same name and the extension .ALL. (You can view the .ALL files by selecting /File List Other from within 1-2-3.)

Don't forget that when you use Allways, you're creating a special format file that's synchronized with the 1-2-3 worksheet file. This means that after you have created a format for your worksheet with Allways, you must resave your worksheet in 1-2-3; otherwise all of your formatting work will be lost. Also, if you detach Allways while you are working on a worksheet in 1-2-3 (a worksheet that has a companion Allways file), Allways may become unsynchronized with the 1-2-3 file, so that formats end up getting used with the wrong cells or ranges. For example, if you detach Allways, and then insert two rows in your 1-2-3 worksheet, Allways will not be able to update its formatted .ALL file for the worksheet; thus fonts, underlining, shading, or other elements originally established for say, row 12, will still be applied to row 12 even though the corresponding data has now moved to row 14.

NOTE: Once you issue a command through Allways, you may not be able to undo the last action within 1-2-3. As discussed earlier, issuing a 1-2-3 command updates the current snapshot of the worksheet; selecting an Allways command has the same effect. Therefore, if you bold a cell in Allways, and then return to 1-2-3, Undo will not work. If you try to use it, 1-2-3 will display the message: "Undo request blocked by add-in (Allways)."

To demonstrate Allways' capabilities, we'll retrieve the budget worksheet used earlier.

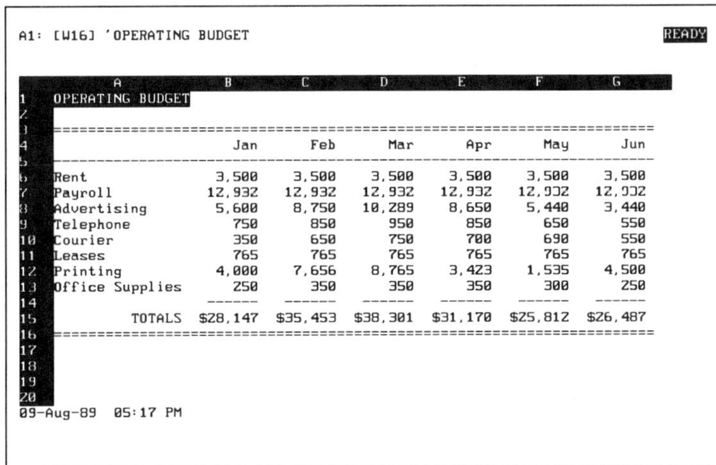

A1: [W16] 'OPERATING BUDGET READY

OPERATING BUDGET

	Jan	Feb	Mar	Apr	May	Jun
Rent	3,500	3,500	3,500	3,500	3,500	3,500
Payroll	12,932	12,932	12,932	12,932	12,932	12,932
Advertising	5,600	8,750	10,289	8,650	5,440	3,440
Telephone	750	850	950	850	650	550
Courier	350	650	750	700	690	550
Leases	765	765	765	765	765	765
Printing	4,000	7,656	8,765	3,423	1,535	4,500
Office Supplies	250	350	350	350	300	250
TOTALS	$28,147	$35,453	$38,301	$31,170	$25,812	$26,487

09-Aug-89 05:17 PM

Figure 11.5
Worksheet viewed within 1-2-3.

When you invoke Allways from 1-2-3 with the budget worksheet on screen, the worksheet is brought into the Allways environment. The cell pointer maintains its position on the worksheet in the Allways screen, but the appearance of the worksheet has changed dramatically. This is because you have shifted to graphics mode. (If your monitor does not support graphics mode, your screen display will appear the same. The Allways indicator will appear in the upper right-hand corner, but you won't see any font or other format changes). That's because all cells within the worksheet are currently formatted for the default font. If you are using a laser printer, the default font will be Triumvirate, which is a relative of Helvetica (see Figure 11.6). Before you begin changing fonts, adding rules, adding graphs, or highlighting cells or ranges, you may want to customize Allways for your display.

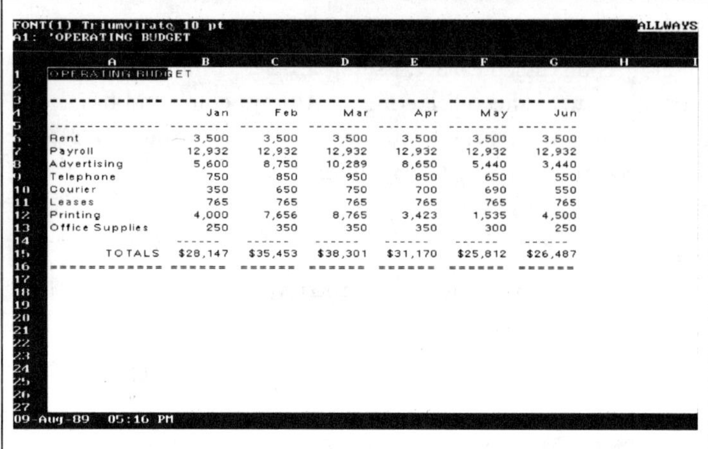

	Jan	Feb	Mar	Apr	May	Jun
Rent	3,500	3,500	3,500	3,500	3,500	3,500
Payroll	12,932	12,932	12,932	12,932	12,932	12,932
Advertising	5,600	8,750	10,289	8,650	5,440	3,440
Telephone	750	850	950	850	650	550
Courier	350	650	750	700	690	550
Leases	765	765	765	765	765	765
Printing	4,000	7,656	8,765	3,423	1,535	4,500
Office Supplies	250	350	350	350	300	250
TOTALS	$28,147	$35,453	$38,301	$31,170	$25,812	$26,487

Figure 11.6
Worksheet created within 1-2-3 and displayed in Allways.

Changing the Display

To change the way Allways appears on your screen, select the /Display command. Allways will offer you four options: Mode, Zoom, Graphics, and Colors. Each is described below. Your default settings appear in a box, much as setting sheets are used in 1-2-3 to show defaults and user selections.

Mode Allows you to choose either text or graphics display. In graphics display, you will see fonts and shading as they will actually appear on the printed page. In text display, the worksheet appears the same as it would in 1-2-3 (although the Allways indicator and font display will still be shown).

Zoom Enlarges or reduces cells to a specified percentage of the normal display (if you're in graphics mode). The fixed zoom reductions and enlargements include: Tiny (60 percent of normal size); Small (84 percent of normal size); Large (120 percent of normal size); and Huge (140 percent of normal size). The greater the reduction from the normal size cell, the more cells you'll see on a page. The opposite holds true for the enlarged cells. With an IBM 8513 monitor, for example, the tiniest reduction will allow you to display 45 rows per screen, although they will be only marginally legible. At the other end of the scale, the Huge option reduces your display to 18 rows. The choice is completely personal.

Graphs Gives you the option of actually displaying graphs on screen or displaying hatch marks. Select Yes to select graphs and No to display the hatch marks. Depending on your system, drawing shaded boxes may be considerably quicker than displaying the actual graph.

Colors Allows you to select colors for the background, foreground, and cell-pointer. Again, the choice is up to you (assuming that you have a monitor that can display the available color choices).

When you're done selecting display options, choose Quit. Your display choices will remain in effect until you reset them. Whatever options you choose, you're ready to structure the 1-2-3 worksheet displayed in the Allways screen and use the various formatting commands.

WORKSHEET STRUCTURE COMMANDS

Columns Allways allows you to specify the width of columns, just as 1-2-3 does. Unlike 1-2-3, though, it displays a vertical bar that moves to the left or right as you press the cursor keys. You can also indicate a column width in fractional characters. The default width depends on the default font, and is based on the size of a digit character (1 through 0). If you have a large font, you might want to use fractional column settings to keep the columns at a desirable width. (See Figure 11.7.)

To restore the original column width, select Reset.

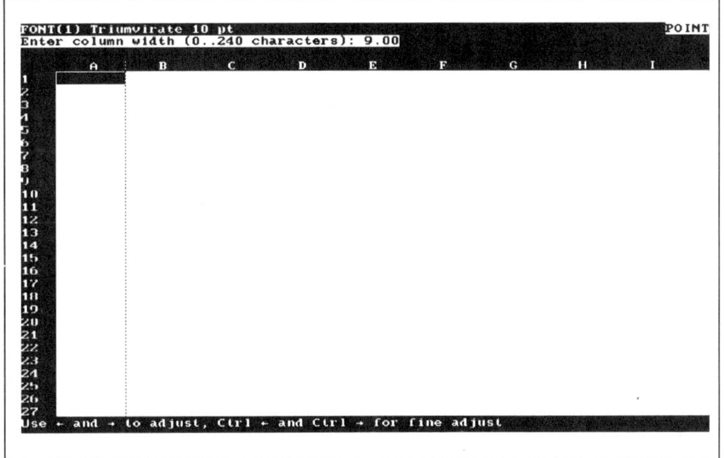

Figure 11.7 Column width markers.

Rows Allways allows you to control the row height, which is fixed within 1-2-3. The Allways default row-height is Auto, which means that the program will adjust the height of the row based on the size of the font. This creates a page in which the line spacing between each typed line (the "leading") is appropriate for the type font being used.

You can also manually set the row height by selecting Set-Height. Allways will then prompt you to enter the height of the row in "points," from 1 to 12. One point equals 1/72 of an inch. In general, you would want to adjust row height when you are using solid rules between portions of a spreadsheet, or you want to make the overall worksheet "tighter" than the automatic settings provide. Figure 11.8 shows lines ranging in thickness from one point to twelve points.

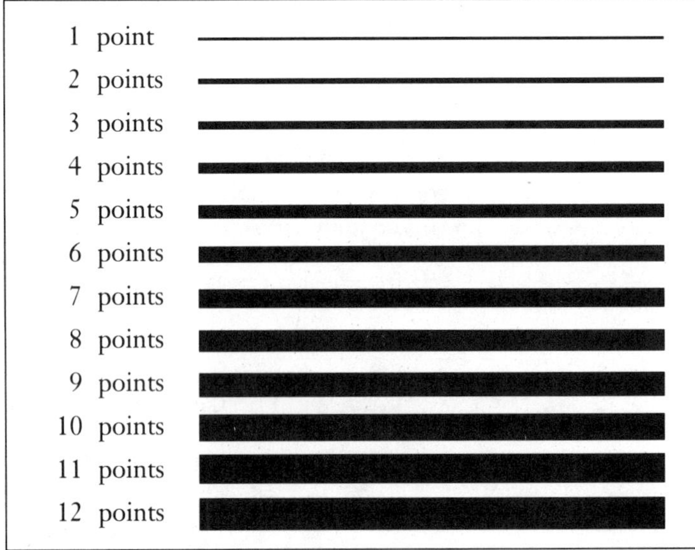

Figure 11.8
Point sizes available for row height.

Page The Page command allows you to specify precisely where page breaks occur by row, column, or both. When you add a page break by row, a horizontal dotted line appears on the screen at the designated row. When you add a page break by column, a vertical line appears at the designated column. To set both a row and column page break, first set the row break and then set the column break, and both page breaks will be displayed on your screen (see Figure 11.9).

To delete a row or column page break, select Delete and move the cell pointer below or to the right of the dotted line. Press ENTER and the page break line will disappear.

Once you've created a worksheet structure for printing, the next step is to format specific cells and ranges. This entails changing type fonts, adding rules, shading, and other design elements.

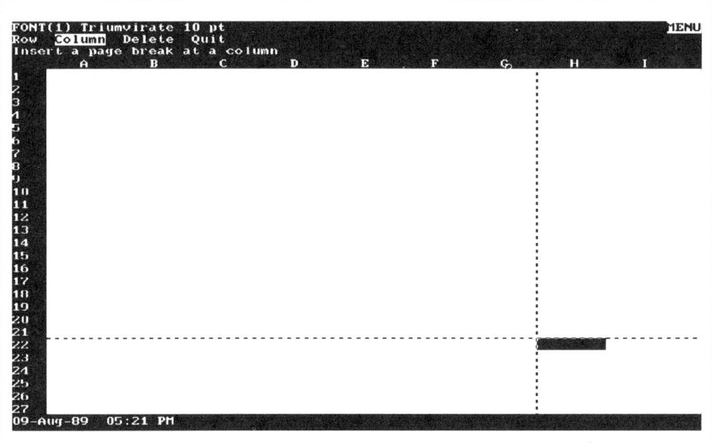

Figure 11.9
Row and column page break markers.

FORMATTING COMMANDS

The real power of Allways lies in its ability to transform ho-hum cell and range contents into highly stylized displays that have a typeset look and feel. We will slightly modify the budget worksheet by removing all separator lines; these will be replaced with more attractive, less "computer-looking" rules. The rest of this section will discuss the formatting options in the order in which they appear on the format menu. Before describing the menu options though, we need to discuss the range concept as it is used in Allways.

Creating Ranges in Allways As with 1-2-3, all formatting is done through range. One difference between 1-2-3 and Allways is that with Allways you can paint a range first, and then select a Format command to apply to the range.

If you have selected a formatting command before creating the range, 1-2-3 will prompt you to specify the range by typing in the coordinates, entering a range name, or painting the range. You don't need to anchor the first cell of the range—just move the cursor to include all the cells you want formatted. If the highlight is currently on the wrong cell, press ESC and move the cell pointer to the desired location. Then anchor the cell with a period (.) and paint the range. Press ENTER when you are done and the range will adopt whatever formatting command you've issued.

To create a range before selecting a formatting command, you must anchor the upper-left corner with a period (.) and then paint the range with the cursor. Do *not* press ENTER once you've painted the range; Allways will simply beep at you. Instead, issue a formatting command through the menu or by means of the special key combinations described. When the formatting is complete, the range will remain highlighted on the screen. Press ESC or one of the cursor keys to clear it from the screen.

The GOTO (F5) key is a convenient way of moving about the Allways screen. You can enter a cell address or a range name to go to. If you've named ranges within the 1-2-3 worksheet, pressing F3 will display a list of the names in a pop-up window. Highlight the desired range and press ENTER, and the pointer will move to the first cell in the range. This is extremely handy when you are dealing with a large worksheet that has scrolled off the screen.

You can also press the F3 key and invoke the range name window when you use any of the formatting commands described below and are prompted for a range. This is extremely convenient and is another good reason to use named ranges whenever possible.

Now that you've seen how ranges work within Allways, it's time to look at some of the formatting options.

About Fonts

Before explaining how fonts are used, let's see exactly what a font is. There is some degree of confusion in the general public about this, considering that the terms font and typeface are used interchangeably. In point of fact, typeface is a part of a definition of a font.

A font is a set of characters, including letters, numbers, and special symbols, such as the pound or number sign (#) the dollar sign ($), the copyright sign (©), etc. Fonts are defined by four factors including:

Pitch The number of characters per inch (cpi). This is only relevant to monospaced fonts; with proportionally spaced fonts, the number of characters per inch will vary with the combinations of characters being printed.

Point Size The vertical height of the character. Font height is measured in terms of *descenders* and *ascenders*. If you imagine a lowercase p, the round part or body sits on what is known as the *baseline*. The downward stroke that extends beneath the baseline is the descender. In contrast, the upward stroke of a lowercase h is called the ascender. The vertical height of a font is measured from the bottom of the lowest descender to top of the highest ascender, in points. One point equals approximately 1/72 of an inch. See Figures 11.10a and b.

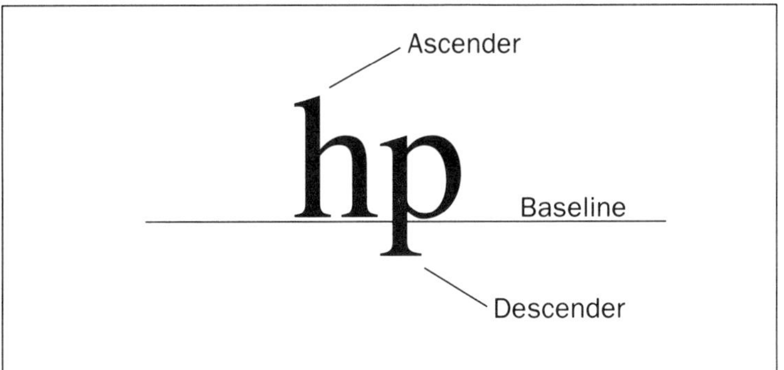

Figure 11.10a
Ascender and descender.

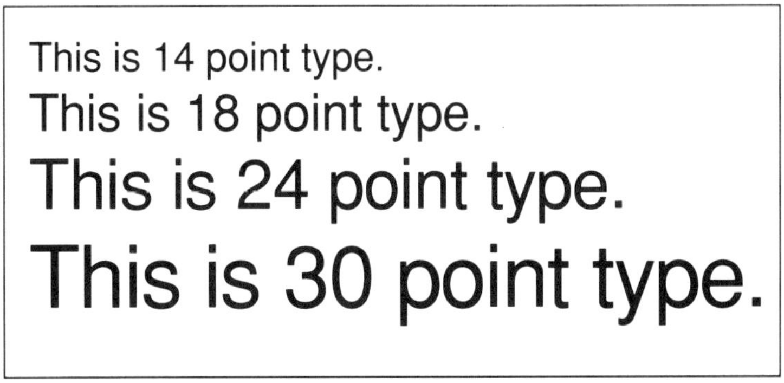

This is 14 point type.
This is 18 point type.
This is 24 point type.
This is 30 point type.

Figure 11.10b
Various point sizes.

Style The first style is called upright (sometimes called Roman or, in the case of Allways, Normal). The opposite style is slanting (i.e., Italic.) Figure 11.11 shows the difference in the two styles.

Stroke Weight A measure of the thickness of stroke of character. The most common stroke weights are light, regular (also called medium), or bold. See Figure 11.12.

Typeface The artistic design of the characters, such as Courier, Triumvirate, and Times Roman.

The above criteria define unique fonts or sets of characters. A group of fonts, related by the typeface criteria, compose a font *family*. In addition, be aware of the difference in fixed pitch and proportional fonts. Fixed or "monospaced" means that each character is assigned the same amount of space. Proportional means that the space assigned to different characters varies, depending on the shape of the characters, giving a smoother feel and texture. Proportional spacing

This is Roman (upright) type.

This is Italic (slanted) type.

Figure 11.11
Roman versus italic styles.

```
This sentence is printed in Courier 10, a
fixed pitch font.
```

This sentence is printed in Times Roman, a proportional font.

Figure 11.12
Comparison of fixed and proportional type.

is a major feature that gives professionally printed material its "typeset" appearance. (See Figure 11.12 for a comparison.)

A confusing aspect of the spacing issue is that fixed fonts are measured by characacters per inch (cpi), while proportional fonts are measured in terms of character height by points (1 point = 1/72 of an inch.). Therefore, a 10-pitch fixed font is actually larger than a 12 pitch fixed font (more characters are crammed into into the same amount of space, so the characters must be smaller). However, a 10 point proportional font will be smaller than a 12 point proportional font, because the width of the characters will necessarily increase with character height. Yes, it can get confusing.

Finally, the names given to a particular font family may vary between software and font designers. This is because certain names, such as Helvetica and Times Roman have been trademarked by a particular typographic design company (Helvetica and Times Roman are trademarks of Linotype). Many designs that appear virtually identical will be given different names to avoid infringing on these trademarks.

Using Fonts

The Allways /Format Font command displays both additional menu options, and a pop-up window containing eight different typefaces (see Figure 11.13).

The following actions can be used with the available fonts.

Use This command changes the typeface of the contents in a cell or range. Highlight the desired typeface and point size, and press ENTER. Allways will prompt you to type in a range (if you haven't already painted one).

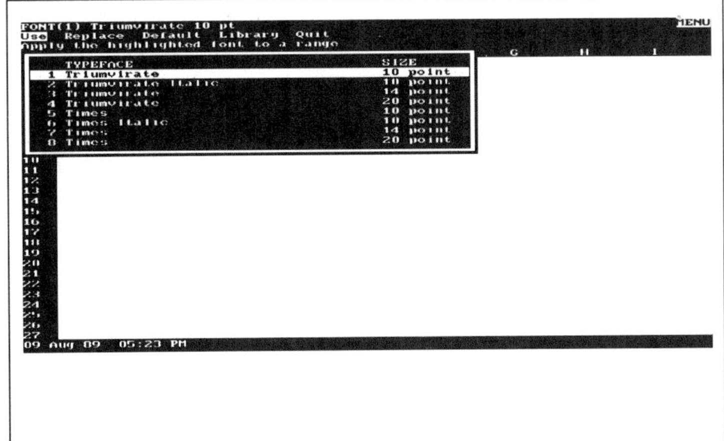

Figure 11.13
Available fonts window.

OPERATING BUDGET

	Jan	Feb	Mar	Apr	May	Jun
Rent	3,500	3,500	3,500	3,500	3,500	3,500
Payroll	12,932	12,932	12,932	12,932	12,932	12,932
Advertising	5,600	8,750	10,289	8,650	5,440	3,440
Telephone	750	850	950	850	650	550
Courier	350	650	750	700	690	550
Leases	765	765	765	765	765	765
Printing	4,000	7,656	8,765	3,423	1,535	4,500
Office Supplies	250	350	350	350	300	250
TOTALS	$28,147	$35,453	$38,301	$31,170	$25,812	$26,487

Figure 11.14
The title appears in 14 point Triumvirate; cells A6 through A13 appear in 10 point Triumvirate Italic.

For example, let's say that you wanted to use a large typeface for the title of the budget worksheet. You could select 14 point Triumvirate and then specify cell A1 as the range to format. When you press ENTER, the text in cell A1 will appear in the selected font.

Next, you might want to format the line items in the same point size as the rest of the worksheet (10-point), but in a different type style. Select 10-point Triumvirate Italics, and format cells A6 through A13 (see Figure 11.14). The text is quite readable as is, and we'll use other formatting commands to enhance the months and highlight the totals, as explained in later in the chapter.

Replace This option allows you to swap the fonts shown in the available font window with printer-based fonts as well as with "soft fonts" provided by Allways and stored on your hard disk. Allways will allow you to have a maximum of eight different fonts on a page. By using the Replace feature, you can include a different constellation of typefaces to meet your needs.

Each printer will offer its own range of additional fonts. In the case of an HP LaserJet Series II, the additional printer fonts include the built-in Courier regular and bold (heavy), as well as the highly condensed Line Printer font. These are shown in Figure 11.15 along with the various Allways soft font listings.

To change a font, first select /Format Font, then highlight the font in the available font window that you would like to swap. For example, let's say that you want to use only various sizes of Triumvirate, and want to expand the range of available point sizes. Place the highlight over font 5, the first Times (Roman) typeface, then select Replace. The available font window will appear shadowed on the screen, and a replacement font window will be displayed. Highlight Triumvirate (soft) and press ENTER. Now the replacement font window will appear shadowed, and a new window with various point size options will be displayed. Highlight the point size you'd like to add to the available font window listing, say, 8-point, and press ENTER. The available font window will once again be displayed, this time with the font 5 listed as Triumvirate 8-point.

You can use this technique to rearrange the available font window so the typefaces appear in increasing size. In fact, you can reorder the window any way you like to fit your needs. Just remember, the exact configuration of available

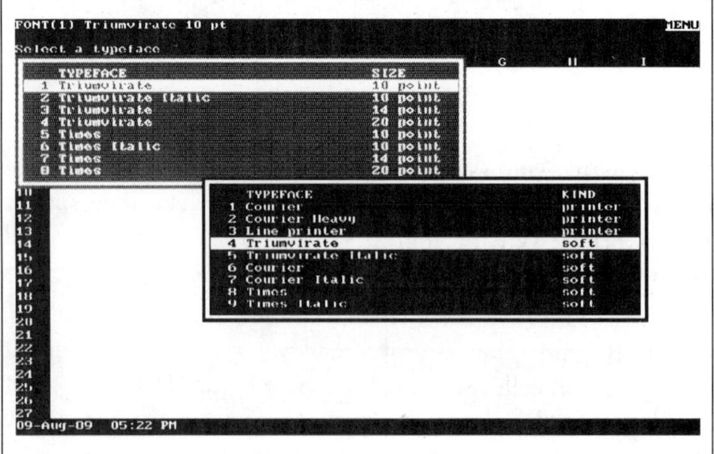

Figure 11.15
Alternate font selections for font window.

fonts will depend on your hardware and/or selected font cartridges. (See the /Print Configuration Cartridge option below). The descriptions in this section are based on a Hewlett-Packard LaserJet Series II; nevertheless the principles discussed apply to all printers.

Remember, Font 1 is the default—any font not explicitly formatted with another font will default to Font 1. Also, any changes made to the available font window applies only to the current worksheet you are formatting. If you want that font set to be your new default font set (i.e., the one that will appear each time you format a new worksheet), you must use the Default command.

Default A default font setting is used in three instances. First, it is the setting used in any cell or range that has not been explicitly set to something else. Second, it is the setting used when you select /Format Reset. Third, it is the setting used when you create a new worksheet. To make your replacement fonts "stick" as your default, select /Font Default Update. This will cause Allways to display your modified available font window each time you invoke the program (making it the default font set). If, during the font replacement process you wish to return to the default font set, select /Font Default Restore, and the available font window will return to your default settings.

Library In addition to creating custom available font windows, you can create a "library" of font sets, each labeled with a name. The libraries are stored on disk and can be retrieved at any time. Here's how to make and use a library:

1. Create a custom configuration of fonts in the available font window using the Replace command.
2. Select /Font Library Save. Allways will switch back to text mode and prompt you for the name of the library. For purposes of illustration, we'll call the font set "budget," assuming that it will be used with budget-related worksheets and will therefore contain the fonts you'll want to use for titles, body text, totals, etc. Type in the name and press ENTER. Allways will append the extension ".AFS." (If you already had a library called budget, Allways would ask you if you want to Cancel the Save operation or Replace the budget library.)
3. The next time you're formatting a budget worksheet, select /Font Library Retrieve, and Allways will display a list of libraries that you've created through the above procedure. Highlight the desired library and press ENTER. Allways will return to the worksheet view screen, displaying the available font window. The typefaces in the window will be those that you chose for the library.

Quit This option clears the menu from the control panel.

Setting Bold

To bold a cell or range of cells, select /Format Bold Set. Allways will then prompt you for the range of cells to make bold (if you haven't already indicated a range). In our example, the bold command has been applied to the month headings (see Figure 11.16).

Note that bold will operate on whatever typeface happens to be in the cell. The text formatted for Triumvirate Italics will become Triumvirate Bold Italics if the Bold command is applied to it. To change text from bold to regular weight, select Bold Clear for the specified range.

Adding Underlines

The underline commands—single and double—are mainly used under columns of numbers that have been added, or to emphasize a certain amount in a report or a balance sheet. This is *not* the same as adding a line in a cell. The single Underline feature adjusts the length of the line to the number of characters in the cell, which means that the cell can't be empty. The double underline feature runs the entire length of the cell and can be used with empty cells.

Adding Color

Allways allows you to assign a rich assortment of colors to ranges. The ability to print the colors, of course, will depend on your hardware. When you select Color, the program displays a window of choices. After selecting a color, indicate the range just as you would for other formatting options.

OPERATING BUDGET

	Jan	**Feb**	**Mar**	**Apr**	**May**	**Jun**
Rent	3,500	3,500	3,500	3,500	3,500	3,500
Payroll	12,932	12,932	12,932	12,932	12,932	12,932
Advertising	5,600	8,750	10,289	8,650	5,440	3,440
Telephone	750	850	950	850	650	550
Courier	350	650	750	700	690	550
Leases	765	765	765	765	765	765
Printing	4,000	7,656	8,765	3,423	1,535	4,500
Office Supplies	250	350	350	350	300	250
TOTALS	$28,147	$35,453	$38,301	$31,170	$25,812	$26,487

Figure 11.16

The monthly headings appear in bold.

Creating Lines

With Allways, you can create a variety of lines for use as separators, or for outlining whole ranges. You can even draw individual lines around all cells in a range to create a grid-like effect. Here are your choices:

Outline Use this to draw a line around all sides of a cell or range—in other words, a box around a cell or group of cells. For example, in the budget worksheet, you might want to draw a box around the March total, since it is the highest value. Select Format Line Outline, then specify cell D15 as the range. The results are shown in Figure 11.17.

OPERATING BUDGET

	Jan	Feb	Mar	Apr	May	Jun
Rent	3,500	3,500	3,500	3,500	3,500	3,500
Payroll	12,932	12,932	12,932	12,932	12,932	12,932
Advertising	5,600	8,750	10,289	8,650	5,440	3,440
Telephone	750	850	950	850	650	550
Courier	350	650	750	700	690	550
Leases	765	765	765	765	765	765
Printing	4,000	7,656	8,765	3,423	1,535	4,500
Office Supplies	250	350	350	350	300	250
TOTALS	$28,147	$35,453	$38,301	$31,170	$25,812	$26,487

Figure 11.17

Cell outline for March total.

OPERATING BUDGET

	Jan	Feb	Mar	Apr	May	Jun
Rent	3,500	3,500	3,500	3,500	3,500	3,500
Payroll	12,932	12,932	12,932	12,932	12,932	12,932
Advertising	5,600	8,750	10,289	8,650	5,440	3,440
Telephone	750	850	950	850	650	550
Courier	350	650	750	700	690	550
Leases	765	765	765	765	765	765
Printing	4,000	7,656	8,765	3,423	1,535	4,500
Office Supplies	250	350	350	350	300	250
TOTALS	$28,147	$35,453	$38,301	$31,170	$25,812	$26,487

Figure 11.18

Example of outlines placed around all cells.

Left Places a line along the left side of the cells in a range.

Right Places a line along the right side of the cells in a range.

Top Use this command to draw a line along the top of each cell in a range.

Bottom Draws a line along the bottom of each cell in a range. If you're going to use top or bottom lines to create separator lines, you'll probably want to manually reduce the row height as explained above.

All This option places an outline around each cell in a range, as shown in Figure 11.18.

OPERATING BUDGET

	Jan	Feb	Mar	Apr	May	Jun
Rent	3,500	3,500	3,500	3,500	3,500	3,500
Payroll	12,932	12,932	12,932	12,932	12,932	12,932
Advertising	5,600	8,750	10,289	8,650	5,440	3,440
Telephone	750	850	950	850	650	550
Courier	350	650	750	700	690	550
Leases	765	765	765	765	765	765
Printing	4,000	7,656	8,765	3,423	1,535	4,500
Office Supplies	250	350	350	350	300	250
TOTALS	$28,147	$35,453	$38,301	$31,170	$25,812	$26,487

Figure 11.19

Example of shading in March total cell.

OPERATING BUDGET

	Jan	Feb	Mar	Apr	May	Jun
Rent	3,500	3,500	3,500	3,500	3,500	3,500
Payroll	12,932	12,932	12,932	12,932	12,932	12,932
Advertising	5,600	8,750	10,289	8,650	5,440	3,440
Telephone	750	850	950	850	650	550
Courier	350	650	750	700	690	550
Leases	765	765	765	765	765	765
Printing	4,000	7,656	8,765	3,423	1,535	4,500
Office Supplies	250	350	350	350	300	250
TOTALS	$28,147	$35,453	$38,301	$31,170	$25,812	$26,487

Figure 11.20

Heavy rule created by solid shade and reduced row height.

To remove a line from a range, select the Clear option, then specify the type of line you would like to remove. Allways will then prompt you for the range.

Using Shading

Shading is an extremely useful way of highlighting certain features, or creating thick rules. You can also use it to create a "drop shadow" effect. Three options are available:

Light This option places a light screen (dot pattern) in the specified cell or range. It is an effective way of highlighting data. To make the text stand out against the background, you might want to make it bold. In Figure 11.19, the March budget total has been given a shade as well as an outline, making it stand out even more.

Dark This is identical to the above option, except that the dot pattern is heavier. Here, contrast with the text becomes very important, and you should make sure that the text is large and heavy enough to stand out. Otherwise, the text may get lost in the pattern.

Solid If you want to fill in a cell as a solid area, select this option. Generally, this is most useful if you want to create a thick rule. For instance, to create a thick rule between the months and the first line item row in our budget worksheet, you could place an underline in the top or bottom of the cell in between, then choose Bold Set for the line. However, that would only create a "hairline" rule. A better way is to fill in the cells with a solid shade, then use the Worksheet Row Set-Height feature to reduce the height of the shaded cells until they become a rule of the desired thickness. Figure 11.20 shows the results of the technique.

Note: Shading is a fun toy as well as a serious tool. Many people are like kids in a candy store when they discover the option. Unfortunately, shading is something that gives true meaning to the slogan, "less is more." Use it sparingly and it will be effective; overuse it, and it will become an eyesore.

To remove any shading, select the Clear command. Allways will prompt you for the type of shading you would like to remove, and then a range in which the shading will be cleared.

SPECIAL COMMANDS

Copy and Move Allways offers you two special commands for quickly formatting worksheets: Copy and Move. Like 1-2-3, these commands require a FROM (source) range and a TO (target) range. Unlike the 1-2-3 commands, the Allways

Copy and Move commands do not manipulate data; they transfer FORMATS from the source to the target range. The Copy command clones the format, while Move transfers a format, resetting the source range to the default format.

Justify This command rejustifies text within a specified range, in the same fashion as the 1-2-3 /Range Justify command. The difference is that the Allways command takes into account the various character widths of a proportional font, while 1-2-3 does not. This command is unique in that it actually alters the cells in the corresponding 1-2-3 worksheet by moving the text.

Import Allways has a provision through the Import command to adopt the overall format of another worksheet. When you use the Import command, all formats and graphs in the current worksheet will be reset, and the formats and graphs of the other worksheet will be adopted. Remember, you're not importing data, but rather the formats of equivalent cells. When you select the command, Allways displays a list of the available worksheet files.

By now you have learned all of the available worksheet structuring and formatting commands, which will enable you to create high quality, professional-looking text. The next section explains how to use the Graph commands, to give your worksheets an additional design element.

THE GRAPH COMMANDS

Allways brings the welcome addition of being able to print graphs within 1-2-3, and best of all, being able to combine text and graphs on the same worksheet (see Figure 11.21). To use the graph command, you must first create a graph within 1-2-3 and then save it. Allways identifies graph files by their .PIC extension. Once you've created a graph in 1-2-3 and have invoked Allways, you can use the following commands to print the graph or combine it with worksheet text and print the two as a single document.

Adding or Removing a Graph

The first step in using Allways to print graphs is to select a graph via the Add command. When you select /Graph Add, Allways will display a list of graphs in the default directory. Highlight the graph you wish to print and press ENTER.

Allways will then prompt you for the range in which the graph should be placed. You can either type in the range address (or range name), press F3 to specify a named range from the list, or paint the range. You are probably best off painting the range so that you can see the exact shape of your printed graph. With Allways, the graph is like water—it will adapt to the shape of the container.

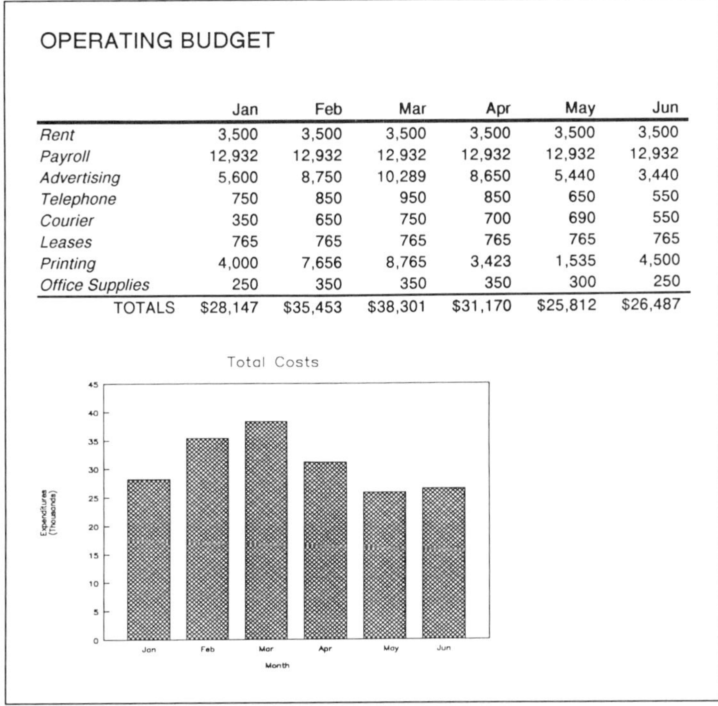

OPERATING BUDGET

	Jan	Feb	Mar	Apr	May	Jun
Rent	3,500	3,500	3,500	3,500	3,500	3,500
Payroll	12,932	12,932	12,932	12,932	12,932	12,932
Advertising	5,600	8,750	10,289	8,650	5,440	3,440
Telephone	750	850	950	850	650	550
Courier	350	650	750	700	690	550
Leases	765	765	765	765	765	765
Printing	4,000	7,656	8,765	3,423	1,535	4,500
Office Supplies	250	350	350	350	300	250
TOTALS	$28,147	$35,453	$38,301	$31,170	$25,812	$26,487

Figure 11.21

Combined worksheet and graph.

If you aren't careful, you might wind up with a mis-shaped graph. In fact, you can even mash an entire graph into a single cell, although it won't be legible.

If your Display Graph option is set for Yes, Allways will display the graph. If it is set for No, Allways will display a hatched pattern rather than the graph itself.

You can add more than one graph to a worksheet. If you do have multiple graphs in a worksheet, you might want to use the /Graph Goto command, which opens a window with the name of all graphs used in the worksheet. When you highlight a graph and press ENTER, the pointer will jump to the graph in question.

If you decide that you don't want a particular graph to appear in your worksheet, select the /Graph Remove command. Allways will display a list of every graph that has been added to the worksheet. Highlight the graph file to be removed and the graph image will vanish.

At this point, you can print the document containing the graph (see Printing With Allways). Alternately, you can modify the graph, as explained below.

Changing Settings

The ability to change the graph settings is a very powerful feature. In fact, it all but eliminates the need to use PrintGraph, because it allows you to make alterations to the graph settings right on the spot. (One advantage of PrintGraph is that you can queue a number of jobs to be printed, whereas with Allways you would have to load multiple graphs into a single document with separating page breaks to achieve the same effect.) When you select the Settings command, Allways will display a sheet similar to those in 1-2-3.

The following Graph Setting options are available:

PIC-File This command allows you to swap the current graph (i.e., the graph in which the pointer is located) with another .PIC file. When you choose Settings PIC-File, Allways displays a list of available graphs. Highlight the graph you wish to swap and press ENTER; the selected graph will appear in place of the current graph.

Fonts The Fonts command allows you to change the fonts used for the first and second titles. When you select 1 or 2, for first and second title, respectively, Allways displays a window with the available fonts. Highlight the desired font and press ENTER.

Scale The Scale option allows you to enlarge or reduce the fonts in a graph by selecting a scale from .5 to 5.0. A scale of 1 is the normal size. Be aware that large scaling factors might cause words and characters to overlap in the axes labels.

Colors If your printer can output in color, you can assign various colors to the X and the A through F ranges. Select a range, and Allways will display a window with the available colors. Highlight a particular color, and that color will be assigned to the range.

Range This command allows you to move the graph to a new range. When you select this command, Allways will ask you to indicate a new range for the graph. The graph will then be moved to the new range. (Remember, the graph will adopt the shape of the new range).

Margins You can specify the position of the graph within a range with respect to the top and bottom, and right and left sides. This command allows you to finely adjust the graph by specifying the margins in inches with two decimal places. Select the margins from the options of Left, Right, Top, and Bottom. Be careful: If you select a margin wider or longer than the page, the graph will be "pushed off" the page. Even if the graph isn't shoved off the page, it might be distorted or compressed. Figure 11.22a shows the effect of a zero margin, while Figure 11.22b shows the results of changing the left margin to 2.5 inches.

Default This option enables you to either restore the default graph settings, or to change the default graph settings to the current graph settings.

This concludes our discussion of the Allways Graphs commands. The next section covers the Layout commands, which are used to specify the structure of the worksheet.

LAYING OUT A PAGE

While you can print a page as is, without additional specifications, you can also control the position of a worksheet through the various Layout options.

Page-Size

Allways allows you to specify the physical dimensions of the paper you are using by choosing from options in a pop-up window. If you select the last option, Custom, Allways will prompt you to enter the page width from 0.25 to 99.99 inches.

Margins

You can specify left, right, top, and bottom margins for the worksheet with respect to the outer edges of the paper. You can enter a value from 0.00 to 99.00 inches.

Titles/Borders

These have the same function as the Title and Border commands used with 1-2-3's /Print command. The Titles command allows you to specify Headers and Footers. The Borders command allows you to choose the rows that will be printed on the top of each page (Top), the columns that will appear on the left side of each page (Left), or the rows that will appear at the bottom of each page (Bottom). The Borders Clear command allows you to remove a specific border, or all borders, in one fell swoop.

Options (Line Weight and Grid)

You can select the weight of lines created through the format Underline or Line commands. Three weights are available: Normal, Light, and Heavy.

The Grid command allows you turn on or turn off a worksheet-wide grid (see Figure 11.23). This is similar to the /Format All command, but it enables you to create a grid without formatting the entire worksheet.

The grid pattern will flow around any graphs embedded in the worksheet.

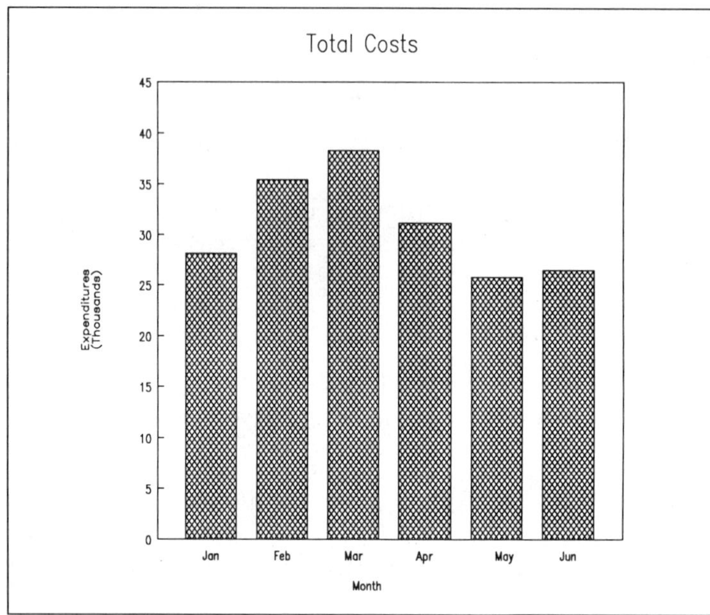

Figure 11.22a
Margin settings at 0 inches.

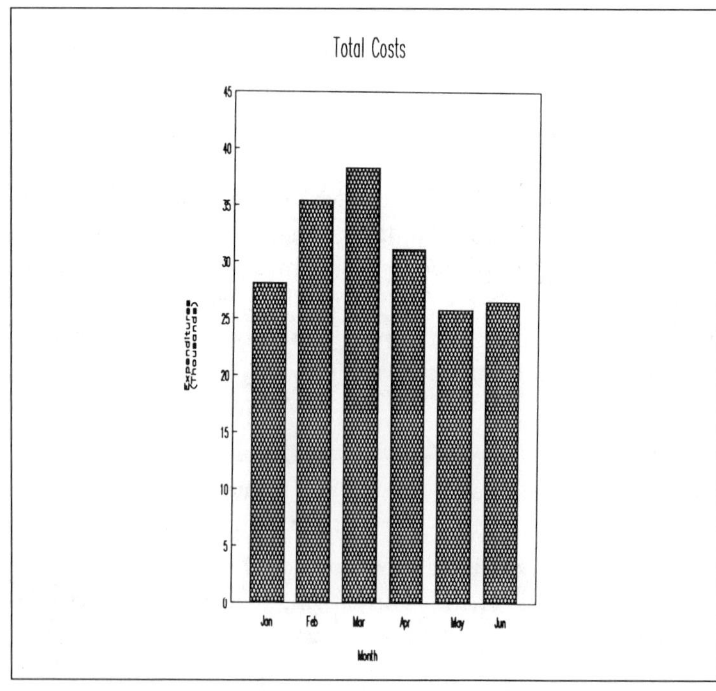

Figure 11.22b
Margin settings at 2.5 inches.

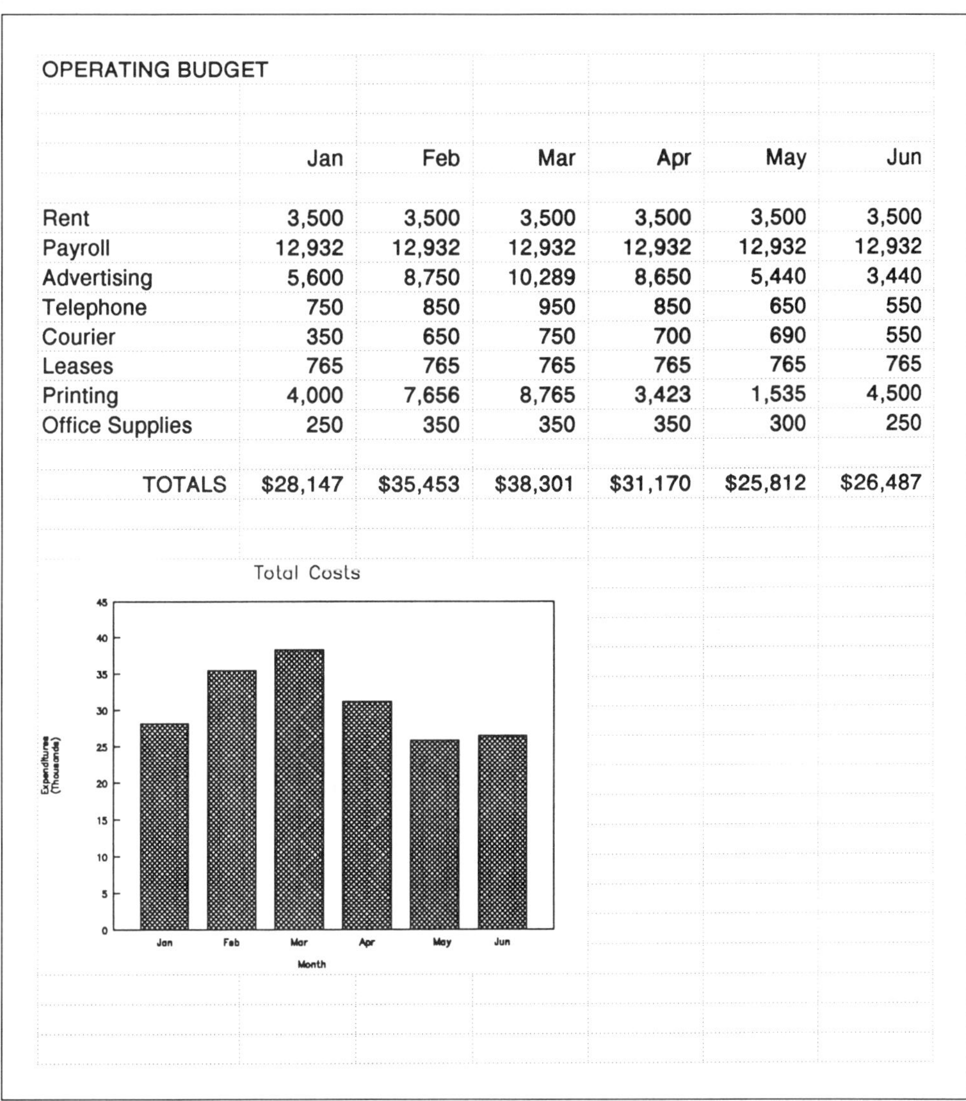

OPERATING BUDGET

	Jan	Feb	Mar	Apr	May	Jun
Rent	3,500	3,500	3,500	3,500	3,500	3,500
Payroll	12,932	12,932	12,932	12,932	12,932	12,932
Advertising	5,600	8,750	10,289	8,650	5,440	3,440
Telephone	750	850	950	850	650	550
Courier	350	650	750	700	690	550
Leases	765	765	765	765	765	765
Printing	4,000	7,656	8,765	3,423	1,535	4,500
Office Supplies	250	350	350	350	300	250
TOTALS	$28,147	$35,453	$38,301	$31,170	$25,812	$26,487

Figure 11.23
Worksheet-wide grid.

Default

As with many other settings in Allways, you can either restore the default settings, or save the current settings as the default settings.

Library

Just as you can create Font Libraries, you can create libraries of layout settings. To create a library, select Library Save, and Allways will prompt you to enter a library file name. Allways will add the extension .ALS to the file. The next time you wish to use the layout settings, select Library Retrieve and Allways will display a list of library files. Highlight the desired files and press ENTER. The settings sheet will be redisplayed with the layout specifications in the Library file. The Library Erase command allows you to specify a library to remove.

At this point, you have might have formatted a worksheet, added a graph, and selected layout options. Now you are ready to actually print the worksheet.

PRINTING WORKSHEETS

The print concept in Allways is similar to that used in 1-2-3. Select a range by choosing Range Set, then type in a range name or address, press F3 to select from a list of named ranges, or paint the range. Allways will show you the range on the screen, inserting dotted lines to indicate page breaks. This shows you exactly what will be printed, so you don't have to worry about columns or rows being wrapped to the next page. The designated print range will be highlighted, just as it is in 1-2-3. To reset the range, select Range Clear. When the range has been set, select Go, and the print job will begin.

Allways does, however, introduce several unique printing commands. These include:

File

Whereas 1-2-3 allows you to create ASCII files with the extension (.PRN), the Print File command in Allways allows you to create an "encoded" file with the extension (.ENC). ASCII files do not contain any formatting features (fonts, colors, etc.) or graphic elements, while Encoded files preserve all features that would normally appear on your printed reports. The encoded file increases your flexibility by allowing you to print your worksheets at a later time or on a different computer. The codes used in the file will depend on the capabilites of the currently selected printer.

ASCII files can be printed on any computer by means of the DOS PRINT command, or imported into a word processor that can accept ASCII text (all major word processors do). Encoded files, on the other hand can only be printed by a printer that can interpret the embedded codes. Each type of printer uses a different set of codes, so an encoded file prepared for one type of printer generally cannot be printed on a different type. For example, a file prepared for a laser printer will print out as gibberish on a dot matrix.

To print an encoded file, you must use the DOS COPY command, and copy the file to your output port. For example, if you have a laser printer attached to LPT1:, you could print an encoded file with the following command:

```
copy file2.enc/b lpt1
```

(The /b parameter tells DOS to print the entire file).

To create an encoded file, select /Print File, and Allways will prompt you to enter the file name. If it already exists, you will be prompted to Cancel or Replace the file.

Print Configuration

This menu option allows you to control various aspects of your hardware, including:

Printer If you installed more than one printer when you set up Allways, they will be displayed in a window when you select the Printer option.

Interface You can choose from among six parallel ports (parallel 1 and 2, and, for networks, LPT1 through LPT4), and two serial ports (COM1 and COM2), which will be displayed in a window when you select the Printer Interface command.

Cartridge This command displays a window with the available cartridges for your selected printer (e.g., the 22 cartridges available for the Hewlett-Packard LaserJet printers). Select the one that you have in your cartridge bay(s). Allways only makes use of a single cartridge, even if your printer has two cartridge slots.

Orientation Choose between "portrait" mode or "landscape" mode. This refers to the alignment of the print across the face of the paper. Portrait means printing vertically on an 8.5 x 11 inch sheet of paper, while landscape refers to printing horizontally on an 8.5 x 11 inch sheet.

Resolution Allways gives you the choice of printing at four different resolutions: 75, 100, 150, and 300 dots per inch (dpi). Highlight the desired resolution in the window that Allways displays when you select the Resolution command.

With laser printers, the resolution only affects your graphics output. Your ability to print a full page at the maximum resolution will depend on how much memory you have in your printer. If you choose too high a resolution for your available memory, your graphic printout may be truncated. One way to solve the problem is to reduce the size of the graph or select a lower resolution.

Bin Allways allows you to choose between manual feed and automatic feed through a paper tray (depending on your printer). You can also select between multiple bins for printers that have more than one paper tray.

Allways and Undo

One final point needs to be reiterated before you begin experimenting with Allways: the effect of Allways on Undo. Be aware that once you format a cell or range within Allways, you may not be able to undo the last action within 1-2-3—any Allways command action will block the undoing of the previous 1-2-3 command. For example, if you bold a cell in Allways, and then return to 1-2-3, Undo will not work. If you try to use it, 1-2-3 will display the message, "Undo request blocked by add-in (Allways)."

This completes our tour of Allways. As you can see, it is an extremely sophisticated program. The best way to learn it is through repeated exposure with many different types of worksheets.

Using a 1-2-3 Worksheet

A WORKING MODEL

If you've had some prior experience with 1-2-3, this chapter will reinforce your knowledge and show you some new tricks. If you're new to 1-2-3 and have followed the tutorial in the previous chapters, this chapter will pull it all together, enabling you to observe a simple 1-2-3 application in action.

The worksheet model used in this chapter is based on an entity called The West Side Aquarium (we couldn't bear the thought of creating an example based on the "Widget Corp"). The worksheet was developed to answer the question: Does the aquarium have enough cash to cover operating costs during the year? To find out, the worksheet records all major categories of revenues and expenses, totals them for each month, and then computes the available net cash. To this end, the worksheet consists of four major sections (see Figure 12.1). Section 1 includes cash flow information, based on total revenues and expenses for the year. The difference is reported on the Net Cash line (in row 11).

Section 2 contains revenue information, broken down into six categories: Admission fees, Contributions, Government support, Membership dues, Misc, and Publications. A series of @SUM formulas in line 24 produces the total revenues for each month; each @SUM function sums up the itemized revenues in rows 17 through 22. The total revenue for January (in cell C24), for example, is represented as @SUM(C17..C22). The Grand Total (in cell C26) is computed by an @SUM formula that spans the range of monthly revenue totals—C24 through N24.

Section 3 reports on projected expenses, breaking out the maintenance costs for the Aquarium's main visitor center, the Dolphin Arena, the "Gator Pit," the Shark Pond, and the Marine Science Center. The total expenses in line 38 sum up the itemized costs in rows 31-36, month by month (derived in the same fashion as the total revenues in Section 2). The Grand Total for projected expenses is in cell C40.

One twist in Section 3 is the use of a file link in row 36, which draws a feed cost amount from cell I17 in a separate file, called FEED. The FEED worksheet, which uses a number of very useful database analysis functions, is discussed in detail later in the chapter.

Finally, Section 4 is the report section of the worksheet, and it contains statistical information about the status of the aquarium.

To assist in navigation around the worksheet and to illustrate the use of the GOTO key (F5), each section of the worksheet has been assigned a range name. These are as follows:

WEST SIDE AQUARIUM
Financial Projections

CASH FLOW PROJECTIONS

	Jan	Feb	Mar	Apr	May	Jun	Jul	Aug	Sep	Oct	Nov	Dec
Total Revenues	626,138	698,528	789,715	696,628	752,122	802,801	824,991	788,498	686,803	680,860	696,504	749,953
Total Expenses	610,474	613,612	632,224	680,769	687,184	776,296	808,066	791,744	748,643	681,170	679,000	635,857
NET CASH	$15,665	$84,917	$157,491	$15,859	$64,938	$26,505	$16,925	($3,245)	($61,840)	($310)	$17,504	$114,096

PROJECTED REVENUES

	Jan	Feb	Mar	Apr	May	Jun	Jul	Aug	Sep	Oct	Nov	Dec
Admission fees	75,266	74,734	146,194	161,392	193,792	214,592	220,799	233,859	193,726	207,600	126,585	78,483
Contributions	163,096	176,293	179,630	80,264	90,370	136,930	130,526	115,529	111,550	109,630	91,554	123,830
Government support	241,059	285,932	292,599	253,279	240,812	196,594	212,801	165,000	159,000	157,414	215,926	247,592
Membership dues	111,262	119,259	120,592	159,266	177,400	183,266	186,592	195,059	153,274	147,000	159,260	281,259
Misc	2,860	3,051	4,767	6,674	10,487	18,019	19,068	18,591	15,254	11,279	72,587	2,955
Publications	32,594	39,259	45,933	35,754	39,260	53,400	55,205	60,460	54,000	47,938	30,592	15,834
Total Revenues:	626,138	698,528	789,715	696,628	752,122	802,801	824,991	788,498	686,803	680,860	696,504	749,953
GRAND TOTAL:	$8,793,542											

PROJECTED EXPENSES

	Jan	Feb	Mar	Apr	May	Jun	Jul	Aug	Sep	Oct	Nov	Dec
Main Visitor Center	312,543	312,543	312,543	312,543	367,453	433,222	446,544	412,565	376,655	312,543	312,543	312,543
Dolphin Arena	105,734	118,940	120,589	167,562	105,913	111,659	113,859	115,200	178,858	176,975	178,858	173,387
Gater Pit	26,493	24,374	27,023	28,126	29,672	33,117	30,997	31,792	25,169	24,904	25,169	16,594
Shark Pond	37,459	39,770	41,260	38,473	40,513	37,994	43,407	44,726	46,130	46,199	40,599	27,394
Marine Sciences Center	128,244	117,984	130,809	134,066	143,633	160,305	173,259	187,461	121,832	120,549	121,832	105,940
Fish Feed	902	902	902	902	902	902	902	902	902	902	902	902
Total Expenses:	610,474	613,612	632,224	680,769	687,184	776,296	808,066	791,744	748,643	681,170	679,000	635,857
GRAND TOTAL:	$8,345,039											

STATISTICAL REPORT

Total Annual Revenues	8,793,542
Total Annual Expenses	8,345,039
Profit/Loss	448,504
Minimum Monthly Cash	(61,840)
Maximum Monthly Cash	157,491
Minimum Monthly Revenues	626,138
Maximum Monthly Revenues	824,991
Average Monthly Revenues	732,795
Minimum Monthly Expenses	610,474
Maximum Monthly Expenses	808,066
Average Monthly Expenses	695,420

Figure 12.1
Aquarium Model.

Range Name	Worksheet Area	Cell Address
Cash	Net Cash	(A5..N11)
Rev	Revenues	(A14..N26)
Exp	Expenses	(A28..N40)
Stats	Statistical Report	(A42..C57)

To move the pointer to any of these designated ranges, press the F5 key followed by the range name. The cursor will then move to the designated cell.

BUILDING AND FORMATTING THE WORKSHEET

If you want to build the Aquarium model yourself (which is advisable if you're new to 1-2-3), a listing of the contents of each cell is presented in Appendix A. To speed things up, use the following techniques:

Worksheet Construction

1. Set the column widths as follows:

Column A	16
Column B	17
Column C–N	11

2. Enter all the text.
3. Create the double separator rules as follows. In cell A4, enter:

   \=

   This will repeat the equals sign throughout the width of the cell. Copy the cell A4 to the range B4..N4. Now copy from A4..N4 to A13, then to A27, and finally to A41. This will instantly place the double separator lines in the correct place.
4. Create the first single separator line in row 7 by using the same techniques described above (using a hyphen rather than an equals sign). Copy the single lines to rows 16, 30, and 43.
5. Use the/Range Name Create command to create the ranges Cash, Rev, Exp, and Stats as shown in the table above. Type in the appropriate range addresses or paint the range areas. In addition, create the following range names to expedite writing the formulas used in the report section:

Netcash (C11..N11)

Revtot (C24..N24)

Exptot (C38..N38)

6. Enter the figures shown in Appendix A, or devise your own.

Worksheet Formatting

1. Format the entire worksheet for comma, no decimal places—only the net cash and grand totals have dollar signs (a mass of dollar signs makes the report difficult to read.) Reformat the range netcash as Currency, 0 decimal places. Since you've named the range, you can enter the name netcash when prompted for a range to format, or press the F3 key, which will display a list of all named ranges in the worksheet. Highlight netcash and press ENTER.
2. Finally, reformat cells C26 and C40, as currency, no decimal places.

Formulas

1. Enter the formula `+C24` in cell C8—this instructs 1-2-3 to place the total monthly revenues for January in cell C8. Copy the formula in C8 to cells D8 through N8. Enter the formula `+C38` in cell C9, then copy it in cells D9 through N9 so that the appropriate monthly expenses appear in the Cash Flow Projections section.

   Finally, in cell C11 enter the formula `+C8-C9`. Copy this formula to the range D11..N11. The formulas are now in place for the Net Cash Flow section of the worksheet.
2. Enter the formula `@SUM(C17..C22)` in cell C24. This sums all the revenue line items for the month of January. Copy the formula to cells D24 through N24.
3. In cell C26, enter the formula `@SUM(C24..N24)` to total all the monthly revenues.
4. In cell C38, enter the formula `@SUM(C31..C36)`, then copy it to cells D38 through N38. This totals all the expense line items for each month.
5. Enter the formula `SUM(C38..N38)` in cell C40, to generate a grand total for expenses.

6. Save your worksheet under the name AQUARIUM (or a file name of your choosing) and clear the screen by selecting /Worksheet Erase Yes. Now create a blank "dummy" worksheet called FEED. (This is necessary, because you are about to reference the FEED file in AQUARIUM, and 1-2-3 will not let you reference a file that does not yet exist.)

   Save the blank worksheet as FEED. Now retrieve the AQUARIUM file, and enter the formula <<FEED>>$I17 in cell C36. This will reference the total consumption figure that you will later compute in cell I17 of the FEED file. It is important to make the column portion of this cell absolute, since you will be copying it from cell C36 to the range D36 through N36. If you left the address relative, 1-2-3 would increment the column address from I17 to J17 to K17, and so on, in the cells D36 through N36 and the results would be erroneous.

   Since FEED is empty, the cells in AQUARIUM that reference FEED will evaluate to 0. Once you've constructed the FEED file described below, the links in AQUARIUM will be automatically updated each time AQUARIUM is retrieved.

7. Enter the following formulas for the Statistical Report. As you can see, the use of range names makes the formula writing a breeze.

Total Annual Revenues	`+C26`
Total Annual Expenses	`+C40`
Profit/Loss	`+C44-C45`
Minimum Monthly Cash	`@MIN(NETCASH)`
Maximum Monthly Cash	`@MAX(NETCASH)`
Minimum Monthly Revenues	`@MIN(REVTOT)`
Maximum Monthly Revenues	`@MAX(REVTOT)`
Average Monthly Revenues	`@AVG(REVTOT)`
Minimum Monthly Expenses	`@MIN(EXPTOTAL)`
Maximum Monthly Expenses	`@MAX(EXPTOTAL)`
Average Monthly Expenses	`@AVG(EXPTOTAL)`

At this point, the financial portion of the model is complete. Now we need to create the FEED worksheet to complete the monthly feed costs. Later we provide suggestions for taking advantage of 1-2-3's built-in functions.

THE FEED CONSUMPTION WORKSHEET

As mentioned, the expense line items in row 36 is derived from the worksheet FEED, which calculates the feed consumption for various members of the aquarium population. If you re-created the financial projection worksheet described above, you will need to create the FEED worksheet for the model to be complete. The cell contents are listed in Appendix A for you convenience, and the complete FEED worksheet is shown in Figure 12.2.

The FEED worksheet illustrates a use of the /Data Table 2 command for cross-tabulation. The objective of the FEED worksheet is to compute the monthly feed cost. The basis for the feed cost calculation is a data table—created in 1-2-3—listing the monthly feed consumptions for individual denizens of the deep. The worksheet calculates the average consumption of different kinds of feed (mackerel, tailings, and beef) by each animal group (dolphins, alligators, orcas, and sharks); and then multiplies these averages by the number of representatives in each animal group. (There are two dolphins, three alligators, two orcas, and four sharks.) The resulting figure is the total consumption of each kind of feed each month. Finally, it multiplies the volume of feed consumption by the cost per unit to produce a gross cost. This is the figure that appears in cell I17 and that is referenced by the AQUARIUM worksheet.

Here are the details (refer to Figure 12.2):

1. The data table range is established in cells A2 through D14. That table includes the four field name labels: Name, Type, Feed, and Pounds.
2. The Input 1 and 2 cells are assigned to the empty cells A19 and B19, with the field names corresponding to each variable placed directly above them. In this case we are analyzing animal Type and kind of Feed. (Together, the field names and the empty input cells will constitute the criteria range for the @DAVG formula.) Cells A17 and B17 simply label each input cell.
3. The rules for structuring a /Data Table 2 command are as follows: Input variable 1 (in our case, animal types) should be in the left column of the output table, and input variable 2 (in our case, feed type) should be in the top row of the output table, starting one cell above and to the right of the variable 1 column. The formula for evaluating the variables must be placed at the intersection of the row and column variables (in the upper-left hand corner of the table). In our example, dolphins, alligators, orcas, and sharks, have been placed in column F, while the Feed types—mackerel, tailings, and beef—start in cell G2. At the intersection of the two variable lists, in

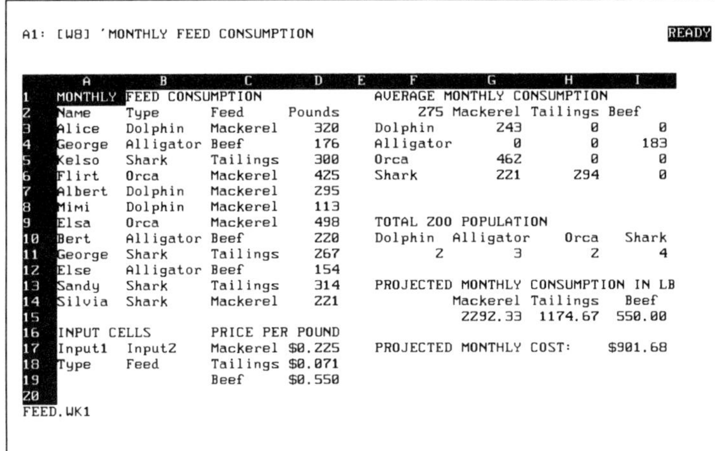

A1: [W8] 'MONTHLY FEED CONSUMPTION READY

	A	B	C	D	E	F	G	H	I
1	MONTHLY FEED CONSUMPTION					AVERAGE MONTHLY CONSUMPTION			
2	Name	Type	Feed	Pounds		275	Mackerel	Tailings	Beef
3	Alice	Dolphin	Mackerel	320		Dolphin	243	0	0
4	George	Alligator	Beef	176		Alligator	0	0	183
5	Kelso	Shark	Tailings	300		Orca	462	0	0
6	Flirt	Orca	Mackerel	425		Shark	221	294	0
7	Albert	Dolphin	Mackerel	295					
8	Mimi	Dolphin	Mackerel	113					
9	Elsa	Orca	Mackerel	498		TOTAL ZOO POPULATION			
10	Bert	Alligator	Beef	220		Dolphin	Alligator	Orca	Shark
11	George	Shark	Tailings	267		2	3	2	4
12	Else	Alligator	Beef	154					
13	Sandy	Shark	Tailings	314		PROJECTED MONTHLY CONSUMPTION IN LB			
14	Silvia	Shark	Mackerel	221			Mackerel	Tailings	Beef
15							2292.33	1174.67	550.00
16	INPUT CELLS		PRICE PER POUND						
17	Input1	Input2	Mackerel	$0.225		PROJECTED MONTHLY COST:		$901.68	
18	Type	Feed	Tailings	$0.071					
19			Beef	$0.550					
20									

FEED.WK1

Figure 12.2 Food consumption worksheet.

cell F2, the following formula is inserted (see step 5 for an explanation):

```
@IF(@ISERR(@DAVG(A2..D14,3,A18..B19),0, @DAVG(A2..D14,3,A18..B19))
```

4. The /Data Table 2 command instructs 1-2-3 to evaluate this formula for each animal type (variable 1) and for each type of feed (variable 2). Each combination of animal type and feed type is substituted into the criteria range (Input cells 1 and 2); and for each substitution the @DAVG formula is evaluated using the specified database (e.g., A2..D14), the specified field (e.g., Pounds—offset 3), and the criteria range with the inserted values (e.g., A18..B19). The formula results are placed in the data table. For example, given the animal type, Dolphin, in cell F3 and the feed type, Mackerel, in cell G2, the @DAVG function shows an average monthly consumption of 243 pounds of mackerel per dolphin in cell G3.

5. The @DAVG formula simply averages the amount of each feed type consumed by each member of the four animal groups. The formula only looks complex because of the embedded @IF and @ISERR functions. They have been included to test for error conditions that occur when a given set of criteria finds no matches in the database. For example, dolphins and orcas don't eat beef; if 1-2-3 were to proceed with the @DAVG function as is, it would have divide by zero producing an ERR result in the table. To avoid the display of ERR in the table, the @IF and @ISERR functions cause the formula to display zeros instead. The structure of the formula with the ERR test is as follows:

The @IF function tests for a logical condition. If the @DAVG function reports an error, the condition is true, and 1-2-3 is instructed to place a 0 in the cell (as opposed to an ERR). If the condition is false, 1-2-3 is instructed to enter the results of the @DAVG calculation.

6. Once the average monthly food consumption (per animal in each animal group) is computed with the @DAVG formula, the next step is to determine the projected monthly consumption of each type of feed—in pounds —for all animals. This is accomplished by using the /Data Matrix Multiply command and multiplying the number of animals in the aquarium population (F11 through I11) by the average monthly consumption matrix in the range G3 through I6 (i.e., multiplying the number of mackerel-eaters by the average mackerel consumption, then doing the same for fish tailings and beef). The resulting projected weekly consumption for each type of feed is reported in cells G15 through I15.

   When you invoke /Data Matrix Multiply, 1-2-3 will prompt you for the first range to multiply. It is very important to stipulate the aquarium population row (F11 through I11) as the first range, and the feed consumption table (G3 through I6) as the second range. Since the /Matrix Multiply command produces an output matrix with as many rows as the first matrix and as many columns as the second, the order in which you select your matrices is critical. (See /Data Matrix Multiply in the Reference Section for details about the math calculations used.)

7. The next step in the process is to determine the projected monthly cost. This is again accomplished by a /Data Matrix Multiply command; this time we multiply the projected monthly consumption by the price per pound of mackerel, fish tailings, and beef, and report the resulting monthly food cost in cell I17. Here, the first data matrix range is monthly consumption (one row—G15 through I15) and the second data matrix range is the price per pound (a single column—D17 through D19), yielding a single cell, I17.

NOTE: This worksheet is command-driven. In other words, you must actually execute the /Data Table 2 and the /Data Matrix Multiply commands to obtain the results. If you make any changes to the worksheet you must re-execute the commands in the sequence described above.

As this model demonstrates, you can use /Data Table commands with cross-tabulation to summarize a database according to the values it contains, and the /Data Matrix Multiply command to manipulate the resulting table in a fashion that would be extremely laborious if done manually. With a large data range, such computations might be even be impossible. Before applying any of the data tables on a large scale basis, we recommend that you experiment with small, manageable databases such as the one used above; if it works on a small scale, it will work on a large scale, too.

WHAT-IF ANALYSIS

The greatest value of a worksheet is the ability to try out different scenarios and see their effects on the bottom line. For example, as you can see in the Net Cash results (row 11) in Figure 12.1, the aquarium is projecting a serious cash shortage in September, and minor shortfalls in August and October. What can we do about the shortfall? Boost revenues or reduce expenses?

The simplest way to adjust the numbers is to simply add to the revenues or subtract from the expenses until the numbers turn positive. This would yield a set of target figures that would have to be obtained to keep the numbers positive. More likely, you'll want to work with percentages. For example, you might want to know the effect of boosting admission fees by 10 percent in August through October. Perhaps you can secure a special event that will attract more people, or maybe you can generate another 12 percent in membership or contributions by sponsoring a special campaign.

Before engaging in the what-if analysis session, you may want to place the cell pointer in cell B8 and then select /Worksheet Title Both. This will lock in the months and the line items on the left side of the worksheet. Then you can move about the worksheet—to the Net Cash figure for the month of September, for example—without losing track of which month or line item you're viewing (see Figure 12.3).

One way to do what-if analysis is the "brute force" method. Simply edit each cell and enter the multiplier factor, then observe the results. For example, you could edit cell K17, which corresponds to admissions fees in September, so that the contents read: 193726*110% The fees will change to $213,039 and the shortfall in September (cell K11) will be reduced from $61,840 to $42,467 (see Figure 12.4).

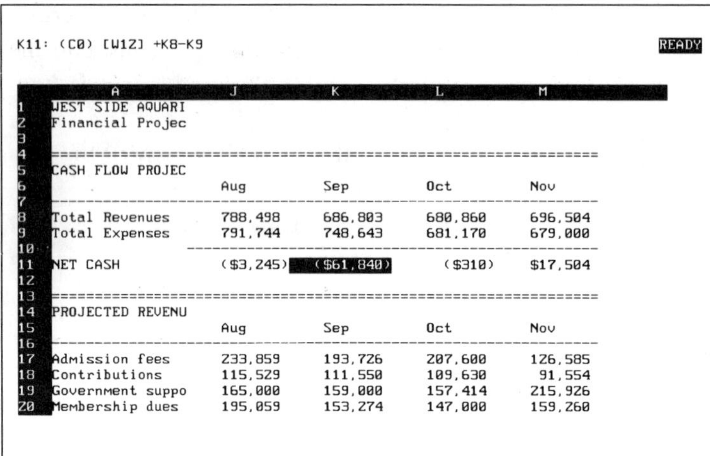

K11: (C0) [W12] +K8-K9 READY

	A	J	K	L	M
1	WEST SIDE AQUARI				
2	Financial Projec				
3					
4	====	====	====	====	====
5	CASH FLOW PROJEC				
6		Aug	Sep	Oct	Nov
7	----	----	----	----	----
8	Total Revenues	788,498	686,803	680,860	696,504
9	Total Expenses	791,744	748,643	681,170	679,000
10		----	----	----	----
11	NET CASH	($3,245)	($61,840)	($310)	$17,504
12					
13	====	====	====	====	====
14	PROJECTED REVENU				
15		Aug	Sep	Oct	Nov
16	----	----	----	----	----
17	Admission fees	233,859	193,726	207,600	126,585
18	Contributions	115,529	111,550	109,630	91,554
19	Government suppo	165,000	159,000	157,414	215,926
20	Membership dues	195,059	153,274	147,000	159,260

Figure 12.3
Horizontal and vertical title lock allows you to keep track of rows and columns while performing what-if analysis.

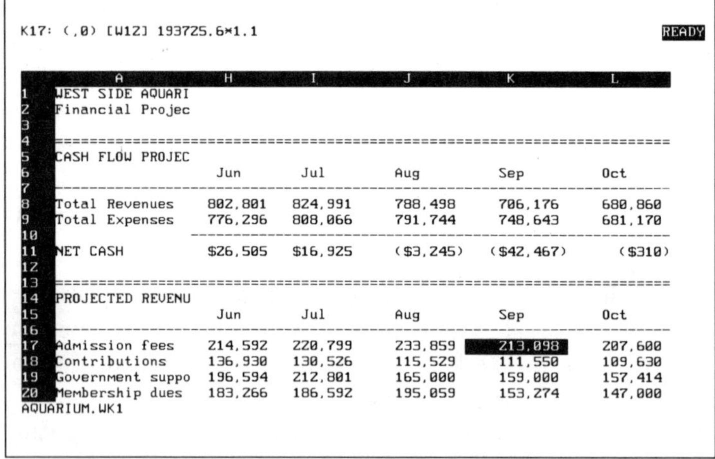

K17: (,0) [W12] 193725.6*1.1 READY

	A	H	I	J	K	L
1	WEST SIDE AQUARI					
2	Financial Projec					
3						
4	====	====	====	====	====	====
5	CASH FLOW PROJEC					
6		Jun	Jul	Aug	Sep	Oct
7	----	----	----	----	----	----
8	Total Revenues	802,801	824,991	788,498	706,176	680,860
9	Total Expenses	776,296	808,066	791,744	748,643	681,170
10		----	----	----	----	----
11	NET CASH	$26,505	$16,925	($3,245)	($42,467)	($310)
12						
13	====	====	====	====	====	====
14	PROJECTED REVENU					
15		Jun	Jul	Aug	Sep	Oct
16	----	----	----	----	----	----
17	Admission fees	214,592	220,799	233,859	213,098	207,600
18	Contributions	136,930	130,526	115,529	111,550	109,630
19	Government suppo	196,594	212,801	165,000	159,000	157,414
20	Membership dues	183,266	186,592	195,059	153,274	147,000

AQUARIUM.WK1

Figure 12.4
Effects of what-if analysis on bottom line for September.

If you want to compare the value prior to the inclusion of the 110% adjustment to K17, press UNDO (ALT-F4), assuming it's been enabled. The trouble with this approach is that you constantly have to edit each cell, which becomes time consuming when you want to vary a number of line items. Here are two alternative approaches.

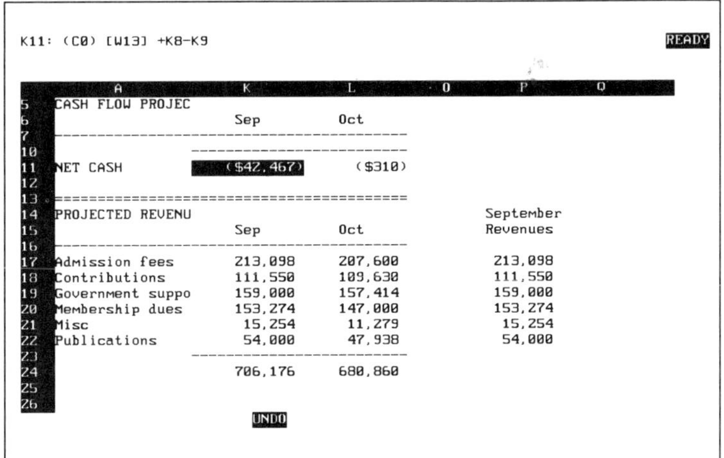

Figure 12.5
Step one in the adjustment cell technique is to create a duplicate column of numbers to the side of the worksheet. (Columns M and N are hidden.)

Adjustment Cell Technique 1 (ACT1): Gross What-If Analysis

ACT1 involves copying the original data in a column to a blank portion of the worksheet, then multiplying the original data by an adjustment factor, and placing the new figure back in the worksheet by means of a formula. In this way, you can simply enter a new adjustment without having to edit the formula for each cell in the column of data to be evaluated.

To use this technique with the aquarium model, copy the data from the September revenues column and place it to the right of the worksheet in column P (see Figure 12.5).

For convenience, select a cell—such as K14—that you can see on screen above the September figures in column K. This cell will contain your what-if adjustment factor. Format cell K14 for percent, 0 decimal places. Change the value in cell K17 to this formula:

```
K$14*P17/100
```

In other words, multiply the amount in cell P17 (the duplicate column with the original worksheet figures for September) by the adjustment factor in K14. The formula also instructs 1-2-3 to divide the result by 100; this allows you to type in a value in K14 as a percentage, without having to enter a decimal value. For example, if you want to adjust by a factor of 90%, you can type 90 into K14 rather than .9, and to adjust by 110% you can type in 110 rather than 1.10.

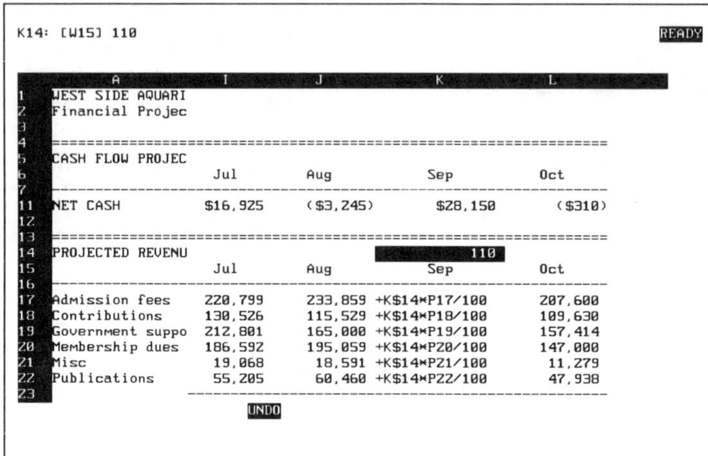

Figure 12.6
With the adjustment cell, you can quickly change an entire group of values with a single multiplier factor.

Copy the formula from K17 down through K22. Note that the row component of the K14 cell reference must be absolute (e.g., K$14); otherwise, when you copy the formula down the column, the row number will increment in the copy, creating erroneous results. (In Figure 12.6 we have formatted the formulas as text, so that you can read the cell contents in each case.)

With this adjustment cell technique you can now see what an across-the-board increase in revenues will do to the bottom line. As you can see in Figure 12.6, a 10 percent increase puts the aquarium squarely in the black for September. You could also use an adjustment cell for expenses, placing it in cell L15, and play with the two multiplier factors until the scenario is realistic.

Adjustment Cell Technique 2 (ACT2): Individual Cell Analysis

While the ACT1 analysis allows you to quickly change an entire group of values and determine the effect on the bottom line, in many cases you will want to fine-tune the analysis by adjusting individual values, especially if it is unrealistic to achieve an across-the-board increase in revenues (or decrease in expenses). ACT2 is useful in such cases. It entails copying the original data to a blank portion of the worksheet, and then entering formulas that allow you to see the adjustment factor in individual cells. The objective of ACT2 is to allow you to perform what-if analyses on individual entries with individual adjustment factors, rather than evaluating all entries in a column with a common factor.

You can do this with the aquarium model by duplicating the September revenue column in column P as in the ACT1 example, and then inserting a new

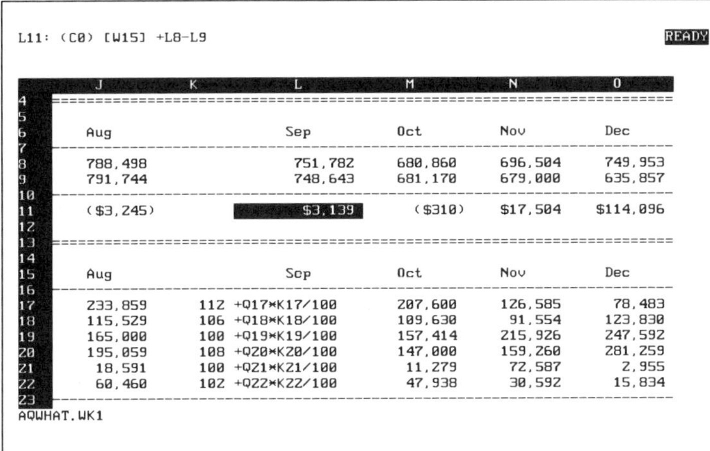

Figure 12.7
With multiple cell adjustments, you can analyze numerous scenarios for changing the bottom line.

column before the September column. (You may want to extend the separator lines to close up the spaces created by the new column.) Now enter the following formula in L17:

```
+Q17*K17/100
```

This simply instructs 1-2-3 to multiply the original values for Admission Fees, contained in cell Q17 (the column address is now moved over one column to the right because you inserted a column) by whatever adjustment factor value is contained in cell K17. Now copy the formulas down through cells L18..L22. (See Figure 12.7.)

The advantage of this technique is that you can evaluate different increments for each line item. For example, you might determine that admission fees could be raised by 12 percent and that contributions could be raised by 6 percent, but that given the current administration's budget-slicing mentality, government support will not likely increase at all. Further, membership dues could probably be increased by 8 percent, miscellaneous revenues are not likely to increase, and publications could increase a maximum of 2 percent. With this scenario, the effect on the bottom line is still positive; the aquarium will go from a major shortfall to a minor cash surplus.

As you can see, ACT2 is powerful way of conducting what-if analyses on detailed sections of the worksheet and can be used to formulate a specific action plan. This, of course, is the goal of creating the worksheet in the first place: to determine where the aquarium is heading financially, and what can be done to keep it afloat.

You could conceivably create an adjustment cell for every month and every line item in the worksheet, although there's a practical limit to the number of adjustments that will be useful in a given analysis. The general rule is simply to zero-in on those elements that you can control or predict, and determine best and worst case scenarios. You can then take the appropriate action to maximize profits or avoid disaster.

Now that we've seen the numbers side of the worksheet, let's see what a visual representation can tell us. The next section builds on the graphing tools you've learned to use in Chapter 9.

SHOWING THE STORY WITH PICTURES

There are many combinations that could be graphed in this report, such as Monthly Revenues, Monthly Expenses, Net Cash, the individual line items, total expenses versus total revenues, as well as the 11 statistical computations from the report section. In fact, you could create quite a visual potpourri from the available data. The point of graphing, though, is to create meaningful graphs that give people an instant sense of an important trend or situation. Therefore, when deciding what to graph, ask yourself the following questions:

- What are the key numbers?
- What trends will be instantly evident if depicted graphically?
- What relationships between groups of data will become clearer if depicted in graphic format?

In the case of the aquarium worksheet, the most important set of numbers is the amount of monthly available cash. Bar and line graphs, such as the ones shown in Figures 12.8a and b, really "say it all"; where are we today and where are we going tomorrow. The graphs clearly highlight the fact that some action has to be taken to avoid the shortfalls in August, September and October.

Of course, there are other important relationships that could have been graphed as well. For example, revenues and expenses could have been graphed as trend lines, or individual line items could have been compared on a monthly basis.

Now that you've collected all this valuable data, you may want to present it to others in your company, in which case you'll need to do some formatting—there are too many numbers jam-packed in a small space for people to get an instant sense of the situation. This calls for a 15-minute makeover.

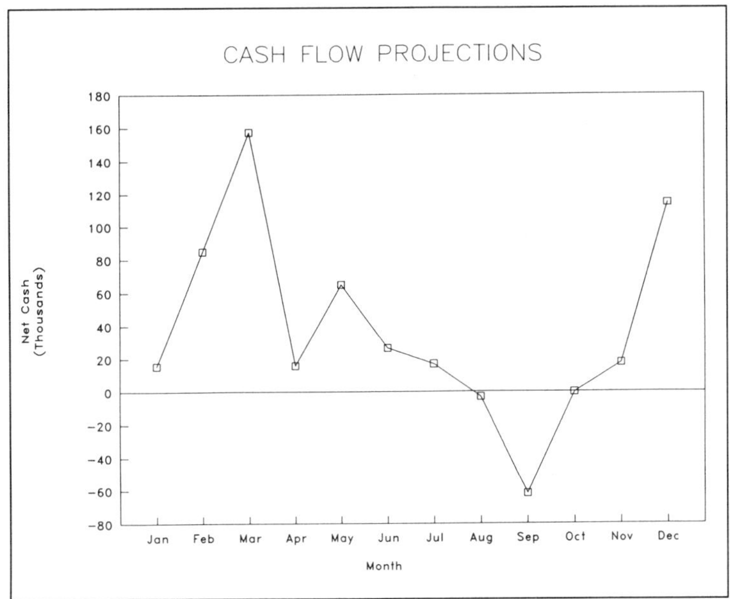

Figure 12.8a

Cash flow Line graph.

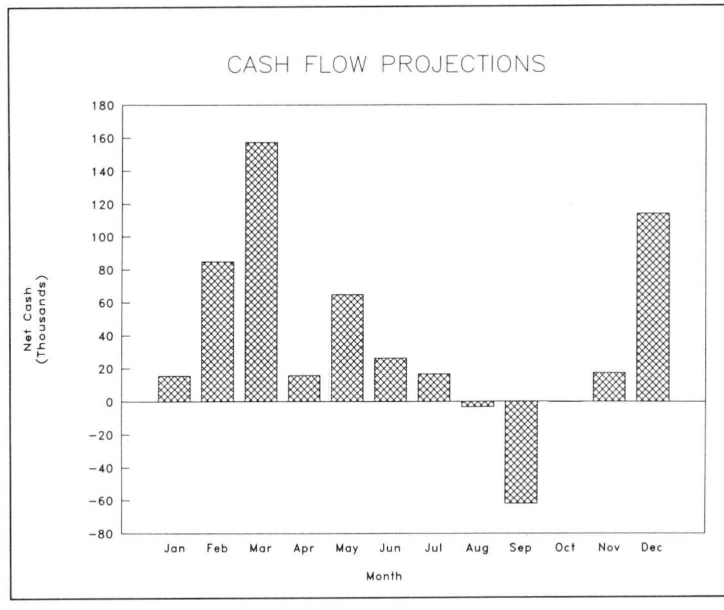

Figure 12.8b

Cash flow Bar graph.

CREATING A PRESENTATION QUALITY REPORT

The aquarium worksheet is quite wide and, with most printers, will have to be printed in Landscape (lengthwise) mode on 8.5 by 11-inch paper. The problem with printing in Landscape mode is that even with the condensed Line Printer font available in many printers, you won't be able to output the bottom report section. One solution is to use a font cartridge that contains a very small typeface. The printout shown in Figure 12.1 was printed in Portrait mode with an HP LaserJet Series II printer using the JetFont Cartridge and its specialized Lotica 30 cpi typeface. Although the worksheet is legible, it could be greatly improved upon by using Allways, the spreadsheet publisher add-in described in Chapter 11. If nothing else, the use of a proportional font will allow us to use a larger type size and still print the worksheet in Portrait (widthwise) mode. Let's see what else we can do with Allways to turn this ho-hum, microscopic specimen into a report with some pizzazz and sparkle, by using Allways capabilites to change fonts, add lines and other graphic elements, and combine text and graphs. To begin, attach and invoke the Allways add-in.

Change the Column Widths

To change column widths, use the /Worksheet Column Set-Width command in Allways. Leave columns A and B in their default width, and set Column C to 10.00 characters, which is necessary to accommodate the Grand Total amount. Change columns D through N to 8.25 characters. To change columns D through N, place the cell pointer in column D, anchor it with a period, then continually press the right cursor to extend the highlight until it covers the cells in column N, then select the /Worksheet Column Set-Width command.

To fit all of the text on a single sheet in Portrait orientation, you will have to set your left and right margins to 0. You'll still have about a quarter of an inch on each side. If you want more of a margin, you'll have to use Triumvirate 6 point as your default font (Font 1—see next section). While this will give you plenty of white space, 6 point type (also known in graphic arts circles as "mouse type") is difficult to read. Also when you reproduce it, the spaces tend to fill in, so that the legibility rapidly degrades over successive generations of photocopying.

Change the Default Font for the Body Text

Next, we'll change the font to the largest size that will include all columns on a single sheet of 8.5 by 11-inch paper in Portrait orientation. This happens to be Triumvirate 7 point. Select /Format Font Replace, and select Triumvirate 7 point as your default font (Font 1). This will create the worksheet shown in 12.9.

WEST SIDE AQUARIUM
Financial Projections

CASH FLOW PROJECTIONS	Jan	Feb	Mar	Apr	May	Jun	Jul	Aug	Sep	Oct	Nov	Dec
Total Revenues	626,138	698,528	789,715	696,628	752,122	802,801	824,991	788,498	686,803	680,860	696,504	749,953
Total Expenses	610,474	613,612	632,224	680,769	687,184	776,296	808,066	791,744	748,643	681,170	679,000	635,857
NET CASH	$15,665	$84,917	$157,491	$15,859	$64,938	$26,505	$16,925	($3,245)	($61,840)	($310)	$17,504	$114,096

PROJECTED REVENUES	Jan	Feb	Mar	Apr	May	Jun	Jul	Aug	Sep	Oct	Nov	Dec
Admission fees	75,266	74,734	146,194	161,392	193,792	214,592	220,799	233,859	193,726	207,600	126,585	78,483
Contributions	163,096	176,293	179,630	80,264	90,370	136,930	130,526	115,529	111,550	109,630	91,554	123,830
Government support	241,059	285,932	292,599	253,279	240,812	196,594	212,801	165,000	159,000	157,414	215,926	247,592
Membership dues	111,262	119,259	120,592	159,266	177,400	183,266	186,592	195,059	153,274	147,000	159,260	281,259
Misc	2,860	3,051	4,767	6,674	10,487	18,019	19,068	18,591	15,254	11,279	72,587	2,955
Publications	32,594	39,259	45,933	35,754	39,260	53,400	55,205	60,460	54,000	47,938	30,592	15,834
Total Revenues:	626,138	698,528	789,715	696,628	752,122	802,801	824,991	788,498	686,803	680,860	696,504	749,953
GRAND TOTAL:	$8,793,542											

PROJECTED EXPENSES	Jan	Feb	Mar	Apr	May	Jun	Jul	Aug	Sep	Oct	Nov	Dec
Main Visitor Center	312,543	312,543	312,543	312,543	367,453	433,222	446,544	412,565	376,655	312,543	312,543	312,543
Dolphin Arena	105,734	118,940	120,589	167,562	105,913	111,659	113,859	115,200	178,858	176,975	178,858	173,387
Gater Pit	26,493	24,374	27,023	28,126	29,672	33,117	30,997	31,792	25,169	24,904	25,169	16,594
Shark Pond	37,459	39,770	41,260	38,473	40,513	37,994	43,407	44,726	46,130	46,199	40,599	27,394
Marine Sciences Center	128,244	117,984	130,809	134,066	143,633	160,305	173,259	187,461	121,832	120,549	121,832	105,940
Fish Feed	902	902	902	902	902	902	902	902	902	902	902	902
Total Expenses:	610,474	613,612	632,224	680,769	687,184	776,296	808,066	791,744	748,643	681,170	679,000	635,857
GRAND TOTAL:	$8,345,039											

STATISTICAL REPORT	
Total Annual Revenues	8,793,542
Total Annual Expenses	8,345,039
Profit/Loss	448,504
Minimum Monthly Cash	(61,840)
Maximum Monthly Cash	157,491
Minimum Monthly Revenues	626,138
Maximum Monthly Revenues	824,991
Average Monthly Revenues	732,795
Minimum Monthly Expenses	610,474
Maximum Monthly Expenses	808,066
Average Monthly Expenses	695,420

Figure 12.9

Font 1 changed to 7 point Triumvirate.

Changing Headers and Section Text Fonts

With a densely packed worksheet, we want to be careful not to introduce too many graphic elements, so we'll just bold the monthly headings, rather than switching to a different size or style of type. An easy way to format the three rows of monthly headers is to paint a range encompassing the first row, then select /Format Bold Set (or press ALT-B). Next, highlight the range and select /Special Copy. (You can't just select the three rows of headers as a continuous range, because you will also bold the intervening body copy.) Press ENTER to accept the range as the copy FROM range. When prompted to enter a range to copy TO, move the cursor to the Jan header in the next row. Press ENTER, and the format will be copied to all of the monthly headers in the row. (Remember, the /Special Copy command doesn't copy data, just formats.) Repeat the procedure for the third row of monthly headers.

Next, use the /Format Font command to make the following changes. While we are trying to minimize the number of fonts in this cramped report, we still need to use typography to distinguish segments of the reports and components of the various segments. We also want items such as the Grand Total amount to stand out:

Section Headers:	8 point bold Triumvirate
Line Items:	7 point bold Triumvirate italics
Total Expenses:	7 point bold Triumvirate
Total Revenues:	7 point bold Triumvirate
Grand Total:	7 point bold Triumvirate

By using the /Special Copy command, you only have to use the /Format commands four times. All other font changes can be done by copying formats from section of the worksheet to the next. The results of your font formatting are shown in Figure 12.10.

Rules and Shading

Now let's get rid the all the dashed rules in the worksheet so we can replace them with solid rules. From within 1-2-3, use the /Range Erase command to eliminate the rules in rows 4, 13, 27, 41, 43, and 59. Use the /Worksheet Delete Row command to remove all remaining separator lines in rows—we'll be using Allway's built-in line generator to place rules at the bottom of cells, so we don't need to have additional space for them.

WEST SIDE AQUARIUM
Financial Projections

CASH FLOW PROJECTIONS

	Jan	Feb	Mar	Apr	May	Jun	Jul	Aug	Sep	Oct	Nov	Dec
Total Revenues	626,138	698,528	789,715	696,628	752,122	802,801	824,991	788,498	686,803	680,860	696,504	749,953
Total Expenses	610,474	613,612	632,224	680,769	687,184	776,296	808,066	791,744	748,643	681,170	679,000	635,857
NET CASH	$15,665	$84,917	$157,491	$15,859	$64,938	$26,505	$16,925	($3,245)	($61,840)	($310)	$17,504	$114,096

PROJECTED REVENUES

	Jan	Feb	Mar	Apr	May	Jun	Jul	Aug	Sep	Oct	Nov	Dec
Admission fees	75,266	74,734	146,194	161,392	193,792	214,592	220,799	233,859	193,726	207,600	126,585	78,483
Contributions	163,096	176,293	179,630	80,264	90,370	136,930	130,526	115,529	111,550	109,630	91,554	123,830
Government support	241,059	285,932	292,599	253,279	240,812	196,594	212,801	165,000	159,000	157,414	215,926	247,592
Membership dues	111,262	119,259	120,592	159,266	177,400	183,266	186,592	195,059	153,274	147,000	159,260	281,259
Misc	2,860	3,051	4,767	6,674	10,487	18,019	19,068	18,591	15,254	11,279	72,587	2,955
Publications	32,594	39,259	45,933	35,754	39,260	53,400	55,205	60,460	54,000	47,938	30,592	15,834
Total Revenues:	626,138	698,528	789,715	696,628	752,122	802,801	824,991	788,498	686,803	680,860	696,504	749,953
GRAND TOTAL:	$8,793,542											

PROJECTED EXPENSES

	Jan	Feb	Mar	Apr	May	Jun	Jul	Aug	Sep	Oct	Nov	Dec
Main Visitor Center	312,543	312,543	312,543	312,543	367,453	433,222	446,544	412,565	376,655	312,543	312,543	312,543
Dolphin Arena	105,734	118,940	120,589	167,562	105,913	111,659	113,859	115,200	178,858	176,975	178,858	173,387
Gater Pit	26,493	24,374	27,023	28,126	29,672	33,117	30,997	31,792	25,169	24,904	25,169	16,594
Shark Pond	37,459	39,770	41,260	38,473	40,513	37,994	43,407	44,726	46,130	46,199	40,599	27,394
Marine Sciences Center	128,244	117,984	130,809	134,066	143,633	160,305	173,259	187,461	121,832	120,549	121,832	105,940
Fish Feed	902	902	902	902	902	902	902	902	902	902	902	902
Total Expenses:	610,474	613,612	632,224	680,769	687,184	776,296	808,066	791,744	748,643	681,170	679,000	635,857
GRAND TOTAL:	$8,345,039											

STATISTICAL REPORT

Total Annual Revenues	8,793,542
Total Annual Expenses	8,345,039
Profit/Loss	448,504
Minimum Monthly Cash	(61,840)
Maximum Monthly Cash	157,491
Minimum Monthly Revenues	626,138
Maximum Monthly Revenues	824,991
Average Monthly Revenues	732,795
Minimum Monthly Expenses	610,474
Maximum Monthly Expenses	808,066
Average Monthly Expenses	695,420

Figure 12.10

Worksheet after additional font changes.

Switch to Allways, and change the row height of row 3 to 3 points by selecting /Worksheet Row Set-Height. Then select /Format Shade Solid and fill in the entire rule to create a handsome separator line that will clearly define the top boundary of the body of the report. Do the same for Rows 10, 22, and 34, but set the row height to 1 point. Finally, create another 3 point rule on line 53, which will serve to define the bottom boundary of the report.

We'll use Allways' line feature to separate the monthly headers, and the shading feature to highlight the various totals. First, let's tend to the monthly headers. Block out the range C5 to N5, which contains the headers, and select /Format Lines Bottom. Allways will separate the headers from the data with a hairline rule. Copy the format to the other three monthly header rows.

Next, paint the range from C8 through N8, which needs to stand out from the rest of the data. Use the /Format Shade Light command to apply a thin dot screen behind the numbers. Repeat this for rows 19 and 31. The results of this formatting and adding the rules are shown in Figure 12.11.

The Title

Next we'll spiff up the title, with a "drop shadow" effect (i.e., a title that appears to float in space, creating a shadow underneath it (see Figure 12.12). In actuality, Allways has no built-in drop shadow capabilities, but you can simulate the effect by using the following technique.

From within 1-2-3, insert a blank row on top of the title, and insert a blank column to the left and right cells containing the title. Make sure that a blank row exists under the title. From within Allways, draw an outline around the title, encompassing the left blank column and the top blank row. Now shrink the column to the right until it is 0.50 characters. Fill the column with a solid shade (/Format Shade Solid) up to the next top row of the outline. You do not want to add solid fill to the very top portion of the column, in order to create a "perspective" appearance. Adjust the row height of the top row so that a fraction of an inch exists between the solid fill and the top of the outline. Next, adjust the row height underneath the outline so that it is approximately 2 points high. Fill the bottom row with a solid fill, but do not extend the fill across the blank column on the left edge of the outline. The effect will be an outline floating in space above the page with the solid fill appearing as a shadow.

Add a Graph

The final touch for this worksheet involves adding the graph shown in Figure 12.12. (We'll use the line graph, since we want to emphasize the trend in the cash position from month to month.) There's a convenient place for the graph on the right side of the report. The graph will give the viewer an instant glimpse of the situation (see Figure 12.12). His or her eye will then be drawn to the highlighted figures, which reveal the details underlying the trend.

ON YOUR OWN

The preceding makeover suggestions were purely subjective—there are few absolutes or "rights" and "wrongs" in spreadsheet publishing. Nevertheless, our makeover does encompass certain guidelines that help ensure balanced looking

WEST SIDE AQUARIUM
Financial Projections

CASH FLOW PROJECTIONS

	Jan	Feb	Mar	Apr	May	Jun	Jul	Aug	Sep	Oct	Nov	Dec
Total Revenues	626,138	698,528	789,715	696,628	752,122	802,801	824,991	788,498	686,803	680,860	696,504	749,953
Total Expenses	610,474	613,612	632,224	680,769	687,184	776,296	808,066	791,744	748,643	681,170	679,000	635,857
NET CASH	$15,665	$84,917	$157,491	$15,859	$64,938	$26,505	$16,925	($3,245)	($61,840)	($310)	$17,504	$114,096

PROJECTED REVENUES

	Jan	Feb	Mar	Apr	May	Jun	Jul	Aug	Sep	Oct	Nov	Dec
Admission fees	75,266	74,734	146,194	161,392	193,792	214,592	220,799	233,859	193,726	207,600	126,585	78,483
Contributions	163,096	176,293	179,630	80,264	90,370	136,930	130,526	115,529	111,550	109,630	91,554	123,830
Government support	241,059	285,932	292,599	253,279	240,812	196,594	212,801	165,000	159,000	157,414	215,926	247,592
Membership dues	111,262	119,259	120,592	159,266	177,400	183,266	186,592	195,059	153,274	147,000	159,260	281,259
Misc	2,860	3,051	4,767	6,674	10,487	18,019	19,068	18,591	15,254	11,279	72,587	2,955
Publications	32,594	39,259	45,933	35,754	39,260	53,400	55,205	60,460	54,000	47,938	30,592	15,834
Total Revenues:	626,138	698,528	789,715	696,628	752,122	802,801	824,991	788,498	686,803	680,860	696,504	749,953
GRAND TOTAL:	$8,793,542											

PROJECTED EXPENSES

	Jan	Feb	Mar	Apr	May	Jun	Jul	Aug	Sep	Oct	Nov	Dec
Main Visitor Center	312,543	312,543	312,543	312,543	367,453	433,222	446,544	412,565	376,655	312,543	312,543	312,543
Dolphin Arena	105,734	118,940	120,589	167,562	105,913	111,659	113,859	115,200	178,858	176,975	178,858	173,387
Gater Pit	26,493	24,374	27,023	28,126	29,672	33,117	30,997	31,792	25,169	24,904	25,169	16,594
Shark Pond	37,459	39,770	41,260	38,473	40,513	37,994	43,407	44,726	46,130	46,199	40,599	27,394
Marine Sciences Center	128,244	117,984	130,809	134,066	143,633	160,305	173,259	187,461	121,832	120,549	121,832	105,940
Fish Feed	902	902	902	902	902	902	902	902	902	902	902	902
Total Expenses:	610,474	613,612	632,224	680,769	687,184	776,296	808,066	791,744	748,643	681,170	679,000	635,857
GRAND TOTAL:	$8,345,039											

STATISTICAL REPORT

Total Annual Revenues	$8,793,542
Total Annual Expenses	$8,345,039
Profit/Loss	$448,504
Minimum Monthly Cash	($61,840)
Maximum Monthly Cash	$157,491
Minimum Monthly Revenues	$626,138
Maximum Monthly Revenues	$824,991
Average Monthly Revenues	$732,795
Minimum Monthly Expenses	$610,474
Maximum Monthly Expenses	$808,066
Average Monthly Expenses	$695,420

Figure 12.11 Worksheet after adding solid rules and the separation of headers and totals.

reports in which important data is highlighted, and that the overall document is framed in an aesthetically pleasing manner.

Above all, be careful about your use of type fonts. As you experiment with your own layouts and designs, keep in mind the following tried and proven graphic design tips regarding the use of typography. Type is more than just a collection of strokes; it is a means of communicating a message. The right choice of type will convey your message forcefully and with the greatest impact; the wrong type or wrong mix of type may result in a spreadsheet document that is hard to read, or worse, not read at all.

WEST SIDE AQUARIUM
Financial Projections

CASH FLOW PROJECTIONS

	Jan	Feb	Mar	Apr	May	Jun	Jul	Aug	Sep	Oct	Nov	Dec
Total Revenues	626,138	698,528	789,715	696,628	752,122	802,801	824,991	788,498	686,803	680,860	696,504	749,953
Total Expenses	610,474	613,612	632,224	680,769	687,184	776,296	808,066	791,744	748,643	681,170	679,000	635,857
NET CASH	$15,665	$84,917	$157,491	$15,859	$64,938	$26,505	$16,925	($3,245)	($61,840)	($310)	$17,504	$114,096

PROJECTED REVENUES

	Jan	Feb	Mar	Apr	May	Jun	Jul	Aug	Sep	Oct	Nov	Dec
Admission fees	75,266	74,734	146,194	161,392	193,792	214,592	220,799	233,859	193,726	207,600	126,585	78,483
Contributions	163,096	176,293	179,630	80,264	90,370	136,930	130,526	115,529	111,550	109,630	91,554	123,830
Government support	241,059	285,932	292,599	253,279	240,812	196,594	212,801	165,000	159,000	157,414	215,926	247,592
Membership dues	111,262	119,259	120,592	159,266	177,400	183,266	186,592	195,059	153,274	147,000	159,260	281,259
Misc	2,860	3,051	4,767	6,674	10,487	18,019	19,068	18,591	15,254	11,279	72,587	2,955
Publications	32,594	39,259	45,933	35,754	39,260	53,400	55,205	60,460	54,000	47,938	30,592	15,834
Total Revenues:	626,138	698,528	789,715	696,628	752,122	802,801	824,991	788,498	686,803	680,860	696,504	749,953
GRAND TOTAL:	$8,793,542											

PROJECTED EXPENSES

	Jan	Feb	Mar	Apr	May	Jun	Jul	Aug	Sep	Oct	Nov	Dec
Main Visitor Center	312,543	312,543	312,543	312,543	367,453	433,222	446,544	412,565	376,655	312,543	312,543	312,543
Dolphin Arena	105,734	118,940	120,589	167,562	105,913	111,659	113,859	115,200	178,858	176,975	178,858	173,387
Gater Pit	26,493	24,374	27,023	28,126	29,672	33,117	30,997	31,792	25,169	24,904	25,169	16,594
Shark Pond	37,459	39,770	41,260	38,473	40,513	37,994	43,407	44,726	46,130	46,199	40,599	27,394
Marine Sciences Center	128,244	117,984	130,809	134,066	143,633	160,305	173,259	187,461	121,832	120,549	121,832	105,940
Fish Feed	902	902	902	902	902	902	902	902	902	902	902	902
Total Expenses:	610,474	613,612	632,224	680,769	687,184	776,296	808,066	791,744	748,643	681,170	679,000	635,857
GRAND TOTAL:	$8,345,039											

STATISTICAL REPORT

Total Annual Revenues	$8,793,542
Total Annual Expenses	$8,345,039
Profit/Loss	$448,504
Minimum Monthly Cash	($61,840)
Maximum Monthly Cash	$157,491
Minimum Monthly Revenues	$626,138
Maximum Monthly Revenues	$824,991
Average Monthly Revenues	$732,795
Minimum Monthly Expenses	$610,474
Maximum Monthly Expenses	$808,066
Average Monthly Expenses	695,420

Figure 12.12 Main title with drop shadow and additional graph augments the usefulness of the report.

The following list of rules for selecting and using type in 1-2-3 reports is by no means exhaustive, but it will get you started in the right direction. (For a basic course in graphic design for non-designers, you might want to take a look at *Instant PageMaker* by Thompson, Randall, and Bennett (Brady), or visit the graphic arts section of your library or bookstore.) In the meantime, consider the following:

1. Select serif typefaces for large blocks of text—they're more readable. For blocks of numerical text, a sans serif face, such as Triumvirate, will be quite readable, and will preserve a tight columnar appearance.
2. Distinguish column and row headings with different weights or sizes of text. When labels and numeric data contrast with text, the distinction makes the page more visually interesting. Contrast is an acceptable way to draw attention to key areas of the report.
3. Use extreme caution when mixing serif typefaces. Unless you've had some experience with graphic design, the best advice for mixing typefaces, especially serif typefaces, is don't. Serif typefaces can clash like uncomplimentary colors. Besides, most type families provide enough variation between the various stroke weights, styles, and sizes to provide visually pleasing and lively 1-2-3 reports.

One exception to this rule is the use of a sans serif typeface for headlines and numeric text. For these purposes, you're best off using a typeface like Triumvirate, which like basic black, goes with almost everything.

Again, there are few rights and wrongs in graphic design, although certain tried and tested ideas, such as those listed above, will maximize your chances of creating a successful report. Above all, experiment and see for yourself what works and what doesn't; after all, success ultimately lies in the eye of the beholder.

Now that you've seen a working model in action, and have followed the step-by-step production of a document using Allways, the final step in this session is to write down the assumptions and the logic that lie behind your current worksheet—this will be invaluable as your skills increase and you create large and intricate models.

DOCUMENTING YOUR WORKSHEETS

Up to now, the models used in this book have been simple and the formulaic connections between cells and ranges has been obvious. As as you develop more complex and larger models whose inner workings are not obvious at first blush, you will want to document the underlying logic and structure in a worksheet "dossier." Whether you keep the dossier in a word processing file, or a paper notebook, or best of all, in a blank area of the worksheet itself, the following kinds of information should be included:

Model Purpose or Function Give a statement of the purpose or function of the model. This is especially important if other people will be using your worksheet—anyone should be able to understand what the model does from this nutshell description. For the aquarium cash flow model, the description might read:

"Projects monthly cash flow based on data from the expense and revenue sections. Line item 45 of the expense sections references FEED.WK1, which uses the /Data Table 2 and Matrix Multiply commands to determine the monthly feed consumption of various inhabitants of the aquarium. The bottom section (A42..C57) contains a statistical analysis based on the data in the worksheet."

Linked Files List any outside worksheet files that are referenced in the main worksheet. In the case of the aquarium file, FEED.WK1 is the only file. You should create a separate set of documentation for the FEED file, since it is a worksheet in its own right.

Range References It is extremely useful to know what each range does and where each range is in your worksheet. Fortunately, 1-2-3 makes it easy to print tables to document your worksheet ranges (with /Range Name Table)—this prints the coordinates of each range, to which you can add your own brief description after the table is created. In our example, the range name table and descriptive notes could appear as follows:

Range Name	Coordinates	Content
CASH	A5..N11	Cash flow areas
EXP	A28..N40	Expense section
EXPTOTAL	C38..N38	Total monthly expenses
NETCASH	C11..N11	Total monthly cash flow
REV	A14..N26	Revenue section
REVTOT	C24..N24	Total monthly revenues
STATS	A42..C57	Statistical analysis area

In addition to using the /Range Name Table command to document your range name addresses, you should also document the information below, without fail. Your efforts will pay off handsomely when you need to modify or debug your worksheet:

1. The purpose, function, or use of the range.
2. Formulas or other ranges that depend on this range.
3. Formulas or ranges on which this range is dependent.
4. Any other significant feature such as the date of last update.

However you decide to document your ranges, the goal is to be able to reconstruct your thinking a week, a month, or a year later if you need to go in and perform surgery on the worksheets that contain the various ranges. Moreover, this is an essential means for conveying the logic and design of your worksheet to others who may follow.

Named Graphs List all named graphs, using the /Graph Name Table command, which lists the graph name, the type (i.e., "B" for bar, "L" for line, and the first line of the title). Add a brief description of what the graph does. For example:

Graph Name	Type	Title	Description
MONTHLY	L	CASH FLOW PROJECTION	Shows net cash
EXPENSES	B	EXPENSE COMPARISON	Compares expense totals
REVENUE	B	REVENUE COMPARISON	Compares total Revenue

Finally, in addition to capturing the above basic information, we recommend creating a worksheet "plumbing chart" for complex models. The chart should show the general flow of information into and out of various files/and or worksheets. You need not be an artist or use complex flow-charting techniques. A simple schematic will suffice. The plumbing chart should complement all of the information in your worksheet dossier, so that it provides a snapshot of the entire model.

Keep the plumbing chart in a notebook nearby, combined with a hard copy of your worksheet "dossier." As you modify or add to the model, you should reprint the dossier and update the plumbing chart.

If all this sounds like a lot of work, consider the Randall-Bennett Law of Memory Drain:

The larger your worksheet, the greater the chance you'll forget what's in it.

So rather than risk a mental Divide Overflow error, write down the worksheet essentials and print them out. A year from now when you go back and modify your twenty-one file model, you'll thank yourself. Again and again and again.

If you've worked through the tutorial and/or this chapter, you're ready to tackle macros, which enable you execute complex series of keystrokes with a single command or key combination. The next chapter gives you an in-depth course into the use and construction of macros. Following the macro section, you'll find an exhaustive reference section that contains information about every single 1-2-3 command. This should serve as a guide when you've graduated from this book; even the most advanced 1-2-3 aficionados forget a command or two occasionally, so don't worry about learning everything in one sitting—you can't, and more importantly, you don't need to. Start with the subset of commands and functions you know, and add to that repertoire as your needs require, supplementing your hands-on knowledge with the Reference section.

Using Macros With Release 2.2

INTRODUCTION TO MACROS

One of the most powerful features of 1-2-3 is its macro language. In their simplest form, macros serve as "typing alternatives" that greatly facilitate data entry.

For example, a macro can be written that automatically inserts the words "Robert L. Smith" every time ALT-S is pressed. Likewise, the combination ALT-F could be designated to insert the phrase, "FY 1987" into the current (or otherwise designated) cell. Obviously, pressing ALT plus a key is much faster than typing out entire words or phrases.

In the same fashion, 1-2-3 macros can be used to quickly enter a sequence of 1-2-3 commands. Simply enter the commands or their special macro representations into a text cell and assign the cell a macro range name or a special macro-starting name that consists of ALT plus an alphabetic key. Thereafter, you can execute the sequence of commands by pressing the macro ALT-key combination. Alternatively, you can use the RUN (ALT-F3) key to run a macro that has been assigned a range name (more on this later).

For example, suppose you were constantly formatting individual cells in a worksheet for currency format with no decimal places. The command sequence would be:

```
/Range Format Currency 0 ENTER ENTER
```

This action requires seven keystrokes for each occurrence. Wouldn't it be easier to create a macro that performs the same function almost instantly when you press, say, the ALT-C combination?

There's no "magic" to this formatting trick. You need only enter the same commands into a single cell, assign it a special macro starting key combination, and you're all set. To create the macro, you would enter the following sequence:

```
/rfc0~~
```

where the tilde (~) is the special character representing the ENTER key.

Once you've entered the cell contents, you will need to assign the cell a special macro starting name. These are any of the 26 letters of the alphabet preceded by a backslash (\). For example, you could assign the above macro the name \C by using the /Range Name command, entering:

```
\C
```

and then highlighting the cell that includes the macro keystrokes. Each time you press ALT-C, 1-2-3 would invoke the currency formatting command.

Mimicking Keystrokes, Introducing Special Commands

As you can see from the simple example above, the keystrokes used in macros can be identical to those used when you enter commands from the keyboard. In addition, 1-2-3 provides equivalents for the cursor keys {UP}, {DOWN}, {RIGHT}, and {LEFT}, for each function key, as well as for special advanced commands that can only be executed from within a macro. These special commands can prompt users for data to be entered in specific cells, generate menu structures that execute custom-designed command sequences, control the screen (freeze or clear the control panel, turn off the row and column borders, etc.), and carry out many other functions that cannot be done with standard keyboard commands.

Here's a sampling of some of the types of commands available in the macro language. (A complete listing of all macro commands and keystrokes can be found in Tables 1, 2, and 3.)

{EDIT} = (F2) When {EDIT} is used in a macro, the contents of a cell are displayed above the control panel and 1-2-3 enters the EDIT mode. For example, a macro might have the line:

```
{RIGHT}{DOWN}{EDIT}
```

This would move the pointer one cell to the right, then one cell down, and display the contents of that cell in the control panel for editing. If a formula is in the cell and you wanted to recalculate just that cell, you would add a tilde at the end of the line, as in:

```
{RIGHT}{DOWN}{EDIT}~
```

Now you have a macro that recalculates the formula occupying the cell one cell down and to the right of the current position.

{GOTO}=(F5) Just as the (F5) key is a convenient shortcut for moving the pointer to a desired cell location, the {GOTO} macro command can be embedded in a macro to move the pointer without indicating a specific pattern of {RIGHT},{LEFT}, {DOWN}, etc. The {GOTO} command is followed by a cell address or name, as in:

`{GOTO}D45~{EDIT}~` or `{GOTO}RANGENAME~{EDIT}~`

which would move the cursor to cell D45 or the top left of the range named RANGENAME and then recalculate the formula in that cell.

{CALC}=(F9) Use this command when you want the macro to recalculate the worksheet when it is set for manual calculation. This is especially useful in macros that initiate printing, to ensure that all calculations are updated before the print job is started. For example, the macro:

```
{CALC}/pprDATA~agpq
```

tells 1-2-3 to first recalculate the worksheet, then select the print range called DATA, align the printer, and then begin printing.

{BS}=(Backspace) The {BS} command has two uses in macros. Its primary use is to delete the character to the left of the cursor position when you are in the EDIT mode. It can also be used to clear the current range setting when you are redefining a range name or specifying a range to print or graph. This latter technique is frequently used to define the cell pointer location at the start of a macro so that it can be returned at the conclusion as in:

```
/rncHERE~{BS}~
```

which defines the current cell as the range named "HERE," regardless of the previous definition of "HERE."

{DEL}=(Del) Use this command to delete characters above the cursor. The {DEL} command is often used in macros to strip off the leading label prefix and turn a label into a value as in:

```
{EDIT}{HOME}{DEL}~
```

{ESC}=(Esc) You can use the {ESC} command to "back out of" or cancel a command or clear the control panel, as in:

```
/ppag{ESC}{ESC}{ESC}
```

It is also useful in combination with the {?} pause for displaying messages as in:

```
'Position cell pointer and press ENTER to continue
{?}{ESC}
```

{?} The bracketed question mark causes the macro to pause for a user's input, followed by ENTER. The most common use for {?} is for user responses to prompts or range specifications for command sequences as in:

```
/ppr{BS}{?}~agpq
```

which prompts the user to type in or "paint" the range to be printed, and then executes the print command.

Thinking in Macro Logic

As with any programming language, 1-2-3 macros have an underlying structure or grammar. It is essential that you begin to think in terms of the underlying logic in order to obtain the best results from 1-2-3's macro language. With the exception of some of its special functions, which are described in detail later, all the commands used in a macro are identical to those that are available to you via the keyboard and 1-2-3 menus. When you run a macro, you are instructing 1-2-3 to execute the specified commands exactly as if you had entered them manually.

The key to "macro-thinking" is to understand how to accomplish the desired objective using the command menus. If, for example, you wanted to enter the phrase "Gross National Product" repeatedly in a spreadsheet, you could create a simple typing macro as follows:

```
\G  Gross National Product~
```

In this example, \G represents the macro starting range name assigned to the cell to its right, and the ~ (tilde) is the special macro symbol for ENTER. To execute this macro, you would place the cell pointer on the desired cell and press the macro initiator ALT-G key combination.

It is easy to see the logic of the macro because it clearly parallels the process that you would use to enter the phrase manually: You would begin by typing the phrase and conclude by pressing the ENTER key. The macro represents the same two steps.

If you wanted to create a more complicated macro, say, one that moves the cursor to the upper right-hand corner of the active area of the worksheet, you must first think of the process you would use to perform the task manually and then enter those steps into the macro. To move the cell pointer to the upper right-hand corner, try the following procedure:

1. Move the cell pointer to the bottom right-hand corner of the worksheet by pressing the END-HOME key combination.
2. Move the cell pointer one column to the right, which *must* be blank, since it is outside the active area of the worksheet. Do this by pressing the → cursor key.
3. Move the cell pointer to the top row of the worksheet by pressing the END-↑ key combination. This will move the cursor to the top row because the current column is blank. If it wasn't blank, the cell pointer may be stopped prior to reaching the top row.
4. Finally, move the cell pointer back to the last column of the active worksheet, by moving it one column to the left by pressing the ← cursor key.

To create a macro that could perform this task repeatedly upon demand, enter the corresponding macro commands into the worksheet and assign them a macro name. See Figure 13.1. Thereafter, you could move the cell pointer to the upper-right corner of the worksheet, by simply pressing the ALT-U key combination assigned to this macro.

Note that each keystroke in the macro was entered in a separate cell in a column. It could have been entered in a single cell and produced the same results. The practice of separating the individual steps of the macro into individual lines in the worksheet however, makes the logic crystal clear and makes it easier to debug complex macros. Also, note how the macro uses the commands available to it in a creative fashion that will perform as expected under all conditions.

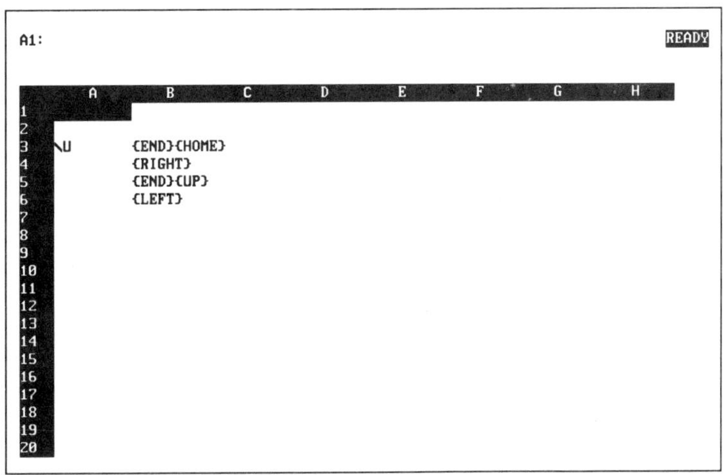

Figure 13.1
Simple movement macro.

The final step in creating a macro is to test it under a variety of expected and unexpected conditions. The extent of your testing will depend on the potential havoc that the macro might wreak on your worksheet once it's turned loose on live data. For example, a macro that moves, copies, or erases data should be tested under all possible scenarios.

WHEN NOT TO USE MACROS

Macros can be used to perform many different types of functions. In general, they should be used when you need to perform a particular task repeatedly or when it is important to perform a particular series of tasks in a precise sequence. In the former case, the macro permits you to quickly repeat the steps at the touch of only two keys. In the latter context, a macro permits you to carefully create a complex sequence of keystrokes, save them, and then test the results until you are certain that they produce the desired results every time.

Macros can also produce some results that you cannot perform manually. The macro menu commands, for example, allow you to create custom 1-2-3 style menus with your own designated options and commands. By using menus designed for a particular application, you can create complex application templates that perform specific tasks or calculations totally under your control. The user makes selections from the custom menus or enters data under the cursor control of the macro. Such prompted data entry commands allow you to specifically request data from the user and then test that data for reasonableness prior to actually placing it in the worksheet and using it as the basis for calculations.

While it is easy to see that there are many applications that can be run under macro control, not *all* situations warrant a macro. In fact, there are often unexpected liabilities that macros bring to the worksheet, such as a reduction in processing speed. While simple macros appear to be virtually instantaneous, they actually perform their tasks relatively slowly by computer standards. This is because they are "interpretive commands." In other words, 1-2-3 must translate the English command into a computer-executable command each time the macro is performed. This process can degrade performance if 1-2-3 must go through the same sequence many times to produce a particular result. It is often better to try to obtain the desired results by formula rather than by macro. For example, suppose that you created a worksheet that contained a column of numbers representing account balances. Also suppose that you wanted to highlight those accounts that contained a negative balance. You could construct the macro in Figure 13.2, which tests each value in column C and places the flag "OVER-DRAWN" in column D for those accounts with negative balances. The logic in this macro is as follows:

1. Place the cell pointer at the top of the data in column C.
2. Name the current cell and the cell below it as a two-cell range named "HERE". This will be used for the end of data test later in steps 5 and 6. The {BS} command clears any previous definition of the range name "HERE".
3. Name the current cell "HERE2" for the subsequent {IF} test, then move the cell pointer to the column D and erase any current message. This is necessary so that previous "OVER-DRAWN" messages can be erased prior to retesting the balance.
4. Test the value of the current cell (HERE2). If it is less than zero (i.e., negative), move to column D and insert the message "OVER-DRAWN" and then move back to column C.
5. Move the cell pointer down a row and test for the end of data. The test looks for the presence of a blank cell in the range named "HERE" by testing the @COUNT value. If one of the two cells in the range "HERE" is blank, the count will equal 1. Otherwise, it will equal 2. Note that it is necessary to test a two-cell range because of a quirk in 1-2-3 that causes a single blank cell to count as 1. If the end of the data has been reached, the macro deletes the range names "HERE" and "HERE2," returns to the top of column C, and quits.

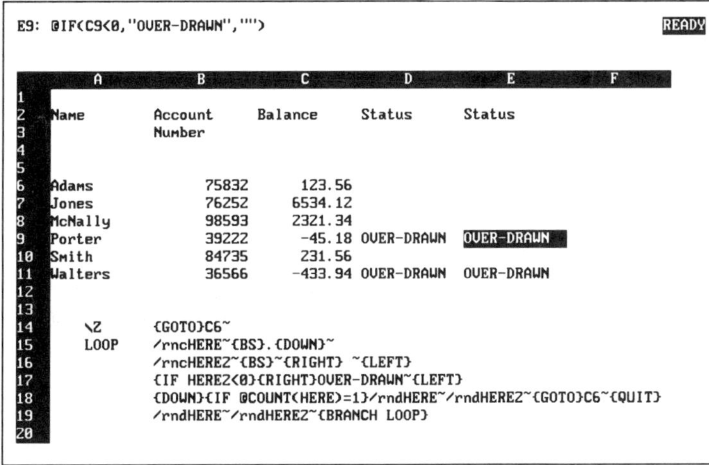

Figure 13.2
Irrational Looping Macro.

6. If there is more data, it deletes the name “HERE” and loops back to the beginning to test the next value.

On an IBM AT, running at 8 MHz, this macro took almost 17 seconds and processed only 6 records. If the table contained 1000 records, the process would take about 45 minutes. By comparison, the cell E6 contains a simple formula:

```
@IF(C6<0,"OVER-DRAWN","")
```

which accomplishes the same results virtually instantaneously. And since it is a formula, it is automatically recalculated each time the variables change, unless you have set recalculation to manual.

As you can see, there are cases when macros are not the best solution. Therefore, whenever you are about to write an extremely complex macro, first consider the alternatives of achieving your goal with the built-in commands and formulas at your disposal.

TYPES OF MACROS

Macros tend to fall into three basic categories. The first are macros whose function is to quickly execute a series of keystrokes. These might be macros for typing frequently used words or phases, or macros that select a sequence of options from the 1-2-3 menu. Examples would be macros that automatically align the printer and print the current print range, or macros that total the column above the cell pointer.

The second category of macros include those that branch to separate processes, depending on the value or contents of a particular cell. These macros differ from the first category in that they perform a logical branch as they operate. Typical of the second type of macro would be macros that perform data verification tests that test the value of data input by the worksheet user and report any errors. The 1-2-3 menu macros are branching macros. In this case, the logic for the branching process is provided by the user when he makes a menu selection.

The third category of macros includes iterative or looping macros. These macros perform the same sequence of tasks for a specified number of times either by counting the iterations or by testing for the end of data to process. Data conversion or testing macros are typical of the third type. The “OVER-DRAWN” flag example described above is an example of the looping macro.

Let’s consider these various types of macros in more detail.

Basic Macros

Simple macros can be as short as a single word or several lines long. The key is that they perform a simple series of consecutive tasks, either entering information, moving the cell pointer, or selecting options from the 1-2-3 menus. The following are examples of each of these:

```
\U  United States of America
```

By pressing the macro initiator ALT-U, you will enter the phrase United States of America in the current cell.

Pressing the macro initiator ALT-D will move the cell pointer down five rows.

```
\D  {DOWN 5}
```

This macro moves through the regular sequence of menu commands— /Print Printer Align Go Quit—to print the current range.

```
\P  /ppagq
```

Branching Macros

Branching macros differ from simple macros in their ability to perform different tasks, depending on the value of a given cell or range. They also include macros that branch according to user input or menu selection. Menu macros will be discussed in detail later on. Here, we'll look at branching by value testing, which entails testing the value of any cell or range against a fixed value or the value of another cell or range. It is also possible to create an IF-THEN-ELSE branching macro or simply an IF-THEN branch.

1-2-3 macros branch via the use of an {IF} or a {BRANCH} command. The {BRANCH} command is also referred to as an *absolute* branch since it branches without testing, while the {IF} command is used for *conditional* branching, depending on the values being tested.

As its name implies, conditional branching operates by comparing two values and then performing one of two actions depending on the comparison. With 1-2-3, the structure of the command is as follows:

```
\Z  {IF condition} AFFIRMATIVE ACTION
    NEGATIVE ACTION
```

where the action to perform under true conditions follows the test on the same line as the IF command, and the alternative action follows on the line below. The condition of the test can take any valid numerical or string comparison. If the condition is true, the test branches to the affirmative action. If it is false, it skips the affirmative action and proceeds to the negative action on the line below it.

The OVER-DRAWN macro described above demonstrates two common uses of IF-THEN branching logic.

1. `{GOTO}C6~`
2. `/rncHERE~{BS}.{DOWN}~`
3. `/rncHERE2~{BS}~{RIGHT} ~{LEFT}`
4. `{IF HERE2<0}{RIGHT}OVER-DRAWN~{LEFT}`
5. `{DOWN}{IF@COUNT(HERE)=1}/rndHERE~/rndHERE2~{GOTO}C6~{QUIT}`
6. `/rndHERE~/rndHERE2~{BRANCH LOOP}`

Lines 1 through 3 position the cursor. Line 4 shows a simple value comparison. If the value of the range "HERE2" is negative, the macro will perform the steps to the right of the test. Since the affirmative test does not contain a secondary branching statement, the macro will continue to perform the negative action upon completion of the affirmative action. This is often referred to as an IF-THEN branch.

Line 5 demonstrates an IF-THEN-ELSE branch. In this case, the affirmative action contains an absolute branch away from the negative action in line 6. The {QUIT} command terminates the macro as soon as a positive test is reached in line 5.

NOTE: If the affirmative action does not explicitly branch away from the negative action with a {BRANCH}, {RETURN}, or {QUIT} command, the macro will proceed to process the negative action after the affirmative action, since it is on the next line of the macro. This may not be a desired result. You must be sure of your intent and include or exclude such a secondary branch as necessary.

Looping Macros

The OVER-DRAWN macro also demonstrates the principal idea behind the looping macro. There are two basic types of looping macros: those that repeat a specific number of times, and those that continue until they hit a boundary or run out of data. It is also possible to create an endlessly looping macro that will continue until a conditional branch within the loop branches out of the loop, or you stop it by pressing ESC or CTRL-BREAK.

The OVER-DRAWN macro runs until it reaches a blank cell indicating that it has run out of data. This is a very common macro technique that uses an {IF}

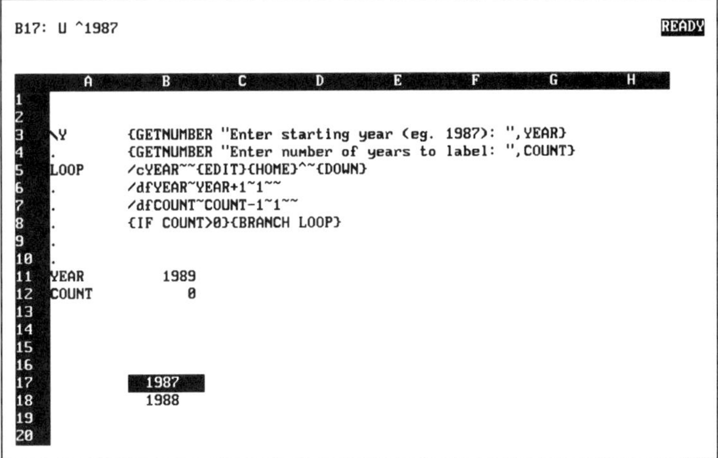

Figure 13.3
Looping Macro.

branch to test for the end of the data as indicated by the @COUNT(HERE) value. If the count of the two-cell range, "HERE," equals 1, then the bottom cell must be blank, indicating that the macro has reached the end of the data. When the test is true, the macro quits; otherwise, it branches back to the beginning. Note that the macro doesn't go all the way to the top, but only to the beginning of the portion that you want to repeat. If the macro had branched to the very top, it would reposition the cell pointer at the top of the column of data each time it looped and would go nowhere.

The second form of looping macros cycles for a specific number of times. This is usually accomplished by storing a counter in a named range and incrementing it once during each iteration of the loop until it reaches a specified value, and thus terminates the macro. The macro shown in Figure 13.3 inserts a column of year labels starting in the current cell and continuing for as many years as specified by the user.

This macro asks the user to supply the starting date and the total number of dates to be entered. It places these values in data ranges called YEAR and COUNT. It then copies the value from the range called YEAR into the current cell and converts it to a centered label. Now comes the tricky part: By using the /Data Fill command, the macro replaces the value in the range YEAR with the previous value plus one, thereby incrementing it to the next year. Then, again using the /Data Fill command, the macro decrements the value in the range COUNT. Finally, the macro performs the loop test. If the value in the range COUNT is greater than zero, the macro branches back to the top.

The looping point is *not* the very beginning of the macro since you do not need to re-enter the starting data. By testing a decrementing counter for greater than zero, the process will continue until the initial value is consumed. In this example, the initial value is set by the user in step 2. It is also possible to have the macro set the initial value directly if the value will always be the same.

For example, suppose you wanted to create a table that contained data for each of the twelve months of the year. You could create a looping macro that would be preset to iterate 12 times, once for each month of the year. While it is possible to increment the counter and test against the desired value (either fixed or user supplied), this is slower than testing a single cell against zero.

Another way to create looping macros is to use the {FOR} command with a subroutine. The {FOR} command allows you to specify the starting count, ending count, and the step increment. It then performs the designated subroutine repeatedly until the counter exceeds the stop count, after which it returns control to the command following the {FOR} command.

Menu Macros

One of the major benefits of 1-2-3's macro capability is its ability to create menu structures in the same format as the 1-2-3 command menu. This allows developers to create templates with the familiar Lotus-style menu. The menu macros are set up in the same fashion as above, but use the special macro command:

```
{MENUBRANCH menu-name}
```

to initiate the menu macro.

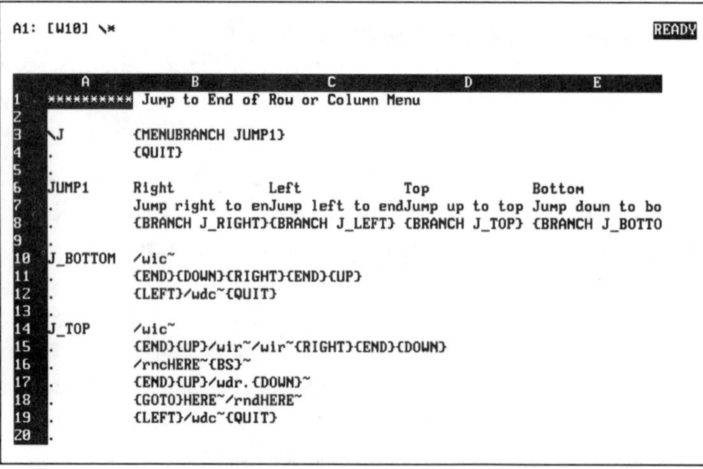

Figure 13.4
Menu Macro.

Figure 13.4 shows a menu macro that allows the user to select between four cursor movement commands that move the cursor to the end of the current row or column without regard to intervening blank cells. The figure includes the menu and two of the four subroutines. Notice that the menu appears in the top two lines of the control box in the same fashion as the regular 1-2-3 command menu. By selecting one of the options, either by pointing or pressing its first letter, you will initiate the appropriate subroutine listed below the menu option.

Self-Modifying Macros

One of the unique programming techniques for 1-2-3 macros is self-modification. Since a macro is nothing more than a series of special text cells in the worksheet, they can be modified during the execution of the macro, which in turn will alter the actions of subsequent steps. A simple example of this is shown in Figure 13.5.

This macro duplicates the GOTO (F5) key; it asks the user to enter the name or address of the cell he wants to move to and then moves the cell pointer there. The key feature of this macro is that it places the results of the initial request into the body of the macro and uses it as the object for the {GOTO} command. In this fashion, the macro modifies itself. The actual code of the macro is altered by the macro as part of its operation. The modified code is then executed. Relying on user data input to modify the code of a macro is a very common macro technique in 1-2-3.

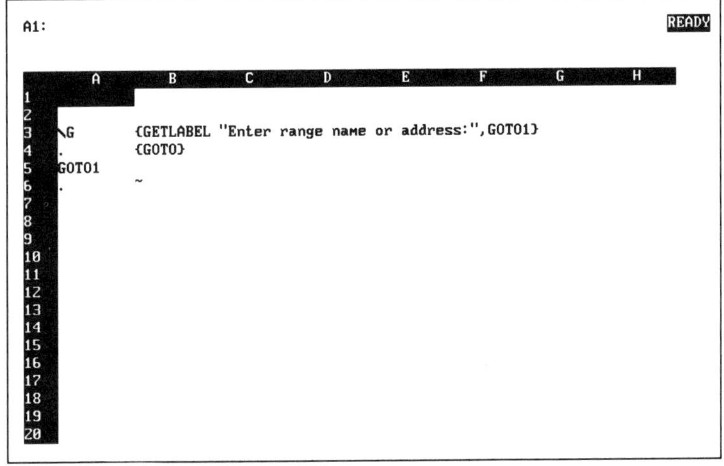

Figure 13.5
Self-modifying Macro.

Toggle Macros

One of the benefits of using macros in 1-2-3 is that macros can anticipate the next logical request of the user and prepare to handle the command. For example, if the user requests that 1-2-3 shift into manual recalculation mode, the most likely following command regarding recalculation mode would be to shift it back to automatic. Another example would be the command to lock the titles in a worksheet; the next logical command would be to unlock them. The problem with each of these is that they are commands that are several steps long, and the command to undo the initial command is different than the initial command. Wouldn't it be helpful if you could set up a macro "smart" enough to realize that after toggling a feature on, the next time it is called it should toggle the feature off? Figure 13.6 shows one such macro for the recalculation mode toggle.

Notice that the macro has one action cell and two data cells. As the last step of each command sequence, the macro copies the opposite command into the action cell. The next time the macro is called, the opposite command will be executed and the action cell reset for the first command again. While this toggle macro is very simple, it is possible to create an extremely complex macro using the same technique. For example, the toggle command could branch to entirely different subroutines by toggling the {BRANCH} commands. It is also possible to include more than two commands, so long as they proceed in sequence.

This concludes our tour of the various types of macros. Now we'll consider the process of actually writing macros.

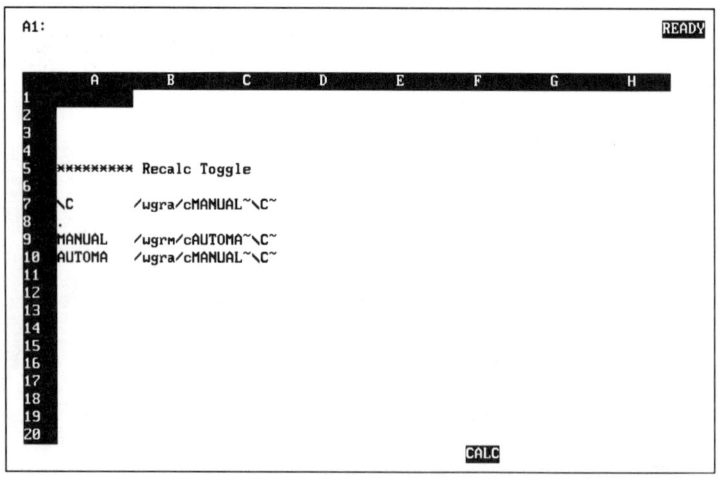

Figure 13.6
Toggle Macro.

WRITING MACROS

Creating Macros Automatically

While previous versions of 1-2-3 had their own macro language, Release 2.2 adds a new twist; the Learn feature. While in macro LEARN mode, 1-2-3 will "watch over your shoulder" and record your keystrokes for you, writing them to a designated range of cells in the current worksheet. The Learn feature requires two steps—first you must designate a learn range in which to store the captured keystrokes and then you must activate the LEARN mode by pressing the LEARN key (ALT-F2).

The Learn feature is extremely useful for creating simple cursor movement and typing macros, where simple repetition is all that is desired. It can also be used to create the basis of more complex macros since the resulting learn range can be edited to correct errors or add any of the advanced macro commands.

To use the Learn feature, you must first define a learn range by selecting /Worksheet Learn. You should define a range that is one column wide and as many cells long as the steps you intend to record. After you have defined the range, you can turn on the Learn feature whenever you are ready to start recording by pressing ALT-F5. 1-2-3 will record each entry you make in a separate cell of the learn range until you turn off the Learn feature by pressing ALT-F5 a second time, cancel the current learn range, or completely fill the current learn range.

To replay the captured keystrokes, name the first cell of the learn range with a macro range name as you would any macro and then start it either directly (with one of the special macro-starting names i.e., \A for ALT-A) or indirectly with the RUN (ALT-F3) key. You can edit the captured keystrokes as you would any cell with the EDIT (F2) key and insert or delete cells from the range.

For example, to capture the keystrokes to move the cell pointer to the upper rightmost cell in the active portion of the worksheet:

1. Find a free area of the current worksheet below or to the right of the data, to be used for the learn range. It should be at least 10 rows long.
2. Designate the learn range by selecting /Worksheet Learn Range and painting the range or entering its address.
3. Activate the Learn feature by pressing ALT-F5.
4. Execute the desired steps of the macro by pressing in sequence:

END-HOME	To move to the bottom right of the active worksheet.
→	To move to the next open column (outside the active area).
END-↑	To move to the top of the worksheet.
←	To move back into the active area of the worksheet.

5. Press ALT-F5 to turn off the Learn feature.
6. Name the top cell of the learn range with the special macro starting name \R, to permit its initiation by pressing ALT-R. Use the /Range Name Create command.
7. Test the new macro. Press the HOME key to place the cell pointer in cell A1 and then initiate the macro with ALT-R. The cell pointer should move to the upper-right corner of the active area of the worksheet.

If you run out of room in the learn range while recording a macro, 1-2-3 will display the error message "Learn range is full". You can increase the size of the learn range without losing any keystrokes, by immediately pressing ESC to clear the error message and then redefining the learn range to a larger size by selecting /Worksheet Learn Range, and restarting the Learn feature. Do not delete the learn range column while in LEARN mode, otherwise 1-2-3 will terminate LEARN mode.

Note that the LEARN mode captures the keystrokes as they are executed on the current worksheet. This is usually helpful, since the current worksheet will be modified as if the macro were being executed upon it. This can produce a problem if you make an error that damages the current worksheet, or that affects the learn range. Be sure that you save your worksheet before activating LEARN mode.

Entering Macros Manually

Label Prefix When you enter a macro into a worksheet you are simply entering a series of ordinary text cells that have been assigned a special macro initiator name as a range name. Since macros are text cells, it is necessary to ensure that they are given a label prefix if they do not start with a letter. This is especially important if the cell starts with a 1-2-3 command beginning with a slash (/) command. If you forget to enter the label prefix, 1-2-3 will bring up the main menu when you press the (/) key, causing the steps of your macro to be executed immediately rather than entered into the cell as intended. Since the label prefix does not appear in the 1-2-3 display, we will generally not include it in illustrations of specific macros; just don't forget that it needs to be there.

Multiple Cell Macros To enter a multiple cell macro, you must enter the individual cells into a single continuous column of text cells. The macro will continue to process cells in the column until it reaches a blank cell. When naming the macro with a macro initiator, it is only necessary to name the top cell of the column. The two exceptions to the single column rule are menu macros, which can be up to eight columns wide, and data cells, which can be located anywhere as long as they are assigned range names.

As your macros become more complex and use logical branching, menus, self-modification, and looping, it will become more important to follow strict

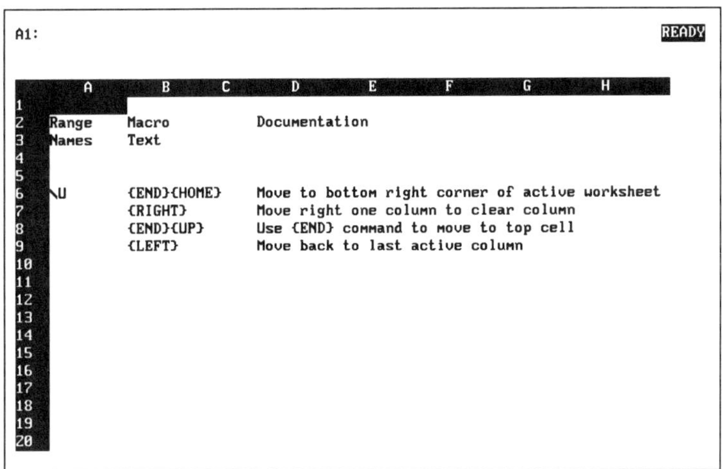

Figure 13.7 Macro Documentation.

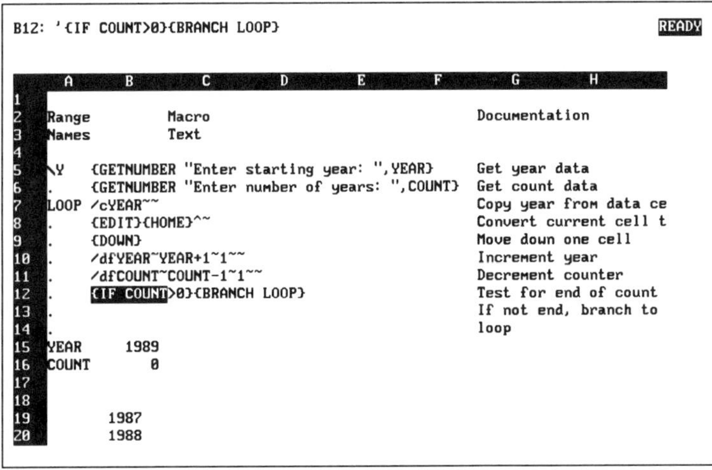

Figure 13.8 Macro Layout.

rules of structure to permit easier understanding of the logic. Branching will also dictate the need for blank lines separating the different sections of macro code associated with each branch.

1-2-3 provides a very useful command for naming ranges: /Range Name Labels Right. This command causes 1-2-3 to name the cell to the right of the current cell with the name contained in the current cell. This means that you should place all range names, including the special macro initiator name, in the column to the left of the actual macro text. Following the same logic, it is a good practice to place any text documenting your macros in a column to the right of the macro text. Figure 13.7 shows the macro that moves the cell pointer to the upper right-hand corner of the active area of the worksheet. Note that the range name is placed in column A, the macro in column B, and the documentation in column D.

With more complex macros, it is often difficult to fit all three columns of text on a single screen. You might have to cursor over to the documentation to read it. (See Figure 13.8.) In any case, establish a rational structure and stick to it.

Special Characters Since macros are entered as text files, you will encounter some keyboard commands that are not normally associated with text characters. For example, 1-2-3 has established the convention of using the tilde (~) character in macros to represent the ENTER key.

For example, the macro to enter the words "United States of America" in the current cell must end with an ENTER. It would be typed in as follows.

```
\U   'United States of America~
```

where the terminal tilde (~) represents the ENTER.

The same convention applies to menu options, where pressing the ENTER key selects the default option. For example, if you want to create a macro to set the format of the current cell to currency with two decimal places, you could write the macro as follows:

```
\C   '/rfc~~
```

where the first tilde (~) selects the default decimal setting of two decimal places and the second tilde (~) selects the default location as the current cell.

While the tilde convention seems quite simple, it can cause problems for new macro users. It is so simple that it is very easy to forget. If you forget to include a tilde as the terminator for one command, it will continue to read the next statement of the macro as part of the current command. This can produce some truly bizarre results that can be very hard to debug. In addition to the special tilde character for the ENTER key, there are other special macro commands for the many special function keys. Table 13.1 lists the keyboard commands and their purpose. They break down into three types: function keys, editing keys, and cursor movement keys.

To enter one of the special 1-2-3 macro commands into a macro, type the command surrounded by the curly brackets {} into the text cell of the macro. The command will be executed as if you had pressed the equivalent key at that point in the execution of the macro. 1-2-3 recognizes the curly bracket as a text character. Therefore, it is not necessary to precede it with a label prefix when entering a special macro command as the first character of a cell.

Selecting 1-2-3 Menu Options

It is possible to include any of the 1-2-3 menu commands and options in your macros. To do so, include the first letter of the command as a method of selecting that option. You must precede the menu selection with the slash character (/), which instructs 1-2-3 to bring up the main menu. (If the slash is the first character in a macro cell, don't forget to precede it with a label prefix.) To enter the command sequence to format the current cell as currency with zero decimal places, you would enter the commands: /Range Format Currency, then select zero decimal places by entering a 0 and finally select the default range as the current cell by pressing the ENTER key. To enter this sequence of commands as a macro, you would type in only the first letter of each command as follows:

```
\C   '/rfc0~
```

Note the label prefix, the initial slash command, the first letters of the three level of the menu, the entry of the 0 for the number of decimal places and the tilde (~) for the final ENTER. You can also select various commands from the main menu by pointing to them and pressing the ENTER key. The same applies to macro commands, so it would be possible to enter the same macro as:

```
\C   '/{RIGHT}~~{RIGHT}{RIGHT}~0~
```

where the first {RIGHT} and the first tilde select the command, Range, which is the second command from the left of the main menu. The second tilde selects the leftmost command of the range submenu or the Format command. Finally, the last two {RIGHT}s and the next tilde select the Currency option from the Format menu; the 0 and the final tilde act as before. While it is possible to create a macro in this fashion, we strongly urge against it as it depends on 1-2-3 maintaining consistent menu structures in the future (almost impossible for them to guarantee) and makes the resulting macros almost impossible to debug. After a while, you will be able to read /RFC0~ as clearly as English, but no one can read /{RIGHT}~~{RIGHT}{RIGHT}~0~ as anything but gibberish.

Table 13.1: Keyboard Macro Commands

Keystroke	Command
(↓)	{DOWN} or {D}
(↑)	{UP} or {U}
(←)	{LEFT} or {L}
(→)	{RIGHT} or {R}
ABS (F4)	{ABS}
APP1 (ALT-F7)	{APP1}
APP2 (ALT-F8)	{APP2}
APP3 (ALT-F9)	{APP3}
BACKSPACE	{BACKSPACE} or {BS}
BACKTAB	{BIGLEFT}
BIG LEFT (CTRL-←)	{BIGLEFT}
BIG RIGHT (CTRL-→)	{BIGRIGHT}
CALC (F9)	{CALC}
CTRL-BREAK	{BREAK}
DEL	{DELETE}
EDIT (F2)	{EDIT}
END	{END}
ENTER	~ (tilde)
ESC	{ESCAPE} or {ESC}
GOTO (F5)	{GOTO}
GRAPH (F10)	{GRAPH}
HELP (F1)	{HELP}
HOME	{HOME}
INS	{INSERT}
NAME (F3)	{NAME}
PgDn	{PGDN}
PgUp	{PGUP}
QUERY (F7)	{QUERY}
TABLE (F8)	{TABLE}
{WINDOW} (F6)	{WINDOW}
/	/ or < or {MENU}
<	/ or < or {MENU}
~	{~}
{	{{}
}	{}}

Placing Macros in Your Worksheet

As with previous releases of 1-2-3, there are several different theories for the best location to place a macro in a worksheet, e.g., below and to the right, starting in cell AA1, upper left of the worksheet, below the active area of the worksheet. The primary concern in locating a macro is that it not be damaged by the worksheet user inserting or deleting rows or columns of data. Obviously, deleting a row that contains part of a macro will damage the macro. Inserting a blank row into a macro will also damage it by causing it to terminate prematurely. In the same fashion, inserting or deleting columns might damage a macro placed below the active area of the worksheet.

With Release 2.2 there is a new option nicknamed Hyperspace. The Macro Library Manager add-in allows you to store your common macros in a part of memory and in a special file on disk so that you can use them with any worksheet. Equally important, they cannot be damaged by actions performed in the current worksheet. They can even be used to erase the current worksheet or load another—an action that is impossible for macros stored within a specific worksheet.

The Macro Library Manager is a 1-2-3 add-in that allows you to store one or more macros or other named ranges (containing data or formulas) in a special part of memory and in special library files. You can store up to 16,376 cells in each library file and can load as many as 10 library files into memory at the same time. In general, you will want to create individual library files that contain common or related macros or data.

Once you have saved a macro to a library file and/or have loaded a previously saved file into memory, the named macros within that library are available for use as if they were contained in the current worksheet. However, since they are not physically located within the current worksheet, they cannot be damaged by actions within the current worksheet.

Let's look at a pair of simple macros that are generally hazardous to themselves (as well as other macros within the current worksheet)—they insert and delete rows. We will create them in the current worksheet, save them to a macro library called UTILITY.MLB, and then try executing them within the current worksheet. This example assumes that you have properly installed the Macro Library Manager add-in.

1. Start with an empty worksheet by selecting the command /Worksheet Erase Yes.
2. Enter the first macro in cells A1 and B1. We will place the macro name in cell A1 and the macro itself in cell B1.

3. Enter the second macro in cells A3 and B3. Remember to skip a row between the macros so that the INSERT macro doesn't flow into the DELETE macro. See Figure 13.9.
4. Assign a macro range name to each of the macros. You can assign single letter macro starting names or more revealing text names. Since these macros are potentially destructive we recommend assigning them text names. We have placed the names in Column A; this lets us use the /Range Name Labels Right command to assign the names to the cells in column B.
5. Invoke the Macro Library Manager by pressing its assigned Add-In key (e.g., ALT-F8). At the main Macro Library Manager menu, select Save, specify a macro library name, `UTILITY`, and press ENTER.
6. Specify the range to save to the library by typing `A1..B3`, and press ENTER. Select whether you want to assign a password to the library or not.
7. Notice that as the macros are saved to the library they are removed from the current worksheet. You can recall them with the Edit command on the Macro Library Manager menu.
8. Now comes the fun part. Type a label in cell A1 so that you can keep track of the cell (e.g., "This is cell A1"). Then run the INSERT macro by pressing the RUN key (ALT-F3), highlighting the INSERT macro name on the list, and pressing ENTER. You see that cell A1 has moved down to cell A2 because a new row has been inserted. Now try running the

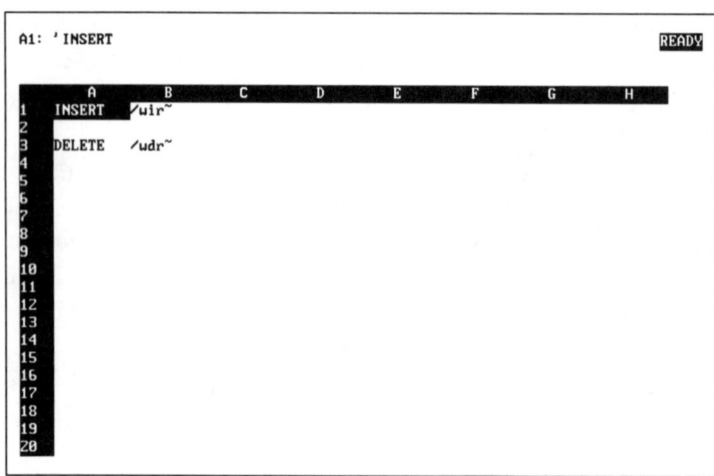

Figure 13.9
INSERT and DELETE macros before saving to library.

DELETE macro to delete row 1. Notice that the cell in A2 has moved back to cell A1. Try the DELETE macro once again and delete the row containing the label.

The use of the Macro Library Manager is much more powerful and sophisticated than this simple example warrants. For more ideas on how to use this new feature to its fullest potential, refer to the Macro Library Manager discussion under the /Add-In section of the Reference guide.

Naming Macros

You can assign up to 26 different macros a special macro initiator name. These macro initiator names consist of the backslash key followed by one of the 26 letters of the alphabet. The names are special because you can execute the macro simply by pressing the ALT key in combination with the assigned letter of the alphabet.

In Release 2.2, you can assign any range name to a macro by pressing the RUN (ALT-F3) key, highlighting that range name on the list and pressing ENTER. This greatly expands the number of macro initiator names that you can assign to include any valid range name. This, in turn, means that you can assign more meaningful names to macros such as DATA_ENTRY or EDIT_DATA as compared to simply \D or \E.

In general, you should assign one of the 26 special macro initiator names to macros that you use frequently and that are not hazardous to your work if they are invoked by error. Imagine the sinking feeling you'd get after accidentally pressing ALT-W to execute a worksheet erase command when all you wanted to do was enter a capital W in the current cell!

To avoid such a disaster, you should assign more informative long names to macros that you use infrequently or macros that have potentially fatal consequences. If you make a practice of starting all macro names with a special character combination, like M_NAME, all your macros will be listed together when you press the RUN (ALT-F3) key. If you started all macro range names with an asterisk, not only would they all be listed together, but they would be at the head of the list of range names. If you wish, you can even assign both types of initiating names to the same macro.

To name a macro you need to assign a range name to the top cell of the macro. You can expand the range to include the entire macro, but the upper-left corner of the range must be the top cell of the macro. We have found that it is easiest to place a label in the cell to the left of the macro containing the names of the named cells of the macro. You can then use the command /Range Name

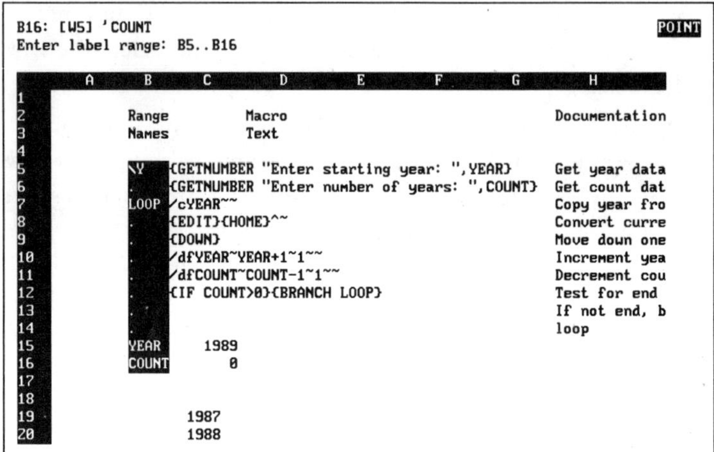

Figure 13.10
Using /rnlr to name macro cells.

Labels Right to actually name the cells while providing a visual label of the cell names. If your macro has more than one named cell—for looping, branching, or data cells—its a good idea to place a place-holding character such as a period (.) in the cells that do not have assigned names. See Figure 13.10.

If you use the place-holding character, you will create a complete column of name labels in the column to the left of the column of the macro. You can then use the END-DOWN key combination to name all cells in the macro as follows. Start to name the top cell of the column (the special macro initiator name) by placing the cell pointer on the top cell and pressing /Range Name Labels Right and before you press ENTER, press END-DOWN to highlight the entire column of range names. Then press ENTER to conclude the naming command.

Congratulations! You have just named all the labeled cells in the column.

ADVANCED MACRO COMMANDS

In addition to the keyboard macro commands, Release 2.2 adds a set of sophisticated advanced macro commands. These perform such functions as logical branching, creating menus, obtaining user input, reading and writing to text files, controlling the display screen, and manipulating database tables. The Advanced Macro Commands are listed in summary form in Table 13.2 and described in more detail in the following section.

Table 13.2 Advanced Macro Commands

Command	Description
{subroutine}	Calls a specified subroutine with the specified arguments and returns control to the command following the subroutine call upon completion of the subroutine
{?}	Pauses the macro execution to allow you to move the cell pointer. Use the {?} command when you want to pause to select a menu option, move the cell pointer to another location, or enter data into the current cell.
{BEEP}	Sounds the computer bell (beeper). Used to signal the user that the macro has finished, requires user input or has determined that an error occurred.
{BLANK}	Erases the contents of a cell or range.
{BORDERSOFF} and {BORDERSON}	Turns off and on the display of the worksheet frame including column numbers and row letters. Identical to {FRAMEOFF} and {FRAMEON}.
{BRANCH}	Transfers control of the current macro from the current cell and column of macro commands to another cell and column of commands starting in the designated cell.
{BREAK}	Returns macro control to READY mode.
{BREAKOFF}	Disables the CTRL-BREAK key so that it cannot be used to terminate macro control. Used to prevent users from accidently or purposely exiting a macro and changing data, formula, or the macro itself.
{BREAKON}	Reactivates the CTRL-BREAK key after it has been disabled by the {BREAKOFF} command
{CLOSE}	Closes an open text file.
{CONTENTS}	Copies the contents of one cell to another cell as a label, converting values to labels according to a specified format and width. Used to convert values to labels for use with string formulas.
{DEFINE}	Declares arguments passed from the calling {subroutine} command for use by the subroutine macro. Arguments passed from the calling routine must be defined before they can be used by the subroutine.
{DISPATCH}	Redirects the macro processing to a variable location specified in the cell named as the argument. Used to branch to differing sections of macro code based on the specified cell location.
{FILESIZE}	Determines the size of the open text file and places the results in a specified cell.
{FOR}	Repeatedly executes a specified subroutine a specified number of iterations.
{FORBREAK}	Terminates the {FOR} loop prematurely, returning control to the calling macro just after the {FOR} command.

Table 13.2 *continued*

{FORM}	Controls user input into a defined range of unprotected cells
{FRAMEOFF} and {FRAMEON}	Turns off and on the display of the worksheet frame including column numbers and row letters. Identical to {BORDERSOFF} and {BORDERSON}.
{GET}	Pauses to get a single keystroke entry from the user and store the keystroke in the specified location as a left-aligned label containing the macro name of the key pressed.
{GETLABEL}	Prompts the user to enter a label and stores that label in the designated location.
{GETNUMBER}	Prompts the user to enter a number and stores that number in the designated location.
{GETPOS}	Reads the current byte-pointer location in the current open text file and places the numeric value in the designated cell.
{GRAPHOFF} and {GRAPHON}	Displays the current or named graph as a full screen view.
{IF}	Performs conditional branching within a macro, passing control to the command to its right in the same cell if the condition is true, and to the cell immediately below it if the condition is false.
{INDICATE}	Controls the contents and appearance of the state indicator in the upper-right corner of the screen.
{LET}	Enters a number or label in the specified cell or range.
{LOOK}	Reads the typeahead buffer and copies the first key into the specified cell.
{MENUBRANCH}	Initiates a designated macro menu by displaying the menu items in the control panel and then branching to the macro commands associated with the menu option selected by the user.
{MENUCALL}	Initiates a designated macro menu by displaying the menu items in the control panel and then calls the macro commands associated with the menu option selected by the user as a subroutine, returning to the next command after the {MENUCALL} command when the subroutine is complete.
{ONERROR}	Branches to a designated macro location immediately upon detecting an error condition. Stores the 1-2-3 error message in a designated cell.
{OPEN}	Opens a named text file in one of four read/write access modes: read-only(r), read-write(w), modify(m), and append(a).

Command	Description
{PANELOFF} and {PANELON}	The {PANELOFF} command locks the control panel at its current state, or clears and locks the panel for the duration of the macro or until a {PANELON} command is executed.
{PUT}	Places a number or label in a cell specified by its offset from the top-left corner of a specified range.
{QUIT}	Terminates the current macro and returns control to the user.
{READ}	Reads a specified number of bytes from the currently open text file, copies into the specified cell and move the byte-pointer forward the same specified number of bytes.
{READLN}	Reads the rest of the current line from the currently open text file, copies it into the specified cell, and moves the byte-pointer forward to the next line of the text file.
{RECALC} and {RECALCCOL}	Recalculates a designated portion of the worksheet when recalculation mode is set to manual.
{RESTART}	Clears the subroutine stack so that the macro is no longer returned to the calling macro location at the conclusion of the subroutine.
{RETURN}	Returns control from a subroutine to the calling macro immediately without completeing the subroutine.
{SETPOS}	Moves the byte-pointer to the specified byte position in the open text file.
{SYSTEM}	Suspends 1-2-3 and executes the designated operating system command.
{WAIT}	Pauses the macro execution until the specified time, while displaying the WAIT indicator.
{WINDOWSOFF} and {WINDOWSON}	The {WINDOWSOFF} command locks the worksheet display in its current state for the duration of the macro or until a {WINDOWSON} command is executed.
{WRITE}	Writes the specified string to the open text file.
{WRITELN}	Writes the specified string to the open text file and adds a carriage return and line feed.

{Subroutine}

Purpose Calls a specified subroutine with the specified arguments and returns control to the command that follows the subroutine call, when the subroutine is completed.

Syntax {subroutine argument1, argument2, ... argumentn}

Arguments

subroutine — the range name assigned to the top cell of the subroutine. Although you can use a cell address, it is less flexible than a named range. If you move the subroutine by inserting or deleting rows or columns, the subroutine call will no longer work since the cell reference would have changed. Named ranges are automatically updated.

argument1 ... argumentn — any number, string, formula, or cell reference. Passed to the subroutine command {DEFINE}, which evaluates and stores the arguments. If you specify one or more arguments, you must include a {DEFINE} command in your subroutine before you reference one of the arguments. You can include up to 31 arguments.

Usage When you call a subroutine, 1-2-3 completes the entire subroutine (and any branches or subroutines called by the first) before returning control to the command immediately following the subroutine call. Subroutines differ from branches in that they automatically return control to the calling macro after completion, while branches must explicitly redirect control at their end or the macro will terminate.

Subroutines are typically used for generic functions such as testing data input for allowable entries or highly repetitive tasks.

You can nest subroutines by calling a second from within the first. 1-2-3 will complete the second before returning control to the first, which it will then complete before returning control to the initial calling routine. The area of memory where 1-2-3 stores the information about the calling routines (so that it can return control) is called the *subroutine stack*. If you want to break out of the return control of the subroutine stack (e.g., to branch to another macro), you must clear the subroutine stack with the {RESTART} command.

Example To test the input obtained by a {GETNUMBER} command and placed in the cell NUMB for validity as a month of the year (i.e., between 1 and 12), you might use the following macro:

```
INPUT       {GETNUMBER "Enter month (1-12): ",NUMB}
            {TESTNUMB}
TESTNUMB    {IF NUMB>12#OR#<1}{RESTART}{BRANCH ERROR}
```

Cautions Do not assign one of 1-2-3's key words to the range name of a subroutine. The subroutine calling structure {name} can create macro commands out of some potential range names. For example the name "quit" would produce the command {QUIT} and would terminate your macro instead of calling the named subroutine.

{?}

Purpose Pauses the macro execution to allow you to enter data or move the cell pointer. Use the {?} command when you want to pause to select a menu option, move the cell pointer to another location, or enter data into the current cell.

Syntax {?}

Arguments None.

Usage The {?} pause command pauses the macro execution at the specific point in which it is placed. If your macro is in the process of making menu selections when it encounters the {?} command, the current menu is displayed (assuming you have not turned off the display with {PANELOFF}). You can move the menu pointer to select the menu option of choice. When you press ENTER, the macro continues, using that selection. If the menu selection is waiting for input (e.g., a range name or specification), you can either type in the name, paint the range, or use the NAME key (F3) to list the range names. When you conclude the specification by pressing ENTER, the macro continues. If your macro is not in the process of a menu selection or data request, the current cell will be highlighted, allowing you to move the cell pointer to another location or enter data. If you want the data to be entered into the current cell, you must be sure to include the macro ENTER character (~) after the {?} command.

Examples To enter data into the current cell, use:

```
{?}~
```

To select a format for the current cell, use:

```
/rf{?}~{?}~~
```

To select the range and assign it the currency format with two decimal places use:

```
/rfc2~{?}~
```

To select both the range and the format, use:

```
/rf{?}~{?}~{?}~
```

To select the format and then prompt for the range name, use:

```
/rf{?}~{?}~{NAME}
```

The {?} command can also be used to pause the macro to allow the user to read a help, error, or other message. If the message screen was assigned the range name HELP1, the command would be:

```
{GOTO}HELP1~{?}{ESC}
```

Notes The {GETLABEL} and {GETNUMBER} commands offer greater control and features for data entry than the {?} command.

Cautions The {?} command will not prevent a user from initiating a command when he should be entering data. This can produce bizarre results when the macro continues, thinking that it is at one logical position in the menu when in fact the user has moved to another. Likewise it does not restrict where he can place the data entered or move the cell pointer. You may want to use one of the above commands to prevent accidental misplacement.

{BEEP}

Purpose Sounds the computer bell (beeper). Used to signal the user that the macro has finished, requires user input, or has determined that an error occurred.

Syntax {BEEP x}

Arguments

x — OPTIONAL—the pitch of the beep from 1–4, with 1 being the highest and 4 the lowest. Tone 2 is the default. If you enter a number greater than 4, 1-2-3 divides by 4 and uses the remainder.

Usage To sound the bell at the end of a macro, place {BEEP} in the last cell of the macro.

Example {BEEP 1}{BEEP 2}{BEEP 3} sounds the bell three times using different tones.

Notes If you have turned the bell off with /Worksheet Global Default Other Beep No, the bell will not sound.

Cautions Using the bell excessively is annoying to users, and eventually defeats its purpose as a warning device.

{BLANK}

Purpose Erases the contents of a cell or range.

Syntax {BLANK location}

Arguments

location — any cell or range address, or named range.

Usage To erase the contents of a specific cell use the address as in {BLANK A25}. To erase the contents of a named range of cells, use {BLANK rangename}. To erase the contents of the current cell, use the @CELLPOINTER function as in:

```
{BLANK @CELLPOINTER("coord")}
```

Notes The {BLANK} command does not alter the format of the cell.

{BORDERSOFF} and {BORDERSON}

Purpose Turns off and on the display of the worksheet frame including worksheet letter, column numbers, and row letters.

Syntax {BORDERSOFF} and {BORDERSON}

Arguments None.

Usage To turn the worksheet frame off use the {BORDERSOFF} command. To turn it back on use {BORDERSON}.

Example To display a donor order form without worksheet frames (as in Figure 13.11) you would change the main macro command to read:

```
{BORDERSOFF}
/riA1..E20~
{BORDERSON}
```

Notes {BORDERSOFF} and {BORDERSON} are identical in function to {FRAMEOFF} and {FRAMEON}.

If you have turned off the screen display with the {WINDOWSOFF} command, the {BORDERSOFF} and {BORDERSON} commands will not take effect. You must first execute the {WINDOWSON} command to reactivate the screen and the frame command will take effect.

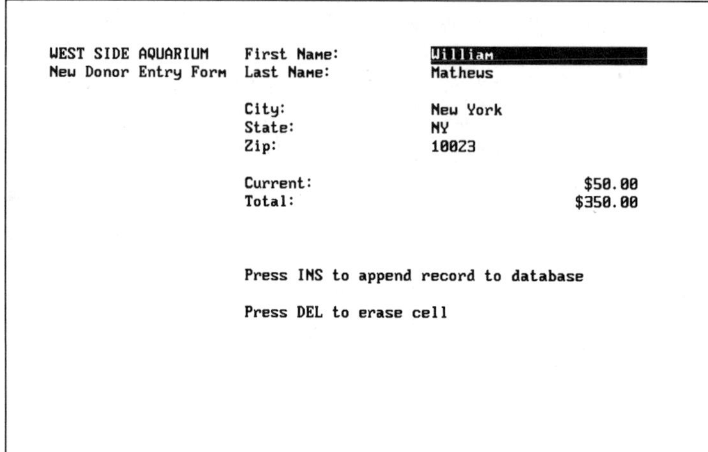

Figure 13.11 Input screen displayed with {BORDERSOFF}.

{BRANCH}

Purpose Transfers control of the current macro from the current cell and column of macro commands to another cell and column of commands starting in the designated cell.

Syntax {BRANCH location}

Arguments

location — any cell or range address, or named range containing macro commands. If you specify a range, 1-2-3 will branch to the top-left cell of the range.

Usage Use the {BRANCH} command to branch to another macro or a different position in the current macro based on the results of a condition test using the {IF} macro command.

Example The following macro branches to the macro starting in the cell named TRUTH if the cell named FACT evaluates to a value of logical true; otherwise it branches to the macro starting in the cell named LIE:

```
{IF FACT=@TRUE}{BRANCH TRUTH}
{BRANCH LIE}
```

Notes The {BRANCH} command can be used to create a looping macro by redirecting control to the same column of macro commands above the {BRANCH} command. Such a loop will cycle endlessly unless there is another conditional {BRANCH} command (located between the looping branch command and its target location) that redirects the processing flow out of the loop, or the user presses CTRL-BREAK to cancel the macro process.

The {BRANCH} command is different than the {subroutine} calling command. The former is an absolute branch with no designated return. The latter will return control to the original calling macro at the point just after the subroutine call when it reaches a {RETURN} command or when it reaches the end of the subroutine.

The {BRANCH} command is different than the {GOTO} command. The former controls the flow of logic of the macro itself, while the latter moves the cell-pointer from cell to cell as part of a macro command.

The {BRANCH} command performs the same function as the /XG command.

Cautions Be careful of creating endless looping macros after you have set {BREAKOFF}. If you enter an endless loop, you will have to reboot your computer to escape, losing the worksheet in memory.

{BREAK}

Purpose Returns to the READY mode under macro control, without interrupting the macro.

Syntax {BREAK}

Arguments None.

Usage In your macros you will often need to escape from the depths of a menu tree and return to READY mode before pursuing a different course of macro commmands. The easiest way to accomplish this is to use the {BREAK} command. To return to the READY mode from within a 1-2-3 menu, insert the {BREAK} command in the appropriate location.

Example

```
/ppag{BREAK}
```

The {BREAK} command returns macro control to the READY mode after completing a /Print command.

{BREAKOFF}

Purpose Disables the CTRL-BREAK key so that it cannot be used to terminate macro control. Used to prevent users from accidentally or purposely exiting a macro and changing data, a formula, or the macro itself.

Syntax {BREAKOFF}

Arguments None.

Usage To prevent the use of the CTRL-BREAK key to terminate macro control, place the {BREAKOFF} command at the beginning of the macro. If you are using an autoexec macro, be sure to make it the first command. If your macro returns control to the user at the end of the process, be sure to turn CTRL-BREAK back on with {BREAKON}.

Example `{BREAKOFF}`

macro commands

`{BREAKON}`

Caution Do not place a {BREAKOFF} command in your macro until you are certain that it does not have an endless loop. If you enter an endless loop with {BREAKOFF} activated, you will have to reboot your computer to stop the loop.

{BREAKON}

Purpose Reactivates the CTRL-BREAK key after it has been disabled by the {BREAKOFF} command.

Syntax {BREAKON}

Arguments None.

Usage Used to reactivate the CTRL-BREAK key at the end of a macro process to allow the user to terminate a macro loop, or to break out of the macro itself and maneuver about the worksheet without macro control.

{CLOSE}

Purpose Closes an open text file.

Syntax {CLOSE}

Arguments None—closes the current open text file.

Usage You can only close a text file after it has been opened with the {OPEN} command. If you do not close the text file before the end of the macro, the file will remain open until closed by another close command, or until another text file is opened with the {OPEN} command (1-2-3 automatically closes the current open text file when it opens another), or you exit 1-2-3 (1-2-3 automatically closes open text files before terminating). If you try to close a file that is not open, 1-2-3 ignores the {CLOSE} command.

Example To open the text file "text.prn" with write access, insert the phrase "This is the text", and then close the file, use:

```
{OPEN text.prn,w}
{WRITE "This is the text"}
{CLOSE}
```

Caution 1-2-3 never processes any macro code that appears on the same line and to the right of the {CLOSE} command.

{CONTENTS}

Purpose Copies the contents of one cell to another cell as a label, converting values to labels according to a specified format and width. Used to convert values to labels for use with string formulas.

Syntax {CONTENTS target,source,width,format}

Arguments

target — any cell, address, or named range.

source — any cell, address, or named range.

width — OPTIONAL—the width used to determine the display of the converted value. Similar in concept to column width, though the width is used only when making the value to label conversion, determining how many characters are displayed or if the value should be displayed as asterisks. The actual width of the target cell will be used to display the resulting label.

format — OPTIONAL—the format to use when converting values to labels. You can select any one of the standard value formats by entering the code from the following table:

Code	Format
0 to 15	Fixed format—0 to 15 decimal places
16 to 31	Scientific format—0 to 15 decimal places
32 to 47	Currency format—0 to 15 decimal places
48 to 63	Percent format—0 to 15 decimal places
64 to 79	Comma format—0 to 15 decimal places
112	+/− format
113	General format
114	D1 format (DD-MMM-YY)
115	D2 format (DD-MMM)
116	D3 format (MMM-YY)
117	Text format
118	Hidden format
119	D6 format (HH:MM:SS AM/PM)

Code	Format
120	D7 format (HH:MM AM/PM)
121	D4 format (Long Intn'l)
122	D5 format (Short Intn'l)
123	D8 format (Long Intn'l)
124	D9 format (Short Intn'l)
127	Current worksheet global format

Usage Used to convert values to labels for use with string formulas and self-modifying macros. Can be used to convert values to labels that are then appended to other labels for reports.

Example If the cell named SOURCE contained the value @TODAY and the current system date was 5-MAY-89, then the macro command:

```
{CONTENTS TARGET,SOURCE,10,114}{CALC}
+"This report was prepared on "&TARGET&" just for you."
```

would convert the current system date is the cell named SOURCE into date D1 format (with a width of 10) and append it to the text to produce the following label in the current cell:

```
This report was prepared on 5-MAY-89 just for you.
```

Notes 1-2-3 does not automatically recalculate the worksheet after the {CONTENTS} command even in automatic recalculate mode. To be sure that changes made by the {CONTENTS} command are reflected in the worksheet prior to continuing with your macro, insert either a tilde (~) or the {CALC} command after the {CONTENTS} command.

{DEFINE}

Purpose Declares arguments passed from the calling {subroutine} command for use by the subroutine macro. Arguments passed from the calling routine must be defined before they can be used by the subroutine.

Syntax {DEFINE location1, location2, ... locationn}

Arguments

location 1–n — any cell, address, or named range. The number of locations must match the number of arguments passed by the calling routine. If not, 1-2-3 will terminate the macro. You can also provide an optional suffix identifying the type of argument passed. Use either :value or :string (the default) or any contraction of the suffixes down to :v or :s.

Usage In order to pass an argument from the calling routine to a subroutine with the {subroutine argument1, argument2 ... argumentn} command, you must define the locations for 1-2-3 to store the passed values and labels. This instructs the subroutine where to look for the passed values or labels when it needs them. Therefore, the {DEFINE} should be among the first commands in the subroutine. If you attempt to use a passed argument before it is defined, 1-2-3 will terminate the macro.

If you append a suffix to the location, 1-2-3 will process the passed argument before storing it. If you append :string to a location and then pass a string, a value, a formula, or a cell reference, 1-2-3 will store the argument as a left-aligned label. If you append :value, 1-2-3 will do one of the following depending on what type of data you pass to the subroutine:

value	1-2-3 stores the value.
label	1-2-3 stores the label.
formula	1-2-3 evaluates the formula and stores the value.
cell reference	1-2-3 stores the contents of the cell, if it contains a value or a label. It evaluates the formula and stores the value, if it contains a formula.

Examples Suppose you wanted to create a subroutine that calculated the area of a circle when you passed it the radius as an argument. The following macro calls the subroutine CIRCLE and passes the value 25. The {DEFINE} command stores the value in the cell named RADIUS and indicates that it is a value. Since it is already a value, no changes are made. Finally, the {LET} command computes the area and stores the results in the range named AREA.

```
\C        {CIRCLE 25}

CIRCLE    {DEFINE RADIUS:value}{CALC}
          {LET AREA,@PI*RADIUS^2}
```

What if we called the same subroutine, but this time passed it a formula:

```
\B        {CIRCLE DIAMETER/2}

CIRCLE    {DEFINE RADIUS:value}{CALC}
          {LET AREA,@PI*RADIUS^2}
```

Since we defined the argument as a value, 1-2-3 will evaluate the formula (taking the value in the range DIAMETER and dividing it by 2, before storing the results in radius. This shows the power of subroutines (albeit simplistic) and their ability to perform the same function on a variety of data passed from different calling routines.

Cautions 1-2-3 does not automatically recalculate the worksheet after the {DEFINE} command even in automatic recalculate mode. To be sure that changes made by the {DEFINE} command are reflected in the worksheet prior to continuing with your macro, insert either a tilde (~) or the {CALC} command after the {DEFINE} command.

{DISPATCH}

Purpose Redirects the macro processing to a variable location specified in the cell named as the argument. Used to branch to differing sections of macro code based on the specified cell location.

Syntax {DISPATCH location}

Arguments

location — any *single* cell address or *single* cell named range.

Usage The {DISPATCH} command works like a sort of hyper {BRANCH} command. Instead of branching to the location specified as the argument, it branches to the location contained in the location specified as the argument. In this way, the {DISPATCH} command allows you to select one of several different branches according to the contents of the cell you specify as the location. Combined with an {IF} or series of {IF} commands you can construct a multi-branching "CASE" command by storing one of the different initial cells for several different macro routines in the specified cell location. 1-2-3 will then read the stored initial cell name or address and branch to it.

Example Suppose you wanted to branch to one of three different macro processes depending on whether a bill is 30, 60, or 90 days old. You could use the following macro structure:

```
{IF @TODAY-BILL_DATE>=30}{LET NOTICE,"DAY30LOGIC"}
{IF @TODAY-BILL_DATE>=60}{LET NOTICE,"DAY60LOGIC"}
{IF @TODAY-BILL_DATE>=90}{LET NOTICE,"DAY90LOGIC"}
{DISPATCH NOTICE}
```

where BILL_DATE holds the billing date, and DAY30LOGIC, DAY60LOGIC and DAY90LOGIC are the first cells of the different processing macros.

Cautions If the specified location is more than a single cell, the {DISPATCH} command branches to the top cell in the range specified as the location rather than the cell name contained in the cell specified as the location.

{FILESIZE}

Purpose Determines the size of the open text file and places the results in a specified cell.

Syntax {FILESIZE location}

Arguments

location — any cell, address, or named range. If the range is more than a single cell, 1-2-3 places the results in the top-left cell of the range.

Usage The {FILESIZE} command determines the size in bytes and places the resulting number in the specified cell. You must first open the file of interest with the {OPEN} command and should be sure to close it with the {CLOSE} command.

Example To determine the size of the file named WHALES.TXT and place the results in a cell named SHAMU use the following command:

```
{OPEN WHALES.TXT,R}
{FILESIZE SHAMU}{BRANCH ERROR}
...
```

Notes If the {FILESIZE} command executes properly, 1-2-3 continues to process the cell immediately below it, skipping any remaining commands in the same cell as the {FILESIZE} command. This feature can be used as a branch to test if the command completed successfully. If yes, continue below; if no, branch to an error message.

{FOR}

Purpose Repeatedly executes a specified subroutine a specified number of iterations.

Syntax {FOR count,start,stop,step,subroutine}

Arguments

count — any cell, address, or named range. The location where the counter is stored.

start — any number—must be less than or equal to stop for the subroutine to execute. The initial value of the counter.

stop — any number—must be greater than or equal to start for the subroutine to execute. The value against which the counter is tested. If the counter is less than or equal to the stop number, the subroutine is executed.

step — any number—the amount that the counter is incremented each time the subroutine is executed.

subroutine — any cell, address, or named range containing the first cell of the subroutine macro as its top-left cell.

Usage The {FOR} command is used to create looping macros that execute a specified number of times. They can be used to perform successive approximation routines or other repetitive tasks.

Examples To execute the subroutine GUESS twenty-five times using the cell named TEMP as the counter location use:

```
{FOR TEMP,1,25,1,GUESS)
```

To execute it continuously use a zero step value. Note that you will have to provide an alternative method of stopping the macro using {FORBREAK} or {QUIT} within the subroutine.

```
{FOR TEMP,1,25,0,GUESS}
```

Notes 1-2-3 does not automatically recalculate the worksheet after the {FOR} command, even in automatic recalculate mode. To be sure that changes made by the {FOR} command are reflected in the worksheet prior to starting the subroutine, insert either a tilde (~) or the {CALC} command at the top of the subroutine.

{FORBREAK}

Purpose Terminates the {FOR} loop prematurely, returning control to the calling macro just after the {FOR} command.

Syntax {FORBREAK}

Arguments None.

Usage Used with a conditional test such as {IF} to break out of the subroutine and return to the calling macro based on the tested condition.

Examples Suppose your subroutine performed a successive approximation calculation and you wanted to repeat the calculation as many as 100 times or until the difference in successive approximations stored in the cell named DELTA was less than 1.

```
\A          {FOR TEMP,1,100,1,GUESS}

GUESS       perform calculation
            {IF DELTA<1}{FORBREAK}
```

Cautions Only place the {FORBREAK} with subroutines called by {FOR} looping commands. Placing it in a main macro or a subroutine called by another type of command (e.g., {subroutine}) will cause premature termination of the macro.

{FRAMEOFF} and {FRAMEON}

Purpose Turns off and on the display of the worksheet frame including worksheet letter, column numbers, and row letters.

Syntax {FRAMEOFF} and {FRAMEON}

Arguments None.

Usage To turn the worksheet frame off use the {FRAMEOFF} command. To turn it back on use {FRAMEON}.

Examples To display a donor order form without worksheet frames (as in Figure 13.11) you would change the main macro command to read:

```
{FRAMEOFF}
/riA1..E20~
{FRAMEON}
```

Notes {FRAMEOFF} and {FRAMEON} are identical to {BORDERSOFF} and {BORDERSON}.

If you have turned off the screen display with the {WINDOWSOFF} command, the {FRAMEOFF} and {FRAMEON} commands will not take effect. You must first execute the {WINDOWSON} command to reactivate the screen and the frame command will take effect.

{GET}

Purpose Pauses to get a single keystroke entry from the user and stores the keystroke in the specified location as a left-aligned label containing the macro name of the key pressed.

Syntax {GET location}

Arguments

location — any cell, address, or named range.

Usage Used to capture single keystroke responses to prompts such as Y/N confirmations or selecting an option from a numbered or lettered list. Can also capture function and cursor keys and store their macro names. Some cursor movements (e.g. last cell – END+cursor key) require two distinct keystrokes and would therefore require two {GET} commands with different storage locations.

Examples The following macro displays an exit confirmation message in the range DISPLAY and stores the response in the cell CONFIRM.

```
{GOTO}DISPLAY~
{GET CONFIRM}
{IF @UPPER(CONFIRM),"Y"}{BRANCH EXIT}
{RETURN}
```

Cautions 1-2-3 does not automatically recalculate the worksheet after the {GET} command, even in automatic recalculate mode. To be sure that changes made by the {GET} command are reflected in the worksheet prior to continuing with your macro, insert either a tilde (~) or the {CALC} command after the {GET} command.

{GETLABEL}

Purpose Prompts the user to enter a label and stores that label in the designated location.

Syntax {GETLABEL prompt,location}

Arguments

prompt — any literal string, formula that evaluates to a string, or reference to a cell containing a label. The prompt can be as long as will fit in a single line in the control panel. The actual number of characters will depend on the display you are using.

location — any cell, address, or named range. If the range contains more than one cell, the response is placed in the top-left cell of the range.

Usage When 1-2-3 encounters the {GETLABEL} command it displays the prompt in the control panel and pauses to allow the user to enter a response. When the user presses ENTER, 1-2-3 places the response in the designated location as a left-aligned label. If the user presses ENTER without entering any response, 1-2-3 still enters a single left label prefix in the designated location.

Examples

```
{GETLABEL "How are you feeling ? ",RESP1}
{GETLABEL "What can I do for you ? ",RESP2}
{GETLABEL NEXT_QUESTION,RESP3}
```

Notes Corresponds to the /XL command.

Cautions The {GETLABEL} only accepts labels and will convert numbers to labels. While this is often desired for numbers such as dates, zip codes, and telephone numbers (how often have you entered a date, only to have it calculated into a ridiculous fraction?), it can cause difficulties when you may want numerical data entered. In those cases use {GETNUMBER}.

1-2-3 does not automatically recalculate the worksheet after the {GETLABEL} command, even in automatic recalculate mode. To be sure that changes made by the {GETLABEL} command are reflected in the worksheet prior to continuing with your macro, insert either a tilde (~) or the {CALC} command after the {GETLABEL} command.

{GETNUMBER}

Purpose Prompts the user to enter a number and stores that number in the designated location.

Syntax {GETNUMBER prompt,location}

Arguments

prompt — any literal string, formula that evaluates to a string, or reference to a cell containing a label. The prompt can be as long as will fit in a single line in the control panel. The actual number of characters will depend on the display you are using.

location — any cell, address, or named range. If the range contains more than one cell, the response is placed in the top-left cell of the range.

Usage When 1-2-3 encounters the {GETNUMBER} command it displays the prompt in the control panel and pauses to allow the user to enter a response. When the user presses ENTER, 1-2-3 tests to make sure the entry is a number, a formula that evaluates to a number, or a cell reference to a cell containing a number or numeric formula. If you enter a label, a formula that evaluates to a string, or a cell reference to a cell containing a label or string formula, 1-2-3 enters ERR in the designated location.

Examples

```
{GETNUMBER "How old are you ? ",RESP1}
{GETNUMBER "How much do you weigh ? ",RESP2}
{GETNUMBER NEXT_QUESTION,RESP3}
```

Notes Corresponds to the /XN command.

Cautions 1-2-3 does not automatically recalculate the worksheet after the {GETNUMBER} command, even in automatic recalculate mode. To be sure that changes made by the {GETNUMBER} command are reflected in the worksheet prior to continuing with your macro, insert either a tilde (~) or the {CALC} command after the {GETNUMBER} command.

{GETPOS}

Purpose Reads the current byte-pointer location in the current open text file and places the numeric value in the designated cell.

Syntax {GETPOS location}

Arguments

location — any cell, address, or named range. If the range contains more than one cell, the byte-pointer location is placed in the top left cell of the range.

Usage Used to store the current read or write location in the current open file in order to return to the same location at a later time.

Example

```
{OPEN FISH.TXT,r}
{GETPOS, POSITION}{BRANCH ERROR}
...
```

Notes You must first open the text file with the {OPEN} command before using the {GETPOS} command.

If the {GETPOS} command executes properly, 1-2-3 continues to process the cell immediately below it, skipping any remaining commands in the same cell as the {GETPOS} command. This feature can be used as a branch to test if the command completed successfully. If yes, continue below; if no, branch to an error message.

{GRAPHON}

Purpose Displays the current or named graph as a full screen view.

Syntax {GRAPHON name,nodisplay}

Arguments

name — OPTIONAL—any named graph in the active worksheet. If no name is supplied, the current graph is displayed (except in combination with the nodisplay option).

nodisplay — OPTIONAL—requires that a name be supplied. Makes the named graph the current graph without displaying it.

Usage The {GRAPHON} command can be used to produce three different results, depending on the arguments supplied. Using {GRAPHON} without any arguments displays the current graph. Using {GRAPHON} with just the name makes the named graph the current graph and displays it. Using {GRAPHON} with both the name and the nodisplay option makes the named graph the current graph but doesn't display it.

When graphs are displayed, 1-2-3 continues with the macro execution and will remove the graph and redisplay the worksheet when it encounters one of the following commands: {GRAPHOFF}, {INDICATE}, {?}, {GETLABEL}, {GETNUMBER}, {MENUCALL}, {MENUBRANCH}, /XL, /XM, /XN or reaches the end of the macro.

To maintain the graph on the screen, you must create an endless loop, combined with a test to see if a key has been pressed. When a keystroke is detected, use {GRAPHOFF} to turn off the graph display and redisplay the worksheet.

Example To display the named graph EGRETS until any key is pressed, use:

```
\G          {BLANK TEST}
            {GRAPHON EGRETS}
CONTINUE    {LOOK TEST}
            {IF TEST=""}{BRANCH CONTINUE}
            {GRAPHOFF}
```

{IF}

Purpose Performs conditional branching within a macro, passing control to the command to its right in the same cell if the condition is true, and to the cell immediately below it if the condition is false.

Syntax {IF condition}

Arguments

condition — generally any formula that evaluates to a logical value of true (1) or false (0), a cell reference to a cell containing such a formula or value. Logical formulas contain one or more of the logical operators:

=, <, >, <=, >=, <>, #AND#, #OR#, #NOT#

Conditional arguments can also contain any other type of formula, number, string, or cell reference though they often would have no logical meaning. For example, {IF "whale"} is legal but has no meaning, since the logical value of a string is always 0, which always means false. In addition, blank cells, ERR, and NA equal 0 and evaluate to false.

Usage The {IF} command is among the most important for building macros. It is the simplest method for the macro to make a decision based on user input, the value of certain cells, or the equivalency of two strings. In its simplest form, you can compare two numbers and branch to two different sections of macro code or subroutines based on that comparison. More complex conditional formulas can include any number of Boolean operators and 1-2-3 functions, but basically they all work the same way:

If it's true, continue to the right.

If it's false, skip to the next cell.

Examples Suppose you want to use one of two different bonus calculations depending on whether January sales exceed $50,000:

```
{IF JANSALES>50000}{BRANCH HIGHBONUS}
{BRANCH LOWBONUS}
```

It is possible to create more than two options by using the {DISPATCH} command and a {IF} sieve. Suppose you wanted to branch to one of three different macro processes depending on whether a bill is 30, 60, or 90+ days old, you could use the following macro structure:

```
{IF @TODAY-BILL_DATE>=30}{LET NOTICE,"DAY30LOGIC"}
{IF @TODAY-BILL_DATE>=60}{LET NOTICE,"DAY60LOGIC"}
{IF @TODAY-BILL_DATE>=90}{LET NOTICE,"DAY90LOGIC"}
{DISPATCH NOTICE}
```

where BILL_DATE holds the billing date, and DAY30LOGIC, DAY60LOGIC, and DAY90LOGIC are the first cells of the different processing macros.

The {IF} command is often used as an exit test for an endless looping command. The following macros enters data in a column until the user enters a blank.

```
INPUT     {BLANK TEMP}
          {GETLABEL "Enter data: ",TEMP}
          {IF TEMP=""}{QUIT}
          {LET @CELLPOINTER("coord"),TEMP}
          {DOWN}
          {BRANCH INPUT}
```

You could replace the {QUIT} command with another {BRANCH} command or a {RETURN} command to continue with the macro after the input process was complete.

{INDICATE}

Purpose Places the message of your choice in the mode indicator box at the upper right of the screen.

Syntax {INDICATE string}

Arguments

string — OPTIONAL—any string, or cell reference to a cell containing a string. The string can be as long as will fit on one line of the control panel. The actual size limit will vary with the type of display you are using. If you enter an empty string "", the mode box will disappear. If you enter no string argument, you return control of the mode indicator to 1-2-3.

Usage The mode indicator can be used to inform the user about the current status of the macro. For example, you could change it to:

```
"Processing data, please wait"
```

during a long recalculation.

Examples To display the above message, use:

```
{INDICATE "Processing data, please wait"}
```

To display the message contained in the named range MESSAGE, use:

```
{INDICATE MESSAGE}
```

To erase the mode indicator from the screen, use:

```
{INDICATE ""}
```

To return control to 1-2-3, use:

```
{INDICATE}
```

Notes If you are performing a lengthy looping calculation, you can create a temporary PROGRESS cell that stores the loop counter as a percent of the stop value. By including the {INDICATE} inside the loop and referencing the string conversion of the PROGRESS, you will display the percent completion in the indicator window. For example, the following macro shows the percent completion of a {FOR} loop and then returns control of the indicator to 1-2-3 when the loop is complete.

```
START       1
STOP        500
STEP        1
COUNTER
\I          {FOR COUNTER,START,STOP,STEP,LOOP}
            {INDICATE}
```

```
LOOP        {recalculate LOOP}{INDICATE @STRING(100*
            COUNTER/STOP)& " % Complete"}
            other loop commands
```

{LET}

Purpose Enters a number or label in the specified cell or range.

Syntax {LET location,entry}

Arguments

location — any cell, address, or named range. If the range contains more than one cell, 1-2-3 places the entry in the top-left cell.

entry — any number, literal string, formula, or cell reference to a cell containing one of these. If the entry is a formula, 1-2-3 evaluates the formula and enters the value in the cell.

Usage The {LET} command is the macro equivalent of the equals sign. It places the value or label that you supply in the designated cell. It makes the cell "equal" to your entry.

Examples Here are several examples:

```
{LET C2,C3*C4}
```

places the product of the contents of two cells in a third.

```
{LET REV_LABEL, "Year to Date Revenues"}
```

places the label "Year to Date Revenues" in the cell named REV_LABEL.

```
{LET DEAL,COST=PRICE}
```

places the results of the logical comparison of the cell contents of COST and PRICE into DEAL. If cost and price are both values and they are equal, the logical value true (1) will be placed in DEAL. If they aren't equal, the value false (0) will be placed in the cell. If they are both strings, the same logic applies. If one is a string and the other is a value, then they can't be equal and a logical false is inserted.

Cautions 1-2-3 does not automatically recalculate the worksheet after the {LET} command, even in automatic recalculate mode. To be sure that changes made by the {LET} command are reflected in the worksheet prior to continuing with your macro, insert either a tilde (~) or the {CALC} command after the {LET} command.

{LOOK}

Purpose Reads the typeahead buffer and copies the first key into the specified cell.

Syntax {LOOK location}

Arguments

location — any cell, address, or named range. If the range contains more than one cell, 1-2-3 copies the keystroke in the top-left cell.

Usage Used to test for keystrokes made while the macro was not in interactive mode, i.e., busy doing something else. For example, if the macro was processing a {FOR} loop, you could use the {LOOK} command at the end to see if the user pressed any keys during the processing period and branch the macro accordingly. 1-2-3 uses the typeahead buffer to store keystrokes made since the last interactive command ended and the next one begins. 1-2-3 uses the contents of the typeahead buffer when processing keystrokes for the {?}, {FORM}, {GET}, {GETLABEL}, and {GETNUMBER} commands so that you do not have to manually prepare for them if one of these commands is the next command. If no keystrokes have been pressed since the last interactive command, {LOOK} returns a null string, i.e., just a left-aligned label prefix.

Examples Suppose you had a looping macro and needed to determine if the user had pressed a key during the process before continuing. You don't want to just let the pressed key be passed to the next interactive command (e.g., {?} or {GET}), but want to branch to a separate procedure called EVALUATE, if a key had indeed been pressed. You could use the following:

```
...
end of looping macro
{BLANK TEMP}
{LOOK TEMP}
{IF TEMP<>""}{BRANCH EVALUATE}
continue processing
...
```

{MENUBRANCH}

Purpose Initiates a designated macro menu by displaying the menu items in the control panel and then branching to the macro commands associated with the menu option selected by the user.

Syntax {MENUBRANCH location}

Arguments

location — a cell, address, or named range specifying the top-left corner of a macro menu. (See below for description of macro menus.)

Usage Used to display a user-defined macro menu and then act upon the user's selection by branching to the macro commands that start immediately below the second line of the menu prompt. Since this command BRANCHES to the selected commands, 1-2-3 passes macro control to the selected commands. (This is in contrast to the subroutine call logic of the {MENUCALL} command below.) You must explicitly redirect the macro control to the next process after the completion of the commands associated with the user's selection. If no redirection is provided, the macro ends when the selected process is completed.

Menu Structures The {MENUBRANCH} and its cousin {MENUCALL} allow you to create menus that appear and operate in the same fashion as 1-2-3's own menus. You can define both the top-line selection item prompts and the associated second-line detailed prompt. When a user selects an option, the menu macro either branches to the associated macro commands (if you use {MENUBRANCH}) or calls them as a subroutine (if you use {MENUCALL}). When creating menus, the following design rules should be followed.

1. Select a location to place the menu macro. It will require at least three rows and as many columns as there are options in the menu plus one blank cell to mark the end of the menu (up to the maximum of eight). If you define the full eight options, you do not need to leave the next cell blank. You should generally segregate your macros in a separate area of the worksheet.

2. Construct your menu by placing the menu choices in the first row of the menu macro range. The first choice should be placed in the top-left cell of the named range assigned to the menu. Each of the menu options should start with a different letter of the alphabet; otherwise, you will not be able to use the process of pressing the first letter of an option as a method of selecting that option. If more than one option has the same first letter, pressing that letter will always select the leftmost option, starting with the selected letter. Use single words as menu options or hyphenate multiple word options. While 1-2-3 will accept any length menu option (up to the width of the screen), you should try to keep them brief and clear.

Directly below each menu option you can enter the text of the second line of the menu that is displayed as each individual option is highlighted. You can include as much text as will display on your screen, though again it is better to be brief and clear. If the menu will branch to a submenu, you can follow 1-2-3's style of placing a copy of the first line of the submenu, showing its options, in the second-line prompt of the calling menu.

3. In the third line, enter the first macro command to be executed when the option is selected. This can be any macro command, but is usually a {BRANCH} or {subroutine} command that directs the processing to a specified macro procedure or subroutine. You can list an entire macro procedure in the column below each menu option, but this is often a messy style. Long macro commands will be visually truncated (but still operate correctly) if there is a command in the adjacent cell to its right.

Examples Figure 13.12 shows a menu that allows the user to select from among three options: Enter, Print, and Quit. The Enter option branches to the INPUT macro, which in turn recalls the MAINMENU to redisplay the menu. The Print option lists the print commands directly under the menu option. Even though there isn't an explicit {BRANCH} statement for the print option, it is still a logical branch since the {MENUBRANCH} command was used to initiate the menu. The Input option is really a double branch—first to the command under the option and then to the INPUT macro. The Print option also redirects the command back to the MAINMENU when it is finished. The final option, Quit, terminates the menu and the macro control with the {QUIT} command. The

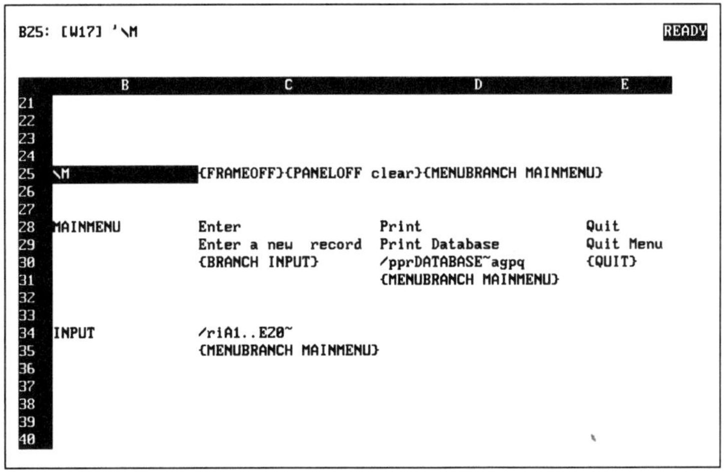

Figure 13.12 Menu controlling input and printing—using {MENUBRANCH}.

{QUIT} command is superfluous since the menu and, therefore the macro, will terminate at the end of any branch that doesn't explicitly direct the control to another macro or menu, or redirect the control back to the calling menu as the Enter and Print options do. It is, however, good programming practice to explicitly terminate branches when you want them to terminate. Then if you call the subroutine with a {subroutine} or {MENUCALL} command, they will still terminate as desired instead of returning to the calling routine. See {MENUCALL} below.

Notes If the user presses ESC or CTRL-BREAK while a macro menu is displayed, the menu is cancelled and control is passed to the command following the command ({MENUBRANCH} or {MENUCALL}) that activated the menu.

You can use a menu to display a message in the control box. By creating a single-option menu, you can use the full first and second line of the menu for a two-line message. The first line will be highlighted and the second will appear in normal text. Since there is only one option, pressing ENTER will automatically select it and continue processing the commands below it.

The first option is always the default option, highlighted when the menu is first displayed. You should use this fact to place the most likely or least destructive option in this location. This forces the user to explicitly choose another option.

Cautions Don't place any leading spaces in the menu option names or the select-by-first-character technique won't work. Don't branch to a menu with {BRANCH} or {subroutine} or 1-2-3 will treat the menu prompts as labels to be typed into the current cell.

{MENUCALL}

Purpose Initiates a designated macro menu by displaying the menu items in the control panel; then calls the macro commands associated with the user's selected menu option as a subroutine; and finally returns to the next command after the {MENUCALL} command when the subroutine is complete.

Syntax {MENUCALL location}

Arguments

location — a cell, address, or named range specifying the top-left corner of a macro menu. (See {MENUBRANCH} above for description of macro menu.)

Usage Used to display a user-defined macro menu and then act upon the user's selection by calling to the macro commands that start immediately below the second line of the menu prompt as a subroutine. Since this command CALLs to

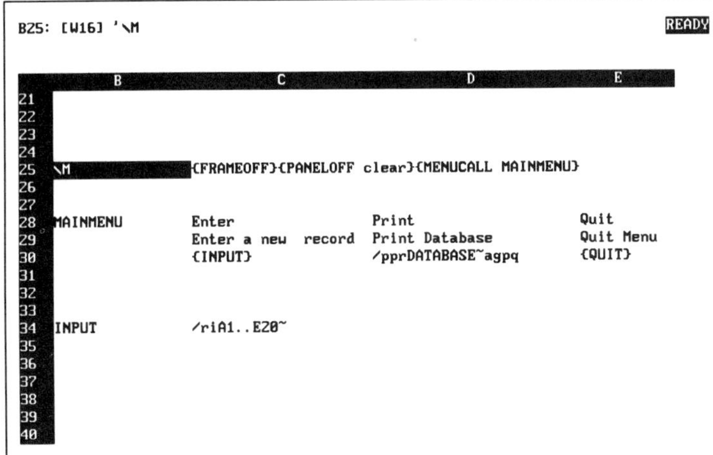

Figure 13.13 Menu controlling data input and printing using {MENUCALL}.

the selected commands, 1-2-3 passes macro control to the selected commands and then returns to the calling location after the subroutine completes (as contrasted to the branching logic of the {MENUBRANCH} command above). See {MENUBRANCH} for a discussion of menu structures.

Example Figure 13.13 shows the same menu as shown in Figure 13.12, adapted for use with the {MENUCALL} command. Notice the repositioning of the commands used to redirect control back to the main menu.

Notes If the user presses ESC or CTRL-BREAK while a macro menu is displayed, the menu is cancelled and control is passed to the command following the command ({MENUBRANCH} or {MENUCALL}) that activated the menu.

You can use a menu to display a message in the control box. By creating a single-option menu, you can use the full first and second line of the menu for a two-line message. The first line will be highlighted and the second will appear in normal text. Since there is only one option, pressing ENTER will automatically select it and continue processing the commands below it.

The first option is always the default option, highlighted when the menu is first displayed. You should use this fact to place the most likely or least destructive option in this location. This forces the user to explicitly choose another option.

Cautions Don't place any leading spaces in the menu option names or the select-by-first-character technique won't work. Don't branch to a menu with {BRANCH} or {subroutine} or 1-2-3 will treat the menu prompts as labels to be typed into the current cell.

{ONERROR}

Purpose Branches to a designated macro location immediately upon detecting an error condition. Stores the 1-2-3 error message in a designated cell.

Syntax {ONERROR branch-location,message-location}

Arguments

branch-location — a cell, reference or named range containing the macro commands to be executed in case of an error.

message-location — OPTIONAL—a cell, reference, or named range where 1-2-3 will store the 1-2-3 error message generated by the error.

Usage Used to trap errors and remedy them without interrupting the macro control. Most frequently used when user-supplied data is used to perform a command (such as opening a file into memory) that can generate an error if data is entered incorrectly or the requested item is not available. Rather than let the error terminate the macro, the {ONERROR} command can direct the user to perform corrective action and then repeat the command that generated the error.

Only one {ONERROR} command can be active at any one time. Once activated, {ONERROR} remains in effect until an error occurs, another {ONERROR} command is executed, or the macro ends.

Example Figure 13.14 shows a macro that erases a user-specified range. Note that it uses the self-modification strategy of placing the entered range name into the path of the macro at the cell named RANGE. If an error occurs, as it would if the range requested did not exist, 1-2-3 branches to the ERROR macro, which in turn displays the ERR_MENU menu. The macro uses a two-option menu to allow the user to try again or cancel the procedure. In the second line of the menu, cells C15 and D15 display the error message generated by 1-2-3. Cell C15 is the designated message-location named MESSAGE and cell D15 simply copies the label. This causes the error message to appear on the second line of the menu in the control box, allowing it to be displayed without moving the cell pointer from the current position in the worksheet.

Notes {ONERROR} is not designed to trap macro syntax errors. They are reported as they occur and the macro process is terminated.

If you use the {ONERROR} command to loop back to the step that generated the error, be sure to reset the {ONERROR} command by issuing it again. Be sure to give the user the option of quitting out of the correction loop if he is unable to correct the error.

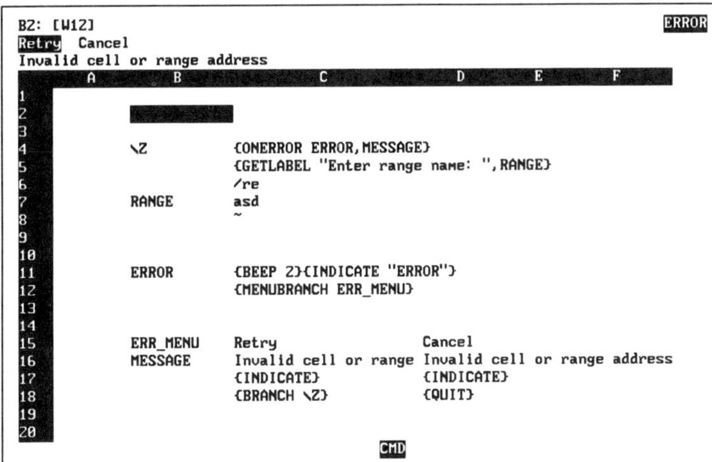

Figure 13.14

Error trapping with {ONERROR}.

Cautions {ONERROR} clears the subroutine stack, which prevents it from returning to the calling location after completion. If an error occurs while the macro is in a subroutine, you must explicitly return it to the calling macro.

1-2-3 does not automatically recalculate the worksheet after the {ONERROR} command even in automatic recalculate mode. To be sure that changes made by the {ONERROR} command are reflected in the worksheet prior to continuing with your macro, insert either a tilde (~) or the {CALC} command at the beginning of the macro code in the branch-location.

{OPEN}

Purpose Opens a named text file in one of four read/write access modes: read-only(r), read-write(w), modify(m), or append(a).

Syntax {OPEN name,access}

Arguments

name — full file name including the extension (e.g., donors.txt or penguins.prn) or a cell reference to a cell containing a full file name. If the file is not in the current directory of the current drive, you must preface the file name with the full path including the drive name and the directory name (e.g., "A:\data\penguins.prn") and you *must* enclose the file name in quotes.

access — one of four letter codes that correspond to the four access modes as follows:

r — read only access—opens an existing file for read only; you cannot write, modify, or append. Places the byte-pointer at the beginning of the file.

w — write access—opens a new or an existing file for write access, placing the byte-pointer at the beginning of the file. If you open an existing file with the w option, 1-2-3 will overwrite the old file with the new file, effectively deleting all of the existing data in the file. To add to or modify data in an existing file, use the a and m access codes instead.

m — modify access—opens an existing file for read and/or write access. Places the byte-pointer at the beginning of the file. Does not delete current data, but will allow you to overwrite existing data.

a — append access—opens an existing file for read and/or write access. Places the byte-pointer at the *end* of the current data, allowing you to easily append data to it.

Usage Before you can read or write to a text file from within 1-2-3, you must first open the file with the {OPEN} command. After opening the file, you can use the {READ}, {READLN}, {WRITE}, and {WRITELN} commands depending on the access requested at the time you opened the file. If you requested r access, you will only be able to use {READ} and {READLN}; otherwise you can use all four commands. When you are finished with the text file you must explicitly close it with the {CLOSE} command. 1-2-3 does not close open files at the end of the macro. It does close them at the end of a session (though it is not a good practice to leave files open).

Text files are valuable for keeping track of values or transactions that accumulate over time. The append option makes it very easy to append new entries to the end of a file. You might want to use one to maintain an audit trail of a transaction processing macro.

Examples {OPEN penguins.prn,w} opens a new file called penguins.prn with read and write access. If an existing file were named penguins.prn, it would be overwritten, erasing any data contained in the file.

```
{OPEN penguins.prn,r}
```

opens the existing file, penguins.prn, for read-access only.

```
{OPEN penguins.prn,m}
```

opens the existing file, penguins.prn, with read and write access, placing the byte-pointer at the beginning of the file.

```
{OPEN penguins.prn,a}
```

opens the existing file, penguins.prn, with read and write access, placing the byte-pointer at the end of the file.

Notes Remember to close a file when you are finished with it with the {CLOSE} command.

Cautions If you open an existing file with write access (w), you will erase the current contents of the file. If you want to append data to the file, use append (a) access. If you want to modify existing data use modify access (m). Only use write access (w) if you really want to start with an empty file.

{PANELOFF} and {PANELON}

Purpose The {PANELOFF} command locks the control panel at its current state or clears and locks the panel for the duration of the macro or until a {PANELON} command is executed.

Syntax {PANELOFF clear} and {PANELON}

Arguments

clear — OPTIONAL—used to clear the control panel before locking it.

Usage The {PANELOFF} command is frequently used to prevent the wildly changing menus of an active macro from distracting the user while the system is under macro control. To lock the control panel in its current state, use {PANELOFF}. To clear the control panel before you lock it, use {PANELOFF clear}. To reactivate the control panel, use {PANELON}.

Example To lock the panel in a clear state during the execution of a macro

```
{PANELOFF clear}
...
macro commands
...
{PANELON}
```

Notes To lock the window in addition to the control panel, use {WINDOWSOFF}. To control the status indicator, use {INDICATE}.

{PUT}

Purpose Places a number or label in a cell specified by its offset from the top-left corner of a specified range.

Syntax {PUT location,column-offset,row-offset,entry}

Arguments

location — any range address or name that contains the target cell.

column-offset — any number or a cell reference to a cell that contains a number representing the number of columns from the leftmost column in the range in which to place the entry. The leftmost column of the range has an offset of 0.

row-offset — any number or a cell reference to a cell that contains a number representing the number of rows below the top row of the range in which to place the entry. The top row of the range has an offset of 0.

entry — any number, literal string, formula, or cell reference to a cell containing one of these. If the entry is a formula, 1-2-3 evaluates the formula and enters the value in the designated cell.

Usage The {PUT} command is very similar to the {LET} command. It performs the same function, but instead of placing the entry in an explicitly named location, it places it in a location specified by its relative position to the top-left cell of the specified range.

Example To place the contents of the cell called GROUPER into the cell two columns over and four rows down within the range called FISH you would use:

```
{PUT FISH,2,4,GROUPER}
```

Cautions 1-2-3 does not automatically recalculate the worksheet after the {PUT} command even in automatic recalculate mode. To be sure that changes made by the {PUT} command are reflected in the worksheet prior to continuing with your macro, insert either a tilde (~) or the {CALC} command after the {PUT} command.

{QUIT}

Purpose Terminates the current macro and returns control to the user.

Syntax {QUIT}

Arguments None.

Usage Used to provide an immediate exit from a position in the macro back to interactive READY mode. Often used as the branch action for an {IF} command.

Example To exit the macro if the value of cell PASSWORD is not equal to "Octopus" use the macro:

```
{IF PASSWORD<>"Octopus"}{QUIT}
```

Notes Corresponds to the /XQ command.

While it is not necessary to place a {QUIT} command at the end of every branch that you want to be a terminus for your macro, it is a good practice. If the given branch is accessed via a {subroutine} call or a {MENUCALL} command, it would not terminate the macro without the {QUIT} command. If it is accessed via a {BRANCH} or {MENUBRANCH} command, the {QUIT} command is superfluous but not damaging. Besides, it makes your intentions explicitly clear that you want to terminate your macro at the end of the specific branch.

{READ}

Purpose Reads a specified number of bytes from the currently open text file, copies them into the specified cell and moves the byte-pointer forward the same specified number of bytes.

Syntax {READ byte-number,location}

Arguments

byte-number — any number from 0 to 512, a formula evaluating to a such a number, or a cell reference to a cell containing such a number or numeric formula. A negative number or number greater than 512 is equated to 512. If the number exceeds the number of bytes remaining between the current byte-pointer and the end of the file, 1-2-3 copies all the remaining bytes.

location — any cell, address, or named range. If the range contains more than one cell, 1-2-3 copies the bytes in the top-left cell.

Usage Used to read data from a text file into the current worksheet.

Example To read 10 bytes from the current open file into the cell named SHARKS:

```
{READ 10,SHARKS}
```

Notes You must open a file with the {OPEN} command before you can read it.

{READ} copies the carriage and line feed characters at the end of each line of the text file. If you want to skip these characters, use {READLN}.

If 1-2-3 does not execute the {READ} command, (e.g., you forgot to open a file), it processes the command to the right of the {READ} command in the same cell. If it does execute correctly, 1-2-3 moves directly to the next cell below the {READ} command. This can be used as a specialized {IF} type condition test, allowing you to branch to an error correction routine if the {READ} fails.

Cautions 1-2-3 does not automatically recalculate the worksheet after the {READ} command, even in automatic recalculate mode. To be sure that changes made by the {READ} command are reflected in the worksheet prior to continuing with your macro, start the next line of the macro with either a tilde (~) or the {CALC} command.

{READLN}

Purpose Reads the rest of current line from the currently open text file, copies it into the specified cell, and moves the byte-pointer forward to the next line of the text file.

Syntax {READLN location}

Arguments

location — any cell, address, or named range. If the range contains more than one cell, 1-2-3 copies the bytes in the top-left cell.

Usage Used to read data from a text file into the current worksheet one line at a time. The {READLN} reads from the current byte-pointer position to the end of the current line. If the byte-pointer is not at the beginning of the current line, the bytes that precede it will not be copied. The {READLN} then moves the byte pointer to the beginning of the next line. It does not copy any of the line feed or carriage return characters to the worksheet.

Example To read the rest of the current open line into the cell named SHARKS:

```
{READLN SHARKS}
```

Notes You must open a file with the {OPEN} command before you can read it.

{READLN} does not copy the carriage and line feed characters at the end of each line of the text file. If you want to copy these characters, use the {READ} command.

If 1-2-3 does not execute the {READLN} command, (e.g., you forgot to open a file), it processes the command to the right of the {READLN} command in the same cell. If it does execute correctly, 1-2-3 moves directly to the next cell below the {READLN} command. This can be used as a specialized {IF} type condition test, allowing you to branch to an error correction routine if the {READLN} fails.

Cautions 1-2-3 does not automatically recalculate the worksheet after the {READLN} command even in automatic recalculate mode. To be sure that changes made by the {READLN} command are reflected in the worksheet prior to continuing with your macro, start the next line of the macro with either a tilde (~) or the {CALC} command.

{RECALC}

Purpose Recalculates a designated portion of the worksheet when recalculation mode is set to manual.

Syntax {recalculate location,condition,iterations}

Arguments

location — any cell, address, or named range containing the cell(s) to be recalculated.

condition — OPTIONAL—generally any formula that evaluates to a logical value of true (1) or false (0), a cell reference to a cell containing such a formula or value. Logical formulas contain one or more of the logical operators

=, <, >, <=, >=, <>, #AND#, #OR#, #NOT#

Conditional arguments can also contain any other type of formula, number, string, or cell reference though they often would have no logical meaning. For example, {IF "walrus"} is legal but has no meaning, since the logical value of a string is always 0, which always means false. In addition, blank cells, ERR and NA equal 0 and evaluate to false. 1-2-3 will continue to recalculate the designated range until the condition evaluates to true.

iterations — OPTIONAL—any number, formula evaluating to a such a number, or cell reference to a cell containing such a number or numeric formula. Instructs 1-2-3 to repeat the recalculation the specified number of times.

Usage Used to recalculate a designated portion of the current worksheet when the recalculation mode is set to manual. Can significantly speed up recalculation when the user can determine which cells need to be recalculated. You can select to recalculate the specified range row by row by selecting {RECALC}, or column by column by selecting {RECALCCOL}. You should recalculate by rows if the dependent formulas are located below and/or to the left of the cells on which they depend. If the dependent formulas lie above or to the right of the cell on which they depend, you should select {RECALCCOL}.

Examples To recalculate the range TURTLES in a rowwise fashion, use:

```
{recalculate TURTLES}
```

To recalculate the range APPROX in columnwise fashion,until the cell named DELTA contained within the range APPROX is less than 10 or a maximum or 100 recalculations, (e.g., a successive approximation calculation), use:

```
{RECALCCOL APPROX,DELTA<=10,100)
```

Notes If you exclude the condition argument and include the iterations argument, you must be sure to insert all the argument separators, for example:

```
{recalculate RANGE,,25}
```

If the condition references a cell containing a formula, and the formula needs to be updated during each recalculation iteration before the condition is tested, it must be located within the location range.

Cautions 1-2-3 does not recalculate any formulas outside the designated range. It is your responsibility to insure that all such formulas are properly updated with the {CALC} command within the macro or by pressing the CALC key (F9) when the macro is finished.

{RESTART}

Purpose Clears the subroutine stack so that the macro is no longer returned to the calling macro location at the conclusion of the subroutine.

Syntax {RESTART}

Arguments None.

Usage The {RESTART} command is only used in subroutines called by other macro commands. In normal operation, control is returned to the calling location at the conclusion of the subroutine. If you branch from the subroutine, control is returned to the calling location at the conclusion of the branch. But what if you want to permanently branch out of a subroutine as the result of an error or some other condition? The {RESTART} command clears the subroutine stack (the part of memory where the calling location's address is stored), thus eliminating the link back to the calling location and allowing the macro to end or branch freely.

If 1-2-3 encounters a {BRANCH} command after the {RESTART} command in the subroutine, 1-2-3 will follow the branch and will *not* return to the subroutine's calling macro command at the conclusion of the branch.

If 1-2-3 does not encounter a {BRANCH} command after the {RESTART} and before reaching the end of the subroutine, the macro will terminate at the end of the subroutine.

If there is more than one subroutine call stored in the stack (in the case of nested subroutines), the {RESTART} command clears them all.

Examples To branch from a subroutine called PROCESS to an error message macro called ERR_MESS in the case of an error code of true in the cell named ERR_CODE you would use:

```
PROCESS   ...
          {IF ERR_CODE=@TRUE}{RESTART}{BRANCH ERR_MESS}
          ...
```

To terminate the macro at the conclusion of PROCESS, you would use:

```
PROCESS   ...
          {IF ERR_CODE=@TRUE}{RESTART}
          ...
```

{RETURN}

Purpose Returns control from a subroutine to the calling macro immediately without completeing the subroutine.

Syntax {RETURN}

Arguments None.

Usage If you want to exit from a subroutine to the calling routine before the normal end of the subroutine, use the {RETURN} command. If the subroutine was initiated by a {subroutine} call or {MENUCALL} command, control is passed to the next command in the calling routine. If the subroutine was initiated by the {FOR} command, control is passed to the {FOR} command. The iteration counter is incremented and, if further iterations are still required, control is passed back to the subroutine, otherwise it is passed on by the {FOR} command to the next command in the calling macro.

Example To return from a subroutine called PROCESS to its calling program in the case of an error code of true in the cell named ERR_CODE you would use:

```
PROCESS   ...
          {IF ERR_CODE=@TRUE}{RETURN}
          ...
```

Notes If {RETURN} is encountered in the main body of the macro instead of in a subroutine, it is the equivalent of {QUIT} and terminates the macro.

{SETPOS}

Purpose Moves the byte-pointer to the specified byte position in the open text file.

Syntax {SETPOS offset}

Arguments

offset — any number, formula evaluating to a such a number, or cell reference to a cell containing such a number or numeric formula. The offset number specifies the byte position relative to the first byte of the file. The first byte will have an offset of 0. The last byte will have an offset equal to one less than the value returned by the command {FILE-SIZE}. Negative offset numbers will be treated as 0.

Usage Used to move the byte-pointer to a specified location in the open text file before a {READ} or {WRITE} command. You must open the file with the {OPEN} command before you can use {SETPOS}.

Example To move the cell pointer to the byte position 10 in the currently open text file, use:

```
{SETPOS 10}
```

Notes If 1-2-3 does not execute the {SETPOS} command (e.g.,you forgot to open a file), it processes the command to the right of the {SEPOS} command in the same cell. If it does execute correctly, 1-2-3 moves directly to the next cell below the {SETPOS} command. This can be used as a specialized {IF} type condition test, allowing you to branch to an error correction routine if the {SETPOS} fails.

Cautions It is possible to move the byte-pointer beyond the end of the file. You can use the {FILESIZE} command to determine the limit (one less than the filesize), and the {GETPOS} command to determine the current byte-pointer location in order to test the offset number before executing the {SETPOS} command.

{SYSTEM}

Purpose Suspends 1-2-3 and executes the designated operating system command.

Syntax {SYSTEM command}

Arguments

command — any string contained in quotes or cell reference to a cell containing such a string. The string can be any valid system command or batch file.

Usage Used to execute other programs and commands without leaving 1-2-3 or macro control. This could be used to format disks or backup data under macro control. Alternatively, it could permit you to run your word processor from within 1-2-3 Release 2.2 while you are writing a book about it.

Example To format a disk in drive a:, use:

```
{SYSTEM "format a:"}
```

Notes If the executed command sets a system error level, you can test for it using the @INFO("osreturncode") function.

If you want to leave 1-2-3 temporarily and go to the operating system's command mode (the DOS prompt), use the /S command.

Cautions When operating with the DOS operating system, do not use the {SYSTEM} command to load memory-resident or terminate-and-stay-resident (TSR) programs. If you do, you may interfere with 1-2-3's memory management program and crash the system.

{WAIT}

Purpose Pauses the macro execution until the specified time, while displaying the WAIT indicator.

Syntax {WAIT time}

Arguments

time — any number, formula evaluating to a such a number, or cell reference to a cell containing such a number or numeric formula representing some time in the future. If the time specified has already passed, 1-2-3 ignores the {WAIT} command.

Usage Used primarily to pause the operation of a macro for a specified period of time to display a message. To specify a period of time to wait, combine the @NOW function with the @TIME function to specify a point in time a fixed period of time away form the current time. See the example.

Examples To provide an automatic rest break, use the following:

```
{BEEP 3}{BEEP 2}{BEEP 3}
{WAIT @NOW+@TIME(0,5,0)}
{ESC}
```

{WINDOWSOFF} and {WINDOWSON}

Purpose The {WINDOWSOFF} command locks the worksheet display in its current state for the duration of the macro or until a {WINDOWSON} command is executed.

Syntax {WINDOWSOFF} and {WINDOWSON}

Arguments None.

Usage The {WINDOWSOFF} command is frequently used to prevent the wildly changing worksheet displays of an active macro from distracting the user while the system is under macro control. To lock the display in its current state use {WINDOWSOFF}. To reactivate the worksheet display movement use {WINDOWSON}.

Example To lock the screen during the execution of a macro:

```
{WINDOWSOFF}
...
macro commands
...
{WINDOWSON}
```

Notes Locking the screen speeds up macro execution as 1-2-3 doesn't have to rewrite the screen after each command.

To lock the control panel in addition to the display screen, use {PANELOFF}. To control the status indicator, use {INDICATE}.

{WRITE}

Purpose Writes the specified string to the open text file.

Syntax {WRITE string}

Arguments

string — any string contained in quotes, or formula that evaluates to a string, or a cell reference to a cell that contains a label or formula that evaluates to a string.

Usage Used to write the specified string starting at the current byte-pointer location. 1-2-3 converts the string from the LMBCS code that it uses to store characters internally to the codes required by the operating system for text files and then places the converted string in the file starting with the first character at the current position of the byte-pointer. 1-2-3 then moves the byte-pointer to the position beyond the last character written.

Examples To write "Mako" to the new file SHARKS.TXT use:

```
{OPEN SHARKS.TXT,w}
{WRITE "Mako"}
{CLOSE}
```

To append "Great White" to the same file:

```
{OPEN SHARKS.TXT,a}
```

```
{WRITE "Great White"}
{CLOSE}
```

Notes You must open a file with the {OPEN} command using one of the three write access codes: w—write, m—modify, or a—append.

If 1-2-3 does not execute the {WRITE} command (e.g., you forgot to open a file), it processes the command to the right of the {WRITE} command in the same cell. If it does execute correctly, 1-2-3 moves directly to the next cell below the {WRITE} command. This can be used as a specialized {IF} type condition test, allowing you to branch to an error correction routine if the {WRITE} fails.

{WRITELN}

Purpose Writes the specified string to the open text file and adds a carriage return and line feed.

Syntax {WRITE string}

Arguments

string — any string contained in quotes, or a formula that evaluates to a string or a cell reference to a cell that contains a label or formula that evaluates to a string.

Usage Works exactly the same as the {WRITE} command, except it adds a carriage return and line feed to the end of the specified string. See {WRITE}.

Example To write "Lemon" to the new file SHARKS.TXT use:

```
{OPEN SHARKS.TXT,w}
{WRITELN "Lemon"}
{CLOSE}
```

To append "Tiger" to the same file:

```
{OPEN SHARKS.TXT,a}
{WRITELN "Tiger"}
{CLOSE}
```

Notes You must open a file with the {OPEN} command using one of the three write access codes: w—write, m—modify, or a—append).

If 1-2-3 does not execute the {WRITE} command (e.g., you forgot to open a file), it processes the command to the right of the {WRITE} command in the same cell. If it does execute correctly, 1-2-3 moves directly to the next cell below the {WRITE} command. This can be used as a specialized {IF} type condition test, allowing you to branch to an error correction routine if the {WRITE} fails.

/X Commands

1-2-3 Release 2.2 continues to support the /X commands introduced with Release 1A. Each of the commands has an equivalent {} advanced macro command described below. The advanced macro functions perform all the functions of the /X command and add additional features in a few cases. In general, you should avoid using the /X commands altogether and especially if they might be called in a situation other than the READY mode as they can produce unexpected results. The /X commands are offered only to maintain compatibility with Release 1A macros. We strongly recommend that you cease using them.

Table 13.3 below lists each /X command and refers you to the appropriate {} advanced macro command. You are advised to read the associated section as the table only lists the differences between the /X command and its associated {} advanced macro command.

Table 13.3 /X Commands

/XC	{subroutine}	Subroutine call Identical in function except the /XC command cannot pass arguments to the subroutine as the {subroutine argue1,argue2,...,arguen} form of the {subroutine} is able to do.
/XG	{BRANCH}	Branch Identical in function.
/XI	{IF}	Condition test Identical in function.
/XL	{GETLABEL}	Label input Identical in function.
/XM	{MENUBRANCH}	Display menu and branch to selection Note there is no /X equivalent to {MENUCALL}.
/XN	{GETNUMBER}	Number input Identical in function.
/XQ	{QUIT}	Terminate macro and return to READY mode Identical in function.
/XR	{RETURN}	Return from subroutine Identical in function.

▸ Add-In

Purpose

Used to attach, detach, invoke, and clear 1-2-3 add-in applications.

Description

With Release 2.2, Lotus has included the Add-In manager as part of its main program. In previous releases, it was available as an added product. The integration of the Add-In manager has reduced the amount of memory required for the manager and gives you direct access to the manager via the /Add-In option on the main menu. (You can still access the Add-In manager via the ALT-F10 key combination unless you redefine that key combination). The Add-In manager allows you to attach properly installed add-in applications or @functions.

Release 2.2 has two add-in applications included with the package: Allways and Macro Library Manager. Allways is a spreadsheet publishing system that extends your ability to print presentation quality worksheets and graphs. The Macro Library Manager allows you to store macros in a special portion of main memory and in special library files so that they can be used with any worksheet. (Previously, both add-ins were separately sold programs.) Release 2.2 also includes one add-in @function @D360, which calculates the difference between two dates based on a 360 day year.

Defaults

None.

Usage

To use an add-in application, you must first install it according to the instructions provided with the program. (You probably installed Allways and the Macro Library Manager when you installed 1-2-3.)

After they've been installed, add-in applications are ready to be attached; you must attach an add-in before you can use it. The attachment process links the application to 1-2-3. This link allows you to call up the add-in with an assigned key (or with the /Add-In Invoke option), and it also allows the add-in to read the current worksheet.

To attach an add-in application, select the Attach option from the /Add-In menu, point to the add-in you wish to attach, and press ENTER. (See Figure Add.1.) Next, you will be prompted to assign an ALT-function key combination to the add-in—to invoke it without using the 1-2-3 menu. If, for example, you assign the number 7 to the add-in, you will be able to call it up with ALT-F7 from your worksheet.

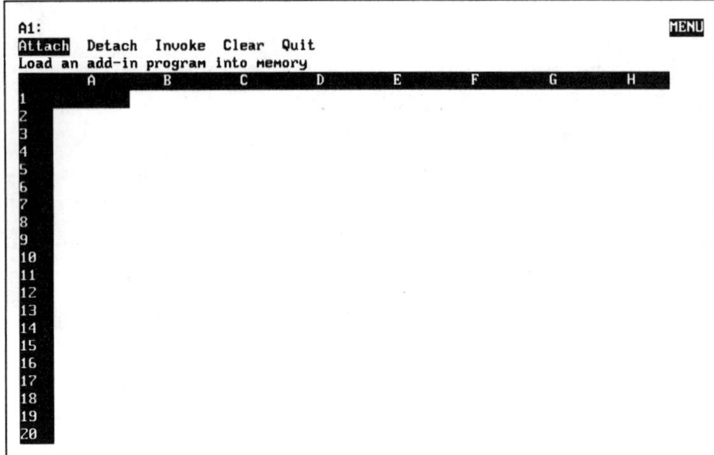

Figure Add.1
Add-In Main Menu.

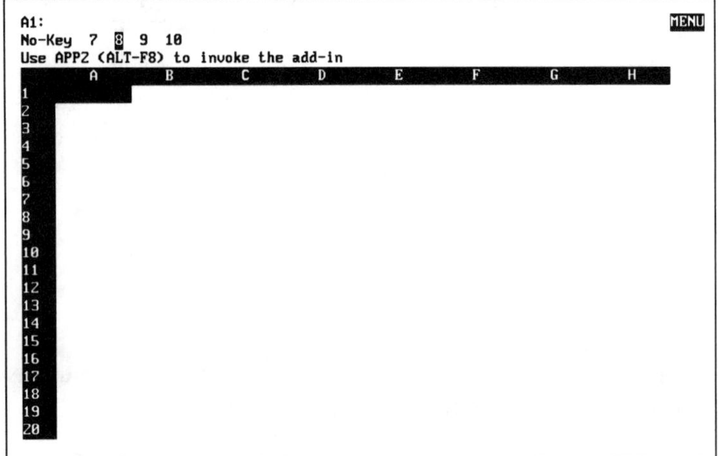

Figure Add.2
Assigning a key combination for invocation.

Select one of the available key combinations from the menu or, if you do not wish to assign a key, select the No-Key option (see Figure Add.2). If you do not assign a key to the add-in, it can only be invoked with the Invoke option from the /Add-In menu.

To invoke an add-in application that you have attached, press the assigned key combination (e.g., ALT-F8) or select the Invoke option from the /Add-In menu, point to the application's name and press ENTER. The add-in program's main menu will then be displayed. See Figure Add.3.

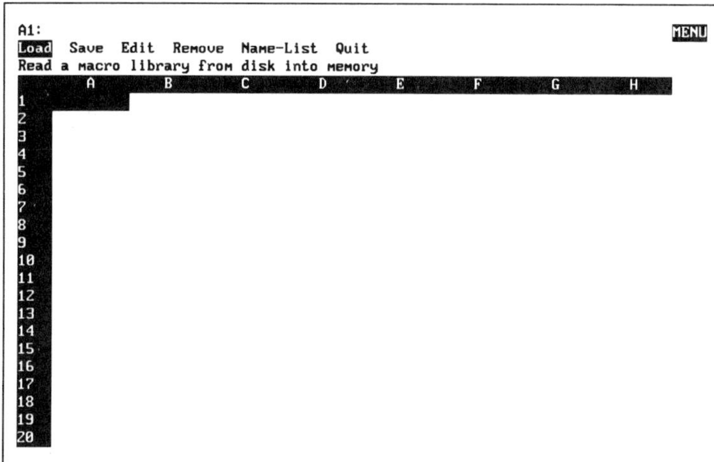

Figure Add.3 Macro Library Manager Main Menu.

Examples

To attach the Allways spreadsheet publisher, assign it the key combination ALT-F8, and then invoke it:

1. Select the command /Add-In Attach.
2. Point to ALLWAYS and press ENTER.
3. Select 8, for the APP2 key combination (ALT-F8).
4. To invoke ALLWAYS, either select the Invoke option from the /Add-In menu, point to ALLWAYS, and press ENTER; or press ESC to return to READY mode and press the ALT-F8 key combination.

Notes

When you attach an add-in application, you use additional memory. This may reduce the size of the worksheet you can work with. You can detach add-ins that you are not using to free up some memory. Also, if you have enabled the Undo feature, you can free up additional memory by disabling it.

Add-In Attach

Purpose

Used to attach an add-in application to 1-2-3 by loading it into memory and linking it to 1-2-3. When you attach an application, you may assign a keystroke combination (ALT plus a function key) that can be used to invoke it.

Description

To use an add-in program, you must first install it, then attach it as described below, and finally you must invoke it. Once attached, an application will remain in memory until it is specifically removed with /Add-In Detach or Clear or until you end the 1-2-3 session.

Defaults

None.

Usage

To attach an application, you must first be sure that it has been properly installed. If you are attaching one of the two add-ins included with Release 2.2 (Macro Library Manager and Allways), they were installed when you first installed 1-2-3 and set up Allways. Other add-in applications provide their own instructions for installation.

The next step is to select /Add-In Attach. 1-2-3 will display a list of all the available installed add-in applications. (If you are using a two-diskette system, the disk that contains the installed add-in application must be located in one of the two disk drives.) Either point to one of the applications or type in its name and press ENTER. 1-2-3 will prompt you to select one of the available key combinations to invoke the application. You can select from among the remaining keys (keys already assigned to other applications will not be listed on the menu), or you can select No-Key. If you select the latter, the only way to invoke the application is by using the Invoke option on the /Add-In menu.

Notes

To automatically attach one or more applications each time you start up 1-2-3, use the /Worksheet Global Default Other /Add-In Set option.

The number of add-in applications and the maximum size of your worksheet will depend on the total amount of memory you have available. If 1-2-3 determines that it does not have enough memory left to attach another add-in, it will display an error message. If you have attached too many add-in applications, you may not be able to reload a worksheet that you were once able to load. In either case you may have to detach one or more add-in applications to free up memory. Alternatively, you can turn off the Undo feature (if Undo is on) to release some memory for the additional add-in or worksheet.

Add-In Clear

Purpose

Removes all add-in applications from memory. Used to clear memory for a large worksheet or to free up memory for other add-in applications.

Description

The Clear option removes all add-in applications from memory, making more memory available for large worksheets or other add-in applications. All assigned add-in key combinations (ALT-F7 through ALT-F10) are also freed up and can be reassigned.

Defaults

All attached add-ins.

Usage

To clear all attached add-in applications from memory, select /Add-In Clear.

Notes

To detach a single add-in application without affecting the others, use /Add-In Detach.

Add-In Detach

Purpose

Used to remove an attached add-in application from memory and release the key combination assigned to that add-in.

Description

The Detach option removes the designated application from memory, freeing the assigned memory for use by other add-in applications or large worksheets.

Defaults

None.

Usage

To detach an attached add-in application, select /Add-In Detach. 1-2-3 will list all attached add-in applications. Either point to the desired application name or type it in at the prompt and press ENTER. The selected add-in will be removed from memory and the associated key combination (if one was assigned) will be released for assignment to another add-in application. Before you can invoke the detached add-in in the future, you must re-attach it with the Attach option.

Notes

If you want to detach all attached add-in applications, you should use the Clear option.

Add-In Invoke

Purpose

Used to start up an attached add-in application. This is the final step in activating an add-in. Generally, the main menu of the add-in application appears, and you are free to select from the options displayed.

Description

Before you can invoke an add-in application, be sure that it has been properly installed, and that you have attached it via the Attach command. (If you are using a two diskette system, the diskette containing the add-in program must also be in one of the two disk drives.) You can invoke any attached add-in application by selecting the Invoke option from the /Add-In menu. If you have assigned one of the four key combinations (ALT-F7 through ALT-F10) to the application, you can also invoke the application with the appropriate key combination.

Defaults

None.

Usage

To invoke an attached add-in application via the menu, simply select /Add-In Invoke. 1-2-3 will list the available attached add-in applications. Point to the desired application or enter its name at the prompt and press ENTER. The main menu or main screen of the add-in application will then be displayed.

Notes

The Invoke option can be used to invoke any attached add-in application, whether or not you have assigned a key combination to it. If you did not assign a key combination to a particular add-in at the time of attachment, selecting /Add-In Invoke is the only method for invoking that add-in.

The Invoke option is the recommended routine for activating add-in applications from within a macro. It is the only way that you can be sure to activate the correct add-in application.

Macro Library Manager

Purpose

The Macro Library Manager is an add-in application that allows you to store macros, data, and formulas in a special part of RAM memory and in special library files on disk. The macros, data, and formulas can then be loaded and used in any worksheet.

Description

The Macro Library Manager must be attached and invoked according to the procedures outlined in the /Add-In command section. Once invoked, you can store ranges of data (that can contain formulas), or ranges that contain named macros—the ranges are stored in a *macro library*. A macro library occupies a reserved space in main RAM memory and is also saved to a special disk file with an .MLB extension. You can save as many macro libraries as you wish. Each can contain as many as 16,376 cells. You can load as many as 10 macro libraries into memory at a time, assuming that you have sufficient main RAM memory to hold them all.

There are several reasons to use the Macro Library Manager for storing your macros or data:

1. Once you store a macro or macros in a library, they can be called from within any active worksheet. This means that you can develop a library of utility macros, such as ones that create standard worksheet layouts, insert common column or row headers, or perform complex calculations. The individual macros can then be called from within any worksheet, without the need to copy the macro itself into that worksheet. This not only saves space in the worksheet, it also works much faster. In the same fashion, you can store common data or formulas in a macro library and then reference them from within a given worksheet. For example, suppose you had a range containing a complex tax table. You could store the range in the macro library manager and then use it to look up the applicable tax rate without having to copy the data into the current worksheet.
2. Some macros are hazardous to themselves and can disrupt their own operation. For example, a macro that inserts or deletes rows from a worksheet could disrupt its own operation depending on where it is placed in the worksheet. If the inserted row fell in the middle of the macro, it could cause premature termination. If the deleted row fell within the macro, it could cause a critical step in the macro to be skipped. By moving the macro into the macro library, it is immune from its own actions and can insert or

delete rows with impunity. It can even erase the current worksheet or load another. You might create a macro that would sequentially load, recalculate, and resave a series of worksheets that were linked together in a daisy chain (where worksheet A depends on worksheet B, which depends on worksheet C, which depends on worksheet D, and so on) so that a change in the lowest worksheet is reflected in the top worksheet. This process would be impossible to perform directly with a macro loaded into one of the worksheets.

3. You can use the macro library as a temporary storage area for data you want to transfer between worksheets. Suppose you have calculated a particular series of values that you want to copy from one worksheet to another. You could save the range to the macro library, load the second worksheet and then recall the range from the library into the desired location. This is quicker and simpler than saving the first file to disk and then performing a /File Combine Copy command.

The Macro Library Manager has its own main menu that appears when you invoke the add-in application. See Figure Add.3. The options on the menu allow you to Save a range to a named library, Edit a range in a named library, Load a library, List the named ranges in a library, and Remove a named library from memory. Each of these commands is discussed in detail in the sections that follow. Before you move on to the specific commands, however, you need to know some basic rules about how the Macro Library Manager operates.

1. Each macro library can store 16,376 cells or two columns that are 8,188 rows long. The macro library reserves memory and disk space for *every* cell in the range that you store there. Because the macro library does not use a sparse matrix storage technique (a technique that allows you to store only cells with data), it is best to store your macros and data with as few blank cells as possible to avoid wasting memory and disk space.
2. 1-2-3 Release 2.2 can load as many as 10 separate macro libraries into memory at the same time. The actual number of libraries that you will be able to load depends on the total amount of memory you have available, the number and size of other attached add-in applications, the size of the worksheets you plan to load, and whether you have the Undo feature enabled. If you do not have sufficient memory to load a library, 1-2-3 will issue an error message. You will have to remove one or more macro libraries already in memory, detach one or more other add-in applications, or disable the Undo feature.

3. A macro library is *not* a worksheet and does not have cell addresses. Any cell addresses that appear within the macro library will be assumed to refer to the current worksheet. If you want to refer to other data that is stored in the macro library, you must assign it a range name. For example, if you are saving a macro or a formula that makes reference to a cell that is *also* saved in the *same* library, you must refer to that cell by an assigned range name. Its cell address will be lost as soon as it is saved to the library and removed from the worksheet in which it was created.
4. You cannot save a range to a macro library that contains a reference to another worksheet. If you attempt to save such a link, 1-2-3 will issue an error message.
5. When you edit a macro library, the contents of the macro library are copied to the current worksheet. If one or more range names in the macro library also exist in the current worksheet, 1-2-3 will warn you that a conflict exists and will ask you if you want the named ranges in the macro library to take precedence (Overwrite) or if you want the existing range names in the worksheet to take precedence (Ignore).
6. When a range name is used more than once in different libraries that are loaded into memory, or when a range name is used in a library and also in the current worksheet, 1-2-3 will search for the corresponding range in the following order:
   a. In the current worksheet,
   b. In the Macro Library first loaded into memory,
   c. In the Macro Library next loaded into memory, and so on.

   If 1-2-3 finds a named range in the current worksheet, it will ignore a range with the same name in the library. If it finds a range name in one library, it will ignore the named range in a subsequent library. It is essential that you use range names that are unique. You can use the Macro Library Manager command Name-List to list the named ranges in the library and the 1-2-3 command /Range Name Table to list the named ranges in the current worksheet.
7. You can reference a named range within a macro library from the worksheet only as the starting name for the macro or as an argument for an advanced macro command. For example, {LET DOLPHIN, 45} would assign the value 45 to the named range DOLPHIN in the macro library. You cannot use a library range name as the object of a 1-2-3 menu command such as /Copy or /Move.

8. You can use advanced macro commands to move data to and from a named range in a macro library. For example, the macro command {LET DOLPHIN, A25} would copy the contents of the cell A25 in the current worksheet into the range named DOLPHIN. You can also use advanced macro commands to alter a named range in a library. {BLANK DOLPHINS}, for example, will erase the contents of the range named DOLPHINS.
9. You can use the advanced macro commands to branch to subroutines that are located within the same library, in a different library, or located in the current worksheet. This allows you to create utility macros and/or menus that perform standard actions, place them in a library, and then call them from other macros located in a library or from a macro located in the current worksheet. Suppose you created a utility macro to format a diskette and create a backup of your worksheet. You could store the macro in a utility library and then call the subroutine as an option for any of the macros you create in your worksheets.
10. You can save formulas in a library. However, formulas contained in a library can *only* refer to ranges or cells also saved in the same library. Formulas in libraries *cannot* refer to ranges or cells located in the current worksheet or other libraries. Formulas contained in a library are automatically recalculated when the formula is saved to the library, or when a macro instruction changes a cell in the library, or when the macro executes either the {RECALC} or {RECALCCOL} command.
11. If the macro in a macro library contains a /File Retrieve command, it will continue to run after the new worksheet is loaded unless the worksheet contains an autoexec macro (\0). In that case, the autoexecute macro will be executed and the library macro will be terminated. You can avoid this by turning the autoexecute macro feature off via the /Worksheet Global Default Autoexec No option. If you want to make the changed Autoexec setting permanent, be sure to use the Update option after making the change.

Using The Macro Library Manager

The key to using the Macro Library Manager is to understand the sequence of operation. You must first create your macros or your data ranges in the current worksheet. When you are certain that you have them working correctly, you should attach the Macro Library Manager using the /Add-In Attach command.

Then invoke the Macro Library Manager with the assigned key combination (ALT-F7 through ALT-F10) or with /Add-In Invoke. The next step is to use the Save option on the Macro Library Manager menu to save the range in your current worksheet that contains all the named macros and/or data ranges to a library file. The saved range will be copied into memory and to a .MLB file on disk. The range will then be removed from the current worksheet. You can start a given macro from the saved library in one of two ways. If you assigned the macro one of the 26 special macro initiator keys (ALT-A through ALT-Z) you can start the macro with the specified key combination. Otherwise you can press the RUN key (ALT-F3), highlight the appropriate macro name from the list of names (or just type it in), and press ENTER.

You can remove a macro library from memory with the Remove option. This removes the copy of the library in memory, but does not remove it from disk. You can reload the library at a future time with the Load option. You can edit the macros or data ranges in the library with the Edit option.

You can easily use the macro manager on a network so that several users can have access to the same macro libraries simultaneously. You must be careful, however, when saving or editing macro libraries; be sure that only one user is editing and saving a particular library at one time. If one user edits and saves a library with a given name and a second user simultaneously edits and saves a library with the same name, the initial user's changes will be overwritten.

Macro Library Manager Edit

Purpose

Used to copy the contents of a macro library into the current worksheet to edit or delete macros or named ranges.

Description

The only way to modify the contents of a macro library file is to use the Edit option. When you do, the entire contents of the macro library file are copied into the current worksheet. You can then edit or delete any macros or named ranges in the library and resave the edited library contents using the Save option.

Defaults

The current cell pointer location in the current worksheet.

Usage

To edit a macro library, you must load it into memory using the Load command (see below). Then you must decide if you want to edit the library within the current worksheet or whether you want to clear the worksheet first with /Worksheet Erase Yes to be sure that there are no extraneous ranges or macros that may be accidently resaved to the library. In the former case, select a clear area of the current worksheet in which to place the library macros and named ranges. Be sure that the area below and to the right of the specified location is clear or can be overwritten. The Edit command will copy the entire macro library into the designated location and overwrite any data in its way.

Initiate the command by selecting Edit. 1-2-3 will prompt you for the name of the macro library to be edited. Highlight the appropriate library name (or type it in) and press ENTER. If the library is password-protected, you will be prompted to enter the password. (Remember that passwords are case-sensitive.)

If one of the range names in the macro library is the same as one in the current worksheet, 1-2-3 will warn you that there is a duplication of range names. You will be asked if you want to Overwrite the existing range name in the worksheet or Ignore the one in the library. Finally, you will be prompted to specify the upper-left corner of the range in the current worksheet into which you want to copy the library.

Examples

To edit the macro called INSERT in the library called UTILITY:

1 Clear the current worksheet by saving it (if desired) and then selecting /Worksheet Erase Yes.
2. Invoke the Macro Library Manager by pressing the assigned key combination or by selecting the command /Add-In Invoke. Highlight MACROMGR from the list of attached add-ins and press ENTER.
3. Select the Load option and specify the UTILITY library.
4. Select Edit and specify the UTILITY library.
5. If the macro library is password-protected, enter the password at the prompt.
6. Since you have cleared the worksheet, you should not have any duplicate range names. If you didn't clear it and you do have duplicate names, you will be prompted to select Overwrite (if you want the range name in the library to take precedence) or Ignore (if you want to ignore the library range name).

7. Specify where in the current worksheet you want the macro library to be placed and press ENTER. The default is the current cell pointer location.
8. Edit the macros or data ranges as desired.
9. Resave the library contents by selecting the Save option.

Notes

If you want to include the same data in several worksheets, you can save the data to a library, and then repeatedly use the Edit command to copy the common data to each of the worksheets in succession.

Cautions

When you edit a macro library, it is copied into the current worksheet in the designated range. It will overwrite any data in its way. Be certain that the area below and to the right of the designated range can be overwritten before you invoke this command.

Macro Library Manager Load

Purpose

Used to load an existing library file (with an .MLB extension) from disk into memory for use or for editing.

Description

You must load a macro library file into memory before you can use any of the macros or data that it contains. The Load command places the specified library into memory in sequence after the last library loaded.

Defaults

None.

Usage

Select the Load option from the Macro Library Manager menu. (If you are working with a dual drive system, make sure that the disk that contains the desired library is located in one of the two disk drives.) 1-2-3 will display the macro libraries contained in the current directory. If you want to select from another drive or directory, press the ESC key to clear the current directory and type in the alternative one. Select the desired library by highlighting it from the list (or by typing in its name) and pressing ENTER. If you have already saved or loaded a library file with the same name into memory, 1-2-3 will ask if you want to replace the version in memory, you can select either Yes or No as desired.

Examples

To load the library called UTILITY into memory:

1. Invoke the Macro Library Manager. (Either press the assigned key combination or select /Add-In Invoke, point to MACROMGR from the list of add-ins, and press ENTER.)
2. Select Load and specify the UTILITY library at the prompt.

Notes

You must load a library file before you can use any of the macros or data ranges it contains and before you can edit it.

Cautions

If you load too many macro libraries, you may not be able to attach another add-in application and/or you may be restricted in the size of worksheet you can load. You may want to remove one or more macro libraries from memory with the Remove option if this occurs.

Macro Library Manager Name-List

Purpose

Lists the range names in a specified library. This is useful for ensuring that macro library range names do not duplicate the named ranges in other libraries or in the current worksheet.

Description

Unlike the /Range Name Table command, the Name-List command only lists the range names and provides no description of their size. Since they are saved in a library they have no cell references.

Defaults

The current cell pointer location.

Usage

To create a list of the range names in a library, you must first load it into memory. Select an unprotected area of the current worksheet for the output location. Be sure that the output location can be overwritten. Select the Name-List command. At the first prompt, select the desired library name from the list of the libraries loaded into memory. At the second prompt specify the desired output location.

Examples

To list the range names in the UTILITY library starting in cell F4:

1. Invoke the Macro Library manager by pressing the assigned key combination or selecting the command /Add-In Invoke, pointing to MACROMGR, and pressing ENTER.
2. Load the library by selecting the Load option and specifying the UTILITY library at the prompt.
3. Initiate the Name-List command.
4. At the prompt for the library name, point to the name UTILITY and press ENTER.
5. At the prompt for the output location, type `F4` and press ENTER.

Notes

The most common use of the Name-List command is to ensure that different libraries that have been loaded at the same time do not have duplicate range names.

Cautions

The Name-List command creates a table one column wide with as many rows as there are named ranges in the library. This table will overwrite any data in its way, so be sure that the column below the designated output cell is blank or can be overwritten before invoking this command.

Macro Library Manager Quit

Purpose

Exits the Macro Library Manager add-in application and returns you to the READY mode of 1-2-3.

Description

Exits the Macro Library Manager without detaching it. In order to reactivate it, you must either press the assigned key combination or select the Invoke option from the /Add-In menu.

Defaults

None.

Usage

To exit the Macro Library Manager add-in application, select the Quit option.

Notes

Quitting the Macro Library Manager does not remove the loaded libraries from memory, nor does it detach the add-in application. You can still use the macros and named ranges from the library.

If you want to remove a given library, use the Remove option described below. If you want to remove the entire add-in application from memory, use the /Add-In Detach command.

Macro Library Manager Remove

Purpose

Used to remove a single library from memory in order to free up additional memory for other libraries, other add-in applications, or larger worksheets. Leaves a copy of the library on disk, so that it can be loaded again in the future.

Description

The Remove option simply clears the library from RAM memory. Any range names and macros contained in the library will become undefined and formulas that reference them will show as ERR.

Defaults

None.

Usage

To remove a library from memory, select the Remove option from the Macro Library Manager menu and select the desired library file from the list of those in memory.

Examples

To remove the macro library UTILITY from memory:

1. Invoke the Macro Library Manager by pressing the assigned key combination or selecting the command /Add-In Invoke, pointing to MACROMGR and pressing ENTER.

2. Remove the library by selecting the Remove option and specifying the UTILITY library at the prompt.

Notes

To remove the library file from disk, use the /File Erase Other command. Press ESC to edit the file extension. Enter `*.MLB`, press ENTER and then select the library file to be deleted.

Macro Library Manager Save

Purpose

Used to copy a section of the current worksheet into both a library in main RAM memory and a library file (.MLB) on disk.

Description

The Save option copies the designated range from the current worksheet to both the active memory and to disk. The range will then be erased from the current worksheet. All references to named cells or ranges contained in the range being saved will then refer to named ranges in the library and no longer to the cells in the worksheet. If the library already exists, you will be asked to confirm your desire to overwrite it. You can save a library with a password. Once assigned, you must use the password to Save or Edit the library, but you do *not* need the password to load the library. This allows developers to create libraries for others that they can freely use, but that cannot be altered.

Defaults

None.

Usage

To save a range of cells and named ranges to a library, first determine the range you wish to save. Try to keep the physical size to a minimum by eliminating blank cells in the range. Initiate the command by selecting Save from the Macro Library Manager menu. Specify the name of the macro library to be saved either by pointing to an existing name or entering a new name and pressing ENTER. If the library already exists, you will be asked to confirm your desire to overwrite the older version or to terminate the save process. Next, you will be prompted to specify the range to be saved. The range should encompass all cells and named ranges, including both data and macros that you wish to save to the library. You can either specify the save range by an assigned name or by its range address;

however, all ranges referred to in the macros and formulas in the saved range must use assigned range names. Cell addresses have no meaning in the library, except to refer to cells in the current worksheet.

Examples

To save the range A1..F12 containing the named macros INSERT and DELETE and the data range MONTHS (containing the twelve month names in a column) to the library named UTILITY:

1. Invoke the Macro Library Manager by pressing the assigned key combination or selecting the command /Add-In Invoke, pointing to MACROMGR, and pressing ENTER.
2. Select the Save option.
3. Either point to the library name UTILITY if it already exists or type it at the prompt and press ENTER.
4. If the library already exists, select Yes to confirm your desire to overwrite it.
5. Specify the range to be copied to the library by pointing to or typing the range `A1..F12` and pressing ENTER.
6. If you want to save it with a password, select Yes at the password prompt, otherwise select No. If you select Yes, enter your password and be sure to remember it, since you can't edit the library without it. Also, remember that passwords are case-sensitive.

Notes

If you want the Macro Library Manager to load a particular library into memory each time the manager is invoked, assign the name AUTOLOAD.MLB to the library. The macros contained in the library will be immediately available for use, though they will not autoexecute (even if you assign one the \0 autoexecute name).

Each library can store 16,376 cells or two columns 8,188 rows long. The macro library does not use the sparse matrix storage technique of the worksheet file (only storing cells that contain data). Instead, it reserves memory and disk space for each cell in the range. It is helpful to store your macros and data as densely (fewest blank cells) as possible to avoid wasting memory and disk space.

Purpose

The add-in application Allways allows you to control the printing of worksheets and graphs. The added features of Allways greatly enhance the printed output of 1-2-3 Release 2.2. With Allways you can specify font faces and sizes, spacing, and shading; you can add boxes and lines, include graphs within the printed page, and add color to your printed output (assuming you have a color printer).

Description

The Allways program, like the Macro Library Manager, is an add-in application that has been bundled with Release 2.2. As such, it works from within 1-2-3 after you have properly installed it, attached it, and invoked it. See Chapter 11 for detailed explanations about these procedures. In general, you will install Allways (using the AWSETUP program) at the same time you install 1-2-3, Release 2.2. Unless you need to change your hardware configuration (e.g., to add or change a printer selection), you will not need to alter or reinstall Allways thereafter. On the other hand, you will need to attach the Allways add-in application each time you start up 1-2-3, and you will have to invoke it each time you want to use it to print a worksheet or graph. If you wish, you can use the /Worksheet Global Default Other Add-In Set command to instruct 1-2-3 to attach Allways automatically each time you load 1-2-3.

Please note that while Allways supplants the /Print command and the PrintGraph utility for most printing requirements, it does not eliminate their usefulness. They are both fully supported in Release 2.2 and can be used in the same fashion as previous releases. This is especially important for users who have developed macros that use the /Print commmand and wish to use them with Release 2.2. Printing macros continue to operate as they did in previous releases.

Once invoked, Allways presents your current worksheet on the screen in WYSIWYG (What You See Is What You Get) format. It uses the graphics display mode of your computer to show the exact type face size, positioning, and other special effects that will be printed when you select the Print option from the Allways command menu. (Allways can be used without a graphics monitor, but will not display in WYSIWYG format.) The WYSIWYG display allows you to view the printed appearance of your worksheet (and/or graphs) before you commit them to paper. This makes it much easier to design your worksheet reports. Figures Add.4 and Add.5 show the difference between 1-2-3's text display of a worksheet and Allways' WYSIWYG graphics display.

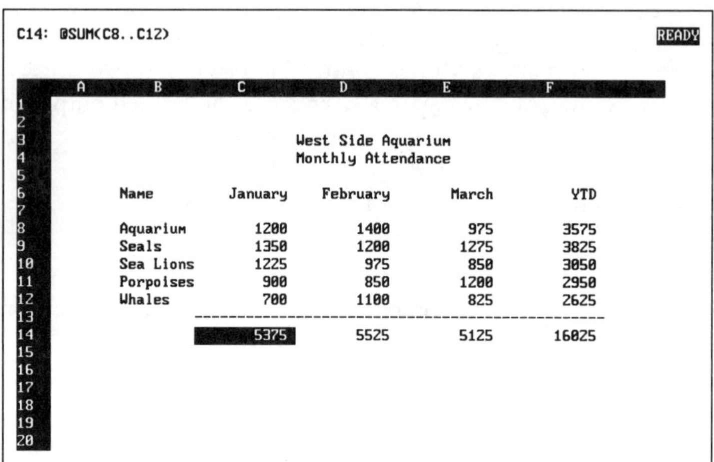

Figure Add.4
Worksheet display before invoking Allways.

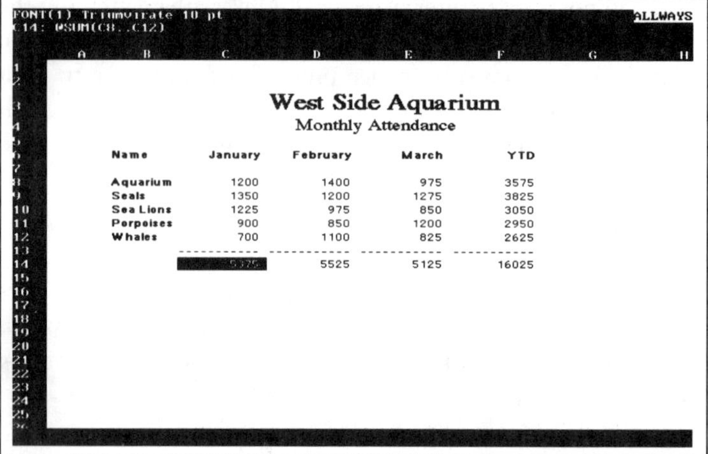

Figure Add.5
Worksheet display after invoking Allways.

In addition to the WYSIWYG display of the worksheet, Allways displays its own command menu when you press the slash (/) command key (see Figure Add.6).

The command menu works exactly like the standard 1-2-3 menu system. You can make selections either by highlighting an option and pressing ENTER or by pressing the first letter of that option. Besides using 1-2-3's horizontal menu system, Allways introduces pull-down menus. These are used for selecting options from a list of similar options. For example, Figure Add.7 shows a pull-down menu for the selection of font face and size.

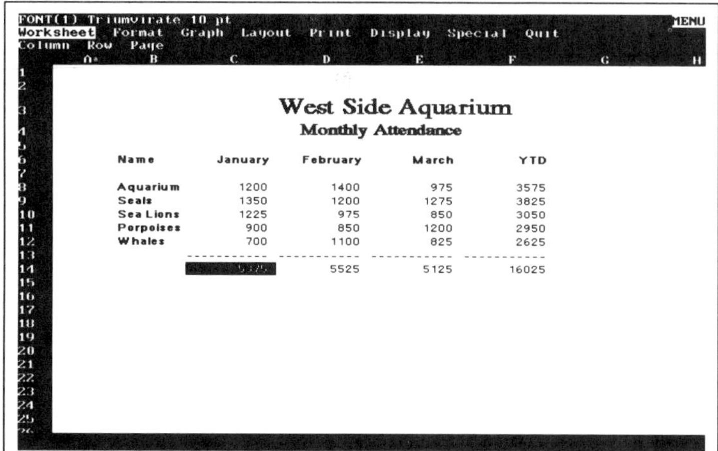

Figure Add.6

Allways Main Menu.

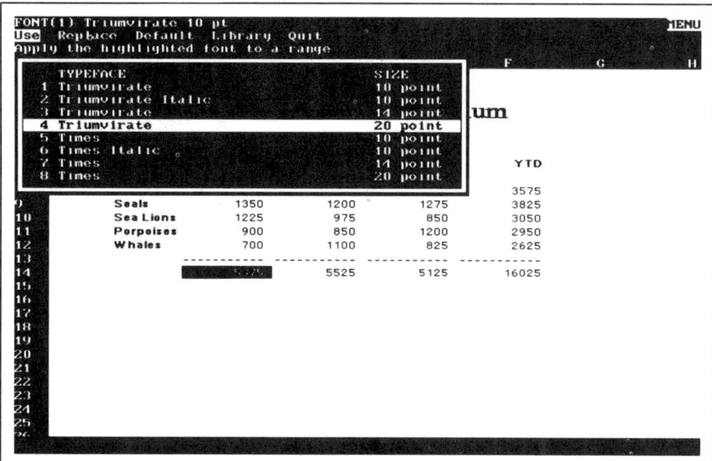

Figure Add.7

Allways Pull-down Menu.

The Allways pull-down menus operate somewhat differently than those used by most other programs in that, in some cases, you can still select from the horizontal menu *after* you have made the selection from the pull-down menu. For example, in Figure Add.7, the pull-down menu was displayed when /Format Font was selected, then option 4—Triumvirate 20 Point—was chosen with the down cursor key. At that point you could either press ENTER to accept the default command Use or select one of the other commands (i.e., Replace) to execute on the selected font.

The Allways system allows you to control many features of your printed output. The following describes the most significant options.

Fonts Fonts are generally characterized by four variables: Face, Point Size, Stroke Weight, and Slant Angle. The Face describes what the characters look like. For example, a given face may or may not include serifs, the small horizontal strokes at the top and bottom of each letter that facilitate reading blocks of text. The text of this book uses a serif face, while the headings and figure captions use a sans serif (without serif) typeface. Common serif typefaces are Courier and Times, while Helvetica and Triumvirate are common sans serif typefaces.

The Size of a single character is most often described by its height as measured in points (one point is about 1/72 of an inch). For example, Triumvirate 12 point is about 12/72 or 1/6 of an inch high. Fixed pitch fonts (with characters that are all the same size), can be measured in terms of pitch or characters per inch. For example, typewriters typically use Courier 10-pitch type.

The Stroke Weight is usually categorized as normal or bold, though some fonts come in thinner or light stroke weights or heavier or extra bold stroke weights. The Slant Angle is generally divided between italic or non-italic (often called Roman).

Allways supports any font that your printer is capable of printing either directly or via supported cartridges. In addition, Allways is supplied with its own set of soft fonts, including: Courier, Times (serif), and Triumvirate (sans serif). You can select from a variety of sizes—from 5 to 24 points. Allways groups a set of eight fonts together into a Font Set. You can select from the eight fonts in a given font set and use them for different sections of your worksheet. You can change the fonts included in the current font set by replacing one of the current fonts with a new font. The changed font set will be stored with the current worksheet. You can also store different Font Sets on disk and recall them at a later time or for use with a different worksheet. You can even change the default font set (the font set first displayed for a new worksheet).

The font labeled number 1 is the Default Font for the current worksheet. Any text that is not explicitly assigned a different font will use the Default Font. The Default Font in Figure Add.7 is Triumvirate 10 Point.

Column Width You can alter the column widths within Allways in much the same fashion as you do in 1-2-3; however, you have much finer control. Column widths are measured in numbers of characters. You can define the column width either as a whole number of characters (e.g., 9 or 12) or include a fractional character (e.g.,

9.33 or 12.5). The width of a single character is defined in terms of the width of a single digit in the default font (font number 1). Thus, the actual width of a column will depend on the number or fractions of characters assigned as well as the size of the default font.

Row Heights The heights of individual rows depend on the size of the font(s) used in the row. Initially all row heights are set to Auto. This causes Allways to assign a row height (measured in points) that is one or two points greater than the largest font used in that row. You can also set the row height manually to create special effects or to fine-tune the printed image.

Label Alignment Like 1-2-3, Allways allows you to center, right- or left-justify the text in a cell. Unlike 1-2-3, Allways will permit the text to overlap the left or right edge of a cell in order to properly center or right-justify the text. This is especially important if you are using different sized text in centered or right-justified titles or labels. Just as 1-2-3 allows a long left-justified label to spill over into empty cells to the right, Allways allows large or long labels to spill over into cell(s) to the left and/or to the right to achieve proper alignment. When you right-align a label with the double quote label prefix ("), Allways includes a space to the right of the label in the same fashion as 1-2-3. This facilitates the positioning of labels over columns of numbers that are automatically right-aligned with a single space. Allways adds an additional form of right alignment using the vertical bar label prefix (¦). This prefix causes Allways to right-align without the additional space.

You cannot change the label alignment directly in Allways. You must set and change them from within 1-2-3. You can edit the label in the current cell to change its label prefix ('—Left, "—Right, or ^—Center). Alternatively, you can change the label prefix in a range of cells with the command /Range Label Left/Right/Center. You can change the default label prefix with the command /Worksheet Global Label-Prefix Left/Right/Center.

Lines, Boxes, and Shading Allways provides a wide array of highlighting tools, including the ability to surround cells with single or multiple cell boxes, underline text, and add a shaded background. These can be used individually or in combination to highlight data ranges or other areas of the printed output.

Graphs One of the greatest enhancements offered by Allways is the ability to print a graph from within 1-2-3 without having to save the graph, exit from 1-2-3, and start up PrintGraph. In addition, Allways allows you to include one or more graphs directly in the formatted page, so that you can mix data and graphs on the same page. While Allways does not add to the number of available graph types, it does provide additional control over the sizing and format of printed graphs (especially the text for graph labels and titles).

Usage

To use Allways, you must first install it, and attach it to 1-2-3. These procedures are described in detail in Chapter 11. The key to using Allways successfully is understanding how it works. Allways is a print formatting program. With one minor exception (Justification), Allways *does not alter your worksheet file*. Instead, Allways creates a separate file with the same name as the 1-2-3 .WK1 file but with an .ALL extension. This Allways file contains all the formatting information that you specify in Allways and it is saved at the same time that you save the worksheet file in 1-2-3. When you invoke Allways, it reads the *data* from your worksheet file and the *format* from the corresponding Allways file. It uses this combination of information to display the worksheet on the screen in the WYSIWYG format and to print the data on your printer.

If you alter data in the worksheet (e.g., change a value from 5 to 10), Allways will change the value to correspond to the worksheet, but will not change the format for that cell. Allways uses some of the formatting information that is prescribed in 1-2-3. For example, Allways uses the label prefix specified in 1-2-3 to determine the alignment of labels. Similarly, Allways uses the cell format established in 1-2-3 to determine the number of decimal places and presentation to use for data in a particular cell or range of cells. There is no way of controlling these features from within Allways. Therefore, you must use a combination of controls from 1-2-3 and Allways to achieve your desired results. You will find that you will switch back and forth between 1-2-3 and Allways, using the separate formatting features from each to produce your output.

Since Allways creates its own file that attaches a format that you select to each of the cells in the print range, you must keep the format file and the worksheet file in synch. This means that you must have Allways active each time you operate on a worksheet that has been formatted with Allways. If you don't and you alter the structure of your worksheet, Allways will not know that you modified the worksheet structure in its absence. For example, suppose that you specified Triumvirate 20-point type for the title of a table of figures in cell C5 of a worksheet and saved your worksheet before exiting 1-2-3. The next time you worked on the worksheet, however, you neglected to attach Allways (or you detached it to free up memory space for the Undo feature or for a large worksheet). Now, suppose that you inserted a new row in the worksheet, pushing the data table and its title down one row (to C6). Since Allways was not attached at the time of the change, it did not alter its corresponding format file. The next time you load the worksheet, attach Allways and invoke it, you will notice that the Triumvirate 20-point type specification is still assigned to cell C5, instead of cell C6 where the title is now located. The two files are out of synch. The only effective way to repair the damage is to go to your backup to find a matching pair of worksheet and Allways files or to manually reformat the new worksheet file to create a new "in synch" format file. To avoid such problems, you may want to use the auto-attach feature and have Allways attached at the beginning of each session (using the /Worksheet Global Default Other Add-In Set command).

The usual sequence of events for using Allways is to create your worksheet in 1-2-3, format individual cells and ranges in the usual fashion, and position your data in the layout you wish to use for printing. When your data is ready, invoke Allways. Use the function key combination (ALT-F7 through ALT-F10) that you assigned when you attached Allways or use the /Add-In Invoke command. Once invoked, Allways will display the current section of the worksheet in WYSIWYG format using the default fonts and formats. (See Figure Add.5.) You can move around the screen using the cursor keys and F5 GOTO key in the usual fashion. You can call up the Allways main menu by pressing the slash (/) key as in 1-2-3. (See Figure Add.6.) Then you can select ranges and formats or add graphics as you wish. Each change will be displayed on screen (if you have a graphics monitor). After you complete your formatting, you can print the desired range. After you complete the formatting session, be sure to return to 1-2-3 (press ESC from the Allways READY mode) and save the worksheet file. This will cause the Allways format file to be saved to disk as well.

While the Allways commands work in much the same fashion as the 1-2-3 commands and use the same grammar and syntax, there is one key difference. You can specify a range within Allways *before or after* you select the command or format. Thus you could specify the range A5..C12 from the Allways READY mode simply by pressing the period anchor key (.) and highlighting the range A5..C12 . You could then select one or more commands to set the font type and/or size, shading, and so on. This greatly facilitates the process of setting more than one formatting feature for the same range of cells.

Notes

Allways requires a hard disk and 512K of main memory. It *cannot* be run on systems with less than these requirements.

Cautions

Allways does not save the formats you establish until you save the corresponding worksheet to disk. If you change an Allways format and then fail to save the worksheet to disk, the format changes will be lost—even if you made no change to the worksheet itself. This becomes critical when you realize that the wonderful new Release 2.2 feature that warns you if you try to quit without saving a changed worksheet does *not* consider format changes in Allways when it checks for changes to the worksheet. This means that 1-2-3 will *not* warn you if you try to quit without saving your format changes.

Allways affects the way the Undo feature works in 1-2-3. Since Allways must keep track of the changes you might make in 1-2-3, such as inserting or deleting rows or columns, it must prevent you from using the Undo feature to reverse these changes. This is because Allways cannot determine from the 1-2-3 Undo feature what exactly is being undone. It therefore simply blocks any attempt to Undo a change that it must keep track of. Such changes include row and column insertions and deletions, and the /File Save or /File Retrieve commands. You can still undo any changes that are irrelevant to Allways. For instance, if you erase data in a cell or move it to a different cell, Allways does not need to make any changes to its .ALL file and will let you undo one of these commands.

Allways Display Color

Purpose

Used to alter the colors for the worksheet display on a color monitor.

Description

With color monitors, you can control what colors are displayed for the cell background, foreground, and the cell pointer.

Defaults

Background—Black
Foreground—White
Cell-Pointer— Blue

Usage

To change one or more of the display colors, select /Display Color. Then select one of the three areas: Background, Foreground, or Cell-Pointer. Allways will display a pull-down menu of color options appropriate for the selected area. Select one and press ENTER.

Notes

Display colors do not affect the color of printed output. This is controlled by the /Format Color command.

Allways Display Graphs

Purpose

Determines whether graphs within the current document are displayed on screen in actual form or simply as a shaded box.

Description

Allways can display graphs that have been placed in the current document either as actual graphs or as shaded boxes. The advantage of the shaded box is that it greatly improves the response time for moving about the screen and making changes that require Allways to redisplay the screen. The advantage of the actual graph display is that you can see exactly how the graph will appear with your text. You can easily switch between these modes using the /Display Graph command.

Defaults

Graphics mode on.

Usage

To switch from displaying actual graphs to displaying a hatched box, select /Display Graph No. To redisplay the actual graph, select /Display Graph Yes.

Notes

On text-only monitors or on graphics monitors with Allways set to text mode, graphs are displayed as a series of Gs (the letter).

You can use the GRAPH (F10) key to switch between actual graph and shaded box displays.

Allways Display Mode

Purpose

Used to switch between graphics and text mode while in Allways.

Description

If you are using a graphics monitor, you can display your worksheet in WYSIWYG format using the monitor's graphics display mode. This allows you to see exactly how your worksheet will be printed, including large font sizes, boxes, and shading. If you want to view the worksheet in its normal text mode (as it appears in 1-2-3), you can select the Text option. To return to graphics mode, reselect the Graphics option. If you have a text mode only monitor (e.g., IBM Monochrome), you can only display your worksheet in text mode, though it will print with the full graphics format supported by your printer.

Defaults

For graphics monitors the default mode is graphics mode. For monochrome monitors the default (and only) mode is text mode.

Usage

To switch between graphics mode and text mode, select /Display Text. To switch back again, select /Display Graphics.

Notes

You can also use the DISPLAY (F6) key to switch between display modes.

Allways Display Zoom

Purpose

Used to alter the display size when in graphics mode.

Description

In graphics mode, you can alter the size of the display between 60% and 140% of normal size. This allows you to increase the size of the display to work with small fonts or to reduce the size of the display to get an overall view of the page layout.

Defaults

Normal size.

Usage

To alter the size of the display, select /Display Zoom and then one of the following options:

Tiny	60% of normal
Small	84% of normal
Normal	100% of normal
Large	120% of normal
Huge	140% of normal

Notes

You can also use the REDUCE (F4) and ENLARGE (ALT-F4) keys to cycle up and down through the different display sizes.

Allways Format Bold

Purpose

Used to bold (or unbold) the text in a cell or range of cells.

Description

The /Format Bold command, like many of the format commands, works as a toggle; it either Bolds normal text or Unbolds text that is already bold.

Defaults

Bolds normal text or Unbolds bold text.

Operates on the current cell or the predefined range.

Usage

As with many of the Allways format commands, you can specify the range to be bolded before or after invoking /Format Bold. If you specify a range before selecting the command, Allways does not prompt you for the range to be bolded. If you do not specify a range, you are prompted for one. To Bold the range A5..F12, select /Format Bold. At the prompt, specify the range by name, address, or by painting it, and press ENTER. Alternatively, you could specify the range before selecting /Format Bold by pressing the ANCHOR key (.) and highlighting the range. Then when you select /Format Bold, Allways will operate on the preselected range.

Notes

You can also use the BOLD (ALT-B) key to bold the current cell or currently selected range.

If you press the BOLD key after selecting a cell or range that is already bolded, it will be unbolded.

Allways Format Color

Purpose

Used to specify the color of text in a cell or in a range of cells when it is printed on a color printer.

Description

The /Format Color command allows you to select from seven different colors for printing. You can also select the Red-on-Negs option, which prints negative numbers in red and positive numbers in black. The ability to print the selected color depends on your printer. If you select white, the data will not be printed. The color choices are as follows:

1. Black
2. Red
3. Green
4. Blue
5. Cyan
6. Magenta
7. White
8. Red-on-Negs

Defaults

Black

Usage

To change the color of the values or labels in a cell or range of cells, select /Format Color. Select the desired color from the pull-down menu and specify the cell or range of cells at the prompt by name, address, or by painting it. If you have already specified a range before invoking the /Format Color command, it will not prompt you for a range and will operate on the pre-specified range.

Allways Format Font

Purpose

Used to assign fonts to individual cells or to a range of cells and to control the set of fonts available for selection.

Description

The /Format Font command has several subsidiary commands used to assign fonts to worksheet data and to control font options. The most common command is the Use option which assigns a particular font from the current font set to a cell or range of cells. The other commands (Replace, Default, and Library) are used to control the current font set. You can change the available fonts, save a font set to a library, restore a font set from a library, and modify or restore the system default font set.

When you assign a font to a portion of your worksheet, you can only select from the eight fonts in the current font set. When you first attach Allways, the current font set is the default font set. Each time you format a worksheet with Allways for the first time, Allways uses the default font set as the current font set. If you want to modify the current font set, you can use the Replace command. From that point on, the modified font set will be associated with the current worksheet and will be saved with it. When you load another worksheet, you will load *its* associated font set. In this way, the current font set can be unique for each worksheet. If you want to save the modified font set in a library for use with other worksheets, use the Library commands. If you want to restore or modify the default font set, you can use the Default command.

Default Controls the default font set, the set used each time Allways is attached to 1-2-3. The default font set will be used for all new worksheets until you modify the font set with the /Format Font Replace command. The /Format Font Default command has two subsidiary options: Restore and Update. The Restore option replaces the current font set with the default font set. This is useful for resetting the current font set to the default after making changes. The Update option saves the current font set as the default to be used for future sessions. The initial default font set created when you installed Allways consists of several sizes of Times and Triumvirate fonts. You can change this by using the Update option.

Library The Library option allows you to save the current font set to a library disk file. This, in turn, allows you to retrieve a specified font set from the library for use with other worksheets. For example, suppose you created a new font set using the Replace option—a font set composed entirely of different font sizes in the Times font family. You want to use this font set with several different worksheets. By saving the font set definition to the library with the Save option, you can later retrieve the same font definition into another worksheet with the Retrieve option. When you retrieve a font set, Allways substitutes the new fonts for the old fonts, according to the number assignments in each font set (i.e., cells formatted with font number 3 in the old set will be assigned to font number 3 in the new set.) The Erase option allows you to discard font sets in the library that are no longer useful. Please note that when you erase a font set from the library, you do not affect that font set's use and association with any worksheets that have been saved with that font set. Nor do you affect the fonts themselves.

Quit Allows you to return to the Allways READY mode.

Replace The Replace option is used to alter individual fonts in a font set. To replace a particular font in the current font set, highlight its name in the pull-down menu and select Replace. You will be presented with a list of available fonts for your particular printer. Highlight your replacement choice and press ENTER. The new font will replace the old font in the list of available fonts in the current font set. The new font will be assigned to all cells that were previously assigned to the old font.

Use Use is the most commonly used option. It assigns a particular font to a cell or range of cells. As with many format commands, you can specify the range before or after you select Use. If you specify the range before selecting /Format Font Use, you will not be prompted for a range and Allways will apply the selected font to the specified range. If you have not specified a range, Allways will prompt you for one after you select Use.

You can also use the special key combinations ALT-1 through ALT-8 to assign any one of the eight fonts to the currently selected cell or range of cells.

Allways Format Lines

Purpose

Used to add lines, boxes, and grids to your worksheet.

Description

Allways allows you to place a line along each of the four edges of a cell. You can place top, bottom, left, or right edge lines in one or more cells, or you can use one of the two special box and grid generating commands—Outline or All. The lines generated by these commands actually lie *between* adjacent cells so that a line across the bottom of one cell is redundant with a line across the top of the cell below it. This means that you can place a given line in either of the two adjacent cells. The only time this becomes significant is when a given cell lies at a page break. If a given cell is located on the last line of a page, a line placed underneath it will be placed on the same page, while a line placed at the top of the next cell will be placed at the top of the following page.

You can place a given edge line in contiguous cells and create a continuous line. Specify a range before you select /Format Line, and you can easily assign the same line to all the cells in a range and create a continuous line through the range.

The line options Top, Bottom, Left, and Right place lines along the associated edge of each cell in the specified range. The Outline option might be better named Box (though it can't because Box starts with the same letter as Bottom), since it really creates a box around the exterior of a multi-celled range. Likewise, the option All might be better named Grid, since it places a box around each cell in the range creating a miniature grid. See Figure Add.8.

The Clear option allows you to remove one or more lines from the edge(s) of the cells in a range. When you select the Clear option, you will be asked to specify what edges to clear or whether you wish to clear All lines.

Defaults

Current cell or currently specified range.

Usage

To create a line, box, or grid, specify the range of cells to receive lines before or after you select /Format Lines. If you specify a range before initiating the command, Allways will act upon the designated range. If you do not specify a range beforehand, Allways prompts you for it. Type in the range name, or address, or paint it.

Notes

To change the thickness of the lines, use /Layout Options Line-Weight.

You can also use the key combination ALT-L to cycle through the three options: Outline, All, and No lines for the current specified range or cell.

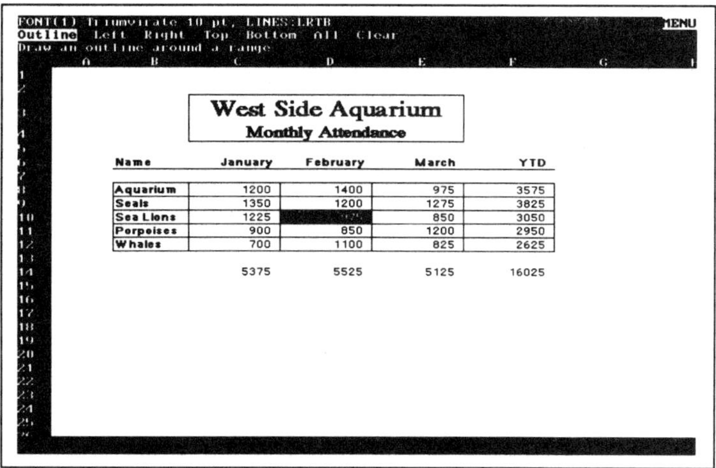

Figure Add.8
/Format Lines.

Allways Format Reset

Purpose

Used to reset the formatting for a cell or range of cells to the current defaults.

Description

When you reset the format settings for a specified range of cells, the font will be set to the default font (#1), the color will be set to black, and any bolding, underlining, lines, or shading will be removed.

Defaults

The current cell or specified range of cells.

Usage

To reset the format settings for a range of cells, select /Format Reset.

Allways Format Shade

Purpose

Used to add shading to a cell or range of cells.

Description

The /Format Shade command places one of three shading patterns behind the text of a cell. The Light and Dark shading options can be used to highlight text, while the Solid option will obscure text and is most often used to create solid dark lines. By shading a series of adjacent cells in a column or row and then altering the row height with /Worksheet Row Height Set or the column width with /Worksheet Column Width Set, you can control the thickness of a horizontal or vertical rule. Obviously, the cells used to create such a rule must be left empty in the 1-2-3 worksheet. Figure Add.9 illustrates the use of Light shading to highlight the title and YTD figures and the use of the Solid option to create a bolder underline below the column headings for the attendance data.

Defaults

No shading.

The current cell or specified range.

Usage

To add shading to a cell or range, you can specify the range of cells to be shaded

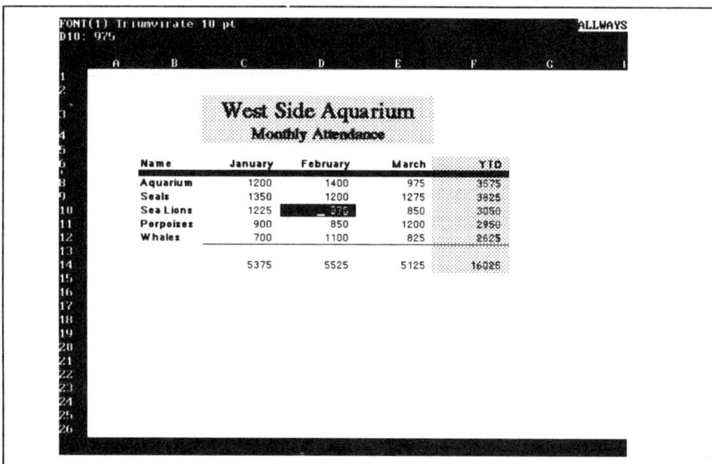

Figure Add.9
/Format Shade

before or after you select the command. If you specify a range before initiating the command, Allways will act upon the specified range. If you do not specify a range beforehand, Allways prompts you for it. Type in the range name or address, or paint it.

Notes

You can also use the key combination ALT-S to cycle through the four options, Light, Dark, Solid and No Shading for the current specified range or cell.

Allways Format Underline

Purpose

Used to underline the contents of a cell with a single line or the entire cell width with a double line.

Description

The /Format Underline command has two options: Single and Double. The two options operate somewhat differently. The Single option underlines only the contents of the cell (text or numbers); the Double option underlines the entire cell regardless of its contents or lack thereof. The Single line option is usually used to underline text, while the Double line option is most often used at the end of a column of numbers that are being totaled.

Defaults

The current cell or specified range.

Usage

To underline a cell or range or cells, specify the range of cells to be underlined before or after you select the command. If you specify a range before initiating the command, Allways will act upon the specified range. If you do not specify a range beforehand, Allways prompts you for it. Type in the range name or address, or paint it. To create a single line underline under the text only, select Single. To create a double line underline across the entire cell, select Double. To clear the underline specification from a range of cells, select Clear.

Notes

The single line underline will be printed in the same color as the text it underlines.

Allways Graph

Purpose

Used to insert 1-2-3 graphs into a printed report.

Description

The /Graph commands work in much the same fashion as the Lotus PrintGraph utility. It prints graphs that have been created in 1-2-3 and saved to disk as a .PIC file (i.e., using the 1-2-3 /Graph Save command). You must save the graph before it can be recognized by the Allways /Graph command. Unlike the PrintGraph utility, Allways /Graph commands are accessible from within 1-2-3 and allow you to place one or more graphs directly into your printed output.

You can position graphs anywhere on the worksheet by specifying a range of cells. Be sure to leave these cells blank or the graph will overwrite any data contained there. When you specify the location range, you are also establishing the basic size and proportions of the graph (though you can modify them with some of the /Graph commands). You can see the graph on the Allways display screen if you have a graphics monitor. You can also display the graph as a shaded box. While the latter option is not as elegant, it greatly reduces the time required to redraw the screen whenever you move the cell pointer or otherwise modify the screen. You can toggle between displaying the graph and the shaded box by pressing the GRAPH (F10) key.

Usage

The basic procedure for adding graphs to printed worksheets is to create the graph in 1-2-3, name it so that you can modify it in the future, and save it to a

.PIC file with the 1-2-3 /Graph Save command. Allways uses the .PIC file as its source for the graph's image. If you want to modify the contents of the graph, you must modify it within 1-2-3 and you must resave it with the /Graph Save command. Allways automatically uses the most recently saved .PIC file for a particular graph.

To place the graph, specify a range of cells. The graph will be automatically sized to fit the selected range. After placement, you can modify many of the attributes of the graph such as scale, margins, fonts, and colors. You can also use other Allways features such as line drawing, shading, and different font sizes to enhance the appearance of your graphs. In fact, you may find it advantageous to delete the titles from your graph and reset them as text within Allways, since Allways provides higher resolution text printing than the 1-2-3 graph file.

Allways Graph Add

Purpose

Used to insert a graph into a designated area in your worksheet for printing.

Description

The /Graph Add command is the primary command for placing 1-2-3 graphs into a worksheet. The size and the positioning of the graph is determined by the range you specify for the Add command.

Defaults

The graph is sized to fill the specified range.

Usage

Before you can place a graph, you must create it; this is done from within 1-2-3. You must also save the 1-2-3 graph to a .PIC file using 1-2-3's /Graph Save command. This saves the current image of the graph to a disk file. Please note that this is not the same as the /Graph Name command, which simply saves the current graph settings.

Allways uses the graphic file on disk as its source for the image, *not* the current graph within 1-2-3. This allows you to place more than one graph within a single worksheet when you print it. It also means that when you alter a graph in 1-2-3, you must be sure to resave it to disk. Allways will use the most recently saved version of the graph when it prints it.

To place a graph, you can either specify the location range before or after selecting the /Graph Use command. If you specify it before the command, Allways does not prompt you for the range; otherwise, it does. For example, suppose you wanted to place a graph below a table of numbers that showed the relative contribution of each aquarium display. (See Figure Add.10.) You would first need to create and save the graph to a .PIC file in 1-2-3. See /Graph in the Reference section and Chapter 9 for details about creating graphs in 1-2-3. Once the .PIC file is saved to disk, you are ready to place it in Allways. Select /Graph Add. Allways will display all the .PIC files in the current directory. If you want to look at a different directory, press the ESC key to clear the directory specification and enter the full path of the directory you want. Select a graph file by highlighting the graph name (or by typing in the name at the prompt) and press ENTER. Specify the range where you want to place the graph—by name, by address, or by painting it. Allways will place the graph accordingly and will display its contents or a shaded box representation of the graph, depending on the current setting of the Allways graph mode.

Notes

If you want to change the size or shape of the graph in row or column increments, use the /Graph Settings Range. You can adjust and fine-tune the graph dimensions by altering the column widths or row heights with /Worksheet Column Set-Width and /Worksheet Row Set-Height. You can modify the placement of the graph within the range by altering the margins with /Graph Settings Margins.

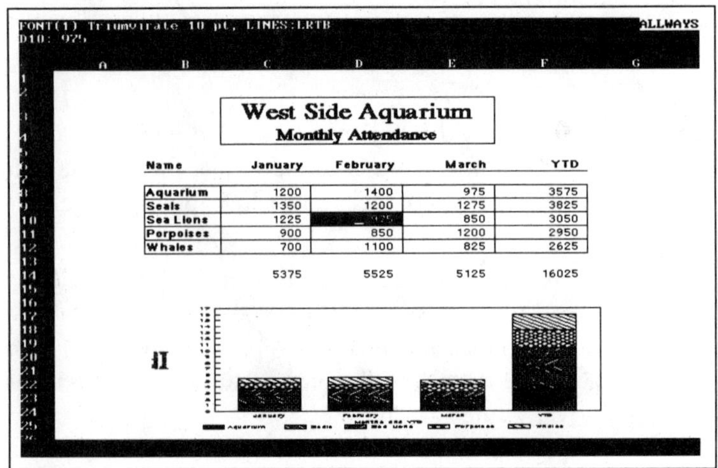

Figure Add.10
/Graph Add.

Cautions

If you alter the contents of a graph in 1-2-3, be sure to resave the graph image to a .PIC file so that Allways will reflect the changes. Allways automatically uses the most recently saved version of the .PIC file when it next prints out the graph.

Allways Graph Fonts-Directory

Purpose

Used to specify the location of the PrintGraph font files (*.FNT).

Description

Allways uses the PrintGraph font files (*.FNT) to generate the text portions of the graphs it displays and prints. 1-2-3 allows you to place these files in a directory other than the directory that contains the 1-2-3 program files. If you have stored the font files in a separate directory, you must tell Allways where to find them. If you have not moved these files, you do not need to change the default setting for the Font-Directory that was established when you installed Allways (i.e., the 1-2-3 program directory).

Defaults

The 1-2-3 program directory.

Usage

You do not need to change the font directory from the default unless you have moved the PrintGraph font files (*.FNT) from the 1-2-3 program directory. If you have moved the files, select /Graph Font-Directory, type in the full path name for the new directory, and press ENTER.

Allways Graph Goto

Purpose

Used to move between multiple graphs within a worksheet on the Allways display.

Description

Allways permits you to place more than one graph in a worksheet. The /Graph Goto command lets you move between graphs. Select Goto and specify the desired graph by name. Allways will then move the cell pointer to the upper-left corner of the range containing the named graph.

Defaults

None.

Usage

To move the cell pointer to the upper-left corner of a named graph, select /Graph Goto. Allways will display the full name of each of the graphs placed in the current worksheet in a pull-down menu. Highlight the name of the graph that you want to move to, and press ENTER. Allways will reposition the cell pointer in the top-left cell of the range containing the graph.

Allways Graph Remove

Purpose

Used to remove a named graph from the current worksheet.

Description

When Allways places a graph in a worksheet, it simply keeps track of the graph's .PIC file name and then reads the associated graph image from the .PIC file. When you want to remove a graph from the worksheet, Allways deletes its own reference to the .PIC file. It does not alter the .PIC file on disk. Once you have removed a graph from Allways, the graph will not be displayed or printed with the worksheet; however, it still exists and can be re-added at a later time or placed in another location.

Defaults

None.

Usage

To remove a currently displayed graph, select /Graph Remove. Allways will display a list of all the graphs attached to the current worksheet in a pull-down menu. Highlight the name of the graph that you wish to remove and press ENTER. The graph will be removed and the associated range of cells will be left empty.

Allways Graph Settings

Purpose

Used to modify the appearance of a graph that has been placed in the current worksheet.

Description

The graph settings are similar to the settings that are controlled in PrintGraph. They allow you to alter the colors, fonts, margins, and scale of the graph. In addition, you can use the settings to move the graph to a new range in the worksheet, change the graph file that is displayed, or restore the graph settings to their defaults. When you select /Graph Settings, Allways will display a graph settings sheet showing the current settings for the selected graph. If the cell pointer is located within the range of a graph, the settings sheet for that graph will be displayed immediately. If the cell pointer is not located in a graph's range, Allways will prompt you to select from one of the graphs that have been added to the current worksheet. Simply highlight the name of the graph whose settings you wish to review or alter, and its settings sheet will be displayed. You can then select the individual setting that you want to change. You can alter any of eight graph settings.

Color The /Graph Settings Color command allows you to set the colors for the individual ranges in the graph. If you have a printer that is capable of printing in color, Allways will use the selected color. When you select the color option, you will have to first select the range (X, A–F) that you want to change from a pull-down menu and then select the desired color.

Default The /Graph Settings Default command allows you to return the graph settings to the current default values. (Initially the default settings are: BLOCK1 font, font scaling equal to one, color equal to black ,and margins equal to zero.) You can also modify the default settings by saving the current graph settings as the new default. To return the current graph settings (after they have been modified) to the default settings, select /Graph Setting Default Restore. To change the default settings, modify the current settings as desired and then select /Graph Settings Default Update to copy the current settings to the default.

Fonts The /Graph Settings Fonts command allows you to alter the type style used for the text of the graph. (Font 1 is used for the first line of the title and Font 2 is used for all other text in the graph). To alter the type, select /Graph Settings Fonts and select which of the two fonts you wish to alter (1 or 2). Then select which of the available font types you want to use. If you want to alter the size of the font, use the /Graph Settings Scale command. If you want to improve the type quality of the titles, you can delete the titles from the graph (this must be done from within 1-2-3 and the graph must be resaved to disk), and then insert new titles in the worksheet within Allways and format them. Since Allways uses higher resolution type fonts, you can achieve significant improvements, especially with larger font sizes.

Margins The /Graph Settings Margins commands allow you to alter the position and size of the graph within the range of cells that you originally assigned to the graph in the Allways environment. These commands help you fine-tune a graph's size and position in the worksheet. This is especially useful when you are combining graphs with text and you are not free to alter the row or column sizes in order to control the graph size and shape. The Margins command has four sub-options for the Left, Right, Top, and Bottom margins. Bear in mind that the margins are set in inches from the corresponding edge of the range that contains the graph (or defines its position). This contrasts with the commands that alter column width and row height, which are set in characters and points, respectively.

PIC-File The /Graph Settings PIC-File command allows you to change the .PIC file that is used for a selected graph without altering any other settings. This is particularly useful if you want to use the Allways graph printing facility as a replacement for the 1-2-3 PrintGraph program. By establishing a standard set of settings, and then simply swapping the .PIC files, you can print a series of graphs in the same style, without leaving 1-2-3.

Quit Exits the /Graph Settings menu.

Range The /Graph Settings Range command allows you to alter the range used to define the location and size of the graph. Use this option if you want to resize the graph in units of rows or columns, or if you want to reposition the entire graph. You can use the cursor keys to stretch the graph to its new dimensions or position, or you can simply type in a new range address or name. If you want to alter the dimensions of the graph in units finer than one row or column, you should use the Margins command described above.

Scale The /Graph Settings Scale command is used to alter the size of the text used in the graph. You can enter a scale factor of 0.5 to 3 for either Font 1 (used for the first line of the title) or Font 2 (used for all other text). The scale factors are relative to the standard size font used by the PrintGraph utility. Thus, a scal.e factor of 0.5 will produce text one-half the size of PrintGraph, while a scale factor of 2.5 will produce text that is two-and-a-half sizes larger than that produced by PrintGraph. The font sizes used by PrintGraph tend to be rather small to avoid overlapping text in the scale and legends. You can improve the legibility of your graphs by increasing the scale factor (especially for Font 2). However, you will need to be careful that the resulting text does not overlap if your text elements are long.

Allways Layout

Purpose

The layout commands are used to control the appearance of the entire worksheet on the printed page.

Description

While the /Format commands control the appearance of single cells or ranges of cells, the /Layout commands control the overall appearance of the worksheet. For example, you can control the size of the page, the margins, page titles, and the use of borders for the entire print job. It is also possible to store the current layout in a library for future reuse or to restore the layout to the default layout. The layout commands are as follows:

Borders The /Layout Borders command works in the same fashion as the 1-2-3 /Print Printer Options Borders command. It allows you to specify a range of cells you want to appear at the top, left, or bottom of every page. This is particularly useful if you are printing a multi-paged, multi-columned worksheet.

By setting up a border, you can have Allways print the column and/or row headings on each page of the report. Allways adds a new Borders feature to 1-2-3— you can create a border for the bottom of each page. To define a border, select /Layout Borders and the type of border you want to define (Top, Left, or Bottom). You then specify the rows or columns to be used for the border, just as you would any range. The Borders command will treat the defined range somewhat differently than other commands in that it will use the entire row for a top or bottom border, regardless of how many columns you included in the range definition. The actual number of columns used for a given page of output depends on how many columns of the print range are printed on that page. Only the border columns that correspond to the columns of printed data will appear on that page. Likewise, for the left border; only the rows that correspond to the actual rows of data that are printed on a particular page will appear on that page.

You should exclude any rows or columns that you wish to use as borders from your print range, otherwise they will appear twice in the printed output—once as a page border and once as the print range data.

The Clear option deletes one or more border specifications. You can select to clear an individual border (Top, Left, or Bottom) or to clear them all (All). If you remove a border definition, you may want to re-include the data from the border in the print range, otherwise it will not get printed.

Default The /Layout Default command allows you to return the layout setting to current default values. (Initially these are: 8.5 by 11-inch page size, one-inch margins, normal line weights, no grid lines, and no settings for titles or borders). You can also modify the default settings by saving the current layout settings as your new default. To return the current layout settings (after they have been modified) to the default settings, select /Layout Default Restore. To change the default settings, modify the current settings to the desired values and then select /Layout Default Update to copy the current settings to the default.

The default settings are used each time you use Allways with a new worksheet. You should set the default layout to the settings that you use most frequently; you can then alter various default settings as necessary for special printouts. If you use several different layouts frequently, you should use the Library command described next.

Library The /Layout Library commands allow you to save a particular layout setting to a named file and retrieve it at a later time. This feature permits you to create a series of standard layouts that can be easily recalled for future use. For example, you may want to create a layout for use with standard sized paper in portrait orientation, you may want to create a second layout for use with legal-sized paper in landscape orientation. By saving each layout to a library file, you can easily retrieve either one as appropriate. When used in combination with the default layout described above, you can improve the efficiency of your use of layouts.

The Library commands consist of three options: Save, Retrieve, and Erase. As their names imply: The Save option saves the current layout to a named library; the Retrieve option retrieves a previously named and saved layout and makes it the current layout; the Erase option erases a named layout. If you try to save a layout with a name that already exists, Allways will ask if you want to replace the existing layout with the new one or cancel the save request.

Margins The /Layout Margins command allows you to set the margins of your printed output. The margins are set in inches from their respective sides of the page; they are initially set at one-inch. This is different from the 1-2-3 method that defines margins in characters and lines, and measures the right margin from the left edge of the page. You can define the margins in inches and fractions of inches.

Options The /Layout Options command is used to control two features, the weight of lines and the printing of a background grid pattern. The Line-Weight option controls the weight of all lines in the worksheet created with the /Format Lines command. Curiously it does not control the weight of the grid lines, which are fixed as hair lines. You can select from three line weights: Light, Normal, and Heavy.

The Grid option places a fine-lined grid throughout the worksheet. This is useful if your worksheet is large and needs such lines to facilitate viewing. If you want to include grid lines in only one portion of the worksheet, you should use the /Format Lines All command. You can also use the ALT-G key combination to toggle the grid lines on and off. Grid lines will not appear in the range that you have specified for graphs. By increasing the range assigned to a graph and also increasing its margins, you can exclude the grid lines from a larger area around a graph.

Page-Size The /Layout Page-Size command allows you to select from a pull-down menu that lists the page sizes supported by your printer. If you need to work with another page size, you can select the Custom option, which will prompt you to enter alternative page dimensions in inches.

Quit Exits the Layout menu.

Titles The /Layout Titles command is used to place a header or footer at the top or bottom of each page of the printed output. Allways uses the same special header and footer symbols as 1-2-3. The @ (at sign) will insert the current system date in the designated location (using the default 1-2-3 data format); the # (pound sign) will insert the current page number. The header or footer consists of three separate sections: a left-justified section, a center-justified section, and a right-justified section. When you are entering the text for a header or footer you must separate the contents of each of these sections with the vertical bar character (¦). For example, entering the header:

```
@¦West Side Aquarium¦Page #
```

will place the header:

07-Aug-89 West Side Aquarium Page 1

on the top of each page, with the page number incrementing for subsequent pages and the date reflecting the current system date.

If you don't want to enter text for a particular section of the header or footer, just leave that section blank, but be sure to include the vertical bar separator if you want to place text to the right of the blank section. To enter a header or footer, select /Layout Titles Header (or Footer) and enter the desired text. If you want to clear a header or footer, select the Clear option and then specify which option you want to clear.

Allways uses three lines for the header and three for the footer. After you add either a header or a footer, check the pagination of your document, since the change in spacing may cause an undesired page wrap. The headers and footers use Font 1.

Allways Print

Purpose

Used to print the formatted worksheet and/or graph to the designated printer or file.

Description

The Print commands are used to control the printing process. They control what gets printed, the initiation of the printing process, and the selection and configuration of the printer used to print the worksheet and/or graph. In general, once you have specified the printer configuration you will not need to alter it unless you change printers or page orientation (portrait or landscape).

The usual sequence of events requires you to specify a range you to print with the /Print Range command and then initiate the printing process with the Go command. Once you have specified a print range, it remains in effect until you specify another print range.

Allways Print Configuration

Purpose

Used to specify the printer to be used for a print job and its configuration.

Description

If you have more than one printer installed, you can select which printer you wish to use for a particular print job. If you have multiple printers or if you have a single printer that supports multiple configurations (e.g., both portrait and landscape orientation), you may also wish to alter the printer configuration. The configuration tells Allways how to access your printer (interface), what optional resources are available (e.g., cartridges,) and what settings you wish to use for variable features (orientation and bin). The configuration commands are as follows:

Bin The Bin selection option allows you to choose between alternative paper sources on printers that support multiple bins. It also allows you to select manual feeding for printers that support that option. To select a bin, initiate the command with /Print Configuration Bin and select the desired bin from the pull-down menu.

If you want to hand-feed paper to your printer (using paper sizes other than the installed tray), you must select the manual feed option in Allways. Otherwise, because Allways explicitly controls the paper feeding process and specifies paper sizes, it will assume that it is still using the same paper tray and send the wrong message to the printer. This can cause a paper "jam" when the printer senses the wrong paper size compared to the specification in the system.

Cartridge Many printers such as laser printers use optional font cartridges to increase the number of fonts available for printing. In order for Allways to use these fonts, you must inform it that a particular cartridge is installed on your printer. When you select the /Print Configuration Cartridge command, Allways will present you with a list of font cartridges that it recognizes for your selected printer. Of necessity, this list must be fixed and may not include all cartridges available for your printer. If you cannot find your font cartridge, you may want to experiment with the selection of cartridges that are similar. Allways only permits you to select one font cartridge, even though your printer may allow you to use two cartridges simultaneously.

Interface You must tell Allways how to talk to your printer. Specifically, you must tell Allways which interface or port is used to connect your printer. The default interface is Parallel 1, which is the most common interface used by personal computers. If you select a serial interface, you must initialize the serial interface with the DOS MODE command before you start 1-2-3 and Allways. See your printer manual for more detailed requirements on initializing your serial port. If you are using Allways with a network and have difficulty accessing the network printer, try altering the interface selection.

Orientation Many printers (such as the H-P LaserJet) explicitly control the orientation of the printed output. You can select to print vertically on the page (portrait) or sideways (landscape). The latter is especially useful for long multi-columned reports. The default orientation is portrait. You will only be offered the landscape option if your printer supports that option. In many cases, the printer requires different font cartridges to support the landscape orientation for some fonts. This means that the number of available fonts may change if you change the orientation.

Printer The /Print Configuration Printer command allows you to select a printer from those you installed at the time you installed Allways. You must specifically install your printers in Allways, even if you have already installed them in 1-2-3. This is because 1-2-3 and Allways use different print drivers. If you can't find the desired printer in the list of available printers, you will have to go back and install it using the AWSETUP program. Refer to Chapter 11 for instructions on installing Allways. Use the Change Selected Equipment option from the Install program's main menu.

When you change the selected printer for a formatted worksheet, you may alter the fonts that are available. If you have selected a font that is not available on the new printer, Allways will try to substitute the closest available font.

Resolution Many printers support different print resolutions when printing in graphics mode. This only affects the printing of graphs since Allways uses hardware-supported fonts or downloaded soft fonts for all of the text. In any case, the choice of resolution affects your printed graphs in three ways. The most obvious is the quality of the output. The H-P LaserJet supports resolutions from 75 dots-per-inch (dpi) to 300dpi. Graphs printed at 300 dpi are much sharper than those printed at 75dpi. The amount of time it takes to print a graph increases with the resolution, since it takes more time to transmit the larger amount of data to the printer. With page printers like the LaserJet, higher resolutions also require more printer memory. This is because the printer must store the entire page image before it begins the printing process. If your printer does not have enough memory to print a particular graph, it will be truncated. You can alleviate this problem by adding more memory to your printer (this seems to be the solution to all computer problems), reducing the size of the graph being printed, or reducing the resolution of the graph.

Allways Print File

Purpose

Used to direct print output to a disk file rather than to a physical printer.

Description

The /Print File command allows you to create an encoded print file (.ENC) on disk. A file can be printed at a later time by copying the file to the port attached to the designated printer. For example, suppose you wanted to print several different worksheets or graphs on a shared printer that was not currently available. You could use the /Print File command to create a series of encoded print files stored on disk. Later, when the printer becomes available, you could print the files by simply copying them to the printer with the DOS COPY command.

Another use of the /Print File command is to create print files for printers not directly connected to your computer. Suppose you worked in an office environment where you used a dot-matrix printer while a colleague down the hall had a PC connected to a laser printer. Your dot-matrix printer provides adequate quality for everyday use, but you want to use your colleague's laser printer to print a worksheet and graph for a presentation. If your colleague also has 1-2-3 Release 2.2 and Allways installed on his machine, you could copy the .WK1 and .ALL files to his machine and print the report directly. Alternatively, you could install the laser printer in Allways on your computer (even though it is not actually attached to your computer), generate an encoded print file of the report using the laser printer driver, and then simply copy the print file to your colleague's computer and then to his printer. In the case of some networks, this is the easiest way to address a shared printer attached to another PC on the network.

The encoded print files prepared by Allways are very different from the ASCII files printed by the 1-2-3 /Print File command. First, they contain all the formatting information required to print the desired worksheet on the selected printer and second, they can contain graphs. ASCII files don't contain any print formatting codes and cannot contain graphs. Third, ASCII files are independent of the type of printer installed, while encoded print files are almost entirely dependent on the selected printer. Different printers use different control codes to convey formatting information such as font type, spacing, orientation, etc. Allways therefore refers to the printer driver for your selected printer to decide which codes to include in the encoded print file. Therefore, if you prepare an encoded print file using one type of printer, you will generally not be able to print that file on a different type of printer. Instead of getting a carefully formatted document, you will get gibberish.

Defaults

Allways uses the printer driver for the currently selected printer.

Usage

To create an encoded print file, first be sure you have selected the desired printer with the /Print Configuration Printer command. Then specify the range to be printed with the /Print Range command. Finally, select /Print File. Allways will prompt you for the name of the file to be created. If you specify an existing encoded print file name, Allways will ask if you want to replace it.

You can print the encoded file from DOS by using the COPY command. You should use the /b argument, to ensure that the file is properly transmitted. For example, to print the file named REPORT.ENC to a printer attached to lpt1, you would use the command:

```
copy report.enc/b lpt1:
```

Allways Print Go

Purpose

Used to initiate the printing process.

Description

The /Print Go command is the action command of the printing process. You must first specify the range to be printed with the /Print Range command, then you can print it by selecting the Go option. If you want to terminate the printing process, you should press the CTRL-BREAK key.

Defaults

The currently defined print range.

Usage

To print the current print range, select /Print Go. Unlike printing in 1-2-3, you do not have or need an Align command on the Allways menu. Allways always starts on a new page. You do need to ensure that the printer is physically aligned to the top of a new page before you select the Go option.

Allways Print Range

Purpose

Used to define the range of the current worksheet to be printed.

Description

The print range specifies what portion of the current worksheet (and any graphs) you want to print as part of the current print request. The print range is saved with the .ALL file and remains the default print range for all future print requests for the worksheet until you respecify it. When you specify the print range, Allways encloses it with a dotted line border (see Figure Add.11). It also shows you where the page breaks will occur based on the current page layout settings. In Figure Add.12, the intermediate dotted line between column D and E shows that Allways placed a page break there after we altered the left and right margins to 2.5 inches, and left only 3 inches for the text on each page. The page break indicators are one of the most valuable enhancements of Allways, since they remove the hit-and-miss formatting problem of 1-2-3's /Print command, where you can't tell very easily what 1-2-3 will print on a given page. Allways updates the page break indicators as you change settings that affect pagination, such as margins, column widths, row heights, and so on.

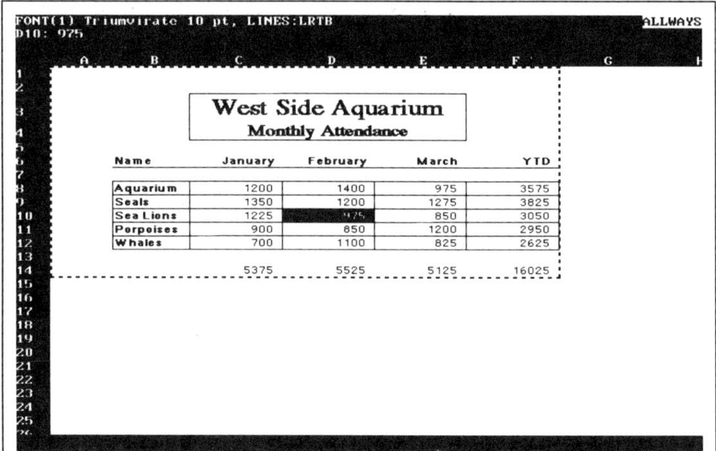

Figure Add.11
/Print Range.

Defaults

The last defined print range.

Usage

To define a print range, select /Print Range Set and specify the range at the prompt by address, name, or by painting it. The range will remain in effect for that worksheet until it is redefined. To clear a print range, select the /Print Range Clear option.

Notes

If you have added borders to your print request with the /Print Layout Borders, you must be sure to remove the border text from the print range, otherwise it will be printed twice. Conversely, if you clear your borders, you should add the text back to the print range.

Allways Print Settings

Purpose

Used to specify several print job options including the number of copies, the starting and ending page numbers, and whether to pause between pages.

Description

The print settings control the current print job options. They remain in effect for the current Allways session *only*. They are not saved with the .ALL file, so they

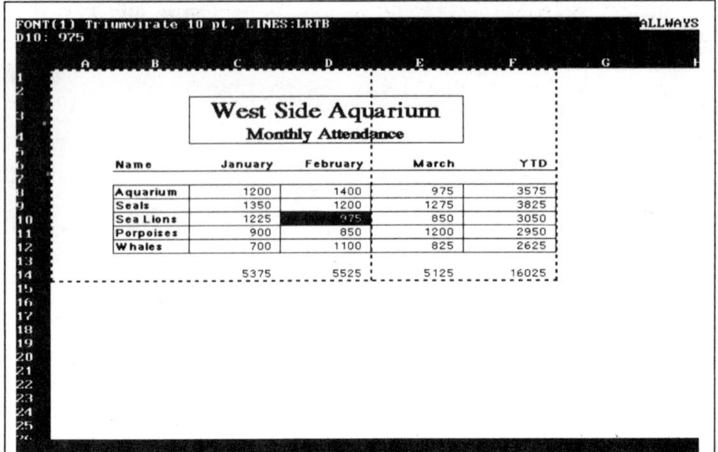

Name	January	February	March	YTD
Aquarium	1200	1400	975	3575
Seals	1350	1200	1275	3825
Sea Lions	1225	975	850	3050
Porpoises	900	850	1200	2950
Whales	700	1100	825	2625
	5375	5525	5125	16025

Figure Add.12 Intermediate page break markers.

will revert to their defaults when you next load 1-2-3 and Allways. The settings are as follows:

Begin Sets the page number on which to begin printing. The Begin setting refers to the physical page number in the sequence of pages to be printed. This option is usually used to pick up an aborted print job in the middle, skipping pages that have already been printed correctly. This is in contrast to the First page option described below, which specifies the starting page number to be printed in headers and footers. The default setting is 1.

Copies Sets the number of copies of the print job to be printed, allowing you to print multiple copies automatically. The default is 1.

End Specifies the last page to be printed as part of the current print job. The ending page number refers to the physical page number in the sequence of pages to be printed and corresponds to the Begin page number option described above. The default is 9999, which should cover most print jobs.

First The First page option allows you to specify what number is to be printed on the first page of the print job. This allows you to assign page numbers different than the physical page number. You might want to use this feature if you were planning to insert the Allways printed output into the middle of a report and wanted to place the proper sequential page numbers on the Allways output. This contrasts with the Begin option, which always refers to the physical page number. The default is 1.

Quit Exits the /Print Settings menu.

Reset Resets the print settings to their defaults.

Wait This option causes Allways to pause after each page is printed to allow you to change paper or to manually insert a new page. The default is No.

Allways Quit

Purpose

Used to exit Allways and return to 1-2-3.

Description

The /Quit option is one of three ways you can exit from Allways back to 1-2-3. In addition, you can press ESC from the Allways READY mode (indicated by the text ALLWAYS in the upper-right corner) or press the ALT-key combination used to start the Allways add-in (e.g., ALT-F8 if you assigned the ALT-F8 key to start up Allways).

Usage

To exit Allways from the menu, select /Quit. Otherwise press ESC or the assigned control key combination from the Allways READY mode.

Allways Special

Purpose

The /Special commands allow you to perform special functions in Allways including copying, moving, or importing formats, and justifying text based on its assigned font.

Description

The Special commands handle the tasks of replicating or moving formats from one cell or range of cells to another cell or range of cells, including a command for copying formats from one worksheet to another. The /Special Justify command performs the same function as the 1-2-3 command /Range Justify, but includes the logic to handle various type sizes so that better results are produced when printed with Allways.

Allways Special Copy

Purpose

Used to copy the format from a cell or range of cells to another cell or range of cells.

Description

The /Special Copy command copies formats, but does *not* copy the contents of the cells. It is very useful for formatting various portions of a worksheet identically. The /Special Copy command copies the following features: font, boldface, underlining, lines, color, and shading. As with 1-2-3, you can copy the format of a single cell to a range of cells, the format of a range of cell to a range of similar size, the format of a single column of cells to a range with the same number of rows but multiple columns, or the format of a single row of cells to a range with the same number of columns but multiple rows.

Defaults

The current cell or currently specified range.

Usage

To copy the format of a single cell, place the cell pointer on the cell whose format you wish to copy and select /Special Copy. At the first prompt for the FROM range, press ENTER to select the current cell. At the second prompt for the TO range, specify the range to which you wish to copy the format by address, name, or by pointing.

To copy the format of a multiple cell range, select /Special Copy. At the first prompt, specify the FROM range by address, name or by pointing. At the second prompt, specify the upper left-hand cell of the TO range by address, name, or by pointing.

To copy the format of one column to several columns, select /Special Copy. At the first prompt, specify the FROM range as a single column range by address, name, or by pointing. At the second prompt, specify the TO range as a single row of cells by address, name, or by pointing.

To copy the format of one row to several rows, select /Special Copy. At the first prompt, specify the FROM range as a single row range by address, name, or by pointing. At the second prompt, specify the TO range as a single column of cells by address, name, or by pointing.

Allways Special Import

Purpose

Used to copy the format from one worksheet to another.

Description

The /Special Import command is really a super copy command. It copies the format from a worksheet saved to disk to the current worksheet. This is especially useful if you have a series of identical worksheets such as regional budget reports that you want to print in the same format. When you import a new format, it replaces all the formats of the current worksheet. Even cells that were not explicitly formatted in the source worksheet will cause the corresponding cells of the target worksheet to be reformatted to the default format of the source worksheet.

Defaults

None.

Usage

To copy the format of one worksheet to another, complete the format specification of the source worksheet and then save it to disk with the 1-2-3 command, /File Save. Load the second worksheet and invoke Allways. Select /Special Import, point to the name of the source worksheet (or type in its name) and press ENTER. If you want to change directories, press ESC and edit the path.

Notes

The source and the target worksheets should have the same layout in 1-2-3, or the /Special Import command is likely to place the imported formats into the wrong cells of the target worksheet. For example, if the target worksheet has one less row between two sections of the worksheet than the source worksheet, the imported format will be placed one row too low on the lower section. While this might not cause a problem, and can be moved in any case, it is usually easier if you ensure that the layouts are the same before you import the format.

Cautions

You should always save your worksheet prior to importing another worksheet's format. If you don't like the results of the import process, you can revert to the old format by reloading the previous version. Remember that Allways commands can not be undone by pressing the UNDO key.

Allways Special Justify

Purpose

Used to reformat a column of text to produce proper line wrapping for justified text.

Description

The /Special Justify command works in the same fashion as the 1-2-3 command /Range Justify. The key difference is that the Allways version takes into consideration the size of the assigned font at the time when the justification is made and the column widths that have been specified in Allways. This produces much more accurate justification when the results are printed by Allways.

Defaults

The currently specified range.

Usage

To justify text in Allways, you must specify the entire range of the text to be justified. Allways will not extend the justified text beyond the specified range. This prevents the justified text from overwriting data in cells below the justify range. If you do not specify a large enough range, Allways reports an error. To justify a column of text, first be sure that you have specified the desired font and column width, then place the cell pointer in the top cell of the column. Initiate the command by selecting /Special Justify and specify the range to be justified *or* the range into which justfied text is to be placed. (Specify whichever range is larger.) If the justified text requires fewer cells than before, the remaining cells will be left empty. If it requires more, you must include the additional cells in the range specification. If you do not specify enough additional space, Allways reports an error.

Notes

If you change the font specification after you have justified the text, you will have to rejustify it to make sure that it is correct.

Allways can only deal with one font specification when justifying text, so it will convert all fonts in the range to be justified to the font specified in the first cell of the range.

Allways allows you to include blank rows in the range to be justified. Blank rows will be treated as if they contain spaces and will not be removed.

Cautions

The /Special Justify command is the only command that writes changes back to the 1-2-3 .WK1 file. Be sure that you back up your .WK1 file before commencing the justification process. If you do not like the results, you can recall the previous version. Remember, you cannot undo an Allways command with the UNDO key.

Allways Special Move

Purpose

Used to move the format of one cell or range of cells to another cell or range of cells.

Description

When you move a format, the target cell(s) is set to the format of the source cell(s) and the source cells are reset to the default format. The /Special Move command can be used to reposition formats that were incorrectly placed by the /Special Import command.

Defaults

The current cell or specified range.

Usage

To move the format of a cell or range of cells, select /Special Move. At the first prompt for the FROM range, specify the cell or range of cells by address, name, or by pointing and press ENTER. At the second prompt, specify the upper-left corner cell of the TO range by address, name, or by pointing and press ENTER.

Allways Worksheet Column

Purpose

Used to set the column width.

Description

Allways maintains its column width specification separately from 1-2-3. This allows you to alter the position of columns for printing purposes without altering the structure of the underlying worksheet. In addition, Allways allows you to specify the column widths in single characters or fractions of characters. The width of a character is defined as the width of a single digit in the default font (Font 1). This provides much finer control of the column width. Allways also allows you to define or reset the column widths of one or more columns at the same time. If you specify a multiple column range with the ANCHOR key (.) before selecting /Worksheet Column, Allways will alter all the column widths simultaneously.

The /Worksheet Column Reset-Width command restores the Allways column width to the 1-2-3 column width. Again, you can reset one or more columns simultaneously.

Defaults

The current cell or specified range.

Usage

To change the column width of one or more columns, place the cell pointer in the leftmost column to be altered. If you want to alter more than one column at the same time, press the ANCHOR key (.) and highlight the range to be altered. Initiate the command by pressing /Worksheet Column Set-Width. Either type in the desired column width (you can specify up to two decimal places) or use the cursor keys to expand or contract the column(s). Use the left and right cursor keys to contract and expand in single character units, or use the CTRL-left cursor and CTRL-right cursor to contract and expand in units of 1/10th of a character.

To reset the column widths to their 1-2-3 widths, select /Worksheet Column Reset-Width.

Allways Worksheet Page

Purpose

Used to insert a page break at the designated row or column.

Description

Allways automatically places page breaks so that a maximum amount is printed on each page. If you want to separate two elements of the worksheet onto different pages you can insert a forced page break. You can define the forced page break-based either on the row position or the column position. This allows you to print long multiple row reports on separate pages or long multiple column reports on separate pages. You can even define a forced row *and* a forced column page break.

Defaults

The current cell.

Usage

To insert a forced page break, select /Worksheet Page. Select either Column or Row, depending on the orientation of the break desired. At the prompt, specify the column or row by pointing to it and then press ENTER. To delete an existing forced page break, select /Worksheet Page Delete, point to the break to be deleted by highlighting the cell below or to the right of the break and press ENTER.

Allways Worksheet Row

Purpose

Used to set the row height of a specified row or rows.

Description

The /Worksheet Row command allows you to specify the row height for one or more rows. Allways defaults to a row height that is set to Auto; automatically sets the row height one or two points larger than the largest sized font used in the row. This generally produces the best results. You can, however, control individual row heights by specifying the desired point size.

Defaults

Auto— one or two points larger than the largest font used in the row.

Usage

To change the row height of one or more rows, place the cell pointer in the top row to be altered. If you want to alter more than one row at once, press the ANCHOR key (.) and highlight the range to be altered. Initiate the command by pressing /Worksheet Row Set-Height. Either type in the desired row height in points or use the cursor keys to expand or contract the row height(s).

To reset the row height to the default, select /Worksheet Column Auto.

Notes

Remember that Allways selects the largest font in a row when determining the Auto row height. If you specify all the text in a row to a point size smaller than the default font (Font 1) size, the row will still be sized for the default. This is because Allways considers the entire row (all the way to column IV) when looking for the largest font specification. Unless you specified the entire row (column A..IV) to smaller font size, Allways will find a cell formatted to the default and use the larger font to determine the row height. If your default font is the smallest font in your font set, this is not a problem. If it is *not* the smallest, be sure to format rows of smaller fonts in their entirety if you want the smaller row height in Auto mode, or you can specify the smaller height manually.

▸ Copy Commands

Purpose

Used to copy a cell or range of cells *from* one location in a worksheet *to* a new location in the same worksheet. You can move a single copy or multiple copies of your source cell(s).

Description

/Copy operates differently depending on whether you are copying cells that contain formulas or cells with labels or values.

Labels and Values When copying labels and values, /Copy makes exact duplicates of the source cell(s) at the target location; the contents of each cell and its format is copied.

Formulas When you copy a formula, /Copy automatically adjusts any relative cell references in the formula to reflect the new location. For example, consider the formula in cell E14 (Figure Copy.1) that sums the contents of the column above it: @SUM(E8..E12). The formula contains the relative cell reference E8..E12. Should you copy the cell E14 to cell F14, the formula references in E14 are automatically adjusted to correspond to the new location in column F. The formula now reads @SUM(F8..F12) and it produces the sum of column F.

This feature is extremely important for copying formulas throughout a worksheet. (For example, if you are summing many columns, such as monthly sales figures, you need only write the formula below the first column and then copy it to all the remaining columns. The summation formula will be adjusted for each column

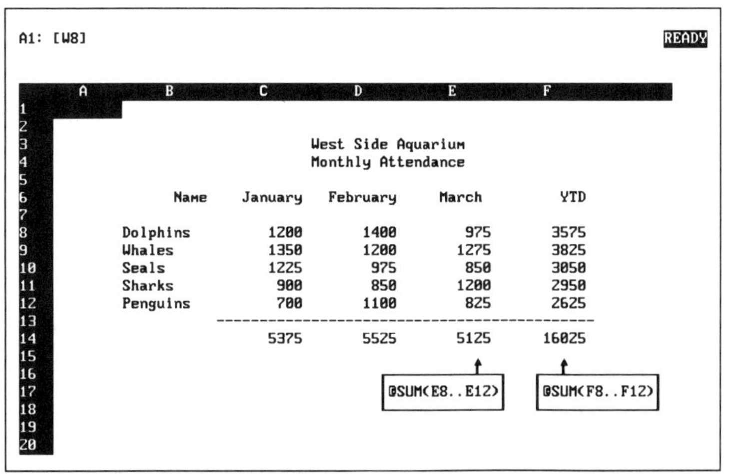

Figure Copy.1
Relative Addresses.

such that it sums the column above it.) When copying absolute or mixed addresses in a formula, the absolute portion remains fixed, while the relative portion will be adjusted. For example, suppose you had a fixed growth rate entered into cell C4 that you wanted to multiply times each of the monthly sales figures located in a row A7..L7. You would enter the formula +$C$4*A7 in cell A9. When you copy it to cells B9 through L9, the reference to the cells in row 7 will change appropriately, while the references to the fixed growth rate in cell C4 will remain fixed in each of the copies.

The /Copy command works quite differently from the /Move command. The /Move command makes no changes to the formulas as they are moved. It presumes that you want the same formula and references simply relocated to a new position.

Defaults

Copies the current cell.

Usage

The /Copy command follows the standard 1-2-3 prompt structure: You are asked to specify a FROM range for the copy and then a TO range. The FROM range is the source cell or range of cells you wish to copy; the TO range is the target cell or destination range for the copy. You can copy a single cell to another single cell or a range of cells to a comparable range of cells. You can also perform multiple copies with the /Copy command, replicating a single cell in multiple cells or a range of cells into a larger range of cells.

Copying a Single Cell to Another Single Cell Position the cell pointer on the cell that you wish to copy (the source cell). Press /C to start the /Copy command. At the copy FROM prompt, press the ENTER key to select the current cell default as the source cell. At the copy TO prompt, enter the cell address (or range name) of the target location, or move the cell pointer to the target location. Press ENTER to complete the /Copy command. The contents of the source cell will be copied to the target cell.

Copying a Single Cell to Multiple Cells When you copy a single cell to a multiple cell range, the single cell is replicated in each of the cells in the target range. To copy a single cell to a range of cells, position the cell pointer on the source cell and select /Copy. At the copy FROM prompt, press the ENTER key to accept the current cell default as the source cell. At the TO prompt (for the target range), move the cell pointer to the upper-left corner of the range of cells into which you want to copy the source cell. Press the period key (.) to anchor the target range, and use the cursor keys to expand the target range to the desired dimensions. Finally, press ENTER to execute the /Copy command. The cell pointer is returned to the source cell. Alternatively, at the Copy TO prompt you can type in the range address (or range name) of the target range.

Copying a Range of Cells to a Comparable Range of Cells To make one copy of a range of cells elsewhere in the worksheet, you can specify your target range simply by moving the cell pointer to the top-left corner of the target range. (You need not type in or highlight the complete target range.) To do the range copy, first position the cell pointer on the cell marking the upper-left corner of the range of cells you wish to copy (the source range). Press /C to initiate the /Copy command. At the FROM prompt, type in the source range address (or name) or paint the source range with the cell pointer and press ENTER. At the copy TO prompt, move the cell pointer to the upper-left corner of the target range and press ENTER to complete the copy process. (You can also type in the address or name of the cell marking the upper-left corner of the target range.)

Copying a Range of Cells to a Larger Range of Cells Position the cell pointer on the cell marking the top-left corner of the range of cells you wish to copy (the source range). Press /C to initiate the /Copy command. At the copy FROM prompt, move the cell pointer and paint the range you wish to copy (or type in the complete range address or range name of the source range) and press ENTER. At the copy TO prompt, move the cell pointer to the top left corner of the new target range. Press the period key (.) to anchor the target range, then use the cursor keys to expand the target range to the desired dimensions. (You may also type in the complete address or name of the target range.) Finally, press the ENTER key to execute the command. The cell pointer will return to the top-left corner of the source range, as soon as the copy is complete.

The source range will be replicated into the target range according to the following rules:

1. If the source range is a single cell, it will be replicated as often as required to completely fill the target range both vertically and horizontally.
2. If the source range is one-dimensional (a single row or column) it may be copied to multiple rows or multiple columns. That is, if the source range contains a row of cells and is copied to a range containing more than one row, the source range is copied to each row of the target range. The dimensions of the target range are defined by the number of columns in

the source range and the number of rows in the target range. (Formulas with relative addresses will be adjusted accordingly.)

3. If the source range is two-dimensional (contains more than one row and more than one column), it can be copied only once, regardless of how much larger the specified target range may be.

Examples

To copy the contents of the current cell E14-@SUM(E8..E12) to another single cell F14. (See Figures Copy.2a-c.) Note the change in the relative addresses in the formula:

1. Move the cursor to cell E14.
2. Select /Copy.
3. Press ENTER at the copy FROM prompt.
4. Move the cell pointer to the target location, F14.
5. Press ENTER to complete the copy.

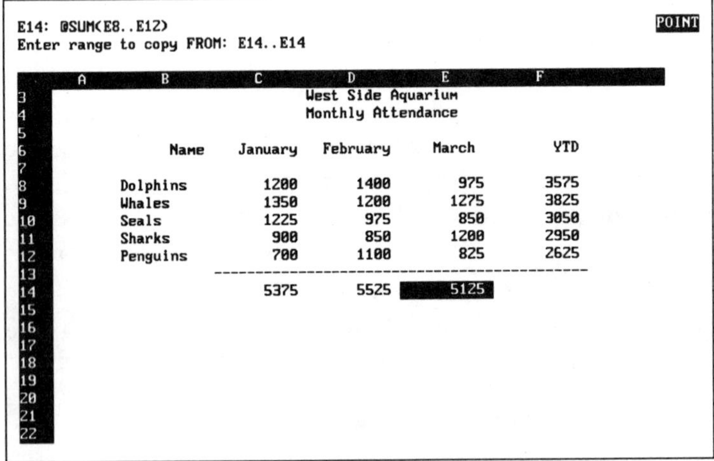

Figure Copy.2a
/Copy FROM Range.

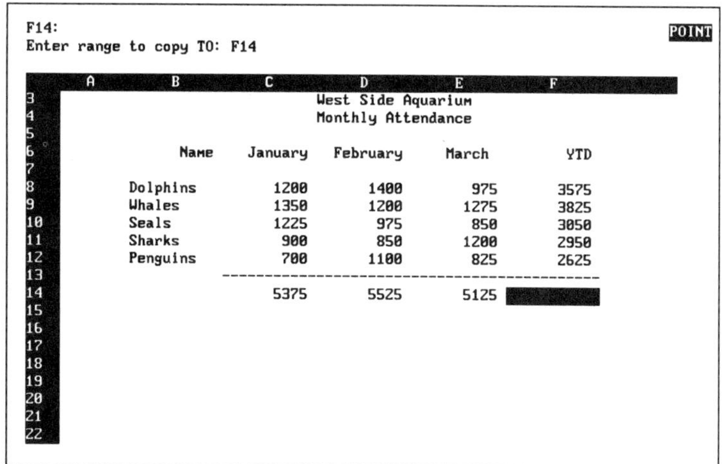

F14:
Enter range to copy TO: F14

POINT

	A	B	C	D	E	F
3				West Side Aquarium		
4				Monthly Attendance		
5						
6		Name	January	February	March	YTD
7						
8		Dolphins	1200	1400	975	3575
9		Whales	1350	1200	1275	3825
10		Seals	1225	975	850	3050
11		Sharks	900	850	1200	2950
12		Penguins	700	1100	825	2625
13			----------	----------	----------	----------
14			5375	5525	5125	
15–22						

Figure Copy.2b
/Copy TO Range.

F14: @SUM(F8..F12)

READY

	A	B	C	D	E	F
3				West Side Aquarium		
4				Monthly Attendance		
5						
6		Name	January	February	March	YTD
7						
8		Dolphins	1200	1400	975	3575
9		Whales	1350	1200	1275	3825
10		Seals	1225	975	850	3050
11		Sharks	900	850	1200	2950
12		Penguins	700	1100	825	2625
13			----------	----------	----------	----------
14			5375	5525	5125	16025
15–22						

Figure Copy.2c
/Copy Results.

To copy the range of cells A14..E17 to a range of equivalent size, starting with cell C47 in the upper-left corner:

1. Select /Copy.
2. Type `A14..E17` at the Copy FROM prompt and press ENTER.
3. Type `C47` and at the Copy TO prompt press ENTER.

You have assigned the range A1..F3 the name Dolphins (using the /Range Name Create command). To make a single copy of the range Dolphins in the range M1..R3 named Mammals:

1. Select /Copy.
2. Type `Dolphins` at the copy FROM prompt and press ENTER.
3. Type `Mammals` (or type in M1) at the copy TO prompt and press ENTER.

Notes

If you copy a formula that contains relative or mixed addresses, it will be altered in the copy. The formula in its new location will reference new cells that are in the same relative position to the new location as the old references were to the source cell. For example, the formula @AVG(A1..A20) in cell A22 would be changed to @AVG(B2..B21) if it were copied to cell B23. The formula AVG (A$1..A$20) in cell A22 would be changed to @AVG(B$1..B$20) if it were copied to B23.

If you wish to copy a cell containing a relative or mixed reference to a new location without altering the references, you can either convert it to an absolute reference before copying it and then convert both the source and the copy back to relative or mixed addresses as necessary. Alternatively, you can convert the formula to a label by inserting a label prefix in front of it, perform the copy and then remove both label prefixes.

Cautions

The /Copy command will copy data over existing data without providing any warning. Be sure that the target location is large enough to accommodate the source range before initiating /Copy.

▸ Data Commands

Purpose

/Data commands are used to sort, extract, parse, analyze, or otherwise manipulate database information in 1-2-3; they can also be used to generate tables of data.

Description

The /Data commands fall into three main categories: those that manipulate the structure of a data table, (such as Sort, Matrix, or Parse); those that assist in data analysis by making calculations on or extracting data from the database (such as Query, Regression, or Distribution); and those that generate new data in tabular form (such as Fill or Table).

Before you use the /Data commands it is best to clearly understand and distinguish between database tables and data tables. (This is particularly important if you are going on to Release 3.)

Database Tables A database table is an organized collection of information stored in 1-2-3's rows and columns. Each 1-2-3 row represents a single record; each column within each row represents a single field within each record. A telephone book, for example, can be considered a database table. Each row in the book contains a listing (or record). Each listing is divided into three columns (or fields): one that contains the last name, followed by the first name; a second that contains an abbreviated address; and a third that contains a seven-digit telephone number.

The place occupied by each piece of information in a telephone database table tells you what kind of information it is, as well as information about the individual in question. In a 1-2-3 database table, the columns separate categories (or fields) of like information. The rows separate each information record. At the head of

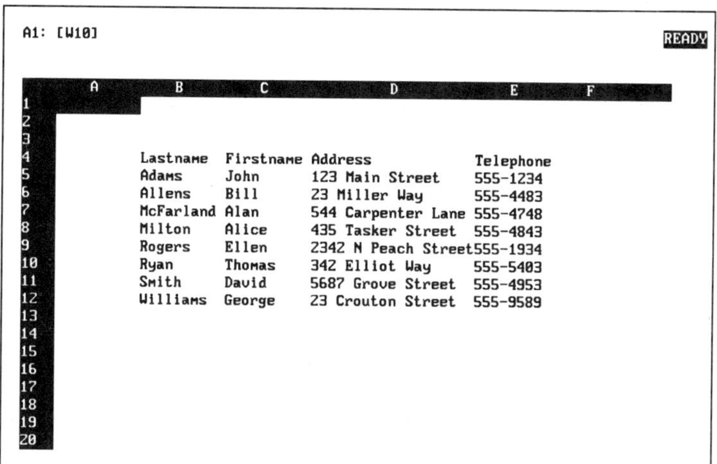
A1: [W10]
READY

Lastname	Firstname	Address	Telephone
Adams	John	123 Main Street	555-1234
Allens	Bill	23 Miller Way	555-4483
McFarland	Alan	544 Carpenter Lane	555-4748
Milton	Alice	435 Tasker Street	555-4843
Rogers	Ellen	2342 N Peach Street	555-1934
Ryan	Thomas	342 Elliot Way	555-5403
Smith	David	5687 Grove Street	555-4953
Williams	George	23 Crouton Street	555-9589

Figure Data.1
A Database Table.

each column in a 1-2-3 database table (that is, in the top row of the table) you must include the field name labels for the fields in the table; each field name label must be unique.

Data Tables Data tables, like database tables, are structured tables of data, but data tables need not contain field names in the top row of the table. Thus, a database table is a class within the larger category of data tables. Just as: All robins are birds, but not all birds are robins; so all database tables are data tables but not all data tables are database tables. We will use the term data table in its most generic form, simply meaning a rectangular structured set of data.

The /Data commands include:

/Data Distribution	Creates a frequency distribution of the data in a data table.
/Data Fill	Fills a defined range with a sequence of values, dates, or times.
/Data Matrix	Inverts or multiplies matrices. Used to solve simultaneous equations.
/Data Parse	Separates a single column of long labels (often the result of a /File Import) into discrete columns of data.
/Data Query	Locates or extracts records from a data table.
/Data Regression	Performs multiple-regression analysis on data in a database table.
/Data Sort	Sorts data in a database table.
/Data Table	Creates a table of results by substituting one or more variables into one or more formulas. Used for "what-if" and sensitivity analysis.

Notes

The field names in a database table must be unique. They must be placed in the row immediately above the first record. 1-2-3 database tables can include up to 256 fields (or columns) and up to 8,191 records (or rows).

Cautions

Many of the /Data commands generate new tables of data that will overwrite any data or macros located in the output range. Be certain that the output range is sufficiently large to accommodate the requested data before performing the /Data command.

Data Distribution

Purpose

Used to show how often values in defined categories (or bins of values) occur in a range. Frequency distributions are vital to data analysis; by arranging similar values into groups you can often create more meaningful graphs of database information.

Description

/Data Distribution uses an input range called the Values range and a special two-column output range called the Bin range. The values range is a the range of data that you want to analyze. The Distribution command counts only numeric values in the values (or input) range; any blanks, labels, or formulas with ERR or NA results in the input range are ignored. The output or Bin range consists of two adjacent columns. The left column contains the user-defined bin values in *ascending* order (you may want to use the /Data Fill option to create evenly distributed bins). The right column will contain the frequency counts for each bin generated by 1-2-3.

The frequency reports for each bin value include all numbers greater than the previous bin value and less than or equal to the current bin value. For example, if the bin values in rows 1, 2, and 3 are 150, 200, and 250 respectively, the frequency count returned for line 3 will include all values greater than 200 and less than or equal to 250.

Usage

First, make sure that all the values you want to analyze are in a single range. Second, select an output range consisting of two adjacent columns (allow one row more than the number of bins you want to define); type in your bin values in the left column of the output range. Bin values must be unique and placed in ascending order. No blank entries or labels may be included in the column of bin values. Formulas can be used as bin values as long as the formula results are unique and in ascending order. Do not include formulas that evaluate to ERR or NA in the bin output range.

Initiate the /Data Distribution command. You will be asked to specify the two ranges. First specify the values range by name, address, or by painting the range, then specify the bin range as the left column of the output range containing the bin values only. Do not specify a two-column range. 1-2-3 will generate the frequency counts in the column to the right of the bin values (see Figure Data.2).

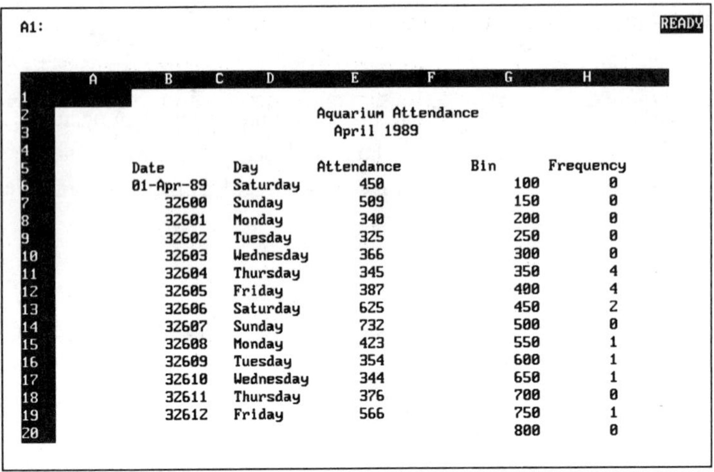

A1: READY

Aquarium Attendance
April 1989

Date	Day	Attendance	Bin	Frequency
01-Apr-89	Saturday	450	100	0
32600	Sunday	509	150	0
32601	Monday	340	200	0
32602	Tuesday	325	250	0
32603	Wednesday	366	300	0
32604	Thursday	345	350	4
32605	Friday	387	400	4
32606	Saturday	625	450	2
32607	Sunday	732	500	0
32608	Monday	423	550	1
32609	Tuesday	354	600	1
32610	Wednesday	344	650	1
32611	Thursday	376	700	0
32612	Friday	566	750	1
			800	0

Figure Data.2
/Data Distribution.

The value placed in the row below your last bin value reports the number of values that are larger than the largest bin value you specified, if any.

Examples

To determine the frequency distribution of daily attendance for the first two weeks of April (as in Figure Data.2), then graph the results:

1. Plot the values range and be sure that all the values you need are within the range.
2. Plot a location for the output range, two columns wide and one row longer than the number of bins you plan to define.
3. Enter your bin values in the left column of this output range. Use the /Data Fill command if appropriate. (In the example above, you would fill the range G6..G20, specifying a starting value of 100, a step value of 50, and a stop value of 800.)
4. Select /Data Distribution.
5. Specify the values range by typing (or painting) `E6..E19`.
6. Specify the bin range by typing (or painting) `G6..G20`.
7. The results are placed in column H.
8. To create a bar graph of these results, place the cursor in cell G5 and select /Graph Type Bar.
9. Select X range and specify the bin values in column G, G6..G20.

10. Select A range and specify the frequencies in column H, H6..H20.
11. Select Options Titles and enter the titles. (Select First to enter the first line of your graph heading: Aquarium Attendance. Select Second to type in the second line of your graph heading: April 1989, and so on for the X and Y axis labels.)
12. Select Quit.
13. Select View to display the graph. See Figure Data.3.

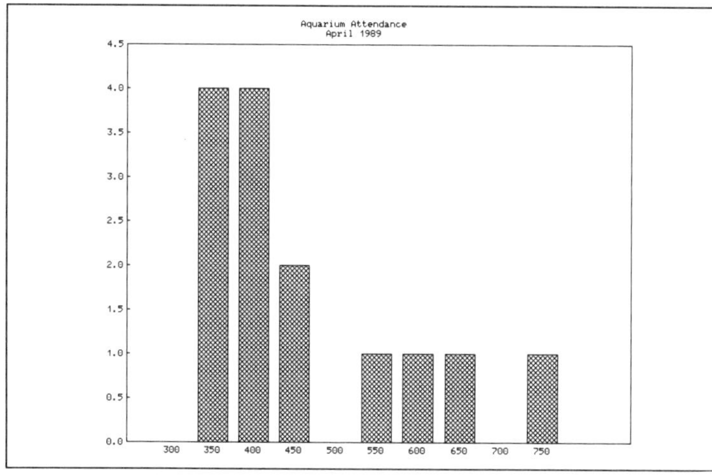

Figure Data.3
Graph of /Data Distribution.

Notes

To quickly create a range of bin values with equally spaced intervals, use the /Data Fill command. Also, consider extracting portions of your complete database (using /Data Query Extract) to obtain a frequency distribution of subcategories of data.

Cautions

The /Data Distribution command will overwrite the column to the right of the bin range. Be sure that this column is empty or can be overwritten.

The bin range must contain only unique values or formulas that evaluate to unique values and they must be entered in ascending order. Otherwise, the /Data Distribution command may generate unreliable results.

Data Fill

Purpose

Used to create a series of equally incremented values in a defined range within the current worksheet. You simply specify a starting value, an ending value, and an incremental step so that 1-2-3 can generate the series. Values can be numbers, dates, or times (in Lotus' Date-Time numerical format or in a date time @function). This is extremely useful for creating column or row headings, or input value ranges for /Data Table commands.

Description

/Data Fill first prompts you to specify the target range that you wish to fill. You are then asked for a starting value, an incremental step, and an ending value. 1-2-3 will fill the target range with the appropriate sequence of values. Note that if your target range is more than one row or column, 1-2-3 will fill the range with values column by column.

Defaults

Starting Value = 0 or last specified value

Increment step = 1 or last specified value

Stop Value = 8191 or last specified value

Usage

To fill a range with a sequence of values, select /Data Fill and specify the fill range (by name, address, or by painting the range). Enter the start value, step value, and stop value at the prompts. Alternatively, you can enter references to cells containing values or formulas that evaluate to values.

Examples

To fill the range A1..A26 with the values 0 to 25, incremented by 1:

1. Select /Data Fill.
2. Type `A1..A26` (or paint it) to specify the fill range.
3. Press ENTER to accept the default starting value of 0.
4. Press ENTER to accept the default step value of 1.
5. Press ENTER to accept the default stop value of 8191.

See Figure Data.4.

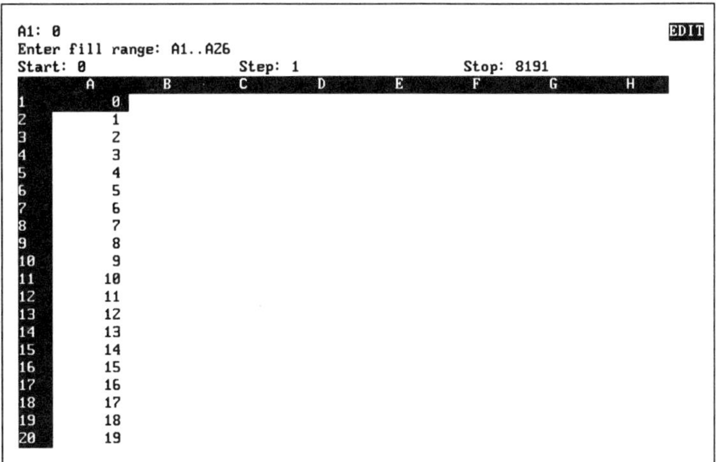

Figure Data.4
/Data Fill.

To fill the range named PENGUINS with the values from 100 to 1000 in increments of 50:

1. Select /Data Fill.
2. Type `PENGUINS` to specify the fill range.
3. Type `100` and press ENTER for the starting value.
4. Type `50` and press ENTER for the step value.
5. Type `1000` and press ENTER the stop value.

Notes

The start, step, and stop values can be entered as numbers; or they can reference a cell that contains a formula that evaluates to a value. They can also reference a range of cells by address or by name. If you specify a range of cells, 1-2-3 then uses the value of the top left cell of the range as the specified value. This feature is often used in macros when you want to store the starting, ending, or step value in a cell and then use the specified value to generate a series of values to be used as the input values of a /Data Table command or as column or row headings.

If you specify a negative step value, the stop value must be less than the start value.

If the fill range is smaller than the number of values between the specified start and stop value (given the incremental step you specify), 1-2-3 fills only the specified fill range, terminating the sequence before the stop value.

If the data fill sequence does not completely fill the fill range that you specfiy, 1-2-3 will nevertheless stop at the stop value without filling the entire range.

Cautions

/Data Fill will overwrite the contents of the fill range with the specified sequence of values without regard for the current contents of the fill range. Be certain the fill range is clear or can be overwritten before initiating this command.

Data Matrix

Purpose

Many physical and financial relationships can be described by simultaneous linear equations. If you can define as many independent equations as you have independent variables, it is possible to solve the equations for a solution (though not necessarily a unique solution), using the two /Data Matrix commands, Invert and Multiply. Invert and Multiply are particularly valuable in scientific or engineering calculations and in economic analysis.

Usage

The procedure for solving the equations is to place the coefficients of your formulas in one matrix and the constants in a second matrix. Invert the first matrix using the /Data Matrix Invert command; then multiply the inverted matrix by the matrix of constants with the /Data Matrix Multiply command. This will produce the solution values for your variables. (See Figure Data.5.)

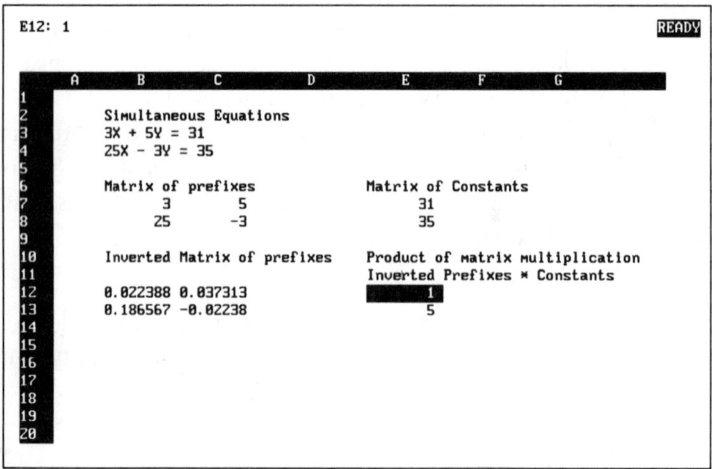

Figure Data.5 Solving Simultaneous Equations.

Examples

Consider the problem of solving for the optimal mixture of two types of fish food, X and Y, for feeding the aquarium's neon tetras. Each neon tetra must receive 31 units of vitamin A weekly for optimal growth and should also get 35 units of vitamin B for optimal coloring. Fish Food X provides 3 units of vitamin A per ounce and fish food Y provides 5 units of Vitamin A per ounce. Fish food X provides 25 units of vitamin B per ounce, while fish food Y actually causes a reduction of vitamin B by 3 units per ounce. What is the optimal weekly mixture of fish food X and fish food grain Y?

As you might have already guessed, this problem can be described by simultaneous equations (two independent equations and two independent variables in this case). Vitamin A's contribution is shown as 3X+5Y=31 while vitamin B's is shown as 25X−3Y=35. To find the values of X and Y that will solve the equations 3X+5Y=31 and 25X−3Y=35:

1. Enter the formulas in cells B3 and B4 as labels for reference.
2. Enter the coefficients of X (3 and 25) and Y (5 and −3) in a matrix from B7..C8.
3. Enter the constants (31 and 35) in a matrix from E7..E8.
4. Select /Data Matrix Invert.
5. Select the matrix of coefficients, B7..C8 as the input range.
6. Point to B12 to select the upper-left corner of the output range.
7. Select /Data Matrix Multiply.
8. Point to B12..C13 to select the inverted matrix of coefficients as the first input matrix.
9. Point to E7..E8 to select the matrix of constants as the second input matrix.
10. Point to E12 to specify the upper-left corner of the output range.
11. The resulting optimal mix is 2 ounces of fish food X and 5 ounces of fish food Y.

Notes

In order to invert a matrix, it must be a square matrix. However, not all matrices can be inverted and therefore, not all simultaneous equations can be solved in this fashion.

In order to multiply two matrices, the number of columns in the first matrix must equal the number of rows in the second. For example, in the problem described above, the first matrix had two columns while the second had two rows. (Be sure your data is set up properly.)

Cautions

The /Data Matrix Invert command creates an output matrix equal in size to the source matrix. 1-2-3 will overwrite any data that may lie in the output location with no warning. Be certain that the output location is clear or can be overwritten before invoking this command.

/Data Matrix Multiply creates a product matrix equal in size to the number of rows in the first source matrix range and the number of columns in the second source matrix range. 1-2-3 overwrites any data that lies in the output location with no warning. Be certain that the output location is clear or can be overwritten before invoking this command.

Data Matrix Invert

Purpose

Used to invert a matrix, this command is most often used in combination with /Data Matrix Multiply to solve simultaneous equations.

Description

The matrix inversion command inverts square matrices (equal number of rows and columns) of up to 80 rows and columns in size. The inverse of a matrix is the same size as the original matrix. When you multiply a matrix by its inverse the result is an identity matrix in which all elements are 0, except for the first element in the first row, the second element in the second row, etc., which are all 1.

Defaults

None.

Usage

To invert a matrix, first make sure that your output location is clear and of equal size as your source matrix. Choose /Data Matrix Invert. Specify the source matrix range by name, by address, or by painting it. Then specify the output range. (You need only point to the upper left cell of the output range.)

Examples

To invert the matrix residing in cells B7 to C8 of Figure Data.5 and place the inverted matrix in B12 through C13:

1. Check the output range to make sure that it can be overwritten.
2. Select /Data Matrix Invert.
3. Type (or paint) `B7..C8` to specify the source range.
4. Type (or paint) `B12..C13` to specify the output range.

Notes

Not all square matrices can be inverted. If you attempt to invert a matrix that has no inverse, 1-2-3 will generate an error message.

Cautions

/Data Matrix Invert creates a matrix of equal size as the source matrix in the output location; it will overwrite any data that may lie in the output location without any warning. Be certain that the output location is clear or can be overwritten before invoking this command.

Data Matrix Multiply

Purpose

Used to multiply two matrices together to produce a third matrix with as many rows as the first matrix and as many columns as the second. /Data Matrix Multiply is often used as a second step in the solution of simultaneous equations. It is also used to figure an expected outcome, given a set of possible outcomes and a corresponding set of probabilities.

Description

You can use /Data Matrix Multiply to multiply two matrices only if the number of rows in the first matrix is equal to the number of columns in the second. In matrix multiplication, the product matrix is computed by summing the products of each member of the source row in the first matrix by its associated member in the source column of the second matrix. (This can be tedious work if you must do it manually for large matrices.) For example, in Figure Data.6, the first matrix is located in cells A1..B4, a 2x4 cell matrix. The second matrix is located in cells D1..G2, a 4x2 cell matrix. The product of these matrices is a 4x4 cell matrix located in cells D8..G12. The value in the first cell of the product matrix (D8) is the sum of the products (A1 * D1) and (B1 * D2). The value in the second cell of the product matrix (E8) is (A1*E1)+(B1*E2), etc. until the first column in the output range is complete. Then, the value for the first cell of the second column in the product matrix is the sum of (A2 * D1) and (B2 * D2); the second cell in the second column is (A2 * E1) + (B2 * E2), and so on.

Defaults

None.

Usage

First, when multiplying two matrices make sure that the number of columns in the first matrix equals the number of rows in the second matrix. Next, be sure that the output range is clear. The product matrix will require a range equal to the number of rows of the first source matrix and the number of columns of the second matrix. Select /Data Matrix Multiply and specify the first matrix range by name, by address, or by painting it. Specify the second matrix range (by name, by address, or by painting the range). Finally, specify the output range for the product matrix; you need only indicate the upper-left corner.

Examples

One of the common uses for matrix multiplication is the calculation of expected outcomes. For example, given the probability of various hatching sizes for turtles (the result of statistical analysis), what is the expected hatching size for a given pair of turtles? (See Figure Data.7.)

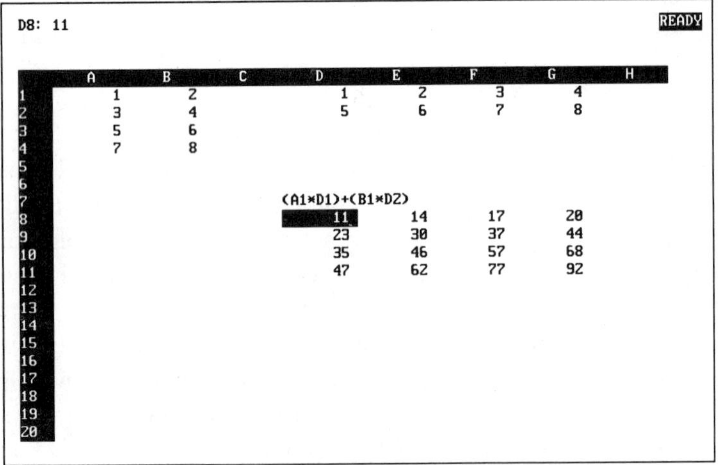

Figure Data.6 /Data Matrix Multiply.

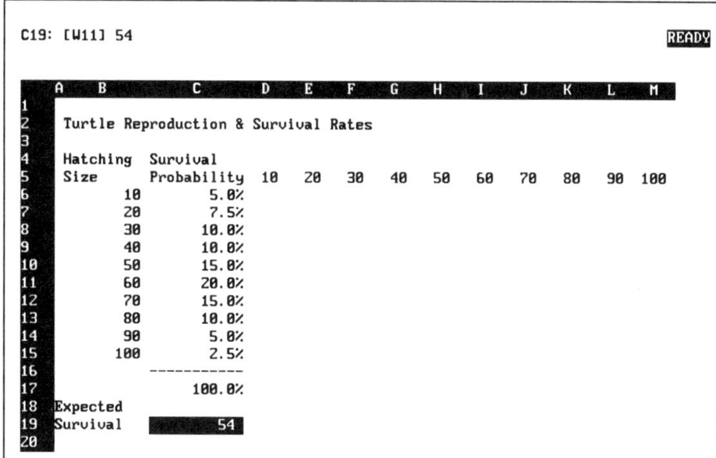

Figure Data.7
Expected Outcome.

1. Place the hatching sizes and their associated probabilities in adjacent columns (the hatching size is just being used as a label here).
2. Copy the column of hatching sizes to a row. You can use /Range Transpose. See Figure Data.7.
3. Select /Data Matrix Multiply.
4. Specify the Row Matrix first, with `D5..M5`.
5. Specify the Column Matrix, `B6..B15`.
6. Specify the output matrix, `B19`.

The results indicate that we can expect an average hatching size of 54 turtles.

Cautions

1-2-3 differentiates the order in which you specify the matrices to be multiplied. If you specify a 1 x 10 (1 row by 10 columns) matrix to be multiplied by a 10 x 1 (10 rows by 1 column) matrix, the result will be a 1 x 1 matrix, as described in the example above. If, on the other hand, you specified a 10 x 1 (10 rows by 1 column) matrix times a 1 x 10 (1 row by 10 columns), you would get a 10 x 10 output matrix. Be sure that you are multiplying your matrices in the correct order.

The /Data Matrix Multiply command creates a matrix of size equal to the number of rows in the first source matrix range and the number of columns in the second source matrix range. 1-2-3 will overwrite any data that may lie in the output location with no warning. Be certain that the output location is clear or can be overwritten before invoking this command.

Data Parse

Purpose

When external data is imported as text, it is brought into the worksheet as a single column of long labels, although each label contains multiple fields of data. /Data Parse separates these long label entries into discrete columns, so that each column represents a single data field—value, date, time, or label.

Description

/Data Parse creates a format line (that the user can modify) based on its analysis of a designated cell in the input column of labels. The format line separates out the discrete elements of the long label and identifies each element in the long label as a particular data type: value, date, time, or label. Once you have an acceptable format line, /Data Parse will break up each long label accordingly and place each data element into its appropriate column in the output range.

Defaults

/Data Parse uses the following hierarchy to generate the format line when it interprets an ambiguous data element in the input range:

1. Value
2. Date
3. Time
4. Label

This means that when you choose /Data Parse Format-Line, 1-2-3 will treat 8/89 (which could be a date or a value) as a value when creating the format line. You are given the opportunity to edit the format line and specify a date format, if necessary.

Usage

The procedure for parsing a column of data involves several steps. They will be described here in general; refer to the following sections for details on each /Data Parse command. The first step in parsing long labels is to create the format line. When you initiate the parse command, the parse setting screen will be displayed showing the last settings specified. If you want to view the worksheet, press the WINDOW key, F6, to clear the setting screen. Place the cell pointer on the first cell of the column of labels you wish to parse. Initiate the command /Data Parse

Format-Line Create. 1-2-3 will create a format line: a continuous string of field symbols indicating column widths, data types, etc. The label prefix for the format line is a split vertical bar (¦). (See the /Data Parse Format-Line section below).

You can edit this line with /Data Parse Format-Line Edit if you choose to. Once you are satisfied with the format line, define your input range (the entire column of long labels) and be sure to include the newly created format line at the top of the range with the /Data Parse Input-Column command. Next, specify your output range with /Data Parse Output-Range. Finally, start the parsing process with the /Data Parse Go command.

Examples

To parse the column of labels containing the name, weight, and the date of measurement of each orca (killer whale) into three columns of data corresponding to each data field:

1. Place the cell pointer on the top label in the single column range to be parsed.
2. Select /Data Parse Format-Line Create. Note the initial symbols L (for label block), press F6 to clear the Parse Settings window and then choose V (for value) and D (for date block). Also note the # and > extension symbols that define the width of each block.
3. You may use /Data Parse Format-Line Edit to edit the line, although this is optional.
4. Select /Data Parse Input-Column.
5. Specify the input column range including the format line with `A6..A9`.
6. Select /Data Parse Output-Range.
7. Specify the output range with `C5`.

See Figures Data.8a–c.

Notes

The format line created by 1-2-3 is based on the first line of the input column range. If there is any ambiguity in the data elements in the first line, or, if there is considerable variation in the size of the individual fields in subsequent lines of the input column, you may need to edit the format line with the /Data Parse Format-Line Edit command. You may also need to add some spaces to various shorter entries in the input column so that the data lines up properly with the

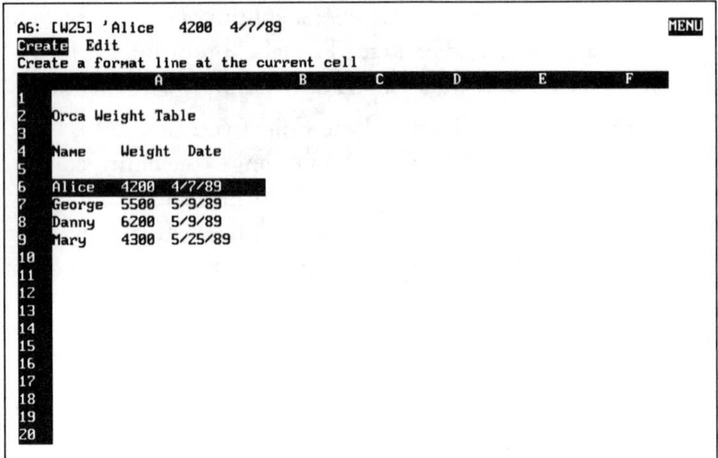

Figure Data.8a
Creating a format line.

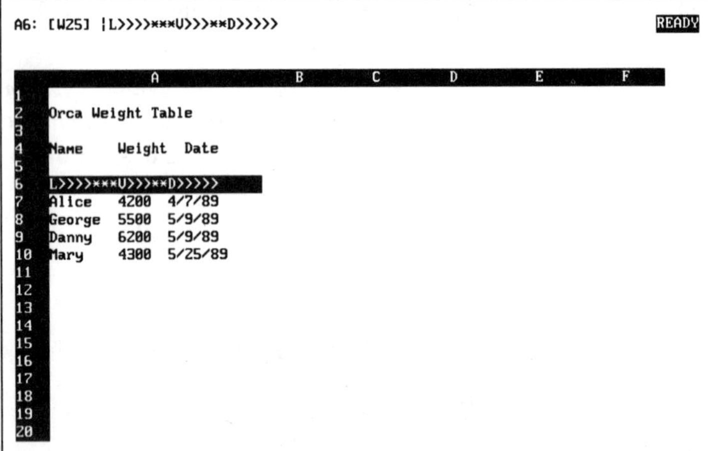

Figure Data.8b
Parsing Format Line.

format line above. 1-2-3 compares each line of the input column with the format line and breaks it into fields accordingly; if a given line is significantly longer or shorter, 1-2-3 may parse it incorrectly.

Cautions

/Data Parse creates an output range equal in size to the number of rows in the input column range and the number of columns defined by the format line. 1-2-3 will overwrite any data that lies in the output location with no warning. Be certain that the output location is clear or can be overwritten before you invoke this command.

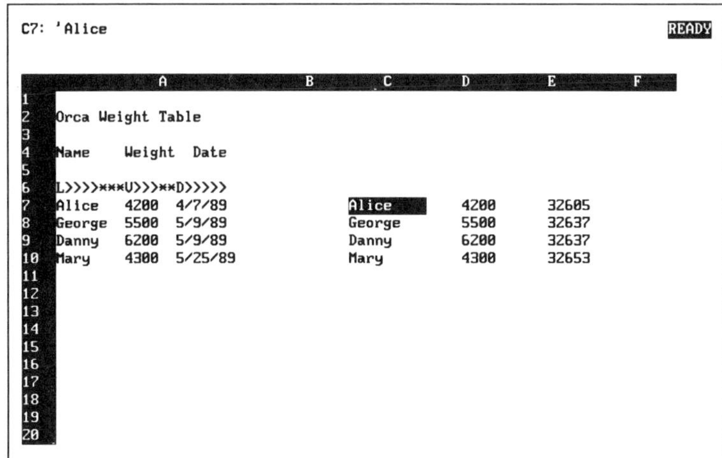

Figure Data.8c
Parsed Data.

Data Parse Format—Line Create

Purpose

Used to have 1-2-3 create a format line derived from its interpretation of the selected long label in the input column range. The format line is used as a template to parse each subsequent long label in the input column range. You may need more than one format line in the input column—one for the parsing of headings and another for the parsing of data entries.

Description

The format line is a single label cell that contains a series of format symbols. These symbols define the model that 1-2-3 will use to split each long label in the input column into separate cells, labels, numbers, times, or dates. The symbols that may be used in a format line include:

D	Initial symbol for a date block
L	Initial symbol for a label block
T	Initial symbol for a time block
V	Initial symbol for a value block
S	Initial symbol that tells 1-2-3 to skip the associated data block in the output. (The symbol is not generated by 1-2-3; you have to edit a format line to include the Skip symbol.)
>	Extension symbol used to define the size of the data block.

* Blank space extension symbol used to accommodate entries that are longer than the defined block.

A data block must start with one of the five initial symbols followed by a series of extension symbols, either > or *. (See Figure Data 8.d.) /Data Parse will generate fields in the output range that are at least as long as the block specified by the initial symbol and the > or * symbol.

Defaults

If /Data Parse Format-Line Create encounters an ambiguous data element in the long label you specify, it uses the following hierarchy to generate the format line:

1. Value
2. Date
3. Time
4. Label

Thus, 1-2-3 will treat the ambiguous 8/89 (date or value) as a value when creating the format line. To specify a date format instead, you will have to edit the format line that 1-2-3 creates.

Usage

To have 1-2-3 create a "best guess" format line for the input column range, place the cell pointer on the top cell in the input range and select /Data Parse Format-Line Create. (Your default input column and output range parse settings will flash to the screen in a window covering your data. Press F6 to clear them.) 1-2-3 inserts a new line above the first line of the input column range and creates the format line; 1-2-3 resorts to its hierarchy of field types when it encounters ambiguous data. You can edit the format line using the /Data Parse Format-Line Edit option.

Examples

To create the format line for the input column range of names, addresses, and phone numbers (see Figure Data.8e):

1. Place the cell pointer in the top cell of the input column range.
2. Select /Data Parse Format-Line (press F6 to clear the parse settings window) and then choose Create. (See Figure Data.8e.)

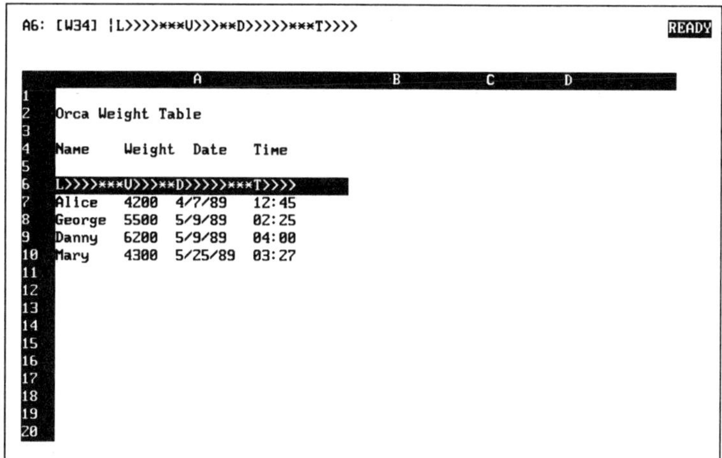

Figure Data.8d
Parsing Format Line.

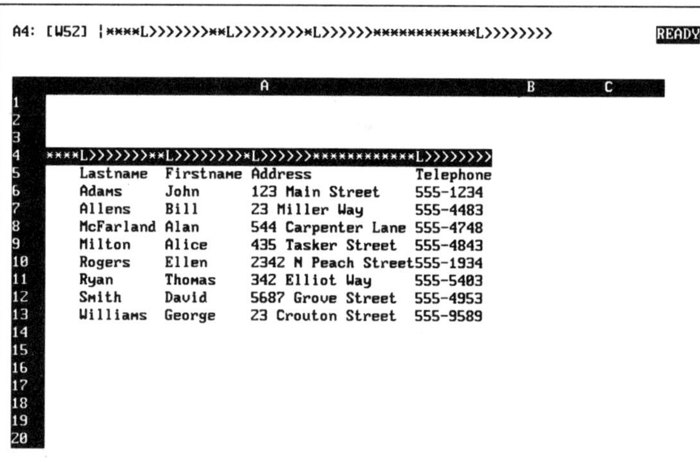

Figure Data.8e
Creating Format Line.

Notes

The format line created by 1-2-3 is based on the first line of the input column range. If there is ambiguity in any data elements in the first line, or, if there is considerable variation in the size of the individual fields in subsequent lines of the input column, you may need to edit the format line with the /Data Parse Format-Line Edit command. You may also need to add some spaces to various shorter entries in the input column so that your data lines up properly under the format line above. 1-2-3 compares each line of the input column with the format line and breaks it accordingly. If a given line in the column is significantly longer or shorter, 1-2-3 may parse it incorrectly.

It is possible to use more than one format line for a given column of long labels to accommodate changes in label size or content. To insert a second format line, place the cell pointer on the top cell of the new format and initiate the command /Data Parse Format-Line Create. A new line will be inserted and the new format line will be generated from the highlighted cell. You can then edit the new format line with /Data Parse Format-Line Edit.

Cautions

/Data Parse Format-Line Create inserts a new row into the current worksheet. This may interrupt other data tables or macros located in the current worksheet.

Data Parse Format—Line Edit

Purpose

Used to modify the field divisions specified in a format line before executing the /Data Parse Go command. Editing may be required to resolve data types, to skip a given field, or to make adjustments for variable data block field sizes.

Description

/Data Parse Format-Line Edit can be used to edit a format line created by /Data Parse Format-Line Create or to type in a format line from scratch. The format line symbols are described in detail in /Data Parse Format-Line Create. (See Figure Data 8.e.)

Defaults

The last created format line.

Usage

To edit the format line, place the cell pointer on the cell that contains the format line, and select /Data Parse Format-Line Edit. (Press F6 to clear the Parse settings window.) Modify the line as required and press ENTER when done. While in edit mode, several control keys are available for moving about the column of data so that you can compare the format line with various lines of the input column. The Up and Down (and PgUp and PgDn) cursor keys scroll the input column range up and down accordingly. HOME returns you to the top cell of the input column. ESC erases the format line contents. CTRL-BREAK cancels the changes you have made to the format line and returns you to READY mode.

Examples

To edit the format line in Figure Data.8e so that 1-2-3 will skip the telephone field:

1. Place the cell-pointer on the cell containing the format line.
2. Select /Data Parse Format-Line Edit.
3. Replace the "L" for the telephone field with an "S" for skip. (See Figure Data 8.f.)
4. Select /Data Parse Go.

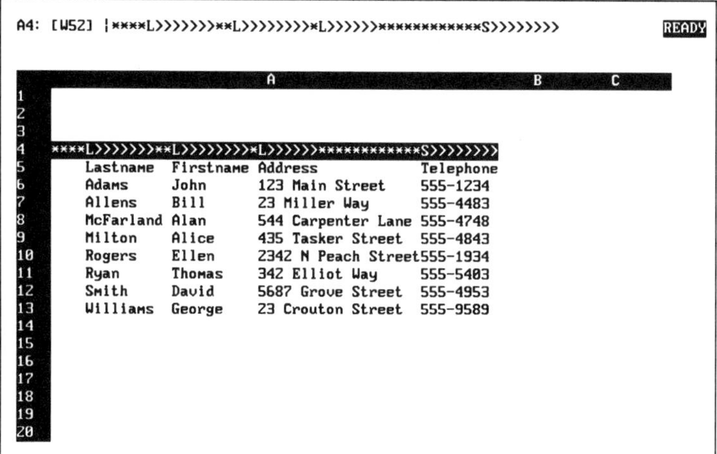

Figure Data.8f
Editing the Format Line.

Notes

In addition to editing the format line generated by 1-2-3, you may have to edit individual lines of your input column range if some fields vary significantly in size. 1-2-3 sets the format line to correspond to the top line of your column of data. If a subsequent line has significantly different spacing, you may have to edit both the data and the format line so that the data is correctly parsed.

It is possible to use more than one format line for a given column of long labels to accommodate changes in label size or content. To insert a second format line, place the cell pointer on the top cell of the new format and initiate the command /Data Parse Format-Line Create. A new line will be inserted and the new format line will be generated from the highlighted cell. You can then edit the format line with /Data Parse Format-Line Edit.

Data Parse Go

Purpose

Used to execute the parsing of each text line in the input column according to the format line displayed at the top of the input column. When there is more than one format line in the input column, each text line is split according to the format line directly above it.

Description

/Data Parse Go executes the parsing process after you have created (or edited) the format line and defined the input and output ranges.

Defaults

The last defined input column and output range. The format line located in the top cell of the input column or the top of the current section of the column if there is more than one format line.

Usage

Before you can use the /Data Parse Go command, you must create a format line that 1-2-3 can use to interpret the long labels in the input column. (Use the /Data Parse Format-Line command.) You must specify the input column and output range with the /Data Parse Input-Column and /Data Parse Output-Range commands. You are then ready to perform the parsing with /Data Parse Go.

Examples

To execute the parsing of the input column named ORCAS into the output range starting in cell C5 using the parsing format defined in the top line of the input column range. (See Figures Data.8a–c.)

1. Select /Range Name Create.
2. Type `ORCAS` at the prompt. Specify the range A6..A9.
3. Select /Data Parse Input-Column to specify the input column.
4. Type `ORCAS` and press ENTER.
5. Select /Data Parse Output-Range to specify the output range.
6. Type or point to `C5`.
7. Select /Data Parse Go.

Notes

You must define an input column, an output range, and the parsing format line before selecting /Data Parse Go.

Cautions

/Data Parse Go requires an output range equal in size to the number of rows in the input column and the number of columns specified by the format line. 1-2-3 overwrites any data that may lie in the output location with no warning. Make sure that the output location is clear or can be overwritten before invoking this command.

Data Parse Input—Column

Purpose

Used to specify the input column range for the /Data Parse commands.

Description

The input column range must be a single column and must contain the format line as the top cell of the range.

Defaults

The current cell.

Usage

To select the input column range, place the cell pointer on the format line at the top of the column of long labels you want to split into separate fields. Choose /Data Parse Input-Column and specify the column range by name, by address, or by painting it.

Examples

To select the input column range containing the names, weights, and dates of the orca population shown in Figure Data.8b:

1. Place the cell-pointer on the format line in cell A6.
2. Select /Data Parse Input-Column.
3. Specify the range with `A6..A9`.

Notes

If the input range contains blank cells, they are ignored by the parsing commands and subsequent cells are moved up in the output range.

Data Parse Output—Range

Purpose

Used to specify the output range for the /Data Parse commands.

Description

The output range will be as long as the number of non-blank rows in the input column range and as many columns wide as the number of data blocks specified in the format line.

Defaults

The current cell.

Usage

To select an output range, choose /Data Parse Output-Range and, at the prompt, specify the range by name, by address, or by painting it. (You need only specify the top-left cell of the output range.)

Examples

To select the output range for the orca population shown in Figure 8b:

1. Select /Data Parse Output-Range.
2. Point to C5 to specify the output range.

Cautions

/Data Parse will overwrite any data that may lie in the output location without warning. Be certain that the output location is clear or can be overwritten before invoking this command.

Data Parse Reset

Purpose

Releases the currently defined input column range and the output range so that they can be redefined.

Description

/Data Parse Reset clears the currently selected input and output ranges; the new range default becomes the current cell. (Press F6 if you need to see your current Parse settings.)

Defaults

Current input column and output range settings.

Usage

To reset the input column range and the output range, select /Data Parse Reset. If you want to reset only one of the ranges, you can simply reselect the /Data Parse Input-Column or Output-Range command and redefine the associated range.

Data Query

Purpose

The /Data Query commands perform three distinct functions: to find (and then edit) records in a database table that match a specified criteria; to delete records that match a specified criteria; and to extract records that match a specified criteria from the input database table and list them in a new output database table. When finding matching records, you have the option to edit them or simply locate them.

Description

The /Data Query commands are used together to define an Input range, a Criteria range, an Output range (if required), and then, finally, to specify an action: Find, Del(ete), Extract, or Unique. The current settings for the /Data Query command are listed in the setting sheet. (See Figure Data.9.) The current setting sheet is shown each time the /Data Query command is selected. (Press F6 to clear the Query Settings window from the screen. Press F6 again to redisplay it.)

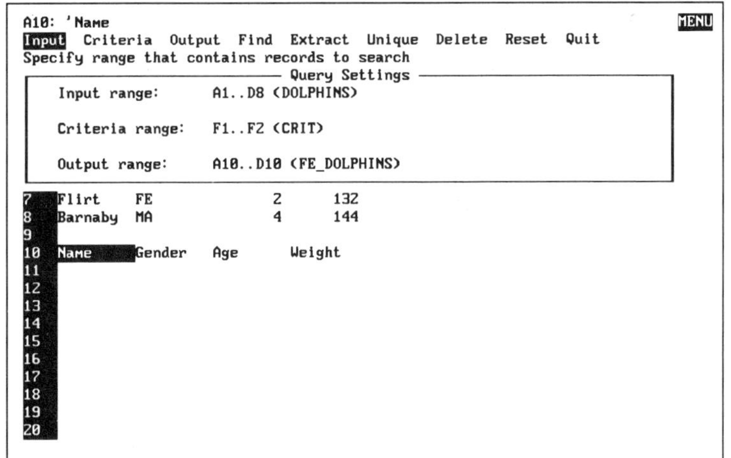

Figure Data.9
/Data Query Setting Sheet.

Usage

To use the /Data Query commands, you must first specify two ranges, the Input range and the Criteria range, using /Data Query Input and /Data Query Criteria. If you intend to extract records from the input database range to another table, you must also define an Output range with /Data Query Output. It is easiest to assign range names to all your ranges and to refer to them by name throughout the /Data Query process. After you have defined the input, criteria, and, if necessary, the output range you can then choose one of the /Data Query action commands such as Find, Extract, or Unique.

Examples

To extract the records of female dolphins from the data table called DOLPHINS (see Figure Data.10) to the output range called FE_DOLPHINS:

1. Select /Range Name Create.
2. Type `DOLPHINS` and press ENTER.
3. Type `A1..D8` to specify the range address.
4. Select /Range Name Create to assign an output range name.
5. Type `FE_DOLPHINS` and press ENTER.
6. Type `A10..D10` to specify the range address.
7. Copy the field names from the top of the input range to the output range.
8. Move the cell pointer to F1.
9. Type `GENDER` in cell F1.
10. Type `FE` in cell F2 to complete the criteria range.
11. Select /Range Name Create to assign a criteria range name.
12. Type `CRIT` and press ENTER.
13. Select range `F1..F2`.
14. Select /Data Query Input to specify input range.
15. Type `DOLPHINS` and press ENTER.
16. Select /Data Query Output to specify output range.
17. Type `FE_DOLPHINS` and press ENTER.
18. Select /Data Query Criteria to specify criteria range.
19. Type `CRIT` and press ENTER.
20. Select /Data Query Extract.

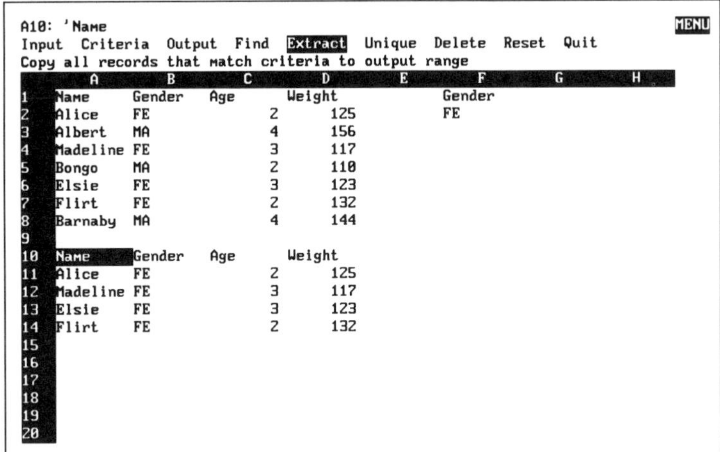

Figure Data.10
/Data Query Extract.

Notes

You can use the QUERY key (F7) to repeat the last query action performed. For example, you can perform an extract with a given criteria, then change the criteria by modifying the cells in the criteria range and repeat the extract with the new criteria by pressing F7.

Cautions

The /Data Query Extract command overwrites any data in the output range without warning. Be sure that the selected output range is clear or can be overwritten before you invoke this command.

Data Query Criteria

Purpose

Used to select a criteria range (that you have already created in the worksheet) for the performance of a /Data Query Find or /Data Query Extract command.

Description

The criteria range is used to specify the kind of records you wish to locate in your data query. It consists of two or more rows. The first row in the criteria range contains one or more field names—field names that correspond to those used in the input database table. (You need only specify the relevant field names to direct your query; you do not have to include all the input database field names.)

The second and subsequent row(s) under the field names contain the selection criteria against which each record in the input database range is compared for selection. If you enter more than one criteria in a given row, they are connected by a logical AND. Thus, for a record to be selected as a match, it must meet all criteria entered in a single row. If you enter more than one row of criteria, they are connected by a logical OR. For a given record to be selected it must meet the criteria in either row. In Figure Data.11 the criteria range (A11..B13) specifies that the selected records meet the following conditions: a. The individual lives in NY AND has given over $1,000; OR b. the individual lives in PA AND has given over $1,000.

If you are working with any *label* matches, you must use the multiple row and column entries technique for your criteria as described above. The same method is also easiest and clearest when you wish to find matching *values* or values that can be expressed in simple formulas using the logical operators <, <=, >=, >, <>, and =. The logical formula +F2>1000 in Figure Data.11 is a good example. Note that when you use logical operators you must reference the *first field entry* in the column you wish to have searched. You may also wish to use the /Range Format Text command to see your logical formulas on screen; otherwise, 1-2-3 will return a value 0 (if false) or 1 (if true) to the formula cell, depending on whether the condition is true or false for the field entry that is specified in the formula.

If you are comparing values and wish to devise complex formula criteria, you can use the logical operators *and* the Boolean operators #AND#, #NOT#, and #OR# to create fairly involved data tests. In such cases you can enter your criteria

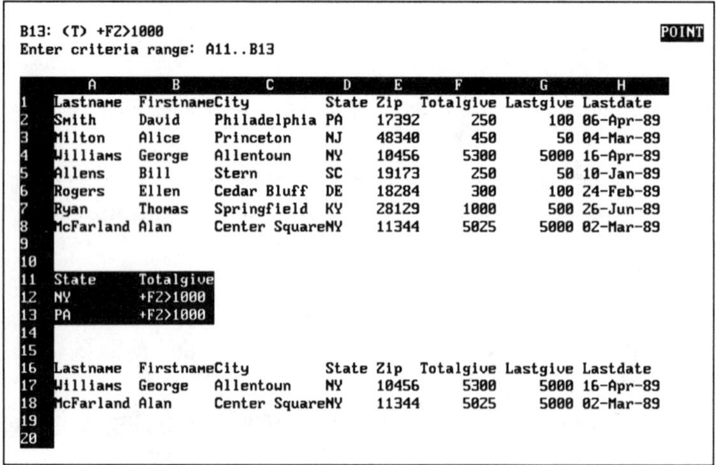

```
B13: (T) +F2>1000                                                    POINT
Enter criteria range: A11..B13

       A         B          C          D     E       F         G        H
1   Lastname  FirstnameCity          State Zip   Totalgive Lastgive Lastdate
2   Smith     David     Philadelphia PA    17392       250       100 06-Apr-89
3   Milton    Alice     Princeton    NJ    48340       450        50 04-Mar-89
4   Williams  George    Allentown    NY    10456      5300      5000 16-Apr-89
5   Allens    Bill      Stern        SC    19173       250        50 10-Jan-89
6   Rogers    Ellen     Cedar Bluff  DE    18284       300       100 24-Feb-89
7   Ryan      Thomas    Springfield  KY    28129      1000       500 26-Jun-89
8   McFarland Alan      Center SquareNY    11344      5025      5000 02-Mar-89
9
10
11  State     Totalgive
12  NY        +F2>1000
13  PA        +F2>1000
14
15
16  Lastname  FirstnameCity          State Zip   Totalgive Lastgive Lastdate
17  Williams  George    Allentown    NY    10456      5300      5000 16-Apr-89
18  McFarland Alan      Center SquareNY    11344      5025      5000 02-Mar-89
19
20
```

Figure Data.11
Criteria range.

formula in a single cell anywhere within the criteria range. For example, in Figure Data.11, you could combine two value tests in the form +F2>1000#AND#G2>500. Note that in such formulas, you must also reference the first field entry (e.g., F2 and G2) in the columns you want to have searched. The Boolean operators *cannot* be used with label criteria alone or to link label and value criteria. (For example, you cannot use a state criteria of +D2=NY=#OR#+D2=PA.) See below for a detailed discussion on formats required for label, value, and formula criteria (and their combinations).

Defaults

The criteria range last defined.

Usage

To define a criteria range, you must first prepare the data to be included in the range. The first line of the range must contain the database fields you wish to test against, one field name per column. Specify the field names exactly as they appear in the database table. Below the first row of field names you may enter one or more rows of criteria. Criteria in a single row are connected by a logical AND. Rows of criteria are connected by a logical OR. You can include label criteria, value criteria, or formula criteria (described below) in any of the cells of your criteria range and fine-tune your selection with amazing precision. (Remember that when you use logical and Boolean operators, you must reference the first field entry in the column you want to search.) In Figure Data.11, for example, +F2>1000 tells 1-2-3 to search the Totalgive column starting with the first row of data entries—row 2.Once you have specified your criteria, select /Data Query Criteria. (Press F6 to clear the Query settings window.)

Next, specify the criteria range; include both the row of field names and all rows of criteria. The selected criteria range will remain in force for the current 1-2-3 session or until you specify another criteria range. Note that you can change the contents of the criteria range, without altering the default range setting itself. The changes to your criteria selection can then be used for the next /Data Query command, or, if you press the QUERY key (F7), to repeat your last /Data Query command. Remember, though, that if you *extend* the criteria entered into the criteria range, you must also *extend* the criteria range setting. Any criteria lying outside the defined range is not considered.

There are three types of criteria that can be specified (and combined) in your criteria range: label, value, and formula criteria. They are defined below.

Label Criteria When you set criteria for labels, 1-2-3 searches for data entries in the input range that match your label criteria exactly, with the same spelling and spacing. These "exact match" searches are among the simplest kinds of data queries. (1-2-3 does not require that capitalization or label format prefixes be identical.)

If you want to accept partial matches in your label criteria, you can use the DOS wildcard characters ? and *. The ? symbol allows any single character to be substituted in its place. (The criteria par? would select pare, park, and part as matches, but would not select pert or parasol.) The * symbol may be replaced by any number of adjacent characters; the * can only occur at the end of a label criteria. (Thus, par* would match parasol or part, but not pert.) In addition, preceding a label with the tilde (~), indicates "not equal"; the resulting criteria will select a criterium of all records except those that match the criteria. For example, ~NY would select all records except those from NY.

Finally, you can combine these wildcard symbols and logical operators to produce complex criteria. For example, the criteria ~n* will select all records except those that start with the letter n.

1-2-3 is generally not case sensitive, but, if you change the collating sequence to ASCII during the installation process, 1-2-3 will become case sensitive and will distinguish between Rob and rob. If, on occasion, you wish to perform a case-sensitive search (and you have not changed the collating sequence to ASCII), you can include the function @EXACT, e.g., @EXACT(A2), "El Greco") within the criteria range.

Value Criteria 1-2-3 matches values based on the internally stored values not on the formatted display. This means that $100.00, 100.000, and 1E+02 will all match 100. On the other hand, this can produce errors if displayed results have been rounded. If, for example, 1-2-3 displayed the results of a calculation as 100, having rounded off the stored value 100.00000000123, you would not get a match. To avoid this error, give the value criteria some leeway so that you can get the matching values you want. Use the logical operators >, <, >=, and <= to create criteria with some room for error such as +F2>=99.999999 or +F2<=100.00001.

To specify a particular date, you can use the @DATE formula. For example, the criteria +H2=@DATE(89,5,1) would find all those records in the database table that have a date in column H of May 1, 1989. Likewise, including the criteria +H2<=@DATE(89,5,1) in the criteria range would find all those with a date on or before May 1, 1989.

Formula Criteria If you want to create complex criteria that manipulate data before testing for matches or that specify relationships between one or more fields, you can create criteria based on formulas. The formulas can refer to labels or values. For example, if your input database range contains the fields Month, ProjSales, and ActSales in columns C, D, and E, you could create the criteria +E2>D2 to find records where actual sales exceeded projected sales or +C2=12 to find results for the month of December. You can combine such formulas with the Boolean logical operators #AND#, #OR#, and #NOT# to create complex relations such as +E2>D@#AND#C2=I2. You can even combine #AND# and #OR# criteria; +E2>=D2#AND#(C2=1#OR#C2=2) will select all records where actual sales were greater than or equal to projected sales for the months of January and February.

Examples

To set the criteria range to State equals either New York or Pennsylvania in the DONORS database (see Figure Data.11):

1. Select an available area of the worksheet.
2. Enter the field names of the database in a row.
3. Enter the criteria `NY` in the row under the field name State.
4. Enter the criteria `PA` in the row under NY.
5. Select /Data Query Criteria.
6. Highlight the complete three-row range and press ENTER.

Notes

When specifying a formula criteria it is often useful to set the format to text so that the criteria is displayed. Otherwise, 1-2-3 returns a 1(true) or a 0 (false) in the formula cell, having checked to see whether the formula is true or false for the first record in the database.

Criteria ranges are not case sensitive unless you have reset the collating sequence to ASCII during the install process.

Data Query Extract

Purpose

Used to extract records from the input database table range and copy them to the output range. By specifying which fields you want to copy (when you define your output range) and which records you want to select (when you define your criteria range), you can carefully control how the records are extracted.

Description

/Data Query Extract is an action command that requires several setup procedures. You must first specify the input range, the output range, and the criteria range before you issue the Extract command.

Defaults

The input, output, and criteria ranges last defined. (Press F6 to see your default Query settings.)

Usage

To extract the records from a database table, first specify your source database table as the input range. Next, select an output range and specify in the top row of the output range the field name labels that you want included in the extract. By including the appropriate field names in the top row of your output range, you have precise control over which fields are extracted from the input range. See the section on /Data Query Output for more information on output ranges. Next, you must specify the criteria range. Here again you can create sophisticated combinations of criteria for the selection of records from the input range. See the sections on /Data Query Criteria and /Data Query Output for more information. Finally, you can execute the extract command by selecting /Data Query Extract.

Examples

To extract the records of those donors whose home state is New York or Pennsylvania and who have donated more than $1,000 from the data table called DONORS, and to copy (or extract) them to the output range called NY_DONORS (see Figure Data.11):

1. Select /Range Name Create to assign a range name to you input database table.
2. Type `DONORS` and press ENTER.
3. Type (or paint) `A1..H8` and press ENTER.
4. Select /Range Name Create to assign an output range name.
5. Type `NY_DONORS` and press ENTER.
6. Type (or paint) `A16..H16` and press ENTER.
7. Copy the field names of those fields you wish to extract to the output range A16..H16.
8. Select a clear location for the criteria range.

9. Type `STATE` in cell A11.
10. Type `Total Give` in cell B11
11. Type `NY` in cell A12.
12. Type `PA` in cell A13.
13. Type +F2>1000 in cells B12 *and* B13.
14. Select /Range Name Create to assign a criteria range name.
15. Type `CRIT` and press ENTER.
16. Type (or paint) `A11..B13` and press ENTER.
17. Select /Data Query Input and specify your input range name.
18. Type `DONORS` and press ENTER.
19. Select /Data Query Output and specify your output range name.
20. Type `NY_DONORS` and press ENTER.
21. Select /Data Query Criteria and specify your criteria range name.
22. Type `CRIT` and press ENTER.
23. Select /Data Query Extract to perform the extract.

Notes

You can use the QUERY key (F7) to repeat the last query action performed. For example, you can perform an extract with a given criteria, then change the criteria by modifying the cells in the criteria range and repeat the extract with the new criteria simply by pressing F7.

Cautions

The /Data Query Extract command overwrites the data in the output range without warning. Be sure that the selected output range is clear or can be overwritten before you invoke this command.

Data Query Input

Purpose

Used to select the input database table range for a /Data Query Extract or /Data Query Find command. The input database table range must be in 1-2-3 database table form (i.e., the first row of the data table must contain the field names).

Description

The input range contains the source data from which data is extracted (with /Data Query Extract) or in which a particular record is found (with /Data Query Find). Before you can select a database table as the input range for an extract, you must ensure that it conforms to the 1-2-3 database table format: where the top row contains the field names, and each subsequent row contains a single record with all the appropriate data elements for each field. The database table *must* be continuous and must *not* contain any blank records.

Defaults

The input range last defined. (Press F6 to see your default Input Range setting.)

Usage

To specify an input range, check that the database table conforms to the 1-2-3 format requirements, then initiate the command with /Data Query Input. Identify the input database table by its assigned name, by address, or by painting the range. Be sure to include the first line of the database table containing the field names as the first line of your input range.

Examples

To specify the range named DONORS as the input range for an extract:

1. Select /Data Query Input.
2. Type `DONORS` to specify the range by name.

See Example under /Data Query for complete sample.

Notes

The input range must include the field names of the database table in the first row.

The input range may contain less then the full number of rows in the database table, but it must include at least the first record below the row of field names.

Data Query Output

Purpose

Selects the output location to hold all records extracted from a database table via the /Data Query Extract and /Data Query Unique commands. (In each case, the top row of the output location you specify must contain the field names that you want to include in the extraction.)

Description

The top row of the output range must contain the field names for each field in the source database table you want included in your extraction. If you specify a single row output range, 1-2-3 will use as many rows below the field names as necessary to display the extracted records. This may cause a loss of data if there is any data located below the output range. If you specify a multiple row output range, 1-2-3 will only write to the output range if it is large enough to hold all qualifying records. If there is not enough space, 1-2-3 will issue an error message.

Defaults

The last specifyied output range. (Press F6 to see your default Output Range.)

Usage

To define an output range, first prepare its top row by typing in each field name you wish to have extracted from the database table. The field names must be spelled exactly as they appear in the database table and in the criteria range. Skip any field names that you do not wish to include in the output range.

Examples

To set up a single row output range as shown in Figure Data.11:

1. Copy the field names from the input range with the /Copy command.
2. Select /Data Query Output.
3. Type or paint `A16..H16` to specify the output range and press ENTER.

Notes

The field names in the output range must match the field names in the input and criteria ranges exactly in spelling and spacing.

Cautions

Make certain that the output range will not overlap the input or the criteria range. In general it is best not place the output range directly below the input range unless you are certain that you will not be adding records to the input range.

If you specify a single row output range, 1-2-3 will overwrite as many rows below the field names as necessary to extract all matching records from the input range. Make sure that you have adequate clear space below the output range for the extracted data.

If you specify a multiple line output range, 1-2-3 will only use those lines specified. While this will protect you from accidentally overwriting data below the extract range, it may not accommodate all records that qualify for the extract. In this case, 1-2-3 will report an error.

Data Query Quit

Purpose

Used to exit from the /Data Query menu

Description

The Quit option returns you directly to the READY mode without traversing the intervening menus. It does not cancel the existing /Data Query settings

Notes

To reset the /Data Query settings to blank, use /Data Query Reset.

Data Query Reset

Purpose

Used to cancel the existing /Data Query setting for Input, Output, and Criteria ranges. They are set to blank and must be redefined before you can re-execute the /Data Query command.

Description

The /Data Query Reset command clears the existing defined ranges, allowing you to redefine them without the previous range specification appearing as the default. This will make redefining them somewhat easier. If you only want to redefine one of the ranges, you would be better off simply redefining the single range by re-selecting the associated option from the menu rather than resetting all of them.

Cautions

The reset option resets all three /Data Query ranges. You should be certain that you want to clear all of them before you initiate this command.

Data Query Unique

Purpose

Used to extract unique records from an input database table to an output range. This command is identical to the /Data Query Extract command, except that it eliminates duplicate records and sorts the output.

Description

/Data Query Unique is one of the action commands that requires preliminary setup procedures in order to operate successfully. You must first specify an input range, output range, and a criteria range before executing the Unique command.

Defaults

The input, output, and criteria ranges last specified.

Usage

To extract unique records from a database table, you must first specify the source database table as your input range. You must then specify your output range location, and type in the field names you wish to include in the top row of the output range. Depending on which field names you include in the output range, you can control which fields are extracted from the input range. (See /Data Query Output and /Data Query Criteria.)

By specifying which fields you want to include in your output range, you also define how "uniqueness" is determined. 1-2-3 refers only to the fields you have specified in the output range when it compare records together to see if they are identical. Therefore, if two records in the input table are identical except for one field and you have included that field in your output range, 1-2-3 considers them unique and copies both records to the output range. On the other hand, if the one field in which they differ is *not* included in your output range, 1-2-3 considers the two records as identical and copies only the first record to the output range. See the section on /Data Query Output for more information on output ranges.

You must next specify a criteria range. Here again, you can create complex and sophisticated criteria for the selection of records from the input range. (See the section on /Data Query Criteria for more details.) Finally, you are ready to execute the unique extraction command by selecting /Data Query Unique.

Examples

Suppose you want to have a celebration benefit party for all donors that live in New York State and who have written donation checks for $500 or more in the past three years. To send these donors their invitations, you want an alphabetical address list. To extract the unique records of those New York donors who have contributed $500 or more at one time from the database table called DONORS to the output range called NY_GUESTS starting in A1..E1:

1. In cells A1..E1, type in these field names (one per cell): Name, Address, City, State, Zip.
2. Select /Range Name Create to assign an output range name.
3. Type `NY_GUESTS` and press ENTER.
4. Type (or paint) `A1..E1` and press ENTER.
5. Type `STATE` in cell G1 for the criteria range field name.
6. Type `NY` in cell G2.
7. Type `Contribution` in cell H1.
8. Type `+F2>500` in cell H2.
9. Select /Range Name Create to assign a criteria range name.
10. Type `GALA_CRIT` and press ENTER.
11. Type in (or paint) `G1..H2` and press ENTER.
12. Select /Data Query Input to select input range.
13. Type `DONORS` and press ENTER.
14. Select /Data Query Output to specify output range.
15. Type `NY_GUESTS` and press ENTER.
16. Select /Data Query Criteria to specify criteria range.
17. Type `GALA_CRIT` and press ENTER.
18. Select /Data Query Unique to perform the extract.

Notes

You can use the QUERY key (F7) to repeat the last query action performed. For example, you can perform a unique extract with a given criteria, then change the criteria by modifying the cells in the criteria range and repeat the unique command with the new criteria by simply pressing F7.

Cautions

The /Data Query Unique command overwrites any data in the output range without warning. Be sure that the selected output range is clear or can be overwritten before invoking this command.

Data Regression

Purpose

/Data Regression is a statistical command used to perform multiple linear regression. Linear regression allows you to determine how much one variable in a data set (the dependent or Y-range variable) is affected by one or more other variables in the data set (the independent or X-range variables(s)). The Regression option allows you to predict a value for the dependent variable, based on a set of values for one or more independent variables. Regression analysis has many applications, including relating production costs to production levels, net sales to price, advertising to market size, etc. The results of the regression analysis can be used for forecasting to project linear historical data into the future. The /Data Regression command also provides statistics showing the strength of the correlation between the dependent and independent variables.

Description

/Data Regression consists of several commands used to specify input ranges (/Data Regression X-Range and Y-Range), the output range (/Data Regression Output-Range), and the intercept specification (/Data Regression Intercept). When all these are properly set, the execution command /Data Regression Go performs the regression analysis. The input ranges specify your independent variable(s) and the dependent variable; the output range specifies where to place the tabled results of the regression analysis. The regression output table includes the following statistics:

Name	**Description**
Constant	The Y-Intercept, the value of the dependent variable when all independent variable(s) are equal to zero.
Degrees of Freedom	The total number of observations (rows of data) subtracted by one more than the number of independent variables.

Name	Description
Number of Observations	The number of rows of data, or the total number of values in the X or Y range.
R2 Value	Also called the coefficient of determination. This value tells what percentage of the variation in the dependent variable is directly affected by the variation in the independent variable. The reliability of the regression is expressed in a value from 0–1. If the R2 value is less than zero, you must have specified that the Y-Intercept should be equal to zero in a situation that was inappropriate. Recompute the regression using the /Data Regression Intercept Compute option.
Standard Error of Coefficient	Estimate of the standard deviation for the sampling distribution of the X coefficient.
Standard Error Y estimate	Standard error of the Y value generated by the analysis (determines how reliably each independent variable can be used for prediction).
X coefficients	The slope for each regression line formed by each independent variable. (An X coefficient shows how much the dependent variable changes given a one-unit change for the independent variable).

Defaults

The previously defined X-Range, Y-Range, Output-Range, and Intercept. If you do not specify the Intercept calculation technique (Zero or Compute), 1-2-3 defaults to Compute. (Press F6 to see your default Regression settings.)

Usage

To use the /Data Regression commands, you must first ensure that the data to be analyzed is arranged into parallel columns. The X-range is used to specify the range of values for the independent variables. The values for each independent variable must be in a single column. If there is more than one independent variable, they must be placed in adjacent columns.

The range of values for the dependent variable is specified by the Y-range; it must contain the same number of rows of data as the independent variable. You can either specify that 1-2-3 calculate the Y-intercept (the value of the dependent variable if all the independent variables are equal to zero), or you can force the Y-intercept to be zero. (You should not do the latter unless the dependent variable should be zero when all the independent variable(s) are zero.)

After specifying your X- and Y-ranges and your Y-intercept as input data, you must specify an output location for the 1-2-3 regression table. The Output range requires nine rows and at least four columns. Each additional independent variable will require an additional column for the Output range. (See Figure Data.12).

You can specify the single cell upper-left corner of the output range and 1-2-3 will use as many cells as required to display the results. You must be careful since this may accidentally overwrite data. Alternatively, you can specify the entire output range and 1-2-3 will alert you with an error message if it is too small.

The final step in the regression process is to select the Go option. This executes the regression analysis and paces the results in the output range.

When you select the /Data Regression command, 1-2-3 displays the current setting sheet for the regression analysis. (See Figure Data.13.) The settings sheet shows the current settings for the X-range, the Y-range, the Output range and the method of calculation for the intercept. (Press F6 to clear the Regression settings window.)

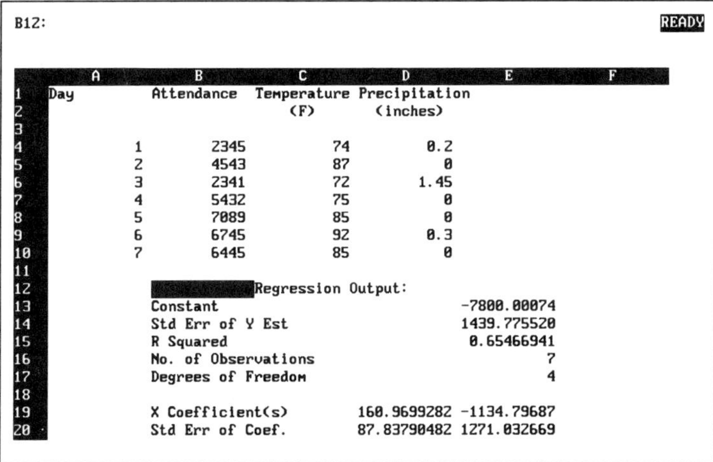

B12: READY

	A	B	C	D	E	F
1	Day	Attendance	Temperature	Precipitation		
2			(F)	(inches)		
3						
4	1	2345	74	0.2		
5	2	4543	87	0		
6	3	2341	72	1.45		
7	4	5432	75	0		
8	5	7089	85	0		
9	6	6745	92	0.3		
10	7	6445	85	0		
11						
12			Regression Output:			
13		Constant			-7800.00074	
14		Std Err of Y Est			1439.775520	
15		R Squared			0.65466941	
16		No. of Observations			7	
17		Degrees of Freedom			4	
18						
19		X Coefficient(s)		160.9699282	-1134.79687	
20		Std Err of Coef.		87.83790482	1271.032669	

Figure Data.12
/Data Regression.

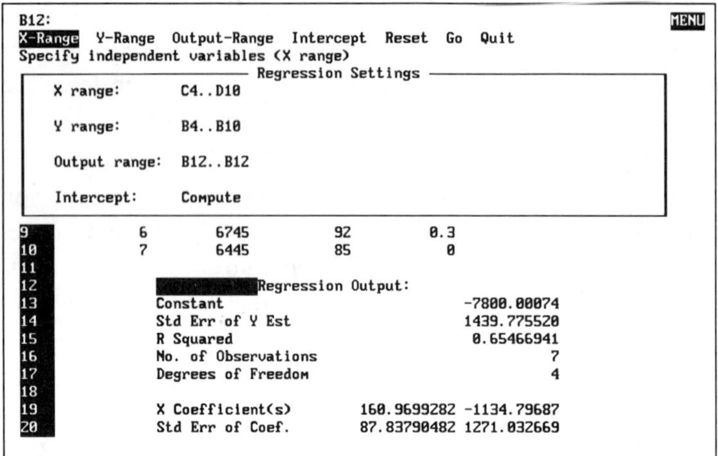

Figure Data.13
/Data Regression Settings Sheet.

Examples

You suspect that weekday attendance at the aquarium is a function of the weather. You know that weekend aquarium attendance is not so directly tied to the weather, so you have eliminated weekends from your calculation. You have collected the daily attendance for the first seven weekdays of April and also noted the weather based on highest daily temperature and total daily precipitation. (You would probably want to use more data to increase the accuracy of your study, but we'll only use seven observations for this example.)

1. Place the data into parallel columns, with the dependent variable on one side and the independent variables in adjacent columns (see Figure Data.12).
2. Select /Data Regression X-Range to specify the columns of independent variables (temperature and weather). (Press F6 to clear the Regression settings window.)
3. Type (or paint) `C4..D10` and press ENTER.
4. Select /Data Regression Y-Range to specify the column of dependent variables (days of the week).
5. Type (or paint) `B4..B10` and press ENTER.
6. Select /Data Regression Intercept Compute to specify the intercept to be computed.
7. Select /Data Regression Output-Range to specify the output range.

8. Type (or point to) `B12`.
9. Select /Data Regression Go to execute the analysis.

Now you can use the results of the regression to project what the attendance will be tomorrow (assuming it's a weekday) based on the weather forecast. Suppose that the weather forecast calls for 85 degrees and no precipitation. The projected attendance would be:

Constant + (X1*Temp) + (X2*Precip) = Forecast

(-7800) + (161*85) + (-1134*0) = 5882

You could add the forecast to your worksheet by adding the weather forecast and the formula in the last column, as shown in Figure Data.14. Please note that absolute addressing has been used for the constant and coefficients. This ensures that they will remain as the referenced cells even if the formula is moved.

Notes

You should rcfcr to a statistics textbook for further information about the use of regression analysis and the data produced by the /Data Regression command.

The /Data Regression Intercept command gives you two options. You can specify that the Y-intercept be set to zero, forcing the value of the dependent variable Y to be zero when the independent variable(s) are equal to zero, or you can allow 1-2-3 to compute the optimal Y-intercept. You may want to force the Y-intercept to be zero if you know from experience or theory that it must pass through zero.

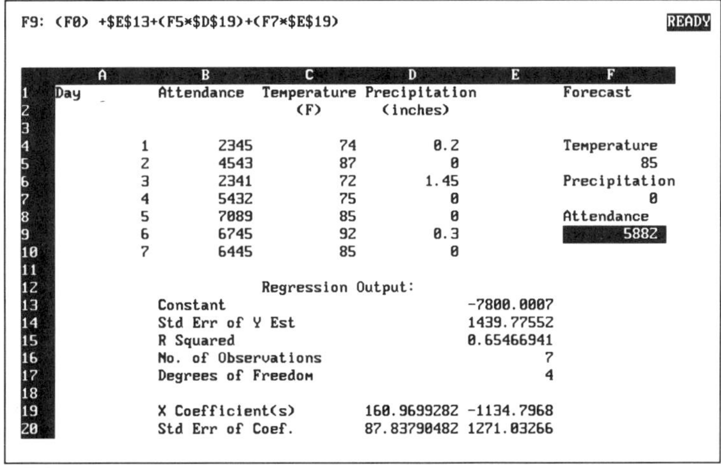

F9: (F0) +$E$13+(F5*$D$19)+(F7*$E$19) READY

	A	B	C	D	E	F
1	Day	Attendance	Temperature	Precipitation		Forecast
2			(F)	(inches)		
3						
4	1	2345	74	0.2		Temperature
5	2	4543	87	0		85
6	3	2341	72	1.45		Precipitation
7	4	5432	75	0		0
8	5	7089	85	0		Attendance
9	6	6745	92	0.3		5882
10	7	6445	85	0		
11						
12			Regression Output:			
13		Constant			-7800.0007	
14		Std Err of Y Est			1439.77552	
15		R Squared			0.65466941	
16		No. of Observations			7	
17		Degrees of Freedom			4	
18						
19		X Coefficient(s)		160.9699282	-1134.7968	
20		Std Err of Coef.		87.83790482	1271.03266	

Figure Data.14
Forecast.

You should not select the Zero option unless you are certain. If the remaining data does not support your selection of the zero intercept, 1-2-3 will report a negative value for R2.

Cautions

Before you use the results of the regression analysis to project data, you should be certain that you understand the limitations of the regression analysis technique. For example, the data being analyzed is assumed to be linearly related. If your data is not linear, regression analysis may produce spurious results. An example of non-linear data would be the aquarium's attendance as a function of the day of the week or year. Attendance that regularly goes up on weekends or during the summer is cyclical or time-series related and should not be treated as linear data. (We have tried to eliminate that factor in our example by ignoring weekends and concentrating on data in a single season.)

The /Data Regression command creates an output table nine rows long and at least four columns wide (each independent variable beyond two variables generates an additional column of output). The regression table will overwrite any data in the output range without warning, so be careful that the output range is clear or can be overwritten.

Data Sort

Purpose

Used to rearrange the rows of a table of data. They may be sorted numerically or alphabetically in ascending or descending order. Typically, it is used to sort a list of names and related data (such as addresses or phone numbers) into alphabetical order, or to resort an alphabetical list according to a numerical field (like size of donation).

Description

The /Data Sort command physically rearranges the records (rows) of the data table. It uses the sort keys to determine the order of the records. If you specify more than one sort key, 1-2-3 will first sort all records according to the primary sort key; in those cases where two or more records have identical values under the primary sort field, 1-2-3 will use the secondary sort key to determine their order.

1-2-3 sorts records within a given sort key depending on the type of data contained in the sort key column and on the collating sequence (or sort order) you selected when you installed 1-2-3. The default collating sequence is numbers first. You also have the option to select numbers last or ASCII as your collating sequence when you install 1-2-3. These three options produce the following sort orders when you select an Ascending sort. (Note that the only difference between Numbers First and Numbers is simply the order of 3 and 4 in the hierarchy.)

Numbers First (Default)—Ignores Capitalization

1. Blank Cells
2. Labels beginning with spaces—number of spaces, followed by numbers in numerical order then letters in alphabetical order
3. Labels beginning with numbers—numerical order
4. Labels beginning with letters—alphabetical order
5. Labels beginning with characters other than numbers or letters—ASCII value of character (e.g., "{go to}" would follow the label "90 West")
6. Values—numerical value

Numbers Last—Ignores Capitalization

1. Blank Cells
2. Labels beginning with spaces—number of spaces, followed by letters in alphabetical order then numbers in numerical order
3. Labels beginning with letters—alphabetical order
4. Labels beginning with numbers—numerical order
5. Labels beginning with characters other than numbers or letters—ASCII value of character
6. Values—numerical value

ASCII Order—Uppercase Before Lowercase

1. Blank cells
2. All labels—the ASCII value of each character
3. Values—numerical value

Defaults

The Data Range, Primary-Key, and Secondary-Key last defined. (Press F6 to display your default sort settings window. Press F6 again to return to the worksheet display.) 1-2-3 defaults to Numbers First sort order unless you specified either the Numbers Last or ASCII collating sequence during installation. There is no way to change the collating sequence except to re-install 1-2-3. Oddly, 1-2-3 defaults to Descending sort order (perhaps showing Lotus's preference for showing the big numbers first), so you must select Ascending to get typical alphabetical order sorts.

Usage

The /Data Sort command uses several commands to define the range of data to be sorted (/Data Sort Data-Range) and to specify which field(s) are to be used to define the sort order. You specify the primary and secondary key with the commands /Data Sort Primary-Key and /Data Sort Secondary-Key. After you have specified the data range and the sort key(s), simply select /Data Sort Go to execute the sorting process.

Examples

To sort the list of donors in the DONORS database table (see Figures Data.15a–b) in alphabetical order by last name and then by first name:

1. Select /Data Sort Data-Table to specify the range to be sorted. (Press F6 to clear the default sort settings window.)
2. Type (or paint) `A2..H8`.
3. Select /Data Sort Primary-Key to specify the primary key.
4. Select any cell in the last name column (A2 through A8).
5. Select /Data Sort Secondary-Key to specify the secondary key.
6. Select any cell in the first name column (B2 through B8).
7. Select /Data Sort Go to execute the sort process.

Notes

If the data table you wish to sort is a database table (i.e., it includes field names as the first row of the table), be sure to *exclude* the field names from the Data-Range and Key specifications otherwise the field names will be sorted along with the data.

To eliminate a sort key that is no longer desirable, you could reset the entire sort process with the /Data Sort Reset option and respecify each of the ranges. Alternatively, you could edit the undesirable key to make it identical to the key that precedes it in the sort process. This effectively eliminates any effect of the undesired key.

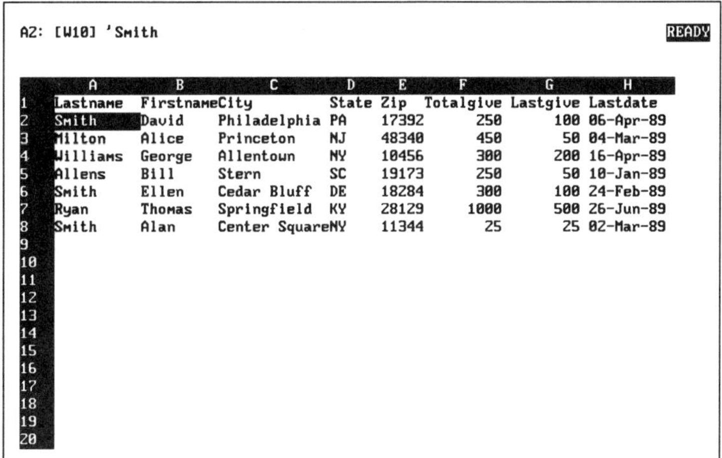

A2: [W10] 'Smith READY

	A	B	C	D	E	F	G	H
1	Lastname	Firstname	City	State	Zip	Totalgive	Lastgive	Lastdate
2	Smith	David	Philadelphia	PA	17392	250	100	06-Apr-89
3	Milton	Alice	Princeton	NJ	48340	450	50	04-Mar-89
4	Williams	George	Allentown	NY	10456	300	200	16-Apr-89
5	Allens	Bill	Stern	SC	19173	250	50	10-Jan-89
6	Smith	Ellen	Cedar Bluff	DE	18284	300	100	24-Feb-89
7	Ryan	Thomas	Springfield	KY	28129	1000	500	26-Jun-89
8	Smith	Alan	Center Square	NY	11344	25	25	02-Mar-89

Figure Data.15a
Donors database before sorting.

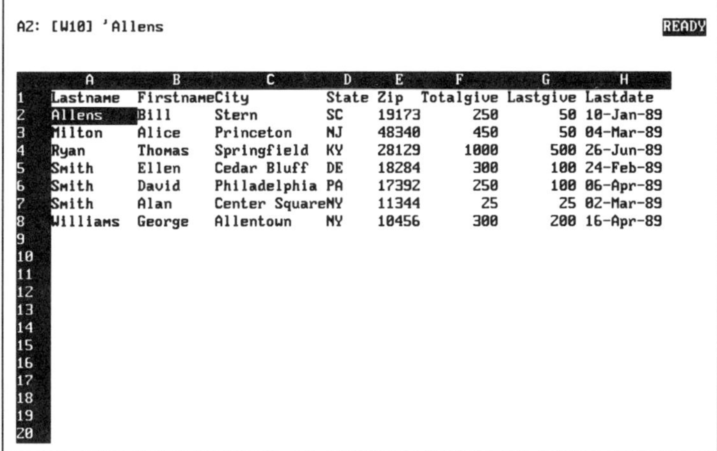

A2: [W10] 'Allens READY

	A	B	C	D	E	F	G	H
1	Lastname	Firstname	City	State	Zip	Totalgive	Lastgive	Lastdate
2	Allens	Bill	Stern	SC	19173	250	50	10-Jan-89
3	Milton	Alice	Princeton	NJ	48340	450	50	04-Mar-89
4	Ryan	Thomas	Springfield	KY	28129	1000	500	26-Jun-89
5	Smith	Ellen	Cedar Bluff	DE	18284	300	100	24-Feb-89
6	Smith	David	Philadelphia	PA	17392	250	100	06-Apr-89
7	Smith	Alan	Center Square	NY	11344	25	25	02-Mar-89
8	Williams	George	Allentown	NY	10456	300	200	16-Apr-89

Figure Data.15b
Donors database after sorting.

Cautions

The /Data Sort command physically rearranges the records of the data table. There may be no way to resort the data to reproduce the original order. If you have the Undo option enabled, you can undo the sort process by immediately pressing UNDO (ALT-F4). In general, you should be sure to backup your worksheet before sorting any data tables. You can also add a new field to the data table that contains the record number before the sort process using the /Data Fill command. You can then use this field as the primary key to re-sort the records back into their original position.

Be very careful when sorting data containing formulas with relative addresses. 1-2-3 will reset the addresses according to the new position of the record in the table. While this is often desirable, it may not be. If you do not want 1-2-3 to adjust the addresses in the formulas in the data range, reset them to be absolute addresses.

Data Table

Purpose

The /Data Table commands are among the most powerful commands in Lotus 1-2-3. They can be used for two very different purposes:

1. To generate tables of formula results for a series of variable input values.
2. To cross-tabulate a database table by one or more fields.

As their names imply, the two /Data Table commands (1 or 2) can be used for one or two variable analyses. Each can also be used in two ways: to perform "what-if" analyses or to do cross-tabulations. We have arranged our discussion of the /Data Table commands as follows:

/Data Table 1—What-If

/Data Table 1—Cross-Tabulate

/Data Table 2—What-If

/Data Table 2—Cross-Tabulate

Description

The /Data Table—What-If command structures require you to supply one or more sets of possible values to substitute in for the variables in one or more functions or formulas. 1-2-3 will then generate a table of formula or function results based on the several values you supply. Figure Data.16 shows a simple /Data Table 2 application where, for a $100,000 loan, the @PMT formula has been used to generate the monthly payment figure for a variety of Terms and Interest rates. You can see that each entry in the body of the table consists of the results of substituting the Term (at the top of each column) and the Percent (at the left of each row) in the formula that appears in the upper-left corner of the table. This is the basic structure for all What-If uses of the /Data Table commands.

The /Data Table—Cross-Tabulate command structures allow you to cross-tabulate the values in a database table, generating totals for combinations of field values. For example, Figure Data.17 shows a database table that contains feed

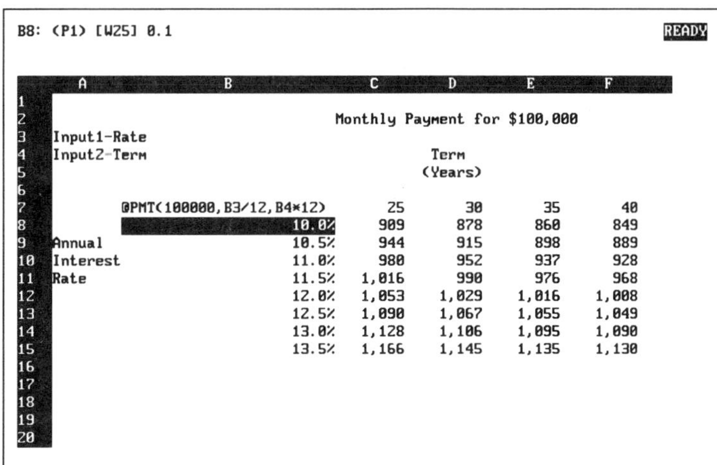

B8: (P1) [W25] 0.1 READY

	A	B	C	D	E	F
1						
2			Monthly Payment for $100,000			
3	Input1-Rate					
4	Input2-Term			Term		
5				(Years)		
6						
7		@PMT(100000,B3/12,B4*12)	25	30	35	40
8		10.0%	909	878	860	849
9	Annual	10.5%	944	915	898	889
10	Interest	11.0%	980	952	937	928
11	Rate	11.5%	1,016	990	976	968
12		12.0%	1,053	1,029	1,016	1,008
13		12.5%	1,090	1,067	1,055	1,049
14		13.0%	1,128	1,106	1,095	1,090
15		13.5%	1,166	1,145	1,135	1,130
16						
17						
18						
19						
20						

Figure Data.16
/Data Table 2—What-If.

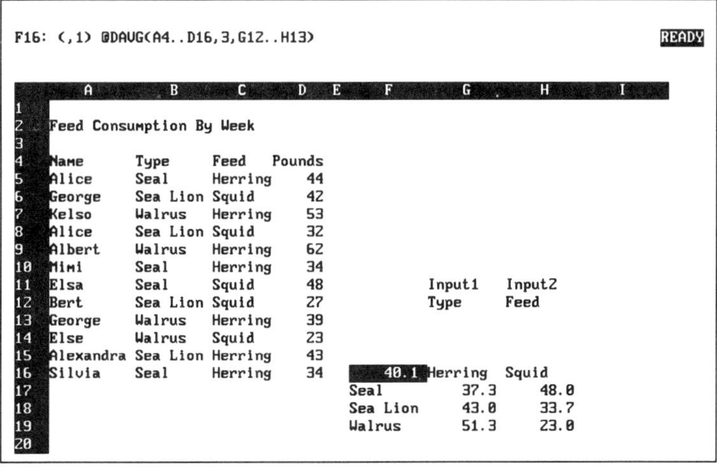

F16: (,1) @DAVG(A4..D16,3,G12..H13) READY

	A	B	C	D	E	F	G	H	I
1									
2	Feed Consumption By Week								
3									
4	Name	Type	Feed	Pounds					
5	Alice	Seal	Herring	44					
6	George	Sea Lion	Squid	42					
7	Kelso	Walrus	Herring	53					
8	Alice	Sea Lion	Squid	32					
9	Albert	Walrus	Herring	62					
10	Mimi	Seal	Herring	34					
11	Elsa	Seal	Squid	48			Input1	Input2	
12	Bert	Sea Lion	Squid	27			Type	Feed	
13	George	Walrus	Herring	39					
14	Else	Walrus	Squid	23					
15	Alexandra	Sea Lion	Herring	43					
16	Silvia	Seal	Herring	34		40.1	Herring	Squid	
17						Seal	37.3	48.0	
18						Sea Lion	43.0	33.7	
19						Walrus	51.3	23.0	
20									

Figure Data.17
/Data Table 2—Cross-Tabulation.

consumption figures for various animals. Using the /Data Table 2 command in its cross-tabulation mode, it is possible to determine the consumption of each type of feed by type of animal.

The upper-left corner of the worksheet contains a database table consisting of the name and type of animal, followed by the type of feed and the weekly consumption. Because the data is not well organized, it would be difficult to determine the total weekly herring consumption, or the total weekly consumption of herring by sea lions. The cross-tabulation table command makes short work of these questions. The command generates the two-dimensional matrix presented in the lower-right corner of the worksheet and shows the sum of feed consumptions for each category. The top-left cell of the matrix (F16) shows the grand total for the input range.

Usage

The first two steps in using the /Data Table commands are deciding which of the two commands to use and setting up your formulas, input ranges, and input cells properly. For example, if you want to perform a what-if analysis and vary just one variable, you should use the /Data Table 1 command. Likewise, if you want to cross-tabulate a database table and summarize only one variable, you would again use /Data Table 1. To vary two variables in a what-if analysis or to cross-tabulate two fields in a database table, you would use /Data Table 2.

When performing a what-if analysis with either /Data Table 1 or 2, you must supply one or more formulas. The formula(s) must appear in a specific location in the data table (depending on how many formulas or how many variables you are working with). (I.e., the top-left corner for /Data Table 2, and along the top row for /Data Table.1) Each formula must reference one or more empty input cell(s) used as temporary storage locations for a series of input variables. The formula is calculated for every combination of the input variable(s).

When performing a cross-tabulation calculation, you must supply a database @D-function (e.g., @DSUM or @DAVG). The function is calculated for all records in the input database range that match each combination of input variables.

Key Terms

Data Table The area of the worksheet that contains the results generated by the /Data Table command. Its size and shape are determined by the definition and placement of the input values and formulas (see below). The range containing the Data Table is called the Table Range.

Table Range The range containing the Data Table. The Table Range includes your column(s) of input variables, and your column(s) of output results generated by the /Data Table commands. The Table Range is one row and one column larger than the Results Area (see below), since it includes the row and column containing the Input value ranges (see below).

Variable The portion of the formula in a what-if analysis that is changed. The variable in the formula references an Input Cell (see below). In Figure Data.16 the input cells are B3 and B4. The input cell is then sequentially filled by each of the values specified in the Input Value range.

Input Cell A temporary cell location that 1-2-3 uses to swap in the several values in the Input Value range and generate the corresponding results. The input cell contains no actual data; it is simply an empty cell that is referenced in the formula and that is also assigned to a range of Input Values. When you execute a /Data Table Command for what-if analysis, 1-2-3 sequentially inserts each of the values from the input value range into the input cell and evaluates the formula, placing the results into the corresponding cell of the results area. For example, in Figure Data.16, the result of inserting 30 years and 11.5% interest into the @PMT formula yields $990 which is placed at the intersection of the column with the heading 30 and the row with the heading 11.5%. Because 1-2-3 copies data into the input cell during the execution of the /Data Table command, it must be unprotected. (See /Range Unprotect.)

The input cells are physical cell locations in the current worksheet that must be kept clear of all data, formulas, and data tables (cells B3 and B4 in Figure Data.16). They must especially be clear of the input ranges and the results area. Further, you must ensure that you properly reference the correct input cell in your formula(s) and when you assign a value range to the input cell. It is easy to confuse input cells in a multiple-variable formula, so it is often helpful to label the cell with a notation above or to the left of the cell.

Input Value Range A range of possible values you specify for a variable in your formula. 1-2-3 will substitute each value in the input range for the formula variable and produce a corresponding result. An input value can either be a value or a formula that evaluates to a value. When you execute a /Data Table command, 1-2-3 sequentially places each value from the input value range into the input cell associated with that range; it evaluates the formula for that value and places the results in the results area (see below). Thus, a table is formed where each input value has a corresponding results value. The same principle holds true for multiple sets of input values and formulas. In Figure Data.16 the range B8..B15 and C7..F7 are the input value ranges.

Results Area The output area that contains all the results generated by 1-2-3 as it systematically evaluates the formula(s) for each input value (or set of values).

Notes

It is possible to change the input values by editing them or modifying the source data for formulas in the input values and then recalculating the data table. You can use the DATA key (F8) to re-execute the last /Data Table command without having to recall the entire menu.

Cautions

It is often difficult to see if you have misconstructed a /Data Table command, and generated incorrect results. You should verify the results by carefully checking several figures in the results area.

It is very important to ensure that your input cells are clear of data, formulas, and your input and results ranges. You might label your input cells to be sure that they are properly referenced and to be sure that they stay clear.

The /Data Table commands generate a table of results determined by the size of the columns and rows specified for input. The tables generated by 1-2-3 will overwrite any data in the output range with no warning. Be certain that the output range is clear or can be overwritten before invoking these commands.

Data Table 1—What If

Purpose

Used to generate results for one or more formulas while changing the value of a single variable. This is extremely useful for performing simple what-if analyses. For example, with /Data Table 1, you might generate a table of monthly mortgage payments based on a series of different annual interest rates, or a table of future values based on various terms or interest rates.

Description

/Data Table 1 is the simpler of the two data table commands. It allows a series of values for only one variable, but it can evaluate more than one formula at a time for that single changing variable. Common formulas include: @PMT, @FV, and @PV. The series of input values and formulas for /Data Table 1 are arranged so as to form a table frame. The input values are placed in a column to the left. The formula(s) are placed in a row along the top. In Figure Data.18, the first formula is placed one cell to the right and above the column of input values in column C; the second formula is placed in column D. The results of /Data Table 1 are presented in the results area to the right of the column of input values and below the formula(s) row. For each input value and each formula, the corresponding result value is located at the intersection of the input value row and the formula column.

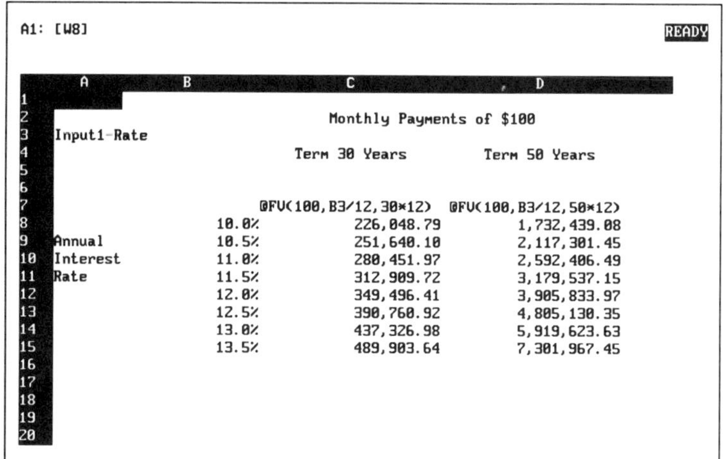

A1: [W8] READY

Monthly Payments of $100

Input1-Rate

Row	A	B	C	D
4			Term 30 Years	Term 50 Years
7			@FV(100,B3/12,30*12)	@FV(100,B3/12,50*12)
8		10.0%	226,048.79	1,732,439.08
9	Annual	10.5%	251,640.10	2,117,301.45
10	Interest	11.0%	280,451.97	2,592,406.49
11	Rate	11.5%	312,909.72	3,179,537.15
12		12.0%	349,496.41	3,905,833.97
13		12.5%	390,760.92	4,805,130.35
14		13.0%	437,326.98	5,919,623.63
15		13.5%	489,903.64	7,301,967.45

Figure Data.18
/Data Table 1—What-If.

Defaults

The input value range, input cell, formula(s), and table range last defined.

Usage

The first step in using /Data Table 1 for What-If analysis is to select a location for the table range: the input values column, the formula row, and the results area. You will also need to plot a location for the input cell that is outside the table range. Place a label above or to the left of the input cell, not only to designate it as the input cell but also to reference the name of the variable it represents. The input cell B3 in Figure Data.18, for example, is labeled in cell A3 as Input1-Rate. Enter the values to be evaluated in a column starting in the second row of the output area. (You may wish to use the /Data Fill command to generate an equally incremented column of values.) The formula(s) are placed in the top row of the output area, with the first formula in the first cell above and to the right of the column of input values. Be sure your formulas reference the correct location for the input cell. In Figure Data.18, you can see that the input cell B3 is referenced as the annual interest rate in the @PMT formulas.

You may want to format your formulas as Text to see them on screen (as shown in the example). Otherwise, the formulas will often evaluate to ERR, because they refer to an empty input cell. (This does not, of course, affect their ability to generate the data table.) The cell in the top left corner of the output area (just above the column of input values) should be left blank.

Initiate the command by selecting /Data Table 1. At the first prompt, designate the table range by range name, by address, or by painting it. Be sure to include the column of input values and the row of formula(s). At the second prompt specify the input cell you have set aside and labeled. Be sure to reference the actual blank input cell and not its adjacent label. The results generated for each input value and output formula will be placed in the results area to complete the table.

Examples

To re-create the example shown in Figure Data.18, calculate the future value of regularly depositing $100 per month at various interest rates between 10 and 13.5, for a term of 30 years:

1. Type in the interest rates as percentages in a column from B8..B15. You can use /Data Fill with an incremental step of .05 to expedite this. Be sure to format the column for percentages using /Range Format Percentage.
2. Because you will use cell B3 as your input cell, label the cell A3 as "Input1-Rate."
3. Enter the formula, `@FV(100, B3/12,30*12)` including the fixed term and payment amount and referencing the input cell B3 for the interest rates in cell C8. Enter the same formula using 50-year term in cell D8. Note that the interest rate and term are altered to correspond to monthly payments by dividing and multiplying by 12 accordingly.
4. Select /Data Table 1.
5. Type in (or paint) `B7..D15` to designate the table range, including the results area, the input values, and the formulas.
6. Select B3 as the input cell.

Notes

If you want to evaluate a single formula with two independent variables, use /Data Table 2. If you want to perform a cross-tabulation, see /Data Table 1—Cross-Tabulate.

Data Table 1—Cross Tabulate

Purpose

Used to analyze a database table. You identify one field in your data table and a series of particular values for that field; 1-2-3 will take each value you specify, find all matching records for it, and then summarize one or more other fields in the data table based on those matching records. This helps you to see significant patterns in your table that might not be apparent in the raw data. For example, summarizing the data in Figure Data.19 by type of animal shows that seals don't eat as much in terms of poundage compared to walruses.

Description

/Data Table 1 cross-tabulation requires a series of input values for a particular field, one or more database @D function formulas, and a two-celled criteria range—one cell with the field name in question and an empty input cell just below it. The input values define a series of values for a single field in your database. The @D function will calculate a statistic for all records that match the specified input value.

Let's look at Figure Data.19 more closely. The main database table lists weekly food consumption for each animal. Suppose you wish to analyze how many pounds of food are eaten weekly by the three animal types: seals, sea lions, and walruses. You must set up a table range for these statistics: an input column of animal types (e.g., F17..F20) and an @D formula (e.g., G16). (The formula @DSUM (A4..D16,3,G12..G13) follows the standard form for @D functions: for the data table range A4..A16, it sums up the Pounds field—field offset 3—for all records that match the criteria specified in G12..G13.) See the discussion of database functions at the beginning of the @Function section.

Note that your criteria range is apart from the table range and consists of two

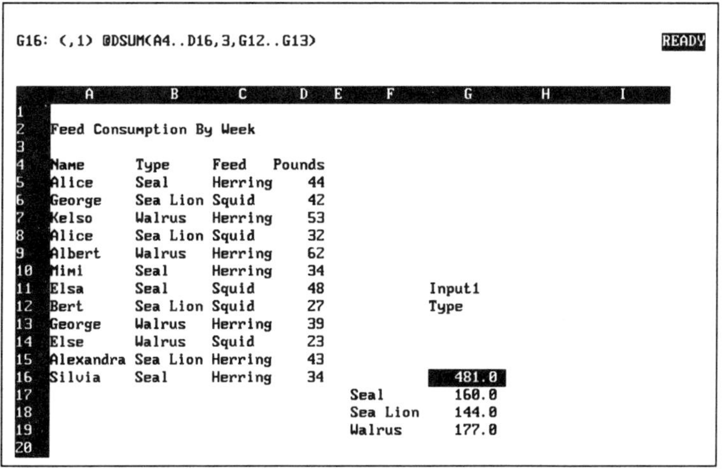

G16: (,1) @DSUM(A4..D16,3,G12..G13) READY

	A	B	C	D	E	F	G	H	I
1									
2	Feed Consumption By Week								
3									
4	Name	Type	Feed	Pounds					
5	Alice	Seal	Herring	44					
6	George	Sea Lion	Squid	42					
7	Kelso	Walrus	Herring	53					
8	Alice	Sea Lion	Squid	32					
9	Albert	Walrus	Herring	62					
10	Mimi	Seal	Herring	34					
11	Elsa	Seal	Squid	48			Input1		
12	Bert	Sea Lion	Squid	27			Type		
13	George	Walrus	Herring	39					
14	Else	Walrus	Squid	23					
15	Alexandra	Sea Lion	Herring	43					
16	Silvia	Seal	Herring	34			481.0		
17						Seal	160.0		
18						Sea Lion	144.0		
19						Walrus	177.0		
20									

Figure Data.19
/Data Table 1—Cross-Tabulation.

cells: an empty input cell and directly above, the corresponding field name. Each animal type in your column of input values will be substituted one after another into the input cell; for each specified animal type, then /Data Table 1 will produce the total weight of food consumed in a week.

Defaults

The input value range, input cell, formula(s), and table range last defined.

Usage

The first step in using /Data Table 1 for cross-tabulation is to select a location for the output table range. The rectangular area for the table range includes your column of input values at the left, and your row of @D formula(s) at the top. Note that your @D formulas are placed one row above and one column to the right of your input values.

You will also need to select a location outside the table range for an empty input cell. Also, in the cell directly above the blank input cell you must specify the field name label for the series of input values. The label should appear exactly as it appears in the database table. Each input value will be substituted into the input cell. The blank input cell, together with the field name above it, will serve as the criteria range for the @D formula(s) you wish to use. You may wish to place a label above the field name and the empty input cell, to designate them as such. Remember, you *must* reference the full two-line criteria range (field name and blank input cell) in your formula, and specify the one empty input cell when executing the /Data Table 1 command. In Figure Data.19, for example, cell G13 is the blank input cell, and G12..G13 is the criteria range referenced in the @D function formula.

Type in the input values (or labels) you wish to have summarized in the left column of the table range. (Start in row two of the table.) These values or labels will be used as criteria for selecting which records will be included in each calculation. Type in the database @D formula(s) in the top row of the table range. (Start in column two of the output table.) Be sure the formulas correctly reference the database table in question and the criteria range (containing the field name and the empty input cell). In Figure Data.19, you can see that the input cell is part of the range G12..G13 that is referenced as the criteria range for the @DSUM formula.

The cell in the top-left corner of the output table range should be left blank. Initiate the command by selecting /Data Table 1. At the first prompt, designate the complete output table range by range name, by address, or by painting it. At the second prompt, specify the empty input cell. Be sure that you reference the single blank cell below the field name (and label), *not* the full criteria range or the cells containing the label itself. For each input value, a corresponding formula result will be placed in the results area. Finally, the formula results for all records in the database table will be placed in the cell containing the formula. In Figure Data.19, for example, 481 represents the number of pounds of food consumed per week by all of the animals.

Examples

To calculate the total weekly feed consumption for each type of animal, reproducing the table in Figure Data.19:

1. Be sure that your source data is in a properly formatted 1-2-3 database table.
2. Select a suitable output location for the table range.
3. Place the input values (or labels) in a column along the left edge of the table range. Be sure that labels are spelled exactly as they appear in the database table. You can use the ? and * wildcard characters. (For example, Sm* will summarize all values for records beginning with Sm in the designated field in the criteria range—Smith, Smyth, Smiley, and so on.)
4. Designate the empty cell, G13, as an input cell. In G12, just above the input cell, enter the field name. Type it exactly as it appears in the database. In cell G11, attach a label to the input cell: Input1.
5. Enter the @D function formula(s) in a row at the top of the table range. In the formula, be sure to designate the full database table (including the field labels) as the input range; specify the field offset for Pounds–3; and specify the full two-line criteria range, including the blank input cell (e.g., @DSUM(A4..D16, 3, G12..G13).)
6. Select /Data Table 1 to initiate the command.
7. Type (or paint) `F16..G19` to designate the table range (including the results area, the column of input values, and the row of formula(s)).
8. Type `G13` to specify your (empty) input cell.

Data Table 2—What If

Purpose

Used to generate the results of one formula while simultaneously changing the value of two variables; /Data Table 2 produces a two-dimensional table of results corresponding to each combination of the changing variables. This is extremely useful for performing what-if analyses. For example, you could generate a table of monthly mortgage payments based on a series of different annual interest rates and terms.

Description

/Data Table 2 is perhaps the most useful of the two data table commands. It alters two independent variables, evaluating the designated formula for each combination of values. The results of the /Data Table 2 are presented in the area that is to the right of the column of input values for variable 1 and below the row of input values for variable 2. (See Figure Data.20.)

Defaults

The previously defined input value ranges, input cells, formula, and table range.

Usage

The first step in using the /Data Table 2 What-If command is to select a location for the output or results area, called the *table range*. The area required for the table range includes the left column of input values for variable number 1, the top row of input values for variable number 2, and a cell at the top-left corner of the table that contains the formula to be evaluated. Outside this table range you need to specify two empty input cells, one for each input variable. You may wish to put a label above or to the left of the input cells. In Figure Data.20, for example, cell B3 is labeled as Input1-Rate and cell B4 is labeled as Input2-Term. Enter the values to be evaluated for variable one in the leftmost column of the output table area. Enter the values to be evaluated for variable two in the top row of the output area, starting one cell above and to the right of the variable one column.

Place the formula to be evaluated in the cell located in the upper-left corner of the table range. Be sure that your formula references the designated input cells correctly. In Figure Data.20, you can see that the input cell B3 is referenced as the annual interest rate while cell B4 is referenced as the term in the @PMT formula. You may want to format the formula as Text, as shown in the example, otherwise it

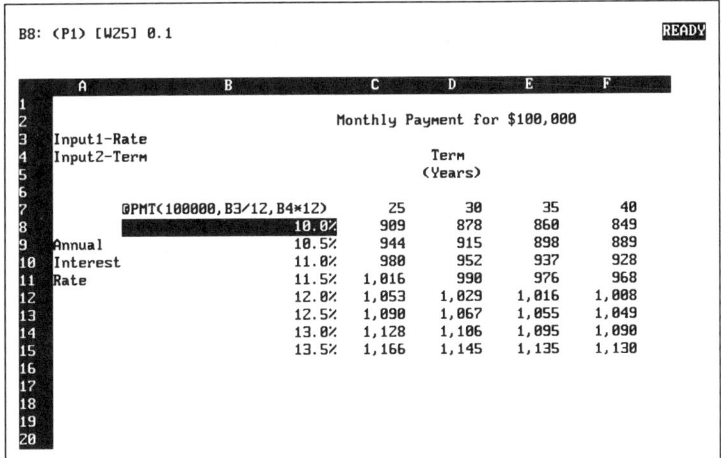

B8: (P1) [W25] 0.1 READY

	A	B	C	D	E	F
1						
2			Monthly Payment for $100,000			
3	Input1-Rate					
4	Input2-Term			Term		
5				(Years)		
6						
7		@PMT(100000,B3/12,B4*12)	25	30	35	40
8		10.0%	909	878	860	849
9	Annual	10.5%	944	915	898	889
10	Interest	11.0%	980	952	937	928
11	Rate	11.5%	1,016	990	976	968
12		12.0%	1,053	1,029	1,016	1,008
13		12.5%	1,090	1,067	1,055	1,049
14		13.0%	1,128	1,106	1,095	1,090
15		13.5%	1,166	1,145	1,135	1,130
16						
17						
18						
19						
20						

Figure Data.20
/Data Table 2—What-If.

may evaluate to ERR. The fact that it evaluates to ERR does not, of course, affect its ability to generate the data table.

Select /Data Table 2 to initiate the command. At the first prompt, designate the table range by range name, by address, or by painting it. Be sure to include the entire column of input values for variable one and the complete row of input values for variable two. At the second prompt, specify the input cell for variable one and then the input cell for variable two. Be sure to reference the blank cells below or to the right of your labels, *not* the label cells themselves. The formula results for each pair of variables will be placed in the results area; at the row and column intersection of variables one and two.

Examples

To re-create the example shown in Figure Data.20, calculate the monthly mortgage payments for a loan of $100,000 at various interest rates between 10 and 13.5, and terms between 25 and 40 years.

1. Enter the interest rates as percentages in a column from B8..B15. You can use /Data Fill and specify an incremental step of .005 to expedite this. Be sure to format the column as percentage using /Range Format Percentage.
2. Select B3 as your input cell for the Rate variable and label the adjacent cell A3 as Input1-Rate.
3. Enter the terms in a row from C7..F7. (Again, you can use /Data Fill to expedite this.)

4. Select B4 as your input cell for the Term variable and label the cell A4 Input2-Term.
5. Enter the @PMT formula in B7, at the top-left corner of the output table range. Include the fixed principal amount and be sure you reference the input cells correctly for rates and terms. (Note that the interest rate and term are altered to correspond to monthly payments by dividing and multiplying by 12 accordingly.)
6. Select /Data Table 2.
7. Type (or paint) `B7..F15` to designate the table range, and press ENTER.
8. Type (or point to) `B3` to designate the input cell number one, and press ENTER.
9. Type (or point to) `B4` to designate the input cell number two, and press ENTER.

Data Table 2—Cross Tabulate

Purpose

Used to analyze a database table by summarizing one field of the table according to value variables in two different fields. This can show patterns in your data, patterns that may not be apparent in the raw data. For example, summarizing the data in Figure Data.21 by type of animal and type of feed, you quickly see that sea lions eat more squid than herring, while walruses eat more herring than squid.

Description

Using /Data Table 2 for cross-tabulation requires two series of input values and a database @ function formula. The command will then perform the designated function formula for all records that match each combination of input values specified in the table. For example, in Figure Data.21, the command calculates the sum (@DAVG) of feed weights for each group of records that match each animal type and feed type combination designated by the input value ranges. Thus, it calculates the average amount of herring consumed by each type of animal—seals, sea lions, walruses, and so on—then it makes the same calculations for squid. The results are displayed in a two-dimensional matrix with as many rows as inputs for variable one and as many columns as inputs for variable two.

Defaults

The input value range, input cell, formula, and table range last defined.

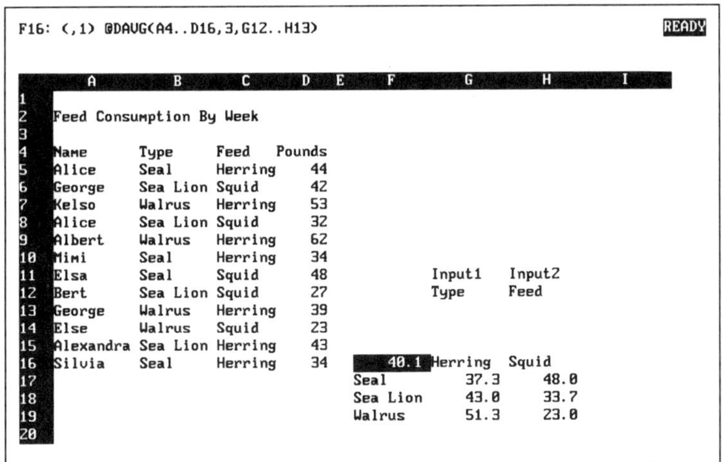

Figure Data.21
/Data Table 1—
Cross-Tabulation.

Usage

The first step in using /Data Table 2 for cross-tabulation is to select a location for the output or results area. The rectangular table range area will include a left column of input values for variable one, a top row of input values for variable two, and a top-left corner cell with the database formula.

You will also need to select a location for your two input cells outside the table range. The input cells for a cross-tabulation must be located directly below cells that contain the appropriate field name labels for each variable. (They should appear exactly as they appear in the database table.) The series of input values will be substituted into the corresponding input cells; the field names, together with the input cells, will serve as a criteria range, referenced by the /Data Table formula. In addition, above the field name, you may wish to label the two input cells. Remember that you must reference the full two-line criteria range (field name and blank input cell) in your @D formula, and that when you execute the /Data Table 2 command, you must reference only the blank input cells for variable one and then for variable two when prompted.

In Figure Data.21, cell G11 labels the input cell, Input1; G12 specifies the field name for variable one (Type, as in column B of the data table); and the empty input cell for variable one is G13. Similarly, the empty input cell H13 is identified by the Input2 label in H11 and by the field name for variable two, Feed, in H12. Thus, G13 and H13 are the empty input cells, and the range G12..H13 is the criteria range referenced by the @D function formula in F16.

Enter the values or labels to be summarized for variable one in the leftmost column of the table range, starting in the second row. Enter the values or labels to be summarized for variable two in the top row of the table range, starting in the second column. The several combinations of these values or labels will be used as the criteria for selecting the records to be included in the formula calculations. Place the database @D formula in the top-left corner of the table range. Be sure to follow the conventional syntax for @D functions: reference the main database table, the field offset (e.g., in Figure Data.21, the offset is 3, for pounds) and the criteria range (containing the two input cells and their corresponding field names). In Figure Data.21, you see that the input cells are part of the range G12..H13 that is referenced as the criteria range for the @DSUM formula. For more information on @D and offsets, see the discussion of database functions at the beginning of @ Function section.

Initiate the command by selecting /Data Table 2. At the first prompt, designate the table range by range name, by address, or by painting it. Be sure to include the entire column of input values for variable number one and the complete row of input values for variable number two. At the second prompt, specify the input cell for variable number one. Be sure to reference the single blank input cell (below the label and field name) and not the full criteria range or the label cell. At the third prompt, specify the input cell for variable number two. The formula results for each pair of input variables will be placed in the results area. The results for all records in the database table will be placed in the cell containing the formula in the upper-left corner of the table range—in this example, the average of pounds of weekly feed consumption for all animals.

Examples

To calculate the average weekly consumption of each type of feed for each type of animal from the database containing each animal's individual feed consumption:

1. Ensure that your source data is a properly formatted 1-2-3 database table.
2. Plot a suitable output location for the table range and results area.
3. Place the input values (labels) for variable number one in a column along the left edge of the table range. Be sure to spell your labels exactly as they appear in the database table. (Note: You can use the ? and * wildcard characters; for example, Sm* will summarize all values for records beginning with Sm in the designated field in the criteria range—Smith, Smyth, Smiley, and so on.)

4. Select a single blank cell as your input cell for variable one. In the cell immediately above, type in the field name for variable number one. (Enter the field name exactly as it appears in the database table.) Label your input cell for variable one as Input1.
5. Place the input values (or labels) for variable two in a row along the top of the table range. Be sure to spell labels exactly as they appear in the database table.
6. Select a second blank cell as your input cell for variable two. In the cell immediately above, type in the field name for variable number two. (Enter the field name exactly as it appears in the database table.) Label your input cell for variable two as Input2.
7. Enter the @D function formula in the top left cell of the table range. Be sure to follow the standard syntax for @D function: reference the main database table, the field offset, and the criteria range (the two empty input cells and their corresponding field names).
8. Select /Data Table 2.
9. Type in (or paint) `F16..I19` to designate the table range.
10. At the prompt for the input cell for variable one, type (or point to) `G13`. Press ENTER.
11. At the prompt for the input cell for variable two, type (or point to) `H13`. Press ENTER.

Data Table Reset

Purpose

Clears the table range, input range, and variable ranges within the current worksheet. This command is useful to clear specification errors or to avoid saving a set of specification defaults with the current worksheet file.

Description

The /Data Table Reset command resets all data table settings to the default current cell.

Defaults

None.

Usage

To reset all /Data Table settings simply select the /Data Table Reset option.

Cautions

Make sure that the cell pointer is located in the correct file for the /Data Table setting you wish to clear before invoking the Reset option.

▸ File Commands

Purpose

Used to save and retrieve worksheet files from disk. As you know, you must save your worksheet files to disk in order to refer to them and use them again later. (The worksheet that you see displayed on the screen is loaded in *memory* and is only temporarily stored there. Unless you save your work to *disk*, it will be lost when you turn off the computer, erase the worksheet, retrieve another worksheet, or exit 1-2-3.) The /File commands also allow you to perform some more specialized operations with worksheet data. You can extract portions of the current worksheet and store them to disk, combine ranges from other worksheets into the current worksheet, control read and write access to files in a multi-user environment, and create or erase files on disk.

Description

When you save a worksheet file to disk, a permanent copy of that file is created. After you have saved a worksheet file, you can retrieve it from disk and bring it into memory at a later time with the /File Retrieve command. You can either retrieve an entire file and replace the current worksheet, or you can combine data from a worksheet on disk into the current worksheet.

In addition, the /File commands allow you to extract and save portions of the current worksheet. You can also import data from other types of data files, using the /File Import command. Finally, the /File commands allow you to manage the worksheet files on disk and in memory and control access via passwords.

Cautions

Until you save a file to disk, it is only stored in temporary memory. If you leave 1-2-3, turn off your computer, load another worksheet file, or erase the current worksheet file prior to saving the data to disk, the data contained in the worksheet will be lost.

File Admin

Purpose

In multi-user environments, it is possible for more than one user to load a given file into memory or to link a file in memory to a given file on disk. In the former situation, care must be taken that only one user be allowed to write any changes to the file back to disk, otherwise changes made by one user will be overwritten by changes made by another user. In the case of linking to files on disk, it is imperative to refresh the link (update the referenced data) periodically to ensure that any changes made to the file on disk are accurately reflected in the linked worksheet.

Description

1-2-3 Release 2.2 uses several /File Admin commands to control the read/write access to files and to automatically refresh links to files on disk. They are:

/File Admin Link-Refresh

/File Admin Reservation

/File Admin Table

File Admin Link—Refresh

Purpose

Used to force recalculation of the current worksheet. All formulas in the current worksheet with links to worksheets stored on disk are updated with the latest data from those worksheets. This ensures that the most current data is used in the current calculations.

Description

In a multi-user environment, it is possible to link cells in one worksheet to worksheets that are controlled by others and have been altered since the links were last evaluated. For example, if you load worksheet A, which linked to cells in worksheet B, those links are evaluated at the time you load worksheet A. But what if another user loads and modifies worksheet B while you are working on A? Worksheet A doesn't know that B has been modified. When you use the Refresh command, you are instructing 1-2-3 to look again at worksheet B to get the latest values for the linked cells. Unless you force the reevaluation of those links, the current worksheet will not reflect those changes. The /File Admin Link-Refresh command forces all links in the current worksheet to be reevaluated, using the most recent data from files on disk.

Usage

To re-evaluate the current links, simply select the command /File Admin Link-Refresh.

Examples

To refresh the links between the current worksheet that consolidates regional sales data located in their own worksheet files with a formula such as the following:

Cell	Contents
C1	+<<east>>B47
C2	+<<central>>B47
C3	+<<west>>B47
C4	@SUM(C1..C3)

Select /File Admin Link-Refresh. The formula will be re-evaluated with the latest value from worksheets east, central, and west.

Notes

1. This command is only applicable for multi-user/network systems where several individuals may be altering one or more of the worksheets linked to the current worksheet on a given terminal. With single-user systems, the command is still accessible, but serves no purpose since only one person is making changes to the data and all links were automatically refreshed when the current worksheet was loaded.
2. /File Admin Link-Refresh is not an automatic command, so it is necessary to reissue the command each time you wish to refresh the links. If you are working with extremely dynamic files and currency is critical, you may be better off combining all the files into a single worksheet and using the file reservation system to control access and limit the privileges of updates to a single user.
3. If a cell in worksheet A is linked to a cell in worksheet B, which in turn is linked to a cell in worksheet C, worksheet B must be refreshed as well as worksheet A.
4. The time required for a refresh to take place is extremely variable, depending on your system, the number of links, and whether the links refer to multiple worksheets.

Cautions

Issuing the /File Admin Link-Refresh command only ensures the currency of the links for the immediate moment. They will be out of date as soon as another user modifies one of the files linked to the current files.

File Admin Reservation

Purpose

Used to control which of several users has the privilege to write changes to a worksheet file to disk in a multi-user/network environment. This prevents multiple users from writing conflicting changes to disk, and preserves the integrity of a worksheet file while still permitting more than one user to read and work with the file.

Description

In a multi-user environment, it is often desirable for more than one user to be able to access the same worksheet simultaneously. For example, different sales people in a company may want to use the same worksheet containing inventory and pricing information. If their PCs were connected to a local area network, they could all use the same worksheet, update inventory levels as they sell items and save their changes to disk so that the other people in the department have an accurate inventory count at all times.

But what if two sales people try to sell the same item simultaneously? If they both try to update the inventory count at the same time, they will produce conflicting updates. Release 2.2 preserves the integrity of worksheet files by allowing many people to access a single file simultaneously, but permitting only one user to write changes to disk.

The key to controlling write access is called a *reservation*. Each file in a multi-user environment has a single reservation. The user who requests and gets the reservation for a file is the only person who can save or write that file to disk. Other users can read the worksheet file simultaneously and make changes in their active worksheet, although they cannot write those changes to disk using the same filename. This prevents the creation of conflicting versions of a file on disk. If you load a file, but do not request or are not granted the reservation for that file, 1-2-3 will display "RO," for "Read Only," at the bottom of the screen.

The /File Admin Reservation command accesses two sub-options: Get and Release.

Get The /File Admin Reservation Get command requests the reservation for the specified file. If no one else already has the reservation, and no one else has changed the file and written their changes to disk since the file was read into memory, the reservation for the file will be granted. If a person requests a reservation and another user already has it, or someone else has made and saved a change to the file since the file was loaded into memory, 1-2-3 will display the appropriate message.

Release This command releases the reservation for the current file so that another user can get it. This is similar to passing on a token for another user to pick up.

Defaults

The first individual to load a given worksheet is automatically granted the reservation for that file.

Usage

To request the reservation for the current file, enter /File Admin Reservation Get. If no one else has the reservation and no one else has changed the worksheet and saved the changes to disk since you loaded your copy of the worksheet, you will be granted the reservation. To release a reservation for another user to request, enter /File Admin Reservation Release.

Examples

To request the reservation for the current file:

1. Select /File Admin Reservation Get.

If you receive the reservation, you will be returned to the READY mode, if you are denied, you will receive an error message.

To release the reservation for the current file:

1. Select /File Admin Reservation Release.

Cautions

The reservation system is used to control access to the file writing privilege for authorized users. It does not control read access, nor does it prevent unauthorized write access. Use the /File Save Password command for these features.

File Admin Table

Purpose

Used to list files in one of several categories: Worksheet, Graph, Print, Linked to the current file, or Other. This command is useful for tracking interrelated files as well as for reviewing the various types of files on the disk.

Description

The /File Admin Table commands create tables of your files in the current worksheet; you can select to have various file types listed. The four-columned table that 1-2-3 produces will list the file name, date and time of its creation, and its size (see Figure File.1).

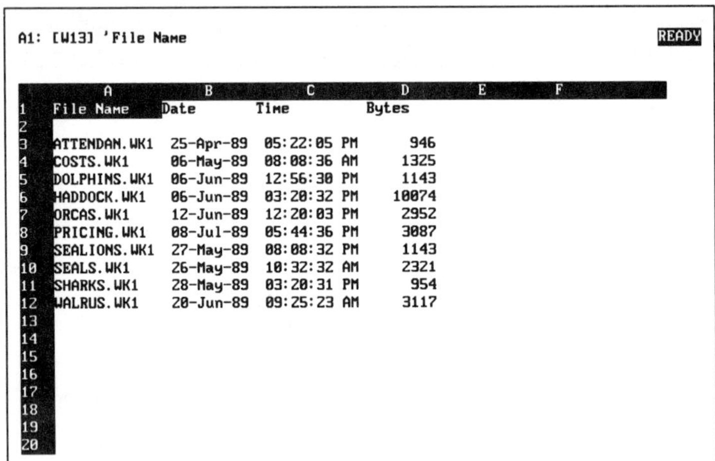

A1: [W13] 'File Name READY

	A	B	C	D
1	File Name	Date	Time	Bytes
2				
3	ATTENDAN.WK1	25-Apr-89	05:22:05 PM	946
4	COSTS.WK1	06-May-89	08:08:36 AM	1325
5	DOLPHINS.WK1	06-Jun-89	12:56:30 PM	1143
6	HADDOCK.WK1	06-Jun-89	03:20:32 PM	10074
7	ORCAS.WK1	12-Jun-89	12:20:03 PM	2952
8	PRICING.WK1	08-Jul-89	05:44:36 PM	3087
9	SEALIONS.WK1	27-May-89	08:08:32 PM	1143
10	SEALS.WK1	26-May-89	10:32:32 AM	2321
11	SHARKS.WK1	28-May-89	03:20:31 PM	954
12	WALRUS.WK1	20-Jun-89	09:25:23 AM	3117

Figure File.1
/File Admin Table.

Defaults

All worksheet files.

Usage

To create a file table, first move the cell pointer to a blank area of the current worksheet. You will need an unprotected range four columns wide and as many rows as required to list all the qualifying files and the subdirectories of the current directory. Initiate the command by selecting /File Admin Table. You will be presented with a menu offering several file types. Each will produce a special table, as described below.

Graph Lists all files in the current directory or diskette with the graphic extension .PIC.

Linked Lists all files linked to the current file by references in formulas.

Other Lists all files (*.*) in the current directory. (You can create your own file specifications using DOS wildcard characters with the Other option.)

Print Lists all files in the current directory with the .PRN extension.

Worksheet Lists all files in the current directory with .WK3, .WK1, or .WKS extensions.

After you have specified the file type, you will be prompted to specify the directory to be listed. The current directory is listed as the default. You can accept it by pressing ENTER, or modify the directory name. (You can also modify the file specification, if you like.) Finally you will be asked to specify the table location. Either enter the name, the address, or point to the target range and press ENTER. File dates and times will be displayed as serial date and time values. All subdirectory names will be displayed at the end of the listing.

Examples

To generate a table of all worksheets in the current directory:

1. Select /File Admin Table Worksheet.
2. Press ENTER to accept the current directory.
3. Specify the output location by name, by address, or by pointing to it.

To generate a table of all files with links to the current file:

1. Select /File Admin Table Linked.
2. Specify the output location by name, by address, or by pointing to it.

Notes

1. To view the file names in the current directory without generating a table, use the /File List command.
2. As their names imply, the date and time columns in the various file listings display dates and time. To properly display this data, however, the date and time columns must be formatted for date and time using the /Range Format Date and /Range Format Date Time commands.

Cautions

The /File Admin Table command generates its output at the current cell pointer location. The resulting table is four columns wide and as long as required to display all the files meeting the selection criteria. The table will overwrite any data in the output range without warning. Be certain that the cell pointer is located in a "safe" location before initiating this command.

File Combine

Purpose

Used to import data from a worksheet file stored on disk into the current worksheet. You can import a range of data, or an entire worksheet file.

Description

The /File Combine command brings any worksheet data that is stored on disk into the current worksheet; the data can be a range from another file, or another entire worksheet. When you use /File Combine, the top-left corner of the imported range or worksheet file will be placed in the current cell.

/File Combine allows you to select from three methods for importing data from another worksheet. The first is a standard Copy—where all contents (except blank cells) from the source on disk will be copied into the current worksheet, overwriting any data that may lie in its way. The second two methods for importing data, Add and Subtract, apply only to numerical values (including formula results) in the source range (or worksheet) on disk. You can add the imported values to the values in your current worksheet, or you can subtract them.

Add Imports values only—of numbers and current formula results—from the range or worksheet on disk and adds them to the numbers or blank cells in the current file. It will not overwrite or alter formulas or text cells in the current file. Thus, if your current worksheet has a value 13, and the imported one has a formula that evaluates to 5, with a /File Combine Add the resulting cell would be 13+5 (value of the formula), or 18. If a formula in the current file depends on cells with numbers that have been altered by the Add option, it will be updated when the file is recalculated. Note that the addition process is one-time *only*; if the data in the file on disk is subsequently changed, the data in the current file will not be altered. In other words, /File Combine Add does not create a dynamic link between two worksheets.

Finally, 1-2-3 copies the format of the incoming data to the cell to which it was added, but does not alter the column size or import any range names from the source worksheet, not even the one named in a Named-Range combine.

Copy Copies data from the specified range, or worksheet file on disk to the current file. The command will copy text, numerical data, and formulas over the contents of the current worksheet. Empty cells from the source will leave the current worksheet cells unaffected. The cell references from the source range or worksheet will be adjusted according to the position of the cursor, whether the references are absolute or not. Once within the overview of the current worksheet, the references will maintain their relative, mixed, or absolute address. /File Combine can be used to copy independent worksheets into a common file.

Subtract Imports the current values of numbers and formulas from the specified range or worksheet on disk and subtracts them from the numbers or blank cells in the current file. The Subtract option will *not* overwrite or alter formulas or text cells in the current file. Formulas in the current file that refer to cells with numbers that have been changed by this option will be updated when the file is recalculated. Like the Add option, Subtract does not provide a dynamic link with the file on disk—the subtraction process will only be carried out once. Also like the Add command, Subtract copies the format of the incoming data to the cell from which it was subtracted.

Defaults

The current cell is the default location for the upper-left corner of the imported data.

Usage

To combine the contents of a file on disk with the current worksheet, first determine if you need to combine the entire file or a range of cells. If you plan to combine an entire file, the data must be arranged in the disk file exactly as you want it in the current file; otherwise it can wreak havoc with your data.

If you are combining a range of data from the file on disk, be sure that before you issue the /File Combine command you know the specific address of the range to be imported. Better yet, give the range to be imported a specific name prior to saving the source file to disk.

When you are certain that the source file is ready, place the cell pointer in the upper-left corner of the target location in the current file. Since the incoming data will overwrite current data, be sure that the target location is correct and make sure that you have backed up the current worksheet.

Start the command by selecting /File Combine. Then, choose one of the three options, Add, Copy, or Subtract, and select either Entire-File or Named/Specified-Range as desired. If you select Entire-File, you will be prompted to select the file name from the list of file names in the current directory. (Press F3 to see a complete list of files on screen.) Point to the desired name and press ENTER or type in the file name at the prompt and press ENTER. If the file is password-protected, you will be prompted to enter the password. Finally, the entire file will be added, copied, or subtracted from the current file, starting in the current cell and extending to the ends of each of the worksheets in the source file.

If you select Named/Specified-Range, you will be prompted to enter the range address or range name of the range to be combined. Type in the name or address and press ENTER. As with the Entire-File option, you will be prompted to select the file name from the list of file names in the current directory. (Press F3 to see a complete list of files on screen at once.) Move the cell pointer to the appropriate file and press ENTER (or simply type in the file name). If the file is protected you will be asked for the password. The specified range will then be brought into the current worksheet. (If the range name does not exist in the specified file, you will be given an appropriate error message.)

Examples

To add the range A1 to F12 in the worksheet named FISH to the range A25 to F37 in the current worksheet:

1. Place the cell pointer in cell A25 of the current worksheet.
2. Select /File Combine Add Named/Specified-Range.
3. Type `A1.F12` and press ENTER.
4. Type `FISH` (or point to the filename FISH) and press ENTER.

To copy the entire file named FISH into the current worksheet starting in cell F25:

1. Place the cell pointer in cell F25 of the current worksheet.
2. Select /File Combine Copy Entire-File.
3. Type `FISH` (or point to the filename FISH) and press ENTER.

Cautions

1. The /File Combine commands change the data in the current worksheet. Be sure to save the current file before you attempt the /File Combine command. If you are using the Undo feature, you can undo the effects of a /File Combine command by immediately pressing the UNDO (ALT-F4) key.
2. In general, do not /File Combine Add ranges that include dates and times, since adding date or time numbers produce meaningless results. (For example, you would be adding large serial numbers rather then measuring lengths of time lapsed. Adding August 15, 1989 to August 16, 1989 produces a ridiculous date far in the future.) You may want to subtract two dates to determine the number of days between them, but proceed

with caution. Remember that the resulting cell will have a date format, so you will have to format it manually.

3. If you import a formula with /File Combine Add or Subtract, it will be converted to its current value first. If you did not recalculate the value of the imported formula in a worksheet set to manual recalculation prior to saving it to disk, it may not represent the true value. Likewise, if the recalculation mode of the current file is set to manual, you will have to recalculate all formulas in the current file after performing a /File Combine Add or Subtract.

File Directory

Purpose

Use this command to temporarily change the default directory for the current 1-2-3 session.

Description

/File Directory changes the default directory where files are saved and retrieved only for the current 1-2-3 session. When you exit and restart 1-2-3, the default directory will revert to the global default directory setting you have specified. To change the *global* default, use the commands /Worksheet Global Default Dir and then /Worksheet Global Default Update.

Default

Current global default directory.

Usage

To change the default directory for the current session of 1-2-3, select /File Directory, type in the full path of the desired directory at the prompt and press ENTER.

Example

To change the default directory from C:\123 to the directory C:\123\DATA\OCTOPUS choose:

1. Select /File Directory.
2. Type `C:\123\DATA\OCTOPUS` and press ENTER.

Cautions

This command will change the directory in which future new files are stored. Be aware, though, that 1-2-3 "remembers" the directory from which it loaded the current worksheet unless you specify otherwise. It will store it again to the same directory even if you have changed your default directory (temporarily or permanently). In order to force 1-2-3 to save a worksheet that was originally from another directory to the new default directory, you must rename the worksheet when you save it, giving it the new directory name. You can also press ESC at the prompt, and the old directory name will be replaced by the new default directory name.

File Erase

Purpose

Used to erase files from disk.

Description

The Erase command performs the same function as the DOS ERASE or DELETE commands. 1-2-3's Erase command, though, will erase only one file at a time. After you choose /File Erase, you must specify a file type (Worksheet, Print, Graph, or Other) and 1-2-3 lists all files in the current directory of that particular type. Highlight the file name that you wish to delete from the list. (You may also type in the name). You will be asked to confirm your decision before 1-2-3 executes your command.

Defaults

The first file of the type specified, as determined by its alphabetical order.

Usage

To delete a file, initiate the command by selecting /File Erase. You must then select which type of files you want 1-2-3 to list for deletion. You can select one of the following four options:

Graph Lists all files in the current directory with .PIC extension.

Other Lists all files in the current directory. You can press ESC and then edit the file specification. You can list files with a particular extension or use the DOS wildcard characters to define the type of files to be listed.

Print Lists all files in the current directory with the .PRN extension.

Worksheet Lists all files in the current directory with .WK3, .WK1, or .WKS extensions.

Once you have selected a file type, 1-2-3 will list all the files in the current directory with the appropriate extension. Either point to the file to be deleted or type in its name and press ENTER. 1-2-3 will ask you to confirm your decision. Select Yes to confirm your choice or No to cancel the command.

Examples

To erase the Graph file named GROWTH.PIC:

1. Select /File Erase Graph. (Press F3 to see a full screen listing of your .PIC files.)
2. Point to the name GROWTH in the listing and press ENTER.
3. Select Yes to confirm your selection.

Notes

1. The /File Erase command erases a file from disk but does not affect the current worksheet in memory.
2. Use the /Worksheet Erase to erase the current worksheet from memory and to open a new blank worksheet.

Cautions

This command permanently deletes the file from the disk. You cannot use the Undo command to reverse this action. There are, however, several third-party utilities that allow you to "un-erase" files that have been deleted in error.

File Import

Purpose

Used to bring data created by other programs into your current worksheet.

Description

The /File Import command can import data into the current worksheet from ASCII or delimited ASCII files. (See Notes below for definitions of these terms.) ASCII files can be produced by most spreadsheet, word processing, and database programs. 1-2-3 creates a non-delimited ASCII file with a .PRN extension when you print to file with the /Print File command. The import process differs in how it handles these two types of files. Further, the Import command allows you to specify whether you want to import the file as text or as numbers. The combinations for importing data are as follows.

Non-Delimited ASCII File Imported as Text When you import a non-delimited file using the Text option, 1-2-3 treats each line of text ending in a carriage return within the source file as a single long label. 1-2-3 will place each line from the source file in a separate cell in the current worksheet. The text lines will form a single column of data. Though the data will appear to be spread over several cells, it is actually located in the left-most cell and spills into the cells to its right.

If the original data contained columns of numbers or text, you can redistribute it into multiple columns of cells in 1-2-3 by using the /Data Parse command. If the data is continuous text, you can modify the line wrapping by using the /Range Justify command.

Non-Delimited ASCII File Imported as Numbers When you import a non-delimited file using the Numbers option, 1-2-3 ignores all text fields. Separate numbers in a single line of the text file will be spread over multiple cells in the corresponding row of the worksheet. Since the file was not specifically delimited (e.g., with commas), 1-2-3 uses the space between numbers as the delimiter.

If the data being imported is in columnar form and one or more entries are left blank, 1-2-3 will interpret the multiple spaces from the source file as a single delimiter. 1-2-3 does not recognize a blank entry in the data source as a separate entity. 1-2-3 simply looks ahead to the next available piece of data from the source and transfers it to the next available column in the worksheet. This can, of course, alter the columnar integrity of the data being imported. To avoid this problem, make sure that the source columnar data has entries in each column of each row and contains no blank entries.

Delimited ASCII File Imported as Numbers Use the Numbers option to import a file delimited by commas, spaces, colons, or semicolons, and with each label enclosed in double or single quotes. 1-2-3 will import these delimited numbers and text and place them in separate columns within the appropriate row (see Figures File.2a–b). The text data is inserted into label cells with your default label prefix; the numbers will be inserted into numerical cells.

Delimited ASCII File Imported as Text If you use the Text option to import a file delimited by commas, spaces, colons, or semicolons, and with each label enclosed in double or single quotes (as with the Numbers option above), 1-2-3 will import both the text and numbers into separate columns and in the appropriate rows. Both text and numbers, however, will be treated as label cells. This means that you will have to convert any cells containing numbers before they can be used for calculations. If you intend to use the numbers for calculations, you're better off using the Numbers option.

Defaults

The current cell.

Usage

Because importing external files will alter the current worksheet, be sure to back up your work prior to importing data. Before you import data, you must determine if the file is properly delimited or if you will have to treat it as a non-delimited file. Most software packages have the ability to export their data as delimited files, and some offer you considerable control as to how the files are delimited. You should select the option that separates each field with a comma, surrounds each text field with quotes, and separates each line or record with a hard return.

If the source file is not delimited, be sure that its columnar data is complete and contains no blanks. Once your source file is ready, move the cell pointer to the top-left corner of the range into which you wish to import the data. Be sure that the spaces below and to the right of the current cell are free to accept new data.

Initiate the command by selecting /File Import and at the prompt select either the Text or Numbers option as appropriate. By default, 1-2-3 will display a list of the files with the .PRN extension (the 1-2-3 text file designator, so named because 1-2-3 creates an ASCII file by "printing" to disk) in the current directory. If you want to list text files with an extension other than .PRN, enter the file name *.XXX, where XXX is the extension you want to list. Point to the file to be imported and press ENTER. If you want to specify the file by name, simply type in the name at the prompt and press ENTER. The file will be imported into the current worksheet starting in the current cell. If you make a mistake and need to use the Undo option, you can undo the import process by pressing UNDO (ALT-F4) immediately.

Examples

Let's say you want to import the delimited ASCII file named OCTOPUS.PRN, which contains both numbers and text data delimited by commas, quotes, and hard returns (Figure File.2a) into the current worksheet starting at cell B5 (Figure File.2b). (This file was produced by exporting a dBASE III file into ASCII format):

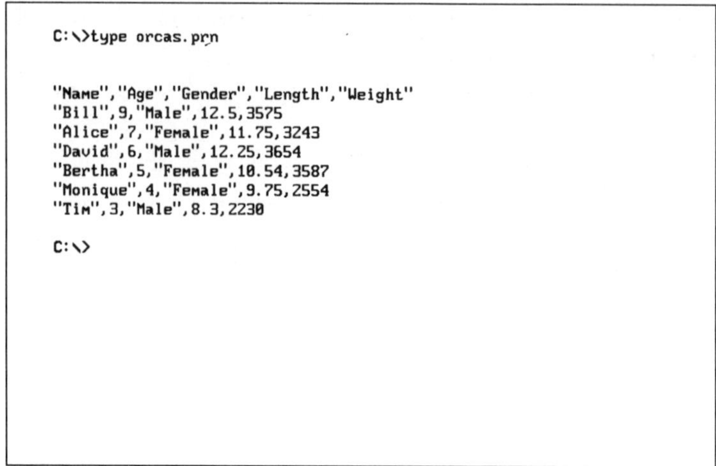

Figure File.2a
Delimited File.

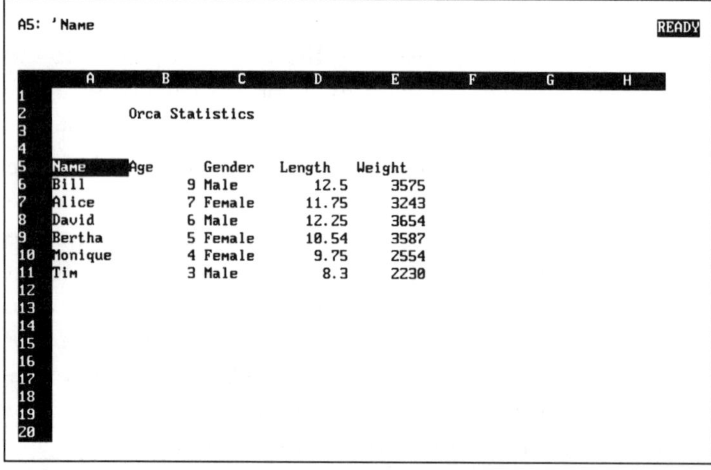

Figure File.2b
Imported file.

1. Move the cell pointer to cell B5 and make sure there is enough space for the imported data.
2. Select /File Import Numbers.
3. Point to the name or enter `OCTOPUS.PRN` and press ENTER.

Notes

ASCII file format is a technical term for generic text files, files that can be easily read by most computer programs. The term ASCII is an acronym for American

Standard Code for Information Interchange. ASCII files are stripped of all special formatting information and codes used by your specific word processor or spreadsheet program; these special codes include items such as tabs or centers, underlining or boldface, headers or footers, etc. ASCII files contain only data, punctuation, and hard returns.

A delimited ASCII file is a file in ASCII file format in which each field or column entry is separated by a delimiter character (typically a comma, space, colon, or semicolon). Each record or row is separated by a hard return. In addition, text fields are usually enclosed in single or double quotes. Most software programs provide a method for exporting their data in delimited file format to facilitate the transfer of the data to other software products.

Cautions

1. When you import files containing numbers, make sure that they do not contain commas separating the thousands. These commas will be treated as delimiters, separating the original number into two numbers. The same holds for other common delimiter characters such as the colon, etc.
2. /File Import changes the data in the current worksheet. Be sure to back up the current file before attempting a /File Import command. If you are using the Undo feature, you can undo the effects of a /File Import command by immediately pressing the UNDO (ALT-F4) key.
3. /File Import places its output in a range large enough to include all data from the imported file, starting at the current cell pointer location. The data will overwrite any data in the output range without warning. Be certain that the cell pointer is located in a safe location before initiating this command.
4. /File Import doesn't import formulas or functions, except as labels. It may be possible to convert the labels back to formulas by removing the label prefix. A better strategy may be to translate the source file with the Lotus 1-2-3 Translate utility. The Translate utility is accessed via the Lotus 1-2-3 Access menu and is capable of translating many file types (e.g., dBASE, DIF, Multiplan, Symphony, etc.) directly into worksheet format.

File List

Purpose

Used to list the files in a particular directory on the screen. By pointing at a specific file name in the list you can also display key information about that file. This can be used to help determine which file should be loaded or imported based on its size or age.

Description

When using /File List, you can specify not only the directory to list, but also the *type* of files you wish to see. For example, you can list all Graph or Print files, all Worksheet files, or all files linked to the current file by formula references. When the selected files are listed to the screen, they temporarily overlay the current worksheet. Use the cursor to point at a particular file name and additional information about the size and age of that file will be displayed on line three of the screen. (As you move the highlight over each file name, the corresponding directory information will be displayed on that line.) Or you can press ESC and edit the directory or file specification using the DOS wildcard characters to expand or narrow the list of files displayed.

Defaults

None.

Usage

To obtain a file listing, select /File List. You will be presented with a menu offering several file types. Each will list files meeting the criteria described below.

Graph Lists all graph files in the current directory with .PIC extension.

Linked Lists all files linked to the current worksheet.

Other Lists all files. You can press ESC and enter a file name or extension using the DOS wildcard characters * and ?. 1-2-3 then lists all files in the current directory that match the file name or extension.

Print Lists all files in the current directory with the .PRN extension.

Worksheet Lists all files in the current directory with .WK1, .WK3, or .WKS extensions.

If you want to change the directory for the file list, press ESC twice and enter the full new directory path and press ENTER. To list detailed information about a file, highlight the file name with the cell pointer.

Examples

To list all worksheets in the current directory:

1. Select /File List Worksheet.
2. Highlight the name of the worksheet of interest to display additional information.

To list all files with links to the current file:

1. Select /File List Linked.
2. Highlight the name of the worksheet of interest to display additional information.

Notes

1. If 1-2-3 can't find any files with the specified extension, it will simply display your current subdirectories.
2. To generate a table of the file names in the current directory in your current worksheet, use the /File Admin Table commands.

File Retrieve

Purpose

Used to load a worksheet from disk into memory; the new file will replace the current worksheet in memory. Any work you have done on the current worksheet since it was last saved will be lost. (Use /File Save before /File Retrieve if you want to keep your work intact.) Use the /File Retrieve command when you want to replace the current worksheet with a previous version of that file, or with another worksheet altogether.

Description

The /File Retrieve command loads worksheets from disk into memory, replacing the current worksheet in memory. If you wish to retain the current worksheet, be sure to save it to disk using /File Save before you retrieve a new worksheet.

Usage

To load a particular file from disk into memory in place of a current file (already in memory), select /File Retrieve. Point to one of the file names from the current directory or enter the name of the file to load and press ENTER. If the file is password-protected, you will be prompted to enter the password. Remember that passwords are case-sensitive.

Examples

To load the file named OCTOPUS in place of the current worksheet:

1. Select /File Retrieve.
2. Type `OCTOPUS` and press ENTER.

Notes

If you do not have enough RAM memory to open the new worksheet in place of the previously current worksheet, 1-2-3 will display the "Memory Full" error message. If you have Undo activated, you can try turning Undo off with /Worksheet Global Default Other Undo Disable. If you have an Add-In attached, you can detach one or more Add-Ins with /Add-In Detach.

If you always load in the same file when you start 1-2-3, you can automate the process by naming the file AUTO123.WK1 and saving it in the default directory. From then on, each time you start 1-2-3, the program will look for and load the AUTO123.WK1 file.

You can retrieve a specified worksheet when you start up 1-2-3 by including the -w prefix and the worksheet name in the startup command. For example to start 1-2-3 and load the worksheet OCTOPUS you would use the command:

```
123 -woctopus
```

Cautions

On a multi-user/network system, if 1-2-3 displays the read only indicator (RO) at the bottom of the screen, it means that you do not have the reservation for the file. You will not be allowed to save any changes that you make to the file to disk unless you obtain the reservation for the file with the /File Admin Reservation Get command.

File Save

Purpose

Used to save a worksheet file from temporary RAM memory to permanent disk storage.

Description

The /File Save command can be used to create a new disk file or replace an existing one. When you save a worksheet file, you will be asked to enter or point to the file name. If you enter a new file name, a new file will be created. If you point to or type in an existing file name, it will be replaced. The save command makes an exact copy of the current file in memory; the range names, current settings, and formats are all saved with the file.

Defaults

The current file will be saved to its previously assigned file name (either the name used when the file was loaded or when it was last saved to disk).

Usage

You can use the /File Save command in either of two situations:

New File If you have a new worksheet that has never been saved before, when you select /File Save, 1-2-3 will display a list of all files in the current directory and prompt you to select or enter a file name. Either point to one of the current names (you will overwrite that file) or type in a new name and press ENTER. 1-2-3 will create a new file with the assigned name.

To save the file to another directory on disk, precede the assigned file name with the complete path and drive name. If you use the name of an existing file, 1-2-3 will assume that you wish to replace that file.

Previously Saved File If the current worksheet has been saved before, 1-2-3 assumes that you want to save it under the same file name; it will supply that name as the default name for the file. You can either point to another file name (to replace that file with the current file), type in a new file name, or accept the default by pressing ENTER. If 1-2-3 looks at the disk and sees that a file with the same name is already there, it offers three options: Backup, Cancel, or Replace. If you select Backup, 1-2-3 renames the old version on disk with the same file name, but with a .BAK extension. Select Cancel to terminate the /File Save command. Select Replace to overwrite the previous disk version.

If the current file has been saved and you want to create a second version of it, save again under a new name, rather than accepting the default name. This technique allows you to create more than one version of the current worksheet.

Passwords

1-2-3's /File Save option allows you to save your file with a password. When you do so, the system saves the file in an encrypted form that cannot be loaded into 1-2-3 without the password, nor can it be read by any other word processor or program. For this reason, passwords provide a high degree of security. Since there is no way to crack the password code, make sure you write down all assigned passwords in a secure location.

Create a New File With a Password To assign a password to a file that you are saving for the first time, initiate the /File Save command in the usual fashion. When you are prompted for the file name, type in the name followed by a single space and then the letter "p". Press ENTER and 1-2-3 will ask you to type in a password. Carefully type the password using up to 15 characters with no spaces. (1-2-3 will not display the password as you enter it.) Remember that passwords are case-sensitive and you must be careful to use capitals consistently.

When you have typed in the password, press ENTER, and 1-2-3 will prompt you to retype the same password for verification. If you enter it exactly the same way as the first time, 1-2-3 will save the file to disk with the desired password. If you enter the password differently, 1-2-3 will display an error message and you will have to start the operation again.

Add a Password to an Existing File To assign a password to a file you previously saved without a password, initiate the /File Save command in the usual fashion. When you are prompted to enter the file name, 1-2-3 will display the current name. Edit the current name to add a space and the letter "p". Press ENTER and 1-2-3 will prompt you for the password as described above. After you have confirmed the password, 1-2-3 will ask you if you want to Backup, Replace, or Cancel. Select Replace to save the file to disk with the desired password. If you select Backup, remember that the backup version with the extension .BAK is *not* password-protected.

Changing an Existing Password To change the password for a worksheet that has already been saved to disk with a password, load the file into memory with /File Retrieve command using the previous password, and initiate the /File Save command in the usual fashion. When you are prompted to enter the file name,

1-2-3 will display the current name followed by the note [Password Protected]. Press ESC or BACKSPACE to delete the note, then press the space bar and enter the letter "p". Press ENTER and 1-2-3 will prompt you for the password. Type in the new password using up to 15 characters with no spaces. 1-2-3 does not display the password as you type. Passwords are case-sensitive, so be careful to use capitals consistently.

When you have entered the password, press ENTER. You will be prompted to retype the password to verify it. If you enter it exactly the same way as the first time, 1-2-3 will ask you if you want to Backup, Replace, or Cancel. Select Replace to save the file to disk with the desired password. If you select the Backup option, remember that the backup version with the .BAK extension will be retained with the old password.

Deleting an Existing Password To delete a password from a password-protected worksheet on disk, load that worksheet file into memory using the /File Retrieve command. (Load it using the existing password.) Then initiate the /File Save command as described above. When you are prompted to enter the file name, 1-2-3 will display the current name followed by the note [Password Protected]. Press ESC or BACKSPACE to delete the note and press ENTER. 1-2-3 will ask you if you want to Backup, Replace, or Cancel. Select the Replace option to write the new version to disk without a password. If you select the Backup option, the new version will not be password-protected, but the backup copy will retain password protection.

Examples

To create a new file named MANTARAY for the current worksheet:

1. Select /File Save.
2. Type `MANTARAY` and press ENTER.

To save the same file under the new name RAYS:

1. Select /File Save.
2. Overwrite the name MANTARAY with the name RAYS and press ENTER.

To update the file RAYS on the disk after correcting the data:

1. Select /File Save.
2. Accept the default current name RAYS by pressing ENTER.
3. Select Replace.

To save the file RAYS with the password Manta:

1. Select /File Save.
2. Accept the default current name RAYS and press the space bar followed by the letter "p" and press ENTER.
3. Type `Manta` and press ENTER.
4. Type `Manta` and press ENTER.
5. Select Replace.

To delete the password Manta from the file RAYS:

1. Select /File Retrieve to load the file.
2. Type `RAYS` and press ENTER (or point at the name and press ENTER).
3. Type `Manta` and press ENTER. This displays asterisks as you type it.
4. Select /File Save.
5. Press ESC to delete the [Password Protected] message.
6. Press ENTER.
7. Select Replace.

Notes

1. If you do not have enough room on the disk to save the file, 1-2-3 will display the "Disk Full" error message. Press ESC to clear the message and either insert another formatted diskette with sufficient space or delete enough files from the hard disk to accommodate the file to be saved.
2. To save the current file as an ASCII text file, use the /Print File command.
3. To save the current file in delimited format use 1-2-3's Translate option.

Cautions

1. The Undo feature cannot undo the /File Save command. If you save an erroneous version of a file on top of the correct version, the correct version will be lost. You will have to restore it from one of your backups. You do have a backup, don't you?
2. Once you save a file with a password you cannot load the file without it. If you can't remember your password, you cannot recover your data. So be sure that you write down all assigned passwords in a secure location.

File Xtract

Purpose

Used to save a range from the current worksheet file to disk. This is most often used to isolate a portion of significant data in your worksheet and save it in a file of its own. If you save the relevant portion of the spreadsheet to a new disk file and then retrieve the new, smaller disk file in place of the old, larger one, you can increase performance and productivity.

Description

The /File Xtract command works exactly like /File Save, except you can designate a range of cells to save and specify how the data should be saved. You can save the range and include all formulas (as they appear on the worksheet), numbers, and labels; or you can save only the values, numbers, and labels in the range. In the latter case, only the current formula results are extracted; they are converted to values in the new file.

Defaults

None.

Usage

To extract a range, initiate the command by selecting /File Xtract. 1-2-3 will first ask you if you want to extract Formulas as well as labels and values, or just Values, where only the current formula results are extracted along with the labels and values in the range.

If you select Formulas, 1-2-3 will extract all formulas in the extract range and will adjust all addresses (relative, mixed, or absolute) to their new position in the extracted file. Once within the extract file, the formulas will maintain the relative, mixed, or absolute address status. If you select Values, all formulas are converted to their current values and only the values are placed in the extracted file.

1-2-3 next prompts you to enter a file name and displays a list of all files in the current directory. Either point to an existing name or enter a new name and press ENTER. If you entered or selected an existing name, 1-2-3 will ask if you want to Backup or Replace the current file or Cancel the extract process. If you select Backup, the current file on disk will be renamed with a .BAK extension before the extract is written to a file with the same name. If you select Replace, the existing file will be written over by the extracted file.

Finally, 1-2-3 will ask you for the range to extract. Specify the range by address, by range name, or by pointing and then press ENTER.

You can assign a password to the extracted file. When you are prompted to enter the file name, enter the name followed by a single space and then the letter "p". Press ENTER and 1-2-3 will prompt you to type in a password. Carefully type in the password, using up to 15 characters with no spaces. 1-2-3 will not display the password as you enter it. Passwords are case-sensitive so be careful to use capitals consistently.

When you have entered the password, press ENTER. You will be prompted to re-enter the same password to verify it. If you enter it exactly the same way as the first time, 1-2-3 will save the file to disk with the desired password. If you enter the password differently, 1-2-3 will display an error message and you will have to start the /File Extract procedure all over again.

Examples

To extract the range B27 to H42 to the new file REPTILES:

1. Select /File Xtract.
2. Type `REPTILES` and press ENTER.
3. Type `B27..H42` and press ENTER.

To extract the range ALLIGATORS to the existing file REPTILES:

1. Select /File Xtract.
2. Type `REPTILES` and press ENTER (or point to the name and press ENTER.)
3. Select Replace.
4. Type `ALLIGATORS` and press ENTER.

To extract the range ALLIGATORS of the current worksheet into the new file CROCODILES with the password Teeth:

1. Select /File Xtract.
2. Type `CROCODILES p` and press ENTER. The "p" indicates a password.
3. Type `Teeth` and press ENTER. Only asterisks will display.
4. Type `Teeth` and press ENTER.
5. Select Replace.
6. Type `ALLIGATORS` and press ENTER.

Notes

1. 1-2-3 saves all file settings and default ranges in the extracted file.
2. If you do not have enough room on the disk to save the extracted file, 1-2-3 will display the "Disk Full" error message. Press ESC to clear the message and either insert another formatted diskette with sufficient room or delete enough files from the disk or diskette to accommodate the file to be saved.

Cautions

1. If you have set the recalculation mode to manual, be sure you recalculate the worksheet by pressing the RECALC (F9) key prior to extracting values. Otherwise the formulas in the worksheet may not be properly converted to their most current values when extracted.
2. If you extract a range as formulas, be sure the extracted range does not contain any formulas or range names that refer to cells in the original worksheet that were not extracted as well.

   If you extract data in a named range, be certain that you also extract all the data that is referenced by the named range, otherwise the extracted range in the new worksheet will not refer to the same data as in the source worksheet.
3. Once you save a file with a password you cannot load the file without it. If you can't remember your password, you cannot recover your data. Be sure you write down all assigned passwords in a secure location.

▸ Graph Commands

Purpose

Used to display numerical data in graphical form on screen and to prepare graphs for printing via the PrintGraph or Allways utilities. Graphs are particularly useful for visually summarizing large quantities of numerical data and for showing the relationships between numerical results.

Description

The Graph commands allow you to select from five basic graph types and then from many other options that will modify or enhance a graph presentation. You can also save the current graph (that is, all the current type, range, and option settings) by assigning them a graph name. Later, you can recall the particular graph (derived from these settings) by name. The primary graph options are as follows:

A–F Used to assign the data ranges (up to six) you wish to graph.

Group Used to specify a single range containing all the graph ranges in adjacent rows and columns.

Name Assigns a name to the current graph settings (e.g., range specifications, graph type, options, etc.) so you can recall them or reference the graph by name.

Options Allows you to modify the way a graph is printed or displayed on screen; you can add or change the titles, legends, colors, hatch patterns, grid lines, and scaling.

Reset Allows you to reset individual or all the current graph settings.

Save Saves the image of the current graph to a disk file in .PIC file format for later printing via the PrintGraph or Allways utilities. This file is also interpretable by other programs such as word processors or desktop publishing programs.

Type Allows you to select from the five basic graph types: line, bar, stacked bar, pie, and XY.

View Displays the current graph on the screen.

X Specifies the range containing the X-axis labels or values.

Graph Types

There are five basic types of graphs: Line, Bar, XY, Stacked Bar, and Pie. Each of these can be modified to include titles, legends, and other features. The permutations and combinations of graph types and features provide a multitude of graphical displays to choose from. We will first discuss the basic graph types and then discuss the features of each /Graph command in the following pages.

Line The line graph is most often used to display data trends over time (see Figure Graph.1, which shows the first screen of monthly expense data represented

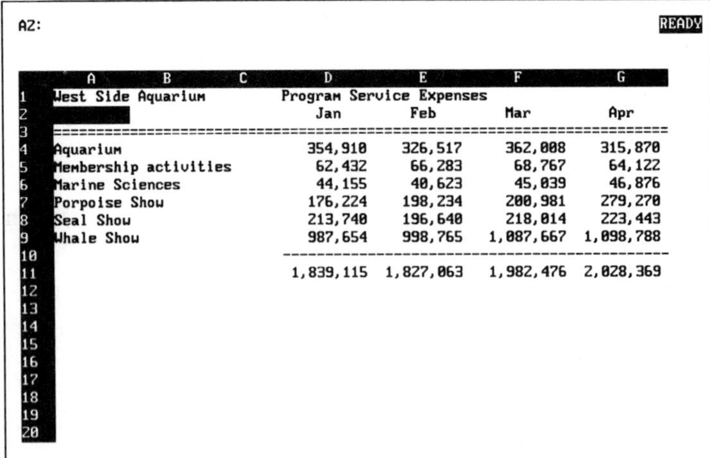

A2: READY

	A B C	D	E	F	G
1	West Side Aquarium	Program Service Expenses			
2		Jan	Feb	Mar	Apr
3	=====================	==========	==========	==========	==========
4	Aquarium	354,910	326,517	362,008	315,870
5	Membership activities	62,432	66,283	68,767	64,122
6	Marine Sciences	44,155	40,623	45,039	46,876
7	Porpoise Show	176,224	198,234	200,981	279,270
8	Seal Show	213,740	196,640	218,014	223,443
9	Whale Show	987,654	998,765	1,087,667	1,098,788
10		----------	----------	----------	----------
11		1,839,115	1,827,063	1,982,476	2,028,369
12					
13					
14					
15					
16					
17					
18					
19					
20					

Figure Graph.1
Expense data.

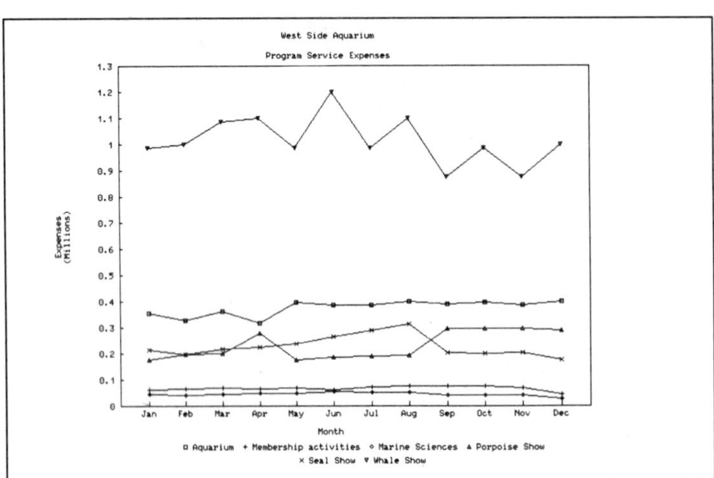

Figure Graph.2
Line Graph of expense data.

in the line graph in Figure Graph.2). The line graph shows how one or more variables change in relation to the change in a single common variable (the X-axis variable). Usually the X variable is time, measured in days, months, or years. You can use any variable for the X-axis as long as its measurement has relation to all the variables in the other data ranges A through F. Figure Graph.2 shows the changes in various aquarium expenses over time. The line graph allows you to quickly grasp the fluctuations within each expense category over the course of the year, as well as to compare each category of expense with one another.

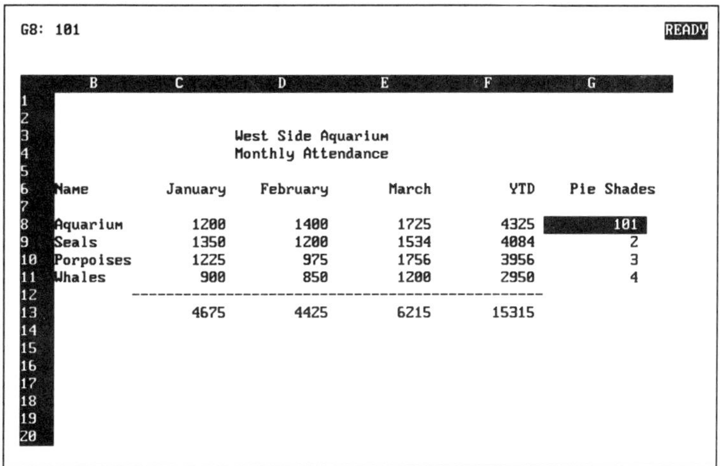

G8: 101 READY

West Side Aquarium
Monthly Attendance

Name	January	February	March	YTD	Pie Shades
Aquarium	1200	1400	1725	4325	101
Seals	1350	1200	1534	4084	2
Porpoises	1225	975	1756	3956	3
Whales	900	850	1200	2950	4
	4675	4425	6215	15315	

Figure Graph.3a
Attendance data.

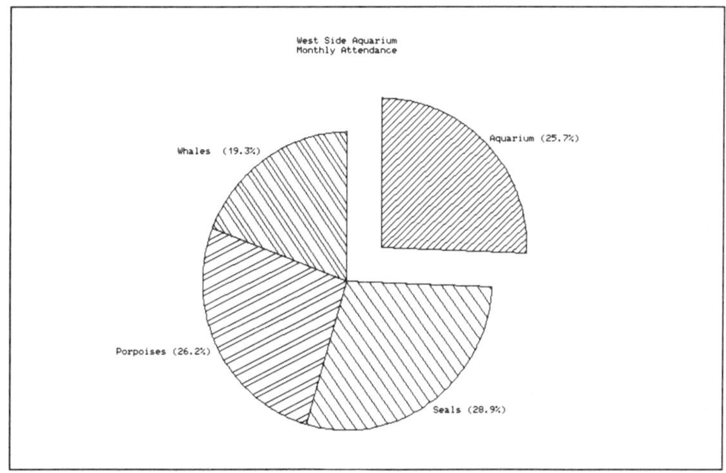

Figure Graph.3b
Pie Graph.

Pie A pie chart takes the separate components of a whole and shows the relative proportion of each component to the whole; each component element is represented as a segment or a "slice" of the pie. In Figure Graph.3a, the attendance of each of the separate displays of the aquarium are listed. In Figure Graph.3b, they are shown as percentages of the total costs. Pie chart segments can either be "exploded" (slightly pulled out from the pie circumference) as shown or kept together. 1-2-3 automatically provides data labels (from your X-range) and calculates the percentages. The percentages displayed on a pie chart are rounded so they may not always add up to 100%.

Stacked Bar The stacked bar graph is used to show component elements in a series of data totals. In Figure Graph.4 (also dependent on the data in Figure Graph.3a), we show the total monthly attendance for the four most popular exhibits of the West Side Aquarium during the first three months of the year. Each separate segment within the stacked bar represents the attendance for one of the exhibits. The total stack adds up to the total attendance for all four exhibits for each month. The stacked bar chart lets you evaluate both the individual attendance variations as month by month *and* the cumulative variations month by month. The comparative attendance, exhibit by exhibit, can also be inferred by the stacked-bar graph, though not as clearly as with a clustered bar graph (see below).

Bar An alternative way to show changes in multiple variables is with the clustered bar graph. (See Figure Graph.5—also based on the data in Figure Graph.3a.) The clustered bar graph doesn't show cumulative values as clearly as the stacked bar graph, but it lets you compare values for each of the component elements—from month to month, from period to period—more precisely.

XY XY graphs are used to show the one-to-one relationship between two variables. One variable is plotted along the X-axis while the associated range value is plotted along the Y-axis. In order to plot reasonable XY graphs, you must sort your data so that it is in ascending or descending order (or you can eliminate the lines connecting the data points). Otherwise, you will create a spider's web for a graph. Figure Graph.6 shows the length versus the weight of each killer whale in the aquarium. As you can see, there is a general relationship between length and weight (with the obvious exception of Bertha).

Usage

To create a graph, first decide what data ranges you wish to represent in your graph and select the graph type that will best display your data. Initiate the command by selecting /Graph, then select Type to choose the desired graph type.

Select the X option and specify the X-axis data either by typing in the address or name of the range or by painting the range. (Note that for a pie chart the X data range is used to specify the labels for each pie segment.) Next specify one to six additional ranges to be graphed; select a range letter (A–F) and then type in (or paint) the range address. (Again, the pie chart follows a slightly different protocol, see below for details.) If the X and A–F ranges are in consecutive rows and columns, you can use the Group option to specify them all at once. Finally, select the View option to display the graph on your screen. Press ESC to return to the /Graph menu. You may then modify any of the features you wish by selecting

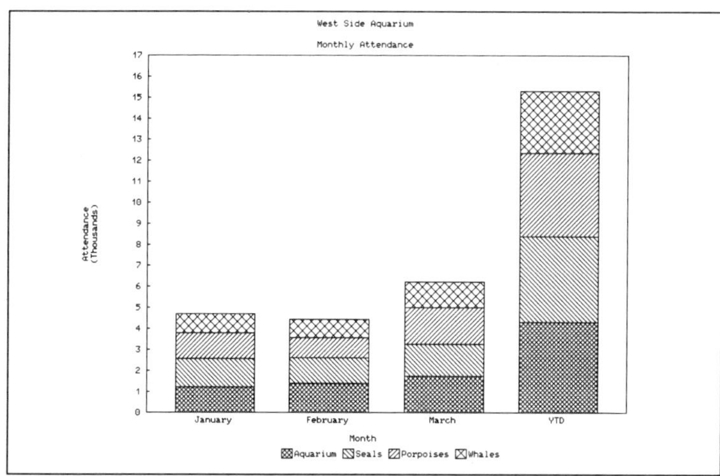

Figure Graph.4
Stacked bar graph.

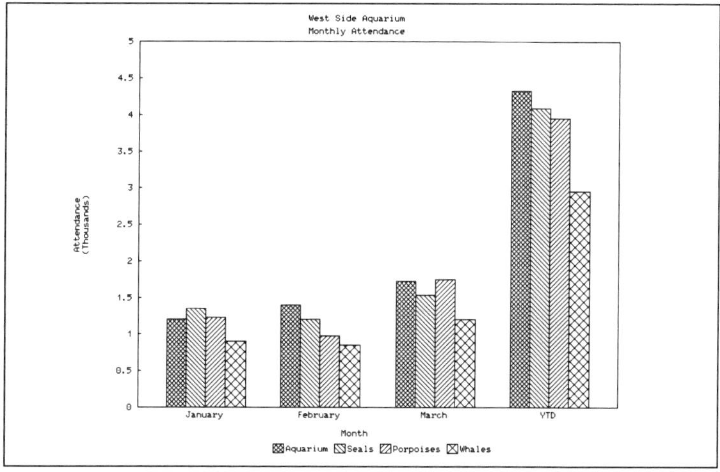

Figure Graph.5
Bar graph.

/Graph Options and redisplay the graph by selecting View again. At any time within the /Graph menu, press F6 to display your current graph settings. Press F6 again to clear the graph settings window from the screen.

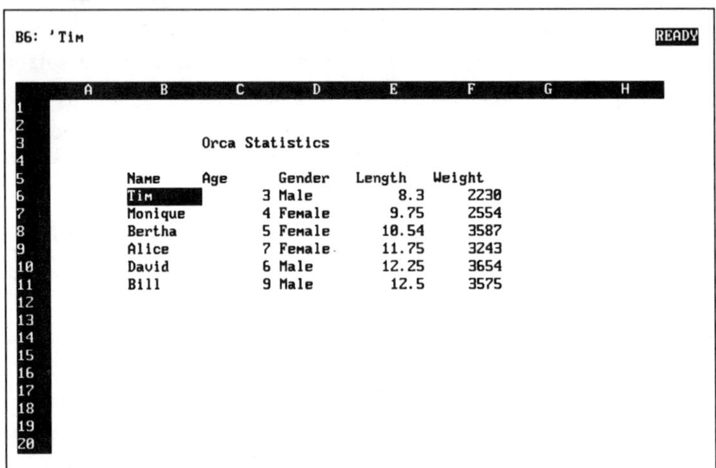

Name	Age	Gender	Length	Weight
Tim	3	Male	8.3	2230
Monique	4	Female	9.75	2554
Bertha	5	Female	10.54	3587
Alice	7	Female	11.75	3243
David	6	Male	12.25	3654
Bill	9	Male	12.5	3575

Figure Graph.6a
Weight versus Length Data.

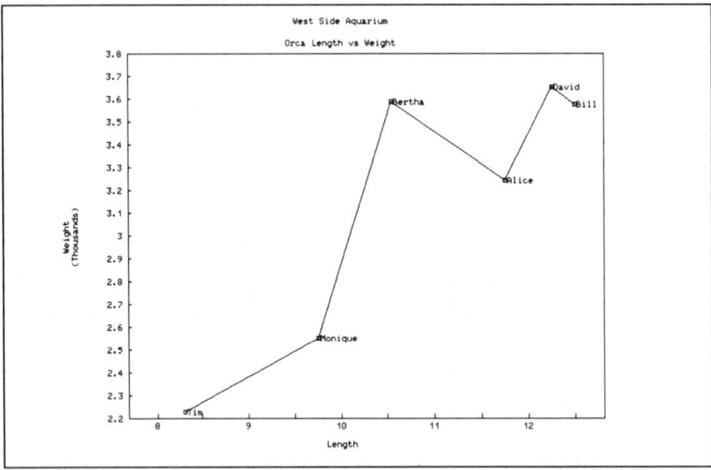

Figure Graph.6b
XY Graph of Weight versus Length.

Graph A–F

Purpose

Used to specify the A through F graph ranges containing the data you wish to graph.

Description

The 1-2-3 /Graph command graphs the currently assigned X and A-F ranges. (Press F6 to see your current graph settings.) To display a graph with the View option or the F10 GRAPH key, you must define the data ranges to be graphed. You can either assign each data range individually or, if they are appropriately arranged in consecutive rows or columns, you can use the /Graph Group option to select them all at once. The different graph types each use the various graph ranges in their own way, but in general, the X range is used to set the X-axis and the ranges A–F are used to specify the dependent variables. The graph range assignments for each graph type are as follows:

Bar Ranges A–F are each assigned a separate bar pattern or color. 1-2-3 displays a separate bar for each value in each range. They are clustered for each value of the X variable, as shown in Figure Graph.5. You can see from the worksheet data that produced this graph in Figure Graph 3.a that the A range is row 8 containing data for the aquarium attendance.

Stacked Bar Ranges A–F will be displayed as segments of each bar. Data range A will be the first (lowest) portion of each bar; data range B will be above data range A, and so on, as shown in Figure Graph.4. (This stacked bar graph uses the same A–D range settings as Figure Graph.5.)

Line Each data range (A–F) is graphed as a separate line; and the values in each range are represented as a set of points on that line. Unique symbols can be used as points on each data range line to distinguish the lines from one another. The points (or the symbols used for each point) can be connected with a line (as shown in Figure Graph.2) or not. Range A contains the data from row 4 in Figure Graph.1 for aquarium, B contains row 5 for membership, C contains row 6, and so on.

Pie 1-2-3 uses the A–B ranges quite differently for pie graphs than for other graph types. It completely *ignores* any settings for ranges C–F. Range A is used to specify the data to be graphed. Range B is used to determine the color or hatching patterns (depending on whether the graph is being displayed in color or in monochrome) for the graph. Range B also determines if the individual slices of the pie should be exploded (as in Figures Graph.3a and b) or not.

The pie chart can include seven colors and/or eight hatching options (seven patterns plus one solid). To select colors or patterns, you must create a range B adjacent to the data in range A; in range B, include a color number (1–8) for each adjacent value in range A. For example, to select color 6 for the second slice, enter 6 in range B, next to the second entry in range A. To explode a slice, increment the color number in range B by 100, i.e. 106. To hide a slice, enter a negative number. In Figures Graph.3a and b, the A range is assigned to column C while the B range is assigned to Column G. Note that by assigning 101 to the first data element, the first slice in Figure Graph.3b is "exploded." To set color or black and white, select /Graph Options B&W or /Graph Options Color.

Defaults

Last A–F range selected.

Usage

To assign a range, select the range letter, type in (or paint) the range address, and press ENTER. You can redefine a range at any time.

Notes

You can clear a particular range by selecting the /Graph Reset option and then the letter of the range you want to clear. You can clear all the ranges (and the rest of the graph options) by selecting the Graph option under Reset.

Cautions

It is easy to misassign the data ranges for a graph. To avoid this problem, name the data ranges with /Range Name Create before starting the Graph command and use the assigned names when assigning the graph ranges.

Graph Group

Purpose

Used to specify all graph data ranges at once. (The data must be structured according to a few simple rules.) This is a quick and easy way to create a graph.

Description

To use the /Graph Group command the data ranges must be arranged in contiguous rows or columns; the X range must be at the top (for data in rows) or at the left of the range (for data in columns). 1-2-3 will assign the first column (or row) of data to the X range, the next to the A range and so on until there is no more data or range F is assigned.

Usage

To use the Group command, first check that your data conforms to the layout requirements described above, and then select /Graph Group. At the prompt, specify all rows and columns of the range by address, by name, or by painting it. Finally, indicate whether you want 1-2-3 to treat the data in rows or in columns. If your X data range lies in a row at the top of the other ranges, select Rowwise; if it lies in a column to the left, select Columnwise.

Example

To specify the data range from A1..F4 with the X range in row 1 and data ranges A–C in rows 2 through 4:

1. Select /Graph Group.
2. At the first prompt, type in `A1..F4` to specify the total range, and press ENTER.
3. Select Rowwise.
4. Select View to see the graph.

Cautions

It is easy to misassign graph ranges if your data table is not set up correctly. Be sure to verify the range assignments before you rely on the resulting graph.

Graph Name

Purpose

Used to save the current graph range, type, and option settings with the worksheet file for later recall. Using named graphs allows you to work with more than one graph in a given worksheet file.

Description

The /Graph Name commands work much like the /Range Name commands. You can Create a name, Use the settings of an existing range, Delete a name, Reset all names, or create a Table of graph names. Once you have created a named graph with /Graph Name Create, the settings, including the data ranges (but not the actual data) and the options and features are saved with the worksheet file under the assigned name. You can recall the named graph using the /Graph Name Use option. This feature allows you to retrieve a named graph with its settings and apply it to a new data range, e.g., retrieve the named graph, reset the data ranges, and then assign new ones.

Usage

Create To create a graph name, first set up the graph exactly as you want it saved, then select /Graph Name Create. At the prompt, type in a new name or point to an existing graph name and press ENTER. (Be careful, if you just press ENTER at the prompt, you may accidentally overwrite a named graph.)

Use To use a named graph, select /Graph Name Use. Type in the assigned graph name or point to it and press ENTER.

Delete To delete a graph name, select /Graph Name Delete and type in the assigned graph name (or point to it). (Press F3 to see a full screen list.) Press ENTER to complete the deletion.

Reset To clear all assigned graph names, select /Graph Name Reset.

Table To create a table of graph names in the current worksheet, select /Graph Name Table. At the prompt, designate a clear area of the current worksheet for the placement of the graph table. The table will require two columns (specifying the graph name and type) and as many rows as there are named graphs in the current file. This command will overwrite any data in the output range with no warning. Be sure that the space is clear or can be overwritten.

Examples

To create the graph name, SHARKS, with the current graph settings:

1. First check the graph settings to be sure they are correct, then select /Graph Name Create.
2. At the prompt type `SHARKS` and press ENTER.

To create a table of the named graphs in the current worksheet:

1. Place the cell pointer in the top-left corner of the range where you want to list the named graphs. Be sure to allow enough space for two columns and as many rows as there are named graphs.
2. Initiate the command by selecting /Graph Name Table.
3. At the prompt requesting the output location, press ENTER to accept the current cell as the default for the output.

Notes

To edit the settings in a named graph, recall the named graph with /Graph Name Use, edit the settings as necessary, and save them under the same name. Select /Graph Name Create and respecify the graph name.

To save a graph for printing or for use outside 1-2-3 with other programs like word processors or desktop publishing systems, use the /Graph Save command.

Cautions

When you Use a named graph, it cancels the current graph settings. If you want to save the current settings, be sure to assign them a graph name before you select Use to work with another.

Graph Options

Purpose

Used to customize the presentation of a graph. You can enhance your graphs by adding titles, colors, data labels, etc.

Description

The main /Graph Option menu is composed of nine sub-options as follows:

B&W Selects Black and White as the color for printing and for displaying graphs. If you have a monochrome monitor, this is the default. The B&W option will automatically assign cross-hatching to the different graph ranges. If you have a monochrome monitor and a color printer, you must select Color (see below) to print in color. The monitor will still display in black and white.

Color Selects colors for displaying and printing graphs (if you have a color printer). If you have a color monitor, this is the default. If you have a color monitor and a black and white printer, 1-2-3 will automatically print in black and white. If you have a monochrome monitor and a color printer, you will have to select /Graph Options Color to have your graphs printed in color. (The monitor will still display in black and white.)

Data-Labels Allows you to assign the data range values (A–F) as labels for their associated data points, or bars on the graph. You can select to place the labels above, below, left, right, or center for line graphs. For Bar graphs, you can place the labels above or below, and with Stacked Bar graphs, 1-2-3 will always center the value inside the corresponding portion of the bar block. If you prefer not to use the data range values as labels, you must specify a Data Label range (equal in

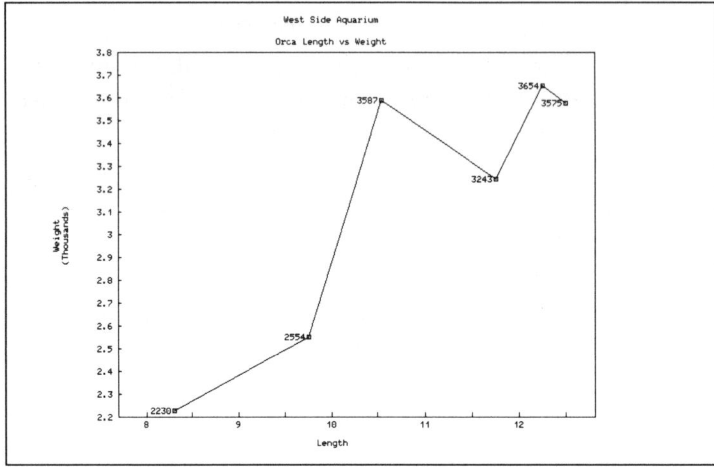

Figure Graph.7
XY Graph using Weights as data labels.

size to the data range), with labels corresponding to each data value. See Figure Graph.6, where the names of the whales have been used as data labels. If you want to assign data labels to all ranges at once, you can use the Group option and select a range of lables of equivalent size to the number of data points.

Format Determines how 1-2-3 will display the lines and symbols for the Line and XY graph types. Select Format, then specify the data range (A–F) you wish to format. (Select Graph to format *all* lines in the graph). You can use Symbols, Lines, Both, or Neither.

Grid Determines whether 1-2-3 displays and prints a grid behind the graph data to make it easier to read the graph data and to compare values for separated data ranges. You can include Horizontal grid lines (originating from the Y-Axis), Vertical grid lines (originating from the X-axis), or Both. The Clear option lets you clear all the grid lines.

Legends Creates legends below the graph, to identify the symbols, colors, or hatching patterns that represent each data range. After you select Legend, you may select a data range (A–F) and then type in the legend text for that data range. Alternatively, you can assign each data range a corresponding legend text cell in the worksheet, and then instruct 1-2-3 to use the contents of that cell as the data legend for the associated range.

You can assign the legend cells in two ways. If you want to assign them individually, select the data range letter (A–F) from the Legends menu, and at the prompt, type in a backslash (\) followed by the cell address. If you have placed all your data legends in a contiguous range (column or row), you can select the Range option and assign them all at once. Specify the range containing the legends; 1-2-3 will use the first legend in the range for data range A, the second for B, and so on. See Figures Graph.2 and Graph.4 where legends have been added to clearly show the identity of each of the data ranges. The legends in Figure Graph.2 are contained in column A of Figure Graph.1. The legends for Figure Graph.4 are contained in column A of Figure Graph.3a.

When specifying legends, it is best to keep them under 19 characters. If the number of legends won't fit on a single line, they will wrap to a second line. Legends that extend beyond the frame will be truncated.

Scale Allows you to specify the scale you wish to use for the X-axis and the Y-axis. You can also control how the X range data is displayed along the X-axis (for line, bar, and stacked bar graphs). To set the scale of one of the axes, select that axis and then choose one of the following options:

Automatic Automatically sets the scaling to include all the data values within the graph display. This is the default setting.

Format Sets the format of the scale labels to one of the standard range formats (comma, currency, fixed, date, general, hidden, percent, +/-, scientific, text, or time). See /Range Format. Figure Graph.8 shows the present value of $100,000 per year for a term of 35 years discounted at various interest rates. The X-axis has been formatted as percentages while the Y-axis has been formatted as currency.

Indicator Determines if the scale indicator is displayed. To display the scale indicator, select Yes. To hide the scale indicator, select No. For example, if you were graphing data with values between 5 and 25, 1-2-3 would apply no scaling. However, if you were graphing numbers between 5,000 and 25,000, 1-2-3 would automatically scale the graph in units of one thousand; in addition, 1-2-3 would automatically insert a scale indicator to identify the order of magnitude—in this case, "Thousands"—between the label for the axis in question and the scale itself. Selecting No does not alter the scale selected, it just hides the scale indicator.

Lower Sets the lower limit of a manually set scale (see below). The default value is 0.

Manual Allows you to create the scale for the selected axis by setting its upper and lower limits. Only data that falls within the limits will be displayed. 1-2-3 does not warn you if one or more data points lie outside the scale range and are not being displayed.

Upper Sets the upper limit of a manually set scale. (The default is 0).

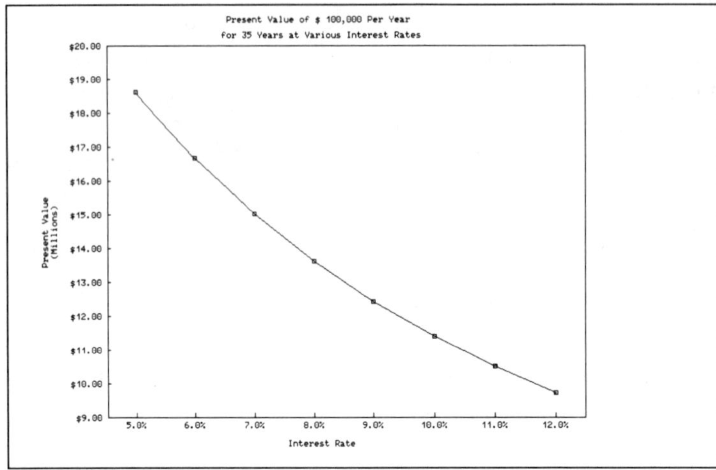

Figure Graph.8
Scale formats set to currency and percent

Skip The Skip option under the Scale menu lets you skip elements of the X range as labels on the X-axis. This can help reduce visual clutter on the X-axis. Select Skip and enter the number of values to skip. For example, if you want 1-2-3 to show only every other X range value, set a skip value of 2.

Titles Used to add titles to the top of your graph, and to its axes. When you select Titles from the Options menu, you will be presented with the following sub-menu:

First Allows you to enter the text of the top (or primary) title line.

Second Allows you to enter a secondary title line at the top of the graph.

X-Axis Allows you to enter the text for the X-axis title.

Y-Axis Allows you to enter the text for the Y-axis title.

Alternatively, you can enter a backslash (\) and a cell reference in place of the text for any of the titles. 1-2-3 will then use the contents of the referenced cell for the text of the title.

Graph Reset

Purpose

Used to clear selected settings or all graph settings and ranges back to their defaults.

Description

The reset option displays a submenu with the following options:

A–F Clears each individual data range (A to F).

Graph Resets the entire graph. Returns all settings back to the defaults.

Options Resets all the current /Graph Options settings to the program defaults.

Ranges Clears all the data ranges (X and A–F) and their corresponding labels as a group.

X Resets the X data range setting.

Usage

To clear a given range or to reset a given option, select /Graph Reset and then select the range or option you wish to reset.

Cautions

Once you have reset an option there is no way to reinstate it unless you have activated the Undo feature or have named the setting with /Graph Name Create. It is often a good idea to name the current setting to a throw-away name (our favorite is ZXC) before resetting any features. You can then restore the former setting by selecting /Graph Name Use and then specifying the throw-away name.

Graph Save

Purpose

Saves the current graph in a file format (.PIC) suitable for printing with either the PrintGraph or Allways utilities or for exporting the graph to other programs.

Description

1-2-3 saves the graph in a picture (extension .PIC) file format. The Save command saves an image of the graph in question; the resulting .PIC file contains no information about the source data range settings, options, etc. This is different from naming a graph. When you name a graph, you are saving the current graph *settings* with a name so that when you save the worksheet you will be able to use the named graph again. You should use Save to export or print a particular graph and use Name to save its settings for later re-creation with different data.

Usage

To save the current graph for printing or exportation, select /Graph Save. At the prompt, type a file name (up to eight characters). 1-2-3 will automatically supply the appropriate extension.

Examples

To save the current graph to the file GUPPIES:

1. Select /Graph Save.
2. At the prompt, type `GUPPIES` and press ENTER.

Notes

The Save option can only be used to save the current graph image for later printing or for exporting; you can not reload the graphic data back into 1-2-3. If you want to save a graph *definition* for later reference in 1-2-3, you should assign it a graph name with /Graph Name Create and then save the worksheet file.

Graph Type

Purpose

Used to select a graph type from the five basic types.

Description

The five basic graph types are described in detail in the introduction of the /Graph section. They include the Line (the program default), Bar, Stacked Bar, Pie, and XY graphs.

Usage

To select a graph type, simply select the desired type from the menu of five options.

Graph View

Purpose

Displays the current graph as a full screen display.

Description

The View option displays the current graph, and temporarily replaces the worksheet on the screen.

Notes

If you do not have a monitor capable of displaying graphics or you have selected a monitor driver that doesn't support graphics, this option will display a blank screen.

If you have not selected enough data ranges for the selected graph type or have not selected any data ranges, this option will display a blank screen.

If only titles, legends, data-labels, and the graph axes are displayed when you select /Graph View, you have probably specified scales settings that do not correspond to your data. Check that your upper and lower limits are correct.

As an alternative to selecting /Graph View, you can press the GRAPH key, F10.

Graph X

Purpose

Used to select the data range for the X-axis scale or labels.

Description

The use of the X data range will vary depending on the type of graph you have selected.

If you have selected a Line, Bar, or Stacked Bar graph, the X range will be used as the X-axis labels; they can contain either labels or values. If your labels are long enough to overlap one another along the X axis, 1-2-3 will automatically stagger them in two lines.

If you have selected an XY graph, the X range must contain values; these will be used to set the X-axis scale and to plot the corresponding values in the A–F data ranges.

If you have selected a Pie graph, the X range will be used as labels for the pie sections; they can contain either labels or values. Note that 1-2-3 automatically calculates the percentages and displays them next to the labels.

Usage

To specify the X data range for your graph, select /Graph X; then specify the range by typing in the range address or name, or by painting the range. Press ENTER.

Default

The last X range assigned.

Example

To select the X range for the data in Figure Graph.9a in order to show how the present value varies according to interest rates:

1. Select /Graph X.

2. Type `B9..B15` and press ENTER.
3. Select A.
4. Type `E9..E15` and press ENTER.
5. Select View to display the graph shown in Figure Graph.9b.

Notes

If the labels in the X-axis are placed too close together, you can use the /Graph Options Scale Skip command to force 1-2-3 to skip the display and printing of some of the labels.

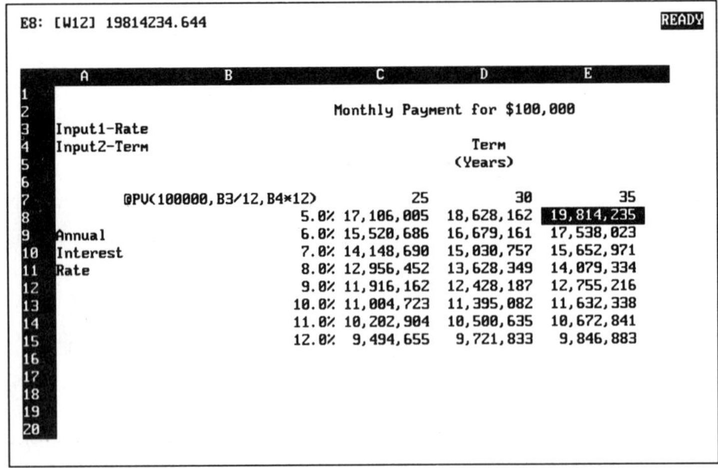

E8: [W12] 19814234.644 READY

	A	B	C	D	E
1					
2			Monthly Payment for $100,000		
3	Input1-Rate				
4	Input2-Term			Term	
5				(Years)	
6					
7		@PV(100000,B3/12,B4*12)	25	30	35
8		5.0%	17,106,005	18,628,162	19,814,235
9	Annual	6.0%	15,520,686	16,679,161	17,538,023
10	Interest	7.0%	14,148,690	15,030,757	15,652,971
11	Rate	8.0%	12,956,452	13,628,349	14,079,334
12		9.0%	11,916,162	12,428,187	12,755,216
13		10.0%	11,004,723	11,395,082	11,632,338
14		11.0%	10,202,904	10,500,635	10,672,841
15		12.0%	9,494,655	9,721,833	9,846,883
16					
17					
18					
19					
20					

Figure Graph.9a
Data for XY graph of Present values.

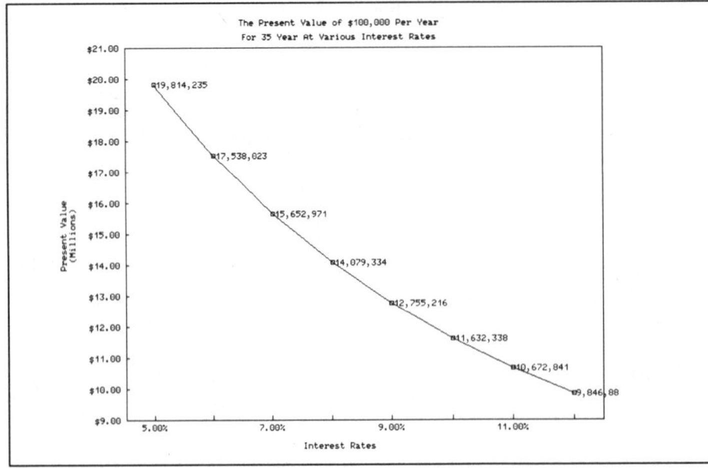

Figure Graph.9b
XY graph of Present values.

Printing Graphs with the PrintGraph Utility

Release 2.2, like its predecessors, cannot print a graph on a printer or plotter with the /Print command. Instead, you must use one of the two graph printing utilities provided with the program—PrintGraph or Allways. This section covers the PrintGraph option. The /Add-In section of the command guide discusses how to use Allways to print graphs. In general, you should use the Allways options if you can. It does require a hard disk and more memory than PrintGraph, but provides greater flexibility and the ability to combine text and graphs on the same page. In either case, you must first save the graph image to a disk file with the /Graph Save command before you can print it. /Graph Save creates a .PIC file that contains the image of the graph; the .PIC file does not contain any reference to the graph settings or the worksheet in which it was created. If you change the data or the graph format, you must resave the graph image to disk in order to print the new image. (Use a new file name if you want to keep the earlier graph image, or the same filename if you want to overwrite the previous .PIC file.)

After you have saved the graph image to disk, you must leave 1-2-3 by selecting the /Quit option. Be sure to save your worksheet to disk before you exit from 1-2-3. If you started 1-2-3 directly from the operating system, you will be returned to the operating system. If you started 1-2-3 from the Lotus Access System, you will be returned to the Access System main menu. In the former case, start PrintGraph by typing `PGRAPH` at the system prompt. In the latter case, start PrintGraph, simply by selecting it from the Access main menu. If you wish, you can also load the Access System from the DOS prompt; type `Lotus` at the system prompt and then select PrintGraph from the Access System main menu.

Once PrintGraph has been started, you will be presented with the main menu of the PrintGraph system. See Figure Graph.10.

The PrintGraph utility works in much the same fashion as the /Print command. You must first select what you want to print with the Image-Select option, then select the Align option to align the printer, select Go to start printing, and then Page to eject the page. In addition, the PrintGraph utility provides many options for fine-tuning the printing process. For example, you can control the size, orientation, colors, and fonts used to print an individual graph. Unlike the /Print command, you can select multiple .PIC files to be printed in sequence. The PrintGraph commands include:

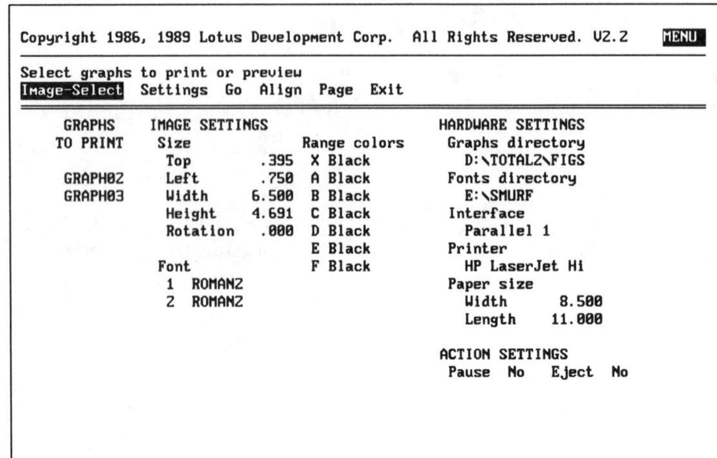

Figure Graph.10
PrintGraph Main Menu.

Image-Select Used to select one or more graphs from the default directory for printing.

Settings Used to specify your printer or plotter type, your default directories, and many of the physical parameters of the printing process such as paper size, colors, and rotation.

Go Used to initiate the printing of the selected graph(s) with the selected options.

Align Used to reset the internal logical page to the top of the page.

Page Used to eject the current page from the printer and re-align the logical page to the top of form.

Exit Used to exit the PrintGraph utility program.

The following sections describe each of the PrintGraph commands in sequence.

Notes

It is not possible to alter the contents of a graph from within PrintGraph. You must return to 1-2-3, modify the graph as desired, resave the graph, exit 1-2-3, and restart PrintGraph.

PrintGraph Align

Purpose

Used to reset the internal logical page to the top of the page.

Description

Internally, 1-2-3 keeps track of how many lines it has sent to the printer and determines when it has reached the end of a page. It will automatically eject the page when it reaches the end of its logical (or internal) page. In order to ensure that 1-2-3's logical page corresponds to the physical page in your printer, you must reset the logical page with PrintGraph's Align each time you adjust the physical page during the PrintGraph session. Thus, whenever you manually eject a page from the printer or realign your paper in the printer, you must also instruct 1-2-3 to reset its logical page with the Align command; this is 1-2-3's internal equivalent to realigning the paper in your printer. If you eject the physical page via the Page option on the /PrintGraph menu discussed below, 1-2-3 automatically aligns to the top of the next logical page.

Defaults

None.

Usage

To reset 1-2-3 to the top of the logical page, select Align.

Notes

Some printers keep track of the page line count on their own; they, like 1-2-3, maintain a logical (or internal) page scheme. If you manually adjust the paper in such printers, you must then be sure that the printer is reset to the top of its logical page as well as aligning 1-2-3 to the top of *its* logical page. This is ususally done by pressing the Top of Form, Form Feed, or Reset button on your printer. This way, the physical paper, and the two logical pages (the printer's and 1-2-3's) are synchronized. If your printer continues to insert "false page breaks" in the middle of printing out your graphs, you may have to deactivate the printer's automatic page break feature. See your printer's manual for more information about your printer.

PrintGraph Exit

Purpose

Used to exit the PrintGraph utility program.

Description

If you started PrintGraph from the system prompt, the Exit option will return you to the system. If you started it from the Lotus Access system, the Exit option will return you to the Access Main Menu.

Defaults

None.

Usage

To exit from PrintGraph, select Exit.

PrintGraph Go

Purpose

Used to initiate the printing of the selected graph(s) with the selected options.

Description

The Go option is the primary action command of the PrintGraph utility. All other PrintGraph commands (except Page and Exit) simply establish your selections for various hardware and style or format options. Until you select the Go option, nothing happens. When you do select Go, the selected graphs will be sent to the selected printer with the selected options.

Defaults

The currently selected graphs, printer or plotter, and settings.

Usage

Before you select the Go option, you must first be sure to select the graphs you wish to print and establish the desired print settings. To start printing the selected graphs, choose the Go option.

Notes

If you are printing on a network, you may have to issue a Page command after the Go command to complete a prior print job and to initiate printing.

To stop the printing of a given graph, press CTRL-BREAK. Do not turn the printer off.

PrintGraph Image—Select

Purpose

Used to select one or more graphs from the default directory for printing.

Description

The Image-Select option allows you to specify which graphs are to be printed by the subsequent Go command. You can select one or more graphs from the current directory. Selected graphs will be printed in the order of selection.

Defaults

Only graphs from the current directory can be selected for a single print job.

Usage

To select graphs, initiate the command by selecting Image-Select. You will be presented with a list of all the graph files (.PIC extension) in the current directory. You can mark one or more graph files by highlighting the file name and pressing the SPACE-BAR. A pound sign (#) will be placed to the left of the selected graph name. You can "unselect" a given graph by rehighlighting its name and pressing the SPACE-BAR again. When you are satisfied with the selected graphs, confirm your selection by pressing ENTER.

Notes

If you want to select graphs from a different directory, use the PrintGraph Settings Hardware Graphs-Directory command to change the current directory. (Note, however, that you can only print graphs from one directory at a time.)

To preview a particular graph, highlight its name and press the GRAPH (F10) key. The selected graph will be displayed on the screen, temporarily replacing the PrintGraph menu. Press ESC to return to PrintGraph. The graph displayed on the screen may not correspond exactly to the options you have selected, since many of these options cannot be displayed on the screen (e.g., special fonts, rotation, and so on).

PrintGraph Page

Purpose

Used to eject the current page from the printer and re-align the logical page to the top of form.

Description

The Page command both ejects the current page from the printer and resets the logical page to the top of the form.

Defaults

None.

Usage

The Page command is especially useful with page printers such as laser and inkjet printers. These printers will not begin to physically print a new page until the complete page has been transmitted to the printer. PrintGraph's Page command finishes the current page by issuing as many line feeds as necessary to complete the page and to advance the paper to the top of the next page. (The actual line count per page is determined by the page length setting—PrintGraph Settings Hardware Size-Paper).

Notes

If you manually eject the page from the printer by pressing the Form Feed button, you must be sure to re-align the logical page by selecting the Align option before you issue the next Go command.

PrintGraph Settings

Purpose

Used to specify your printer or plotter type, your default directories, and many of the physical parameters of the printing process such as paper size, colors, and rotation. You cannot alter the contents of the graphs through the Settings menu.

Description

The Settings options allow you to establish alternative settings for printing the selected graphs. (Your current settings are displayed onscreen when you load PrintGraph.) The initial options are saved in a configuration file called PGRAPH.CNF. You can alter various settings and use them temporarily—for a particular session—without saving them. The next time you load PrintGraph, you will revert to the old defaults. Alternatively, you can change your settings and save them to the PGRAPH.CNF file with the Save option. Thereafter, each time you load PrintGraph, the new settings will be the defaults until you alter them again.

Each of the major Settings options are discussed separately below. They are as follows:

Action Determines whether PrintGraph should automatically eject the page after each graph.

Hardware Specifies the printer type, the printer interface (parallel or serial), the paper size, the directory containing the font files, and the current directory for graph files.

Image Allows you to control the graph size, margins, rotation, fonts, and colors.

Quit Exits the Settings menu.

Reset Resets the current settings to those contained in the default PGRAPH.CNF configuration file.

Save Saves the current settings to the PGRAPH.CNF configuration file.

Notes

PrintGraph prints all selected graphs with the current settings. If you want to print various graphs with different settings, you must select the first graph or group of graphs, establish the desired settings and select Go. Then select the next group of graphs, alter the settings as desired, and select Go a second time. Repeat this process for each desired group and setting. At any time you can instantly change the current settings back to your default (saved) settings with the Reset option.

If you do not save the current settings to the PGRAPH.CNF configuration file with the Save option, when you next load PrintGraph it will revert to the settings you had previously saved as your default.

PrintGraph Settings Action

Purpose

Determines whether PrintGraph should eject the page after each graph and whether it should pause after printing each graph so that you can insert a new page or change the printer/plotter settings.

Description

The Action Eject option allows you to specify if PrintGraph should print each graph on a separate page. If you select Eject Yes, 1-2-3 will automatically eject the current page at the end of the current graph. If you are using continuous paper, it starts the next graph on a new page. If you are using single sheets, it will prompt you for the next piece of paper. If you select Eject No, 1-2-3 will not eject the current page and will print the next graph immediately below it. If 1-2-3 determines that your next graph will not fit on the current page, it will eject the current page regardless of the action setting.

The Action Pause option allows you to specify if PrintGraph should pause before each graph to allow you to change paper, pens, or otherwise adjust the printer or plotter. If you select Yes, 1-2-3 will pause. If you select No, 1-2-3 will not pause.

Defaults

No eject.

No pause.

Usage

The Action commands are most commonly used with plotters or sheet-fed printers that require a page eject at the end of each page or require that you manually adjust each page. You would also use the Pause option if you needed to change settings or pens on a plotter.

To force a page eject at the end of each graph, select Settings Action Eject Yes.

To cause 1-2-3 to pause before each graph, select Settings Action Pause Yes.

To return to the main Settings menu, select Quit.

Notes

In a network environment, the Action Pause Yes command has *no* effect on the printer. It will appear to pause on the screen, but it will not actually stop the printing process.

PrintGraph Settings Hardware

Purpose

Used to specify your printer type, the printer interface, your page length and width, the directory containing the font files, and the current directory for graph files.

Description

The Hardware option is somewhat of a misnomer, since it sets not only printer specifications, but also the default directories for your font and graph files. In general, you will only need to set your printer/plotter specification once (unless you change your hardware). On the other hand, if you use several different directories for your worksheet and graph files, you may need to change the current directory setting for your graph files quite often. There are several different sub-options under the Hardware option as follows:

Fonts-Directory This option is used to specify which directory (and/or drive) contains your font files (*.FNT). PrintGraph uses the font files to create the font faces and sizes that appear in graph titles, legends, etc. On a hard-disk system, 1-2-3 expects that you have stored your font files in the same directory as the 1-2-3 program files (e.g., C:\123). If you are using a two-diskette system, you must insert the PrintGraph disk containing the font files in one of the two drives and you must specify the selected drive (e.g., A:\).

Graphs-Directory This option allows you to specify which drive and directory contains the graph files you wish to print. Graph-Directory is probably the Hardware option that you will change most often if you keep your various graph files in several different subdirectories. (This may be an incentive to store all your .PIC files in one directory.) If, for example, you have stored your graph files on a floppy disk, you must specify the drive containing the data disk (e.g., B:\). If you have stored your graph files in a subdirectory called \123data on your C: drive, you would set the Graphs-Directory to C:\123data.

Interface The interface option allows you to specify which of the eight ports to use for the graph output. Options 1–4 should be used for printers physically attached to the computer, while options 5–8 should be used for logical printers (LPT1 through LPT4) attached to a network.

Options	Port
1	Parallel 1
2	Serial 1
3	Parallel 2
4	Serial 2
5	LPT 1
6	LPT 2
7	LPT 3
8	LPT 4

If you select one of the serial ports (options 2 or 4), you will also need to specify a Baud rate (or the speed in bits per second—you can select from 110 to 19,200) that corresponds to your printer setting. Be sure, also, that the serial port is itself properly initialized to the same baud rate with the DOS MODE command. Furthermore, you must ensure that the printer is set to 8 Data bits, 1 Stop bit, and Parity equal to None. (If you are using 110 Baud, you should use 2 Stop bits). These settings cannot be altered in PrintGraph, so you must be sure that the printer and the port conform to them.

Printer The Printer option allows you to select from among the graphics printers you specified during the installation process. You must have installed a graphics-capable printer in order to print graphs. If you have installed more than one graphics printer, you can select from among them by highlighting the desired printer and pressing the space-bar key. A pound sign (#) will appear next to the selected printer. You can unselect the printer by pressing the SPACE-BAR a second time or select another printer by highlighting the new printer and pressing the SPACE-BAR. After you have selected the printer you wish to use, confirm your choice and return to the Hardware submenu by pressing the ENTER key.

Quit Exits the Hardware submenu and returns to the Settings menu.

Size-Paper Allows you to specify the size of the paper you are using. The default size is 8 1/2 by 11 inches. To change the length, select Length and enter the new length. To change the width, select Width and enter the new width. If you are using continuous feed paper, you must make sure that the form length on the printer conforms to the paper length as well.

PrintGraph Settings Image

Purpose

Used to alter the physical properties of the graph image, including the fonts, color, size, margins, and rotation.

Description

While you cannot alter the contents of the graph within the PrintGraph program (you must return to 1-2-3 to alter these), you can control many of the features affecting its appearance. They are as follows:

Font Allows you to specify two different fonts: one for the top line of the title and one for all other titles, legends and labels. Figure Graph.11 shows the different font options. Figure Graph.12 shows the same graph as in Figure Graph.2 but printed using the Block1 font. Figure Graph.13 shows the same data using Roman2 and Roman1 fonts.

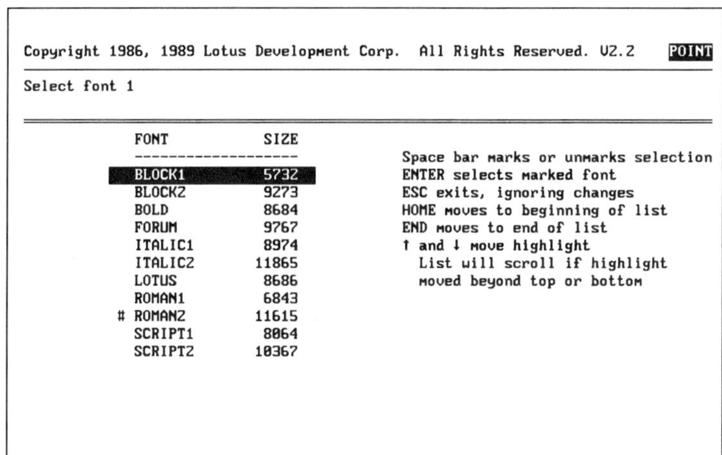

Figure Graph.11
PrintGraph Font Options.

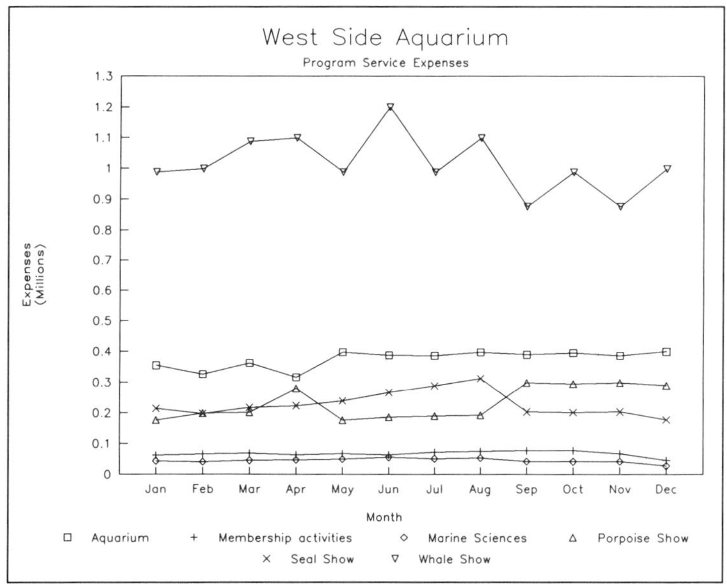

Figure Graph.12
PrintGraph Output using Block1 font.

If you do not specify a second font option, PrintGraph will use the first font option for all text in the graph. Fonts with similar names followed by different numbers have the same face but use different stroke weights. For example, Italics2 has the same face as Italics1, but is heavier and darker. The heavier, second face option is best used on high-resolution printers.

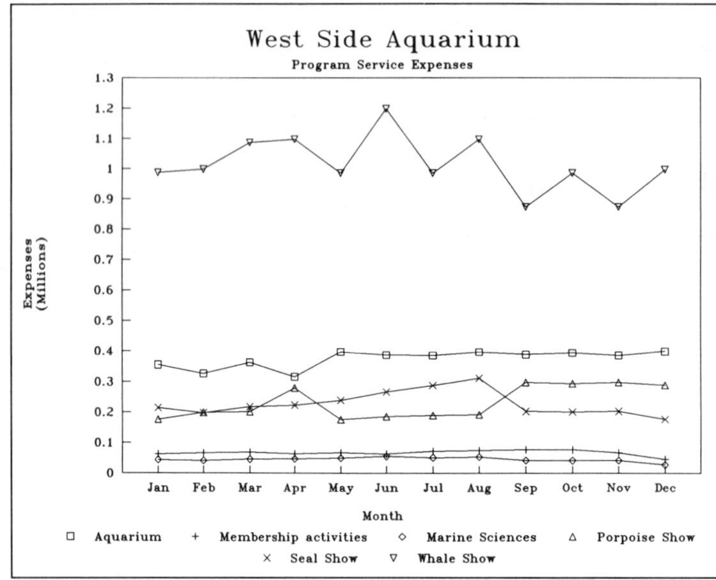

Figure Graph.13 PrintGraph Output using Roman2 and Roman1.

In general, the Block fonts are most reliable on dot-matrix printers. If your printer can be set to high density, the Roman, Forum, and Bold fonts can come out well also. Italic and Script fonts, however, are usually not recommended for dot-matrix printers. Note that PrintGraph can only use its own fonts, and not those of your printer.

To select a font, you must first select Font #1 or Font #2 (#1 is used for the first line of title, #2 all else). Then highlight the desired font and press the SPACE-BAR. A pound sign (#) will appear next to the font name. Press ENTER to confirm your choice. If you want to change your selection, simply highlight another font name and press the SPACE-BAR a second time. If you are using a two diskette system, be sure that your PrintGraph disk is located in the drive you specified as the Fonts-Directory under PrintGraph Setting Hardware Fonts-Directory. If you are using a hard disk system, be sure that you have copied the specified font file (.FNT) into the directory specified under PrintGraph Setting Hardware Fonts-Directory.

Quit Exits the Image option back to the Settings menu.

Range-Colors Allows you to assign different colors to the different data ranges for printers or plotters that can print in color. You must select a color printer via the Settings Hardware Printer option before you can select colors. If your printer or plotter will not print in color, you will only be offered the color black as an option. If you printer or plotter can print in color, only the supported colors will be offered as options. You can select a color for each data range (and its corresponding legend): X and A–F. Your selection for the X range will also be used for the graph frame or grid and all labels—except legends. To select a color, first select the range to be assigned, and then select a color from among those offered.

If you are printing a pie chart in color, the colors are controlled differently: by the numerical values that you assigned in the B range within 1-2-3 (see Graph /A–F) *and* the colors assigned to the data ranges under PrintGraph Settings Image Range-Colors. The B range values also determine what hatching patterns to use (in black and white) and whether the pie slice is exploded. Check the values you assigned in your B range. Thus, when PrintGraph determines what color to use, PrintGraph uses the color assigned to range X for B range values of 1 and 101, A for 2 and 102, C for 3 and 103, and so on. Therefore, you can assign the hatching pattern (1-8), the explosion factor by adding 100, and the color by assigning the desired color to the associated data range.

Image-Size Allows you to specify the size of the graph. You have three options—Full, Half, and Manual:

Full Prints one full size graph per page in landscape mode (rotation = 90 degrees). Prints the largest graph that will fit on an 11 × 8 1/2 sheet of paper. Increasing the paper size will not alter the graph.

Half Prints two half size graphs per page in portrait mode (rotation = 0 degrees). Prints the largest graph that will fit between the left and right margins of an 8 1/2 × 11 sheet of paper, allowing two graphs to be printed on a single sheet. Altering the paper size will not alter the graph size.

Manual Allows you to specify the Height, Width, Left and Top margins in inches. Also allows you to specify the rotation in degrees (counter-clockwise). When setting the dimensions manually, you may want to preserve the standard aspect ratio (the ratio of width to height) of 1.385 to 1. The formula for calculating a width for a given height would be:

Width = 1.385 × Height

The formula for calculating a height for a given width would be:

Height = Width ÷ 1.385

The heights and widths are always determined in relation to the physical paper. If you rotate the graph 90 or 270 degrees, you must interchange the height and width values to maintain the same aspect ratio. If you rotate the graph by some other angle, you must modify the height and ratio to produce square corners and round pies otherwise your graph will be printed as a rhomboid or an ellipse. Figure Graph.14 shows the same graph as shown in Figure Graph.13 rotated 45 degrees to the left. Note the rhomboid shape.

Quit Exits the Settings menu and returns to the main PrintGraph menu.

Reset Allows you to reset all the graph settings to the settings last saved to the PrintGraph configuration file (PGRAPH.CNF) via the Save option.

Save Saves the current graph settings to the PrintGraph configuration file (PGRAPH.CNF). The next time you load PrintGraph, these settings will be used as the defaults. Once you have configured PrintGraph with your desired options (e.g., colors, size, fonts, and rotation) you should save the settings to the configuration file with the Save option. If you are using a two diskette system, you must be sure to place the PrintGraph disk into the designated drive without write protection, before invoking the Save command.

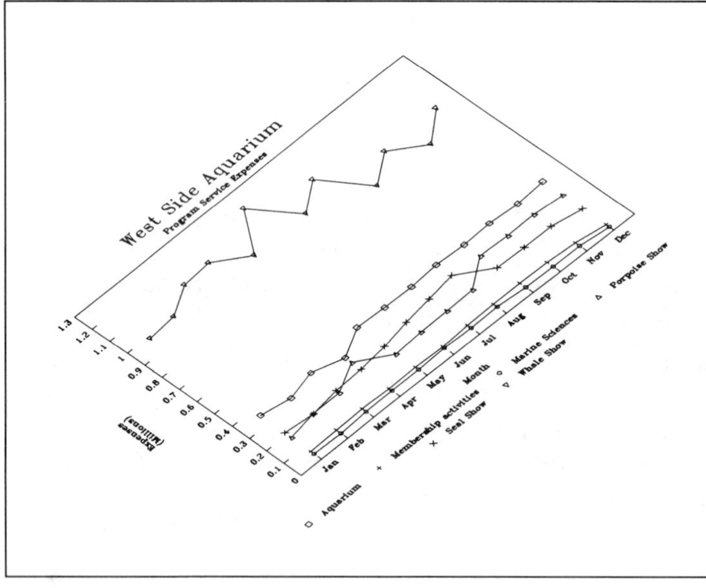

Figure Graph.14
Graph rotated 45°.

▸ Move Commands

Purpose

Used to move (or transfer) a cell or range of cells from one location to a new location in the worksheet.

Description

/Move physically transfers data from one range to another. The source range is left empty. The moved data will overwrite any data in the target range.

Unlike the /Copy command, which takes all relative or mixed cell addresses in the source range and adapts them to the new location, /Move works to keep your original data intact, making as few changes as possible. /Move makes no change to any formulas in the source range that refer to other parts of the worksheet. The formula results are therefore still accurate in the new location. 1-2-3 will update formulas (inside and outside the source range) that contain references to data within the range being moved—again, so that results remain accurate.

The logic and convenience of the /Move command is simple to grasp in theory. In practice, however, it can have unexpected results. You should avoid moving data into any cell that is a defining cell for a formula range or for a named range (i.e., the left or lower-right corner). Otherwise, the formula will evaluate to ERR and the named range will lose its definition. Similarly, if you move data that includes a defining cell for a formula range or for a range name, the resulting formula address will be expanded or contracted accordingly. See Cautions for details.

Defaults

Current cell.

Usage

The /Move command follows the 1-2-3 standard prompt structure: You are first asked what you wish to move (the FROM cell or range) and then asked to specify where you wish to move it (the TO cell or range). If you are moving a single cell, you can make use of the current cell default to facilitate the specification of the source cell.

Single Cell Position the cell pointer on the cell that you wish to move (the source cell). Initiate the /Move command by pressing /M. You are prompted for the range to be moved—the FROM range. Simply press the ENTER key to select the current cell default as the source cell. 1-2-3 will prompt you for the new target location—the TO range. Either move the cell pointer to the target location or type in the new cell address or range name of the target location. Press ENTER to complete the command. The contents of the source cell will be moved to the target cell.

Range of Cells Position the cell pointer on the cell marking the upper-left corner of the range of cells you wish to move (the FROM range). Initiate the /Move command by pressing /M. Either move the cell pointer to paint the range to be moved or enter the complete cell address or name of the range of cells to be moved and press ENTER. Move the cell pointer to the upper-left corner of the target (TO) range, or enter the address or the name of the cell in the upper-left corner of the target range, then press ENTER a second time.

Examples

To move the contents of the current cell to the target location (see Figures Move.1a–c), use the following sequence:

1. Select /Move.
2. Press ENTER.
3. Move the cell pointer to target location.
4. Press ENTER.

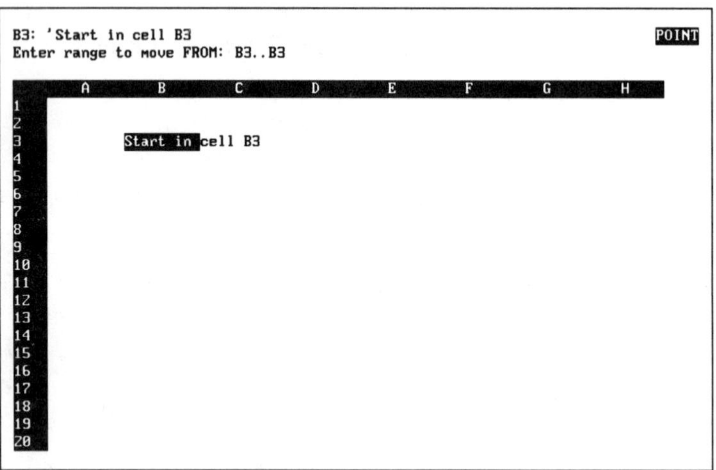

Figure Move.1a
Specifying the FROM Range.

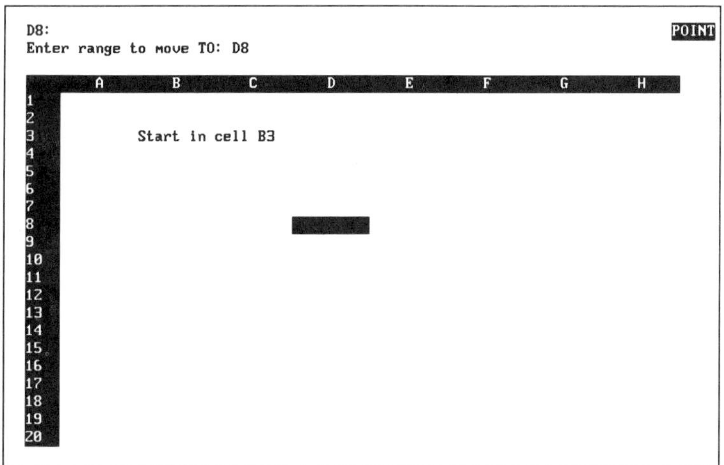

Figure Move.1b

Specifying the TO Range.

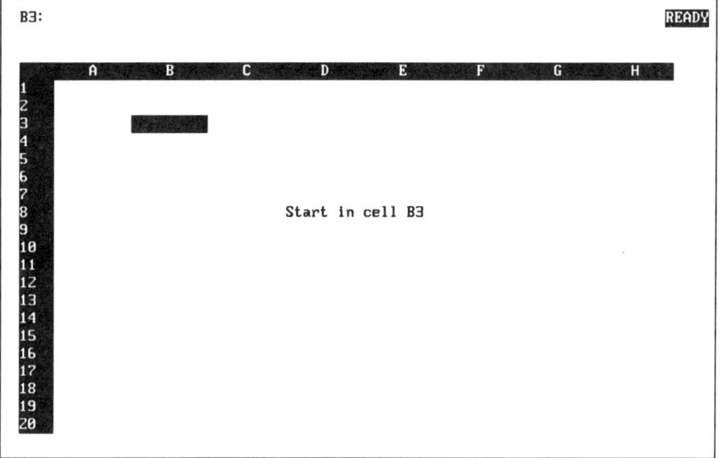

Figure Move.1c

Results of the /Move command.

To move the range of cells A14..E17 to the range of equivalent size starting with cell C47 in the upper-left corner, use the following steps:

1. Select /Move.
2. Type `A14..E17` and press ENTER.
3. Type `C47` and press ENTER.

To move the range named SHARKS to the range of equivalent size starting in the upper-left corner of the range named FISH, use:

1. Select /Move.
2. Type `SHARKS` and press ENTER.
3. Type `FISH` and press ENTER.

Notes

It is critical to understand the difference in the way that /Copy and /Move handle formulas with relative addresses. /Copy automatically adjusts the relative addresses to the new location, while /Move does not. The /Move command does not alter any formulas in the source (or FROM) range that refer to data in other parts of the worksheet. Conversely, any formulas that refer to the moved data automatically are changed to reflect the new location.

Cautions

1. If you move the first or last cell of a range that is referenced by a formula, the range referenced in the formula will be automatically altered to correspond to the new location. This can create gross inaccuracies. Also, if you move data on top of the first or last cells of a range that is referenced in a formula, 1-2-3 changes the range in the formula to ERR and the formula will evaluate to ERR. If a named range was referenced in the formula, 1-2-3 will retain the name in the formula, but will consider it an undefined range, again evaluating the formula as ERR until it is later redefined.

   For example, in Figure Move.2a the formula in cell C14 sums the range from C8..C12. Suppose you realized you had made a data entry error in cell C8; the value 2 should have been placed in column D for February instead of column C for January. January's values should have been 5. It would seem simple enough to move the value from C8 to cell D8 and reenter the value 5 in cell C8. But look what happens in Figure Move.2b. The formula in cell C14 has had its range expanded to include column D as well, producing an erroneous value, while the formula in D14 shows as ERR since one of the end points of its range has been overwritten by the /Move command.

2. The /Move command will overwrite existing data without providing any warning. Be sure that the target location is large enough to accommodate the source range before initiating the command.

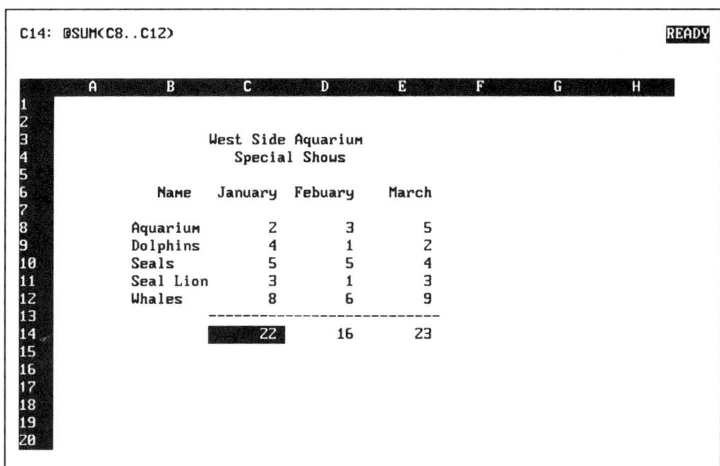

Figure Move.2a
Worksheet before /Move command.

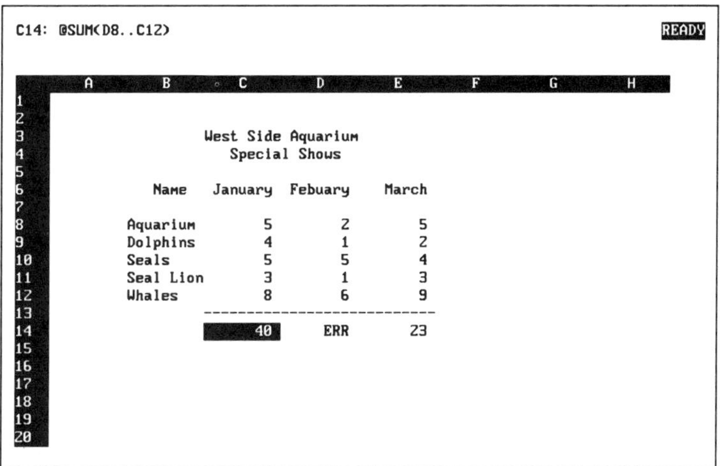

Figure Move.2b
Erroneous results produced by moving a range's end point on top of another range.

▸ Print Commands

Purpose

Used to print out all or parts of your worksheet data. You may print directly to a printer or create a print file on disk. To print with variable fonts and other enhancement features, you may want to use the Allways print utility. To print graphs, you must use the PrintGraph or Allways utility.

Description

Use the /Print menu when you want to create a permanent, hard-copy record of your worksheet or range. The /Print commands allow you to specify which range is to be printed and what device you wish to print to. They also control how the printed output will appear; for example, you can specify your margins, borders, headers and footers, and format.

In addition to printing directly to printers or plotters for hard copy output, 1-2-3 will print to ASCII print (or text) files for easy export to other programs. You can install multiple printer drivers and select from among them when you print.

When you initiate the /Print command and select a destination device (see below), 1-2-3 will display the current print settings on the screen (see Figure Print.1). You can alter any of the settings via the various print options described below.

Style Note

The first level of the /Print menu offers two output options: Printer or File. You *must* select one of these before you can access the main Print menu and any further

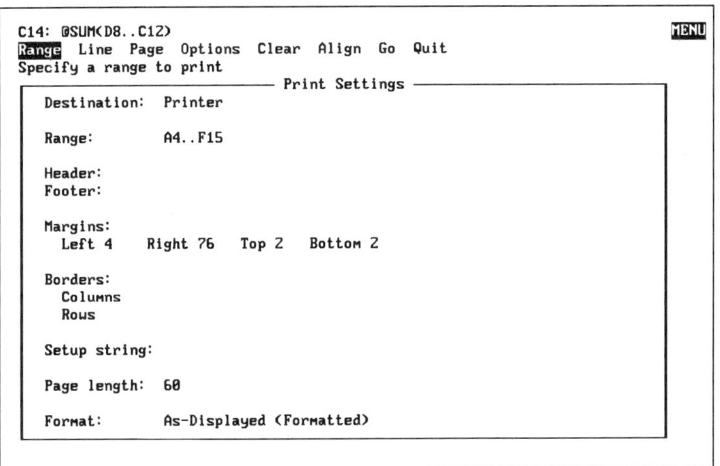

Figure Print.1
Print Settings Screen.

print options. We will represent this stage in the command selection process as [Printer or File]. Thus, the command /Print [Printer or File] Range tells you to select Print, then one of the output options File or Printer, and then Range.

Key Terms

Print Job Other versions of Lotus 1-2-3 (Release 3 in particular) have assigned a special meaning to the term print job as it relates to the background print spooler included with that version. For Release 2.2, however, the term print job has a far more generalized meaning—a set of individual print requests issued in sequence.

Since Release 2.2 can only print a single range at a time, it is quite common to string several print requests together to form a collective print job. The individual elements are not linked in any way except that they will generally use the same print options, will share a sequential set of page numbers (reset with the Align command), and will print out in sequence. You can control the spacing between each range with the Line and Page options.

Print Destination The device or file to which 1-2-3 sends the printed output. You must select a print destination before you can execute a print request. If you select Printer, the current default printer (see below) will be the destination. If you select File, to send your output to a text (ASCII) file, you will be prompted to type in a file name for the print destination. The print destination is also called the *destination device.*

Default Printer The printer that 1-2-3 will use for print jobs directed to the printer. Initially, the default printer will be the first printer installed during the installation process. You can change the default printer with the /Worksheet Global Default Printer Name command.

Current Printer The printer most recently selected in the current 1-2-3 session. At the start of each 1-2-3 session, your default printer is the current printer. You can select another installed printer (instead of the default) as your current printer with the /Worksheet Global Default Printer Name command. When you direct a print job to a printer, 1-2-3 always uses the current printer. If you do not save the new selection with the Update option, 1-2-3 will revert to the old printer when you next load the program.

Print Driver The command file (unique to each printer) that informs 1-2-3 how to control the various print features of a particular printer. For example, the HP LaserJet print driver instructs 1-2-3 how to specify bold or compressed text fonts for the LaserJet, or how to draw lines or other graphics. When you select a printer (or printers) during installation, 1-2-3 copies the necessary print driver(s) to your system disk or hard disk and assigns a name to it (or them). You can then select the appropriate print driver by name.

Print Settings You can specify many different features for a given print job, including margins, headers, footers, page length, and range format. Together these specifications make up the print settings for that print job. Once you have specified a setting, it is saved with the worksheet and remains the default for all future print jobs in that worksheet until you specify another setting. When you choose /Print [Printer or File], a window showing your current print settings appears on screen.

Text File The text and numerical data in a print job can be directed to an ASCII file on disk. ASCII text files *cannot* contain any special printer command codes (or setup strings); they are generic files that can be printed by most any printer. ASCII text files are most often used to transfer data from 1-2-3 to other programs that can also read ASCII files. When spreadsheets are saved as ASCII text files, much of the information about the physical layout of the file is lost.

Logical Page 1-2-3 keeps track of the number of lines that it sends to the printer or to the file. Thus, it is able to automatically insert headers, footers, borders, and page breaks when required, as well as increment the page number. Because it keeps track of the current print position at any time, 1-2-3 maintains its own internal line and page count defined by the options you have specified. This is its "logical page" or reference page. Whenever you alter any print format options, you alter this logical page as well. So, if you change from standard size to legal size paper in your printer, you are increasing the number of *physical* lines per page; you must tell 1-2-3 to increase its *logica*l page size as well. Most importantly, you must insure that 1-2-3 is aligned on its logical page in the same way that the printer is aligned on the physical page. For example, if you manually eject a page from your printer and then re-align the printer to the top of the next page, you must also tell 1-2-3 to re-align itself to the top of its logical page using the /Print [Printer or File] Align option.

Examples

There are two fundamental printing options: printing to a device (Printer) or to a text file (File) [Printer or File]. With either of these two primary options, you can print a range of data from your worksheet. We will look at simple examples of several of these print operations before we discuss each /Print option in detail.

Printing a Data Range on a Printer To print the data range A1..F14 in Figure Print.1:

1. Select /Print Printer to print to the printer.
2. Select Range to specify a range.
3. Define the print range. Type (or paint) `A1..F14` and press ENTER.
4. Check the printer to be sure that it is on-line and the paper is properly aligned to top of physical page.
5. Select Align to reset the logical top of page.
6. Select Go to execute the print request.
7. Select Quit to exit the print menu.

Print a Range to a Text File To print a range to a text file, simply select the File option instead of the Printer option at the top of the /Print menu tree. You will be prompted to type in a file name for the file, or to highlight an existing ASCII text file (ending with the .PRN extension). Otherwise the process is the same as printing a range on a printer. To print the range A1..F14 to the file ATTPRINT.PRN:

1. Select /Print File to print to a file.
2. At the prompt type in the text file name `ATTPRINT` and press ENTER.
3. Select Range to specify a range.
4. Type (or paint) `A1..F14` and press ENTER.
5. Select Align to reset the logical top of page.
6. Select Go to execute the print request.
7. Select Quit to leave the print menu.

Notes

The Allways worksheet publishing utility provides many features to enhance your printed output. Compared to 1-2-3's /Print command, the Allways utility is often easier to use for the same printed results; in addition, Allways provides a broad range of features and effects that are very difficult or even impossible to create with the /Print command. For example, you can easily combine text and graphics on the same page. Because of its simplicity and its added features, we recommend that you learn how to use the Allways utility right away. You will quickly find that you will almost always use it instead of the /Print command. See the beginning of the Reference section for more information about Allways.

Print FIle

Purpose

Used to print to an ASCII text file on disk. The text file *cannot* contain any of the printer formatting codes that you usually issue with the /Print Printer Options Setup command. Use the /Print File option when you want to transfer data from a 1-2-3 worksheet to another program that can read ASCII files.

Description

The ASCII file produced by /Print File contains only alphanumeric characters, spaces, and hard carriage returns.

Defaults

The current print range and option settings.

Usage

To print a range to an ASCII text file, select /Print File; type in the file name at the prompt (or point to an existing file name that you wish to overwrite) and press ENTER. 1-2-3 automatically assigns a .PRN extension to the file. You can subsititute your own extension (but we do not recommend that). Select the range to be printed with the Range option, align the logical page with Align, and execute the print command with Go. If you wish to add other print ranges to the text file, specify each range consecutively, (using the Range option, followed each time by the Go option). Specify your ranges in the order that you wish them to appear. Select Quit to close the print job.

Examples

To print the range OTTER_TEXT to an ASCII text file OTTER.PRN:

1. Select /Print File.
2. Type `OTTER` and press ENTER.
3. Select the Range option, type `OTTER_TEXT` and press ENTER.
4. Select Align to align the logical top of page.
5. Select Go to execute the print request.
6. Select Quit to exit the print menu and save the print file.

Notes

1. Because ASCII text files do not contain any print formatting codes (and thus any setup strings that you may have specified in 1-2-3), they are independent of the currently selected printer.
2. If you are printing a series of ranges, you may wish to include a few line feeds between ranges to add some spacing. (Do this by selecting the Line option once or twice after you issue the Go command for each range.)
3. You may also want to suppress all headers, footers, and page breaks as well as margins when you print to a text file. This way long lines in the print range are not broken. Use the Options Other Unformatted option, and the Options Margin None option to do so.

Print Printer

Purpose

Used to print one or more ranges to the current printer. Printer is the more usual of the two print destination options.

Description

The /Print Printer command directs the current print job to your printer. If you selected drivers for more than one text printer during the installation, the print job will go to the current default printer (specified under the /Worksheet Global Default Printer Name option).

Defaults

The current printer, print range, and options.

Usage

To print a range to the currently selected printer, select /Print Printer. Select Range to define the range to be printed. Align the logical top of page by selecting Align and execute the print request by selecting Go. Select Quit to exit the Print menu.

Examples

To print the range A1..H25 to the current printer:

1. Select /Print Printer.
2. Select Range, type (or paint) `A1..H25` and press ENTER.
3. Select Align to align the logical top of page.

4. Select Go to execute the print request.
5. Exit the print menu by selecting Quit.

Notes

You can change the selected printer by changing the default printer with /Worksheet Global Default Printer Name.

Cautions

Do *not* select Printer as the print destination unless the selected printer driver matches the installed printer. If you mix up drivers and physical printers, you can produce bizarre results as your printer tries to interpret printer command codes intended for a different type of printer. If your printer is printing gibberish, check that the selected printer matches the physical printer and that the communi- cations parameters are set correctly for the serial interface, if you are using one. You can display the printer selection by selecting /Worksheet Global Default Status.

Print [Printer or File] Align

Purpose

Used to re-align 1-2-3's logical top of page. Align resets the logical line count to 0 and page number to one. Align insures that all headers, footers, and page breaks will be properly positioned. Check when you select Align that your printer too is physically aligned at the top of page.

Description

Align performs the logical (or internal) equivalent of aligning the paper in your printer. 1-2-3 keeps track of how many lines it has printed and knows to insert page breaks, etc. when it reaches the end of each logical page. If you do not reset 1-2-3's logical page when you start a print job, 1-2-3 will print out the new job, basing its internal line count on the count left over from the previous job. When you select Align, be sure that your printer is likewise aligned. Most printers will align themselves automatically if you eject the last page with a Page command or by issuing a form feed. If you manually move the page in the printer, you will probably have to manually re-align it as well.

Usage

To re-align 1-2-3 to the top of logical page number one, select /Print [Printer or File] Align.

Examples

After printing a half-page report, you ejected it manually from your printer (i.e., using the printer's line feed button). You now need to prepare for a new report on a new page:

1. Re-align the paper in the printer so that the printer will start at the top of a new page.
2. Select /Print [Printer or File] Align.

Notes

Suppose you are printing several half-page ranges to a print file, and you want each range to be printed on a new page one. Between each Go command you must select Page (to eject the page) and then Align to reset the page number and start on the next page. If you are printing to a file, and have specified that your output is unformatted, Align has no effect.

Print [Printer or File] Clear

Purpose

Used to reset various print options (or all of them at once) to their default settings.

Description

The Clear option clears the current settings for one or more print options; the settings are reset to their defaults. You can reset print options one by one or reset them all at once. You can select to clear the following options:

All Clears the current print range; clears all headers, footers, and borders; resets the format and print options to their global defaults.

Borders Clears all specified borders.

Format Resets the margins, page length, and setup string to their defaults.

Range Clears the current print range.

Defaults

None.

Examples

This is an example to clear the specified borders so that they no longer print:

1. Select /Print [Printer or File] Clear Borders.

Notes

The /Print [Printer or File] Clear command menu does *not* include every possible print option as a separate selection. Thus in some cases, it is easiest to reselect a particular print feature, and reset it manually. For example, the only way to reset a header from the Clear menu is to Clear All. It is much simpler to reselect the header option, delete the existing header and avoid losing all your other settings.

On the other hand, the Clear menu is the only way to reset some print option settings such as Borders.

Clear resets your print option settings to their global defaults. It is possible to alter many of the global defaults via the /Worksheet Global Default command. For example, you can reset the global defaults for margins, page length, and setup string. For other print options the default is to not use the feature in question. For example, the default for borders is no border, the default for headers and footers is no headers or footers.

Print [Printer or File] Go

Purpose

Used to execute the current print request, sending the data to the printer or file.

Description

Go is the action step in the printing process. Before you select Go you must have first specified the range to be printed, aligned the logical page (if necessary), and selected all your printer and format options. In general, you need only specify the range to be printed, the printer, and the format options once for a worksheet. 1-2-3 will remember your selections and save them with the worksheet. You do, however, have to re-align the logical page each time you print. It is a good practice to precede each Go command with the Align command, unless you specifically want to append one print request to its predecessor. If your print job is completed before the end of a page is reached, follow the Go command with a Page command; this ensures that your footer is included on the last page.

Defaults

The print range and formatting options last selected in the current worksheet.

Usage

To issue the Go command, select the destination device [Printer or File], define the range to print, modify any of the format options, and align the logical page. Then select Go.

Examples

To print the range A3..H25 to the ASCII file named WALRUS:

1. Select /Print File.
2. Type `WALRUS` and press ENTER.
3. Select the Range option, type (or paint) `A3..H25` and press ENTER.
4. Select Align to reset the logical top of page.
5. Select Go.
6. Select Quit to exit the print menu and save the print file WALRUS.PRN.

Notes

When you are using a page printer such as a laser printer, it is often difficult to determine the status of your print job if it is less than one page since 1-2-3 does not automatically issue a page eject at the end of the print job. Remember that it will take 1-2-3 only a few moments to prepare a half-page print job and transmit it to the printer, so what may appear to be an unusual delay is really a completed print job that is just waiting for a final page eject. You will have to issue the page eject by selecting the Page option (after you select Go to execute the print request) or by manually ejecting the page from your printer.

Print [Printer or File] Line

Purpose

Used to send a line feed request to the destination device (printer or file). This command is used to insert extra spaces between the ranges of a multiple range print job.

Description

The line feed request sends a hard carriage return code to the printer or print file.

Usage

To insert a line between two ranges of the current print job, begin by specifying the first range of your print job. Next select Align and Go to complete the first print request. Then select /Print [Printer or File] Line. (Reselect it if necessary to include additional lines.) Finally, specify the second range of the print job, and choose Go without Align.

Examples

To insert two lines between the two ranges A1..D5 and P12..T20:

1. Execute the print request for the first range. (Select /Print [Printer or File] Range. Type in (or paint) `A1..D5`. Select Align and then Go.)
2. Select the Line option twice.
3. Execute the print request for the second range. (Select Range and type in (or paint) `P12..T20`. Select Go.) (Do *not* select the Align option before you select Go or 1-2-3 will think it is at the top of a new page.)

Cautions

Do not execute the Align command either before or after the Line command (except at the very beginning of a print job where you have physically aligned the printer to the top of the first page). Otherwise, 1-2-3 will lose track of the line count and will not position the headers, footers, borders, or page breaks correctly.

Print [Printer or File] Options

Purpose

Used to modify and control the way your data is printed. You can add headers, footers, and borders. You can change the page length and margins. You can even issue special printer setup strings to take advantage of some of your printer's enhanced features.

As you look through the Options you may be eager to experiment. Just remember two key points:

1. Options *are* optional.
2. If you choose no options at all you will probably still get what you need—a basic printout.

Description

There are seven primary print options.

Borders Lets you specify one or more worksheet rows (or columns) to appear as headings at the top (or left) of every page and print range in the current print job.

Footer Specifies the text (one line) to be printed one line above the bottom margin specified for each page.

Header Specifies the text (one line) to be printed one line below the top margin specified for each page.

Margins Sets the top, bottom, left, and right margins of each page.

Other Specifies whether to print data as it appears on screen (e.g., with formula results or values) or whether to print formula contents. Also specifies whether to print data with formatting (i.e., using the selected options) or without formatting (i.e., no page breaks, headers, or footers).

Pg-Length Set 1-2-3's logical (or internal) page length in lines based on six lines per inch.

Quit Closes the Options menu and returns you to the main Print menu.

Setup Allows you to specify additional printer command codes that will be sent directly to the printer.

Notes

1-2-3 remembers the current printer settings and saves them with the worksheet. The next time you retrieve the worksheet, the settings you last specified are restored.

The current print settings are displayed on the print settings screen when you initiate the /Print [Printer or File] command.

Print [Printer or File] Options Borders

Purpose

Used to specify rows (or columns) from the worksheet that you wish to incorporate as labels or titles at the top (or left) border of each printed page and/or print range in the print job. These border headings will help identify the contents of each row or column on all of your printed pages.

Description

The Borders option allows you to repeat heading labels or titles on each page of a multi-page printout. If you are printing large numbers of columns or rows, this structures the data on each page of the printout, making the report easier to follow from page to page. Specify Rows for headings at the top of every page if your print range is too long. Specify Coumns for headings at the left of every page if your print range is too wide. Also, if you specify several print ranges in a print job, the Borders option will also repeat these headings at the top (or left) of each print range.

Defaults

Borders off.

Usage

To create borders for your printouts, first decide whether you wish to print a *column* of labels at the left of every page (or print range), or a *row* of labels at the top of every page (or print range) or both. Select /Print [Printer or File] Options Borders. Select either Columns and/or Rows; type in the address or paint the range that you wish to use as a border. You only have to specify one cell in each row of a Rows border and/or one cell in each column of a Column Border. 1-2-3 will include each cell in the border row or column that corresponds to a column or row in the print range. Be sure that your print range does not include the border rows and/or columns that you select; otherwise they will appear twice on the first page(s) of the printout.

Examples

To include rows one through five as a border at the top of each page of your printout:

1. Select /Print [Printer or File] Range to define your print range. Do not include the five rows you wish to use as a border.
2. Select Options Borders Rows.
3. Type in or paint the range `A1..A5` and press ENTER.
4. Select Align, then press Go to execute the print request.

Notes

1-2-3 is set to automatically include only the cells in the border rows or columns that correspond to your print range. This means that you can not exclude a given cell in a row or column border by explicitly excluding it from the border definition. If a cell lies in the border row or column, it will be printed unless you hide it.

1-2-3 will only print the portion of each border that corresponds to the portion of the print range that appears on a given sheet. For example, suppose you have specified a top border that stretches over ten columns and only five columns of your print range will fit on a single page. The first five columns of the border will be printed on the first page; the second five columns will be printed on the next page.

Exclude your border rows or columns from the print range or they will be double printed on the first page. If you are using a named range and you decide to add a border to it, be sure that you eliminate the appropriate border rows or columns from the range so that they will not appear twice in the printout.

The Borders option has no effect on how the borders are displayed on the screen. Use the /Worksheet Titles command to control the way that row and columns of titles can be fixed to remain displayed on the screen.

The only way to clear the current Border setting is to use the /Print [Printer or File] Clear Borders command.

Print [Printer or File] Options Footer

Purpose

Used to place a one-line footer at the bottom of each page of printed output. The footer appears one line above the bottom margin on each page.

Description

The footer text can be up to 240 characters long, but it cannot extend past the right margin of the page. The footer is inserted one line above the bottom margin of the page; and the two lines set above the footer are left blank. The footer appears on every page. It can include text and one or more of several special symbols used to control text placement and to insert incremented data such as page numbers and dates, as well as data from a specific cell. The symbols are as follows:

#	Inserts the current page number in the footer text, starting with page 1.
@	Inserts the current system date in the form DD-MMM-YY or your current International settings for (D4), specified under /Worksheet Global Default Other Clock.
¦	This is a separator character that is used to specify the alignment of your footer text. 1-2-3 lets you divide the footer into three elements: a left-aligned portion, a center portion, and a right-aligned portion. You can include data in any one or all three elements. For example:

Attendance	Left-aligns the footer text
¦ Page #	Centers the page number reference (Page 1, Page 2, etc.)
¦ ¦ @	Right-justifies the date
Attendance¦Page #¦@	Left-, center-, and right-justifies each element
\	The backslash character followed by a cell address or a single cell range name will insert the contents of that cell in a footer. The footer appears as a single left-justified element. You cannot use the \ symbol in combination with any of the other control symbols.

Defaults

No footer.

Usage

To create a footer for your current print job, decide on the contents and their alignment. If you wish to reference the contents of a particular cell in the worksheet, assign it an appropriate range name. Select Options from the main /Print menu, then select Footer. At the prompt, enter the text and symbols comprising the footer.

Examples

To create a footer that contains the worksheet title (Attendance) at the left, the date of printing in the center, and the page number (just numerals) at the right:

1. Select /Print [Printer or File] and specify your print range with the Range option on the main /Print menu. Then select Options Footer.
2. Type in the footer text and control symbols `Attendance¦@¦#` and press ENTER.

Notes

The footer adds three lines to your bottom margin: the line containing the footer itself and two blank lines between the footer and the printed data. You cannot use the backslash cell reference in the footer with any other control characters or text. You could however create complex cell referenced footers by first typing in the components for the footer in individual cells and then concatenating the text in the referenced cell. The referenced cell might look like this: +A1&" "&A2&", "&A3&" "&@STRING(B5,0).

If the last element in a print job does not take up a full page exactly, 1-2-3 will not print the footer on that page. To be sure that 1-2-3 includes the footer on the last page, add the Page command after executing the last element in the print job.

Print [Printer or File] Options Header

Purpose

Used to place a one-line header at the top of each page. The header appears one line below the top margin on each page.

Description

A header line, like the footer, can contain any text you specify as well as various symbols instructing 1-2-3 to insert elements such as the date or page number. 1-2-3 places the header line on the first line below the top margin and leaves the next two lines blank before starting to print the data range.

Defaults

No header.

Usage

Headers are created the same way and use the same symbols as footers.

Examples

To create a header line containing the title "Total 1-2-3" centered within the margins:

1. Select /Print [Printer or File] Options Header. (If a header is already there, type the new one over it.)
2. Type the header line including the placement code as `¦Total 1-2-3` and press ENTER.

Print [Printer or File] Options Margins

Purpose

Used to specify left, right, top, and bottom margins that are different from the global default settings or the margins last specified. (See the Print Settings sheet to check your default margin settings.)

Description

The top and bottom margins are measured in lines from their respective edges of the page. The sum of the top and bottom margins and any headers and/or footers cannot exceed the total page length. The default for the top and bottom margins is two lines from the top and two lines from the bottom of the page.

The left and the right margins are both measured in standard width characters (10 cpi) from the left edge of the page. The default left and right margins are 4 and 76 characters from the left side of the page. The left margin cannot be set higher than the right margin. If you change the character size by specifying a printer setup string for a different sized type, 1-2-3 cannot determine the character size and calculates the margins that will correspond to the type size you selected. You will have to reset the margins to accommodate the number of newly sized characters that would fit in the same space as the standard sized characters.

The None option resets the left, top, and bottom margins to 0 and the right margin to 240. This effectively eliminates the margins from exercising any control. The None option is often used with /Print File to export complete lines of data.

Defaults

The margin setting last specified via the command /Worksheet Global Default Printer Left, Right, Top, or Bottom. When you first take 1-2-3 out of the package, the defaults are:

Top	Two lines from top of page.
Bottom	Two lines from bottom of page.
Left	Four standard characters from left edge of page.
Right	76 standard characters from left edge of the page.

Usage

The most common need for resetting the margins occurs when you change the orientation of the page from Portrait to Landscape. You must reset the right margin and the total page length. To calculate the right margin, you should take the new physical page width (11 inches) and multiply it by the number of standard characters per inch (10 cpi). This means that the maximum right margin would be 110. If you wanted a right margin of at least two characters, you would set the margin to 108.

Examples

To set the right margin to 108 to print a print range in Landscape mode:

1. Select /Print Printer Range and specify the range you wish to print.
2. Select Options Setup and enter the setup string to switch your printer into landscape mode. (See your printer manual for information about its command code sequences.) If you were using an H-P LaserJet printer with a landscape Courier font available, the string would be: \027&l1O (lowercase el, digit 1, capital O).
3. Return to the Options menu.
4. Select Margins Right, type the value `108` and press ENTER.
5. Select Align, then select Go to execute the print request.

Notes

You *must* reset the margins after you have changed the page orientation from Portrait to Landscape or vice versa to represent the new page size in the new orientation.

Print [Printer or File] Options Other

Purpose

Used to control whether 1-2-3 prints the values of formulas (formula results) or the text of the underlying formulas; and whether 1-2-3 prints headers and footers or not.

Description

The Other options really control two main formatting items: how formulas are printed (As-Displayed and Cell-Formulas) and how header/footer printing and spacing should be treated (Formatted and Unformatted). They operate as follows:

As-Displayed Prints the current valuation of the formulas in the print range, using the format established for each cell.

Cell-Formulas Prints the technical details about each cell including: the cell address, the protection status, the format, and the cell contents—number, formula (text) or label. This option is particularly useful for debugging complex worksheets; you can see the actual formulas in each cell as well as the cells that the formulas reference.

Formatted Prints the data range, headers, footers, and borders as specified. Use this option to return to formatted printing after selecting Unformatted.

Unformatted Prints the specified print range without headers, footers, borders, top or bottom margins, and page breaks. This option is most often used when printing text files (/Print File) to export data to another program; this will prevent spaces from occurring in the file that would ordinarily represent page breaks.

Defaults

Formatted and As-Displayed.

Usage

To select a formatting option, select /Print Option Other and select the desired option. To select more than one option, choose Other again and select a second option. The Other options work like toggles. To turn an option off, select the opposite option. (For example, to turn Cell-Formulas off, select As-Displayed.)

Examples

To print the current data range as Cell-Formulas, and Unformatted:

1. Select /Print [Printer or File], and specify your print range. Select Options Other Cell-Formulas.
2. Select Other Unformatted.
3. Select Align, then Go to execute the print request.

Print [Printer or File] Options Page-Length

Purpose

Used to set the length of each page.

Description

The Pg-Length option allows you to adjust the vertical print area on each page. The default page length is 66 standard lines, the most common setting when printing out on 11-inch paper at six lines per inch. The page length that you specify under the Pg-Length option will overrule the global default page length setting, until you select another page length, or clear your current print settings with Clear All or Clear Format. Your current print settings are saved with the file. When you next load 1-2-3, and create a new file, global defaults are restored.

Notes

Most laser printers are unable to print on the top and bottom half-inch of the page. They therefore have a page length of only 10 inches when using 8 1/2 × 11- inch paper. This corresponds to a page length setting of 60 lines.

Print [Printer or File] Options Setup

Purpose

Allows you to send printer command codes directly to the printer. Setup strings are preceded by a backslash (\).

Description

A *setup string* consists of a series of printer control code characters and symbols. Printer control codes are specific to each printer. In general, you will have to refer to your printer's manual to determine the appropriate setup strings to perform the desired command.

Setup strings usually start with the ESC character followed by one or more additional characters. You can either use the actual alphanumeric character (be careful about uppercase and lowercase), or type in the ASCII code equivalent for that character, preceded by the backslash (\) character. Since ESC and the other ASCII characters from 1–31 have no character equivalent, they must be entered as ASCII codes in the setup string. ESC, for instance, must be entered as \027.

For example, you may wish to select a particular font that is not explicitly supported by 1-2-3. The command code for italics print on a Epson Printer is ESC 4. This could be entered as \027\052; 027 is the ASCII code for ESC and 052 is the ASCII code for 4. Each code is preceded by a backslash. Alternatively, you could have entered the code as \0274, typing in the character 4, rather than its ASCII numerical equivalent.

Defaults

No setup string.

Usage

Suppose you wanted to select a Helvetica Bold 14 point font for a headline in a printout using a Hewlett-Packard LaserJet with the B font cartridge. To change the font, you must determine the appropriate command code for the LaserJet printer from the LaserJet manual. It is:

Esc&l0OEsc(0UEsc(s1p14.4v0s3b4T

where Esc refers to the ESC character. (Nobody told you that this would be easy.) Now having determined the code, you must translate it into a 1-2-3 setup string, using the table in Appendix C to find the ASCII replacement for any non-typeable characters (e.g. Esc). As you can see it can be represented by \027 in the 1-2-3 setup string. You can either translate the other characters in the string into their ASCII equivalents, or enter them as themselves. The following codes are identical:

\027&l0O\027(0U\027(s1p14.4v0s3b4T

and

\027\038\108\048\079\027\040\048\085\027\040

\115\049\112\049\052\046\052\118\048\115

\051\098\052\084.

Having determined the desired string, select /Print [Printer or File] Options Setup and type it in as the setup string. The string will be transmitted to the printer each time you select the Go command. This means that you can change the setup string within a given sequence of print requests to add flexibility to your printed output.

Notes

Because of the tedium and potential for making typographical errors, you may want to place your setup strings into macros that will allow you to edit the string until you know it works and then insert it into the setup string whenever you want it by calling the macro.

Cautions

You must be extremely careful about uppercase and lowercase letters and the difference between a lower case el (l) and the digit 1 when you are typing in command codes. Both are used frequently and represent totally different commands.

If you enter a setup string that alters the size of the printer font, 1-2-3 does not know to alter the number of characters per line or lines per page. You must also modify the margins and page length to correspond with the selected font. Each will still be calibrated in the standard character size (10 pitch) and lines per inch (6 lpi).

There are two other ways to enter setup strings to your printer. You can specify a default setup string with the /Worksheet Global Default Printer Setup option (and then selecting the Update option of the Default submenu). The setup string will be sent to your printer each time you print. (This default setup string can be overridden, of course, by the Print [Printer or File] Option Setup command.)

You can also embed setup strings directly in the worksheet to print specific rows in bold or underlined; for example, include the setup string in a row of its own. Precede the setup string with two vertical bars (¦¦). Only the rows that appear below the setup string in the worksheet will be affected by the command. (By the way, you cannot isolate one cell in the row as bold, underlined, italic, etc.) The printer will continue printing with the specified attribute until you turn it off with another setup string in a row of its own, preceeded by two vertical bars (¦¦).

Printer setup strings have no effect when you are printing to a file. Some printers require that you turn them off and back on in order to cancel the effects of your previous setup string; do this to set the printer back to normal or before you issue another setup string.

Print [Printer or File] Page

Purpose

Used to advance the printer to the top of the next page and print the footer on the bottom of the current page. Used to eject the current page from a printer, especially page printers such as laser printers, or to insert pages between ranges in a print job.

Description

The /Print [Printer or File] Page command (with Line and Go) is one of the print action commands. After you have executed a print request with the Go command and you wish to start the next request at the top of a new page, you must issue a Page command. Selecting Page is not the same as issuing a page eject command; rather, guided by 1-2-3's internal line count, Page spaces down the requisite number of lines to reach the top of the next page. (It must do this in order to print the footer on the current page.) If you are printing to a file, 1-2-3 inserts the required number of blank lines and the footer text into the file.

Usage

To instruct the printer to space down to the end of the current page, print the footer on that page, and space to the top of the next page, simply select /Print [Printer or File] Page.

Examples

To start the next section of a print job on a new page:

1. Execute the print request for the first range as described under /Print [Printer or File] Range, ending with the Align and Go commands.
2. Select the Page option.
3. Execute the print request for the second range ending with the Go command. Do not select the Align option before the second element or 1-2-3 will lose track of the line and page count in the current job.

Cautions

Do *not* execute the Align command either before or after the Page command unless you want 1-2-3 to reset the page count to 1. 1-2-3 will automatically reset the logical page to the top of the page when you select the Page option.

Print [Printer or File] Quit

Purpose

Used to exit the Print menu and return to the READY mode.

Description

The Quit option exits the print menu and returns you to the READY mode. Pressing ESC or CTRL-BREAK enough times to return to the top /Print menu is equivalent to selecting Quit.

Print [Printer or File] Range

Purpose

Used to specify the range to be printed.

Description

When you specify a range, you can use its address, or assigned name, or you can paint it.

Defaults

The last selected range.

Usage

To specify a range to be printed, select /Print [Printer or File] Range. At the prompt, specify the range either by typing the range name or address or by painting the range with the cursor keys.

Examples

To specify the range A1..H12:

1. Select /Print [Printer or File] Range.
2. Type the range address `A1..H12` and press ENTER.

Notes

If 1-2-3 can't fit the entire specified print range within the margins of the currently selected printer, it will print the left-over portion on subsequent pages. To increase the number of columns that 1-2-3 will print you can reduce the column widths with /Worksheet Column Set-Width.

1-2-3 does not print hidden cells or columns. Hiding columns is a good way to avoid including parts of a worksheet that are unnecessary for the current printout.

1-2-3 remembers the last range you specified under the /Print menu and saves the specification with the worksheet. If you want to print the same range again, you will not need to type it in again. If you want to change the range, select Range and type in the new range at the prompt. If the data that you want to print includes long labels that "spill over" to columns on the right, be sure to include those columns with overlapping data in your print range.

▸ Quit Command

Purpose

Used to end 1-2-3 session and return to the operating system or Access system command menu.

Description

The Quit option concludes the current session of 1-2-3 and returns you to the operating system or the Access system main menu, depending on how you started 1-2-3. It does not save the current worksheet to disk. It will, however, warn you if the current worksheet has been altered since it was last saved.

Defaults

None.

Usage

To leave 1-2-3, first decide if you want to save the current worksheet. If you do want to save it, use the /File Save option and then select the Quit option. 1-2-3 will ask you to confirm your choice with Yes or cancel it with No. If you have not saved the current worksheet since it was last altered, 1-2-3 will warn you and ask you to confirm your choice a second time with Yes. Again, selecting No will return you to READY mode.

Examples

To exit 1-2-3 without saving the current worksheet, although it has been altered since it was last saved:

1. Select /Quit.
2. Select Yes to confirm your choice.
3. 1-2-3 will warn you that you have not saved the current worksheet since it was altered and will ask you to reconfirm your selection. Select Yes a second time to exit without saving.

Notes

To temporarily return to the operating system without exiting 1-2-3, use the /System option. 1-2-3 will be suspended and you will be presented with the operating system command prompt. To return to 1-2-3 simply type `Exit` at the command prompt.

Cautions

While 1-2-3 will warn you that you are trying to quit without saving your work, it is easy to develop the habit of confirming your decision without thinking. Since this selection terminates 1-2-3 the Undo option will not help you in this circumstance. It is a good idea to develop the habit of always saving your work before you exit 1-2-3. You may want to use a "throw-away" file name for such last minute saves. Our favorite is "ZXC.WK1", since it is easy to type, clearly recognizable and can be used consistently as the throw-away file name for many different programs.

▸ Range Commands

Purpose

The /Range commands are used to manipulate portions of the worksheet as a unit. A range of cells can be as small as one cell, or it may consist of a rectangular block of cells, spanning one or more rows and columns. Range commands control the display and formatting of parts of the worksheet. To control the entire worksheet, use the /Worksheet command menu.

Description

For all options under the /Range command menu (Format, Erase, etc.), you will be asked to specify the range to be manipulated. You can do this in one of three ways: by typing in the range address, by typing in the range name, or by painting the range.

Range Address A range can be described by the cell addresses of any pair of opposite corners of the rectangle. The corners describing the range may be in any order. For example, the range consisting of the first three rows and first four columns in the current worksheet could be described as A1..D3, where cells A1 and D3 represent a pair of opposite corners of the range. You could also use the pairs: A3..D1, D1..A3, or D3..A1 to define the same range.

Regardless of the order in which you specify the range corners, 1-2-3 will convert the range address to show the upper-left corner followed by the lower-right. Thus a range entered as D3..A1 will be displayed by 1-2-3 as A1..D3. The upper-left and lower-right corners of a range are called its *defining* corners.

Range Names You can assign logical text names of up to 15 characters to ranges. These names can then be used in place of addresses when specifying the range in a command or formula. The /Range Name option under the /Range command menu may be used to assign and manage range names. We strongly encourage you to assign and use range names because they greatly reduce the chance of error in specifying ranges for formulas. Figure Range.1 shows the assignment of the range name PENGUINS to the range A1..D3.

In addition, using range names in formulas can help you remember the meaning of that formula. For example, say you wanted to find the sum of a range of 12 cells containing the monthly rainfall amounts in order to determine the annual rainfall level. If the monthly figures were contained in the range A7..L7, you could calculate the sum by entering the formula @SUM(A7..L7). However, several weeks or months later if you try to debug or review your formulas and come across the formula @SUM(A7..L7). What does it really mean?

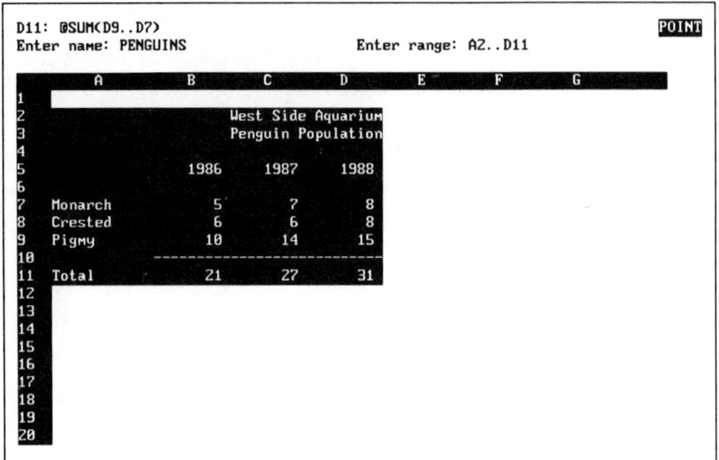

Figure Range.1
Assigning the range name PENGUINS.

Had you named the range of cells containing the monthly rainfall with a meaningful English name, such as MONTHLYRAINFALL, you could write the formula as @SUM(MONTHLYRAINFALL), which clearly declares its intent. Of course, for this approach to be effective, you must correctly specify the range address or dimensions when creating a range name for it.

Painting Ranges When you are about to answer a 1-2-3 prompt in MENU mode and press any one of the cursor movement keys, 1-2-3 switches into POINT mode; in POINT mode you can move the cell pointer freely about the current worksheet. Place the cell pointer on one of the corners of the range you wish to specify. Press the period (.) key to anchor one corner of the range. Now move the cell pointer to the opposite corner of the desired range with the cursor keys. As you move the cell pointer, the rectangle of cells between the current cell pointer position and the anchor cell will be highlighted (or "painted"). When you have highlighted the entire range of cells being defined, press ENTER to conclude the painting process. Note that the complete address is entered into the command prompt.

When you are specifying a range for a formula, you can also paint a range of cells; type in the @function and the opening parenthesis—`@SUM(`—and then use the cursor keys to paint the range. You can end the painting process by pressing ENTER and then conclude entering the formula or save a keystroke by simply pressing the closing parenthesis in the @function (see Figure Range.2).

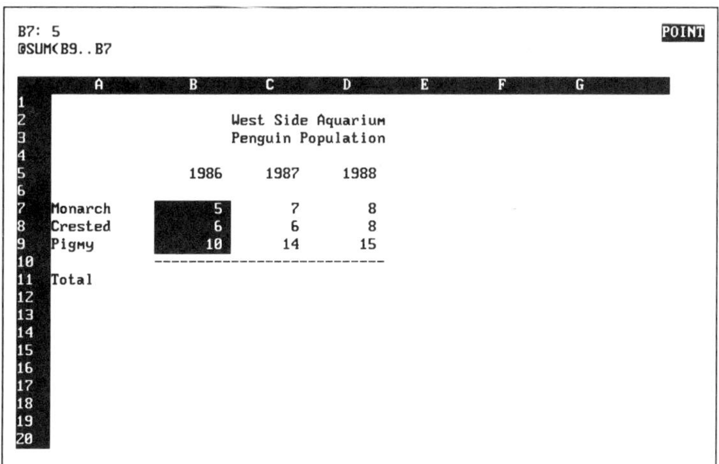

Figure Range.2

Painting a Range in a formula.

Note

Certain commands, such as /Graph, /Data, and /Print, "remember" the most recently defined range and will use it as the default range for their operation unless you respecify it. The "remembered" range will appear on the settings sheet for that command. You can accept the default range by pressing ENTER. You can clear the default (by pressing BACKSPACE or ESC) and then type in a different range.

Range Erase

Purpose

Used to empty a range of cells of its contents.

Description

The /Range Erase command replaces the contents of a cell or range of cells with blank cells, without altering the defined format of the cell(s). /Range Erase is the only way to empty a cell (or cells) of its contents. If you are using the Undo feature, you can press UNDO (ALT-F4) immediately after accidentally erasing a cell or range of cells and restore their contents.

Any formula in the remainder of the worksheet that depends on an erased cell will show up as an ERR. If you erase one of the defining corners of a range (the upper-left or lower-right corner), that range will lose its definition. Any formulas that depend on it will evaluate to ERR. If the range was a named range, you will have to rename and redefine it.

Defaults

The current cell.

Usage

Single Cell Position the cell pointer on the cell you want to erase. Select /Range Erase. Press the ENTER key to select the current cell as the default. The contents of the current cell will be erased.

Range of Cells Position the cursor on the cell marking the upper-left corner of the cell range you wish to erase. Select /Range Erase. Either move the cell pointer to paint the range to be deleted or enter the cell address or range name of the range of cells to be erased and press ENTER. The range of cells will be deleted, leaving the cell pointer in the upper-left corner of the range.

Notes

By turning on global worksheet protection with the /Worksheet Global Protection Enable command every cell in the worksheet is protected, unless it has been explicitly "unprotected" with /Range Unprot. The cell protection status (PR for protected and U for unprotected) is displayed in the first line of the control panel. Enabling protection will prevent you from accidentally erasing the contents of a cell or range of cells. In order to erase a cell that is protected, you must unprotect that cell or range of cells or turn off worksheet protection altogether.

Range Format

Purpose

The various Format options enable you to choose from seven formats for the screen display and printing of a range. Any formatting that you do with /Range Format will override the global default worksheet format.

Description

The /Range Format command alters the way a value or the result of a formula appears on the screen and is printed on a report. The format options do not actually change any numerical values or the number of decimal places that will be used for subsequent calculations (15 significant digits). If you wish, the format displayed on screen or in print can be rounded off in terms of any undisplayed decimal places. (Remember, you may also have to change column size with /Worksheet Column Set-Width in order to see complete decimals or places on screen. Values that are too long to fit in the column width are displayed as asterisks.) Format options include:

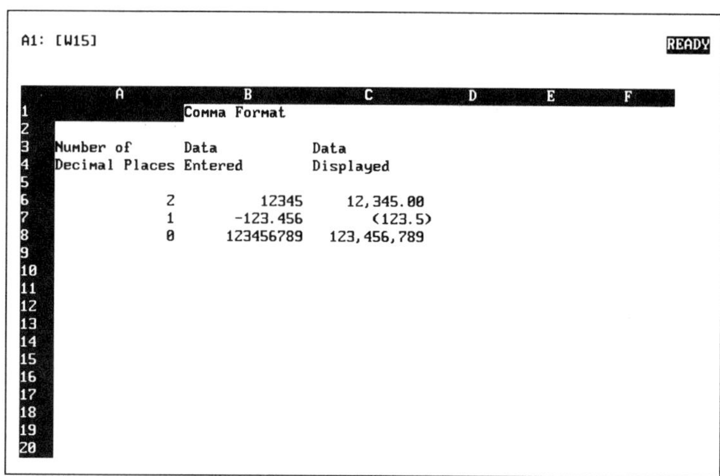

Figure Range.3
Comma format.

, (Comma) Displays numbers with commas separating every third digit to the left of the decimal point, and a specified number of decimal places to the right (up to 15). See Figure Range.3. Negative numbers are displayed with parentheses or a minus sign depending on the global default setting of the Negative option under the /Worksheet Global Default Other International menu. Note that 1-2-3 does not allow you to actually type in values with commas. The only way to include separating commas is with the /Range Format , (Comma) option.

Currency Displays numbers with a leading dollar sign ($), commas separating every third digit to the left of the decimal point, and a specified number of decimal places to the right (up to 15). See Figure Range.4. Negative numbers are displayed with parentheses or a minus sign depending on the setting of the Negative option under the /Worksheet Global Default Other International menu. (You may also change the default currency symbol, and specify its location before or after the currency value using the /Worksheet Global Default Other International Currency option.)

Date Displays valid date serial numbers (1 to 73050, corresponding to dates from Jan 1 1900 to Dec 31 2099) in one of five date formats:

D1	DD-MMM-YY	12-Jan-89
D2	DD-MMM	12-Jan
D3	MMM-YY	Jan-89
D4	Long Int'l	01/12/89
D5	Short Int'l	01/12

Invalid dates are shown as asterisks.

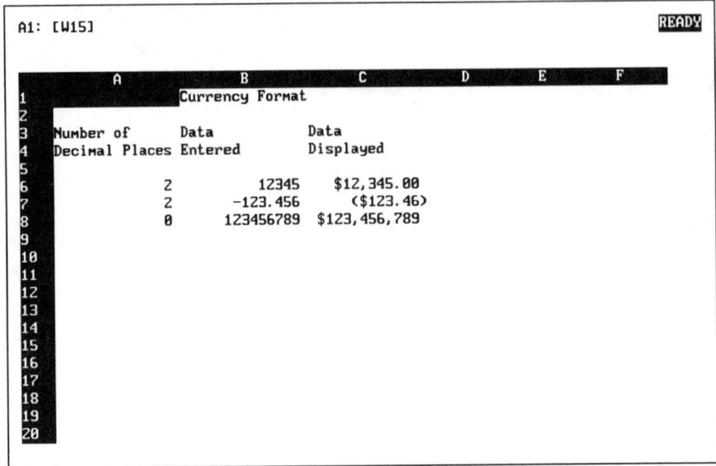

A1: [W15] READY

	A	B	C	D	E	F
1		Currency Format				
2						
3	Number of	Data	Data			
4	Decimal Places	Entered	Displayed			
5						
6	2	12345	$12,345.00			
7	2	-123.456	($123.46)			
8	0	123456789	$123,456,789			
9						
10						
11						
12						
13						
14						
15						
16						
17						
18						
19						
20						

Figure Range.4
Currency format.

Dates are stored by 1-2-3 as integers from 1 to 73050, corresponding to January 1, 1900 through December 31, 2099. You can enter the integer directly as a value or use one of the many date functions to generate the values (e.g., @DATE, @NOW, @TODAY). See Figure Range.5. Note: You will have to adjust the default column width of nine spaces to display data in several of the date formats.

Date Time Displays the decimal portion of positive numbers as time in one of four time formats. Decimals can run from .000, which represents 12:00 AM, to .999, which represents 11:59 PM. Negative decimal values are subtracted from 1.0 to calculate the displayed times as though you were counting backward in time from midnight. See Figure Range.6.

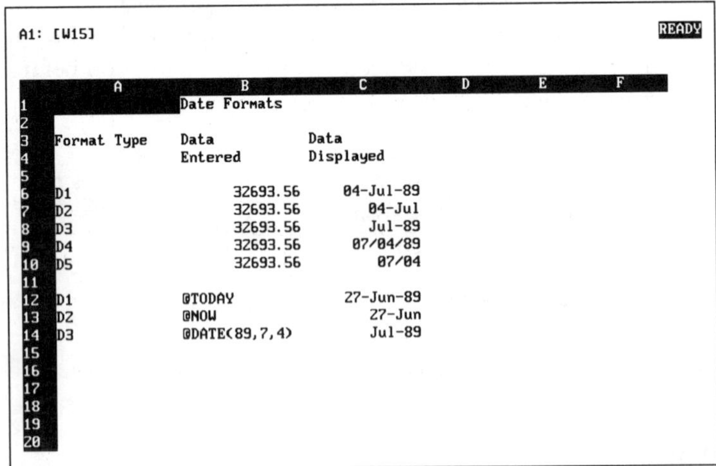

A1: [W15] READY

	A	B	C	D	E	F
1		Date Formats				
2						
3	Format Type	Data	Data			
4		Entered	Displayed			
5						
6	D1	32693.56	04-Jul-89			
7	D2	32693.56	04-Jul			
8	D3	32693.56	Jul-89			
9	D4	32693.56	07/04/89			
10	D5	32693.56	07/04			
11						
12	D1	@TODAY	27-Jun-89			
13	D2	@NOW	27-Jun			
14	D3	@DATE(89,7,4)	Jul-89			
15						
16						
17						
18						
19						
20						

Figure Range.5
Date formats.

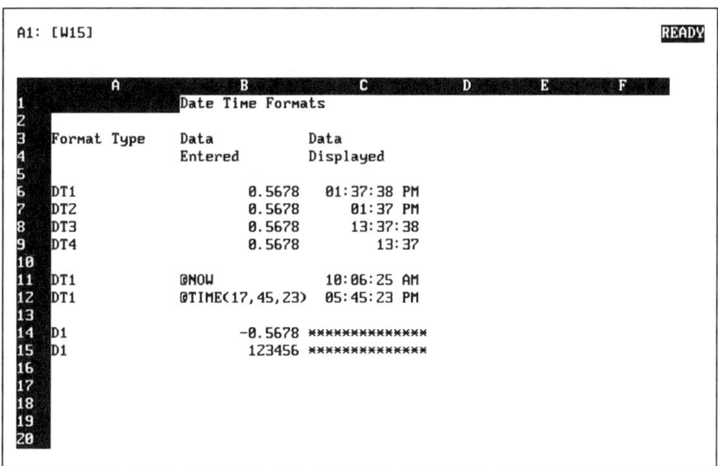

Figure Range.6
Date-Time Format.

Times are stored as decimal values. You can enter the decimal directly as a value or use one of the time functions to generate the value (e.g., @TIME or @NOW.) The four time formats include:

D6 HH:MM:SS (AM/PM) 4:27:45 PM

D7 HH:MM (AM/PM) 4:27 AM

D8 Long Int'l (24Hr) 16:27:45

D9 Short Int'l (24Hr) 15:27

Again, you may have to adjust the default column width of nine spaces to display time in several of the time formats.

You can combine the integer (date) and decimal (time) values into a single value to represent the time on a particular date (e.g., 32640.123 represents 2:57 A.M. on May 12, 1989.) If you format the cell with one of the date formats, the date will be displayed. If you format the cell with one of the time formats, the time will be displayed.

Fixed Displays numbers without commas. Allows you to set the number of decimal places displayed (up to 15 decimal places). Values with more decimal digits than displayed will be rounded. If you set your format for Fixed with two decimal places, even the integer 12 will be displayed as 12.00. Values between –1 and 1 will be displayed with a leading zero (e.g., 0.9). Negative numbers are preceded with a minus sign. If you set the decimal places to zero, no decimal point is displayed. See Figure Range.7.

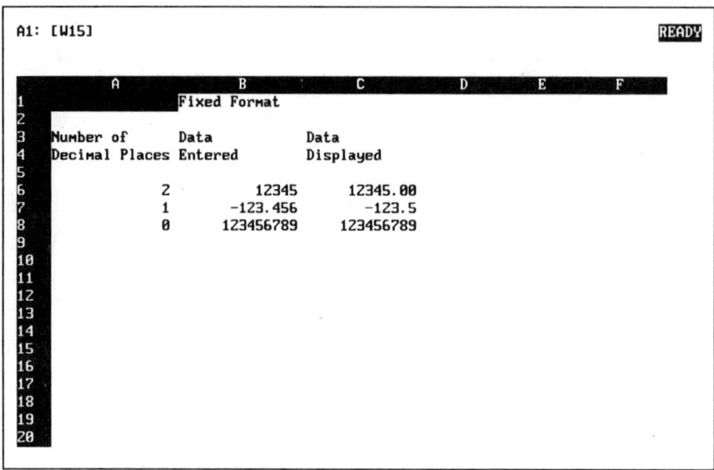

Figure Range.7
Fixed Format.

General A dynamic format that displays values according to the number of digits contained in the value and the size of the column width. If the number of digits to the left of the decimal point exceeds the column width, the number is displayed in scientific notation. If the number of digits to the right of the decimal point exceeds the column width, the decimal is truncated (not rounded), dropping the least significant digits. Negative numbers are displayed with a minus sign and trailing zeros to the right of the decimal are not displayed. See Figure Range.8.

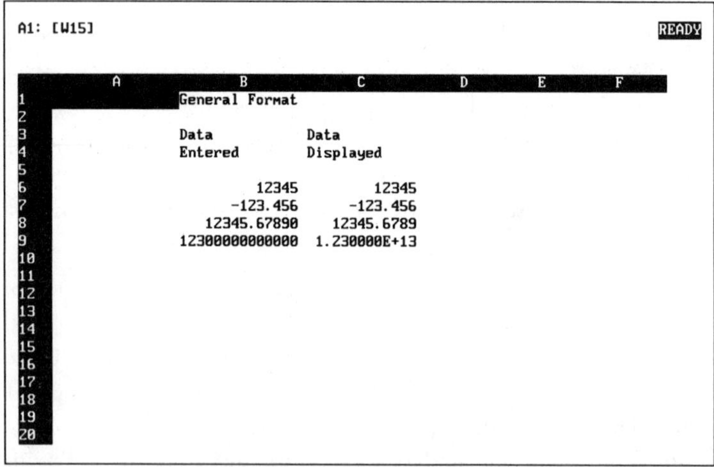

Figure Range.8
General Format.

Hidden Hides the contents of a range by displaying the cells as blank. The contents of the current cell will still be displayed in the control panel unless you also protect the range with the /Range Protect option. See Figure Range.9. To redisplay hidden cells, select another format or choose /Range Format Reset to reset the format to the global default (usually General).

+/– Creates rudimentary horizontal bar graphs for the specified range; where the integer portion of the value entered into the cell is represented by a corresponding number of plus signs. Conversely, negative integers are represented by minus signs. Values between –1 and 1 are represented by a period. If the number of plus or minus signs required to display a particular value exceeds the width of the cell, asterisks are displayed. This is useful for computers with limited graphics capabilities or when quick visual display of a series of values will help identify differences. See Figure Range.10.

Reset Resets the format of a range to the format specified under the /Worksheet Global Default Format command.

Sci(entific) Displays numbers using scientific, or exponential, notation. With scientific format, the mantissa portion can be up to 15 decimal places, while the exponent can range from –99 to 99 (see Figure Range.11).

Text Displays all formulas in the range as text rather than as values. All numerical values in the range are displayed in the General format. This is particularly useful for displaying the formulas used in creating tables with the /Data Table command.

Defaults

When you first use 1-2-3 the default format for all cells in a worksheet is General. The default format for all cells can be changed to any of the above formats via the /Worksheet Global Format command. Thereafter, the format for a particular cell or range of cells can be set (as variations from the default) using the /Range Format command. The default target for the /Range Format command is the current cell. The default number of decimal places displayed is two.

Usage

To format a range of cells, position the cursor on the cell marking the upper-left corner of the range of cells you wish to format. (If you wish to format only a single cell, move the pointer to that cell.) Select /Range Format followed by the first letter or symbol of the desired format, i.e., /RF, for comma format. In many cases 1-2-3 will then prompt you for the number of decimal places to display; press ENTER to accept the two decimal place default or type in your preference.

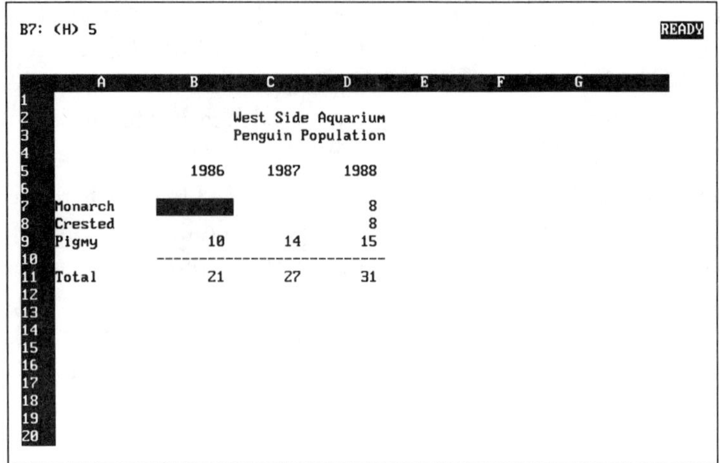

Figure Range.9
Hidden Format—Cell contents displayed in control panel.

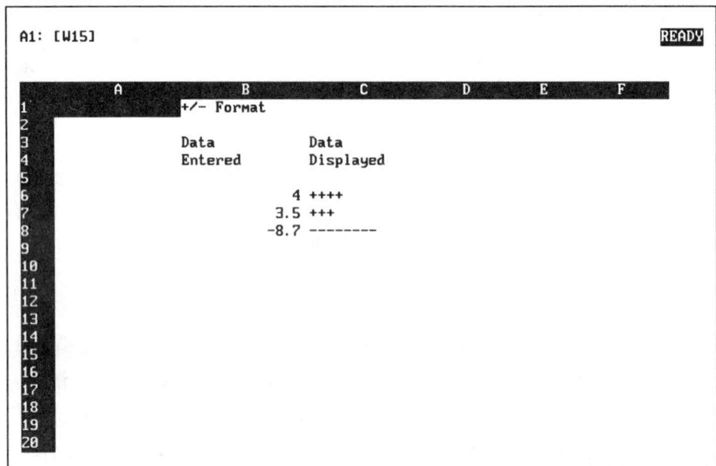

Figure Range.10
+/– Format.

Finally, move the cell pointer to paint the range to be formatted or type in the range name or address and press ENTER. (When formatting a single cell, simply press ENTER to accept the current cell default.)

Examples

To format the current cell as currency with two decimal places:

1. Select /Range Format Currency.
2. Press ENTER to accept the two decimal place default.
3. Press ENTER to accept the current cell default.

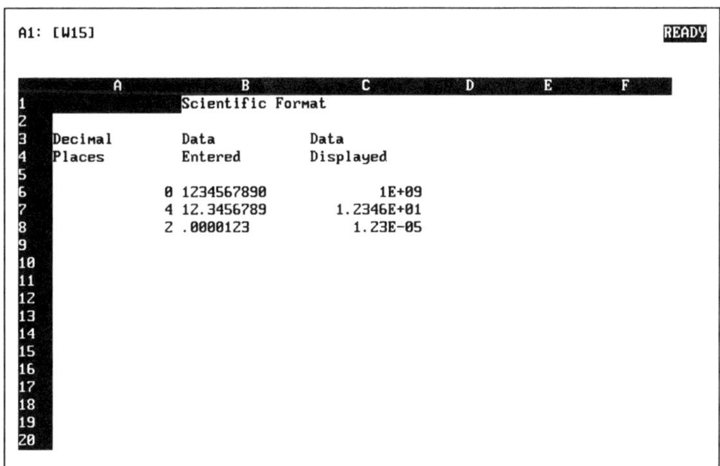

Figure Range.11
Scientific Format.

To format the range of cells A14..E17 as comma with zero decimal places:

1. Select /Range Format ,.
2. Type `0` and press ENTER.
3. Type (or paint) `A14..E17` and then press ENTER.

To format the range of cells previously named INTEREST with the /Range Name Create or /Range Name Labels commands as percent with one decimal place:

1. Select /Range Format Percent.
2. Type `1` to display one decimal place and press ENTER.
3. Type `INTEREST` and press ENTER.

Notes

1. When you move or copy a cell or a range of cells that has been formatted, its assigned format is also copied to the new cell or range of cells.
2. The currency symbol, the Long Intn'l and Short Intn'l date and time formats D4, D5, D8, and D9 (01/27/89, 01/27, 17:45:27, and 17:45), and the symbol used to separate every third digit to the left of the decimal point in comma and currency formats, will be affected by the setting of /Worksheet Global Default Other International.
3. The Comma format is generally a better choice for long columns of dollar figures rather than the Currency format; the repeated dollar sign of the Currency format can appear redundant. You might use the Currency format just for column headers and totals.

Cautions

1. It is easy to accidentally overwrite the contents of cells after you have hidden them using the /Range Format Hidden command, since they appear to be unused. You can prevent this by using the /Worksheet Global Protection Enable command and (if necessary) protecting the hidden cells with the /Range Protect command.
2. 1-2-3 will round the display to the designated number of decimal places (except for the General format, which will simply truncate the decimal display). The underlying value, however, will be retained with 15 decimal places for subsequent calculations. This can mean that columns of numbers may not appear to add correctly.

   For example, Figure Range.12 shows values with 15 significant decimal places in column B. The same figures are also shown in column C in currency format with the normal two decimal places. Note that the sum of each column is the same in row 12. If, however, you manually add the numbers as displayed in column C, you'll find that your figure doesn't agree with the calculation in the worksheet. This is because the 1-2-3 calculation is made on the underlying figure, significant to 15 decimal places, while your manual addition is made on the rounded figure, as displayed. The difference between the two figures is created by the rounding error. 1-2-3 always uses the full 15 places when making subsequent calculations unless you specifically round the underlying figure using the @ROUND function.

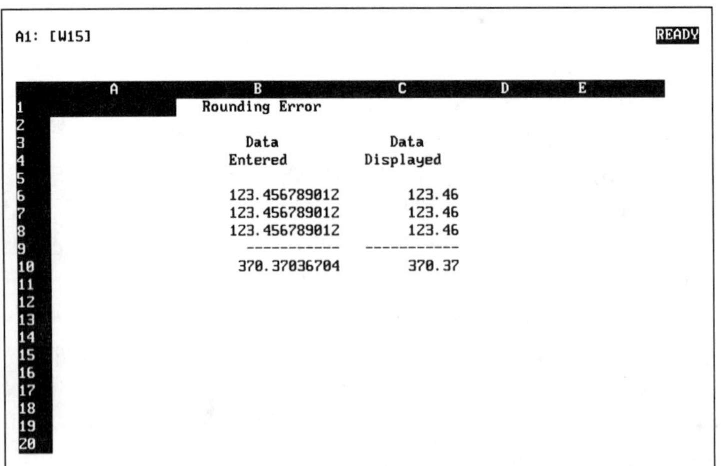

Figure Range.12
Format Rounding Error.

Range Input

Purpose

Used in conjunction with the /Range Unprotect command to create fill-in-the-blank worksheets. This is especially useful for inexperienced users who are less likely to make errors if they can enter data into a predefined form, or into predefined areas.

Description

The /Range Input command limits cursor movements to the unprotected cells within the range defined by the command. This allows you to create data entry or input forms with predefined cells for variable data input. /Range Input allows you to move the cell pointer freely between the unprotected cells within the range by means of the cursor keys, but will not allow the cell pointer to be moved to a protected cell in the input range or to a cell outside of the input range, significantly limiting its movement. This both increases the speed of data entry and also protects the rest of the worksheet from accidental overwriting.

/Range Input is used most frequently with interactive macros, designed to permit controlled user input in various parts of the worksheet. For example, /Range Input can be used for restricted input in one range of the worksheet in a first segment of a macro and then move to another range for further restricted input in a second part of the macro.

Defaults

None.

Usage

The /Range Input command *must* be used in conjunction with the /Range Unprotect command. (Your global worksheet protection setting may be on or off.) You must first create your input form, and set up various cells or ranges of cells for data input. Each cell for data entry (or input) must then be explicitly unprotected using the /Range Unprotect command. Finally, you must turn on /Range Input, by specifying the input range.

The input range should include the entire input form, including both the cells for input and their labels. 1-2-3 will move the input range to the upper-left corner of the display allowing the complete form (or as much as possible) to appear on screen. The cell pointer will be restricted to movement between the unprotected data entry cells and only within the input range. Press ENTER without changing the contents of the current input cell or ESC to terminate the /Range Input Command.

Examples

Suppose you wanted to calculate the present value of a series of equal payments at various interest rates and terms. You might set up the input form shown in Figure Range.13, leaving specific cells for entering the payment, term, and interest rates:

1. Move cursor to B5.
2. Type `Payment:` and press the DOWN arrow key.
3. Type `Interest:` and press the DOWN arrow key.
4. Type `Term:` and press the DOWN arrow key.
5. Type `Present Value:` and press the RIGHT arrow key.
6. Type the present value formula `@PV(C5,C6,C7)` and press ENTER.

Next, you must unprotect the input cells using the /Range Unprotect command; and finally, you must define an input range containing all of the input cells:

7. Select /Range Unprotect.
8. Type (or paint) the range `C5..C7` and press ENTER.
9. Select /Range Input.
10. Type (or paint) the range `A1..C7` and press ENTER.

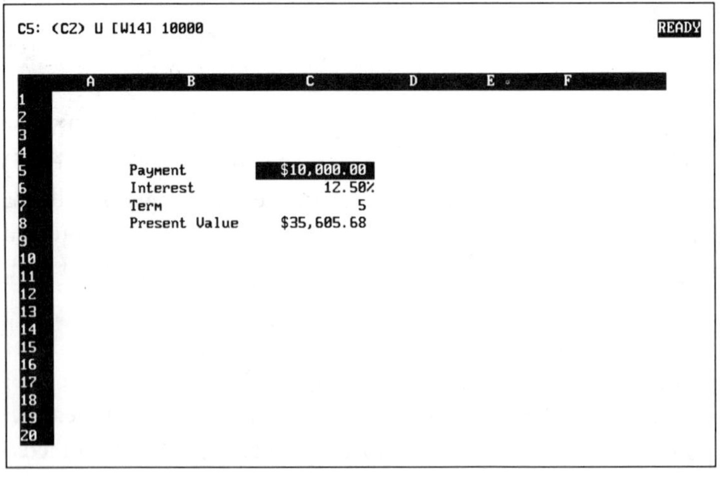

Figure Range.13
/Range Input.

Note that the cell pointer moves to the upper left-most unprotected cell in the input range. By pressing the cursor movement keys, you can move the cell pointer from input cell to input cell. You can enter different values for the payment, term, and interest rate using the cursor movement keys and read the resulting present value in cell C8 (if you have automatic recalculation on). When you are finished, you can terminate the range input by pressing either ENTER (having made no change to the current cell) or ESC.

Notes

1. When you use the /Range Input command in a macro, the macro will pause for user input; free cell pointer movement will be allowed within the input range until the user presses the ENTER or ESC keys. The macro will proceed with the next command. See Chapter 13 for additional information on this form of controlled data input.
2. /Range Input restricts the keys that can be used: a user is limited to ESC, ENTER, F2, F1, HOME, END, ↑, ↓, ←, →, and the standard alphanumeric keys.
3. When you are in /Range Input the ENTER key operates in two ways. If you press ENTER after typing in or editing a data entry, your cell pointer will move on to the next input cell. If you press ENTER without making any changes to the contents of the current cell, you will terminate the /Range Input command.

Range Justify

Purpose

Used to create a uniform line-wrapped paragraph out of a column of text (labels) of variable line lengths.

Description

The /Range Justify command treats a column of labels as a continuous string of text; it then word wraps (or rebreaks the string into fragments of approximately equal line width) to fit the range or range width you specify. This is useful for fitting an explanatory block of text into a fixed width column. /Range Justify can also be used to create memos within 1-2-3 or to justify blocks of text imported into 1-2-3 from ASCII files via the /File Import Text command.

Defaults

None.

Usage

To justify a range of text, you must tell 1-2-3 what text to justify and how to justify it. You identify the text to be justified by placing the cell pointer on the top cell of the column of text before starting the command. 1-2-3 will justify the continuous column of text until it reaches a blank cell or a cell containing a value or formula.

When you start the /Range Justify command, it will ask you to enter the Justify Range. This is the range into which you want 1-2-3 to fit the text. You can either define a text width by highlighting one or more columns; or you can define a two-dimensional range with multiple rows and one or more columns. The key factor is whether the Justify Range is only one row or more than one row. 1-2-3 treats each option differently, as described below. In each case, the width of the text paragraph will be determined by the sum of the column widths in the Justify Range. You may want to adjust the widths of your columns to the desired values with the /Worksheet Column Set-Width or /Worksheet Global Column-Width commands before you use the /Range Justify command.

Single Row Justify Range If you enter a single row Justify Range, 1-2-3 will use the width of the specified row for the line length and will create a paragraph of the entire column of contiguous label cells below the specified row. If the newly justified text requires more rows than the original labels, 1-2-3 will create as many rows of text as required. Any cells containing text, values, or formulas that were located below the text being justified will be pushed down the worksheet so that the new text will not overwrite them. See Figures Range.14a–b.

Multiple Row Justify Range If you enter a multiple row Justify Range, 1-2-3 will automatically justify the text to the width of the range and will not extend the text below the bottom row of the Justify Range. Data below the Justify Range will not be moved; however, any data within the Justify Range may be overwritten. If there is not enough room to include the entire text to be justified, 1-2-3 will report an error. Press ESC to clear the message and enter a larger Justify Range. See Figures Range.15a–b.

Examples

After importing the text shown in Figure Range.15a from your word processor, 1-2-3 stores the resulting text as labels in a single column. You now want to justify the text to a uniform column 27 characters wide, using as many rows as required.

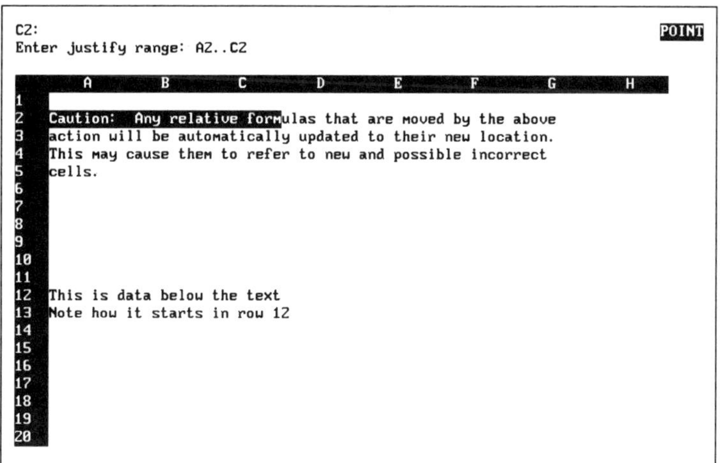

Figure Range.14a
Single Row Justify Range—Before.

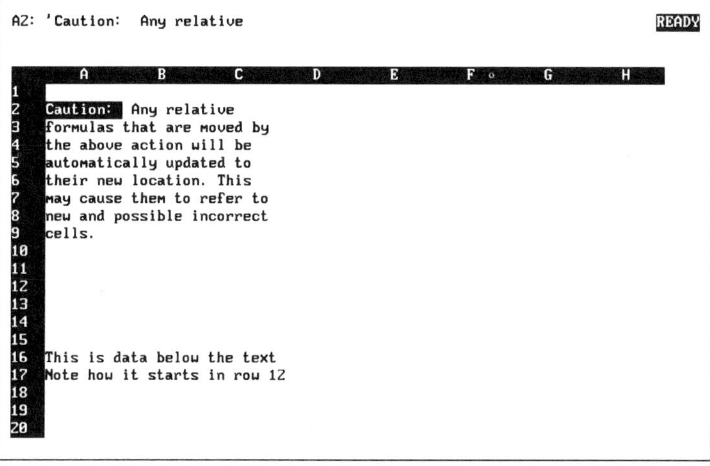

Figure Range.14b
Single Row Justify Range—After.

1. Place the cell pointer on the top cell of the text.
2. Highlight enough cells in one row to produce a collective width of 27 characters. (You may have to alter the width of one or more cells to do so.) If you want to create a single column of width 27, use the command /Worksheet Column Set. Type in 27 and press ENTER.
3. Start the /Range Justify command by pressing /RJ. Enter the Justify Range. If you have created a single column of 27 characters and it is the current column, you can just press ENTER to accept the current column as the default.

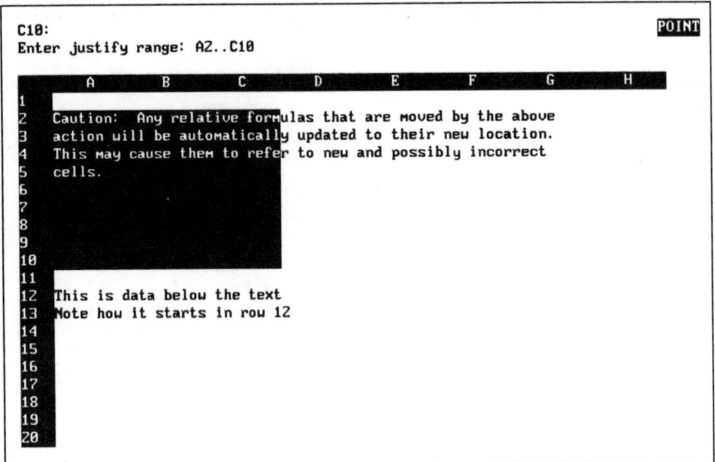

Figure Range.15a
Multiple Row Justify Range—Before.

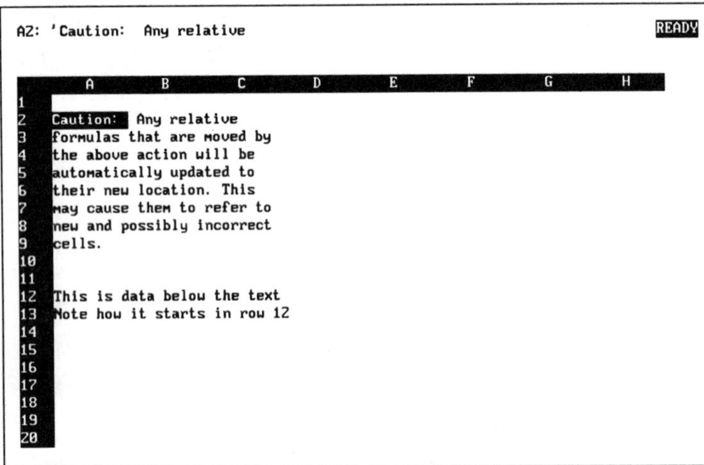

Figure Range.15b
Multiple Row Justify Range—After.

The text will be wrapped into rows of 27 character-width, with as many rows as required to contain the complete text. Any cells containing data located below the justified text will be pushed down the worksheet. See Figure Range.15b above.

Notes

1. Since the /Range Justify command writes your text into new cells, /Worksheet Global Protection must be off before you start this command or the output range must be specifically unprotected.

2. The /Range Justify command automatically left-justifies the labels containing the justified text.

Cautions

Any relative formulas that are moved through the justification process will be automatically updated to their new location. This may cause them to refer to new and possibly incorrect cells.

Range Label

Purpose

Used to change the alignment of label cells within a range to left-aligned, right-aligned, or centered.

Description

This command changes the alignment of the label cells by replacing their current label prefix with a new prefix that you specify (' for left-aligned, " for right-aligned, and ^ for centered). The new label prefix overrides any existing global prefix setting for the cells within the range. The command only affects existing label cells and does not impact new label cells entered subsequently within the range. See Figures Range.16a–b.

Defaults

Current cell, with left alignment.

Usage

If you are re-aligning a range of cells, position the cursor on the cell marking the upper-left corner of the range of the cell you wish to format (or on the single cell that you wish to re-align.) Initiate the /Range Label command by pressing /RL. Select Left, Right, or Center alignment. If you are reformatting a single cell, press ENTER to accept the default. If you are reformatting a range of cells, type in the range address or name, or paint the range with the cursor keys and press ENTER.

Examples

To center the text in the current cell:

1. Select /Range Label Center and press ENTER to accept the current cell as the default.

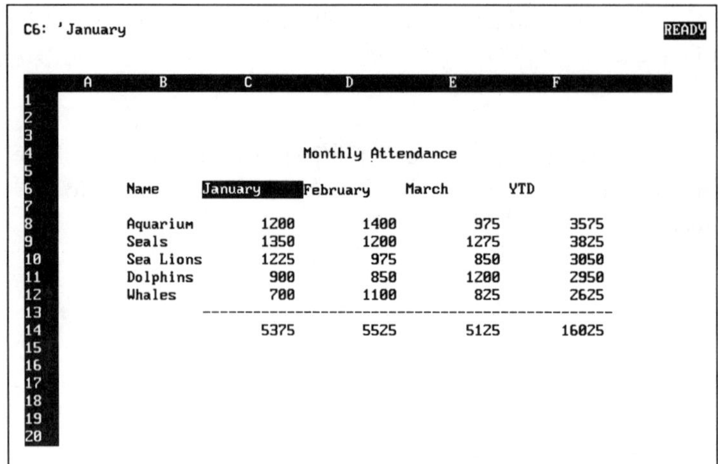

Figure Range.16a
Left-Justified labels.

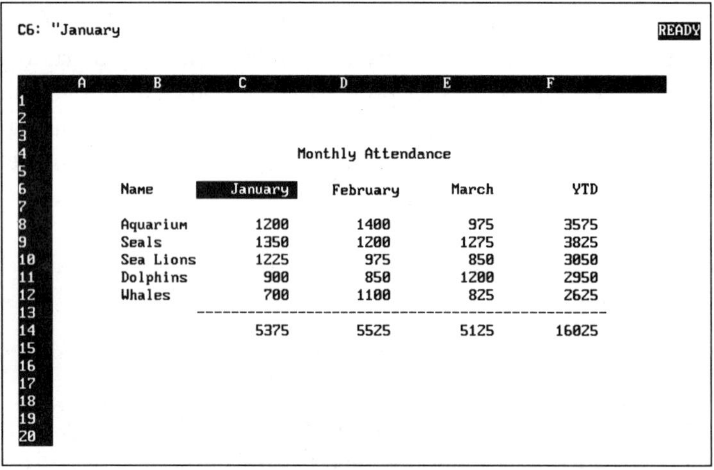

Figure Range.16b
Right-Justified labels.

To right-align the text in the cells within the range of cells A14..E17:

1. Select /Range Label Right.
2. Type in (or paint) the range `A14..E17` and press ENTER.

Notes

/Range Label has no effect on numbers or numerical formulas; these are always right-justified. It also has no affect on the results of string formulas, which are always left-aligned. If the text of a label cell exceeds the width of the cell, it will always appear left-justified. If you enter in a label that begins with a number, you have to attach a label prefix.

There is another range label prefix option, the \ (backslash), which cannot be selected from the Range Label menu. The backslash prefix tells 1-2-3 to repeat the character(s) to fill the cell.

Range Name

Purpose

These commands are used to create range names and also to reference and manage range names. Once named, ranges can be referred to by their assigned name in commands, functions, and formulas.

Description

The ability to assign range names to blocks of cells is an extremely useful and important tool in 1-2-3. Once you have assigned a meaningful English name to a range, you can refer to that range by name—in commands, functions, and formulas—rather than by typing in (or painting) the range address.

A major problem with complex worksheets is that you can lose your orientation and even your train of thought among thousands of near-to-identical cells. By assigning significant names to important ranges that you reference often, you can greatly reduce confusion and the possibility of error. This is especially useful if other people will be navigating your worksheet or if you will have to review a worksheet many weeks or months later. Also, as you begin to create and use macros, you will find that named ranges are indispensable.

Once you have created range names, you can use these names when performing commands. For example, if you were to name a range TOTALS, and another range WHALES, you could print TOTALS, or move WHALES to another part of the worksheet. In the same manner, you can include a range name in functions or formulas in place of its address. Calculating the total number of whales is much clearer with the formula @SUM(WHALES) instead of @SUM(F12..F34).

There are four /Range Name commands used to create, delete, reset, or list range names. Each range name option is discussed on the following pages.

Range Name Create

Purpose

Used to create or redefine a range name. You must supply the desired range address and name as prompted by the command.

Description

/Range Name Create assigns a name to a specific range of cells so you can refer to that range by name instead of by address in commands, functions, and formulas. The named range can consist of a single cell, or a one- or two-dimensional rectangle of contiguous cells in the worksheet. A range name can be any combination of up to 15 characters and numbers. (See cautions below regarding names to avoid.)

Named ranges are dynamic; if you insert new rows, columns, or worksheets into a two-dimensional named range, the range will automatically expand to include them. Likewise, if you delete any rows or columns, the range will contract correspondingly to include only the remaining rows or columns. If you move one of the defining corners of a range (the upper-left or lower-right corner) the range will stretch or shrink according to the new position of the corner cell. If you move data onto the first or last cells of a named range with the /Move command, the range will become undefined and any formula referring to it will appear as ERR.

Defaults

The current cell.

Usage

To create a range name, start the command by typing /RNC. 1-2-3 will display a list of all existing range names. If you want to redefine one of them, point to the desired name with the cursor keys and press ENTER. If you are creating a new name, you can enter any alphanumeric combination up to 15 characters and press ENTER.

Specify the range to which you are assigning the name either by painting it, typing in its range address, or (if you are renaming an already-named range) by supplying the existing range name assigned to the range. If you are redefining an existing name, you will be presented with the current range highlighted on the screen. You can modify it by moving the cell pointer or by typing in a new range address. When modifying the existing range, you can shift the cell pointer to another corner of the range by pressing the period (.) key. When you are satisfied with the new range address, press ENTER.

Examples

To name the range from A4 to C25 as MANTAS:

1. Place the cell pointer on cell A4.
2. Select /Range Name Create.
3. At the prompt for the range name, type `MANTAS` and press ENTER.
4. At the prompt for the range location, paint the range down to cell C25, and press ENTER.

To redefine the range named MANTAS as C4 to F27:

1. Select /Range Name Create.
2. At the prompt for the range name, point to the name MANTAS and press ENTER.
3. At the prompt for the range location, type `C4..F27`, and press ENTER.

To rename the range WHALES as SEALIONS:

1. Select /Range Name Create.
2. At the prompt for the range name, type `SEALIONS` and press ENTER.
3. At the prompt for the range location, enter the name `WHALES`.
4. To delete the old name, select /Range Name Delete.
5. At the prompt for the range name, enter `WHALES` and press ENTER.

Notes

Named ranges are dynamic in size. If you insert or delete rows or columns *within* the boundaries of a named range, the range specification will be automatically updated to include the new rows and/or columns, or to remove the deleted rows, and/or columns. Also, if you move the first or last corner cell of a range, the range address will be updated to reflect the new location. If any formulas refer by address to the range you just named, 1-2-3 will automatically replace the address with the range name.

Cautions

1. Avoid using spaces, punctuation, or any of the special 1-2-3 characters (+ – * / & < > @ or #) in a range name. Also, do not use names that start with a number (15K, for example, cannot be used in a formula) or that correspond

to a cell address (e.g., F24 or IN15.). Do *not* use any of the function names or macro commands as range names. Each of these can cause confusion in 1-2-3 and will produce erratic results.

2. If you move data into the first or last cell of a range with the /Move command or delete the first or last row or column of a range with the /Worksheet Delete command, the range becomes undefined and any functions or formulas that reference that range will show as ERR.
3. Named ranges used in functions or formulas are treated as *relative* addresses. If you copy a formula or function containing a named range, the address will be automatically updated relative to the new location. This may cause the function or formula to produce incorrect results. Given the range A1..A10 named SEALIONS, the formula @SUM(SEALIONS), for example, will produce a different result if you copy it from cell A11 to cell B11. The new formula in B11 will read @SUM(B1..B10).
4. Functions or formulas will treat a named range as *absolute*, if you precede the range name with a $ sign. The function, @PV($PMT,$INT,$TERM), for example, will produce the same results regardless of where you move it because it is absolutely referenced to the ranges named PMT, INT, and TERM. You cannot create a mixed address with a named range.

Range Name Delete

Purpose

Used to delete a single range name.

Description

When you delete a range name, only the name and its link to the defined range are deleted. The data within the range remains unchanged and any references to the previously named range are converted to the range addresses. Typically, you might want to delete range names that are no longer used or that you have since renamed. Unlike previous releases of 1-2-3, when Release 2.2 assigns a new name to a preexisting named range it does not automatically replace the old range name; you must specifically delete the old range name.

Defaults

The current cell.

Usage

Start the command by entering /Range Name Delete. Specify the range to be deleted either by typing in the name or by pointing to the name in the prompt listing. Press ENTER to complete the deletion process. If you delete a range name in error and are using the Undo feature, you can restore the deleted name by pressing UNDO (ALT-F4) immediately after the deletion.

Examples

To delete the range name TURTLES:

1. Select /Range Name Delete.
2. At the prompt for the range name, either enter the name `TURTLES` or point to the name in the prompt listing and press ENTER.

Notes

When a range name is deleted, all functions and formulas that referred to that range are converted to addresses—the last address specified for that range.

Also, if you re-create the deleted range name using the /Range Name Create command, that name will automatically be returned to all the formulas and functions that previously contained the name.

Range Name Label

Purpose

This command allows you to use a label cell in your worksheet as a range name for any adjacent cell. Thus a label cell not only serves to identify the contents of a particular neighboring cell, but it may also be used as a source for the range name for that neighboring cell.

Description

The /Range Name Labels command uses the contents of an existing label cell and assigns it as a range name to a single adjacent cell, immediately above, below, to the right, or to the left of the label cell. This command can also take the labels of an entire row or column and use them as range names for the single cells just above, below, to the right, or to the left of each label.

Defaults

Current cell for the name and the cell to its right for the named range.

Usage

Select /Range Name Label. At the first prompt, select the appropriate direction from the cell(s) to the cell or cells that are to be named with these labels. At the second prompt requesting the label range, specify the range of the label cell(s) by painting the range, typing in the address, or with an existing named range containing the desired label cells. Press ENTER and the new range name(s) will be created.

Examples

To name the cells to the right of the labels in Figure Range.17 with the names contained in the labels:

1. Select /Range Name Labels Right.
2. At the prompt, enter the range containing the range names as `B5..B7`, and press ENTER.

Notes

1. 1-2-3 can use *only* label cells as range names. Cells containing values or formulas are ignored by this command. Verify that the range you define as the source for the range names for the /Range Name Label command contains only labels.
2. If the label contains a name longer than the 15 characters allowed for a range name, 1-2-3 will only use the first 15 characters for the range name.

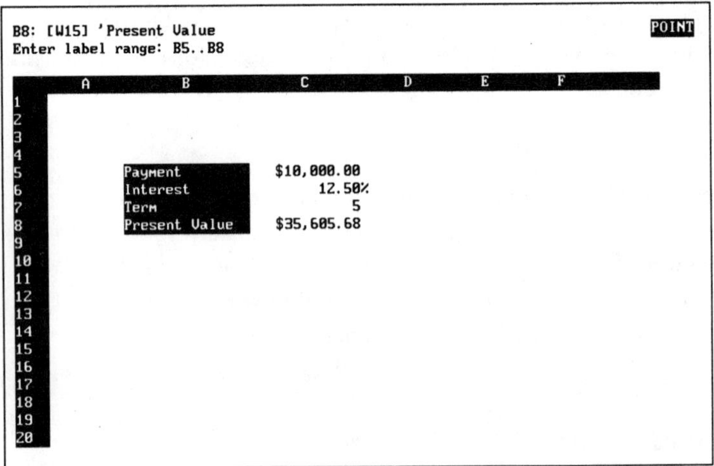

Figure Range.17
/Range Name Labels Right.

Cautions

1. Do not use labels that contain spaces, punctuation, or any of the special 1-2-3 characters: + − * / & < > @ or #. Do not use names that can be interpreted as cell addresses (e.g., F24 or IN15) or names that begin with a number (e.g., 15K). Avoid using function names or macro commands as range names. Each of these can cause confusion in 1-2-3 and will produce erratic results.
2. Editing or erasing the original cell label used for a /Range Name Label command does not alter the previously defined range. You must re-execute the /Range Name Label command after editing the label to have your range name actually correspond to the new label. In addition, this does not delete the old name—the old name must be explicitly deleted with the /Range Name Delete command.

Range Name Reset

Purpose

Used to delete all range names in the current worksheet.

Description

The /Range Name Reset command deletes all range names; it does not delete the data in the named ranges. The Reset option also does not delete references to the named ranges in any formulas or functions in the current worksheet. Instead, any references to deleted range names in formulas and functions are converted to the corresponding range addresses. Thus, if you have assigned the name EELCOSTS to the range A3..A15, the formula @SUM(EELCOSTS) will be converted to @SUM(A3..A15) when you use the /Range Name Reset command.

Defaults

None.

Usage

To delete all range names in the current worksheet, select /Range Name Reset. All range names will be deleted.

Notes

If you delete the range names in error and are using the Undo feature, you can restore the deleted names by pressing UNDO (ALT-F4) immediately after the deletion.

Cautions

The /Range Name Reset command can be extremely destructive to your worksheet if used in error. Therefore, be sure to back up your worksheet before using this command. It is also a good idea to create a range name table listing the range names and their addresses prior to deleting them all. Then you can at least re-enter the range names manually if you later find that the deletion was in error.

Range Name Table

Purpose

Used to generate a two-column table of the range names in the current worksheet and their corresponding addresses. The table can be used to document the ranges used in the worksheet and assist in debugging complex worksheets.

Description

/Range Name Table lists all the range names and their associated addresses in the current worksheet in alphabetical order. See Figure Range.18.

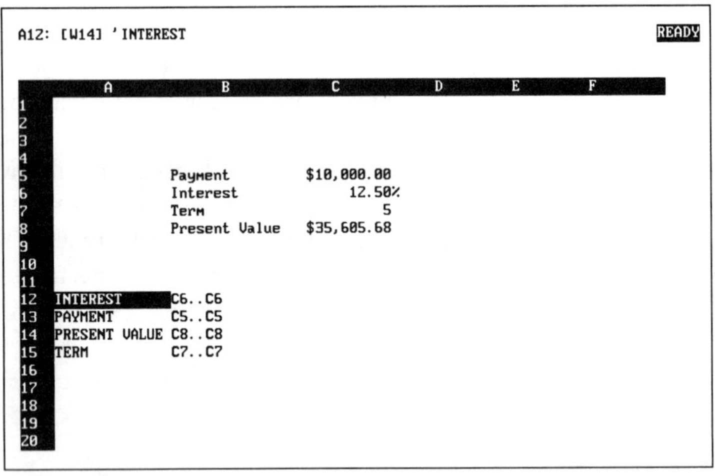

Figure Range.18
/Range Name Table.

Defaults

The table output starts in the current cell.

Usage

To create a range name table, select an output location on the current worksheet, either by address or by range name. Be sure to allow enough room for the resulting two-column table listing so that data is not overwritten. Initiate the command with /Range Name Table. At the prompt for the output range, type in the output location for the table and press ENTER.

Examples

To create a range name table:

1. Select /Range Name Table.
2. Type in the address or name of the output location and press ENTER.

Cautions

The /Range Name Table command creates a table two columns wide and long enough to list all the defined range names in the current worksheet. The resulting table overwrites any data in the output location. Be certain that the output location is large enough to handle the resulting table.

Range Protect

Purpose

When used in combination with /Worksheet Global Protection Enable, this command protects against accidental alteration of data or formulas in a worksheet.

Description

The default state of all individual cells in a worksheet is protection on. The command is used only if you have previously unprotected a cell with the /Range Unprot(ect) command. The /Range Protect option alone is not adequate to protect a range of cells if you have the global worksheet protection setting turned off. Global worksheet protection must be on. Use the /Worksheet Global Protection Enable command.

After global protection is activated, the protection status of a given cell can be determined by looking at the control panel when the pointer is located on the cell in question. If the control panel displays PR next to the cell address, the cell is protected; if it displays U, the cell is unprotected. Unprotected cells are also displayed in color (on color monitors) or highlighted.

Defaults

The current cell.

Usage

To reprotect previously unprotected cells, initiate the command with /Range Protect. At the prompt, type in the range to be protected by address, by name, or by painting it. Press ENTER to complete the range protection.

Examples

To protect the range A3 to D15:

1. Select /Range Protect.
2. Type (or paint) in the range `A3..D15` and press ENTER.

Notes

Protected cells cannot be accessed by the user during /Range Input commands. Consequently, protected cells can be used as secure labels for the unprotected input cells, or they can be used for formulas that you don't want the user to be able to change.

Cautions

The /Range Protect command alone is not adequate to protect a range of cells. Global worksheet protection must also be on. Turn on global protection with /Worksheet Global Protection Enable.

Range Search

Purpose

Use Search to find all occurrences of a given string in labels or formulas. The Search command also offers two modes of operation: a Find mode that simply highlights each occurrence of the string, and a Search and Replace mode that finds each occurrence of a string and replaces it with an alternate string.

Description

The /Range Search command can be used to locate a given string within the range you specify. You can search for letters or numbers in a label cell or formula. You *cannot* search for values. 1-2-3 will search for the string in label cells only, in formula cells only, or in both label and formula cells. Once it finds a match, /Range Search can either highlight each match, or replace the string with a new string.

Defaults

None.

Usage

Search for a string To search for all occurrences of a string within a given range, initiate the command with /Range Search. 1-2-3 will prompt you for the range you wish to search; specify the range by address, by name, or by painting it and press ENTER. If you have already used /Range Search in the current 1-2-3 session, 1-2-3 "remembers" the last range searched and supplies it as the default range. At the next prompt for the search string, type in the text you want to locate and press ENTER. You will then be prompted to select Labels, Formulas, or Both.

If you select Labels, 1-2-3 will search only label cells in the selected range; if you choose Formulas, 1-2-3 will search only cells with formulas. Choose Both to search formulas and labels.

Next, you must select the search mode. To do a simple search without replacement, select Find. 1-2-3 highlights the first cell in the range that contains the search string and displays a mini menu with two options: to move to the Next occurrence of the string or to Quit. If you select Next, 1-2-3 moves on to the next occurrence of the search string. Quit returns you to READY mode. When there are no further occurrences of the search string in the specified range, 1-2-3 reports "String Not Found". Press ESC or ENTER to clear the message and return to READY mode.

Search and replace a string To search for a given string and replace it with an alternative string, select /Range Search, specify the range you wish to search by address or name, or by painting it, and press ENTER. 1-2-3 will ask you for the string that you want to locate; type it in and press ENTER. Again, if you have used the search command earlier, 1-2-3 remembers the last search string and supplies it as the default.

1-2-3 then prompts you to select Labels, Formulas, or Both. If you select Labels, 1-2-3 searches only the label cells in the selected range. Choose Formulas to search only formulas. Choose Both to search formulas and labels. You are then asked to select a search mode. Choose Replace from the menu and 1-2-3 will prompt you for the replacement string. Type it in, press ENTER, and 1-2-3 will begin the search-and-replace operation. 1-2-3 stops at the first occurrence of the search string and offers four options: All, Next, Quit, or Replace.

All Tells 1-2-3 to automatically replace all occurrences of the search string with the replacement string. You will not be asked for confirmation. After making the appropriate substitutions, 1-2-3 returns you to READY mode.

Replace Instructs 1-2-3 to replace the currently displayed instance of the search string with the replacement string and to move on to the next occurrence and offer once again the options: All, Next, Quit, or Replace. The Replace option therefore lets you confirm each individual replacement in context.

Next Tells 1-2-3 to skip the replacement of the current occurrence of the search string and to move to the next instance of the search string. At the next occurence of the string, 1-2-3 will again offer the option: All, Next, Quit, or Replace.

Quit Returns 1-2-3 to READY mode without making any further replacements.

Examples

To search labels for the string Neon Tetra in the range named TROPICAL:

1. Select /Range Search.
2. Type `TROPICAL` and press ENTER.
3. Select Labels.
4. Type `Neon Tetra` and press ENTER.
5. Select Find.
6. The first instance of the string Neon Tetra will be highlighted. To find the next instance, select Next; to quit, select Quit.

To replace all occurrences of the word Dolphin in both labels and formulas in the range MAMMALS with the word Porpoise:

1. Select /Range Search.
2. Type `MAMMALS` and press ENTER.
3. Select Both.
4. Type `Dolphin` and press ENTER.
5. Select Replace.
6. Type `Porpoise` and press ENTER.
7. The first instance of the word Dolphin will be highlighted. Select All to replace that and all subsequent instances.

Notes

The /Range Search command is not case sensitive, it treats uppercase and lowercase letters as the same. The replacement string you specify, however, will be entered exactly as you type it.

Cautions

The /Range Search Both Replace All command may produce unintended results in formulas that contain the search string. This is especially true for short search strings that might be embedded in various range names or addresses. A more cautious approach is to use the Replace option in place of the All option when searching in formulas.

Range Transpose

Purpose

/Range Transpose is a variation of the /Copy command. Use this command to copy a one-or two-dimensional range, and exchange (or transpose) the dimensions: Columns will be converted to rows and vice versa.

Description

If you transpose a two-dimensional range within a worksheet, 1-2-3 converts the rows of data to columns and the columns of data to rows. In two dimensions, Transpose is particularly good for changing data from a standard database format (with field labels at the left and the data in columns to the right) to a standard spreadsheet format (with the field labels in a row at the top and the data in rows below). When formulas are transposed, they are converted to *constant* values—the values that were shown just prior to the shift. This prevents them from losing all meaning in the new location, since their relative position to their referenced cells has been twisted.

Defaults

None.

Usage

To transpose a two-dimensional range in your worksheet from rows to columns, be sure to recalculate the formulas with the CALC (F9) key (if necessary) before selecting /Range Transpose. At the first prompt for the FROM range, specify the range to transpose (by name, by address, or by painting it) and then press ENTER. At the prompt for the TO range, specify the upper-left corner of the output range for the transposed source range and press ENTER. Be sure that the output range does not overlap the source range and that the output range has enough room to contain all the data from the source range after it has been transposed. See Figure Range.19.

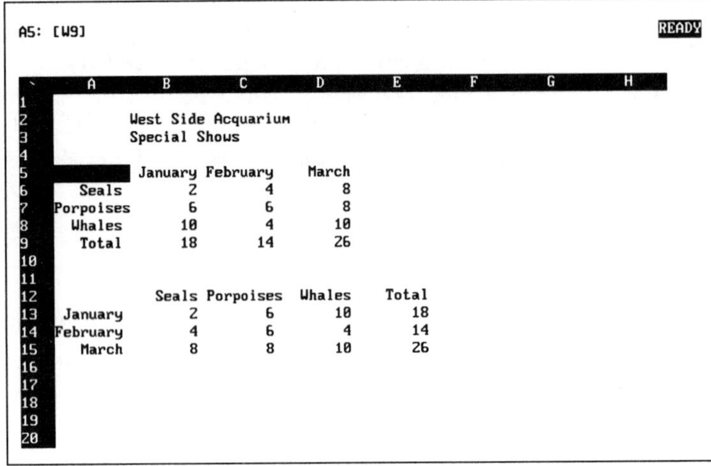

Figure Range.19
/Range Transpose.

Examples

To transpose the range A1 to F4 into the range G1 to J6:

1. Press F9 to CALC, if the CALC indicator is on at the bottom of the screen.
2. Select /Range Trans(pose).
3. Type in (or paint) `A1..F4` and press ENTER.
4. Move the cursor to G1 and press ENTER.

Notes

All formulas are converted to values before they are moved, so be sure to recalculate the values prior to transposition. Each cell retains its format and protection status as it is moved.

Cautions

1. /Range Trans(pose) does not automatically recalculate the values of formulas before converting them to values. If you have set the recalculation mode to Manual, be sure to recalculate your worksheet by pressing CALC (F9) before selecting this command.

2. If you specify overlapping source and output ranges you may lose data. If you have activated the Undo feature, you can use it to undo the resulting mess.

Range Unprotect

Purpose

Most often used in conjunction with /Worksheet Global Protection Enable and /Range Input to permit users to change the contents of certain unprotected cells while preventing them from altering protected cells.

Description

The default state of all individual cells in a worksheet is protection "on." (Meanwhile, the default state of /Worksheet protection is "disable.") You do not need to explicitly set the protection status to "off" unless you plan to use /Worksheet Global Protection Enable or the /Range Input command. The protection status of a given cell can be determined when global protection is turned on. When the pointer is located on a particular cell, the control panel displays PR for protected or U for unprotected to the left of the current cell address. Unprotected cells are also displayed in color or are highlighted.

Defaults

The current cell.

Usage

To unprotect a range of cells, initiate the command with /Range Unprot(ect). At the prompt, specify the range to be unprotected (by address, by name, or by painting it). Press ENTER to complete the range unprotection. All cells in the unprotected range will display a U in the control panel.

Examples

To unprotect the range A3 to D15:

1. Select /Range Unprot(ect).
2. Type in (or paint) `A3..D15` and press ENTER.

Cautions

/Range Protect (the default state) alone is not adequate to protect a range of cells. You must also be sure that worksheet protection is on with the /Worksheet Global Protection Enable command.

Range Value

Purpose

When copying the source range to a target location, this command converts all formulas in the source to unchanging values in the target range.

Description

/Range Value is used to convert formulas in the source range to their current values when copying them to a destination range. The original formulas are not altered unless the output range overlaps the source range, causing the copy to overwrite the original. If the output (TO) range is the same as the source (FROM) range, this command effectively converts all formulas in the range to their current values.

Defaults

The current cell.

Usage

To copy a range to a new location with current formula results rather than the formulas themselves, be sure to recalculate all values with the CALC key (F9). Initiate the command with /Range Value. At the first prompt for the FROM range, specify the source range (by name, by address, or by painting it) and press ENTER. At the second prompt for the TO range, specify the upper-left corner of the output range (by name, by address, or by painting) and press ENTER. The source range will be copied and all of its formulas converted to constant values. If the output range is the same as the input range, the formulas in the source range will effectively be converted to their values.

Notes

To convert a formula to its value in a single cell, you can also highlight the cell to be converted, press EDIT (F2), press CALC (F9), and then press ENTER.

Cautions

/Range Value does *not* automatically recalculate the values of formulas before converting them to values. If you have set the recalculation mode to Manual, be sure to recalculate your worksheet by pressing CALC (F9) before selecting this command.

▸ System Command

Purpose

Used to leave 1-2-3 temporarily. By suspending 1-2-3's operation you can go to the operating system prompt, perform various other tasks, and then return to 1-2-3 where you left off.

Description

The /System command can be used to return to the operating system without terminating 1-2-3. This is especially useful for executing such DOS commands as FORMAT, CHKDSK, and DIR. You can even run other programs such as file managers or word processors from within 1-2-3. Much of this book was written by running WordPerfect from within 1-2-3. To return to 1-2-3, type `Exit` at the DOS prompt.

Defaults

None.

Usage

To temporarily suspend 1-2-3 and return to the operating system, select /System. To return to 1-2-3, type `Exit` at the system prompt.

Cautions

Do not load any Memory-Resident, Ram-Resident, or Terminate and Stay (TSR) programs from the System option. Also, do not run the operating system PRINT command. These kinds of programs are likely to create memory conflicts and prevent you from returning to 1-2-3.

▸ Worksheet Commands

Purpose

Used to control the display of worksheets on screen; the insertion and deletion of rows and columns; and the setting of global defaults for format, label alignment, column widths, etc. /Worksheet commands are commands that are performed in general. They allow you to specify global preferences. These commands affect the way you operate the program, and can apply to the current worksheet as a whole, or to the system as a whole. (These global preference settings can be modified at any time for particular needs in particular circumstances.)

Description

There are 10 basic /Worksheet commands. Each one brings you to various submenus. The individual /Worksheet commands are discussed in detail in the following sections. Here is a summary of each command:

Column Used to set the width of one or more columns. Also can be used to hide one or more columns or to redisplay hidden columns. (Hidden columns are not displayed or printed.)

Delete Used to delete rows or columns from the current worksheet.

Erase Used to erase the current worksheet data from memory.

Global Used to set many of the formatting and other system defaults. Sets the default cell format, label alignment, column width, cell protection status, and the display of zeros. Sets the recalculation mode.

Insert Used to insert columns or rows.

Learn Used to specify a Learn Range that holds the keystrokes recorded with the LEARN key (ALT-F5).

Page Inserts a special page-break character at the current row.

Status Displays the current 1-2-3 status, including memory, global settings, hardware configuration, and circular references.

Titles Used to lock (or "freeze") rows, or columns, or both so that they act as stationary titles on the screen display. Also used to unlock or release titles.

Window Used to control the display. Allows you to split the display horizontally or vertically to display different portions of the worksheet simultaneously. Also used to synchronize or unsynchronize the scrolling of the windows.

Worksheet Column

Purpose

Used to set the width of one or more columns. Also used to hide one or more columns or to redisplay them. Hidden columns are not displayed or printed.

Description

The Column commands only affect the way a column is displayed on the screen or in print. They do not affect any underlying data. Thus, if you choose to hide a column, you can still refer to the data contained in the hidden column, but it will not be displayed or printed. In the same manner, when you change the column width you are not altering the number of digits stored by 1-2-3 for numbers nor the number of characters in a label. It only affects how many digits or characters are displayed or printed. The Column command affects all cells in the column. You *cannot* alter portions of a column independently. There are five Column commands:

Column-Range The Column-Range command allows you specify a column width for several adjacent columns (or a range of columns). Specify the range of columns to reset by address, name, or by painting it; then use Set-Width to set the width of the range to a value other than the default width. (The width is measured by the number of standard-size characters that will fit in a column.) Use Reset-Width to reset the column range to the global default width.

Display The Display command lets you redisplay one or more columns that were previously hidden.

Hide The Hide command removes the designated column(s) from the display and from any printouts of the worksheet. All numbers or formulas contained in the hidden column(s) continue to exist and operate normally.

Reset-Width Resets the column width to the global default.

Set-Width Allows you to specify a width for the current column; either type in the desired number of characters or use the left and right cursor keys to stretch or compress the column one character at a time.

Usage

To set the column width of a given column, select /Worksheet Column Set-Width and then type in the desired character width or use the cursor keys to stretch or compress the column. To set the same width for a series of adjacent columns, select /Worksheet Column Column-Range Set-Width, define the range (you will automatically be in POINT mode), and specify the new character width as desired.

To hide one or more adjacent columns, select /Worksheet Column Hide and specify the column or range of columns you wish to hide (by address or by painting the range). To redisplay one or more hidden columns, select /Worksheet Column Display; all the hidden columns will be temporarily redisplayed, each one with an asterisk next to the column letter in the worksheet frame. Select the column(s) you want to redisplay by typing in their addresses or by pointing to them, and then press ENTER. The remaining hidden columns will again disappear and the unhidden columns will be displayed.

Worksheet Delete

Purpose

Used to delete rows or columns from the current worksheet.

Description

The Delete command lets you select one or more row(s) or column(s) in the current worksheet for deletion. Any data or formulas contained in the deleted range will be erased. Unless you have enabled the Undo feature, there is no way to reverse this step.

When you use the /Worksheet Delete command to delete rows or columns, it may affect the various range addresses you have specified; ranges referred to in formulas or ranges with assigned names. 1-2-3 will *automatically* contract the referenced or named range to exclude the deleted rows or columns.

Usage

Before deleting a row or column you should make sure that you really want to delete it. Remember that if you do not have Undo enabled, you cannot recover a deleted element. Even if you do have the Undo feature enabled you can not recover the deleted element if you have performed other Undo events since the deletion. If you are not certain, save the file to disk prior to using /Worksheet Delete.

To delete a range of row(s) or column(s) from the current worksheet, place the cell pointer in the top row or left-most column to be deleted. Select /Worksheet Delete and then choose the appropriate dimension (Column or Row). Highlight the range of columns or rows to be deleted and press ENTER.

Notes

To remove data from a range of cells without removing the underlying column or row of cells, use the /Range Erase command.

Cautions

If you do not have Undo enabled, you cannot recover a deleted element. Even with Undo enabled, you cannot recover the element if you have performed another Undo action subsequent to deleting the element. Also, sometimes there is not enough memory available to perform an Undo.

Worksheet Erase

Purpose

Used to remove the current worksheet from memory, replacing it with a blank worksheet.

Description

The /Worksheet Erase command completely removes all data from memory and creates a new blank worksheet. It is the equivalent of quitting from 1-2-3 and starting all over again.

Usage

To clear the current worksheet from memory, simply select /Worksheet Erase. You will be asked to confirm your choice. Select Yes to erase the worksheet or No to cancel the Erase command.

Notes

If you have Undo enabled, you can Undo the /Worksheet Erase command.

Cautions

While 1-2-3 does ask you to confirm your choice to clear a worksheet, it is still extremely easy to thoughtlessly erase a worksheet. Use this command with extreme caution.

Worksheet Global

Purpose

Used to set many of the formatting and other system defaults including the default cell format, label alignment, column width, protection status, and the display of zeros. /Worksheet Global also sets the recalculation mode.

Description

The current Global settings are saved with the current worksheet. They will be restored whenever the current worksheet is loaded. They will remain in force for the remainder of the current work session unless you retrieve a worksheet with other settings. The current Global Default option settings can also be saved as the default setting for all future sessions and new worksheets by selecting the /Worksheet Global Default Update option. This saves the current settings to the 123.CNF configuration file. The options for the /Worksheet Global command include:

Col-Width Used to set the global default column width for the current worksheet. All columns will use the global default width unless they are explicitly set to a different column width (e.g., with the /Range Column command). When you select /Worksheet Column Reset-Width, all columns will be reset to the global default width. (The global default column width for new worksheets is nine characters.)

Default Sets the 1-2-3 configuration settings, including: the Autoexec macro; the default directory; the default printer; a default printer setup string; the default clock, international, and beep settings; and Undo. You can save your changes to the default configuration settings in a 123.CNF file for future use.

Format Used to set the global default cell format for the current worksheet. All cells will use the global default unless they are explicitly formatted otherwise. When you select /Range Format Reset, all cells in the range will be reset to the global default format. (The global default format for new worksheets is General.)

Label Used to set the global default label prefix for label alignment (Left=', Right=", or Center=^) in the current worksheet. All label cells will use the global default unless they are explicitly aligned in a different way. (The global default label assignment for new worksheets is left-justified.)

Protection Global Protection works in league with /Range Prot and /Range Unprot to set the global default protection status for the current worksheet. When global protection is enabled, you can specify which cells can be changed with the /Rang Prot and /Range Unprot commands. When global protection is disabled, /Range Prot and /Range Unprot have no effect.

Recalc Used to set the recalculation mode.

Zero Determines how zero values are displayed. You can select to display zero values, a blank cell, or a label of your choice.

The current global settings are displayed in the Global Setting screen, whenever the /Worksheet Global command is invoked. See Figure Worksheet.1.

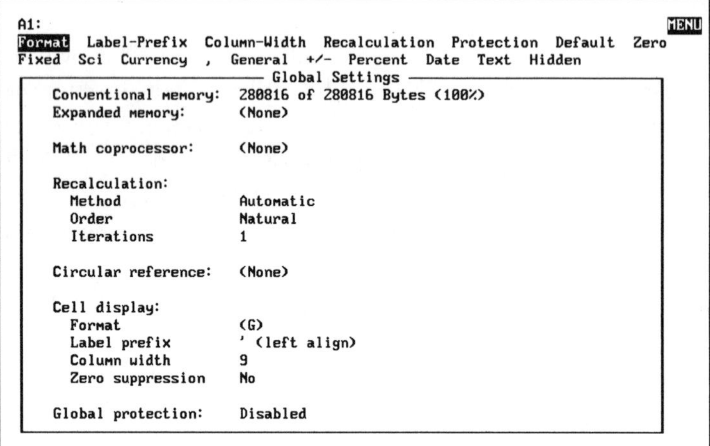

Figure Worksheet.1
Global Settings screen.

Worksheet Global Column-Width

Purpose

Used to set the global default column width for the current worksheet. All columns in the worksheet will use the global default unless they are explicitly set to a different column width (with the /Worksheet Column Set-Width command).

Description

The global default column width is set at 9 characters when you first load the program. You can set it to any value between 1 and 240 for the current worksheet.

Usage

To reset the global column width, select /Worksheet Global Column-Width. At the prompt, type in the new width as a number of characters between 1 and 240. You can also use the left or right cursor keys to dynamically stretch or compress the current setting.

Notes

If you are frequently using dates in Date 1 format (which requires at least 10 characters), you may wish to change the default column width to 10.

Select /Worksheet Column Reset-Width to reset all columns to the global default.

Worksheet Global Default

Purpose

Sets the 1-2-3 configuration settings, including: the Autoexec macro; the default directory; the default printer (and printer setup string, if necessary); the default clock, international, and beep settings; and Undo.

Description

The current Global Default settings are displayed in the Default Settings screen whenever this option is selected. See Figure Worksheet.2.

The /Worksheet Global Default option includes the following options:

Autoexec Used to specify whether 1-2-3 should run the autoexec macro (named \0) when it loads a file that contains one. The initial default setting is Yes. To turn off the autoexec feature, select No. To turn it back on, select Yes. When you change this feature it remains in force for the rest of the current 1-2-3 session (until you select Quit from the main menu). To make the current setting "permanent" and applicable to all future sessions, you *must* save it in your 123.CNF configuration file. To do this, select the Update option from the /Worksheet Global Default menu.

Directory Selects the default directory where 1-2-3 will store and look for worksheets, print files, and graph files. When you first use 1-2-3 the default directory is set to the directory in which you installed the program files. You should change it to another directory to keep your 1-2-3 data files separate from

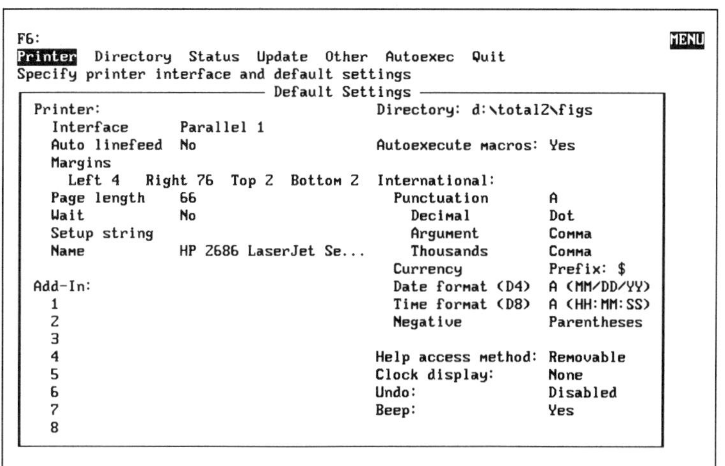

Figure Worksheet.2
Default Settings Screen.

the program files. This makes it far easier to find specific files and to back up your data files regularly.

To change the default directory, select the Directory option and type in the full directory path for the new directory. 1-2-3 will check to make sure the directory exists and will issue an error message if it does not.

To make the new default directory setting "permanent" and applicable to future sessions, you must save it in your 123.CNF configuration file. To do this, select the Update option from the /Worksheet Global Default menu. (To reset the default directory temporarily, consider using the /File Dir command, which is designed to overrule the default directory for the current session only.)

Other Allows you to set the defaults for Clock, International, Undo, and Beep as follows:

Beep Used to turn the computer's bell (or beeper) on or off. When it is set on, the bell will sound whenever 1-2-3 reports an error or encounters a {BEEP} command in a macro. To set the bell on, select Yes. (This is the default). To turn the bell off, select No.

Clock Determines two things: first, whether 1-2-3 should display a clock or file name, or neither in the bottom left corner of the screen. And second, whether your date and time format (when displayed) should appear in the International or Standard forms. The initial default is to display the clock in standard format. You have five options:

Clock Displays the date and time (no file name) at all times using either the Standard or International format (select one or the other).

File name If the current file has been assigned a name, the name is displayed, otherwise the date and time are displayed. (For unnamed files, the date and time are displayed in either Standard or International format—your choice.)

International Sets the date to Long Intn'l (D4) and the time format to Short Intn'l (D9). (The Long Intn'l and Short Intn'l date and time formats are specified via the /Worksheet Global Default Other International Date and Time commands.)

None Turns off both the clock and file name display at the bottom left of the screen.

Standard Sets the date to DD-MMM-YY and the time to HH:MM (AM/PM) formats. This is the initial default format for the file-and-clock indicator. (It is displayed if you select Clock or File name above.)

Help The Help setting determines if the Help file remains in memory after it is first accessed or is removed to free up the memory. If you set Help to Instant, the Help file (once accessed) stays open in memory for immediate access; if you set Help to Removable, 1-2-3 calls Help into memory and then removes it every time the F1 HELP key was pressed. It is usually recommended that users in a two-drive system select Removeable. Otherwise, you will be forced to keep the Help disk in the drive at all times.

International Used to set the currency symbol, punctuation for numbers, date formats, time formats, the argument separator for @functions, and macro commands, and the format of negative numbers. There are five options on the /Worksheet Global Default Other International menu:

Currency Used to set the currency symbol character (and its position—before or after the currency value) for values displayed in the currency format. To change the currency symbol, select the Currency option and enter the desired character or characters (up to 15) at the prompt; then select either Prefix or Suffix to indicate its position. If you want to combine characters (e.g., Y and = to produce a Yen sign), you can use the ALT-F1 Compose key. To produce the Yen character, for example, press ALT-F1, and type in the compose sequence(Y and =) and then press ENTER. (See the LICS code tables in Appendix B for the complete list of characters and compose sequences.)

Date Sets the format for the D4 Long Intn'l and the D5 Short Intn'l date formats. Also sets the format of the date portion of the Clock display (if you select International on the /Worksheet Global Default Other Clock menu). You can select from the following options:

Long International	Short International
A - MM/DD/YY (the default)	MM/DD
B - DD/MM/YY	DD/MM
C - DD.MM.YY	DD.MM
D - YY-MM-DD	MM-DD

Your Date format selection determines which format can be used with the @DATEVALUE( ) function. (See the /Range Format Date Time section for complete information on date and time formats.)

Negative Determines how 1-2-3 displays negative numbers in currency or comma formats. You can select either Parentheses (the default) or the Minus sign.

Punctuation Specifies what characters 1-2-3 will use for the decimal point, the thousands separator, and the argument separator. You can select from the following character combinations:

	Period	Argument	Thousands
A -	.	,	,
B -	,	.	.
C -	.	;	,
D -	,	;	.
E -	.	,	none
F -	,	.	none
G -	.	;	none
H -	,	;	none

If you select options B or F, which set the argument separator to a period, you must be sure to *separate* all range specifications with two periods as in A1..A5.

Time Sets the format for the D8 Long Intn'l and D9 Short Intn'l time formats and the format of the time portion of the clock display. You can select from the following:

Long International	Short International
A - HH:MM:SS (the default)	HH:MM
B - HH.MM.SS	HH.MM
C - HH,MM,SS	HH,MM
D - HHhMMmSSs	HHh,MMm

Your Time format selection determines which format can be used with the @TIMEVALUE( ) function. (See the /Range Format Date Time discussion for complete information on date and time formats.)

Undo Toggles the Undo feature (ALT-F4) on and off. To activate the Undo feature, select Enable. To deactivate, select Disable. The Undo feature is initially turned on.

To make the current Undo setting "permanent" and applicable to future sessions, you will have to reset the 123.CNF configuration file. To do this, select the Update option from the /Worksheet Global Default menu.

When Undo is on, 1-2-3 reserves space in memory to keep a backup copy of the current worksheet. The backup copy is only "one step behind" the current worksheet, and occupies about the same amount of memory as the current worksheet. 1-2-3 can and will use expanded memory for the Undo buffer, if available; but it must use conventional memory if there is no (or little) expanded memory available for use. This can put many constraints in your system, especially when you are working with large or complicated worksheets and you have add-ins installed. Under such circumstances, if you have Undo disabled, and you wish to turn it on, you may have to save your current file, detach your add-ins, and erase your worksheet with /Worksheet Erase. Then, you have to turn on Undo and retrieve your file.

Printer Allows you to specify the default printer and printer interface, default setup strings, as well as printed output settings—margins and page length. These option settings can be overruled temporarily by the /Print [Printer or File] commands for the current print job; but each time you restart 1-2-3, the system will return to these defaults. If you load a worksheet file that was saved with other settings, those previously saved settings take precedence over any default settings selected with /Worksheet Global Default Printer.

You can select the following global printer settings:

AutoLf The AutoLf option allows you to specify whether or not your printer automatically inserts a line feed command at the end of each line of print. If you specify Yes, 1-2-3 will skip sending its own line feed at the end of each line. If you specify No, 1-2-3 will include a line feed command at the end of each line.

If your printed reports are printing out with one line overwriting another, neither the printer nor 1-2-3 is generating the necessary line feed command. You should change the AutoLf option to No to turn on 1-2-3's automatic line feed. If your reports are printing out with double spacing, both the printer and 1-2-3 are generating line feeds; you should change the AutoLf option to Yes to turn off 1-2-3's automatic line feed.

This command may seem to be structured somewhat backwards (selecting No to turn 1-2-3 automatic line feed On). Just remember that you are actually telling 1-2-3 what the capabilities of your printer are. (No, it does not insert a linefeed; or Yes, it does include a line feed.)

Bottom Used to set the bottom margin. The bottom margin is measured in lines from the bottom of the page and can be set to any value between 0 and 32. The initial default is two lines from bottom of the page. (The sum of the top and bottom margins of course cannot exceed the total page length.)

Interface You can select any of the available printer interfaces numbered 1–8. As you move your cursor to each number, the option is defined in the third row of the control panel: 1 is Parallel1, 2 is Serial1, 3 is parallel2, etc. (e.g., parallel or serial ports). The initial default is number 1, LPT1:. Be sure to select the right port to have your printer operate correctly. If you select a serial interface, you will also have to specify the appropriate baud rate for the printer, and you must check that the serial port is correctly initialized for the selected baud rate by executing the proper MODE command from DOS (e.g., MODE COM1:9600,n,8,1,p). See your operating system manual or printer manual for more information about serial ports and MODE commands. Use options 1–4 if your printer is directly attached to your computer and options 5–8 (DOS devices LPT1–4) if you are using a shared printer on a network.

Left The left margin is measured in standard-width characters (10 pitch) from the left edge of the page. The left margin cannot be set higher than the right margin. The left margin can be set to any value between 0 and 240. The initial default is four standard characters from the left edge of the page.

Name Use this command to change the current printer and to select another from a list of those you have installed. (See the Installation section for more information on installing printers.) When you select the Name option, you will be presented with a menu of numbers; each number corresponds to one of the text printers you have installed. The list of available printers is in the order that you installed them. As you highlight any number on the list, 1-2-3 will display the name of the printer and any installed options for that printer on the second line of the selection menu.

Pg-Length Sets the logical page length in lines. The internal page length setting is used to determine where page breaks, headers, and footers are placed in print jobs. The initial default is 66 lines. You can select any value between 1 and 100. In general, the page length should be set to the number of lines per inch that your printer prints times the length of the paper in inches (e.g., 6 lines per inch x 11 inches). Note: Laser printers usually need a page length of 60.

Right The right margin is measured in standard-width characters from the *left* edge of the page. The right margin cannot be set to a value lower than the left margin. The right margin can be set to any value between 0 and 240. The initial default is 76 standard characters from the *left* edge of the page.

Setup Allows you to specify additional printer control commands that will be sent directly to the printer at the start of each print job. Printer control codes are specific to each printer. In general, you will have to refer to your printer's manual to determine the appropriate setup strings to perform the desired command. See the /Print [Printer or File] Options Setup command and Appendix C for more information on printer setup strings.

The printer setup string usually begins with the ESC character, followed by one or more characters. You can either use the actual character (be careful about upper- and lowercase) or type the ASCII numerical code for the character preceded by a backslash (\) character. Since most printer control codes (ESC and the other ASCII characters 1–31) have no character equivalent, they must be entered as ASCII codes.

Suppose you wanted to select a particular font that is not supported by 1-2-3. The command code for italic printing on a Epson Printer is ESC 4. You could type in your setup string as \027\052, the ASCII codes for ESC and 4. Alternatively, you could enter the ASCII code for ESC followed by the character 4 (e.g., \O274).

Top Used to set the top margin. The top margin is measured in lines from the top of the page; it can be set to any value between 0 and 32. The default top margin is two lines from top of the page. (The sum of the top and bottom margins cannot of course exceed the total page length.)

Wait Used to pause the print process after each page so that you can insert single sheets of paper. If you use a single sheet paper feeder or if you often need to pause printing in order to insert a sheet of letterhead stationery or special paper, you should turn this option on. The initial default for this option is off. To turn the option on, select Yes; to turn it off again, select No.

Status Displays the current setting for the worksheet global defaults. (See Figure Worksheet.2.) To see the current settings for recalc, column-width, cell-format, label-prefix, zero-display, protection status, as well as information about the available memory and your computer's processors, select /Worksheet Status.

Update The Update option should be the last step before leaving the /Worksheet Global Default menu. Update saves your changes for future use in the 123.CNF configuration file. If you do not update the configuration file, the changes you make to the global defaults will remain active for the current 1-2-3 session only. (They will, however, be saved with the current file when you select /File Save.) The system will revert to the old global settings the next time you load the program. This may be acceptable if you only want to change an item for the current session. If you want to change a setting just for a particular worksheet file, you are better off making that change "manually," using one of the corresponding /Range, /Print, /Graph, /File, or other /Worksheet commands, rather than using the /Worksheet Global Default menu.

Worksheet Global Format

Purpose

Used to set the default format for cells in the current worksheet.

Description

The /Worksheet Global Format menu offers the same selection of formatting options as the /Range Format menu. The /Worksheet Global Format choices apply to the worksheet as a *whole*, rather than to a portion of a worksheet. Remember, if you explicitly format a range of cells with the /Range Format command, that setting takes precedence over the global format. When you first load the program, the initial global format is General.

The /Worksheet Global Format commands alter the way a value or formula result is displayed on the screen or is printed on a report. The format setting does *not* change the underlying number either in form or in the number of decimal places that will be used for subsequent calculations (15 significant digits). In some instances, the displayed format will round the undisplayed decimal places into those displayed.

The options for /Worksheet Global Format are as follows:

, (Comma) Displays numbers with commas separating every third digit to the left of the decimal point and a specified number of decimal places (up to 15) to the right of the decimal point. Negative numbers are displayed with parentheses or a minus sign, depending on the setting of the parentheses option under the Other option described below. See Figure Worksheet.3.

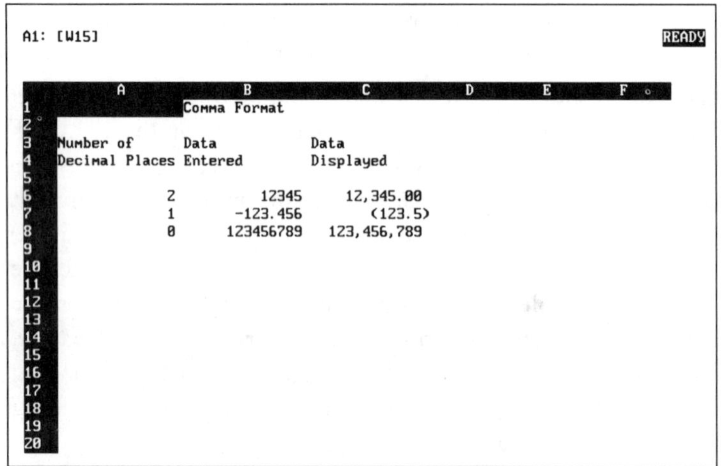

Figure Worksheet.3
Comma Format.

Currency Displays numbers with a leading dollar sign ($), with commas separating every third digit to the left of the decimal point and a specified number of decimal places (up to 15) to the right of the decimal point. Negative numbers are displayed with parentheses or a minus sign, depending on the setting of the Parentheses option under the Other option described below. (Alternate currency symbols—preceding or following—may be specified with the /Worksheet Global Default Other International Currency option.) See Figure Worksheet.4.

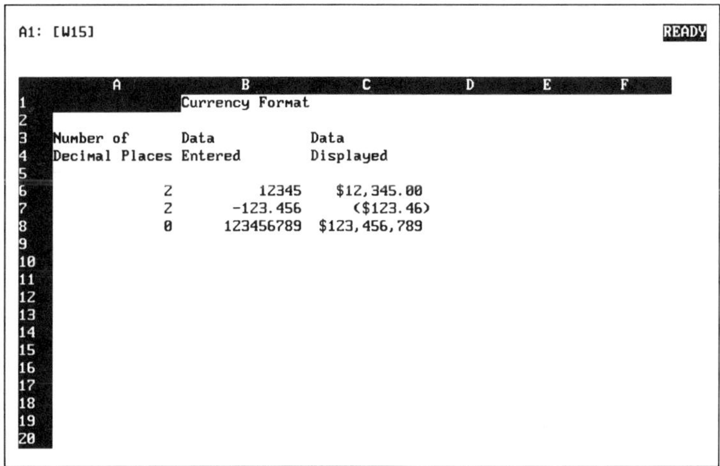

Figure Worksheet.4
Currency Format.

Date Takes valid date serial numbers (1 to 73050, corresponding to dates from Jan 1 1900 to Dec 31 2099) and displays them in one of five date formats:

D1 DD-MMM-YY 12-Jan-89
D2 DD-MMM 12-Jan
D3 MMM-YY Jan-89
D4 Long Int'l 01/12/89
D5 Short Int'l 01/12

The Long Int'l and Short Int'l date formats may be adjusted or reordered through the /Worksheet Global Default Other International Date option. Invalid dates are shown as asterisks. See Figure Worksheet.5.

Date Time Uses the decimal portion of a number to determine a time value for that number; decimals can run from .000 (which represents 12:00 AM) up to .999 (which represents 11:59 PM). 1-2-3 produces a time value for negative numbers by subtracting the decimal portion from one, as though you were going backward in time. The time value is displayed in one of four time formats.

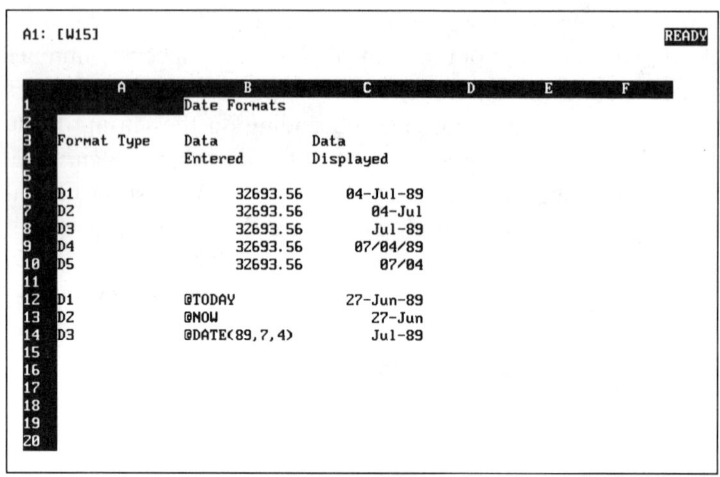

A1: [W15] READY

	A	B	C	D	E	F
1		Date Formats				
2						
3	Format Type	Data	Data			
4		Entered	Displayed			
5						
6	D1	32693.56	04-Jul-89			
7	D2	32693.56	04-Jul			
8	D3	32693.56	Jul-89			
9	D4	32693.56	07/04/89			
10	D5	32693.56	07/04			
11						
12	D1	@TODAY	27-Jun-89			
13	D2	@NOW	27-Jun			
14	D3	@DATE(89,7,4)	Jul-89			
15						
16						
17						
18						
19						
20						

Figure Worksheet.5
Date Formats.

D6	HH:MM:SS (AM/PM)	4:27:45 PM
D7	HH:MM (AM/PM)	4:27 AM
D8	Long Int'l (24Hr)	16:27:45
D9	Short Int'l (24Hr)	15:27

The Long Int'l and Short Int'l time formats may be adjusted through the /Worksheet Global Default Other International Time option. See Figure Worksheet.6.

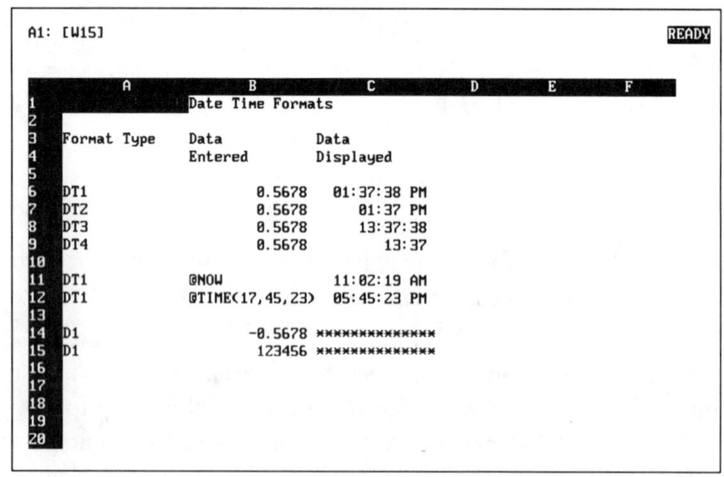

A1: [W15] READY

	A	B	C	D	E	F
1		Date Time Formats				
2						
3	Format Type	Data	Data			
4		Entered	Displayed			
5						
6	DT1	0.5678	01:37:38 PM			
7	DT2	0.5678	01:37 PM			
8	DT3	0.5678	13:37:38			
9	DT4	0.5678	13:37			
10						
11	DT1	@NOW	11:02:19 AM			
12	DT1	@TIME(17,45,23)	05:45:23 PM			
13						
14	D1	-0.5678	*************			
15	D1	123456	*************			
16						
17						
18						
19						
20						

Figure Worksheet.6
Date/Time Formats.

Fixed Displays numbers without commas and allows you to set the number of decimal points displayed (up to 15 decimal places). Values with more decimals digits than displayed will be rounded. If you set your format for Fixed with 2 decimal places, even the integer 12 will be displayed as 12.00. Values between 1 and –1 will be displayed with a leading zero (e.g., 0.7). Negative numbers are preceded with a minus sign. See Figure Worksheet.7.

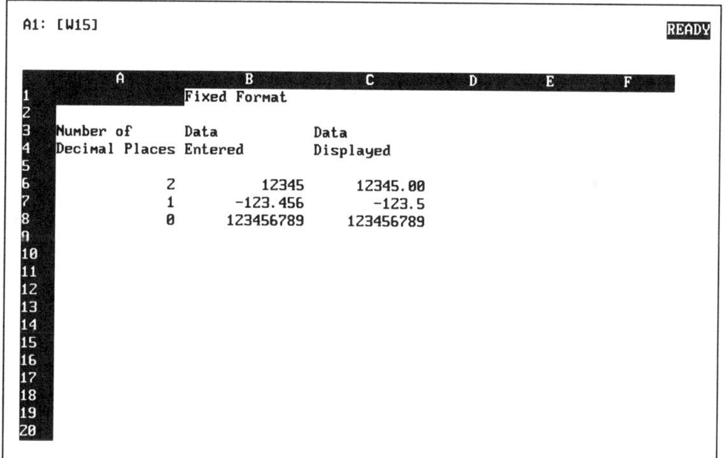

Figure Worksheet.7
Fixed Format.

General A dynamic format that displays a value according to its size (in digits) in relation to the column width. If the number of digits to the left of the decimal point exceeds the column width, the number is displayed in scientific notation. If the number of digits to the right of the decimal point exceeds the column width, the decimal is truncated (not rounded), dropping the least significant digits. Negative numbers are displayed with a minus sign and trailing zeros to the right of the decimal are not displayed. See Figure Worksheet.8.

Hidden Hides the contents of the worksheet, and displays it as blank. The contents of the current cell will still be displayed in the control panel unless you also protect the worksheet. To redisplay hidden cells, simply select another format option. To avoid accidently overwriting the hidden cells, protect the worksheet using /Worksheet Global Protection Enable. See Figure Worksheet.9.

Percent Displays numbers with a percent sign and with as many decimal places (0–15) as you specify. When you type in a percentage value, the decimal point is automatically moved two digits to the right for the display; the entry 0.125, for example, is displayed as 12.5%. (You cannot type 10, meaning 10%—1000% will be displayed.)

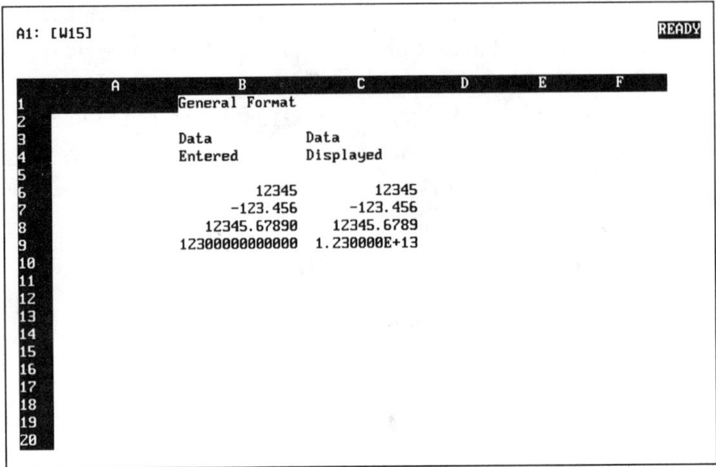

Figure Worksheet.8
General Format.

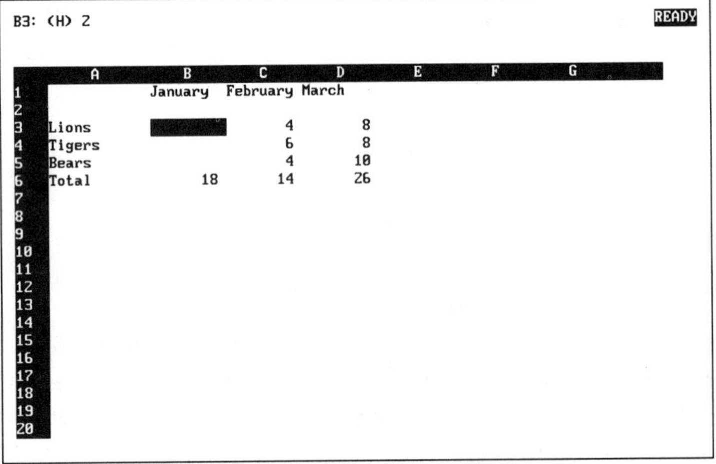

Figure Worksheet.9
Hidden Format — Cell contents displayed in control panel.

+/- A rudimentary bar graph display, showing the number of plus signs corresponding to the integer portion of the value entered into the cell. Conversely, minus signs are displayed for negative integers. Values between −1 and 1 are displayed as periods. If the number of plus or minus signs required to display a particular value exceeds the width of the cell, asterisks are displayed. See Figure Worksheet.10.

Sci(entific) Displays numbers in scientific or exponential notation. The mantissa portion can display up to 15 decimal places, while the exponent can range from −99 to 99. See Figure Worksheet.11.

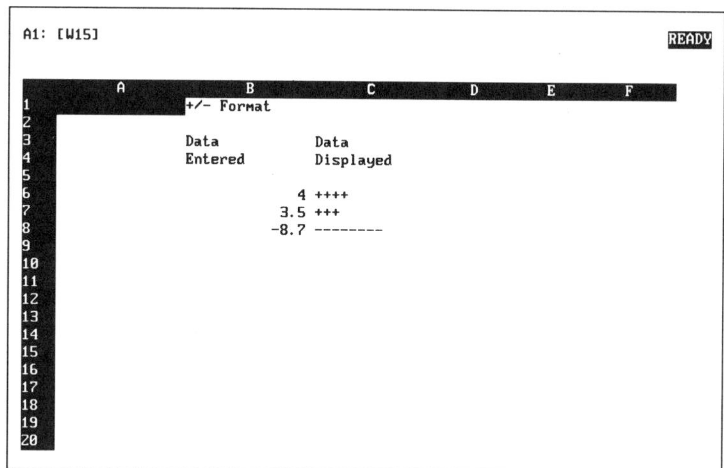

Figure Worksheet.10
+/– format.

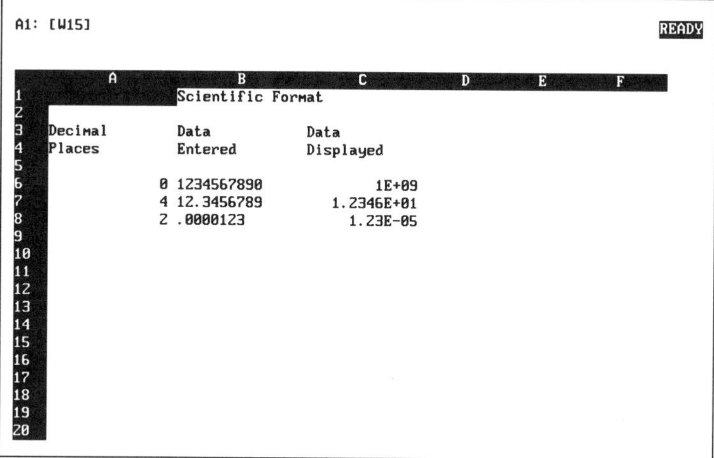

Figure Worksheet.11
Scientific Format.

Text Displays formulas as text. Displays numerical values in the General format.

Usage

To set the Global format, select the option of your choice from the above list. If necessary, 1-2-3 will then prompt you to specify the number of decimal places to display.

Example

To set the Global format to Currency with 2 decimal places:

1. Select /Worksheet Global Format Currency.
2. At the prompt, type 2 and press ENTER.

Notes

Any /Range Format settings you specify will take precedence over the /Worksheet Global Format setting.

Worksheet Global Label

Purpose

Used to set the default label prefix to be applied to all future labels entered into the current worksheet.

Description

The label prefix determines if the label is left-aligned ('), right-aligned (") or centered (^) in the cell. The global prefix setting does not alter existing labels in the worksheet. If you need to change the positioning of any existing labels, use the /Range Label command.

Usage

To change the label positioning of future label entries, select /Worksheet Global Label and then select Left, Right, or Center.

Notes

You can control the positioning of new labels manually by typing in your own label prefix as you enter the text. For example if the global prefix is set to left-aligned ('), you can center a particular label by typing the centering prefix (^) before the text as in: ^This is the label text.

Worksheet Global Protection

Purpose

Used to set the protection status for the current worksheet.

Description

The global protection status is initially turned off, allowing you to freely enter information into, or alter, any cell. If you set it on, with /Worksheet Global

Protection Enable, you will not be able to alter any cells in the worksheet unless they are explicitly unprotected by the /Range Unprot command. You will also be prevented from inserting or deleting rows or columns. When worksheet protection is on, the protection status of the current cell is included in the control panel: PR for cells that are protected under /Range Prot(ect) and U for cells that have been specifically unprotected with /Range Unprot(ect). Note that the default protection status for each individual cell is protected, while the default protection status for the worksheet is disabled.

Usage

To enable worksheet protection, select /Worksheet Global Protection Enable. To disable worksheet protection, select /Worksheet Global Protection Disable.

Cautions

Enabling global protection does not by itself prevent the alteration of all cells in the worksheet; you must also explicitly protect any cells that have been previously unprotected with the /Range Unprot command.

Worksheet Global Recalculation

Purpose

Used to control how 1-2-3 recalculates the worksheet after you have made changes to data or formulas.

Description

The Recalculation menu determines two factors in 1-2-3's recalculation process: when and in what order. You can specify whether you want recalculation to take place automatically (the initial default), or manually, when you press the CALC key (F9). You can also specify whether you wish 1-2-3 to recalculate the worksheet in a natural order (i.e., calculating parent formulas before their dependents) or by columns or rows progressively. You can even control how many times 1-2-3 recalculates each formula during its recalc cycle with the Iteration option. (This is required when performing successive approximation calculations, or for resolving other deliberately created circular references.) The Recalc options include:

Automatic Each time you alter a cell value or formula, 1-2-3 recalculates that cell and all cells that depend on the changed cell. Automatic is the recalc default when you first load the program. Because Release 2.2 now optimizes its recalculation procedures, automatic recalculations take a minimal amount of time.

Columnwise 1-2-3 calculates each column in each worksheet in sequence, starting in column A.

Iteration Allows you to set the number of recalculation passes that 1-2-3 makes for each complete recalculation. You can select any number from 1 to 50, with 1 being the default. 1-2-3 only performs multiple passes when you have specified either columnwise or rowwise recalculation, or if you have specified natural recalculation and there is a circular reference in the worksheet.

Manual 1-2-3 only performs recalculations when you press the CALC key (F9). If 1-2-3 determines that the current worksheet needs to be recalculated due to changes, it will display the CALC indicator at the bottom of the screen. Manual recalculation is often used to speed up macros when the programmer can explicitly control the recalculation via the {CALC} or {RECALC} commands. If you select Manual recalculation, you must be sure to press F9 to recalculate before you print or save the file, or copy formulas as values.

Natural 1-2-3 recalculates all the formulas on which a particular formula depends before recalculating that formula. This option is usually the best selection, unless your particular worksheet structure requires that you calculate by rows or columns. When you first load 1-2-3, Natural is the initial default setting. If you have a circular reference in your worksheet, and your recalculation order is set to Natural, 1-2-3 will not perform a minimal recalculation (just for cells that have changed and their dependents) but a complete recalculation.

Rowwise 1-2-3 calculates each row in each worksheet in sequence, starting in row 1.

Notes

The current recalculation setting is saved with each worksheet. When a worksheet is retrieved, that file's recalculation setting becomes the setting for the session. It will remain in force until another file with another setting is retrieved or until you change the setting via the /Worksheet Global Recalc option.

Cautions

If you have set the recalculation to manual, it is *your* responsibility to recalculate the worksheet prior to printing, graphing, or otherwise exporting the data.

Worksheet Global Zero

Purpose

Determines how values of zero are displayed in the current worksheet. This is useful when you don't want to clutter a worksheet with zero values, or if you want to insert some more meaningful text such as "Missing," and yet still have the cell evaluated.

Description

You can elect to show zero values (or formulas that evaluate to zero) either as a numeric zero in the current cell format, as a blank, or with any designated text string. To specify how zeros should be displayed, select from among the following options:

Label Inserts the label of your choice in cells with zero values. You can enter any text you wish at the prompt and include any of the label prefixes.

No Turns off the special zero display and shows zeros as their numeric value in the format of the cell. This is the initial default.

Yes Shows cells that have values of zero as blanks.

Notes

When you show zero cells as blanks or as a specified text string, you do not alter the underlying value (zero). This can still be used in formulas and counts.

Cautions

If you have selected the Yes option to display zeros as blanks, be careful about overwriting cells that seem to be blank but that really contain zero values. You can determine if the cell is truly blank or contains a zero value by looking at the control panel.

Worksheet Insert

Purpose

The /Worksheet Insert command is used to insert additional blank rows or columns into the current worksheet.

Description

When you use the /Worksheet Insert command to insert rows or columns into a worksheet, it may affect certain range addresses that you have specified: ranges referred to in formulas or ranges with assigned names. 1-2-3 will automatically expand the referenced or named range to include the new rows or columns.

Range addresses will be adjusted even if the cell references in the formula are absolute (preceded with $ signs). For example, if the formula @SUM($A$1..$B$1) was placed in cell C1 and you subsequently inserted a new column to the left of the initial column A, the initial column A will be moved to column B, and B to C, and so on. The formula, now residing in cell D1 will now read @SUM($B$1..$C$1).

Usage

When you select to insert rows, 1-2-3 places them above the current cursor position. When you insert columns, 1-2-3 places them to the left of the current cursor position. To insert rows or columns, you must therefore position the cell pointer in a cell below or to the right of the desired position, then invoke the command. Indicate the number of rows or columns that you wish to insert by highlighting the corresponding number of existing rows or columns in the worksheet.

Example

To insert five new columns to the left of column G:

1. Place the cell pointer in column G.
2. Select /Worksheet Insert Column.
3. Highlight five columns, either to the left or right of column G and press ENTER. The new column(s) will always be inserted to the left of the initial column (i.e., column G).

Notes

Suppose you have budget columns A1..A9, B1..B9, etc.; below each column in cell A10, B10, etc. is a dotted line (e.g., /-); and in cell A11, B11, you have a totaling formula @SUM(A1.A9), @SUM(B1.B9), etc. You find yourself continually having to add new rows to include new line items. Each time you insert a new row, you have to change your @SUM formulas to correspond. There is an easy way around such changing and rechanging. Because range addresses will automatically expand to include a row inserted *within* its span, consider assigning the dotted line originally in cells A10, B10, etc. as part of the range. Then, each time you insert a row above A10, the formulas below will be automatically updated.

Worksheet Learn

Purpose

Used to capture keystrokes into a designated range in the current worksheet so that they can be used to create a macro that will replay the same keystroke sequence.

Description

The /Worksheet Learn command allows you to designate a range (a single column) of cells in the current worksheet where you want to place the captured keystrokes. You can terminate the current Learn Range definition with the Cancel option or erase the contents of the current Learn Range with the Erase option. The Learn command is extremely useful for creating simple cursor movement and typing macros, where simple repetition is all that is desired. It can also serve as a basis for more complex macros; you can edit the resulting Learn Range and correct errors or add advanced macro commands.

Defaults

Current cell.

Usage

To use the Learn feature, you must first define a Learn Range by selecting the Range option. You should define a range that is one column wide and as many cells long as entries you intend to record. After you have defined the range, you can turn on the Learn feature whenever you are ready to start recording by pressing ALT-F5. 1-2-3 will record each entry you make in a separate cell of the Learn Range until you turn off the Learn feature by pressing ALT-F5 a second time, Cancel the current Learn Range, or completely fill the current Learn Range.

To replay the captured keystrokes, name the first cell of the Learn Range with a macro range name as you would any macro and then start it either directly (with one of the special macro starting names (e.g., \A for ALT-A) or indirectly with the RUN (ALT-F3) key (with any range name). You can edit the captured keystrokes as you would any cell with the EDIT (F2) key and insert or delete cells from the range.

To erase the contents of the current Learn Range, select /Worksheet Learn Erase Yes. To cancel the specification of the current Learn Range, select /Worksheet Learn Cancel.

Examples

To capture the keystrokes required to move the cell pointer to the upper right-most cell in the active portion of the worksheet:

1. Determine a free area of the current worksheet below or to the right of the data, to be used for the Learn Range. It should be at least 10 rows long.
2. Designate the Learn Range by selecting /Worksheet Learn Range and painting the range or entering its address.
3. Activate the Learn feature by press ALT-F5.
4. Execute the desired steps of the macro by pressing in sequence:

END-HOME	To move to the bottom right of the active work-sheet.
Right Arrow	To move to the next open column (outside the active area.
END-Up Arrow	To move to the top of the worksheet.
Left Arrow	To move back into the active area of the worksheet.

5. Press ALT-F5 to turn off the Learn feature.
6. Name the top cell of the Learn Range with the special macro starting name \R, to permit its initiation by pressing ALT-R. (Use the /Range Name Create command.)
7. Test the new macro by placing the cell pointer in cell A1 by pressing the HOME key and then initiating the macro by pressing the ALT-R key combination. The cell pointer should move to the upper-right corner of the active area of the worksheet.

Notes

If you run out of room in the Learn Range while recording a macro, 1-2-3 will display the error message “Learn range is full”. You can increase the size of the learn range without losing any keystrokes by immediately pressing ESC to clear the error message, then redefining the Learn Range to a larger size by selecting /Worksheet Learn Range, and restarting the Learn feature.

Cautions

Do not delete the column containing the Learn Range while recording key-strokes, otherwise 1-2-3 will terminate the Learn feature.

Worksheet Page

Purpose

Used to insert the special page break symbol (|::) into a new blank line at the current cursor location. When printing out the worksheet, 1-2-3 will start a new page at that line.

Description

When 1-2-3 is printing out a worksheet and comes to a page break symbol (|::), it will immediately issue a page eject command to the printer. 1-2-3 will start the next line of the worksheet at the top of the next page. When you insert a page break symbol in your worksheet, place it in the leftmost column of the print range in a row by itself, since the entire row is not printed.

Usage

You can enter the page break symbol manually in the leftmost column of the print range, in the spot where you want the next page to start. You can also use the /Worksheet Page command to perform the insertion automatically. The command inserts a new blank row at the current cursor location, moving the current and all subsequent rows down one line, and inserts the page break symbol in the current column. Since the page break symbol *must* be in the leftmost column of the print range, you must place the cell pointer there before you invoke the command. When 1-2-3 inserts the new blank row, it automatically adjusts all ranges and cell references to accommodate the new row.

Notes

The line that contains the page break symbol is not printed; do not insert any data into it unless you specifically do not want that data to print. It will still display on the screen.

Cautions

If you insert the page break symbol manually, do not place it in a line that contains data, since it causes 1-2-3 to ignore all data in the same line when printing.

Worksheet Status

Purpose

The /Worksheet Status command displays a temporary status screen that shows available memory, the type of computer processor(s) in your system, the current recalculation mode, cell formatting information, and information about any circular references. See Figure Worksheet.12.

Description

The status screen can be used to check the global cell format settings, to determine whether the recalculation mode is set to manual or automatic, and/or whether the calculation sequence is natural, rowwise, or columnwise. If you have a circular reference, you can use the status screen to tell you which cell contains the circular reference. The status screen can only display one circular reference at a time. Therefore, if you have more than one circular reference, you will have to view the screen, note the first circular reference, fix it, and then view the status screen again to find the next cell containing a circular reference.

Usage

To view the status screen select /Worksheet Status. Press any key to return to READY mode.

Notes

If you want to view the status of the global default settings for the printer, graphing, international, and file defaults, select /Worksheet Global Default Status.

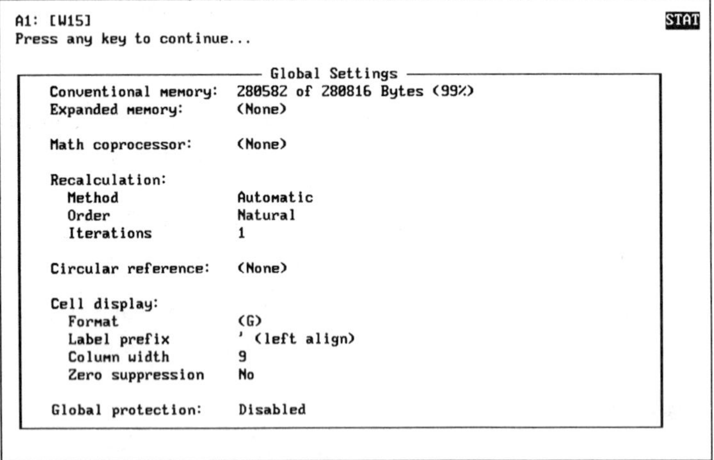

Figure Worksheet.12
/Worksheet Status.

Worksheet Titles

Purpose

Used to lock and unlock one or more rows and/or columns at the top and left of the screen. When the rows and/or columns are locked, they will not scroll off of the screen as you move the cell pointer beyond the confines of the screen. The title-locking feature is especially useful when you are dealing with large tables that extend below or to the right of a single screen. Without locking the titles containing the column and row headers, you could easily lose track of which column or row contained what data. You can also use the titles feature to keep summary data displayed on the top or left of the screen while you add line item data below it. See Figures Worksheet.13a and b.

Description

The /Worksheet Titles command allows you to lock either the Horizontal titles (rows of column headings), Vertical titles (columns of row headings), or Both. The command also allows you to clear all titles by selecting Clear.

Usage

To lock the top five rows of the worksheet as a horizontal title, you must place the cell pointer in the sixth row, i.e. under the desired title, and select /Worksheet Title Horizontal. To lock the fifth row by itself, you must move cursor down until just the fifth row is displayed in the top row of the worksheet (and rows one to four have scrolled off the screen). Then return the cell pointer to row six and select /Worksheet Title Horizontal.

To lock a vertical title, you must position the desired title in the leftmost column of the display and place the cell pointer in the column to the right of the column you wish to lock. To lock both vertical and horizontal titles, position the worksheet so the desired titles are in the leftmost column(s) and the topmost row(s), position the cell pointer below and to the right of the desired row(s) and column(s) and select /Worksheet Titles Both. To clear all titles, select /Worksheet Titles Clear.

Notes

You cannot move the cell pointer into the locked area of the titles with the cursor keys. If you need to move the cell pointer into a cell in the titles area to edit that cell, use the GOTO key (F5) and specify the cell to be edited. 1-2-3 will display a duplicate copy of the titles area below and/or to the right of the titles with the

A8: 1 READY

	A	B	C	D	E	F	G	H
1								
2				West Side Aquarium				
3				Donation History and Projection				
4								
5	Record	Name	Total	Last	Projected	Actual		
6	Number	Lastname	Donation	Donation	1989	1989	Variance	Percent
7								
8	1	Smith	250	100	175	150	-25	-14.3%
9	2	Milton	450	50	88	100	12.5	14.3%
10	3	Williams	300	200	350	150	-200	-57.1%
11	4	Allens	250	50	88	100	12.5	14.3%
12	5	Rogers	300	100	175	150	-25	-14.3%
13	6	Ryan	1,000	500	875	900	25	2.9%
14	7	McFarlan	25	25	44	25	-18.75	-42.9%
15	8	Elliot	250	100	175	150	-25	-14.3%
16	9	Sarnoff	450	50	88	100	12.5	14.3%
17	10	Kalber	300	200	350	150	-200	-57.1%
18	11	Benny	250	50	88	100	12.5	14.3%
19	12	Adams	300	100	175	150	-25	-14.3%
20	13	Dilton	1,000	500	875	900	25	2.9%

Figure Worksheet.13a
/Worksheet Titles before scrolling.

A30: 23 READY

	A	B	C	D	E	F	G	H
1								
2				West Side Aquarium				
3				Donation History and Projection				
4								
5	Record	Name	Total	Last	Projected	Actual		
6	Number	Lastname	Donation	Donation	1989	1989	Variance	Percent
17	10	Kalber	300	200	350	150	-200	-57.1%
18	11	Benny	250	50	88	100	12.5	14.3%
19	12	Adams	300	100	175	150	-25	-14.3%
20	13	Dilton	1,000	500	875	900	25	2.9%
21	14	Fennel	25	25	44	25	-18.75	-42.9%
22	15	Gilbert	250	50	88	100	12.5	14.3%
23	16	Macking	300	100	175	150	-25	-14.3%
24	17	Neubold	1,000	500	875	900	25	2.9%
25	18	Zipfel	25	25	44	25	-18.75	-42.9%
26	19	Simpson	250	100	175	150	-25	-14.3%
27	20	Billings	450	50	88	100	12.5	14.3%
28	21	Randolph	300	200	350	150	-200	-57.1%
29	22	Quincy	250	50	88	100	12.5	14.3%
30	23	Peters	300	100	175	150	-25	-14.3%

Figure Worksheet.13b
/Worksheet Titles after scrolling.

selected cell highlighted. You can now edit the cell. To clear the screen of the duplicate titles, press PgDn followed by PgUp (for horizontal titles) or Tab followed by Shift-Tab (for vertical titles).

If you split the screen display with /Worksheet Windows, the /Worksheet Titles command only affects the worksheet in the current window.

The /Worksheet Titles command only affects the way titles are displayed on the screen. It has no effect on printing. To repeat titles on each page of a printout, use the /Print [Printer or File] Options Borders command.

Worksheet Window

Purpose

Used to change the layout of the windows on the screen by splitting it either vertically or horizontally into two windows.

Description

The /Worksheet Window command allows you to split the display into two separate windows that can display different portions of the worksheet simultaneously. In addition, the Window command controls whether the displays in the multiple worksheet windows scroll together in synch when you move the cell pointer outside the displayed area or not. You can choose among the following options:

Clear Clears any special window display and returns to the full-screen display. 1-2-3 will display the section of the worksheet that was displayed in the top or left window when the Clear command was issued as the worksheet in the full screen window. You need to clear one type of special window before you can create the next. To move from a vertical window to a horizontal window, you would first have to clear the vertical window.

Horizontal Splits the screen horizontally at the current cursor location, placing the top portion of the current worksheet into the top window and the bottom portion in the bottom window. (See Figure Worksheet.14.) You may switch between windows using the WINDOW (F6) key.

Synch Select this option to synchronize the window scrolling in both window displays as you move the cell pointer past the edge of the current window. When you synchronize horizontal windows, 1-2-3 maintains the same columns in each window. When you synchronize vertical windows, 1-2-3 maintains the same rows in each window.

Unsynch Select this option to unsynchronize the scrolling of multiple window displays. When you move the cell pointer past the edge of the current window, only the current window will scroll.

Vertical Splits the screen vertically at the current cursor location, placing the left portion of the current worksheet into the left window and the right portion in the right window. You can move between windows with the WINDOW (F6) key. See Figure Worksheet.15.

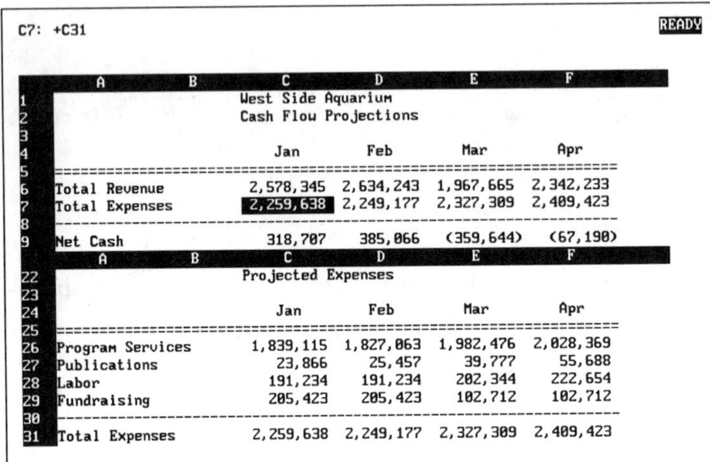

Figure Worksheet.14
Horizontal Window showing two portions of the worksheet.

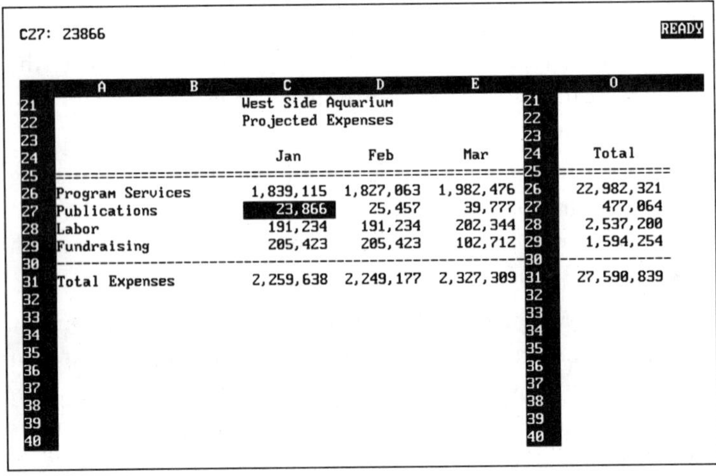

Figure Worksheet.15
Vertical Window showing two portions of the worksheet.

▸ @Functions

Purpose

The @functions are used in formulas to perform predefined calculations such as sums, averages, present values, and so on. They are divided into eight categories:

Database Used to perform statistical calculations and queries on database tables.

Date and Time Used to calculate or generate date and time values.

Financial Used to perform financial calculations such as present and future values of a cash flow.

Logical Used to perform logical comparisons of values and strings.

Mathematical Used to perform standard mathematical calculations on values such as sums, averages, absolute values, and so on.

Special Used to perform such specialized tasks as looking up values in a table.

Statistical Used to perform statistical calculations on ranges of values.

String Used to manipulate labels and other strings such as formulas.

We will first discuss the @functions in general, reviewing the structure and syntax of @functions and the various categories of @functions. This overview will be followed by a Table of @Functions, by category. Finally, each @function will be discussed in detail, alphabetically.

The @functions all use standard syntaxes and can accept either values, strings, or references to other cells as input. They can be used alone or they can be combined with each other or with other mathematical and logical operators to produce formulas. In all cases, the final result of a function or formula is displayed in the cell that contains the function or formula. You can then refer to a function or formula result in other formulas and functions by using its cell reference. It is this feature, the ability to use the contents of referenced cells as data input, that makes @functions a powerful part of the worksheet environment.

Let's look at a simple example. Suppose you wanted to calculate the sum of the monthly attendance figures for several of the exhibits at the aquarium. You could create a formula that added each value in each column. In Figure @Function.1, for example, the value of 5375 calculated at the bottom of column C for January attendance was created by explicitly adding the values above it: 1200+1350+1225+900+700. You can see the formula listed in the control box.

If any of the values in the column were to change, you would have to go and alter that value in the formula. By referencing the cell addresses of the cells in column C, we could improve our situation somewhat. Figure @Function.2 shows the same calculation using the formula: C8+C9+C10+C11+C12.

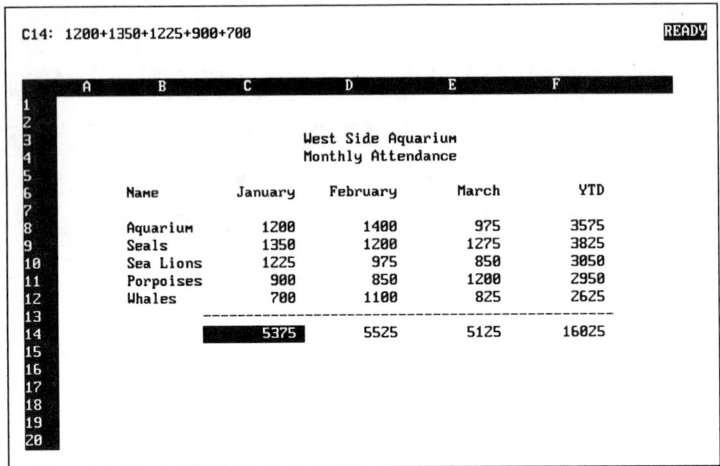

Figure @Function.1 Explicitly summing the column of attendance numbers.

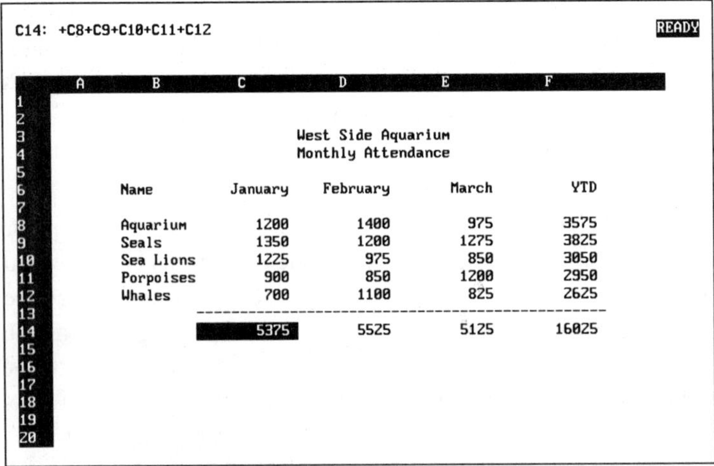

Figure @Function.2 Explicitly summing named cells.

In this way, if any of the figures in the column changed, the change would be reflected in the value of the formula. But what if the column contained hundreds of values? Creating such a formula would be a horrendous process. Here is where @functions come into play. Using the simple @SUM function, we can create the formula shown in Figure @Function.3, where we define the cells to be added as a simple range.

We could have also assigned a range name to the range of cells (C8..C12), the /Range Name Create command, and then used the assigned name in the function instead of the cell addresses. As you can see, the use of the predefined @SUM

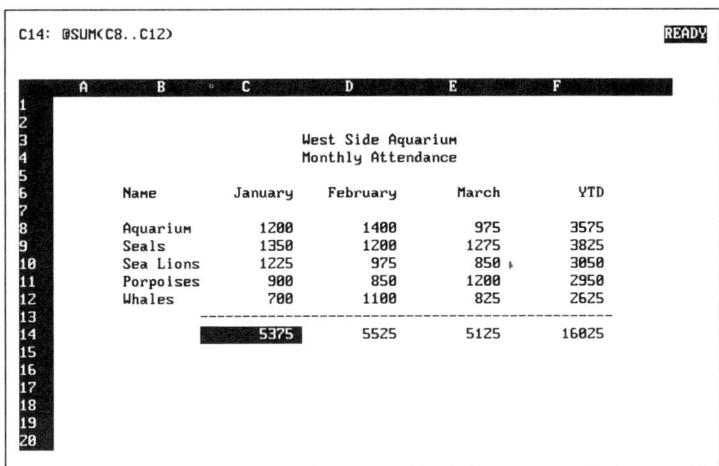

C14: @SUM(C8..C12) READY

West Side Aquarium
Monthly Attendance

Name	January	February	March	YTD
Aquarium	1200	1400	975	3575
Seals	1350	1200	1275	3825
Sea Lions	1225	975	850	3050
Porpoises	900	850	1200	2950
Whales	700	1100	825	2625
	5375	5525	5125	16025

Figure @Function.3 Using @SUM function.

function and the range of cells as the data, quickly produced the desired results. Other @functions use different data arguments, and produce many different kinds of results.

Key Terms

The @functions introduce two new terms and their associated concepts: *syntax* and *argument*. The syntax of an @function determines how you should feed it the data it requires. All @functions share the same syntax as follows:

@NAME(argument1, argument2, ..., argumentn)

They all start with the @ character, followed by the function's name (no spaces) and an opening parenthesis. Within the parentheses lie one or more arguments. The arguments are the data required by the function to calculate its results, they may be values, strings, cell addresses, ranges, or conditions. Different @functions require different numbers and types of arguments. For example, the @SUM function requires only one argument and it can be a value, a cell address, range address, or range name. The Present Value function, @PV, on the other hand requires three arguments: the payment amount, the interest rate, and the term.

The following rules apply to the syntax and arguments of all @functions:

1. Always type the function as @NAME(arguments). You must start with the @ character followed by the name (upper- or lowercase), and the opening parenthesis. You cannot leave any spaces in between these features. Between the parentheses, you enter the arguments, separated by the argu-

ment separator character (initially set by default to the comma and/or semicolon). You may include extra spaces between the arguments so long as the spaces do not interrupt the syntax on a given argument. You must conclude the function with the terminal parenthesis.

2. Value arguments can be entered as values; formulas that evaluate to values; or the range name or address of a range that contains values or formulas that evaluate to values.
3. String arguments can be any literal string, string formula, or the range name (or address) of a range that contains literal strings (labels) or string formulas. Literal strings should be enclosed in quotation marks to differentiate them from numbers, formulas, addresses, or range names. This is especially true if they contain the argument separator characters (, or ;).
4. Location arguments can be any range address, name, or formula that evaluates to a range name or address.
5. Condition arguments can contain any formula that evaluates to a logical yes or no (1 or 0). Such formulas must contain one or more of the logical operators:

    =, <, >, <=, >=, <>, #AND#, #OR#, #NOT#

    or reference a cell that contains a logical formula. A conditional argument can also be any of the other argument types, though they often would have no logical meaning. For example, @IF("whale") is legal but has no meaning, since the logical value of a string argument is always 0.

Standard Features

Most @functions within each of the groups have standard features or requirements. Since the individual functions are listed alphabetically in the detailed section of this chapter, only the standard features of each group are listed here. Be sure to refer back to this section if you have any general questions about a particular type of @function.

Database Functions The database functions require a database table as a source of input. The database functions scan the records of the table, test them against a criteria range, and select the records that match the criteria; they then perform their designated calculations on a specified field of the database with the selected records.

All database functions require three arguments: input, field, and criteria. The *input argument* defines the database table or tables to be scanned.

The *field argument* tells the function which field the function is to operate upon. You designate the field by its column offset from the leftmost column of the input range. For example, if the input range had five columns of data named field1 through field5, you could specify field1 as offset 0 and field3 as offset 2. Remember, you are describing the offset from the first column not the column number. (That is why the first column (field1) has an offset of 0). For example, to sum the selected values in field 3 you would use @DSUM(Input, 2, Criteria).

The *criteria argument* must be a range that 1-2-3 uses to determine which records from the input range are used for the calculation. It consists of one or more field names corresponding to the field names in the input range with one or more criteria entered below their associated field names. You can also create multiple field criteria, multiple value and string criteria, and complex formula based criteria. See the discussion of /Data Query Criteria for more information on the creation of criteria ranges.

Date and Time Functions Date and time are represented in 1-2-3 as decimal numbers. The integer portion represents the date and can lie between 1 and 73050, corresponding to Jan 1, 1900 and December 31, 2099. The decimal portion is used to represent time and can lie between .000000 and .999988, corresponding to 12 midnight and 11:59:59 PM. The Date and Time functions are used to convert from the decimal time numbers to and from the more conventional presentations of dates and time. Date functions ignore the decimal portion of date/time values while time functions ignore the integer portion.

Financial Functions When entering terms and interest rates into financial functions you must ensure that they represent the same unit of time. You cannot mix an annual interest rate with a monthly payment schedule. This usually just involves dividing the rate by 12 and multiplying the term by 12 to convert annual figures to monthly figures. You can enter interest rates either in decimal form or percentage form. For example, 8.7 percent could be entered either as .087 or 8.7%. 1-2-3 assumes that all payments are made at the end of regular intervals and that they are equal.

Logical Functions Most logical functions like @ISERR or @ISNA are used to prevent the display and perpetuation of the ERR or NA message in worksheets that can legitimately be missing values or in which an error condition is a valid state. For example, if you were to calculate the @DAVG of a database that might not have any records that match the criteria, you would generate an error as 1-2-3 tried to calculate the average and divided by zero (average=sum/count, and with no matching records the sum and count both equal 0).

To avoid the ERR message in the cell (and any dependent cells), use the @ISERR function as follows:

@ISERR(@DSUM(range),0,@DSUM(range))

which displays 0 instead of ERR. You could also include a string output in the form:

@ISERR(@DSUM(range), "None",@DSUM(range))

You can also use logical functions to test data input against a range of values and flag errors, or test for valid types of data input with @ISNUMBER or @ISSTRING.

Mathematical Functions Math functions involving trigonometric calculations require the arguments to expressed in radians and not in degrees. You can convert degrees to radians by multiplying the number of degrees by @PI/180, where @PI is the function that calculates the value of PI. To convert radians back to degrees, multiply the number of radians by 180/@PI.

Special Functions 1-2-3 carries error messages (ERR) and not available messages (NA) through all formulas that depend on a cell that evaluates to ERR or NA. All cells containing such dependent formulas will also evaluate to ERR or NA and will display accordingly. The functions @ERR and @NA allow you to set the value of a particular cell to ERR or NA. The former can be used to show dependencies, while the latter can be used to show that the data required to evaluate the dependent formulas is not yet available.

Statistical Functions Statistical functions require a single list of values as their argument to be evaluated. The list can contain one or more numbers, formulas that evaluate to numbers, ranges containing numbers, or ranges that contain formulas that evaluate to numbers. All statistical functions except @COUNT treat labels in argument ranges as having the value of zero. This may cause errors in calculations such as @AVG, since this function will add labels to the count and assign zero to the sum before dividing the sum by the count to determine the average. All statistical functions ignore blank cells.

String Functions String functions that evaluate cells containing blanks, will evaluate to ERR. String functions that use offsets to determine the position of a character in a string always treats the leftmost character as having an offset of zero. The rightmost character will have an offset equal to one less than the length of the string.

Table @Function.1

DATABASE FUNCTIONS

@DAVG	Calculates the mean (average) of the values in the designated field among the records that meet the selected criteria.
@DCOUNT	Counts the number of non-blank cells in the specified field of the input range that meet the criteria.
@DMAX	Returns the maximum value of the specified field from records in the input database table that meet the specified criteria.
@DMIN	Returns the minimum value of the specified field from records in the input database table that meet the specified criteria.
@DSTD	Calculates the Population Standard Deviation of the values in the specified field of the input database table that meet the specified criteria.
@DSUM	Calculates the total of the values in the designated field among the records that meet the selected criteria.
@DVAR	Calculates the population variance of the values in the specified field of the input database table that meet the specified criteria.

DATE FUNCTIONS

@DATE	Calculates the 1-2-3 date-number from the specified year, month, and day.
@DATEVALUE	Converts strings that look like dates into 1-2-3 date-numbers.
@DAY	Calculates the day of the month of the specified date-number.
@HOUR	Calculates the hour of the day of the specified time-number.
@MINUTE	Calculates the minute of the hour of the specified time-number.
@MONTH	Calculates the month of the year of the specified date-number.
@NOW	Returns the current system date and time as a 1-2-3 date- and time-number.
@SECOND	Calculates the seconds (0–59) of the specified time-number.
@TIME	Calculates the 1-2-3 time-number from the specified hours, minutes, and seconds.
@TIMEVALUE	Converts strings that look like times into 1-2-3 time-numbers.
@TODAY	Returns the current system date as a 1-2-3 date-number.
@YEAR	Calculates the year of the specified date-number.

FINANCIAL FUNCTIONS

@CTERM	Calculates the number of compounding periods required for an investment to grow to a specified future value at a fixed interest rate.
@DDB	Calculates the depreciation allowance for a specified period using the double declining balance technique.
@FV	Calculates the future value of a uniform stream of payments, earning a specified interest rate for a specified term.
@IRR	Calculates the internal rate of return from a series of positive and negative cash flows.
@NPV	Calculates the net present value of a stream of cash flows (equal intervals, but not necessarily the same amounts), discounted at a specified interest rate.
@PMT	Calculates the equal period payments to repay a loan at a fixed interest rate, for an ordinary annuity such as a mortgage or car loan.
@PV	Calculates the present value of a uniform stream of payments earning a specified interest rate for a specified term.
@RATE	Calculates the interest rate required to grow a given present value to a given future value over a given term.
@SLN	Calculates the depreciation allowance for a single period using the straight-line depreciation technique.
@SYD	Calculates the depreciation allowance for a specified period using the sum of the year's digits depreciation technique.
@TERM	Calculates the number of periodic payments required to produce a given future value at a given periodic interest rate.

LOGICAL FUNCTIONS

@FALSE	Returns the logical value false (0).
@IF	Evaluates a condition, returning one of two labels or values depending, if it is true or false.
@ISERR	Tests for ERR value.
@ISNA	Tests for NA value.
@ISNUMBER	Tests if a location or formula evaluates to a number.
@ISSTRING	Tests if a location containing a label or a formula evaluates to a string.
@TRUE	Returns the logical value true (1).

MATHEMATICAL FUNCTIONS

@ABS	Calculates the absolute (positive) value of a number.
@ACOS	Calculates the arc cosine of a value.
@ASIN	Calculates the arc sine of a value.
@ATAN	Calculates the arc tangent of a value.
@ATAN2	Calculates the four-quadrant arc tangent of a value.
@COS	Calculates the cosine of an angle.
@EXP	Calculates the value e (approx 2.718282) raised to the power x.
@INT	Calculates the integer portion of a decimal number by truncation at the decimal point.
@LN	Calculates the natural logarithm of a value in base e.
@LOG	Calculates the common logarithm of a value in base 10.
@MOD	Calculates the remainder of a division calculation.
@PI	Generates the value of Pi = 3.14159265358979324.
@RAND	Generates a random number between 0 and 1.
@ROUND	Rounds off a value to a specified number of decimal places.
@SIN	Calculates the sine of an angle.
@SQRT	Calculates the square root of a value.
@TAN	Calculates the tangent of an angle.

SPECIAL FUNCTIONS

@@	Returns the contents of a specified cell.
@CELL	Returns the code, string, or value of the specified attribute for the specified cell.
@CELLPOINTER	Returns the code, string, or value of the specified attribute for the current cell after data entry.
@CHOOSE	Finds a designated value or string in the specified list (e.g., chooses the fifth name in a list of names).
@COLS	Counts the number of columns in a range.
@ERR	Used primarily in logical formulas testing data to generate the special value ERR, when the data is missing or incorrect. The ERR value is carried forward to all formulas dependent on the cell that is valued as ERR.
@HLOOKUP	Used to look up values in a horizontal lookup table and return the contents of a specified cell.

SPECIAL FUNCTIONS *continued*

@NA	Assigns the NA (Not Available) value to cells and dependent formulas.
@ROWS	Counts the number of rows in a range.
@VLOOKUP	Used to look up values in a vertical lookup table and return the contents of a specified cell.

STATISTICAL FUNCTIONS

@AVG	Calculates the average value in a list of values.
@COUNT	Counts the non-blank cells in the designated list.
@MAX	Determines the largest value in a list of values.
@MIN	Determines the smallest value in a list of values.
@STD	Calculates the population standard deviation of a list of values.
@SUM	Calculates the sum of a list of values.
@VAR	Calculates the population variance of a list of values.

STRING FUNCTIONS

@CHAR	Used to enter special and foreign characters.
@CODE	Returns the LICS code corresponding to the first character of the argument.
@EXACT	Compares two strings and determines if they are identical.
@FIND	Finds the position of one string within another.
@LEFT	Extracts the specified number of characters from a string, counting from the left.
@LENGTH	Calculates the number of characters in a string.
@LOWER	Converts a string to all lowercase characters.
@MID	Extracts a specified number of characters from within a string starting at a specified character location.
@N	Tests the value of the first cell in a range and returns that value if it is numeric or the value 0 if it is a label.
@PROPER	Converts the first character of each word in a string to uppercase and all others to lowercase.
@REPEAT	Duplicates the designated string a specified number of times.
@REPLACE	Inserts a specified string into another specified string, starting at a designated position in the second string, replacing a designated number of characters.

Li heap.DBF
Li heapx. "
" C.DBF
A. "

Liheap .DBO

Liheape . DBF
" 93. "
HEAP2.PRG

@RIGHT	Extracts the specified number of characters from a string counting from the right.
@S	Tests the first cell in a range and returns its contents if it contains a label or a blank if it contains a value.
@TRIM	Removes leading, trailing, and surplus (adjacent) interior spaces from a string.
@UPPER	Converts a string to all uppercase characters.
@VALUE	Converts a string that contains only numbers or numeric symbols to their equivalent value.

The Reference section that follows discusses each @function in detail.

@@

Purpose Returns the contents of a specified cell.

Syntax @@(location)

Arguments

location—single cell address, or single cell range whose contents you wish to return.

Usage Usually used as an argument for other functions, when you want to supply the second function with the contents of a specified but variable cell.

Example Suppose you had a list of alphanumeric part numbers in column A and wanted to return the first five characters of a one-part number as determined by its cell address. You could place the formula @LEFT(@@(B1),5) in cell B2. Then each time you entered a cell address in column A (e.g., A6) as a label in cell B1, the first five characters of the associated part number would be displayed in cell B2. (See Figure @Function.4.)

Cautions When the @@ function references a cell containing a formula, you must CALC (F9) to update the @@ function after automatic recalc; otherwise it will evaluate to 0.

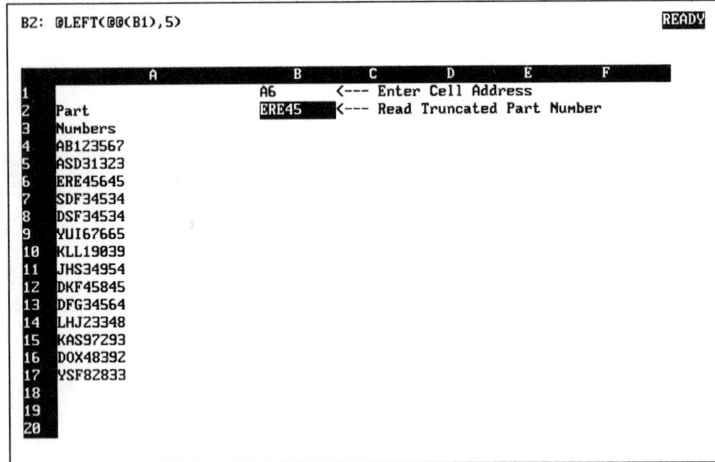

Figure @Function.4
@@Function.

@ABS

Purpose Calculates the absolute (positive) value of a number.

Syntax @ABS(x)

Arguments

x—any value.

Usage The @ABS function is used to convert negative values to positive values. It is often required when calculating the difference between two numbers representing dates. These can lead to negative values simply based on the order in which the difference is calculated.

@ACOS

Purpose Calculates the arc cosine of a value.

Syntax @ACOS(x)

Arguments

x—any value from −1 to 1, representing the cosine of an angle.

Usage The @ACOS function returns the angle whose cosine is represented by the argument value. The resulting angle is measured in radians and can range from 0 to Pi (3.14159...).

Examples

`@ACOS(.5)` = 1.047 radians = 60 degrees

`@ACOS(1)` = 0 radians = 0 degrees

Notes The resulting angle returned by this function is measured in radians. To convert it to degrees, multiply it by 180/@PI.

@ASIN

Purpose Calculates the Arc Sine of a value.

Syntax @ASIN(x)

Arguments

x—any value from −1 to 1, representing the sine of an angle.

Usage The @ASIN function returns the angle whose sine is represented by the argument value. The resulting angle is measured in radians, and can range from −Pi/2 to Pi/2 (Pi = 3.14159...).

Examples

`@ASIN(.5)` = 0.524 radians = 30 degrees

`@ASIN(1)` = −1,571 radians = −90 degrees

Notes The resulting angle returned by this function is measured in radians. To convert it to degrees, multiply it by 180/@PI.

@ATAN

Purpose Calculates the arc tangent of a value.

Syntax @ATAN(x)

Arguments

x—any value, representing the tangent of an angle.

Usage The @ATAN function returns the angle whose tangent is represented by the argument value. The resulting angle is measured in radians and can range from −Pi/2 to Pi/2 (Pi = 3.14159…).

Examples

`@ATAN(.5)` = .464 radians = 26.56 degrees

`@ATAN(-1.5)` = −0.983 radians = −56.31 degrees

Notes The resulting angle returned by this function is measured in radians. To convert it to degrees, multiply it by 180/@PI.

@ATAN2

Purpose Calculates the four-quadrant arc tangent of a value.

Syntax @ATAN(x,y)

Arguments

x—any value.

y—any value, where y/x represents the tangent of the angle. If y=0, @ATAN2 returns 0. If both x and y equal 0, @ATAN2 evaluates to ERR.

Usage The @ATAN2 function returns the angle whose tangent is represented by the argument values y/x. The resulting angle is measured in radians and can range from −Pi to Pi (Pi = 3.14159...), according to the following table:

x	y	@ATAN2(x,y)
Positive	Positive	0 to Pi/2
Negative	Positive	Pi/2 to Pi
Negative	Negative	−Pi to −Pi/2
Positive	Negative	−Pi/2 to 0

Examples

`@ATAN2(.5,1)` = 1.107 radians = 63.43 degrees

`@ATAN(-1.5,1)` = 2.554 radians = 146.31 degrees

Notes The resulting angle returned by this function is measured in radians. To convert it to degrees, multiply it by 180/@PI.

@AVG

Purpose Calculates the average value in a list of values.

Syntax @AVG(list)

Arguments

list—one or more numbers, formulas that evaluate to numbers, ranges that refer to numbers, or formulas that evaluate to numbers, or any combination of the above. The ranges *cannot* contain labels, but can contain blanks.

Usage Calculates the average or arithmetic mean of a set of numbers.

Example To calculate the average value in a range of values from A1..B47, use the formula `@AVG(A1..B47)`.

Cautions If the range(s) specified as the argument for the @AVG contain(s) labels, the @AVG will produce erroneous results.

@CELL

Purpose Returns the code, string, or value of the specified attribute for the specified cell.

Syntax @CELL("attribute",location)

Arguments

attribute—any one of the options listed below contained in quotes.

location —any range name or address.

Usage The @CELL function will return a code, string, or value depending on the attribute requested, as listed in the following table. You can use this function within a macro to verify that data input meets type specifications, or to determine where the user has placed the cell pointer.

Attribute	Returned Code, String, or Value
Address	The cell address.
Col	The column number starting with column A = 1.
Contents	The contents of the cell.
Filename	The name of the file containing the cell.
Format	The cell format in one of the following codes, where ## equals the number of decimal places: C## — Currency F## — Fixed G — General, label or blank P## — Percent S## — Scientific ,## — Comma +/– format D1 through D9 for date and time formats T — Text H — Hidden L — Label A — Automatic 0 — If cell is formatted for parentheses 1 — If cell is not formatted for parentheses
Prefix	The label prefix in one of the following codes: ' — left-aligned " — right-aligned ^ — centered \ — repeating label | — non-printing label Blank label prefix—if cell is empty or contains a value

Protect	The protection status in one of two codes: 1 — protected 0 — not protected
Row	The row number
Type	The type of data contained in the cell in one of the following codes: b — blank cell v — contains a value l — contains a label
Width	The column width

Example To determine the format of cell A25, use the function: `@CELL("format",A25)`

@CELLPOINTER

Purpose Returns the code, string, or value of the specified attribute for the current cell after data entry.

Syntax @CELLPOINTER("attribute")

Arguments

attribute—any one of the options listed under @CELL, contained in quotes.

Usage The @CELLPOINTER function works just like the @CELL function, except that it automatically calculates the value for the current cell. It only updates the calculation when you enter data into the cell or recalculate the worksheet. It will return a code, string, or value depending on the attribute requested (see table under @CELL). You can use this function within a macro to verify that data input meets type specifications, or to determine where the user has placed the cell pointer.

@CHAR

Purpose Used to enter special and foreign characters.

Syntax @CHAR(x)

Arguments

x—Lotus International Character Set (LICS) character code number from 1 to 255.

Usage To enter a special or foreign character into a label in a cell, you can concatenate the results of the @CHAR function to the rest of the label in the form of: `+"label"&@CHAR(x)`.

Notes For more information about the LICS codes and a complete listing, refer to Appendix B.

If your monitor cannot display the selected character, 1-2-3 will try to match it as closely as possible or will display nothing.

@CHOOSE

Purpose Finds a designated value or string in the specified list (e.g., chooses the fifth name in a list of names).

Syntax @CHOOSE(offset,list)

Arguments

offset—a value representing the offset from the first value or string in the list. The first value or string has an offset of 0, while the last value or string has an offset one less than the total number of values or strings in the list.

list —one or more values or strings, ranges that contain values or strings, or any combination of the above.

Usage The @CHOOSE function is used to look up values or strings in a list without having to set up a formal lookup table. To select the third price from the range PRICES, use the formula: `@CHOOSE(2,PRICES)`. Remember: The first entry has an offset of 0.

@CLEAN

Purpose Used to remove certain control characters from a string. The following codes are removed by the @CLEAN function:

ASCII codes 1–32

The Attribute character

The Begin and End attribute characters

The Merge character (LICS–155).

Syntax @CLEAN(string)

Arguments

string—a literal string (enclosed in quotes), a cell, or range reference that contains a label, a formula, or an @function that evaluates to a string.

Example To remove the Escape character from the beginning of a string imported from word processing text file into cell A25, you would use: `@CLEAN(A25)`.

@CODE

Purpose Returns the LICS code corresponding to the first character of the argument. (See Appendix B.)

Syntax @CODE(string)

Arguments

string—a literal string (enclosed in quotes), a cell, or range reference that contains a label, a formula, or an @function that evaluates to a string.

Examples

`@CODE("H")` = 72

`@CODE("Rudolph")` = 82

Note If the referenced cell or range contains a value or is blank, the function evaluates to ERR.

@COLS

Purpose Counts the number of columns in a range.

Syntax @COLS(range)

Arguments

range—any named range or address.

Usage Calculates the width of ranges, for setting margins for printing.

Example `@COLS(A1..F25)` = 6

@COS

Purpose Calculates the cosine of an angle.

Syntax @COS(x)

Arguments

x—any value.

Usage The @COS function returns the cosine of the angle represented by the argument value. The resulting value can vary from −1 to 1.

Examples

`@COS(0)` = 1

`@COS(1.047)` = .5 (1.047 radians = 60 degrees)

Notes To convert an angle measured in degrees to radians for input, multiply it by @PI/180.

@COUNT

Purpose Counts the non-blank cells in the designated list.

Syntax @COUNT(list)

Arguments

list—any combination of ranges.

Usage 1-2-3 considers any cell containing a label, value, or formula to be non-blank, even if the label contains only the prefix, and the formula or function evaluates to ERR or NA. Single-cell addresses count as 1 even if they are blank.

Examples To count the non-blank cells in the range A1..F25 use the formula `@COUNT(A1..F25)`. To count the number of names in the list NAMES use `@COUNT(NAMES)`.

Cautions If you are counting values in a range, be sure that the range does not contain any labels or they will be added to the count.

@CTERM

Purpose Calculates the number of compounding periods required for an investment to grow to a specified future value at a fixed interest rate.

Syntax @CTERM(interest,future-value,present-value)

Arguments

interest —the interest rate for the selected compounding period. Any value above −1, except 0.

present-value—the initial cost or value of the investment, any value.

future-value —the objective value of the calculation, any value.

Note: the present and future values must have the same sign.

Formula $\frac{ln(fv/pv)}{ln(1+int)}$

int = interest rate

pv = present-value

fv = future value

ln = natural logarithm

Example To calculate how long a it would take for a $50,000 investment to reach $100,000 at 12% annual interest, use the formula `@CTERM(12%,100000, 50000)`. You will find that it would take just over six years to reach that objective.

Notes The interest rate must be specified in the same units of time as the compounding periods. You can enter the percentages either in decimal (.12) or percentage (12%) form.

@DATE

Purpose Calculates the 1-2-3 date-number from the specified year, month, and day.

Syntax @DATE(yy,mm,dd)

Arguments

yy —any integer from 1 (year 1900) to 199 (year 2099).

mm—any integer from 1 (January) to 12 (December).

dd —any integer from 1 to 31. The specific integer must be valid for the month selected (i.e., you cannot use 30 or 31 for February, which has only 28 or 29 days).

Usage Used to input or generate dates in 1-2-3 numeric format. You can display the dates using one of the date formats, or perform calculations with them. For example, you could subtract one date-number from another to yield the number of days between them.

Example `@DATE(89,5,25)` = 32653 = 25-May-89

Notes In order for the date to appear in date form, you must format the cell containing the @DATE function with the proper date format using the /Range Format Date. If you do not format the cell, the date number will appear as an integer or decimal value between 1 and 73,050.

Cautions 1-2-3 incorrectly includes February 29, 1900, in its calendar. This will have no effect unless you are making date calculations involving January or February 1900.

@DATEVALUE

Purpose Converts strings that look like dates into 1-2-3 date-numbers.

Syntax @DATEVALUE(string)

Arguments

string—any string or cell reference to a cell containing a label that conforms to one of the 1-2-3 date formats. See /Range Format or /Worksheet Global Format for details about 1-2-3 date formats.

Usage The most common use of the @DATEVALUE function is to convert dates that have been imported from other programs or entered as text. Dates that conform to one of the standard date formats can be converted to their 1-2-3 date numbers. You must still format the cell in which this function is placed in one of the date formats for it to display as a date.

Example `@DATEVALUE("05/25/89")` = 32653 = 25-May-89

Notes You must format the cell containing the @DATE function with the proper date format using the /Range Format Date, for the date to appear in date form. If you do not format the cell, the date number will appear as an integer or decimal value between 1 and 73050.

Cautions 1-2-3 incorrectly includes February 29, 1900, in its calendar. This will have no effect unless you are making date calculations involving January or February 1900.

@DAVG

Purpose Calculates the mean (average) of the values in the designated field among the records that meet the selected criteria.

Syntax @DAVG(input,field,criteria)

Arguments

input —any range containing a database table.

field —any field in the input range specified by its offset from the first field in the range.

criteria—a range with a top row that contains one or more field names (corresponding to the field names in the input range). The criteria are entered in the rows below, with each criteria specification below its associated field name.

Example To calculate the average weight of male walruses in a research study on weight and food consumptions shown in Figure Function.5, you would create the formula: `@DAVG(B3..D70,2,F5..F6)`. This designates the input range as B3..D70, the field to be evaluated as "Weight" (offset two columns from the left-most column in the range), and the criteria range to be F5..F6. The criteria range contains the field name "Sex" and the selection criteria "M". The calculated average is 2,047.

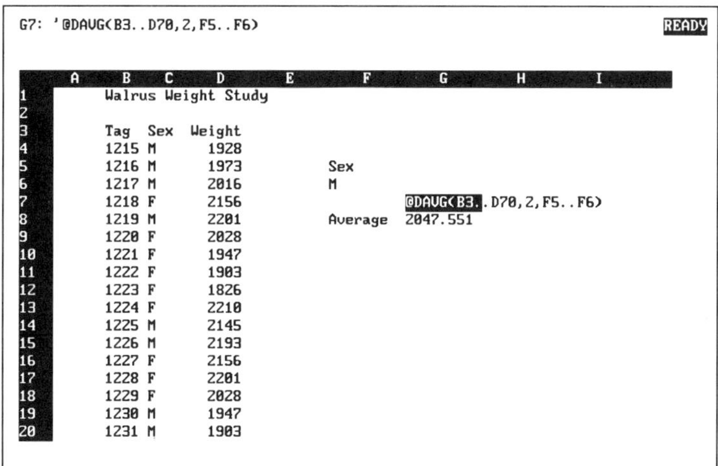

Figure @Function.5
@DAVG.

@DAY

Purpose Calculates the day of the month of the specified date-number.

Syntax @DAY(date-number)

Arguments

date-number—any value between 1 and 73050. 1-2-3 uses only the integer portion of the value for this calculation.

Usage Used to determine the day of the month (1–31) for a given date represented by its 1-2-3 date-number.

Examples

`@DAY(32653)` = 25 (32653 = May 25, 1989)

`@DAY(@DATE(51,5,12))` = 12

`@DAY(@TODAY())` = today's day of the month

@DCOUNT

Purpose Counts the number of non-blank cells in the specified field of the input range that meet the established criteria.

Syntax @DCOUNT(input,field,criteria)

Arguments

input —any range containing a database table.

field —any field in the input range specified by its offset from the first field in the range.

criteria—a range containing one or more field names (corresponding to the field names in the input range). The criteria are entered in the rows below, with each criteria specification below its associated field name.

Usage Used to count the number of records in a database table that meet a specified criteria.

Example Suppose you had a database table containing your address book and you wanted to determine how may of your associates lived in New York state. (See Figure @Function.6.) The input range is the entire data table (A4..F12). The criteria range is A16..A17 and the "State" field is specified by its offset number (from the leftmost column of the input range), in this case 4. The @DCOUNT formula is placed in cell C17, and can be seen in the control panel. It is also listed above cell C17 in cell C16. The formula correctly counts that you have three entries with a state equal to NY.

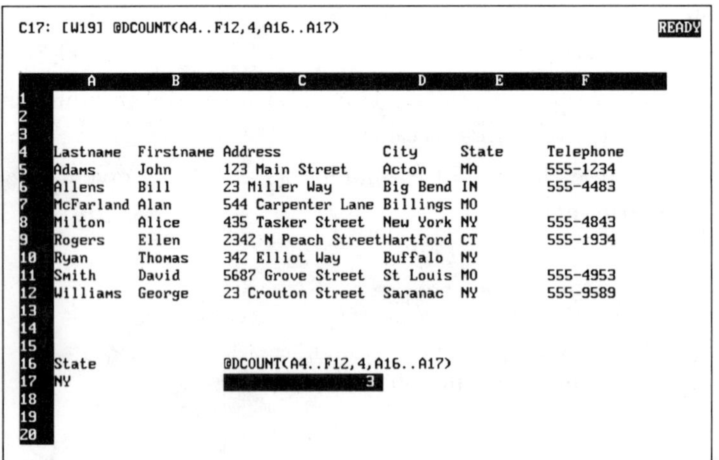

C17: [W19] @DCOUNT(A4..F12,4,A16..A17) READY

	A	B	C	D	E	F
1						
2						
3						
4	Lastname	Firstname	Address	City	State	Telephone
5	Adams	John	123 Main Street	Acton	MA	555-1234
6	Allens	Bill	23 Miller Way	Big Bend	IN	555-4483
7	McFarland	Alan	544 Carpenter Lane	Billings	MO	
8	Milton	Alice	435 Tasker Street	New York	NY	555-4843
9	Rogers	Ellen	2342 N Peach Street	Hartford	CT	555-1934
10	Ryan	Thomas	342 Elliot Way	Buffalo	NY	
11	Smith	David	5687 Grove Street	St Louis	MO	555-4953
12	Williams	George	23 Crouton Street	Saranac	NY	555-9589
13						
14						
15						
16	State		@DCOUNT(A4..F12,4,A16..A17)			
17	NY		3			
18						
19						
20						

Figure @Function.6
@DCOUNT.

Notes In the example, you could have counted any field in the database table. You do not necessarily have to count the same field used for the criteria. With other @D functions you may need to operate on other fields than the criteria field. For @DCOUNT however, using the same field is recommended so that you don't miscount records—records that may qualify on the basis of the tested field, but that may not contain any entry in the field counted. For example, if you counted the field "Telephone", you would only count two records since the telephone field for Thomas Ryan is blank.

@DDB

Purpose Calculates the depreciation allowance for a specified period using the double-declining balance technique.

Syntax @DDB(cost,salvage,life,period)

Arguments

cost —the original purchase cost. Must be greater than the salvage value.

salvage—the residual value of the asset at the end of the period. Must be less than the cost.

life —any value greater than 2. The number of equal periods over which the asset is to be depreciated. It must be expressed in the same time periods as the period (i.e., years or months). The cost is evaluated at period 0 and the salvage is calculated at the period equal to the life.

period —any value greater than 1 and less than the life. The number of the period in question for which you wish to determine the depreciation.

Formula $(bv *2)/n$ bv = book value in a selected period

n = life of the asset

Usage The double-declining balance depreciation technique is an accelerated depreciation calculation that depreciates an asset more quickly in the early years of its life and less in the later. This accelerated depreciation is appropriate for only some assets.

Example Suppose you purchased a manufacturing machine that cost $100,000 and has a useful life of seven years. The residual or salvage value at the end of seven years is estimated to be $15,000. What is the depreciation allowance in year four using the double-declining balance technique? The formula would be `@DDB(100000,15000,7,4)` and would yield the value $10,412.

Notes Not all assets qualify for double-declining balance depreciation schedules. Ask your tax adviser for further information.

If the residual value is low relative to the initial cost, the @DDB calculation may not fully depreciate the asset over the life of the asset.

@DMAX

Purpose Returns the maximum value of the specified field from records in the input database table that meet the specified criteria.

Syntax @DMAX(input,field,criteria)

Arguments

input —any range containing a database table.

field —any field in the input range specified by its offset from the first field in the range.

criteria—a range containing one or more field names corresponding to the field names in the input range, with one or more criteria entered below their associated field name.

Usage Used to find the record containing the maximum value in a numerical field (such as dollars donated) from among those records in the database table that meet the established criteria.

Example Suppose you wanted to determine the maximum contribution made by any donor from the state of New York. Using the database table shown in Figure

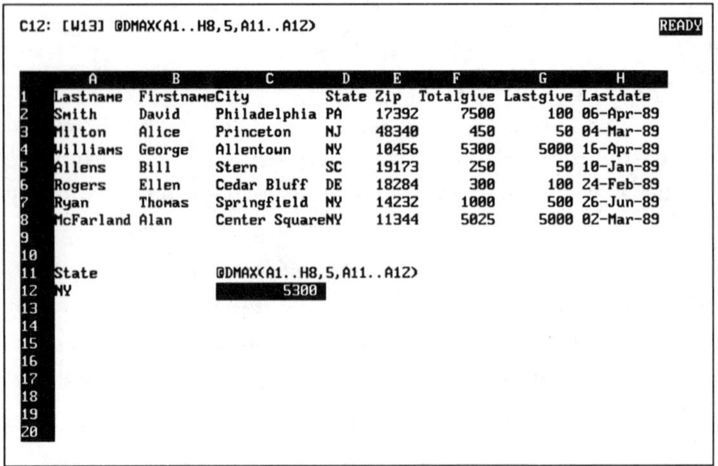

C12: [W13] @DMAX(A1..H8,5,A11..A12) READY

	A	B	C	D	E	F	G	H
1	Lastname	Firstname	City	State	Zip	Totalgive	Lastgive	Lastdate
2	Smith	David	Philadelphia	PA	17392	7500	100	06-Apr-89
3	Milton	Alice	Princeton	NJ	48340	450	50	04-Mar-89
4	Williams	George	Allentown	NY	10456	5300	5000	16-Apr-89
5	Allens	Bill	Stern	SC	19173	250	50	10-Jan-89
6	Rogers	Ellen	Cedar Bluff	DE	18284	300	100	24-Feb-89
7	Ryan	Thomas	Springfield	NY	14232	1000	500	26-Jun-89
8	McFarland	Alan	Center Square	NY	11344	5025	5000	02-Mar-89
9								
10								
11	State		@DMAX(A1..H8,5,A11..A12)					
12	NY		5300					
13								
14								
15								
16								
17								
18								
19								
20								

Figure @Function.7
@DMAX.

@Function.7, enter the formula as: `@DMAX(A1..H12,5, A11..A12)` and place the criteria "NY" below the field name State in the criteria range A11..A12. The value 5 is the field offset of the "Totalgive" column in the input range. If you wanted to check for the maximum donation from an individual from either NY or PA, you could create a multiple criteria range. By entering PA on the line below NY, and expanding the criteria range to A11..A13 to encompass it, you will select the maximum value for donors that match either NY or PA. See Figure @Function.8.

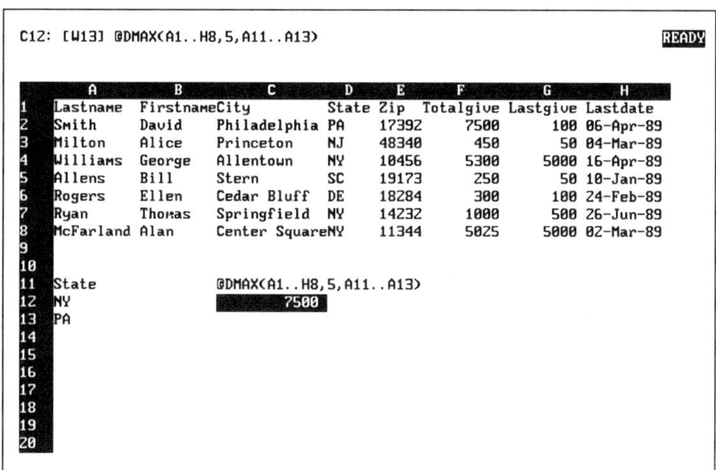

C12: [W13] @DMAX(A1..H8,5,A11..A13) READY

	A	B	C	D	E	F	G	H
1	Lastname	Firstname	City	State	Zip	Totalgive	Lastgive	Lastdate
2	Smith	David	Philadelphia	PA	17392	7500	100	06-Apr-89
3	Milton	Alice	Princeton	NJ	48340	450	50	04-Mar-89
4	Williams	George	Allentown	NY	10456	5300	5000	16-Apr-89
5	Allens	Bill	Stern	SC	19173	250	50	10-Jan-89
6	Rogers	Ellen	Cedar Bluff	DE	18284	300	100	24-Feb-89
7	Ryan	Thomas	Springfield	NY	14232	1000	500	26-Jun-89
8	McFarland	Alan	Center Square	NY	11344	5025	5000	02-Mar-89
9								
10								
11	State		@DMAX(A1..H8,5,A11..A13)					
12	NY		7500					
13	PA							
14								
15								
16								
17								
18								
19								
20								

Figure @Function.8
@DMAX with multiple string criteria.

@DMIN

Purpose Returns the minimum value of the specified field from records in the input database table that meet the specified criteria.

Syntax @DMIN(input,field,criteria)

Arguments

input —any range containing a database table.

field —any field in the input range specified by its offset from the first field in the range.

criteria—a range containing one or more field names corresponding to the field names in the input range with one or more criteria. The criteria are entered in the rows below, each criteria specification below its associated field name.

Usage Used to find the record containing the minimum value in a numerical field, such as dollars donated, from among those records in the database table that meet a specified criteria. Operates in exactly the same fashion as the @DMAX function.

@DSTD

Purpose Calculates the population standard deviation of the values in the specified field of the input database table that meet the specified criteria.

Syntax @DSTD(input,field,criteria)

Arguments

input —any range containing a database table.

field —any field in the input range specified by its offset from the first field in the range.

criteria—a range containing one or more field names in the top row (corresponding to the field names in the input range). The criteria are entered in the rows below, with each criteria specification below its associated field name.

Formula

$$\sqrt{\frac{\Sigma(v_i - avg)^2}{n-1}}$$

n = number of items in list

v_i = the ith item in list

avg = average of values in list

Usage The population standard deviation calculation measures the degree that the individual values in the selected population of values differ from the mean of all values in the total population of the list. A low standard deviation indicates that all selected values lie close to the common mean, which in turn indicates that the mean is a good representation of the selected population. On the other hand, a high standard deviation indicates that one or more values is significantly different than the mean.

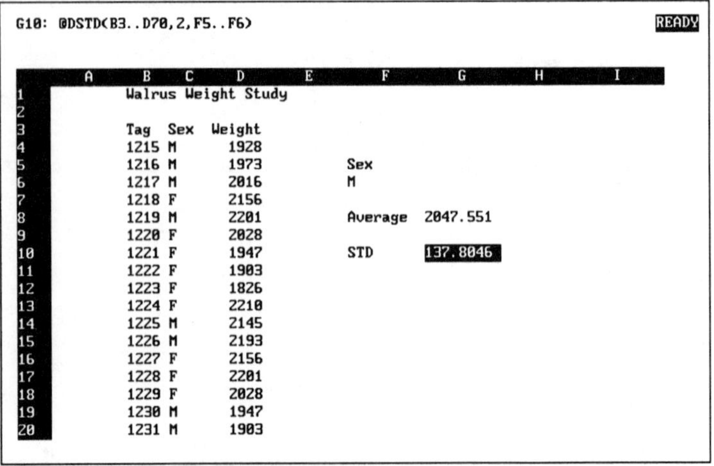

Figure @Function.9
@DSTD.

To use an old statistics example, if a man is standing with one foot in a bucket of ice water and the other in a bucket of boiling water, he is (on average) feeling fine. But he would definitely argue that his standard deviation was high.

Example To determine whether there is a significant difference in the individual weights of male walruses as compared to the mean of all walruses (both male and female) in a research study on weight and food consumptions shown in Figure @Function.9, create the formula: `@DSTD(B3..D70,2,F5..F6)` that designates the input range as B3..D70, the field to be evaluated as "Weight", and the criteria range to be F5..F6. The criteria range contains the field name "Sex" and the selection criteria "M". The calculated standard deviation of 137, while high, is less than that for females, indicating that male walruses are of more uniform weight than female walruses.

@DSUM

Purpose Calculates the total of the values in the designated field among the records that meet the selected criteria.

Syntax @DSUM(input,field,criteria)

Arguments

input—any range containing a database table.

field —any field in the input range specified by its offset from the first field in the range.

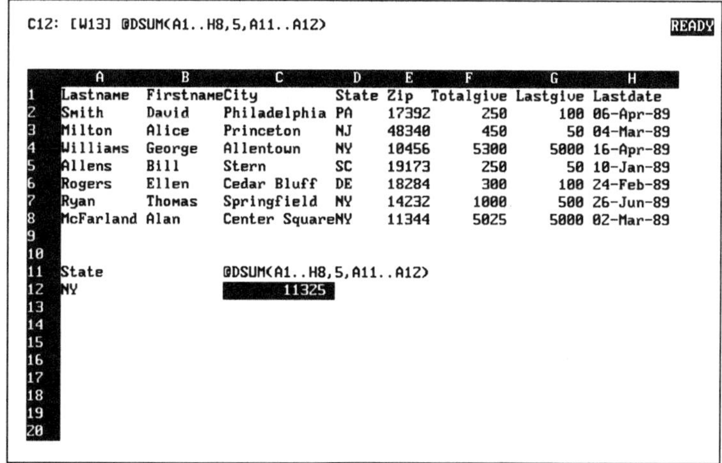
C12: [W13] @DSUM(A1..H8,5,A11..A12) READY

	A	B	C	D	E	F	G	H
1	Lastname	Firstname	City	State	Zip	Totalgive	Lastgive	Lastdate
2	Smith	David	Philadelphia	PA	17392	250	100	06-Apr-89
3	Milton	Alice	Princeton	NJ	48340	450	50	04-Mar-89
4	Williams	George	Allentown	NY	10456	5300	5000	16-Apr-89
5	Allens	Bill	Stern	SC	19173	250	50	10-Jan-89
6	Rogers	Ellen	Cedar Bluff	DE	18284	300	100	24-Feb-89
7	Ryan	Thomas	Springfield	NY	14232	1000	500	26-Jun-89
8	McFarland	Alan	Center Square	NY	11344	5025	5000	02-Mar-89
9								
10								
11	State		@DSUM(A1..H8,5,A11..A12)					
12	NY		11325					
13								
14								
15								
16								
17								
18								
19								
20								

Figure @Function.10
@DSUM.

criteria—a range containing one or more field names in the top row (corresponding to the field names in the input range). The criteria are entered in the rows below, with each criteria specification below its associated field name.

Example To calculate the total donations made by all donors from NY shown in Figure Function.10, create the formula `@DSUM(A1..H8,5, A11..A12)`. Place the criteria "NY" below the field name State in the criteria range A11..A12. The value 5 in the function corresponds to the fifth column from the left of the range on "Totalgive" column. The sum is calculated as $11,325.

@DVAR

Purpose Calculates the population variance of the values in the specified field of the input database table that meet the specified criteria.

Syntax @DVAR(input,field,criteria)

Arguments

input —any range containing a database table.

field —any field in the input range specified by its offset from the first field in the range.

criteria—a range containing one or more field names in the top row (corresponding to the field names in the input range). The criteria are entered in the rows below, each criteria specification below its associated field name.

Formula

$$\frac{\Sigma(v_i - avg)^2}{n}$$

n = number of items in list

v_i = the ith item in list

avg = average of values in list

Usage The population variance calculation measures the degree that the individual values in the selected population of values differ from the mean of all values in the total population of the list. A low variance indicates that all selected values lie close to the common mean, which in turn indicates that the mean is a good representation of the selected population. On the other hand, a high variance indicates that one or more values is significantly different than the mean.

Example To determine whether there is a significant difference in the individual weights of male walruses as compared to the mean of all walruses (both male and female) in a research study on weight and food consumptions shown in Figure @Function.11, use the formula: `@DVAR(B3..D70,2,F5..F6)` that designates

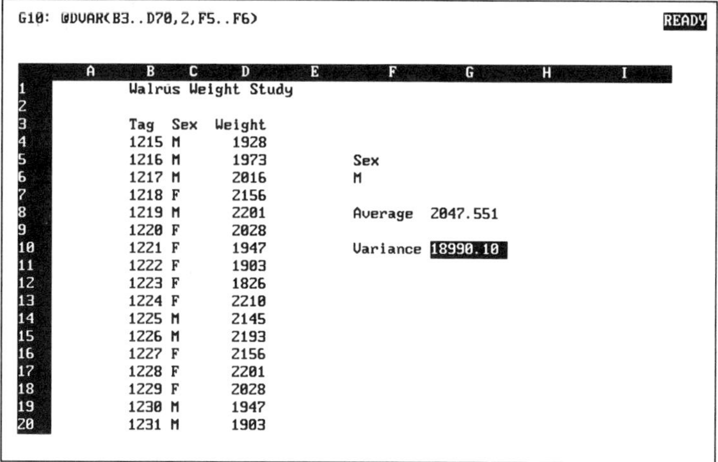
```
G10: @DVAR(B3..D70,2,F5..F6)                                      READY

     A      B    C     D       E       F       G        H       I
1           Walrus Weight Study
2
3           Tag  Sex   Weight
4           1215 M       1928
5           1216 M       1973          Sex
6           1217 M       2016          M
7           1218 F       2156
8           1219 M       2201          Average  2047.551
9           1220 F       2028
10          1221 F       1947          Variance 18990.10
11          1222 F       1903
12          1223 F       1826
13          1224 F       2210
14          1225 M       2145
15          1226 M       2193
16          1227 F       2156
17          1228 F       2201
18          1229 F       2028
19          1230 M       1947
20          1231 M       1903
```

Figure @Function.11
@DVAR.

the input range as B3..D70, the field to be evaluated as "Weight," and the criteria range to be F5..F6. The criteria range contains the field name "Sex" and the selection criteria "M". The calculated variance deviation of 18,990, while high, is less than that for females, indicating that male walruses are of more uniform weight than female walruses.

@ERR

Purpose Used primarily in logical formulas testing data to generate the special value ERR, when the data is missing or incorrect. The ERR value is carried forward to all formulas dependent on the cell valued as ERR.

Syntax @ERR

Arguments—None.

Usage 1-2-3 uses the ripple-effect to carry the error value ERR forward through formulas dependent on a cell that evaluates to ERR. You can use the @ERR function to generate your own ERR value that is also carried forward by the ripple effect. This is often used by formulas that test the validity of data entered by users. If the data passes the test, it is passed on. If it fails the test, the logical formula substitutes the ERR value. This is also passed on indicating that the subsequent formulas are not correct (they, too, will show as ERR) due to the erroneous data.

Example Suppose you wanted a user to enter the number of a month (from 1 to 12) in cell C3. This number is then used by a formula in cell C4. You want to make sure that the user enters a valid month number, since an invalid number (less than 1 or greater than 12 will generate invalid values in the formula in cell C4.

You could create the formula `@IF(C3>=1#AND#C3<=12,C3,@ERR)` and place it in cell F2, away from the prying eyes of the user.

This formula will return the value of C3 and place it in cell F2, if the value entered in C3 is between 1 and 12. If not, it places the value ERR in cell F2. You need only modify the formula in cell C4 to refer to F2 (the test cell) instead of C3 (the data input cell), and it will properly calculate its results when numbers between 1 and 12 are entered in cell C3, but it will evaluate to ERR when any other number is entered.

@EXACT

Purpose Compares two strings and determines if they are identical.

Syntax @EXACT(string1,string2)

Arguments

string1, string2—any literal string (enclosed in quotes), a cell or range reference that contains a label, or a formula or an @function that evaluates to a string.

Usage Often used to compare user input strings against valid responses. This is a more precise version of the string comparison operator (=), since it differentiates uppercase and lowercase characters with and without accents, and leading or trailing spaces. @EXACT returns a value of 1 if the match is exact and a value of 0 if it is not.

Examples

`@EXACT("Hello","hello")` = 0

`@EXACT("Good Bye","Good Bye")` = 1

`@EXACT("Hello Again",C4)` = 1 if the cell C4 contains the string Hello Again, without any leading or trailing spaces. You can use @TRIM to remove any surplus spaces as in:

`@EXACT("Hello Again",@TRIM(C4))` which is no longer sensitive to any surplus spaces in cell C4.

@EXP

Purpose Calculates the value e (approx 2.718282) raised to the power x.

Syntax @EXP(x)

Arguments

x—any value from −11,357 to 11,356.

Usage The value e (approx 2.718282) is used as the base in the system of natural logarithms. Scientific, financial, and statistical formulas often call for the value of e raised to a power (x). This is the value generated by the @EXP(x) function.

Examples

`@EXP(10)` = 22,026

`@EXP(-5)` = 0.60653

Notes 1-2-3 cannot display numbers larger than 1.0E99, this means that values of x greater than 230.259 that would generate values of @EXP greater than 1.0E99 cannot be displayed. They can be used in subsequent calculations, but will appear as asterisks on the screen.

@FALSE

Purpose Returns the logical value false (0).

Syntax @FALSE

Arguments None.

Usage Used in logical formulas to return a value of logical false that can be passed on to other formulas or functions

Example `@IF(C4>=1#AND#C4<=12,@TRUE,@FALSE)` = 0 if the value in C4 is not between 1 and 12, and 1 if it is.

@FIND

Purpose Finds the position of one string within another.

Syntax @FIND(string1,string2,start)

Arguments

string1, string2—any literal string (enclosed in quotes), a cell or range reference that contains a label, or a formula or @function that evaluates to a string.

start—the number of characters from the leftmost character of string2 to start the search, expressed as an offset. For example, the first character has an offset of 0, while the last character has an offset of one less than the length of the string.)

Usage Often used to find and extract portions of labels. By first finding the position of a specific marking character, such as the space between a first and last name, it is possible to extract only a portion of the name. Also used to test for partial string matches.

Example Suppose you wanted to extract the last name from a cell containing the first and last names concatenated together (e.g., "Mary Smith"). You could use the @FIND function to locate the space between the first and the last name, add 1 to it to reach the first letter of the last name, and then extract the rest of the label to produce a string containing just the last name. The formula would look like: :

```
@MID(B4,@FIND(" ",B4,0)+1,@LENGTH(B4)-@FIND(" ",B4,0))
```

Where @FIND(" ",B4,0) finds the space (" ") between the first and last names and @MID extracts from that position + 1, to the end of the label (the total length minus the position of the space).

Notes If @FIND does not find string1 in string2, it returns a value of ERR. If it does find the string, it returns the offset value of the position in string2 where string1 begins. Remember that the offset of the first character is 0.

@FV

Purpose Calculates the future value of a uniform stream of payments, earning a specified interest rate for a specified term.

Syntax @FV(payment,interest,term)

Arguments

payment—any value representing equal payments made at equal intervals.

interest —any value greater than −1 that represents the periodic interest rate earned by the accumulating payments.

term —any value representing the number of payments to be made.

Note: The time period used to express the term and the interest rate *must* be the same as the interval between payments. For example, if the payments are made monthly, the interest rate must be expressed as a monthly interest rate (annual rate/12) and the term must be expressed in numbers of months (number of years*12).

Formula $pmt * \frac{(1 + int)^n - 1}{int}$

pmt = periodic payment
int = periodic interest rate
n = number of periods

Usage Used in financial calculations to determine the value at some point in the future of an investment that requires equal periodic payments and earns a fixed interest on the accumulated payments and interest.

Example Suppose you contributed $25 each month to a Christmas Club fund that paid 7.5 % annual interest compounded monthly. How much would the fund be worth at the end of the year? Let's assume that you will cash it in on January 1 of the following year to pay off your wounded credit cards. Let's further assume that you make the payments at the end of each period. The formula would be: `@FV(25,.075/12,12)` yielding $ 310.53.

Notes The @FV function assumes that each payment is made at the end of the period (e.g., the first payment to the Christmas Club is paid January 31, *not* January 1). If each payment is made at the beginning of the period you must adjust the formula to calculate an annuity due by multiplying it by (1+interest). In the example, the formula would be: `@FV(25,.075/12,12)*(1+(.075/12))`, yielding $312.47.

@HLOOKUP

Purpose Used to look up values in a horizontal lookup table and return the contents of a specified cell.

Syntax @HLOOKUP(x,range,row-offset)

Arguments

x —any value greater than the first value in the lookup range.

range —any range name or address containing a horizontal lookup table.

row-offset —any number less than the total number of rows in the table minus 1. The offset is the number of rows down from the top row that 1-2-3 looks for the contents of a cell to return.

Horizontal Lookup Table—any range that contains values in the top row that increase as you move from left to right. See Figure @Function.12

Usage The most common use of lookup tables is for tax tables where you would look up the applicable tax rate based on taxable income (the values line) and another feature like marital status (the offset). The first step in using the @HLOOKUP function is to ensure that your lookup table is properly designed. It must have only values in the first row of the range (the values row) and these must increase in value from left to right. You need to arrange your data so that you can pinpoint the cell you wish to look up by telling 1-2-3 how many rows down to look, and by asking 1-2-3 to look up the column to use by matching the value entered as the x argument against each value in the values row. (In Figure @Function.12, the attendance values for Whales always lies in the fourth row below the values line. 1-2-3 will test against each value until it reaches the value x, or the value closest to but not larger than x, or until it reaches the last value in the value line (in which case it selects the last column).

Example Using Figure @Function.12, determine the attendance for Whales in month 3. Whales is offset four rows from the value row (row 11), so the formula would be: `@HLOOKUP(3,C7..F12,4)`, which yields the value 1,275.

Notes While the first row of the lookup table must contain values, the rest of the table need not. You can use the @HLOOKUP function to return labels as strings.

```
B17: [W9] @HLOOKUP(3,C7..F12,4)                                    READY

                        Monthly Attendance

   Name          January    February      March       April
                       1           2          3           4
   Aquarium         1200        1400        975        2452
   Seals             900         850       1200        1400
   Sea Lions        1225         975        850        1975
   Whales           1350        1200       1275        2234
   Porpoises         700        1100        825        1856
                 ------------------------------------------
                    5375        5525       5125        9917

   @HLOOKUP(3,C7..F12,4)
        1275
```

Figure @Function.12 @HLOOKUP.

@HOUR

Purpose Calculates the hour of the day of the specified time-number.

Syntax @HOUR(time-number)

Arguments

time-number—Any decimal value between .000000 and .999988. 1-2-3 uses only the decimal portion of the values larger than .999988 for this calculation.

Usage Used to determine the hour of the day (1–23) for a given time represented by its 1-2-3 time-number.

Example `@HOUR(.614583)` = 14 (.614583=2:45 PM)

@IF

Purpose Evaluates a condition, returning one of two labels or values depending if it is true or false.

Syntax @IF(condition,x,y)

Arguments

condition—usually a logical formula or reference to a cell containing a logical formula. Can be any formula that evaluates to a value—any value equal to zero is treated as false; all other values are treated as true. Can even be a string or reference to a cell containing a label, blank, ERR, or NA, though they all evaluate to zero and are treated as false.

x —returned value or label if condition is true.

y —returned value or label if condition is false.

Usage Tests all varieties of conditions, values, or strings against specific values or labels, returning either a default value or a warning label. This is especially useful for verifying user input before processing it.

Example Suppose that you wanted a user to enter the number of a month (from 1 to 12) in cell C3. This number is then used by a formula in cell C4. You want to make sure that the user enters a valid month number, since an invalid number (less than 1 or greater than 12) will generate invalid values in the formula in cell C4. You could create the following formula and place it in cell F2, away from the prying eyes of the user:

```
@IF(C3>=1#AND#C3<=12,C3,@ERR)
```

This formula will return the value of C3 and place it in cell F2, if the value entered in C3 is between 1 and 12. If not, it places the value ERR in cell F2. If you modify the formula in cell C4 to refer to F2 (the test cell) instead of C3 (the data input cell), it will properly calculate its results when numbers between 1 and 12 are entered in cell C3. It will evaluate to ERR when any other number is entered.

@INDEX

Purpose Returns the value in a cell determined by its offset position in a two-dimensional range.

Syntax @INDEX(range,column-offset,row-offset)

Arguments

range —any range address or name.

column-offset—any number less than the total number of columns in the range minus 1. The offset is the number of columns to the right of the first column in the specified range.

row-offset —any number less than the total number of rows in the range minus 1. The offset is the number of rows below the top row in the specified range.

Usage Used to look up the cell contents of a cell specified by its relative position in a two-dimensional range. This is most often used to look up values in a tax table or pricing table.

Example Suppose you had a table of prices for various tools for sale and provided discounts for volume purchases, as shown in Figure @Function.13. You could create a series of @INDEX formulas that took the row and column offset numbers entered into data cells (B14, B15) and returned both the column and row labels (column-offset = 0 and row-offset = 0) as well as one that returned the appropriate price.

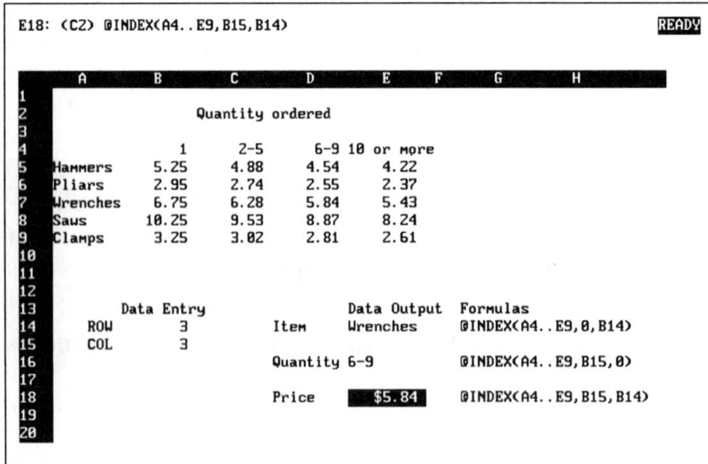

Figure @Function.13
@INDEX.

Notes Use @HLOOKUP or @VLOOKUP if you need to match a value in a row or column instead of providing both relative positions.

@INT

Purpose Calculates the integer portion of a decimal number by truncation at the decimal point.

Syntax @INT(x)

Arguments

x—any value.

Example `@INT(23.7645) = 23`

Notes @INT does not round the value, it truncates it.

@IRR

Purpose Calculates the internal rate of return from a series of positive and negative cash flows.

Syntax @IRR(guess,range)

Arguments

guess—any value—user-supplied first estimate to facilitate the process of successive approximation and to provide a domain in which to seek a solution when more than one solution is possible.

range—any range address or name containing the cash flow values.

Usage Calculates the interest rate that, when applied to the series of positive and negative cash flows contained in the input range, would yield a net present value of zero. The cash flows in the input range *must* contain at least one positive and one negative value. When entering your initial best guess, select a value between 0 and 100%.

Example Suppose you had an opportunity to purchase a lemonade stand from the kid next door for $100. You expect to net, after expenses, $50 at the end of each month for the three months of summer vacation (June, July, and August). You also believe that you can sell the stand back to the same kid for an additional $25 at the end of September. What would the internal rate of return be for the proposed investment? See Figure @Function.14.

As you can see, the proposed investment yields a healthy 29.72% internal rate of return.

Notes Internal rate of return calculations can produce multiple correct results if the cash flow changes directions more than once. One answer is usually more

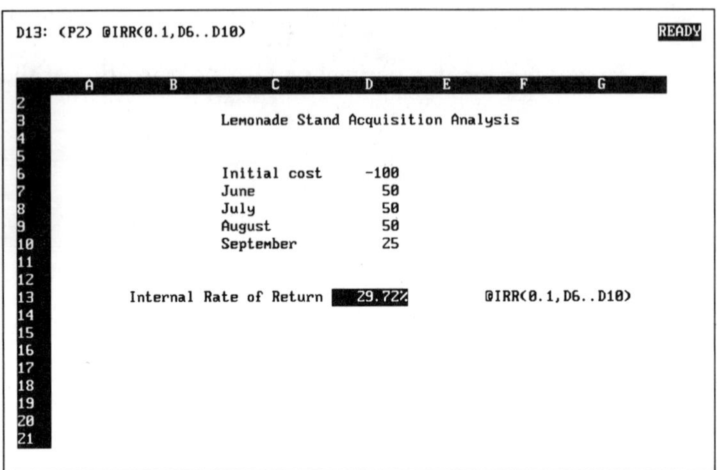

Figure @Function.14
@IRR.

reasonable than the other(s) (i.e., it lies between 0 and 100%). In order to focus in on one of the possible answers, 1-2-3 uses your guess as the starting value. If @IRR returns an unreasonable value, try running it again with another guess.

The @IRR function uses the process of successive approximations to reach its answer. If it can't reach a stable answer to within .0000001 after 30 iterations, it returns the value ERR. You should try a different initial guess and rerun the function.

Cautions The @IRR function assigns the value of 0 to all blank cells in the input range and includes them in its calculation. Be sure that blank cells truly represent zero values for that period. The @IRR function assumes that all cash flows are received at regular, equal intervals. The interest rate is expressed in the same period, i.e., months or years.

@ISAFF

Purpose Used to test if a named add-in function has been defined and is available. This can be used to test for the availability of a given add-in function and branch to an appropriate error message if the function has not been properly installed.

Syntax @ISAFF(name)

Arguments

name—any string contained within quotes, formula, or cell reference that contains a string that corresponds to the name of an add-in function. Do *not* include the leading @ sign when entering the name argument.

Usage The @ISAFF function will return a value of 1 if the named add-in function is loaded and available; it will return a value of 0 if it is not.

Example If you have created an add-in function named "@HIDER" which hides any values that are less than 100, you could test that it is installed and available with the function: `@ISAFF("HIDER")`.

Note The @ISAFF function will return a value of 0 (false) if you test for the existence of a built-in function (e.g., @SUM) since it is a built-in function and not an add-in function.

@ISAPP

Purpose Used to test if a named add-in (AAF or dynamic driver) has been attached and is available. This can be used to test for the availability of a given add-in and branch to an appropriate error message if the add-in has not been properly attached.

Syntax @ISAPP(name)

Arguments

name—any string contained within quotes, formula, or a cell reference that contains a string that corresponds to the name of an AAF or dynamic driver add-in. Do *not* include the leading @ sign when entering the name argument.

Usage The @ISAPP function will return a value of 1 if the named add-in is attached and available; it will return a value of 0 if it is not.

Example The function `@ISAPP("Allways")` will return the value 1 if the add-in Allways has been attached or the value 0 if it has not.

@ISERR

Purpose Tests for ERR value.

Syntax @ISERR(x)

Arguments

x—any string, value location or condition.

Usage Generally used to eliminate ERR messages from appearing on the screen and rippling through dependent formulas. The most common use is to avoid division by zero errors.

Example For example, the @DAVG function calculates the average of a set of records in a database that meet a specified criteria by adding them and dividing by their count. What if no records meet the specified criteria? The @DAVG function will count zero records and sum a zero total. When it divides zero by zero, it generates an ERR value in the cell. If you are using the @DAVG function in a /Data Table command, you can create pages of ERR messages. A less threatening response would be a blank or a zero. You can create that with the formulas `@ISERR(@DAVG(range),0,@DAVG(range))` which displays a zero instead of ERR, or `@ISERR(@DAVG(range),"",@DAVG(range))` which displays a blank instead of ERR.

@ISNA

Purpose Tests for NA value.

Syntax @ISNA(x)

Arguments

x—any string, value, location, or condition.

Usage Generally used to eliminate NA messages from rippling through dependent formulas that aren't effected by the missing data.

Example `@ISNA(A25)` = 1 if A25 evaluates to NA and 0 if it does not.

@ISNUMBER

Purpose Tests if a location or formula evaluates to a number.

Syntax @ISNUMBER(x)

Arguments

x—any string, value, location, or condition.

Usage Most often used in macros to insure that a user has entered the correct type of data into an input cell. For example a section of macro code might read: `{IF@ISNUMBER(A5)}{BEEP}{BRANCH ERROR}`, which beeps and branches to an error correction routine if the user enters a number in a cell that requires a label.

@ISSTRING

Purpose Tests if a location contains a label or a formula evaluates to a string.

Syntax @ISSTRING(x)

Arguments

x—any string, value, location, or condition.

Usage Returns a 1 if x is a string or label, and returns a 0 if x is a value or blank. Most often used in macros to insure that a user has entered the correct type of data into an input cell. For example a section of macro code might read: `{IF @ISSTRING(A5)}{BEEP}{BRANCH ERROR}` which beeps and branches to an error correction routine if the user enters a label or blank in a cell that requires a number.

@LEFT

Purpose Extracts and returns the first specified number of characters from a string.

Syntax @LEFT(string,x)

Arguments

string—any string (not enclosed in quotes), a cell or range reference that contains a label, or a formula or an @function that evaluates to a string.

x —any positive integer. If x is 0, @LEFT returns an empty string. If x is larger than the length of the string, @LEFT returns the entire string.

Usage Used to extract the leading portion of a string, for example the prefix of a file name or a part number.

Examples

`@LEFT(FILE.WK3,4)` = FILE

`@LEFT(ARSD2312-32,4)` = ARSD

Notes @LEFT counts spaces and punctuation as characters.

@LENGTH

Purpose Calculates the number of characters in a string.

Syntax @LENGTH(string)

Arguments

string—any string (not enclosed in quotes), a cell or range reference that contains a label, or a formula or an @function that evaluates to a string.

Usage Calculates the total length of a line before printing or to determine the length of string in order to extract portions of it.

Example `@LENGTH(Octopus)` = 7

Notes @LENGTH counts spaces and punctuation as characters. Use the @TRIM function to trim off leading, trailing, and excess (more than one adjacent) internal spaces.

@LN

Purpose Calculates the natural logarithm of a value in base e.

Syntax @LN(x)

Arguments

x—any positive value.

Examples

`@LN(10)` = 2.30259

`@LN(100)` = 4.60517

@LOG

Purpose Calculates the common logarithm of a value in base 10.

Syntax @LOG(x)

Arguments

x—any positive value.

Examples

`@LOG(10)` = 1

`@LOG(100)` = 2

`@LOG(50)` = 1.69897

@LOWER

Purpose Converts a string to all lowercase characters.

Syntax @LOWER(string)

Arguments

string—any literal string (enclosed in quotes), any cell or range reference that contains a label, or any formula or @function that evaluates to a string.

Example `@LOWER("Spirit of St. Louis")` = spirit of st. louis

@MAX

Purpose Determines the largest value in a list of values.

Syntax @MAX(list)

Arguments

list—one or more values, formulas that return a value, references to ranges that contain values or formulas that return values, or any combination of the above.

Examples

`@MAX(4,5,6,7)` = 7

`@MAX(PENGUINS)` = 14 where 14 is the largest value in a range named PENGUINS.

@MID

Purpose Extracts a specified number of characters from within a string starting at a specified character location.

Syntax @MID(string,start,x)

Arguments

string—any string (not enclosed in quotes), any cell or range reference that contains a label, or any formula or @function that evaluates to a string.

start —any positive integer. If start is larger than the length of the string, @MID returns an empty string.

x —any positive integer or 0. If x is 0, @MID returns an empty string. If x is larger than the length of the string minus start, @MID returns the entire string including and to the right of the character located at the start position (including the starting character).

Examples

`@MID("Spirit of St. Louis",11,2)` = St

`@MID("Spirit of St. Louis",11,47)` = St. Louis

If you don't know what the start position of a string is, you can use the @FIND function to locate it for you. Suppose you wanted to extract the last name from a cell containing the first and last names concatenated together (e.g., "Mary Smith"), you could use the @FIND function to locate the space between the first and the last name, add 1 to it to reach the first letter of the last name, and then use the @MID function to extract the rest of the label, to produce a string containing just the last name. The formula would look like:

```
@MID(B4,@FIND(" ",B4,0)+1,@LENGTH(B4)-@FIND(" ",B4,0))
```

Where @FIND(" ",B4,0) finds the space (" ") between the first and last names and @MID extracts from that position + 1, to the end of the label (the total length minus the position of the space).

Notes @MID counts spaces and punctuation as characters. Use the @TRIM function to trim off leading, trailing, and excess (more than one successive) internal spaces.

@MIN

Purpose Determines the smallest value in a list of values.

Syntax @MIN(list)

Arguments

list—one or more values, or formulas that return a value, or references to ranges that contain values, or formulas that return values, or any combination of the above.

Examples

`@MIN(4,5,6,7)` = 4

`@MAX(PENGUINS)` = 3 where 3 is the smallest value in a range named PENGUINS.

@MINUTE

Purpose Calculates the minute of the hour of the specified time-number.

Syntax @MINUTE(time-number)

Arguments

time-number—any decimal value between .000000 and .999988. 1-2-3 only uses the decimal portion of the values larger than .999988 for this calculation.

Usage Used to determine the minute of the hour of the day (1–59) for a given time represented by its 1-2-3 time-number.

Example `@MINUTE(.614583)` = 45 (.614583=2:45 PM)

@MOD

Purpose Calculates the remainder of a division calculation.

Syntax @MOD(x,y)

Arguments

x—any value.

y—any value except 0.

Formula x–(y*@INT(x/y))

Usage Used primarily to perform day of the week calculations. Since the 1-2-3 date-number system starts on a known day, you can calculate the day of the week; divide the date-number by seven and use the modulus to determine the day according to the following:

0 — Saturday
1 — Sunday
2 — Monday
3 — Tuesday
4 — Wednesday
5 — Thursday
6 — Friday

You can even combine the @MOD function and the @CHOOSE function to perform the entire computation with a formula like: `@CHOOSE(@MOD(A1,7),"Saturday","Sunday","Monday","Tuesday","Wednesday","Thursday","Friday")`, which will display the day of the week of the date number placed in cell A1.

Examples

`@MOD(14,6)` = 2

`@MOD(@DATE(89,5,25),7)` = 5 = Thursday

@MONTH

Purpose Calculates the month of the year of the specified date-number.

Syntax @MONTH(date-number)

Arguments

date-number—any value between 1 and 73,050. 1-2-3 only uses the integer portion of the value for this calculation.

Usage Used to determine the month of the year (1–12) for a given date represented by its 1-2-3 date-number.

Examples

`@MONTH(32653)` = 5 (32653 = May 25, 1989)

`@MONTH(1)` = 1 (1 = Jan 1, 1900)

`@MONTH(@TODAY())` = the current month

@N

Purpose Tests the value of the first cell in a range and returns that value if it is numeric or the value 0 if it is a label.

Syntax @N(range)

Arguments

range—any range address or name.

Usage Most often used in macros to insure that a range contains the correct type of data. For example a section of macro code might read: `{IF @N(OCTOPUS)=0}{BEEP}{BRANCH ERROR}`, which beeps and branches to an error correction routine if the first cell in the range named OCTOPUS doesn't contain a value.

@NA

Purpose Use to assign the NA (Not Available) value to cells and dependent formulas.

Syntax @NA

Arguments None.

Usage 1-2-3 uses the ripple-effect to carry the error value NA forward through formulas that are dependent on a cell that evaluates to NA. You can use the @NA function to generate the NA value in cells that are waiting for data. This is often used by formulas that test the completeness of data entered by users. If the data passes the test, it is passed on. If it fails the test, the logical formula substitutes the NA value. This is also passed on indicating that the subsequent formulas are not complete (they too will show as NA) due to the missing data.

Example Suppose that you wanted a user to enter the numbers in 12 cells of a range corresponding to monthly expenses called EXP-RANGE. The values in the range are used to project future cash flows. You want to ensure that the user inserts values in each of the 12 cells, since an incomplete entry would produce an erroneous projection. You could create a "shadow" range called VALID-EXP that has a cell corresponding to each cell in EXP-RANGE and enter a formula like the following: `@IF(C5="  ",@NA,C5)`, in each of the cells of VALID-EXP. Then reference the projection formula to the range VALID-EXP instead of EXP-RANGE. The formula will show the correct value when values are entered into each cell of EXP-RANGE and will show NA if one or more is left blank. See Figure @Function.15.

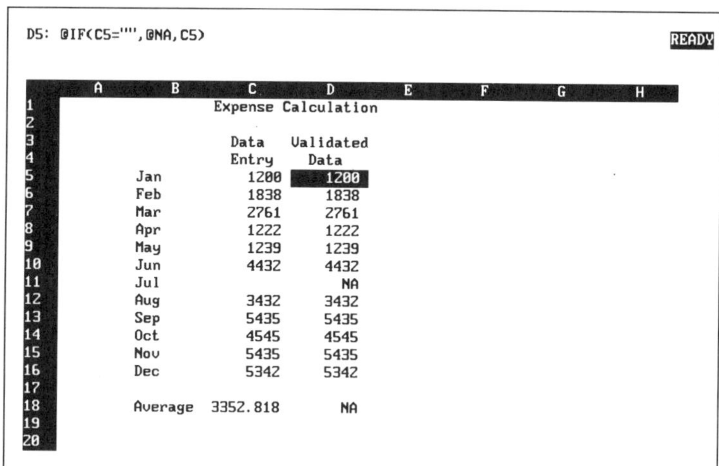
D5: @IF(C5="",@NA,C5) READY

	Data Entry	Validated Data
Jan	1200	1200
Feb	1838	1838
Mar	2761	2761
Apr	1222	1222
May	1239	1239
Jun	4432	4432
Jul		NA
Aug	3432	3432
Sep	5435	5435
Oct	4545	4545
Nov	5435	5435
Dec	5342	5342
Average	3352.818	NA

Figure @Function.15
@NA.

As you can see the @AVG function in cell C18 operating on column C produces a value, even though the entry in cell C11 for July is missing. On the other hand, the formula in cell D18 evaluates to NA, indicating that one or more input cells was left blank.

@NOW

Purpose Returns the current system date and time as a 1-2-3 date- and time-number.

Syntax @NOW

Arguments None.

Usage Used to generate the current date or time for time-stamping a printed report or for determining the time elapsed between a fixed date and the current date (e.g., a payment due date and the current date to determine if a payment is overdue).

Example `@IF(@NOW<duedate,"Overdue","")`

Notes The @NOW function returns a decimal value. The integer portion contains the day-number and the decimal portion contains the time-number. You must format the cell in the appropriate time or date format for the time or date to display.

@NPV

Purpose Calculates the net present value of a stream of cash flows (equal intervals, but not necessarily the same amounts), discounted at a specified interest rate.

Syntax @NPV(range,interest)

Arguments

range —any range containing the stream of cash flows.

interest—any value greater than −1 that represents the periodic interest rate.

Note: The time period used to express the interest rate must be the same as the interval between payments. For example, if the payments are made monthly, the interest rate must be expressed as a monthly interest rate (annual rate/12).

Formula

$$\sum_{i=1}^{n} \frac{v_i}{(1 + int)^i}$$

$v_i \ldots v_n$ = series of cash flows in range
int = interest rate
n = number of cash flows
i = the current iteration (1 through n)

Usage Used in financial calculations to determine the current value of a stream of future payments and/or expenses.

Example Suppose you could purchase a computer for $4,000 that will allow you to earn an extra $100 (typing papers for other students) each month for each of the four years you are in college. You will, of course, want to take the summers off to sit at the beach, so there will be no income for June, July, or August. What is your net present value of this investment using a 10% interest rate for the discounting? (To make it simpler, assume that you pay for the computer at the end of month one and don't earn anything until the end of month two.) See Figure @Function.16.

As you can see, the investment is not very sound from a financial perspective (it cost you $1,072.50), but the computer did help you pass Economics 101 and you did meet Donna. Don't you just love examples with happy endings?

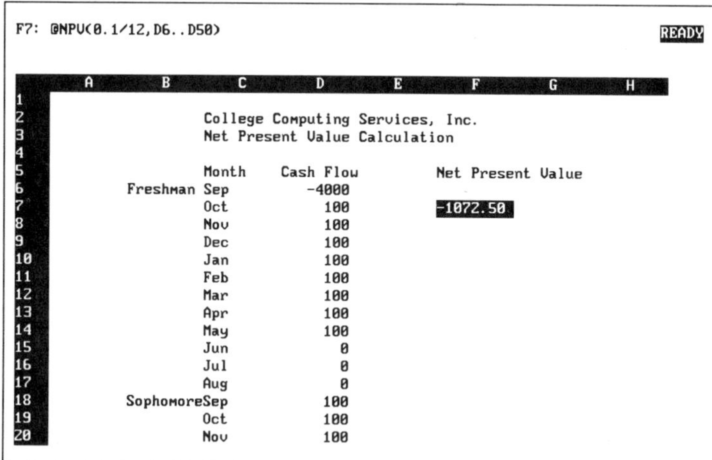

Figure @Function.16
@NPV.

Notes The @NPV function assumes that each payment is made at the end of the period. To evaluate an investment where the first cash flow occurs immediately, you must treat it as independent of the discounted cash flows. For example, if you had to pay for the computer immediately, you would have to remove it from the range of discounted cash flows (replacing it with 0) and add it back into the calculation manually as in: `@NPV(0.1/12,D6..D50)-4000`

@PI

Purpose Generates the value of Pi = 3.14159265358979324.

Syntax @PI

Arguments None.

Usage Used in trigonometric functions and geometry involving circles.

Example To convert radians to degrees multiply the radian value by 180/@PI. To convert degrees to radians, multiply the degree value by @PI/180. To calculate the area of a circle with a radius of 25 inches: `@PI*25^2` = 1963.495 inches.

@PMT

Purpose Calculates the equal period payment to repay a loan at a fixed interest rate (an ordinary annuity such as a mortgage or car loan).

Syntax @PMT(principal,interest,term)

Arguments

principal—any value representing the value of the loan

interest —any value greater than −1 representing the periodic interest rate

term —any value except 0 representing the number of payments to be made.

Note: The time period used to express the interest rate and term must be the same as the interval between payments. For example, if the payments are made monthly, the interest rate must be expressed as a monthly interest rate (annual rate/12) and the term must be expressed as the number of months.

Formula

$$prin * \frac{int}{1-(int+1)^{-n}}$$

prin = principal
int = periodic interest rate
n = term

Usage Used in financial calculations to determine the equal monthly payment needed to amortize a loan.

Example To calculate the equal monthly payment necessary to pay off a mortgage loan of $75,000 over 30 years at the fixed interest rate of 12.5% you would use the formula `@PMT(75000,12.5%/12,03*12)` = $800.44

Notes The @PMT function assumes that each payment is made at the end of the period. If each payment is made at the beginning of the period you must adjust the formula to calculate an annuity due by dividing it by (1+interest). In the example, the formula would be `@PMT(75000,12.5%/12,03*12)/(1+12.5%/12)` = $792.19.

@PROPER

Purpose Converts the first character of each word in a string to uppercase and all others to lowercase.

Syntax @PROPER(string)

Arguments

string—any literal string (enclosed in quotes), any cell or range reference that contains a label, or any formula or @function that evaluates to a string.

Example `@PROPER("spirit of st. louis")` = Spirit Of St. Louis

@PV

Purpose Calculates the present value of a uniform stream of payments, earning a specified interest rate for a specified term.

Syntax @PV(payment,interest,term)

Arguments

payment—any value representing equal payments made at equal intervals.

interest —any value greater than −1 that represents the periodic interest rate earned by the accumulating payments.

term —any value representing the number of payments to be made.

Note: The time period used to express the term and the interest rate must be the same as the interval between payments. For example, if the payments are made monthly, the interest rate *must* be expressed as a monthly interest rate (annual rate/12) and the term must be expressed in numbers of months (number of years*12).

Formula

$$pmt*\frac{1-(int+1)^{-n}}{int}$$

pmt = payment
int = periodic interest rate
n = term

Usage Used in financial calculations to determine the value at the present time of an investment that requires generating periodic payments into the future so that each must be discounted back to present.

Example Suppose a friend asked to borrow $25 to take a date to dinner and offers to repay the loan by giving you a penny a day for the rest of his life. If you expect him to live for only another 20 years (living the fast life takes it toll), should you accept the offer? The formula would be:

```
@PV(.01,.125/365,20*365)
```

yielding $ 26.80 or a net profit of $1.80 over the life of the loan.

Notes The @PV function assumes that each payment is made at the end of the period (e.g., the first penny would arrive tomorrow). If each payment is made at the beginning of the period you must adjust the formula to calculate an annuity due by multiplying it by (1+interest). In the example, the formula would be:

```
@PV(.01,.125/365,20*365)*(1+(.125/365))
```

yielding $ 26.81 or one cent more than the ordinary annuity.

@RAND

Purpose Generates a random number between 0 and 1.

Syntax @RAND

Arguments None.

Usage Used in computer simulations to generate sample data. To generate values other than 0 to 1, multiply the generated value by a factor.

Examples

`@RAND*100`—generates values between 0 and 100.

`@INT(@RAND*100)`—generates integers between 0 and 100.

Notes The @RAND function is recalculated and generates new values each time the worksheet is recalculated. If you want to lock in a set of values, use the /Range Value command to either overwrite the generating function with its current value (a permanent lock) or to copy the current value(s) of the function to another cell or range that leaves the original function(s) intact.

@RATE

Purpose Calculates the interest rate required to grow a given present value to a given future value over a given term.

Syntax @RATE(present-value,future-value,term)

Arguments

present-value—any value except 0.

future-value —any value.

term —any value.

Note: The time period used to express the term will be the same basis for expressing the resulting interest rate. For example, if the term is expressed in months, the interest rate will also be expressed in months.

Formula $\left(\frac{fv}{pv}\right)^{1/n} - 1$

fv = future value

pv = present value

n = term

Usage Used in financial calculations to determine the periodic interest rate that must be earned by an investment to yield a predetermined value at some point in the future. This calculation is frequently used to determine bond yields.

Example Suppose you purchased a savings bond with a face value of $25 that costs you $18.75 today and will mature in 5 years. To calculate the effective yield of the bond you would use the formula: `@RATE(25,18.75,5)`, which yields an effective rate of 5.92%.

@REPEAT

Purpose Duplicates the designated string a specified number of times.

Syntax @REPEAT(string,x)

Arguments

string—any literal string (enclosed in quotes), any cell or range reference that contains a label, or any formula or @function that evaluates to a string.

x —any positive integer.

Usage The @REPEAT function duplicates the specified string the specified number of times.

Examples

`@REPEAT("WOW",5)` = WOW WOW WOW WOW WOW

`@REPEAT("*",20)` = ********************

Notes @REPEAT differs from the backslash (\) repeating label prefix, in that the @REPEAT function duplicates the specified string exactly the specified number of times, while the repeating label prefix duplicates the specified string as many times as necessary to fill the current cell.

@REPLACE

Purpose Inserts a specified string into another specified string starting at a designated position in the second string, replacing a designated number of characters.

Syntax @REPLACE(string1,start,x,string2)

Arguments

string1, string2—any literal string (enclosed in quotes), any cell or range reference that contains a label, or any formula or @function that evaluates to a string. String1 is the string into which string2 is inserted.

start —any positive integer or 0 representing the character offset in string1.

x—any positive integer or 0, representing the number of characters in string 1 that are to be replaced by string2.

Usage The @REPLACE function is used to replace portions of one string with another string. It is easiest to think of the process as inserting the second string at the designated location, and simultaneously removing a designated number of characters from the first string starting in the same location. If you really want to replace a specified string with another specified string, you must construct a complex formula like that shown in Figure @Function.17.

When specifying x, remember that setting x equal to the length of string1 will replace the entire string1. By specifying a start value equal to the length of string1+1, you can append string2 to string1. By making x equal to 0, you will delete no characters of string1, thereby inserting string2 into string1 in its entirety.

Examples

`@REPLACE("Saturday",0,5,"Sun")` = Sunday

To replace the string "fox" anywhere (once) in the string "Mary had a little fox, whose fleece..." with the string "lamb", use the following formula, which both finds the occurrence of the string fox and determines how many characters to delete.

```
@REPLACE("Mary had a little fox, whose fleece...",
@FIND("fox","Mary had a little fox, whose fleece...",0),
@LENGTH("fox"),"lamb")
```

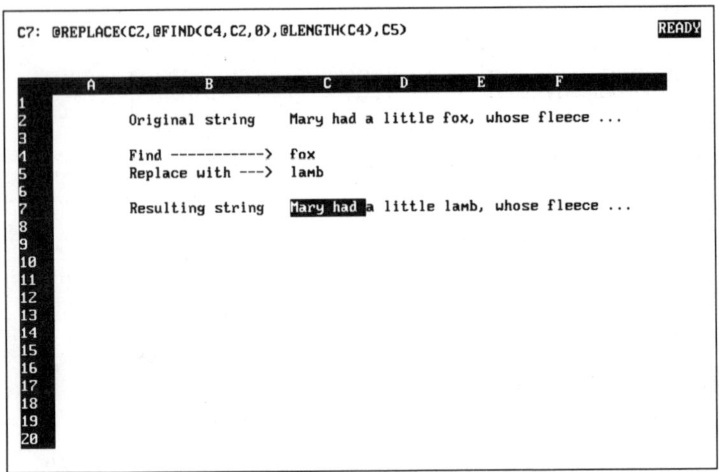

Figure @Function.17 Complex @REPLACE function.

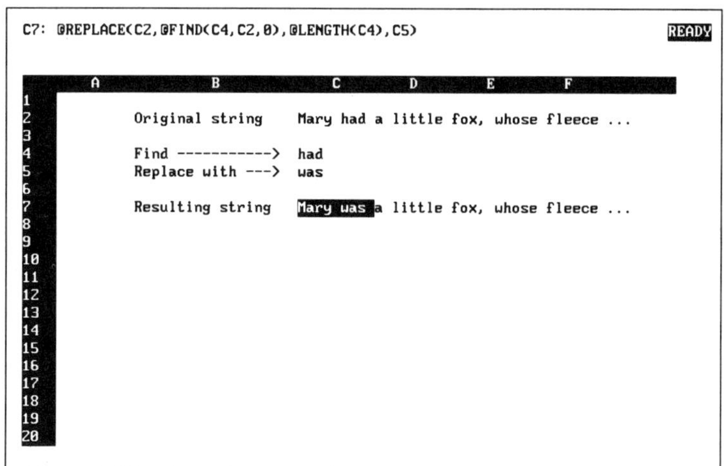

Figure @Function.18
Complex @REPLACE function with second substitution.

Figures @Function.17 and 18 show the same formula in its cell reference form with two different substitutions.

Notes @REPLACE counts spaces and punctuation as characters.

Use the @TRIM function to trim off leading, trailing, and excess (more than one adjacent) internal spaces in either string1 or string2.

@RIGHT

Purpose Extracts and returns the *last* specified number of characters from a string.

Syntax @RIGHT(string,x)

Arguments

string—any string (not enclosed in quotes), any cell or range reference that contains a label, or any formula or @function that evaluates to a string.

x —any positive integer. If x is 0, @RIGHT returns an empty string. If x is larger than the length of the string, @RIGHT returns the entire string.

Usage Used to extract the trailing portion of a string, for example the suffix of a file name or a part number.

Examples

`@RIGHT(FILE.WK3,3)` = WK3

`@RIGHT(ARSD2312-32,2)` = 32

Notes @RIGHT counts spaces and punctuation as characters.

@ROUND

Purpose Rounds off a value to a specified number of decimal places.

Syntax @ROUND(x,n)

Arguments

x—any value, or formula that returns a value, or references to a cell that contains a value or formula that returns a value.

n—any integer between −100 and 100. If n is equal to 0, @ROUND rounds to an integer.

Usage To round a value off, you must specify the number of decimal places you desire. The @ROUND function then rounds the next decimal place to the right of the specified location into the specified location.

Examples

`@ROUND(525.676,-2)` = 500

`@ROUND(525.676,2)` = 525.68

`@ROUND(525.676,0)` = 526

`@INT(525.676)` = 525 (Note the difference.)

Notes Using the @ROUND function is not the same as using either the /Range Format or the /Worksheet Global Format command to set the number of decimal places displayed. While both the function and the commands round the value, the format commands round it just for the display and retain the original value for further calculations. The @ROUND function truly rounds the underlying value. This is not the same as @INT which truncates.

@ROWS

Purpose Counts the number of rows in a range.

Syntax @ROWS(range)

Arguments

range—any named range or address.

Usage Calculates the length of ranges, for printing.

Example `@ROWS(A1..F25)` = 25

@S

Purpose Tests the first cell in a range and returns its contents if it contains a label or a blank if it contains a value.

Syntax @S(range)

Arguments

range—any range address or name.

Usage Most often used in macros to insure that a range contains the correct type of data. For example a section of macro code might read:

```
{IF @S(LOBSTER)=0}{BEEP}{BRANCH ERROR}
```

which beeps and branches to an error correction routine if the first cell in the range named LOBSTER doesn't contain a label.

@SECOND

Purpose Calculates the seconds (0–59) of the specified time-number.

Syntax @SECOND(time-number)

Arguments

time-number—any decimal value between .000000 and .999988. 1-2-3 only uses the decimal portion of the values larger than .999988 for this calculation.

Usage Used to determine the second of the minute (0–59) for a given time represented by its 1-2-3 time-number.

Example `@SECOND(.6455)` = 31 (.6455=2:29:31 PM)

@SIN

Purpose Calculates the sine of an angle.

Syntax @SIN(x)

Arguments

x—any value.

Usage The @SIN function returns the sine of the angle represented by the argument value. The resulting value can vary from −1 to 1.

Examples

`@SIN(0)` = 0

`@SIN(1.047)` = .865927 (1.047 radians = 60 degrees)

Notes To convert an angle measured in degrees to radians for input, multiply it by @PI/180.

@SLN

Purpose Calculates the depreciation allowance for a single period using the straight-line depreciation technique.

Syntax @SLN(cost,salvage,life)

Arguments

cost —the original purchase cost. Must be greater than the salvage value.

salvage—the residual value of the asset at the end of the period. Must be less than the cost.

life —any value except 0. The number of equal periods over which the asset is to be depreciated.

Formula (c-s)/n

c = cost
s = salvage
n = life of the asset

Usage The straight-line depreciation method divides the available depreciation (cost minus salvage) over the useful life of the asset.

Example Suppose you purchased a manufacturing machine that cost $100,000 and has a useful life of seven years. The residual or salvage value at the end of seven years is estimated to be $15,000. What is the depreciation allowance in any given year using the straight-line depreciation technique? The formula would be: `@SLN(100000,15000,7)`, and would yield the value $12,142.86.

Notes Some assets may qualify for accelerated depreciation. Ask your tax adviser for further information.

@SQRT

Purpose Calculates the positive square root of a value.

Syntax @SQRT(x)

Arguments

x—any positive value or 0, any formula that returns a positive value or 0, any references to a cell that contains such a value or to a formula that returns such a value.

Examples

`@SQRT(2)` = 1.41421

`@SQRT(64)` = 6

@STD

Purpose Calculates the population standard deviation of a list of values.

Syntax @STD(list)

Arguments

list—one or more values, or formulas that return a value, or references to ranges that contain values or formulas that return values, or any combination of the above.

Formula $$\sqrt{\frac{\Sigma(v_i - avg)^2}{n}}$$

n = number of items in the list
v_i = the ith item in list
avg = average of values in list

Usage The population standard deviation calculation measures the degree that the individual values in the list differ from the mean of all values in the list. A low standard deviation indicates that all values lie close to the common mean, which in turn indicates that the mean is a good representation of the population. On the other hand, a high standard deviation indicates that one or more values is significantly different than the mean.

Example To determine whether there is a significant difference in the individual weights of walruses as compared to the mean of all walruses in a research study on weight and food consumptions shown in Figure Function.19, you would create the formula:

```
@STD(B3..D70)
```

that designates the input range as B3..D70. The calculated standard deviation is 138.212.

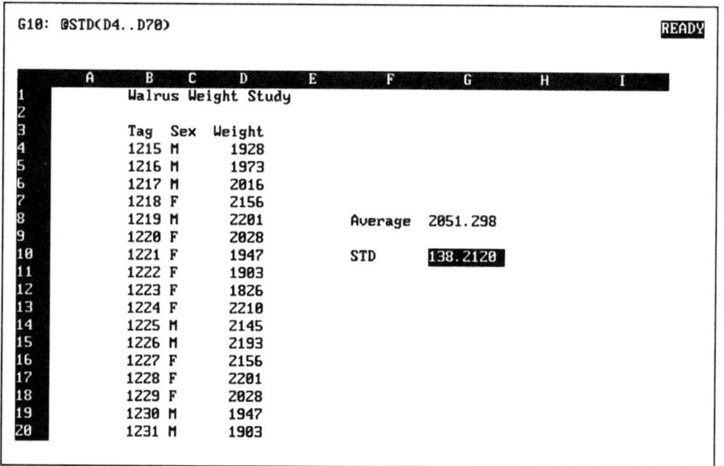

Figure @Function.19
@STD.

@STRING

Purpose Converts a value to a string with the designated number of decimal places.

Syntax @STRING(value,n)

Arguments

value—any value, formula or cell reference that evaluates to a value.

n —any value from 0 to 15.

Usage To convert the value contained in cell A3 to a string with 2 decimal places in cell B3 you would enter the formula:

```
@STRING(A3,2)
```

in cell B3.

Example `@STRING(123.456,2)` = 123.45 (as a string)

Notes The @STRING function truncates the value at the designated decimal place; it does not round it. The @STRING function ignores any formatting characters (e.g., $ or %) when it converts the value to a string.

@SUM

Purpose Calculates the sum of a list of values.

Syntax @SUM(list)

Arguments

list—one or more numbers, or formulas that evaluate to numbers, or ranges that refer to numbers or to formulas that evaluate to numbers, or any combination of the above. The ranges cannot contain labels, but can contain blanks.

Usage Calculates the sum of a set of numbers.

Example To calculate the sum of a range of values from A1..B47, use the formula `@SUM(A1..B47)`.

@SYD

Purpose Calculates the depreciation allowance for a specified period using the sum of the year's digits depreciation technique.

Syntax @SYD(cost,salvage,life,period)

Arguments

cost —the original purchase cost.

salvage—the residual value of the asset at the end of the period.

life —any value greater than or equal to 1. The number of equal periods over which the asset is to be depreciated. Must be expressed in the same time units as the period (i.e. years or months). The cost is evaluated at period 0 and the salvage is calculated at the period equal to the life.

period —any value greater than or equal to 1 and less than the life. The number of the period in question for which you wish to determine the depreciation.

Formula

$$\frac{(c - s) * (n - p + 1)}{(n * (n + 1)/2)}$$

c = cost of the asset

s = salvage value of the asset

p = period for which depreciation is being calculated

n = calculated useful life of the asset

Usage The sum of the year's digits depreciation technique is an accelerated depreciation calculation that depreciates an asset more quickly in the early years of its life and less in the later. This accelerated depreciation is appropriate for some assets.

Example Suppose that you purchased a manufacturing machine that cost $100,000 and has a useful life of seven years. The residual or salvage value at the end of seven years is estimated to be $15,000. What is the depreciation allowance in year four using the double declining balance technique? The formula would be `@SYD(100000,15000,7,4)` and would yield the value $12,142.86.

Notes Not all assets qualify for accelerated depreciation schedules. Ask your tax adviser for further information.

@TAN

Purpose Calculates the tangent of an angle.

Syntax @TAN(x)

Arguments

x—any value.

Usage The @TAN function returns the tangent of the angle represented by the argument value.

Examples `@TAN(0)` = 0

`@TAN(1.047)` = 1.731261 (1.047 radians = 60 degrees)

Notes To convert an angle measured in degrees to radians for input, multiply it by @PI/180.

@TERM

Purpose Calculates the number of periodic payments required to produce a given future value at a given periodic interest rate.

Syntax @RATE(payment,interest,future-value)

Arguments

payment —any value except 0.

future-value—any value.

interest —any value greater than −1.

Note: The time period used to express the interest rate and will be the same basis for expressing the resulting number of periods. For example, if the interest rate is expressed in months, the number of periods will also be expressed in months.

Formula

$$\frac{\ln(1+(fv*int/pmt))}{\ln(1+int)}$$

pmt = periodic payment
fv = future value
int = periodic interest rate

Usage Used in financial calculations to determine the number of payments needed to accumulate a given future value.

Example If you saved $25 a week in a savings account that paid 6.5%, how long would it take for you to accumulate enough money to purchase a $2,000 stereo system. To calculate the time required, use the formula: `@TERM(25,6.5%/52,2000)`, which yields a term of 76 weeks or almost a year and a half.

@TIME

Purpose Calculates the 1-2-3 time-number from the specified hours, minutes, and seconds.

Syntax @TIME(hh,mm,ss)

Arguments

hh —any integer from 0 (midnight) to 23 (11 PM).

mm—any integer from 0 to 59.

ss —any integer from 0 to 59.

Usage Used to input or to generate times in 1-2-3 numerical format. You can display the times using one of the date-time formats, or perform calculations with them. For example, subtracting one time-number from another will yield the elapsed time between them.

Example `@TIME(13,5,25)` = 0.545428 = 1:05:25 PM

Notes You *must* format the cell containing the @TIME function with the proper time format using the /Range Format Date Time command, for the time to appear in time form. If you do not format the cell, the time number will appear as the decimal portion of a decimal value between .000000 and .999988.

@TIMEVALUE

Purpose Converts strings that look like times into 1-2-3 time numbers.

Syntax @TIMEVALUE(string)

Arguments

string—any string or cell reference to a cell containing a label that conforms to one of the 1-2-3 time formats. See /Range Format Date Time or /Worksheet Global Format Date Time for details about 1-2-3 date formats.

Usage The most common use of the @TIMEVALUE function is to convert times that have been imported from other programs or entered as text. Times that conform to one of the standard time formats can be converted to their 1-2-3 time numbers. You must still format the cell that contains this function in one of the time formats so that it will display as a time.

Example `@TIMEVALUE("01:05:25 PM")` = .545428 = 01:05:25 PM

Notes You must format the cell containing the @TIMEVALUE function with the proper time format using the /Range Format Date Time, for the time to appear in time form. If you do not format the cell, the time number will appear as the decimal portion of a decimal value between .000000 and .999988.

@TRIM

Purpose Removes leading, trailing, and surplus (adjacent) interior spaces from a string.

Syntax @TRIM(string)

Arguments

string—any text, or formula that evaluates to a string, or reference to a cell that contains a label or a formula that evaluates to a string. Do *not* enclose the string argument in quotes.

Usage Used to eliminate surplus spaces from a string either for aesthetic purposes or to facilitate string comparisons.

Example `@TRIM ("    Spirit of    St. Louis       ")` yields "Spirit of St. Louis" without any leading, trailing, or excess interior spaces.

@TRUE

Purpose Returns the logical value true (1).

Syntax @TRUE

Arguments None.

Usage Used in logical formulas to return a value of logical true that can be passed on to other formulas or functions.

Example `@IF(C4>=1#AND#C4<=12,@TRUE,@FALSE)` = 0 if the value in C4 is not between 1 and 12 and 1 if it is.

@UPPER

Purpose Converts a string to all uppercase characters.

Syntax @UPPER(string)

Arguments

string—any literal string (enclosed in quotes), a cell or range reference that contains a label, or a formula or @function that evaluates to a string.

Example `@UPPER("Spirit of St. Louis")` = SPIRIT OF ST. LOUIS

@VALUE

Purpose Converts a string that contains only numbers or numeric symbols to its equivalent value.

Syntax @VALUE(string)

Arguments

string—any literal string, or formula that evaluates to a string or reference to a cell that contains a label. The label or string can contain only numbers or numeric symbols.

Examples

`@VALUE("234.78")` = 234.78

`@VALUE("$25.34")` = 25.34

`@VALUE("12.5%")` = .125

Notes You can't include mathematical operators within the string to create formulas. For example `@VALUE("1+1")` will evaluate to ERR while `@VALUE("1"+"1")` will evaluate to 0. You cannot include spaces between leading currency symbols or the value `@VALUE($ 25)` will evaluate to ERR.

@VAR

Purpose Calculates the population variance of a list of values.

Syntax @VAR(list)

Arguments

list—one or more values, or formulas that return a value, or references to ranges that contain values, or to formulas that return values, or any combination of the above.

Formula $\frac{\Sigma(v_i - avg)^2}{n}$

n = number of items in list

v_i = the ith item in list

avg = average of values in list

Usage The population variance calculation measures the degree that the individual values in the list differ from the mean of all values in the list. A low variance indicates that all values lie close to the common mean, which in turn indicates that the mean is a good representation of the population. On the other hand, a high variance indicates that one or more values is significantly different than the mean.

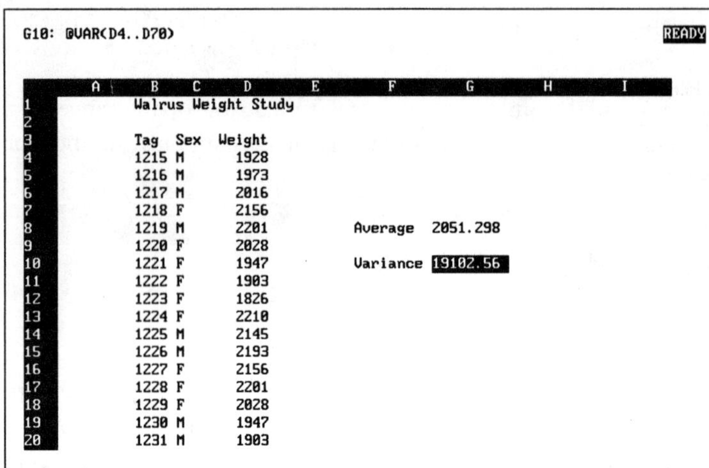

Figure @Function.20
@VAR.

Example To determine whether there is a significant difference in the individual weights of walruses as compared to the mean of all walruses in a research study on weight and food consumptions shown in Figure @Function.20, create the formula:

```
@VAR(B3..D70)
```

that designates the input range as B3..D70. The calculated variance is 19102.56.

@VLOOKUP

Purpose Used to look up values in a vertical lookup table and return the contents of a specified cell.

Syntax @VLOOKUP(x,range,column-offset)

Arguments

x —any value greater than the first value in the lookup range.

range —any range name or address containing a vertical lookup table.

column-offset—any number less than the total number of columns in the table minus 1. The offset is the number of columns to the right of the first column that 1-2-3 looks for the contents of a cell to return.

Vertical Lookup Table—any range that contains values in the leftmost column that increase as you move from top to bottom. See Figure @Function.21.

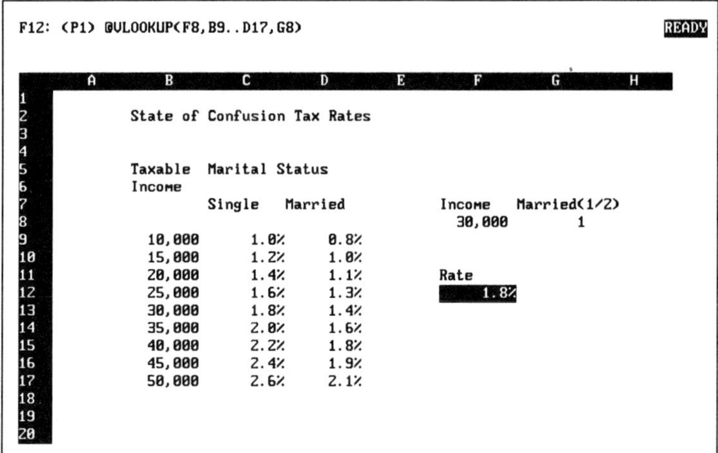

Figure @Function.21
@VLOOKUP.

Usage The most common use of lookup tables is tax tables, where you would look up the applicable tax rate based on taxable income (the values line) and another feature like marital status (the offset). The first step in using the @VLOOKUP function is to ensure that your lookup table is properly designed. It must have *only* values in the first column of the range (the values column) and these must *increase* in value from top to bottom. You need to arrange your data so that you can pinpoint the cell you wish to look up by telling 1-2-3 how many columns to the right to look (in the case of Figure @Function.21, the tax rate for single individuals is always one column to the right, while that for married couples is always two) and by asking 1-2-3 to look up the row to use by matching the value entered as the x argument against each value in the values column. 1-2-3 will test against each value until it reaches the value x, or the value closest to but not larger than x; or until it reaches the last value in the value column (in which case it selects the last row).

Example Looking at Figure @Function.21 determine what the applicable tax rate is for a single person earning $30,000 a year. Using the formula:

```
@VLOOKUP(30000,B9..D17,1)
```

we would get the value 1.8%. Note that the formula in the figure uses cell references to allow you to enter the income and marital status "code" (i.e., offset number 1 or 2) into cells F9 and G9 and it returns the applicable tax rate in cell F13.

Notes While the first column of the lookup table must contain values, the rest of the table need not. You can use the @VLOOKUP function to return labels as strings.

@YEAR

Purpose Calculates the year of the specified date-number.

Syntax @YEAR(date-number)

Arguments

date-number—any value between 1 and 73050. 1-2-3 only uses the integer portion of the value for this calculation.

Usage Used to determine the two- or three-digit year (e.g., 89 for 1989 and 125 for 2025) for a given date represented by its 1-2-3 date-number.

Examples

`@YEAR(32653)` = 89 (32653 = May 25, 1989)

`@YEAR(@DATE(51,5,12))` = 51

`@YEAR(@TODAY())` = the current year

Notes The @YEAR function returns a two- or three-digit number representing the year (0–99 for the twentieth century and 100–199 for the twenty-first century.) Add 1900 to the figure to produce full four-digit years for both.

`@YEAR(32653)+1900` = 1989

Appendix A
Cell Contents: AQUARIUM.WK1 AND FEED.WK1

AQUARIUM.WK1

```
A1: [W16] 'WEST SIDE AQUARIUM
A2: [W16] 'Financial Projections
A4: [W16] \=
B4: [W17] \=
C4: [W11] \=
D4: [W11] \=
E4: [W11] \=
F4: [W11] \=
G4: [W12] \=
H4: [W10] \=
I4: [W10] \=
J4: [W12] \=
K4: [W12] \=
L4: [W12] \=
M4: [W12] \=
N4: [W12] \=
A5: [W16] 'CASH FLOW PROJECTIONS
C6: [W11] ^Jan
D6: [W11] ^Feb
E6: [W11] ^Mar
F6: [W11] ^Apr
G6: [W12] ^May
H6: [W10] ^Jun
I6: [W10] ^Jul
J6: [W12] ^Aug
K6: [W12] ^Sep
L6: [W12] ^Oct
M6: [W12] ^Nov
N6: [W12] ^Dec
A7: [W16] \-
B7: [W17] \-
C7: [W11] \-
D7: [W11] \-
E7: [W11] \-
F7: [W11] \-
G7: [W12] \-
H7: [W10] \-
I7: [W10] \-
J7: [W12] \-
K7: [W12] \-
L7: [W12] \-
M7: [W12] \-
N7: [W12] \-
A8: [W16] 'Total Revenues
C8: (,0) [W11] +C24
D8: (,0) [W11] +D24
E8: (,0) [W11] +E24
```

AQUARIUM.WK1 *continued*

```
F8: (,0) [W11] +F24
G8: (,0) [W12] +G24
H8: (,0) [W10] +H24
I8: (,0) [W10] +I24
J8: (,0) [W12] +J24
K8: (,0) [W12] +K24
L8: (,0) [W12] +L24
M8: (,0) [W12] +M24
N8: (,0) [W12] +N24
A9: [W16] 'Total Expenses
C9: (,0) [W11] +C38
D9: (,0) [W11] +D38
E9: (,0) [W11] +E38
F9: (,0) [W11] +F38
G9: (,0) [W12] +G38
H9: (,0) [W10] +H38
I9: (,0) [W10] +I38
J9: (,0) [W12] +J38
K9: (,0) [W12] +K38
L9: (,0) [W12] +L38
M9: (,0) [W12] +M38
N9: (,0) [W12] +N38
C10: [W11] \-
D10: [W11] \-
E10: [W11] \-
F10: [W11] \-
G10: [W12] \-
H10: [W10] \-
I10: [W10] \-
J10: [W12] \-
K10: [W12] \-
L10: [W12] \-
M10: [W12] \-
N10: [W12] \-
A11: [W16] 'NET CASH
C11: (C0) [W11] +C8-C9
D11: (C0) [W11] +D8-D9
E11: (C0) [W11] +E8-E9
F11: (C0) [W11] +F8-F9
G11: (C0) [W12] +G8-G9
H11: (C0) [W10] +H8-H9
I11: (C0) [W10] +I8-I9
J11: (C0) [W12] +J8-J9
K11: (C0) [W12] +K8-K9
L11: (C0) [W12] +L8-L9
M11: (C0) [W12] +M8-M9
N11: (C0) [W12] +N8-N9
A13: [W16] \=
B13: [W17] \=
C13: [W11] \=
D13: [W11] \=
E13: [W11] \=
F13: [W11] \=
G13: [W12] \=
H13: [W10] \=
I13: [W10] \=
J13: [W12] \=
K13: [W12] \=
L13: [W12] \=
M13: [W12] \=
N13: [W12] \=
A14: [W16] 'PROJECTED REVENUES
C15: [W11] ^Jan
D15: [W11] ^Feb
E15: [W11] ^Mar
F15: [W11] ^Apr
G15: [W12] ^May
H15: [W10] ^Jun
I15: [W10] ^Jul
J15: [W12] ^Aug
K15: [W12] ^Sep
L15: [W12] ^Oct
M15: [W12] ^Nov
N15: [W12] ^Dec
A16: [W16] \-
B16: [W17] \-
C16: [W11] \-
D16: [W11] \-
E16: [W11] \-
F16: [W11] \-
G16: [W12] \-
H16: [W10] \-
I16: [W10] \-
J16: [W12] \-
K16: [W12] \-
L16: [W12] \-
M16: [W12] \-
N16: [W12] \-
A17: [W16] 'Admission fees
C17: (,0) [W11] 75266.4
D17: (,0) [W11] 74733.6
E17: (,0) [W11] 146194.2
F17: (,0) [W11] 161392.2
G17: (,0) [W12] 193792.2
H17: (,0) [W10] 214592.4
I17: (,0) [W10] 220798.8
J17: (,0) [W12] 233859
K17: (,0) [W12] 193725.6
```

```
L17: (,0) [W12] 207599.933
M17: (,0) [W12] 126585.325
N17: (,0) [W12] 78482.9015
A18: [W16] 'Contributions
C18: (,0) [W11] 163096.2
D18: (,0) [W11] 176293.2
E18: (,0) [W11] 179629.5
F18: (,0) [W11] 80263.5
G18: (,0) [W12] 90369.6
H18: (,0) [W10] 136929.6
I18: (,0) [W10] 130526.1
J18: (,0) [W12] 115529.4
K18: (,0) [W12] 111549.825
L18: (,0) [W12] 109629.6
M18: (,0) [W12] 91553.625
N18: (,0) [W12] 123829.5
A19: [W16] 'Government support
C19: (,0) [W11] 241059
D19: (,0) [W11] 285932.4
E19: (,0) [W11] 292599
F19: (,0) [W11] 253279.2
G19: (,0) [W12] 240812.4
H19: (,0) [W10] 196594.2
I19: (,0) [W10] 212801.4
J19: (,0) [W12] 165000
K19: (,0) [W12] 159000
L19: (,0) [W12] 157413.6
M19: (,0) [W12] 215925.6
N19: (,0) [W12] 247592.4
A20: [W16] 'Membership dues
C20: (,0) [W11] 111262.2
D20: (,0) [W11] 119259
E20: (,0) [W11] 120592.2
F20: (,0) [W11] 159265.8
G20: (,0) [W12] 177400.2
H20: (,0) [W10] 183265.8
I20: (,0) [W10] 186592.2
J20: (,0) [W12] 195058.8
K20: (,0) [W12] 153273.6
L20: (,0) [W12] 147000
M20: (,0) [W12] 159260.4
N20: (,0) [W12] 281259
A21: [W16] 'Misc
C21: (,0) [W11] 2860.125
D21: (,0) [W11] 3050.8
E21: (,0) [W11] 4766.875
F21: (,0) [W11] 6673.625
G21: (,0) [W12] 10487.125
H21: (,0) [W10] 18018.7875
I21: (,0) [W10] 19067.5
J21: (,0) [W12] 18590.8125
K21: (,0) [W12] 15254
L21: (,0) [W12] 11278.8
M21: (,0) [W12] 72586.8
N21: (,0) [W12] 2955.4625
A22: [W16] 'Publications
C22: (,0) [W11] 32594.4
D22: (,0) [W11] 39259.2
E22: (,0) [W11] 45933
F22: (,0) [W11] 35754.005
G22: (,0) [W12] 39260.4
H22: (,0) [W10] 53400
I22: (,0) [W10] 55205.4
J22: (,0) [W12] 60460.2
K22: (,0) [W12] 54000
L22: (,0) [W12] 47938.2
M22: (,0) [W12] 30592.2
N22: (,0) [W12] 15833.9165
C23: (,0) [W11] \-
D23: (,0) [W11] \-
E23: (,0) [W11] \-
F23: (,0) [W11] \-
G23: (,0) [W12] \-
H23: (,0) [W10] \-
I23: (,0) [W10] \-
J23: (,0) [W12] \-
K23: (,0) [W12] \-
L23: (,0) [W12] \-
M23: (,0) [W12] \-
N23: (,0) [W12] \-
B24: [W17] "Total Revenues:
C24: (,0) [W11] @SUM(C17..C22)
D24: (,0) [W11] @SUM(D17..D22)
E24: (,0) [W11] @SUM(E17..E22)
F24: (,0) [W11] @SUM(F17..F22)
G24: (,0) [W12] @SUM(G17..G22)
H24: (,0) [W10] @SUM(H17..H22)
I24: (,0) [W10] @SUM(I17..I22)
J24: (,0) [W12] @SUM(J17..J22)
K24: (,0) [W12] @SUM(K17..K22)
L24: (,0) [W12] @SUM(L17..L22)
M24: (,0) [W12] @SUM(M17..M22)
N24: (,0) [W12] @SUM(N17..N22)
B26: [W17] "GRAND TOTAL:
C26: (C0) [W11] @SUM(REVTOT)
A27: [W16] \=
B27: [W17] \=
C27: [W11] \=
D27: [W11] \=
E27: [W11] \=
```

AQUARIUM.WK1 *continued*

```
F27: [W11] \=
G27: [W12] \=
H27: [W10] \=
I27: [W10] \=
J27: [W12] \=
K27: [W12] \=
L27: [W12] \=
M27: [W12] \=
N27: [W12] \=
A28: [W16] 'PROJECTED EXPENSES
C29: [W11] ^Jan
D29: [W11] ^Feb
E29: [W11] ^Mar
F29: [W11] ^Apr
G29: [W12] ^May
H29: [W10] ^Jun
I29: [W10] ^Jul
J29: [W12] ^Aug
K29: [W12] ^Sep
L29: [W12] ^Oct
M29: [W12] ^Nov
N29: [W12] ^Dec
A30: [W16] \-
B30: [W17] \-
C30: [W11] \-
D30: [W11] \-
E30: [W11] \-
F30: [W11] \-
G30: [W12] \-
H30: [W10] \-
I30: [W10] \-
J30: [W12] \-
K30: [W12] \-
L30: [W12] \-
M30: [W12] \-
N30: [W12] \-
A31: [W16] 'Main Visitor Center
C31: (,0) [W11] 312543
D31: (,0) [W11] 312543
E31: (,0) [W11] 312543
F31: (,0) [W11] 312543
G31: (,0) [W12] 367453
H31: (,0) [W10] 433222
I31: (,0) [W10] 446544
J31: (,0) [W12] 412565
K31: (,0) [W12] 376655
L31: (,0) [W12] 312543
M31: (,0) [W12] 312543
N31: (,0) [W12] 312543
A32: [W16] 'Dolphin Arena
C32: (,0) [W11] 105734.4
D32: (,0) [W11] 118940.4
E32: (,0) [W11] 120588.6
F32: (,0) [W11] 167561.724
G32: (,0) [W12] 105913.2
H32: (,0) [W10] 111658.8
I32: (,0) [W10] 113859
J32: (,0) [W12] 115200
K32: (,0) [W12] 178858.02
L32: (,0) [W12] 176975.304
M32: (,0) [W12] 178858.02
N32: (,0) [W12] 173386.8
A33: [W16] 'Gater Pit
C33: (,0) [W11] 26493.25
D33: (,0) [W11] 24373.79
E33: (,0) [W11] 27023.115
F33: (,0) [W11] 28125.6
G33: (,0) [W12] 29672.44
H33: (,0) [W10] 33116.5625
I33: (,0) [W10] 30997.1025
J33: (,0) [W12] 31791.9
K33: (,0) [W12] 25168.5875
L33: (,0) [W12] 24903.655
M33: (,0) [W12] 25168.5875
N33: (,0) [W12] 16593.6
A34: [W16] 'Shark Pond
C34: (,0) [W11] 37459.2
D34: (,0) [W11] 39770.082
E34: (,0) [W11] 41260.2
F34: (,0) [W11] 38473.2315
G34: (,0) [W12] 40512.6
H34: (,0) [W10] 37993.8
I34: (,0) [W10] 43407
J34: (,0) [W12] 44725.8
K34: (,0) [W12] 46129.8
L34: (,0) [W12] 46198.8
M34: (,0) [W12] 40599
N34: (,0) [W12] 27393.6
A35: [W16] 'Marine Sciences Center
C35: (,0) [W11] 128243.8
D35: (,0) [W11] 117984.296
E35: (,0) [W11] 130808.676
F35: (,0) [W11] 134065.8
G35: (,0) [W12] 143633.056
H35: (,0) [W10] 160304.75
I35: (,0) [W10] 173259
J35: (,0) [W12] 187461
K35: (,0) [W12] 121831.61
```

```
L35: (,0) [W12] 120549.172
M35: (,0) [W12] 121831.61
N35: (,0) [W12] 105940.2
A36: [W16] 'Fish Feed
C36: (,0) [W11] +<<FEED.WK1>>$I17
D36: (,0) [W11] +<<FEED.WK1>>$I17
E36: (,0) [W11] +<<FEED.WK1>>$I17
F36: (,0) [W11] +<<FEED.WK1>>$I17
G36: (,0) [W12] +<<FEED.WK1>>$I17
H36: (,0) [W10] +<<FEED.WK1>>$I17
I36: (,0) [W10] +<<FEED.WK1>>$I17
J36: (,0) [W12] +<<FEED.WK1>>$I17
K36: (,0) [W12] +<<FEED.WK1>>$I17
L36: (,0) [W12] +<<FEED.WK1>>$I17
M36: (,0) [W12] +<<FEED.WK1>>$I17
N36: (,0) [W12] +<<FEED.WK1>>$I17
C37: (,0) [W11] \-
D37: (,0) [W11] \-
E37: (,0) [W11] \-
F37: (,0) [W11] \-
G37: (,0) [W12] \-
H37: (,0) [W10] \-
I37: (,0) [W10] \-
J37: (,0) [W12] \-
K37: (,0) [W12] \-
L37: (,0) [W12] \-
M37: (,0) [W12] \-
N37: (,0) [W12] \-
B38: [W17] "Total Expenses:
C38: (,0) [W11] @SUM(C31..C35)
D38: (,0) [W11] @SUM(D31..D35)
E38: (,0) [W11] @SUM(E31..E35)
F38: (,0) [W11] @SUM(F31..F35)
G38: (,0) [W12] @SUM(G31..G35)
H38: (,0) [W10] @SUM(H31..H35)
I38: (,0) [W10] @SUM(I31..I35)
J38: (,0) [W12] @SUM(J31..J35)
K38: (,0) [W12] @SUM(K31..K35)
L38: (,0) [W12] @SUM(L31..L35)
M38: (,0) [W12] @SUM(M31..M35)
N38: (,0) [W12] @SUM(N31..N35)
B40: [W17] "GRAND TOTAL:
C40: (C0) [W11] @SUM(EXPTOTAL)
A41: [W16] \=
B41: [W17] \=
C41: [W11] \=
D41: [W11] \=
E41: [W11] \=
F41: [W11] \=
G41: [W12] \=
H41: [W10] \=
I41: [W10] \=
J41: [W12] \=
K41: [W12] \=
L41: [W12] \=
M41: [W12] \=
N41: [W12] \=
A42: [W16] 'STATISTICAL REPORT
A43: [W16] \-
B43: [W17] \-
C43: [W11] \-
D43: [W11] \-
A44: [W16] '  Total Annual Revenues
C44: (,0) [W11] +C26
A45: [W16] '  Total Annual Expenses
C45: (,0) [W11] +C40
A46: [W16] '  Profit/Loss
C46: (,0) [W11] +C44-C45
A48: [W16] '  Minimum Monthly Cash
C48: (,0) [W11] @MIN(NETCASH)
A49: [W16] '  Maximum Monthly Cash
C49: (,0) [W11] @MAX(NETCASH)
A51: [W16] '  Minimum Monthly Revenues
C51: (,0) [W11] @MIN(REVTOT)
A52: [W16] '  Maximum Monthly Revenues
C52: (,0) [W11] @MAX(REVTOT)
A53: [W16] '  Average Monthly Revenues
C53: (,0) [W11] @AVG(REVTOT)
A55: [W16] '  Minimum Monthly Expenses
C55: (,0) [W11] @MIN(EXPTOTAL)
A56: [W16] '  Maximum Monthly Expenses
C56: (,0) [W11] @MAX(EXPTOTAL)
A57: [W16] '  Average Monthly Expenses
C57: (,0) [W11] @AVG(EXPTOTAL)
A59: [W16] \=
B59: [W17] \=
C59: [W11] \=
D59: [W11] \=
E59: [W11] \=
```

FEED.WK1

```
A1: [W8] 'MONTHLY FEED CONSUMPTION
F1: [W9] 'AVERAGE MONTHLY CONSUMPTION
A2: [W8] 'Name
B2: [W10] 'Type
C2: [W9] 'Feed
D2: [W7] 'Pounds
F2: (,0) [W9] @IF(@ISERR(@DAVG
    (A2..D14,3,A18..B19)),0,
    @DAVG(A2..D14,3,A18..B19))
```

FEED.WK1 *continued*

```
G2: (,0) [W9] 'Mackerel
H2: (,0) [W9] 'Tailings
I2: [W8] 'Beef
A3: [W8] 'Alice
B3: [W10] 'Dolphin
C3: [W9] 'Mackerel
D3: [W7] 320
F3: (,0) [W9] 'Dolphin
G3: (,0) [W9] 242.66666667
H3: (,0) [W9] 0
I3: (,0) [W8] 0
A4: [W8] 'George
B4: [W10] 'Alligator
C4: [W9] 'Beef
D4: [W7] 176
F4: [W9] 'Alligator
G4: (,0) [W9] 0
H4: (,0) [W9] 0
I4: (,0) [W8] 183.33333333
A5: [W8] 'Kelso
B5: [W10] 'Shark
C5: [W9] 'Tailings
D5: [W7] 300
F5: (,0) [W9] 'Orca
G5: (,0) [W9] 461.5
H5: (,0) [W9] 0
I5: (,0) [W8] 0
A6: [W8] 'Flirt
B6: [W10] 'Orca
C6: [W9] 'Mackerel
D6: [W7] 425
F6: (,0) [W9] 'Shark
G6: (,0) [W9] 221
H6: (,0) [W9] 293.66666667
I6: (,0) [W8] 0
A7: [W8] 'Albert
B7: [W10] 'Dolphin
C7: [W9] 'Mackerel
D7: [W7] 295
A8: [W8] 'Mimi
B8: [W10] 'Dolphin
C8: [W9] 'Mackerel
D8: [W7] 113
A9: [W8] 'Elsa
B9: [W10] 'Orca
C9: [W9] 'Mackerel
D9: [W7] 498
F9: [W9] 'TOTAL ZOO POPULATION
A10: [W8] 'Bert
B10: [W10] 'Alligator
C10: [W9] 'Beef
D10: [W7] 220
F10: [W9] 'Dolphin
G10: [W9] 'Alligator
H10: [W9] "Orca
I10: [W8] "Shark
A11: [W8] 'George
B11: [W10] 'Shark
C11: [W9] 'Tailings
D11: [W7] 267
F11: [W9] 2
G11: [W9] 3
H11: [W9] 2
I11: [W8] 4
A12: [W8] 'Else
B12: [W10] 'Alligator
C12: [W9] 'Beef
D12: [W7] 154
A13: [W8] 'Sandy
B13: [W10] 'Shark
C13: [W9] 'Tailings
D13: [W7] 314
F13: [W9] 'PROJECTED MONTHLY
           CONSUMPTION IN LBS
A14: [W8] 'Silvia
B14: [W10] 'Shark
C14: [W9] 'Mackerel
D14: [W7] 221
G14: [W9] 'Mackerel
H14: [W9] 'Tailings
I14: [W8] '  Beef
G15: (F2) [W9] 2292.3333333
H15: (F2) [W9] 1174.6666667
I15: (F2) [W8] 550
A16: [W8] 'INPUT CELLS
C16: [W9] 'PRICE PER POUND
A17: [W8] 'Input1
B17: [W10] 'Input2
C17: [W9] 'Mackerel
D17: (C3) [W7] 0.225
F17: [W9] 'PROJECTED MONTHLY COST:
I17: (C2) [W8] 901.67633333
A18: [W8] 'Type
B18: [W10] 'Feed
C18: [W9] 'Tailings
D18: (C3) [W7] 0.071
C19: [W9] 'Beef
D19: (C3) [W7] 0.55
```

Appendix B Lotus International Character Set

Lotus 1-2-3 Release 2.2 uses the Lotus International Character Set (LICS) to store, display, and print characters. By using the LICS code for a character, it is possible to enter characters that are not available on your computer's keyboard. The 256 LICS codes consist of the values from 0 to 255 that represent three groups of characters: 0–31 are used for controlling printers and other devices and are not available for the user; 32–127 represent the standard ASCII characters, and 128–255 represent international characters and other special symbols.

You can use the LICS characters to enter characters that are not generally available on most keyboards (e.g., the British pound sign (£)). Once entered into a cell, the LICS character will be displayed on the monitor and printed, if the monitor and printer are capable of displaying and printing the designated character. If not, 1-2-3 will display or print a fallback character that closely resembles the designated character.

You can enter the LICS characters into a cell in three ways. You can enter the standard ASCII characters (32-127) by pressing the associated key on the keyboard. You can also use the @CHAR function with the appropriate LICS code for the character desired. For example, @CHAR(163) will produce the British pound sign (£). Or you can use the COMPOSE key (ALT-F1) and type the compose key sequence for the character desired. For example, press ALT-F1 and then type `L=` to produce the British pound sign.

You can create characters that are not contained in the LICS character set if they can be made up of overstruck characters and your printer supports full backspacing. Use the COMPOSE key (ALT-F1) to create a merge character by entering the merge character composition string `mg`. For example, suppose you wanted to create the combined character of a O overstruck by an X. First type the `O`, then create the merge character by pressing the COMPOSE key (ALT-F1) and typing the composition string for the merge character, `mg`. Finally, type the overstriking character `X`. The merge character will appear as a left arrow on your screen, but it will cause the printer to combine the two adjacent characters when it prints by backspacing the printer before it prints the second character.

NOTE: Some personal computers support more than one character set by using a system of code page switching. 1-2-3 supports only code page 437 (English), which is the default. If you have not altered the code page, you will have no problems. If you have, you must return to code page 437 before using 1-2-3 Release 2.2. If you don't know what we're talking about, you probably are using the default and don't need to worry about it.

LICS TABLES

Standard ASCII Characters

Table B.1 defines LICS codes 32 through 127, which represent standard ASCII characters. You can enter any of these LICS characters by pressing the appropriate chatacater key on your keyboard. If you do not have a key on your keyboard for a particular character, you must enter the character by using the @CHAR function and the LICS code listed for the character, or by using the compose sequence listed for the character. You can use more than one compose sequence to create some characters. In these cases, the table lists all possible compose sequences.

Table B.1 Standard ASCII Characters

LICS code	Character	Description	Compose sequence
32	Space	Space	
33	!	Exclamation point	
34	"	Double quotes	
35	#	Pound or number sign	++
36	$	Dollar sign	
37	%	Percent	
38	&	Ampersand	
39	'	Close single quote	
40	(	Open parenthesis	
41	)	Close parenthesis	
42	*	Asterisk	
43	+	Plus	
44	,	Comma	
45	–	Minus	
46	.	Period	
47	/	Slash	
48	0	Zero	
49	1	One	
50	2	Two	
51	3	Three	
52	4	Four	
53	5	Five	
54	6	Six	
55	7	Seven	
56	8	Eight	
57	9	Nine	
58	:	Colon	
59	;	Semicolon	
60	<	Less-than symbol	
61	=	Equal sign	
62	>	Greater-than sign	
63	?	Question mark	
64	@	At sign	aa or AA
65	A	A, uppercase	
66	B	B, uppercase	
67	C	C, uppercase	
68	D	D, uppercase	
69	E	E, uppercase	
70	F	F, uppercase	
71	G	G, uppercase	

72	H	H, uppercase	
73	I	I, uppercase	
74	J	J, uppercase	
75	K	K, uppercase	
76	L	L, uppercase	
77	M	M, uppercase	
78	N	N, uppercase	
79	O	O, uppercase	
80	P	P, uppercase	
81	Q	Q, uppercase	
82	R	R, uppercase	
83	S	S, uppercase	
84	T	T, uppercase	
85	U	U, uppercase	
86	V	V, uppercase	
87	W	W, uppercase	
88	X	X, uppercase	
89	Y	Y, uppercase	
90	Z	Z, uppercase	
91	[	Open bracket	((
92	\	Backslash	//
93	]	Close bracket	))
94	^	Caret	vv
95	_	Underscore	
96	‘	Open single quote	
97	a	a, lowercase	
98	b	b, lowercase	
99	c	c, lowercase	
100	d	d, lowercase	
101	e	e, lowercase	
102	f	f, lowercase	
103	g	g, lowercase	
104	h	h, lowercase	
105	i	i, lowercase	
106	j	j, lowercase	
107	k	k, lowercase	
108	l	l, lowercase	
109	m	m, lowercase	
110	n	n, lowercase	
111	o	o, lowercase	
112	p	p, lowercase	
113	q	q, lowercase	
114	r	r, lowercase	

115	s	s, lowercase	
116	t	t, lowercase	
117	u	u, lowercase	
118	v	v, lowercase	
119	w	w, lowercase	
120	x	x, lowercase	
121	y	y, lowercase	
122	z	z, lowercase	
123	{	Open brace	(-
124	¦	Split vertical bar	^/
125	}	Close brace	)-
126	~	Tilde	--
127	Delete		

International Characters and Special Symbols

Table B.2 defines LICS codes 128 through 255 which represent international characters and special symbols. You can enter any of these characters by using the @CHAR function and the LICS code for the character, or by using the compose sequence listed for the character. Some compose sequences are order-sensitive and you must enter the sequence of keystrokes in the order shown in the table. These cases are marked with an * (asterisk). Do not type the asterisk as part of the compose sequence; it only defines the order-sensitive compose sequences. In addition, you can use more than one compose sequence to create some characters. In these cases, the tables list all possible compose sequences.

Table B.2 International Characters and Special Symbols

LICS code	Character	Description	Compose Sequence
128	`	Grave, uppercase	* ‘ space bar
129	´	Acute, uppercase	* ’ space bar
130	^	Circumflex, uppercase	* ^ space bar
131	¨	Umlaut, uppercase	* " space bar
132	~	Tilde, uppercase	* ~ space bar
133	■	Unknown character (display only)	
134	■	Unknown character (display only)	
135	■	Unknown character (display only)	
136	■	Unknown character (display only)	
137	■	Unknown character (display only)	
138	■	Unknown character (display only)	
139	■	Unknown character (display only)	

140	■	Unknown character (display only)		
141	■	Unknown character (display only)		
142	■	Unknown character (display only)		
143	■	Unknown character (display only)		
144	`	Grave, lowercase	*	space bar ‘
145	´	Acute, lowercase	*	space bar ’
146	^	Circumflex, lowercase	*	space bar ^
147	¨	Umlaut, lowercase	*	space bar "
148	~	Tilde, lowercase	*	space bar ~
149	ı	i without dot, lowercase		i space bar
150	_	ordinal indicator		_ space bar
151	▲	Begin attribute (display only)		ba
152	▼	End Attribute (display only)		ea
153	■	Unknown character (display only)		
154	•	Hard space (display only)		space bar space bar
155	←	Merge character (display only)		mg
156	■	Unknown character (display only)		
157	■	Unknown character (display only)		
158	■	Unknown character (display only)		
159	■	Unknown character (display only)		
160	*f*	Guilder sign		ff
161	¡	Exclamation mark, inverted		!!
162	¢	Cent sign		c| C| c/ or C/
163	£	British pound sterling		L= l= L- or l-
164	„	Open double quotes, low		"^
165	¥	Yen sign		Y= y= Y- or y-
166	Pt	Peseta sign	*	PT pt or Pt
167	§	Section sign		SO so So or s0
168	¤	General currency sign		XO co Co or x0
169	©	Copyright sign		CO co Co or c0
170	ª	Female ordinal indicator		A_ or a_
171	≪	Much less than sign		< <
172	Δ	Delta		dd or DD
173	π	Pi		PI pi or Pi
174	≥	Greater-than-or-equals		>=
175	÷	Division sign		:-
176	°	Degree sign		^0
177	±	Plus-or-minus sign		+-
178	²	2, superscript		^2
179	³	3, superscript		^3

180	”	Close double quotes, low		v
181	µ	Micron symbol or mu	*	/u
182	¶	Paragraph symbol		!P or !p
183	•	Middle dot		^.
184	™	Trademark sign		TM Tm or tm
185	^{1}	1, Superscript		^1
186	º	Masculine ordinal indicator		o_ or O_
187	≫	Much-greater-than symbol		> >
188	¼	One-quarter fraction	*	14
189	½	One-half fraction	*	12
190	≤	Less-than-or-equals sign	*	=<
191	¿	Question mark, inverted		??
192	A	A grave, uppercase		A`
193	Á	A acute, uppercase		A’
194	Â	A circumflex, uppercase		A^
195	Ã	A tilde, uppercase		A~
196	Ä	A umlaut, uppercase		A”
197	Å	A ring, uppercase		A*
198	Æ	AE dipthong, uppercase		AE
199	Ç	C cedilla, uppercase		C,
200	È	E grave, uppercase		E‘
201	É	E acute, uppercase		E’
202	Ê	E circumflex, uppercase		E^
203	Ë	E umlaut, uppercase		E"
204	Ì	I grave, uppercase		I‘
205	Í	I acute, uppercase		I’
206	Î	I circumflex, uppercase		I^
207	Ï	I umlaut, uppercase		I"
208	Đ	Icelandic eth, uppercase		D-
209	Ñ	N Tilde, uppercase		N~
210	Ò	O grave, uppercase		O‘
211	Ó	O acute, uppercase		O’
212	Ô	O circumflex, uppercase		O^
213	Õ	O tilde, uppercase		O~
214	Ö	O umlaut, uppercase		O"
215	Œ	OE dipthong, uppercase		OE
216	Ø	O slash, uppercase		O/
217	Ù	U grave, uppercase		U‘
218	Ú	U acute, uppercase		U’
219	Û	U circumflex, uppercase		U^

220	Ü	U umlaut, uppercase	U"
221	Ÿ	Y umlaut, uppercase	Y"
222	Þ	Icelandic thorn, uppercase	P_
223	β	German sharp, lowercase or beta	ss
224	à	a grave, lowercase	a‘
225	á	a acute, lowercase	a’
226	â	a circumflex, lowercase	a^
227	ã	a tilde, lowercase	a~
228	ä	A umlaut, lowercase	a"
229	å	A ring, lowercase	a*
230	æ	ae dipthong, lowercase	ae
231	ç	c cedilla, lowercase	c,
232	è	e grave, lowercase	e`
233	é	e actue, lowercase	e’
234	ê	e circumflex, lowercase	e^
235	ë	e umlaut, lowercase	e”
236	ì	i grave, lowercase	i‘
237	í	i acute, lowercase	i’
238	î	i circumflex, lowercase	i^
239	ï	i umlaut, lowercase	i"
240	ð	Icelandic eth, lowercase	d-
241	ñ	n tilde, lowercase	n~
242	ò	o grave, lowercase	o‘
243	ó	o acute, lowercase	o’
244	ô	o circumflex, lowercase	o^
245	õ	o tilde, lowercase	o~
246	ö	o umlaut, lowercase	o”
247	œ	oe dipthong, lowercase	* oe
248	ø	o slash, lowercase	o/
249	ù	u grave, lowercase	u‘
250	ú	u acute, lowercase	u’
251	û	u circumflex, lowercase	u^
252	ü	u umlaut, lowercase	u”
253	ÿ	y umlaut, lowercase	y”
254	þ	Icelandic thorn, lowercase	p_
255	■	Unknown character (display only)	

Appendix C
Printer Control Codes

1-2-3 lets you take advantage of special options supported by your printer that are not available through the 1-2-3 menu system. To use these options you must send printer command codes directly to your printer. These codes can be embedded directly in your worksheet, or specified through the /Worksheet Global Default Printer Setup menu, or the /Print Printer Options Setup menu.

Printer control codes are unique to each printer, consult your printer manual to determine the appropriate code for the desired results. In general, a printer code sequence starts with the ESC character, followed by a series of letters, numbers, or other special characters. For example, the command code ESC 4 tells an Epson FX printer to print in italics.

To specify a printer control code in 1-2-3, you must follow two simple rules. First, any character in the code sequence that is a non-keyboard character has to be specified using its three-digit ASCII code equivalent. (Refer to the control-key combinations or simbols with decimal value 0-31 in Table C.1) Second, any ASCII code that you include in the code sequence must be preceded by a back-slash (\). The ESC character, for example, must be entered as `\027`. All typeable characters can be entered directly from the keyboard or using the ASCII code equivalent. For example, the code ESC E can be typed in as \027E or \027\069.

Table C.1 below lists the character numbers (or decimal codes) 0 thorugh 127, their character equivalents in the second column, and the ASCII code setup string equivalents in the third.

Table C.1

Decimal	Character Equivalent	Setup String
1		\001
2		\002
3		\003
4		\004
5		\005
6		\006
7		\007(bell)
8		\008
9		\009(tab)
10		\010(line feed)
11		\011
12		\012(form feed)
13		\013(carriage return)
14		\014
15		\015
16		\016
17		\017
18		\018
19		\019
20		\020
21		\021
22		\022
23		\023
24		\024
25		\025
26		\026
27		\027(ESC)
28		\028
29		\029
30		\030
31		\031
32	space	\032
33	!	\033
34	“	\034
35	#	\035
36	$	\036
37	%	\037
38	&	\038
39	`	\039
40	(	\040
41	)	\041
42	*	\042
43	+	\043
44	‘	\044
45	-	\045
46	.	\046
47	/	\047
48	0	\048
49	1	\049
50	2	\050
51	3	\051
52	4	\052
53	5	\053
54	6	\054
55	7	\055
56	8	\056
57	9	\057
58	:	\058

Decimal	Character Equivalent	Setup String
59	;	\059
60	<	\060
61	=	\061
62	>	\062
63	?	\063
64	@	\064
65	A	\065
66	B	\066
67	C	\067
68	D	\068
69	E	\069
70	F	\070
71	G	\071
72	H	\072
73	I	\073
74	J	\074
75	K	\075
76	L	\076
77	M	\077
78	N	\078
79	O	\079
80	P	\080
81	Q	\081
82	R	\082
83	S	\083
84	T	\084
85	U	\085
86	V	\086
87	W	\087
88	X	\088
89	Y	\089
90	Z	\090
91	[	\091
92	/	\092
93	]	\093
94	^	\094
95	_	\095
96	\	\096
97	a	\097
98	b	\098
99	c	\099
100	d	\101
101	e	\101
102	f	\102
103	g	\103
104	h	\104
105	i	\105
106	j	\106
107	k	\107
108	l	\108
109	m	\109
110	n	\110
111	o	\111
112	p	\112
113	q	\113
114	r	\114
115	s	\115
116	t	\116
117	u	\117
118	v	\118
119	w	\119
120	x	\120
121	y	\121
122	z	\122
123	{	\123
124	|	\124
125	}	\125
126	~	\126
127	DEL	\127

Common Setup Strings for the Hewlett-Packard LaserJet Printer

Table C.2 shows a selection of common setup strings for HP LaserJet printers. Be aware that when you alter type size, 1-2-3 does not automatically alter the number of characters per line or lines per page to fit the new font size. You must also specify the new margin and page length settings to correspond with the selected font.

To print in 12-pitch, you *must* have a cartridge with 12-pitch fonts. To print in 16.66-pitch, you must have a font cartridge with condensed typefaces, or a printer with built-in condensed fonts (LaserJet Series II or LaserJet 2000). To print more than 100 lines per page, select the /Print Printer Options Other Unformatted option. This will bypass 1-2-3's maximum page length of 100 lines per page.

Orientation: Portrait
Paper size: Letter (8 1/2 by 11)
Paper feed: Tray
Lines per page: 60

PITCH	SETUP STRING	RIGHT MARGIN
10 cpi	\027E	80
12 cpi	\027(s)p12H	96
16.66 cpi	\027&k2s	132

Orientation: Portrait
Paper size: Letter (8 1/2 by 11)
Paper feed: Tray
Lines per page: 66

PITCH	SETUP STRING	RIGHT MARGIN
10 cpi	\027&L7.27C	80
12 cpi	\027&L7.27C\027(s0p12H	96
16.66 cpi	\027&L7.27C\027&k2s	132

Orientation: Portrait
Paper size: Letter (8 1/2 by 11)
Paper feed: Tray
Lines per page: 89

PITCH	SETUP STRING	RIGHT MARGIN
10 cpi	\027&L5.39C	80
12 cpi	\027&L5.39C\027(s0p12H	96
16.66 cpi	\027&L5.39C\027&k2s	132

Orientation: Portrait
Paper size: Legal (8 1/2 by 14)
Paper feed: Tray
Lines per page: 78

PITCH	SETUP STRING	RIGHT MARGIN
10 cpi	\027E	80
12 cpi	\027(s0p12H	96
16.66 cpi	\027&k2s	132

Orientation: Portrait
Paper size: Legal (8 1/2 by 14)
Paper feed: Tray
Lines per page: 104

PITCH	SETUP STRING	RIGHT MARGIN
10 cpi	\027&L8D	80
12 cpi	\027&L8D\027(s0p12H	96
16.66 cpi	\027&L8D\027&k2s	132

Orientation: Portrait
Paper size: Legal (8 1/2 by 14)
Paper feed: Tray
Lines per page: 150

PITCH	SETUP STRING	RIGHT MARGIN
16.66 cpi	\027&L4.16C\027&k2s	132

Orientation: Portrait
Paper size: Legal (8 1/2 by 14)
Paper feed: Manual
Lines per page: 78

PITCH	SETUP STRING	RIGHT MARGIN
10 cpi	\027&L84p2H	80
12 cpi	\027&L84p2H\027(s0p12H	96
16.66 cpi	\027&L84p2H\027&k2s	132

Orientation: Portrait
Paper size: Legal (8 1/2 by 14)
Paper feed: Manual
Lines per page: 104

PITCH	SETUP STRING	RIGHT MARGIN
10 cpi	\027&L84p2H8D	80
12 cpi	\027&L84p2H8D\027(s0p12H	96
16.66 cpi	\027&L84p2H8D\027&k2s	132

Orientation: Portrait
Paper size: Legal (8 1/2 by 14)
Paper feed: Manual
Lines per page: 150

PITCH	SETUP STRING	RIGHT MARGIN
16.66 cpi	\027&L84p2H4.16C\027&k2s	132

Orientation: Landscape
Paper size: Letter (8 1/2 by 11)
Paper feed: Tray
Lines per page: 45

PITCH	SETUP STRING	RIGHT MARGIN
10 cpi	\027&L1O	106
12 cpi	\027&L1O\027(s0p12H	127
16.66 cpi	\027&L1O\027&k2s	176

Orientation: Landscape
Paper size: Letter (8 1/2 by 11)
Paper feed: Tray
Lines per page: 66

PITCH	SETUP STRING	RIGHT MARGIN
10 cpi	\027&L1o5.45C	106
12 cpi	\027&L1o5.45C\027(s0p12H	127
16.66 cpi	\027&L1o5.45C\027&k2s	176

Orientation: Landscape
Paper size: Legal (8 1/2 by 14)
Paper feed: Tray
Lines per page: 45

PITCH	SETUP STRING	RIGHT MARGIN
10 cpi	\027&L1O	136
12 cpi	\027&L1O\027(s0p12H	163
16.66 cpi	\027&L1O\027&k2s	226
17.75 cpi	\027&L1O\027&k2s6.75H	240

Orientation: Landscape
Paper size: Legal (8 1/2 by 14)
Paper feed: Tray
Lines per page: 66

PITCH	SETUP STRING	RIGHT MARGIN
10 cpi	\027&L1o5.45C	136
12 cpi	\027&L1o5.45C\027(s0p12H	163
16.66 cpi	\027&L1o5.45C\027&k2s	226
17.75 cpi	\027&L1o5.45C\027&k2s6.75H	240

Orientation: Landscape
Paper size: Legal (8 1/2 by 14)
Paper feed: Manual
Lines per page: 45

PITCH	SETUP STRING	RIGHT MARGIN
10 cpi	\027&L84p2h1O	136
12 cpi	\027&L84p2h1O\027(s0p12H	163
16.66 cpi	\027&L84p2h1O\027&k2s	226
17.75 cpi	\027&L84p2h1O\027&k2s6.75H	240

Orientation: Landscape
Paper size: Legal (8 1/2 by 14)
Paper feed: Manual
Lines per page: 66

PITCH	SETUP STRING	RIGHT MARGIN
10 cpi	\027&L84p2h5.45C	136
12 cpi	\027&L84p2h5.45C\027(s0p12H	163
16.66 cpi	\027&L84p2h5.45C\027&k2s	226
17.75 cpi	\027&L84p2h5.45C\027&k2s6.75H	240

Index

D

E

F

G

Q

R

S

X

Y

Z

ABOUT THE AUTHORS

Peter G. Randall is the president of Ariel Enterprises., a software development and consulting firm. Prior to the start-up of Ariel, he served as President of ESIS International, an international marketing subsidiary of Cigna Corporation. Mr. Randall earned a B.S.E in systems Engineering from Princeton University and M.B.A from the Wharton School of Business. He has written more than 30 major applications for use in business. He coauthored *1-2-3 Ready to Go, dBASE III to Go, The HAL Handbook, 1-2-3 Power Pack, WordPerfect Power Pack, Instant Byline, Simply WorkPerfect, Instant PageMaker, and Total 1-2-3, Release 3* (all published by Brady).

Steven J. Bennett is a professional writer and computer consultant. Educated at the University of Rochester and Harvard University, he has edited and written numerous medical and scientific publications. He has written a number of business books, including: *Playing Hardball with Soft Skills* (Bantam), *Executive Chess* (New American Library), and *Think To Win* (New American Library). He has also coauthored ten Brady Books: *1-2-3 Ready to Go, dBASE III to Go, The HAL Handbook, 1-2-3 Power Pack, WordPerfect Power Pack, Instant Byline, Instant PageMaker, Instant Ventura, Simply WorkPerfect,* and *Total 1-2-3, Release 3.*

Peter G. Randall

Steven J. Bennett